# ROUTLEDGE HANDBOOK OF AFRICAN PEACEBUILDING

Africa lies at the centre of the international community's peacebuilding interventions, and the continent's rich multitude of actors, ideas, relationships, practices, experiences, locations, and contexts in turn shapes the possibilities and practices of contemporary peacebuilding. This timely new handbook surveys and analyses peacebuilding as it operates in this specifically African context.

The book begins by outlining the evolution and the various ideologies, conceptualizations, institutions, and practices of African peacebuilding. It identifies critical differences in how African peacebuilders have conceptualized and operationalized peacebuilding. The book then considers how different actors sustain, construct, and use African infrastructure to identify and analyse converging, differing, or competing mandates, approaches, and interests. Finally, it analyses specific thematic issues such as gender, justice, development, democracy, and the politics of knowledge before ending with in-depth analyses of case studies drawn from across the continent.

Bringing together an international line-up of expert contributors, this book will be an essential read for students and scholars of African politics, post-conflict reconstruction, security, and peace and conflict studies.

**Bruno Charbonneau** is Full Professor of International Studies and Director of the Centre for Security and Crisis Governance (CRITIC) at Canada's Royal Military College Saint-Jean.

**Maxime Ricard** is West Africa Researcher at the Institute for Strategic Research (Institut de recherche stratégique de l'École militaire, IRSEM, France) and holds a PhD in political science from Université du Québec à Montréal. He is also Associate Researcher at the Centre FrancoPaix of the Raoul-Dandurand Chair in Canada.

# ROUTLEDGE HANDBOOK OF AFRICAN PEACEBUILDING

*Edited by*
*Bruno Charbonneau and Maxime Ricard*

LONDON AND NEW YORK

Cover image: UN Photo/Harandane Dicko

First published 2022
by Routledge
4 Park Square, Milton Park, Abingdon, Oxon OX14 4RN

and by Routledge
605 Third Avenue, New York, NY 10158

*Routledge is an imprint of the Taylor & Francis Group, an informa business*

© 2022 selection and editorial matter, Bruno Charbonneau and Maxime Ricard; individual chapters, the contributors

The right of Bruno Charbonneau and Maxime Ricard to be identified as the authors of the editorial material, and of the authors for their individual chapters, has been asserted in accordance with sections 77 and 78 of the Copyright, Designs and Patents Act 1988.

All rights reserved. No part of this book may be reprinted or reproduced or utilised in any form or by any electronic, mechanical, or other means, now known or hereafter invented, including photocopying and recording, or in any information storage or retrieval system, without permission in writing from the publishers.

*Trademark notice*: Product or corporate names may be trademarks or registered trademarks, and are used only for identification and explanation without intent to infringe.

*British Library Cataloguing-in-Publication Data*
A catalogue record for this book is available from the British Library

*Library of Congress Cataloging-in-Publication Data*
Names: Charbonneau, Bruno, editor. | Ricard, Maxime, editor.
Title: Routledge handbook of African peacebuilding/edited by Bruno Charbonneau and Maxime Ricard.
Description: New York: Routledge, 2022. | Includes bibliographical references and index.
Identifiers: LCCN 2021057465 (print) | LCCN 2021057466 (ebook) | ISBN 9780367181949 (hardback) | ISBN 9781032228433 (paperback) | ISBN 9780429060038 (ebook)
Subjects: LCSH: Peace-building–Africa.
Classification: LCC JZ5538. R6875 2022 (print) | LCC JZ5538 (ebook) | DDC 327.172096–dc23
LC record available at https://lccn.loc.gov/2021057465
LC ebook record available at https://lccn.loc.gov/2021057466

ISBN: 978-0-367-18194-9 (hbk)
ISBN: 978-1-032-22843-3 (pbk)
ISBN: 978-0-429-06003-8 (ebk)

DOI: 10.4324/9780429060038

Typeset in Bembo
by Apex CoVantage, LLC

# CONTENTS

*Acknowledgements* *viii*
*List of Contributors* *ix*

    Introduction: Whose Peacebuilding? Power, Politics, Practices    1
    *Bruno Charbonneau and Maxime Ricard*

## PART I
## Institutions      13

1  From Peacekeeping to Peacebuilding: Towards a UN Peace Continuum    15
    *Alexandra Novosseloff*

2  The United Nations and the African Union: Partners or Rivals
    in Peace Operations?    26
    *Arthur Stein and Marie-Joëlle Zahar*

3  Peacebuilding via Security Sector Reform and Governance? The
    Case of West Africa    44
    *Niagalé Bagayoko and Eboe Hutchful*

4  Preventing Conflict-Induced Forced Displacement in Africa:
    UNHCR, the AU and the Rhetoric and Realities
    of 'Root Causes'    57
    *Marina Sharpe*

## PART II
## Themes and Debates                                                                 71

5  African Mediation in High-Intensity Conflict: How African?                        73
   *Laurie Nathan*

6  Justice and Reconciliation in Africa: The Emergence of the African
   Union Transitional Justice Policy                                                 84
   *Tim Murithi*

7  The Politics of Knowledge and an African Transitional Justice:
   Analysing Africa as a Constitutive Outside                                       100
   *Ulrike Lühe and Briony Jones*

8  Local Peacebuilding: The Reflexive Encounter Between a Subaltern
   View and a Practitioner in Côte d'Ivoire                                         114
   *Jeremy Allouche and Patrick Zadi Zadi*

9  Women, Gender and Peacebuilding in Africa                                        128
   *Nina Wilén*

10 Development and Peacebuilding                                                    138
   *Jonathan M. Sears*

11 Peacebuilding and Democracy in Africa                                            155
   *Daniel Eizenga*

12 The Climate Crisis and Its Challenges for African Peacebuilding                  169
   *Bruno Charbonneau, Peter Läderach, Marc-André Boisvert, Tatiana
   Smirnova, Grazia Pacillo, Alessandro Craparo, and Ignacio Madurga*

## PART III
## Case Studies                                                                     189

13 Peace by Delegation? The G5 Sahel's Quest to Build Sustainable Peace             191
   *Ousmane Diallo*

14 Counterinsurgency and Peacebuilding in Somalia and Mali                          206
   *Bruno Charbonneau and Louise Wiuff Moe*

15 Peacebuilding in The Gambia: Sustaining the Gains and
   Addressing Potential Threats to the Process                                      222
   *Festus Kofi Aubyn*

16  The Politics of Transitional Justice and Peacemaking in
    a Non-Transition Context: The Case of South Sudan                235
    *Kuyang Harriet Logo*

17  Peacebuilding in Guinea-Bissau: Challenges and the Way Forward to
    Sustaining Peace and Security                                    247
    *Fiifi Edu-Afful and Ruth Adwoa Frimpong*

18  Stability for Whom and for What? The Ivorian Peacebuilding
    Experience Under Alassane Ouattara                               260
    *Maxime Ricard*

    Conclusion: African Peacebuilding for Whom and for What?
    Bringing the People Back In                                      274
    *Cyril Obi*

*Afterword*                                                          *283*
*Index*                                                              *287*

# ACKNOWLEDGEMENTS

Research is a collective enterprise. Edited volumes are examples of the pleasure and challenges of collaboration between colleagues who share similar interests and expertise, who learn from each other, and who give time and effort toward a common goal. We do not all come from the same background, academic or otherwise, and we do research under different conditions, as we do not have access to the same resources or privileges. Yet, in this book, we share a commitment to African peace, justice, and equality, to African peacebuilding as an endeavour worth pursuing and promoting. The contribution of our colleagues underlines the progress that has been made in the field of African peacebuilding, and the obstacles that endure. As their chapters make clear, progress should not hide the continent's particular place in and contributions to building the world.

As editors, we must first thank warmly our colleagues for their time and efforts in making this book possible. We are grateful to them for the fruits of their labours as they help advance the field in new ways, but also for their patience and swift responses to the editorial queries.

Special thanks to Stéphanie Roullier for her research and technical support, especially in the crazy last days prior to submission, and to Hugo Chouarbi at the Institute for Strategic Research in France for his assistance. We are also grateful to our respective institutions for their assistance and financial support as we worked on this collection, especially the Centre for Security and Crisis Governance (CRITIC) at Canada's Royal Military College Saint-Jean, and the Centre FrancoPaix in Conflict Resolution and Peace Missions at the Raoul-Dandurand Chair in Montréal. Bruno Charbonneau thanks and acknowledges the financial support of the Social Science and Humanities Research Council of Canada. Maxime Ricard would like to thank Shruti Gupta for her everyday support and also all those who contributed to his research in Côte d'Ivoire over the years and continue to help him. Without their generosity, field research would not be possible.

# CONTRIBUTORS

**Jeremy Allouche** is currently a professorial fellow at the Institute of Development Studies, University of Sussex and the Co-director of the Humanitarian Learning Centre. He is on the steering committee of the Sussex African Center and a member of the ESRC-funded STEPS Centre and the Sussex Center for Conflict and Security Research. His current fields of interest are the intersection between development, peacebuilding, humanitarianism, and civilian agency. He is currently leading a GCRF project, 'Islands of Innovation in Protracted Crises: A New Approach to Building Resilience from Below', and an AHRC/DFID project, 'New Community-Informed Approaches to Humanitarian Protection and Restraint'.

**Festus Kofi Aubyn** is the Regional Coordinator, Research and Capacity Building at the West Africa Network for Peacebuilding (WANEP). Before joining WANEP in November 2020, he worked with the Kofi Annan International Peacekeeping Training Centre in Ghana as a senior research fellow for almost a decade. He has participated and presented papers in several international conferences on African peace and security issues. He has several scholarly publications to his credit.

**Niagalé Bagayoko** is President of the African Security Sector Network. She holds a PhD in political science from the Institut d'Études Politiques de Paris (IEP). Her thesis was awarded the first prize of the Institut des Hautes Etudes de la Défense Nationale (IHEDN). She was director of the peacekeeping and peacebuilding program of the Organisation internationale de la Francophonie and a research fellow at the Institute of Development Studies, and at the Institut de recherche pour le développement. She has done extensive field research on security systems in African francophone countries, Western security policies (France, United States, European Union) in Africa, and African conflict-management mechanisms, focusing on the interface between security and development.

**Marc-André Boisvert** is a postdoctoral researcher at Centre FrancoPaix in Conflict Resolution at Université du Québec à Montréal. His work focuses on security governance and civil-military relations in the Sahel and on security sector reforms and armed groups. He is the author of several peer-reviewed publications. Before obtaining his PhD from the University of

East Anglia, he was part of the UN Panel of Experts for Mali and a journalist covering West Africa for more than a decade.

**Bruno Charbonneau** is Full Professor of International Studies and Director of the Centre for Security and Crisis Governance (CRITIC) at Canada's Royal Military College Saint-Jean. He is also Founder and Director of the Centre FrancoPaix in Conflict Resolution of the Chaire Raoul-Dandurand at Université du Québec à Montréal. He specializes in and has published widely on the international politics of conflict management in West Africa and the West African Sahel.

**Alessandro Craparo** is a postdoctoral research fellow at CGIAR and research fellow at Bjerknes Centre for Climate Research (BCCR), Norway. He has worked on bioclimatology globally over the past nine years with a focus on the influence of climate change and variability on plants and biomes. He is working on network and complexity analysis and global environmental change. Together with colleagues at BCCR, he is linking plant-atmosphere processes in the tropics and subtropics with those at higher latitudes.

**Ousmane Diallo** is a researcher for Amnesty International West and Central Africa Regional Office, working on the Sahel (Niger, Mali, Burkina Faso) and Senegal. He is a holder of a PhD in global governance from the Balsillie School of International Affairs, Wilfrid Laurier University. His doctoral thesis was on the response by African security actors to the crisis in Mali.

**Fiifi Edu-Afful** is a senior research fellow at the Faculty of Academic Affairs and Research at the Kofi Annan International Peacekeeping Training Centre. He holds a PhD from the University of Ibadan, Nigeria. He has authored several academic works on peace and security as well as gender. His background is in conflict analysis peace and security. His research mostly focuses on peace operations, violent extremism, and African peace and security mechanism.

**Daniel Eizenga** is a research fellow at the Africa Center for Strategic Studies in Washington, DC. Prior to joining the Africa Center, he was a postdoctoral fellow with the Centre FrancoPaix at Université du Québec à Montréal and a research associate with the Sahel Research Group based at the University of Florida, where he earned an MA and a PhD in political science with specializations in African studies. His research primarily focuses on countering violent extremism in the Sahel and the intersecting roles of civil-military relations, traditional institutions, and civil society across the various regime trajectories of African states.

**Ruth Adwoa Frimpong** is a researcher at the Kofi Annan International Peacekeeping Training Centre. She holds a master's degree in conflict, peace and security from the Kofi Annan International Peacekeeping Training Centre and a bachelor's degree in political science with geography and resource development from the University of Ghana. Her research interest areas include security sector reforms and police governance.

**Eboe Hutchful** is a Ghanaian political scientist and emeritus professor of Africana Studies at Wayne State University in Detroit, Michigan, USA, and Executive Secretary of the African Security Sector Network (ASSN), based in Accra, Ghana. He is a former member of the UN Secretary-General's Advisory Board on All Disarmament Matters and is currently on the Advisory Committee of the Knowledge Platform on Security and Rule of Law (KPSRL), based in The Netherlands. He is a long-time researcher on civil-military relations, security sector reform, and international development issues with many publications in these and related areas.

**Briony Jones** is Reader in International Development in the Politics and International Studies Department of the University of Warwick. She is also Deputy Director of the Warwick Interdisciplinary Research Centre for International Development. Her work sits at the intersection of development, peacebuilding, and transitional justice, with a focus on the politics of societies following large-scale violations of human rights.

**Peter Läderach** is Lead CGIAR Climate Security and for the CGIAR Climate Smart Technologies and Practices Flagship for the Climate Change, Agriculture and Food Security (CCAFS) research program, based in Rome, Italy. He led the expansion of CIAT's (International Center for Tropical Agriculture) climate program to Central America, Africa and Asia, with extensive work experience in more than 15 countries. He has nearly 20 years of research experience in food systems and climate science to support developing countries in alleviating poverty, adapting to and mitigating climate change, building resilience, and protecting the environment. He holds an MSc in geography and a PhD in tropical agriculture (summa cum laude) and has published over 60 peer-reviewed articles, book chapters, and books.

**Kuyang Harriet Logo** teaches international law, international human rights law, and women and child law at the University of Juba. She is an independent consultant working on democratic governance, access to justice and the rule of law. She is currently a fellow of the Rift Valley Institute, a member of the Expert Working Group of the Africa-China-Europe promoting dialogue and cooperation to prevent the diversion of arms and ammunition in Africa, and a research fellow on the Data and Displacement Project of the University of Warwick. Prior to becoming an academic and consultant, she served with the UN Development Programme in the Sudan, South Sudan, and Timor-Leste. She has published on knowledge production and transitional justice, international humanitarian law, customary law, and gender issues.

**Ulrike Lühe** is a senior researcher and program officer at Swisspeace, an associated institute of the University of Basel. Her research focuses on the global politics of transitional justice, particularly through the lens of knowledge and expertise. In addition, she is co-leading an international research project on corporate symbolic reparations and the contribution of corporate actors to transitional justice. She is co-editor of the volume *Knowledge for Peace: Transitional Justice and the Politics of Knowledge in Theory and Practice* and has co-edited a special issue of the *International Journal of Human Rights* titled "Beyond Evidence: The Use of Archives in Transitional Justice."

**Ignacio Madurga** is a visiting researcher at CGIAR FOCUS Climate Security specializing in peace and conflict research. His work mainly focuses on investigating the complex and non-linear interactions between climate, conflict, and socio-economic and political risks and vulnerabilities. He holds a double BA in international relations and economics from the Rey Juan Carlos University of Madrid and a MA with distinction in conflict, governance, and development from the University of York.

**Louise Wiuff Moe** is a research associate at the University of Hamburg. Her research combines theoretical and empirical perspectives on conflict, peace, and security governance, with a regional focus on sub-Saharan Africa. Her recent work explores changing norms and practices of international intervention, the renaissance of counterinsurgency, inter-organizational relations in conflict management in Africa, comparative perspectives on south-south security collaboration, and the climate-security nexus.

**Tim Murithi** is Professor and Head, Peacebuilding Interventions Programme, Institute for Justice and Reconciliation, Cape Town, and Extraordinary Professor of African Studies, Centre for African and Gender Studies, University of Free State, South Africa. He is also a research associate, Institute for Democracy, Citizenship and Public Policy in Africa, University of Cape Town. He was previously Claude Ake Visiting Professor, Department of Peace and Conflict Research, Uppsala University and Nordic Africa Institute, Sweden. He has over 25 years of experience in peace, security, governance, transitional justice, and development in Africa.

**Laurie Nathan** is Professor of the Practice of Mediation and Director of the Mediation Program at the Kroc Institute for International Peace Studies, University of Notre Dame. He was previously director of the Centre for Mediation in Africa at the University of Pretoria. He has been a senior mediation advisor to the UN, a member of the UN Academic Council on Mediation, and lead designer and trainer of the UN High Level Mediation Course. He has published extensively on mediation.

**Alexandra Novosseloff** is a consultant, a non-resident senior fellow at the International Peace Institute in New York, and a research associate at the Centre Thucydide of the University of Paris-Panthéon-Assas (Paris 2). Her latest book is *Le Conseil de sécurité, entre impuissance et toute-puissance* (2nd ed., Éditions CNRS, 2021).

**Cyril Obi** is a program director at the Social Science Research Council, New York, where he leads the African Peacebuilding Network (APN) and (since September 2018) the Next Generation Social Sciences in Africa programs. He has received numerous prestigious international academic awards and fellowships. He is also currently a research associate of the Department of Political Sciences, University of Pretoria, South Africa. He has published extensively in international publications and edited several books. His most recent book is *Developmental Regionalism and Economic Transformation in Southern Africa* (Routledge, 2020), with Said Adejumobi.

**Grazia Pacillo** is a senior economist and evaluator with more than 15 years of experience in research on food and agricultural system resilience, sustainability, and transformation considering interconnected global and regional challenges, notably the climate security crisis. At the CGIAR Focus Climate Security, she leads socio-economic research on the impact of climate change and variability on a diverse set of livelihood systems and outcomes. Her main research interest lies in evaluating the role of climate as a "threat multiplier," exacerbating existing risks and insecurities such as food and nutrition insecurity, poverty, forced migration, gender and other structural inequalities, which in turn can affect the prospect for peace and stability across the world.

**Maxime Ricard** is West Africa Researcher at the Institute for Strategic Research (Institut de recherche stratégique de l'École militaire, IRSEM, France), and holds a PhD in political science from Université du Québec à Montréal. He is also Associate Researcher at the Centre Franco-Paix of the Raoul-Dandurand Chair in Canada. He was coordinator of the Centre FrancoPaix from 2016 to 2021. Before joining academic research, he worked for two years in the field of conflict resolution in Côte d'Ivoire. Specializing in peace and security as well as in African studies, his thesis research focused on order-making and security practices of non-state actors in post-conflict Côte d'Ivoire, including urban and rural vigilantism as well as private security companies.

**Jonathan M. Sears** is Associate Professor of International Development Studies and Associate Dean at Menno Simons College (Canadian Mennonite University at University of Winnipeg). He is an external member of the Centre FrancoPaix (CFP) at Université du Québec à Montréal. From his long-standing interest in Mali, he contributes to reports, policy briefs, bulletins, and articles: through the CFP, *The Conversation–Africa*, and recently "State Legitimacy in Mali: Crisis, Contest, (Re)construction" in a special issue of *Peace Research: The Canadian Journal of Peace and Conflict Studies*. From a multidisciplinary background in political studies, philosophy, and anthropology, he researches governance, development, conflict, and peace in francophone Sahelian Africa and links his research to teaching in development policy, practice, ethics, and theory. As Associate Dean, he oversees programs in conflict resolution studies and international development studies.

**Marina Sharpe** is Assistant Professor of International Studies at Canada's Royal Military College Saint-Jean. Prior roles include senior legal officer with UNHCR's Representation to the African Union and Banting Postdoctoral Fellow at McGill University's Faculty of Law. She is the author of *The Regional Law of Refugee Protection in Africa* (Oxford University Press, 2018) and sits on the editorial board of the *International Journal of Refugee Law*. She holds a DPhil in law from Oxford, where she was a Trudeau Scholar.

**Tatiana Smirnova** is a postdoctoral researcher at Centre FrancoPaix in Conflict Resolution at Université du Québec à Montréal and a research associate at the Sahel Research Group, University of Florida. Her work focuses on different forms of violence in the Sahel. She studies insurrectionary dynamics and the responses of international organizations and foreign forces, with a specialization on Niger and Mali. She has also worked as a consultant for various international non-governmental organizations.

**Arthur Stein** is a PhD candidate at the University of Montreal. His doctoral research focuses on the consequences of armed state support for insurgent groups during civil wars. More broadly, his academic interests focus on the role of non-state armed groups during internal conflicts, their treatment of civilian populations, and their influence on the return to peace and the building of stable institutions. Prior to his doctoral studies, he obtained a master's degree in political science from the Institute of Political Studies in Strasbourg.

**Nina Wilén** is Director of the Africa Programme at Egmont Institute of International Relations and Associate Professor in Political Science at Lund University. She is Editor in Chief of *International Peacekeeping* since 2020, and has authored the books *Justifying Interventions (De)Stabilising Sovereignty* (2012) and *African Peacekeeping* (2021) with Jonathan Fisher. Her research focuses on the politics of peacekeeping, security sector reform, military interventions in conflicts, and gender and the military more broadly. She has published extensively on these topics in international academic journals. She has conducted field research in Niger, Liberia, the Democratic Republic of the Congo, Burundi, Rwanda, and South Africa.

**Patrick Zadi Zadi** is an Ivorian researcher, peacebuilding specialist, and trainer. For the past 11 years, he has been working in Côte d'Ivoire, Mali, and South Sudan in the fields of peacebuilding, local governance, political transition, and project management. He worked in different organizations including ICRC, GTZ, DED (now GIZ), and CITI, a political transitions program funded by USAID. From 2010 to 2011, he was a trainer for the Peace School in Bamako, Mali. His thematic focus is on issues of gender in reconciliation and social cohesion, early warning and conflict prevention, humanitarian relief operations, DDR, CIMIC, and local governance.

**Marie-Joëlle Zahar** is Full Professor of Political Science and Director of the Research Network on Peace Operations at Université de Montréal and Senior Non-resident Fellow at the International Peace Institute. Her current research focuses on UN stabilization missions in Mali and the Central African Republic as well as on UN mediation efforts.

# INTRODUCTION

## Whose Peacebuilding? Power, Politics, Practices

*Bruno Charbonneau and Maxime Ricard*

Peace, conflict, stability, and development have been recurrent themes of post-colonial Africa. After colonial powers withdrew from the continent, the issues of whose peace and whose responsibility it is to enforce, promote, or consolidate have been fundamental questions of peacebuilding initiatives and have been at the centre of the construction of an African peace and security architecture.

A book on *African* peacebuilding is partly the result of the centrality of African experiences, of an international politics that places Africa at the centre of intervention practices. In the twenty-first century alone, Paul Williams calculates that 50 peace operations were deployed on the continent – an expansion in the number, size, and cost of operations that is largely explained by the increasing amount of missions by African regional organizations (Williams 2021). Beyond numbers, a book on African peacebuilding must interrogate and analyse this African specificity: the evolution, the various ideologies and conceptualizations, and the practices of African peacebuilding – both in terms of their African emergence, ideas, and practices and in terms of an international politics that manages African wars and conflicts – of an international politics that has constructed conditions of near-permanent interventions. Africa is a key location for peacebuilding interventions, a spatial and historical imaginary of context-specific sites where one finds a multitude of actors, ideas, relationships, practices, and experiences that shape, in turn, the possibilities of peacebuilding.

A book on African *peacebuilding* must also struggle with a broad term that refers to a variety of practices, to an extensive field of research, to multiple sites, politics, and power relations, embedded in structures and historical legacies. UN Secretary-General Boutros Boutros-Ghali's 1992 report, *An Agenda for Peace*, popularized the idea of a spectrum of activities from preventive diplomacy to peacemaking, to peacekeeping, and to post-conflict peacebuilding (see Novosseloff, this volume). In this framing, the process is linear. Peacebuilding comes after peacemaking and peacekeeping and leads to post-conflict reconstruction, 'as long as the root causes of violent conflict are addressed through development' (Karbo 2018a, 13). In his 1995 *Supplement to An Agenda for Peace*, Boutros-Ghali linked the idea of peacebuilding to the idea of positive peace, linking peacebuilding practices and technologies used to build peace after war to conflict prevention. The elimination of the root causes of conflict was therefore an endeavour to pursue before, during, and after violent conflict – under the label of peacebuilding. The 2000 Brahimi report on peacekeeping reform sought to restrict peacebuilding to post-conflict activities, but in practice, given the 'multiple contributing causes of conflict, almost any international assistance effort that addresses any perceived or real grievance can arguably be called "peacebuilding"' (Barnett et al. 2007, 44). Given the imprecision of the concept, scholars and practitioners often end up taking or assuming an instrumental approach: peacebuilding as it refers to 'the means to institutionalize peace, and remove the root causes of conflict' (McNamee and Muyangwa 2021, 7).

It was against this UN background – and in the context of the demise of the Soviet Union and of the conflicts in Liberia, Sierra Leone, and Somalia – that the Organization of African Unity (OAU) began discussions and negotiations to transform the continental peace and security architecture. In 1992, at the OAU Dakar summit, the report of Secretary-General Salim Ahmed Salim marked the moment by arguing that 'there was an urgent need for the organization to adopt a new security agenda as well as develop an institutional framework' (Muyangwa and Vogt 2000, 8). It led to the 1993 OAU's Continental Mechanism for Conflict Prevention, Management, and Resolution, whose limits and ineffectiveness justified the construction of the African Union (AU) and its array of peace and security institutions – in line with the approach and recommendations of Boutros-Ghali's *An Agenda for Peace* (Kuwali 2018).

With the creation of the AU on 26 May 2001 (and its inauguration in July 2002), there has arguably been much progress toward a form (or forms) of *Pax Africana*. Ali Mazrui's vision and ambition was for a Pax Africana that was 'to be assured by the exertions of *Africans* themselves' and concerned with 'the specifically military aspect of the principle of continental jurisdiction' (Mazrui 2018, 35). Replacing the OAU, the AU was conceived to promote regional integration, continental solidarity, peace, and good governance and to enhance African voices in international relations (for an overview of African regional integration, see Khadiagala 2013). Article 4 of its 2002 Constitutive Act gave the AU an explicit interventionist role in the management of African conflicts and security crises. The AU framework represented 'a milestone in the evolution of a particular kind of legal and philosophical peacebuilding disposition, and the beginning of a narrative of Africa's norms formulation agenda' (Jeng 2012, 9).

## Whose Peace?

Assessments of the progress toward Pax Africana can hardly be isolated from the world, from the ways in which African peacebuilding experiences are embedded in, and are the results of, colonial legacies, international relations, power structures and relationships, hierarchies of knowledge production, and disputed practices. For Devon Curtis, the contested politics and practices of peacebuilding in Africa make it impossible to distinguish the local from the international – or the African from the 'external' – given that 'the local, regional, and global are mutually constitutive'. Peacebuilding in Africa 'is not simply the product of hegemonic external forces, and it is not a failed or incomplete example of something else' (Curtis 2012, 17). The analysis of African peacebuilding cannot deny Africans of their agency or their connections with the world: 'Ultimately post-conflict peacebuilding is a political contest, where peace is not a universally recognized object to discover or impose, but a set of contested ideas and practices' (Curtis 2013, 212; see also Pugh, Cooper and Turner 2008).

If peacebuilding is a political contest about the form of peace to be promoted, imposed, or consolidated, the first question needs to be about whose peace/building we are talking about. Abou Jeng argues that the Eurocentric thinking that informs the dominant conceptualization of peace and peacebuilding – notably its references to order, law, and stability – leads to the marginalization of non-European alternatives, to approaches that are 'either circumscribed to irrelevance or considered incongruent with the institutional and normative configuration of international law' (Jeng 2012, 5; see also Grovogui 2002). Zubairu Wai points to the resilience of the 'colonial library', an 'immense body of texts and systems of representations' that continues to inform the Western imagination about Africa, and thus informs policy (Wai 2018a). At the very least, this means that analysts 'need to be very cognizant of the particular version of peacebuilding that is being institutionalized', as there 'are important differences in how various actors see the complex task of peacebuilding and the many priorities it entails' (Barnett et al. 2007, 37).

Another question that arises is whether, after 20 years, the AU framework still constitutes a 'milestone' or an African version of peacebuilding. Increasing institutional cooperation, the development of joint frameworks, the normalization of joint meetings, and the creation of new institutions have contributed to the AU and UN partnership and the construction of a form of Pax Africana, even if not without challenges and constraints (see Stein and Zahar, this volume). Such practices and their institutionalization contribute to a particular version of peacebuilding, but whose? Beyond institutional, bureaucratic, technical, and operational matters and practices, the fact that the notion of peacebuilding is disputed points to a politics of contested moral economies, to a vision of what constitutes and defines the legitimate political order.

Indeed, for Tony Karbo, the noble aims and ideals of the AU fell short 'in the promotion of democracy and "good governance" on the continent', with the gains of the 1990s and early 2000s 'all but lost' (Karbo 2018b, 458). Thomas Kwesi Tieku (2019) puts it differently, arguing that the AU has been effective in addressing 'the needs of the African political class', mainly 'by socializing them to accept liberal values as the foundation for international cooperation in Africa', by enhancing the influence and power of 'the African political class on the world stage', and by establishing liberal rules and norms for the African continent. In contrast, the 'AU has been less successful in providing services that address many of the expressed needs and concerns of the non-elite in Africa' (Tieku 2019; on the need to study class and privilege in peacebuilding contexts, see De Heredia 2018).

There might be little agreement on what peacebuilding looks like, who it is or ought to be for, and what practices constitute it, but 'the contemporary approach to peacebuilding is reliant on the state as the critical institutional actor' (Jackson 2019, 3). This translates into the ideology of the failed state, a concept that has little to do with the state per se but is 'about the international system and actors intervening in states', helping to avoid contentious legal or bureaucratic issues that might hinder intervention (Woodward 2017, 10). In Africa, the ideology of the failed state strengthens the tendency to internalize the causes of conflict, detaching them from their historical context and global structural condition and thus 'normalizing the historical and structural relations between Africa and Europe' (Wai 2018b, 40). Indeed, in Africa peacebuilding initiatives are limited by the conditions of the post-colonial African state. As Siphamandla Zondi argues, the AU's approach to peacebuilding 'requires the existence of a legitimate government, a functional society and domestic parties for dialogue to begin. Without these conditions, the approach leads to extended peace enforcement rather than peacebuilding' (Zondi 2017, 105). More fundamentally, Zondi emphasizes the morality of the current global order and its effects on African peacebuilding: African peace efforts 'have a fundamental weakness arising from the fact that they take as given the colonial/neo-colonial state and economy established through violent processes of conquest, colonisation and domination; they envisage peace without the decommissioning of the underlying logics of coloniality' (Zondi 2017, 107).

Perspectives on Africa and on the African state have had a governing influence on international relations, and thus on the politics and practices of African peacebuilding. Discourses of state failure, terrorism, and 'ungoverned spaces' inform policy and frame the conditions of possibilities (Smith 2010). Such images and ideologies might be dismissed as 'Western' orientalist representations, but they reflect and inform techniques of governance that tell us a lot more about mechanisms and practices of security and about regional dynamics of intervention and governance than they can about the lived experiences of African peoples who can wage war or be in conflict for a variety of not-so-obvious reasons (Charbonneau 2017). They also generate resources of power and strategic opportunities for African actors as they vie for authority, legitimacy, and wealth under the conditions imposed by international intervention (Charbonneau 2014). Thus, the line between Africa and the international can be blurred. The question of intervention (i.e. the problematic relationship between the sovereignty of a singular state and the sovereignty [authority] of the system of states) is thus avoided, marginalized, and erased as intervention becomes an inescapable condition of the localized political order.

Hence, a critical place to begin the scholarly study of African peacebuilding is to recognize the variety of contending perspectives on Africa as geography, Africa as lived experiences, and peacebuilding. Peacebuilding does not simply respond to conflict, somehow, somewhere, said to be located in(side) 'Africa'. It produces and constitutes the objects and subjects of its interventions, defines the meaning and parameters of the peace, and thus contributes to the constitution and reproduction of states, power relations and structures, and legitimate parameters of peacebuilding practice. In this sense, African peacebuilding is also about the unfinished business of building post-colonial Africa (Zondi 2017).

## Structure of the Book

The book is divided into three parts. Part I focuses on structural and institutional issues; namely, the UN framework, UN-AU partnership, the security sector, and international law. It is meant to outline what are unavoidable aspects of African peacebuilding. Part II examines themes and debates that inform and define the practices and politics of peacebuilding: mediation, justice, knowledge production, local agency, gender, development, and democracy. Part III offers six case studies that analyse the power relations and impact of peacebuilding in the Sahel, Mali and Somalia, The Gambia, South Sudan, Guinea-Bissau, and Côte d'Ivoire. Taken together, the chapters study the evolution of the various ideologies, conceptualizations, and practices of African peacebuilding. They identify critical differences in how peacebuilders have conceptualized and operationalized peacebuilding and how different actors sustain, construct, and use the African peace and security architecture to advance converging, differing, or competing mandates, approaches, and interests.

### *Structures and Institutions*

The African continent is the main location where the UN 'peace continuum' – from prevention to peacebuilding – operates and is being developed. It has evolved through a series of doctrines and crisis management tools. In Chapter 1, Alexandra Novosseloff dissects the conceptual construction of this continuum as it expanded or contracted along with the crises the UN responded to. The gradation of intervention is Boutros-Ghali's *An Agenda for Peace*: from preventive diplomacy to peacemaking, peacekeeping, and post-conflict peacebuilding. Peacebuilding grew in importance, as it was progressively conceived as an exit strategy to build sustainable peace. Yet, institutional and operational barriers remain numerous, with the relationship with UN peacekeeping being particularly troublesome and complex. Novosseloff shows that to solve the problems of operationalizing peacebuilding, the concepts of stabilization and sustaining peace were brought forth but have created other challenges. In theory, a continuum of missions makes sense, but in practice the implementation of an effective peace continuum has led to important obstacles. The transition from crisis management to peacebuilding is often too fast. Ambitious objectives lead to a recurrent discrepancy between assigned mandates and available resources. And as posited above, the ambiguity in what constitutes peacebuilding activities impedes attempts at coordination and burden sharing.

In Chapter 2, Arthur Stein and Marie-Joëlle Zahar examine how such challenges and their solutions arise in the context of UN-AU cooperation. They argue that although the UN and the AU have recognized and make better use of each other's comparative advantages, operational and structural constraints continue to stand in the way of efficient synergies to achieve sustainable peace. Over the years, the AU and the UN have become vital partners in peace operations, but the results vary. Somalia is regularly cited as an example of an encouraging partnership, but Mali and the Central African Republic demonstrate the difficulties and tensions. In several ways, the two organizations have developed a division of labour. The AU conducts more robust operations, counterinsurgency, and counterterrorism efforts, while the UN has resisted going further than stabilization missions, despite its support to AU operations. Notwithstanding remaining challenges, there is no denying the increasing cooperation, joint frameworks, and joint meetings that indicate a mutual desire to continue the development of a relationship. Practices of collaboration contributed to the socialization of UN and AU staff members. Yet, the UN-AU partnership remains limited by structural constraints. Operational impediments such as the sui generis nature of joint operations and the financial conundrum are deep challenges. There are also intractable political and strategic disagreements.

The security sector has been at the core of intervention and peacebuilding activities in Africa. It is a key peacebuilding object of intervention that is meant to build the capacity deemed necessary to sustain peace. In Chapter 3, Niagalé Bagayoko and Eboe Hutchful focus on security sector reform (SSR) for peacebuilding in West Africa. From a governance perspective, the politics of the security sector is characterized by the fragmentation of power and authority at multiple levels. Security sector governance (SSG) is an analytical concept that provides a way to understand the exercise of power and authority over state and human security in a specific context. SSG is facing many challenges in West Africa in terms of political will, security cultures, and the diversity of security actors. West African countries emerging from deep SSR did not show particular improvements in terms of social and development indicators but made gains in terms of democratic stability. Bagayoko and Hutchful posit that SSR is mostly perceived as a technical matter focused on security providers. They argue that SSR could be better connected to the UN's sustaining peace agenda by focusing on civil-military relations, thus increasing democratic governance and civilian oversight of the sector. However, as the West African security environment is characterized by 'asymmetric' threats and conflicts, it is not clear how SSR and SSG can train security forces to deal with such threats. Emerging security risks in West Africa present the possibility that SSR activities will be captured by stabilization and counterterrorism initiatives and training rather than by long-term governance and institution-building objectives.

In Chapter 4, Marina Sharpe asks why root causes of conflict are often addressed only rhetorically. Thirty-nine percent of the more than 65 million forcibly displaced persons in the world are in Africa. Forced displacement in Africa is caused primarily by violent conflict. Yet, she argues, the international and regional organizations tasked to respond do not have peacebuilding mandates. The Global Compact on Refugees adopted by the UN General Assembly in 2018 and the Kampala Convention of the AU in 2009 speak to the issue of root causes to solve sustainably forced displacement. But structural barriers impede the prevention agenda. The mandate of the UN Refugee Agency (UNHCR) and the structure of the AU Commission preclude their meaningful engagement in conflict prevention. To deliver on the 'root causes' rhetoric they advocate, Sharpe argues, UNHCR and the AU Commission must collaborate with actors mandated to prevent and resolve conflict, such as the UN's Department of Political and Peacebuilding Affairs, the AU's Peace and Security Council, and its Peace and Security Department, as well as civil society actors. If the humanitarian imperative constrains collaboration between forced displacement and peacebuilding actors to prevent and resolve conflict, UNHCR and the AU Commission should nuance their messaging accordingly to avoid empty words when the stakes are so high.

## *Themes and Debates*

Part II of the book examines how different themes and debates impact peacebuilding, both in theory and in practice. In Chapter 5, Laurie Nathan delves into the question of whether mediation on the continent has distinct African characteristics. Armed international interventions in the context of high-intensity conflicts usually make the headlines, but mediation is arguably the most common international response to these conflicts. There is strong evidence that African actors lead these mediations and also provide political direction through resolutions of the AU and regional economic communities (RECs). However, the study of strategy, style, and content of mediated agreements suggests that African mediation should be understood in broader global dynamics. African mediation shows a general preference for liberal democratic governance combined with power-sharing agreements. But while mediations expose a de jure liberal and democratic content, de facto practice of governance highlights an illiberal and exclusionary nature. The preference for power-sharing arrangements to manage the distribution of power in a post-conflict society is not particular to Africa but reflects a global trend that does not guarantee stability.

Following from this exploration of African specificity, in Chapter 6 Tim Murithi analyses Africa's role in transitional justice norm setting and norm diffusion. Although the African continent is usually portrayed as an object of external intervention and socio-political engineering, Murithi shows instead how it has played a leading role in the transformation, innovation, and diffusion of the ideas, norms, and practices of justice and reconciliation. The normative pressures on the legal remit of transitional justice exerted by the grassroots experiences of African societies compelled the scope of transitional justice to expand significantly. Transitional justice is now faced with a broad range of challenges including administering justice in a manner that can restore societal trust and promote reconciliation in deeply divided communities. Furthermore, the demands for socio-economic justice have pushed the normative boundaries of transitional justice beyond the confines of its historical origins within the legal sphere. The calls for reparations and restitution have required the development of new approaches that are linked to the peacebuilding and development fields. Although Africa was not the initiator of transitional justice norms, African societies and states innovated by implementing a broader range of approaches and by developing standards that have begun to influence contemporary theory and practice within the field (with sequencing, amnesty, cultural, and cross-border approaches). These African innovations have led to the first regional organization ambition to develop a transitional justice policy by the AU. While the pursuit of justice in the liberal tradition is often considered detrimental (or at times in opposition to) the goals of peace and reconciliation, Africa's experiences challenged this perspective and demonstrated the complementarity between transitional justice and peacebuilding processes.

In Chapter 7, Ulrike Lühe and Briony Jones dig deeper into African contributions to the transitional justice field by exploring the production of the field's knowledge. They point out that the African continent has always been the constitutive outside of transitional justice. They apply a post-colonial lens to the origin myth of transitional justice. This allows them to highlight how the Nuremberg and post–Cold War narratives helped ground transitional justice in a version of international justice that blurs the relationship between transitional justice and colonial governance. Policy and practice hold up certain cases and models rendered legible through a Western gaze and decontextualized from the continent. This has led to a development of transitional justice that goes together with the colonial enterprise, thus sustaining authoritarian and non-democratic practices as transitional justice is instrumentalized by political elites in post-colonial contexts. Transitional justice is tangled up in colonial power systems, forms of governance, and discourse. Thus, according to Lühe and Jones, it might be unable to address historical or ongoing injustices in its current form. Thinking of Africa as a constitutive outside, and thus as integral to the edifice of transitional justice, suggests that the centrality of Africa to the formation of global transitional justice norms has previously been obfuscated. An African transitional justice, as promulgated by the AU policy and the vibrant debates on the continent, is an important step in rendering these contributions visible.

In a similar vein, the focus on 'local' peacebuilding has been conceived as both an example and a necessary African contribution to peacebuilding and peace activities generally. While much of the scholarship emphasized the limits of top-down approaches, there is little critique of bottom-up or local approaches that are presented as alternatives to the former. In Chapter 8, Jeremy Allouche and Patrick Zadi Zadi develop a reflexive analysis of the subaltern view of local peacebuilding and what it means in practice to talk of local peacebuilding for a francophone West African practitioner – an analysis supported by Zadi's experiences in Côte d'Ivoire. The 'local' is both an extraordinarily flexible and a highly contested term. If the local is understood as relational, particular, and contextual, in practice it raises crucial issues related to legitimacy, emancipation, empowerment, and resistance. For Allouche and Zadi, despite all good intentions, a new generation of peacebuilding efforts has retained its top-down and Western-centric characteristics to a large extent, leading to ignoring its social and human consequences on the ground. More fundamentally, local peacebuilding tends to assume a liberal notion of civil society. Allouche and Zadi Zadi analyse two peace initiatives that were successful in addressing land-related violence. They claim that these successes were possible because peacebuilding activities engaged directly with the structural causes of the localized conflict instead of relating to the national context. However, the authors challenge future researchers to define more clearly what subalternity means for peacebuilding, given that international-local encounters are seemingly often instances of the local subversions of international peacebuilding initiatives.

After decades of marginalization, gender and women have become central topics of peacebuilding, both in theory and in practice. How are women and their roles and functions imagined in future African post-conflict societies? In Chapter 9, Nina Wilén analyses the space, wording, function, and roles that peace agreements give to women and gender. She deploys a feminist lens to distinguish four categories of the portrayal of women: vulnerable victims, moral peacebuilders, counting women, and human rights (and women's rights). Complete gender blindness may largely be behind us, Wilén argues, but the peace agreements signed since 2000 reveal several gender dilemmas and gaps. When women are mentioned in peace agreements, they are often given roles that draw heavily on essentialist descriptions and gender stereotypes. The risks include maintaining and reinforcing gender inequality. Men are still the default setting in peace agreements, whereas women are perceived as different and requiring special treatment or special protection. One gender dilemma involves emphasizing women's particular experiences of conflict without reducing them to passive victims. Gendered stereotypical expectations are produced when women bear the burden of morality as the safekeepers of the post-conflict society. Despite a greater representativity of women in the peace accords that Wilén studied, the structural inequalities that women face are rarely addressed by peace negotiations and decision-making organs. Although gender has been mainstreamed, gender dilemmas and gaps remain daunting challenges for African peacebuilding activities.

In Chapter 10, Jonathan Sears argues that the peacebuilding and development paradigm is circular and invites near-permanent interventions into African states and societies. Sustainable peace and development in Africa are framed as an ever-expanding nexus of security, stability, humanitarian relief, and peacebuilding that grows from the post-conflict reconstruction domain. However, this overly ambitious agenda has not adequately addressed structural and pressing challenges. Jonathan Sears frames the crucial importance of the processes of post-colonial, independent state formation in Africa along a 'maximalist-minimalist' axis of state models, with its two poles at odds with one another. These models coexist in governance relationships at the international-national boundary and in domestic state-society relations. On the one hand, the maximalist version aims to capacity-build a state that can provide security and welfare to its citizens. On the other, the neoliberal model of state demands a minimalist state to get on the 'boat' of global capitalism. Yet, as Sears argues, 'the issues are at least as much with the "boat" as with those who are chronically left out'. African leaders have tried over the years to adapt the developmental peacebuilding agenda to expand the role and power of the state, and to deepen Africa's global integration into capitalist circulation, but without addressing the structural impediments to development within the global political economy. Alternatives like the 'local turn' have drawn community leaders into state-led projects that can leverage local capacities, knowledge, and networks for greater effectiveness of interventions but can also align grassroots actors with the ideas and interests of political and economic elites. In specific small-scale contexts, developmental peacebuilding shows micro-level successes. What these small-scale parts add up to, however, can elude effective measurement and persuasive attribution of results in multi-sector and multi-actor initiatives. These difficulties of attributing demonstrable outputs and outcomes are the practical manifestations of fundamental questions of logic and causality in processes of complex social change.

In Chapter 11, Daniel Eizenga analyses the relationship between democracy and peacebuilding in Africa. While many critics underscore the shortcomings of democracy and peacebuilding initiatives, few acknowledge the successes and positive political changes. Eizenga argues that, despite setbacks, peacebuilding and democracy exhibit a robust relationship on the African continent. Sustainable peace and democratic consolidation rarely if ever follow a linear trajectory. Democratic gains continue to be vulnerable to authoritarian elites and tendencies, notably in conflict contexts. Yet, when recovering from conflict, African states that chose the path of sustained democratization improved governance, peace, and prosperity over the long term. While the critiques of democratic peace theory and liberal peacebuilding are well-founded, regular multiparty elections in Africa since the 1990s suggest that the degree of political change that has occurred has been overlooked or underestimated. However, despite a growing number of countries that organize regular national elections, prosperity remains elusive, peace is tenuous, and democratic gains are stymied. Some African elites have flouted the liberal peacebuilding and democratic models as the international context has become more permissive of authoritarian governments and measures. Democratic backsliding presents a real danger for sustainable peace and highlights the importance of substantive democracy promotion within peacebuilding contexts, which in post-conflict settings requires explicit international support and engagement.

In Chapter 12, Bruno Charbonneau, Peter Läderach, Marc-André Boisvert, Tatiana Smirnova, Grazia Pacillo, Alessandro Craparo, and Ignacio Madurga bring together conflict expertise and climate sciences to examine the challenges and risks that the climate crisis represents for conflict, violence, and system fragility. After a brief examination of the literature on the relationship between climate change and armed conflicts, they focus on that relationship in the context of the West African Sahel as they go beyond an abstract discussion of climate-conflict debates. It also enables an analysis of the inherent politics of the academic and policy fields of 'climate security' and how climate security can inform practices of intervention. Second, the chapter presents an overview of the multiple impact pathways through which climate change and variability affect Niger, emphasizing the effects of climate change and variability on local governance practices and mechanisms. These mechanisms, processes, and practices were built historically through consensus, collaboration, competition, and/or conflict, but the climate crisis imposes new stresses as it also accelerates the timeline for their necessary transformation. The authors argue that the extent to which climate variability and stresses affect conflict dynamics is difficult to assess, given that climate variability in Niger has been an environmental background condition for centuries and that Niger's recent instability is inextricably linked to the Malian conflict. Nevertheless, transformation induced by climate change can sustain or exacerbate conflict dynamics just as it can create new ones and cause mass human suffering and misery. One of the key challenges is integrating climate security concerns into peacebuilding activities. What does it mean to do peacebuilding in the era of climate change? The authors conclude that resolving or preventing armed conflicts will require building ecosystem resilience based on the complex interrelationships of biosphere and human systems. To do so, they point to the need for more research (and fine-grained case studies) into unveiling the complexity of climate and security for informed decision-making. This requires not only regular and detailed analyses but also the creation of decision support tools that provide real-time and high temporal and spatial resolution evidence. They also point to the need for better climate security sensitiveness in peacebuilding programs and investments, in particular and most relevant for African peacebuilding, the role of food systems in the climate crisis.

## *Case Studies*

Part III of the book explores context-specific cases of peacebuilding activities and interventions. In Chapter 13, Ousmane Diallo analyses the agency of African actors in the international system through a careful study of the G5 Sahel organization since its inception in 2014. Created in a crowded neighbourhood of regional organizations and international actors, Diallo explores how the G5 Sahel understand its emerging role as a peace and security actor in a rapidly evolving situation. He argues that the approach of the G5 Sahel is state-centric, thus sustaining the idea that peace is attained by capacity-building the state, especially in security and development terms. Its focus on the security-development nexus allows the G5 to development collaboration with international partners that see in the G5 Sahel the 'best fit' organization to secure the region. Yet, as Diallo shows, there is a contrast between the responses of African actors that focus on (state) stability and the micropolitics of violence at the subnational level that the G5 is struggling to address. Moreover, the organization is heavily dependent on its international donors, while its security actions have failed to improve the security situation. Violence in the region of the G5 military operations has steadily increased since 2015, with regular reports of violence against civilians perpetrated by non-state armed groups and the armies of its member states. Building peace involves engaging with local governance politics and with local communities on issues such as justice, accountability, and governance, but it is far from clear that the G5 Sahel contributes to such efforts. Its dependency on international donors limits its possibilities and the development of a distinct G5 voice in policy debates.

In Chapter 14, Bruno Charbonneau and Louise Wiuff Moe compare the cases of Mali and Somalia to analyse the relationship between the doctrines of peacebuilding and counterterrorism. They argue that counterinsurgency is a form of politics that, instead of creating the conditions for peace, dictates the legitimate parameters of politics and peacebuilding practice. Interventions in Afghanistan and Iraq paved the way for a renaissance of counterinsurgency. Colonial and Cold War lessons in fighting irregular enemies were revived, while counterinsurgency was reframed and 'updated' to better align with post–Cold War normative goals related to the promotion of good governance, the rule of law, and sustainable peace. The authors analyse the political logic and effects of counterinsurgency and stabilization thinking on conflict management mechanisms and processes, and on the possibilities of conflict resolution, in Somalia and Mali by interrogating the assumptions that sustain the ideas about the use and the utility of military force. By virtue of its conceptual malleability, stabilization allows the rapprochement of peacekeeping, peacebuilding, counterinsurgency, and counterterrorism practices and doctrines. Stabilization enables and allows the link between violent coercion and enmity by supporting the host state's authority and building its security capacity, or by allowing parallel forces to implement their strategic vision of the conflict. The AU Mission in Somalia (AMISOM) has since its creation in 2007 been a significant entry point for a type of combat-orientated counterinsurgency support channelled to regional and national forces. In addition to support to the efforts directly targeting al-Shabaab, more preventive forms of counterinsurgency-inspired assistance also gained ground, drawing on democratization, peacebuilding, and resilience discourses. In Mali, almost ten years since the launching of the French operation Serval, becoming the regional operation Barkhane in 2014 with an area of operations over the G5 Sahel countries, counterinsurgency also informs international engagement in the country. In Mali, the counterterrorist emphasis has negatively impacted conflict resolution efforts and arguably made things worse. Hence, the 'global approaches' as practiced in Somalia and Mali contribute to the construction and consolidation of local and regional political orders of violence.

In Chapter 15, Festus Kofi Aubyn examines the case of The Gambia; a country that was under the rule of Yahya Jammeh for 22 years. A historic political transition happened when Adama Barrow was elected president in 2016. Unfortunately, this also led to a political stalemate that almost plunged The Gambia into civil war and resulted in January 2017 in the intervention of the Economic Community of West African States (ECOWAS). For Aubyn, the legacy of the former autocratic regime posed a set of peculiar challenges to sustaining peace in what is described as the new Gambia. The exit of Jammeh underlined a legacy of human rights abuses and institutional dysfunction as well as the problem of near-empty national coffers. Peacebuilding in this context requires tackling a broad range of issues such as SSR, constitutional and judicial reforms, socio-economic development, transitional justice, and reconciliation. International support is crucial in this process, as the ECOWAS mission played a crucial role in stabilizing the situation during the electoral stand-off. Aubyn stresses that despite regional and international efforts, the various reform processes and peacebuilding activities must be more visible, participatory, and inclusive to promote local ownership and ensure sustainable peace.

Far to the east of The Gambia, the Sudanese civil war has been one of the longest enduring in Africa. In the South Sudanese context, Kuyang Harriet Logo argues that too little attention has been given to justice and accountability, notably in holding both the Sudanese government and the Sudan People's Liberation Movement responsible for the atrocities they committed. Evidence of large-scale human rights violations prompted key stakeholders to consider the inclusion of transitional justice, especially in the form of hybrid courts in the peace agreements of 2015 and in the revitalized agreement of 2018. Logo demonstrates that while transitional justice, especially accountability for crimes, was regarded as crucial in South Sudan, the inclusion of a transitional justice agenda in peace negotiations in a context where there was no political or democratic transition to speak of was a significant mistake. It resulted in political games that had adverse effects by significantly lowering the prospects for justice. Logo also argues that in the absence of a transition process, political elites put on a façade that gives the impression that they pursue justice while undermining it.

In Chapter 17, Fiifi Edu-Afful and Ruth Adwoa Frimpong discuss one of the world's most fragile states. Since its independence from Portugal in 1974, Guinea-Bissau has suffered from frequent political upheavals. The ECOWAS Mission in Guinea-Bissau (ECOMIB) was deployed on 16 May 2012 to support the transition process. Since then, ECOMIB has supervised the conduct of a relatively peaceful elections in 2014 and has served as an effective deterrent to the political interference of the Bissau-Guinean armed forces. However, the country still faces significant challenges: authoritarian governance, difficult civil-military relations, pervasive corruption, and arms and drugs trafficking that sustain social inequalities. The chapter examines the nature and challenges of the peacebuilding initiatives that were implemented in Guinea-Bissau. Edu-Afful and Frimpong propose a hybrid model based on African perspectives and indigenous approaches to peacebuilding to consolidate peace. They argue that society-centred mechanisms of peacebuilding were effective in preventing retaliation. Geared toward instilling the values of solidarity, truth, social cohesion, and justice, these mechanisms are affordable and accessible to all conflict factions. In Guinea-Bissau, there is seemingly a consensus to remodel African peacebuilding to address historical experiences that, for most, are at the root of political discord and of the problems of the post-conflict state. Analysing the different phases of peacebuilding in Guinea-Bissau and the role of international actors in this process, the authors argue that a viable mechanism to tackle the long-standing issues is not yet in sight but that regional and international support have contributed to limited improvements.

Finally, in Chapter 18, Maxime Ricard looks into what the 'Ivorian experience' can tell us about the nature of contemporary international peacebuilding. Arising out of a political rupture after the fall of Laurent Gbagbo, international peacebuilding under Alassane Ouattara amounted to supporting a cosmetic process of reconciliation. The post-conflict Ivorian experience demonstrated that status quo aspirations are what mainly drive contemporary peacebuilding. The goal of international actors in post-conflict Côte d'Ivoire was to restore the state's authority, but they had little room to manoeuvre because the Ivorian state was not as weak as was assumed. During a nine-year process of peacebuilding and reconciliation, no substantial progress was made on fundamental problems such as the authoritarian exercise of power, widespread poverty, and vast social inequalities. What can be observed in Côte d'Ivoire is a national-international strategy, a nexus of actors and alliances constructed by Alassane Ouattara, who has demonstrated his ability to entice international support. Although the guns have been silenced in Côte d'Ivoire with the support of international actors, the post-conflict Ivorian experience demonstrates the important limits of stabilization agendas as political projects, as elites in positions of power impose a very particular vision of what peace means.

## References

Barnett, M., Kim, K., O'Donnell, M. and Sitea, L., (2007) 'Peacebuilding: What Is in a Name?', *Global Governance*, 13(1), pp. 35–58.

Charbonneau, B., (2014) 'The Imperial Legacy of International Peacebuilding: The Case of Francophone Africa', *Review of International Studies*, 40(3), pp. 607–630.

Charbonneau, B., (2017) 'Whose West Africa? The Regional Dynamics of Peace and Security', *Journal of Contemporary African Studies*, 35(4), pp. 407–414.

Curtis, D., (2012) 'The Contested Politics of Peacebuilding in Africa', in Curtis, D. and Dzinesa, G.A., (eds.) *Peacebuilding, Power, and Politics in Africa*. Athens: Ohio University Press, pp. 1–30.

Curtis, D., (2013) 'Post-conflict Peacebuilding', in Cheeseman, N., Anderson, D.M. and Scheibler, A., (eds.), *Routledge Handbook of African Politics*. New York, NY: Routledge, pp. 202–214.

De Heredia, M.I., (2018) 'The Conspicuous Absence of Class and Privilege in the Study of Resistance in Peacebuilding Contexts', *International Peacekeeping*, 25(3), pp. 325–348.

Grovogui, S.N., (2002) 'Regimes of Sovereignty: International Morality and the African Condition', *European Journal of International Relations*, 8(3), pp. 315–338.

Jackson, P., (2019) 'Peacebuilding Initiatives in Africa', *Oxford Research Encyclopedia, Politics*. [online]. Available at: Peacebuilding Initiatives in Africa | Oxford Research Encyclopedia of Politics (Accessed: 7 July 2021)

Jeng, A., (2012) *Peacebuilding in the African Union: Law, Philosophy and Practice*. Cambridge: Cambridge University Press.

Karbo, T., (2018a) 'Introduction: Towards a New *Pax Africana*', in Karbo, T. and Virk, K., (eds.) *The Palgrave Handbook of Peacebuilding in Africa*. Cham: Palgrave Macmillan, pp. 3–28.

Karbo, T., (2018b) 'Conclusion', in Karbo, T. and Virk, K., (eds.), *The Palgrave Handbook of Peacebuilding in Africa*. Cham: Palgrave Macmillan, pp. 455–465.

Khadiagala, G.M., (2013) 'Pan-Africanism and Regional Integration', in Cheeseman, N., Anderson, D.M. and Scheibler, A., (eds.) *Routledge Handbook of African Politics*. New York, NY: Routledge, pp. 375–389.

Kuwali, D., (2018) 'Squaring the Circle: The Role of the African Peace and Security Architecture', in Karbo, T. and Virk, K., (eds.) *The Palgrave Handbook of Peacebuilding in Africa*. Cham: Palgrave Macmillan, pp. 45–64.

Mazrui, A.A., (2018) 'Towards a Concept of "Pax Africana"', in Karbo, T. and Virk, K., (eds.) *The Palgrave Handbook of Peacebuilding in Africa*. Cham: Palgrave Macmillan, pp. 29–44.

McNamee, T. and Muyangwa, M., (2021) 'Introduction', in McNamee, T. and Muyangwa, M., (eds.) *The State of Peacebuilding in Africa: Lessons Learned for Policymakers and Practitioners*. Cham: Palgrave Macmillan, pp. 3–14.

Muyangwa, M. and Vogt, M., (2000) *An Assessment of the OAU Mechanism for Conflict Prevention, Management and Resolution, 1993–2000*. New York, NY: International Peace Academy.

Pugh, M., Cooper, N. and Turner, M., (eds.) (2008) *Whose Peace? Critical Perspectives on the Political Economy of Peacebuilding*. New York, NY: Palgrave Macmillan.

Smith, M.S., (eds.) (2010) *Securing Africa. Post-9/11 Discourses on Terrorism*. Farnham: Ashgate.

Tieku, T.K., (2019) 'The African Union: Successes and Failures', *Oxford Research Encyclopedia, Politics*. [online]. Available at: African Union: Successes and Failures | Oxford Research Encyclopedia of Politics (Accessed: 7 July 2021)

Wai, Z., (2018a) 'Africa in/and International Relations: An Introduction', in De Heredia, M.I. and Wai, Z., (eds.) *Recentering African in International Relations: Beyond Lack, Peripherality, and Failure*. Cham: Palgrave MacMillan, pp. 1–30.

Wai, Z., (2018b) 'International Relations and the Discourse of State Failure', in De Heredia, M.I. and Wai, Z., (eds.), *Recentering African in International Relations: Beyond Lack, Peripherality, and Failure*. Cham: Palgrave MacMillan, pp. 31–58.

Williams, P., (2021) 'Learning Lessons from Peace Operations in Africa', in McNamee, T. and Muyangwa, M., (eds.) *The State of Peacebuilding in Africa: Lessons Learned for Policymakers and Practitioners*. Cham: Palgrave Macmillan, pp. 15–32.

Woodward, S.L., (2017) *The Ideology of Failed States. Why Intervention Fails*. Cambridge: Cambridge University Press.

Zondi, S., (2017) 'African Union Approaches to Peacebuilding: Efforts at Shifting the Continent Towards Decolonial Peace', *African Journal on Conflict Resolution*, 17(1), pp. 105–131.

# PART I

# Institutions

# 1
# FROM PEACEKEEPING TO PEACEBUILDING

## Towards a UN peace continuum

*Alexandra Novosseloff*

### Introduction

During the Cold War, the UN Operation in the Congo (ONUC) between 1960 and 1964 was the only mission for which UN peacekeepers were deployed to Africa. The deployment of the UN Transition Assistance Group in Namibia in 1989–1990 signalled a change, with the UN Security Council authorizing 15 operations in Africa during the following decade. The 2000s and 2010s continued the trend with a peak in 2015, when 8 of the UN's 16 peacekeeping operations were in African countries, with a total of 96,165 uniformed and civilian personnel serving in these operations (78% of the UN personnel deployed that year). As of the end of November 2021, 6 of 12 operations were in Africa, with 74,329 uniformed personnel deployed (83.7% of the UN personnel). These operations have been very diverse, ranging from observation missions to multidimensional operations, from peacebuilding offices (UNIOGBIS[1]) to technical missions such as the one to confront Ebola outbreaks (UNMEER[2]); from regional offices (in Dakar and Libreville) to support offices for other actors (UNOAU[3] in Addis-Ababa, UNSOS[4]); and from hybrid operations (UNAMID[5]) to special political missions (Somalia) and the most recently created mission (UNITAMS[6] in Khartoum). The UN has deployed all of its tools and cooperated with a variety of stakeholders and non-UN actors such as the African Union (AU) and the European Union, sub-regional organizations such as the Economic Community of West African States (ECOWAS), and numerous governments and non-governmental actors.

With the development of the AU's crisis management mechanisms, the relationship between the AU and the UN has become considerably more important whenever crises occur on the continent, and a significant "peacekeeping partnership" (Williams and Boutellis 2014) has developed. In the beginning, African deployments, mainly oriented by the doctrine of "peace support operations," were conceived as bridging operations to UN peacekeeping missions (Côte d'Ivoire, Liberia) that had been authorized or recognized by the UN Security Council. Increasingly, however, African countries contributing troops have reinforced their commitment to UN missions deployed on the continent, acquiring training, experience, and knowledge that has allowed them to develop their own capacities. Today, African states and organizations are also involved at the political level, whether through bilateral relations, through mediation in which they play the role of special envoys, or through the deployment of small AU political offices alongside larger UN deployments. African states have integrated themselves into a partnership with the UN, not only to share the burden of peacekeeping but also to take part in the management of their own crises.

These developments have taken place in the context of the UN's own evolving doctrines and its development of tools of crisis management in a continuum that has been unclear at times but that the current secretary-general's reforms try to reinvigorate (Novosseloff 2019; Johnstone 2016). The goal of this chapter is to present the evolution of the UN's peacekeeping and peacebuilding doctrines. The focus is on the conceptual construction and evolution of the continuum of crisis management that moves between peacekeeping and peacebuilding – a continuum that expands and contracts depending on the crises that are occurring and their various contexts, and one that remains an implementation challenge for the UN system as a whole.

## The beginning of the conceptualization of a crisis management continuum in *An Agenda for Peace* and its *Supplement* (1992–1995)

Over the years and during the course of operations, the UN and its member states have sought to conceptualize and even to categorize the various types of actions that they carry out in the field, actions that have met with success or, more often, with disappointment. Although doctrines of the use of force have existed for a long time, a typology of international intervention first appeared at the end of the Cold War. It was during the 1956 Suez War that the concept of peacekeeping emerged from a new type of intervention that had well-defined principles (neutrality, consent of the host state, use of force only in self-defence) and that was mainly used for the purpose of settling interstate conflicts. The period at the end of the 1980s quickly moved beyond this initial framework. The security uncertainties generated by the "new international order" led to a multiplication of numerous types of operations (Cambodia, Bosnia-Herzegovina, Mozambique, the Western Sahara, Haiti), most of them within states rather than between states. Since then, the Security Council has continued to expand its definition of what constitutes a threat to international peace and security (UN Security Council 2014; UN Security Council 2011a).[7] In January 1992, it invited "the Secretary-General to prepare his analysis and recommendations on ways of strengthening and making more efficient within the framework and provisions of the Charter the capacity of the United Nations for preventive diplomacy, for peacemaking and for peace-keeping" (UN Security Council 1992). *An Agenda for Peace* was published on 17 June 1992 (UN General Assembly, UN Security Council 1992; UN Security Council 1993).[8]

*An Agenda for Peace* defined for the first time the various possible phases of a crisis management response. These phases correspond to the many possible types of operations that can be deployed in the field or to the numerous tools available to the UN and its member states (see Box 1.1). Thus, this document from the secretary-general paves the way for "a wider mission" for the UN (and for its national and international partners) and defines the "areas for action" that correspond to a "coherent contribution towards securing peace in the spirit of the Charter" and to a gradation of intervention options and peacemaking techniques, ranging from preventive diplomacy to peacebuilding and thus from peacemaking to peacekeeping. It was *An Agenda for Peace* that first conceptualized an integrated vision and approach to peace operations that took into consideration the fact that "peace could not be safeguarded merely through a narrow perspective confined to military issues. . . [T]he maintenance of international peace and security [is] a much wider concept, encompassing political as well as economic, social, humanitarian and environmental issues" (UN General Assembly 1992a, para. 10). *An Agenda for Peace* places particular emphasis on preventive diplomacy as "the most desirable and efficient means of easing tensions before they result in conflict" (UN General Assembly 1992b). Moreover, it attaches particular importance to cooperation with the regional agreements and organizations that are stipulated under Chapter VIII of the Charter and that complement the efforts of the UN (Boutros-Ghali 1949).[9]

Thus, *An Agenda for Peace* paved the way for the creation of parallel forces to peacekeeping operations that were in fact developing at the time, the initial one being NATO's *Sky Monitor* operation to create a no-fly zone in support of the action by the UN Protection Force (UNPROFOR) in 1992 (Resolution 781, 12 October 1992). The first of these operations to be deployed in Africa was the United Task Force (UNITAF), or Operation Restore Hope, conducted by the United States between December 1992 and May 1993 in support of the UN Operation in Somalia (UNOSOM; Novosseloff and Sharland 2019). Finally, *An Agenda for Peace* has also served as a basis of reflection for the development of the doctrines of regional organizations such as the AU. As one ACCORD[10] researcher points out, "the AU approach has benefited from this holistic approach to thinking about peace and this leads to comprehensive peace interventions" (Zondi 2017).

---

**Box 1.1   Definitions in *An Agenda for Peace***

*Preventive diplomacy* is "action to prevent disputes from arising between parties, to prevent existing disputes from escalating into conflicts and to limit the spread of the latter when they occur." It includes measures to help build confidence, improve fact-finding, provide early warnings, reinforce preventive deployments, and establish demilitarized zones.

*Peace-making* is "action to bring hostile parties to agreement, essentially through such peaceful means as those foreseen in Chapter VI of the Charter of the United Nations." It includes introducing mediation and negotiation measures for the peaceful settlement of disputes, increasing recourse to the International Court of Justice, improving the assistance provided to the victims of conflicts, using military force, signing agreements under article 43 with the help of the Military Staff Committee, and creating peace enforcement units.

*Peace-keeping* is "the deployment of a United Nations presence in the field, hitherto with the consent of all the parties concerned, normally involving United Nations military and/or police personnel and frequently civilians as well. Peace-keeping is a technique that expands the possibilities for both the prevention of conflict and the making of peace."

*Post-conflict peace-building* is an "action to identify and support structures which will tend to strengthen and solidify peace in order to avoid a relapse into conflict. Preventive diplomacy seeks to resolve disputes before violence breaks out." It can include "disarming the previously warring parties and the restoration of order, the custody and possible destruction of weapons, repatriating refugees, advisory and training support for security personnel, monitoring elections, advancing efforts to protect human rights, reforming or strengthening governmental institutions and promoting formal and informal processes of political participation." All of these activities are related to security sector reform, maintaining the rule of law, and providing support for democratization. "Preventive diplomacy is to avoid a crisis; post-conflict peace-building is to prevent a recurrence."

Although *An Agenda for Peace* is a major report of the immediate post–Cold War era and reflects the hope generated by the collapse of the bipolar world, its implementation has had little effect. The member states may have thought that the UN had the means to implement this vision of a world where the Security Council would never again "lose the collegiality indispensable to its proper functioning" and where "a strong sense of consensus and common interest" would prevail. And to a certain extent, *An Agenda for Peace* took for granted the continuation of this cooperation and the willingness of member states to act in an orderly and sequenced manner. In January 1995, the *Supplement to An Agenda for Peace* realistically pointed out a number of limitations, particularly in the area of interstate cooperation and with respect to coordination: "[T]he roles of the various players need to be carefully coordinated in an integrated approach to human security" (UN General Assembly, UN Security Council 1995, para. 81). The secretary-general recognized the UN's limitations when it comes to resolving intrastate conflicts where the consent of the parties is precarious and where the collapse of state institutions is total.

## The 2000s: crisis management as a unified whole, peacebuilding as exit strategy

In *An Agenda for Peace*, crisis management is perceived as a *continuum*, but in the Brahimi report it is seen as a unified whole. Peacebuilding is considered part of prevention, the three phases are not necessarily strictly respected, and peacebuilding actions are concomitant with peacekeeping actions. Thus, the Brahimi report takes into account the evolution of operations that are increasingly involved in establishing the rule of law.

Peacekeeping is reinforced in its principles (consent of the parties to the conflict, impartiality, the use of force in self-defence and in the defence of the mandate), but the report points to a number of factors that would make it more effective if they were in place: the existence of a peace process on which a peacekeeping operation could rely, the support of member states, and the adoption of "clear, credible and realistic mandates." The objective must be to constitute a "credible operation" and to provide the UN with the tools to achieve this objective (notably by sending forces that are better equipped and better adapted to the terrain, forces that would constitute a "credible and deterrent" presence). As for peacebuilding, it is defined as "activities undertaken on the far side of conflict to reassemble the foundations of peace and provide the tools for building on those foundations something that is more than just the absence of war." This definition is somewhat broader than the one provided in *An Agenda for Peace* because it specifies that peacebuilding now also includes "promoting conflict resolution and reconciliation techniques" (i.e. peacemaking). According to the Brahimi report, "it is the task of the operation's peacekeepers to maintain a secure local environment for peacebuilding, and the peacebuilders' task to support the political, social and economic changes that create a secure environment that is self-sustaining" (UN General Assembly, UN Security Council 2000, para. 13, 28).

Thus, peacebuilding "works by addressing the deep-rooted, structural causes of violent conflict in a comprehensive manner" (UN 2008)[11] and puts institution building at the center of its action by supporting the restoration and extension of state authority (UN Security Council 2011b). As explained by the High-Level Panel on Threats, Challenges and Change, "the core task of peacebuilding is to build effective public institutions that, through negotiations with civil society, can establish a consensual framework for governing within the rule of law" (UN General Assembly 2004). This means that while peacekeeping is multidimensional and impacts the symptoms as well as the immediate measures of security, peacebuilding focuses on structural causes and sets in place measures to help a state start on or return to the path of development.

In this sense, peacebuilding accompanies and complements peacekeeping. As a result, peacekeepers have increasingly become early peacebuilders by providing a security umbrella for other actors to act by providing complementary assistance to peacebuilding activities, by mobilizing resources for such activities, or by laying the foundations for them to be undertaken on a larger scale. In 2007, the UN Policy Committee approved a relatively vague definition according to which peacebuilding is "a range of measures aiming at reducing the risk of lapsing or relapsing into conflict by strengthening national capacities at all levels for conflict management" (UN 2008, 18). In fact, peacebuilding has become a sub-function of peacekeeping.

Because of this evolution, the concept of peacebuilding has become increasingly unclear. Mixing prevention with post-conflict operations, peacebuilding now encompasses too much and has come to be seen as a part of multidimensional peace operations, but also as something that can be detached from them. Moreover, in 2005 it finally obtained its own institutional structure through the creation of the Peacebuilding Commission, which reports to both the Security Council and the General Assembly and which has its own secretariat (since 2006, it has also had a fund that provides significant assistance to 15 African countries in the process of stabilization; UN n.d.a).[12] According to the 2008 peacekeeping doctrine, "the creation of a new United Nations peacebuilding architecture reflects a growing recognition within the international community of the linkages between the United Nations peacemaking, peacekeeping and peacebuilding roles" (UN 2008). As a result, peacebuilding has come to refer to everything that the UN can undertake to do through its operations and through the actions of its agencies, funds, and programs for stabilizing countries in crisis. Henceforth, "effective peacebuilding strategies" become indispensable for ensuring "durable peace and development" (UN Security Council 2010), and peacebuilding is primarily characterized as long-term action to avoid the recurrence of conflicts.

This goal now has an instrument, "a single intergovernmental organ dedicated to peacebuilding, empowered to monitor and pay close attention to countries at risk, ensure concerted action by donors, agencies, programs and financial institutions, and mobilize financial resources for sustainable peace" (UN General Assembly 2004, para. 225). This intergovernmental organ can also deploy "peacebuilding missions" to consolidate the gains made by previous peacekeeping operations and coordinate with the country team for a more integrated vision of what remains to be done (with the exception of Liberia in 2003 and the Central African Republic [CAR] in 2013, for some of these missions preceded the creation of the Peacebuilding Commission).[13] Examples include the UN Peacebuilding Support Office in Liberia (UNOL) from 1997 to 2003, the UN Integrated Office in Sierra Leone (UNIOSIL) from 2005 to 2008, the UN Peacebuilding Office in the CAR (BONUCA) from 2000 to 2009, UNOGBIS from 1999 to 2009, the UN Integrated Peacebuilding Office in Sierra Leone (UNIPSIL) from 2008 to 2014, and the UN Integrated Peacebuilding Support Office in the CAR (BINUCA) from 2009 to 2014. As of the end of 2020, UNIOGBIS remains the only peacebuilding mission currently deployed.

However, since 2009, the UN has felt the need to clarify the link between peacekeeping and peacebuilding and to operationalize what can be grouped together as peacebuilding activities. In June 2009, the secretary-general wrote a fairly comprehensive report (with an action plan) on "peacebuilding in the immediate aftermath of conflict" (i.e. during "the first two years after the end of major hostilities"), an activity described as "primarily the responsibility of national actors" – a characterization that fundamentally distinguishes it from peacekeeping because the latter is almost exclusively the responsibility of international bodies and partners (UN General Assembly, UN Security Council 2009). The New Horizon initiative (July 2009) then raises the issue of the necessary sequencing of the different phases of a stabilization and peacebuilding process: "Critical peacebuilding roles of UN peacekeepers must be clarified. So too, recurrent gaps and challenges to transition and exit for peacekeeping missions must be addressed" (UN 2009). However, practitioners note that "peacebuilding has become a niche activity instead of being the umbrella that unites UN operations" and that this "has led to fragmented approaches, with each UN department and agency wanting to preserve its own conceptual and operational independence" (Von der Schulenburg 2014, 1). Supporters of peacebuilding find it regrettable that unlike peacekeeping, the former has not been developed as a specific tool even though it has had an institution since 2005 to give it a tangible reality. And all the more so with peacebuilding offices increasingly "competing" with the "special" political missions that began to be developed in 2002 (with the creation of the UN Assistance Mission in Afghanistan [UNAMA]) using an integrated mission concept similar to the peacebuilding office concept.

## The 2010s: from stabilization to sustaining peace, concepts that are difficult to define

To operationalize peacebuilding, it seems to be necessary to leave it behind and invent another concept. Thus, two new concepts have emerged, stabilization and sustaining peace – concepts that attempt to replace the concept of peacebuilding without actually succeeding because it has been institutionalized since 2005. The concept of "sustainable peacebuilding" was at one point put forward, but nothing came of it (De Coning 2010). In January 2015, the secretary-general created a panel of experts to review the peacebuilding architecture, and six months later it issued a 60-page report. The panel recommended that "peacebuilding be treated as the principle that flows through all the UN's engagements: before, during and after potential or real violent conflicts" (Mahmoud and Ó Súilleabháin 2016). However, it questioned the use of the term "peacebuilding," which was perceived as referring to a purely post-conflict intervention. This is how the concept of "sustaining peace" emerged and came to be preferred, so that it also became possible to include preventive measures to stop violent conflict from occurring, the goal being to link preventive actions to consolidation actions in a conceptual whole that comprises any operations whose aim is to bring about "sustainable peace."

According to the advocates of this concept, the UN has focused too long on what causes crises and conflicts and has not paid enough attention to the building blocks of sustainable peace conceived as "the ability to manage and transform conflict in a peaceful and constructive manner." Thus,

> sustainable peace attempts to broaden the peace agenda to include proactive measures aimed at building on peace where it already exists by reinforcing the structures, attitudes, and institutions that underpin it. . . . Whereas the starting point of peacebuilding is conflict and the process is one of transitioning from war to peace, sustainable peace begins with identifying those attributes and assets that have sustained social cohesion, inclusive development, the rule of law, and human security – the factors that together contribute to a peaceful society.
> 
> *(Mahmoud and Makoond 2017)*

The concept also emphasizes the importance of "supporting national actors to develop the resilient national capacities they need to address structural inequalities, exclusion, and other drivers that undermine social cohesion, and if neglected, may over time lead to violent conflict" (De Coning 2018).

The concept of peacebuilding appears very liberal, whereas the concept of sustainable peace seems to refer more to social dimension (Mahmoud and Makoond 2018), trying to transcend the "liberal peace" categorization "to develop more nuanced and empirically informed critical approaches" (Campbell, Chandler and Sabaratnam 2011). However, although it involves a determination to bring states to the point where they no longer need international assistance, sustainable peace comes up against the operational difficulty of doing so. Thus, it is seen as a continuous process and not as a one-off intervention. In fact, the concept of sustaining peace broadens the notion of international security even further and brings crisis management closer to the sphere of development, for its creators see it as cutting across the three pillars of UN work (peace and security, human rights, and development; Rosenthal 2017), and thus they acknowledge that it has a significant connection to the UN's Sustainable Development Goals (SDGs; UN n.d.b). It continues to be a very encompassing concept that seems difficult to operationalize beyond calls, such as Resolution 2282 (27 April 2016) giving it official recognition, for greater cooperation and coordination between the different elements of the UN system, including the Bretton Woods institutions, and between the UN and different regional organizations such as the AU. Be that as it may, the Security Council now refers to the issue of "peacebuilding and sustaining peace" as if the two concepts were interchangeable.

In the meantime, the concept of stabilization has slipped into the debate from the field, but without giving rise to any real discussion. Three of the four current multidimensional peacekeeping operations include a stabilization mandate (Mali, the CAR, and the Democratic Republic of the Congo [DRC]). This concept of stabilization seems to have two interpretations at the UN. The first one is connected to the way military strategists understand security stabilization (robust military interventions). The second one is connected to civilian activities close to development in a post-conflict transition phase (technical and programmatic interventions to address the roots of conflicts) that complement traditional mediation; disarmament, demobilization, and reintegration (DDR); and security sector reform (SSR) activities within the framework of so-called integrated missions (Boutellis 2013). At the UN, stabilization is a concept that combines the extension of state authority with the use of proactive and "robust" forces, the latter having the role of protecting civilians while at the same time targeting non-state actors who challenge the state's monopoly on violence, as well as any support for the restoration of the rule of law and for the strengthening of state capacities. Thus, stabilization is supposed to address the root causes of conflict by supporting the transfer of control of territory from troublemakers to the legitimate authorities of the country (Gorur 2016; De Coning, Aoi and Karlsrud 2017; Curran and Holtom 2015). MONUSCO's[14] International Security and Stabilization Support Strategy (I4S) defines stabilization as

> a process aimed at strengthening mutual trust and legitimacy between the state and society so that they can jointly resolve or mitigate different types of conflicts. The stabilization process should change the relationship between state and society by supporting an ongoing negotiation of the respective responsibilities of state actors and communities, on the basis of which accountability and trust can begin to be built.
> *(MONUSCO n.d.; Novosseloff et al. 2019)*[15]

This suggests that stabilization is "late peacekeeping" or "early peacebuilding," but a concept that is ultimately too inclusive (Gilder 2019), for it introduces more confusion than clarity and may even undermine conflict resolution efforts.

In short, despite numerous efforts and reflection reports (notably in 2015, which is known as the "year of reviews"; Arthur 2018), the 2010s did not succeed in operationalizing the concepts of peacebuilding and sustaining peace or in conceptualizing stabilization activities on the ground in multidimensional peacekeeping operations. It is still too early to assess whether the reforms undertaken by António Guterres since he became head of the UN Secretariat in 2017 will lead to greater synergy among the different pillars of the UN (Cliffe and Gerlach 2019). Indeed, this will be the key challenge during the coming decade. African states have also understood, particularly in light of their deployment in Somalia with the AU Mission in Somalia (AMISOM; Williams 2018), that a purely military or security approach is not sufficient.

## Conclusion

Finding the way to a peace continuum seems to be *the* challenge of the decade ahead, both for the UN and for its partnerships with organizations, coalitions, and member states that act in support of or in parallel to its operations. Until the end of the Cold War, the UN was able to invent multiple tools that could be adapted to specific contexts and crises, but this way of operating seems to have been diluted during the 2000s. The UN has become accustomed to basing its response on the lead department in charge of the crisis and no longer on the context (Johnstone 2016). This approach tends to obscure the variety of tools available to the UN, which means that the idea of a continuum also loses clarity during difficult times of crisis or conflict. But this fragmentation is not merely an issue for the UN. From the Balkans to Afghanistan and from Somalia to the Sahel, three or four years of intervention have often led international actors to lose sight of their initial objectives or to fail to adapt their objectives to the evolution of the crisis or conflict, given that international intervention always changes the course of events.

It is often thought that making peace means winning the war. The evolution of UN concepts from peacekeeping to sustaining peace shows that making peace involves much more and that the silence of weapons is not synonymous with peace – certainly not with sustainable peace in any case. Therefore, it is a question of including military intervention in a more global approach and limiting the duration of the military intervention per se, for the continuum makes it possible to deal with the other aspects of the situation. As Secretary-General Guterres has pointed out, it is a matter of replacing a "crisis continuum" with a "peace continuum," which he defines in institutional terms as the product of "a comprehensive, modern and effective operational peace architecture, encompassing prevention, conflict resolution, peacekeeping, peacebuilding and long-term development" (Guterres 2016). However, this peace continuum could also be defined in temporal terms, in order to allow all the available tools to be applied within a limited time frame, according to the needs of the moment and according to the possible partnerships at a given stage of the crisis or conflict, even if the cumulative results of the various actions carried out are necessarily part of a process that takes place over a long period of time (two or three decades). For the moment, the implementation of this mechanism comes up against three essential obstacles:

- The lack of time given to resolving crises in the totality of their different aspects and to passing the baton by way of the necessary transition to peacebuilding;
- The lack of modesty in the ambitions attributed to this or that instrument or organization, a lack of modesty that leads to a constant discrepancy between the mandates assigned and the resources available; and
- The desire of the various actors to keep the visibility of their activities or actions to themselves, a practice that inevitably undermines the overall coherence of operations and that too often makes efforts to improve coordination and share the burden or the tasks between organizations pointless.[16]

These three aspects of crisis management require deeper reflection, for the continuum also implies giving a clear role to each of the actors involved and first of all to the UN, which is sometimes faced with the more visible military interventions undertaken by others. Indeed, the objective is to align the temporal with the functional so that international interventions can achieve greater effectiveness and so that some of the technical difficulties related to making peace can be at least partially resolved.

## Notes

1 UN Integrated Peacebuilding Office in Guinea-Bissau.
2 UN Mission for Ebola Emergency Response.
3 UN Office to the African Union.
4 UN Support Office in Somalia.
5 UN-AU Hybrid Operation in Darfur.
6 UN Integrated Transition Assistance Mission in Sudan.
7 With Resolution 2177 (September 18, 2014), the Council considered that "the extraordinary scale of the Ebola epidemic in Africa constitutes a threat to international peace and security." With regard to the impact of climate change, the Council, in a presidential statement of July 20, 2011, only "expressed concern that the possible adverse effects of climate change may, in the long term, aggravate existing threats to international peace and security."
8 Between June 1992 and May 1993, the Security Council considered the report and recommended that "all States make participation in and support for international peacekeeping operations an integral part of their foreign and national security policies."
9 This theme was at the heart of Boutros Boutros-Ghali's doctoral thesis in law.
10 African Centre for the Constructive Resolution of Disputes.
11 Defined by the 2008 doctrine (*Peacekeeping Operations: Principles and Guidance*), which also considers that the achievement of a sustainable peace requires progress in at least four critical areas: (1) restoring the state's ability to provide security and maintain public order; (2) strengthening the rule of law and respect for human rights; (3) supporting the emergence of legitimate political institutions and participatory processes; and (4) promoting social and economic recovery and development, including the safe return or resettlement of internally displaced persons and refugees uprooted by conflict.
12 See the website of the Peacebuilding Fund (www.un.org/peacebuilding/fund).
13 Some of these missions were led by an executive representative of the secretary-general (ERSG) who served as both resident coordinator and head of the UN Development Programme (UNDP).
14 UN Organization Stabilization Mission in the Democratic Republic of the Congo.
15 For further discussion on that concept in MONUSCO, see MONUSCO, "International Security and Stabilization Support Strategy, 2013–2017." Available at: https://monusco.unmissions.org/sites/default/files/1._issss_2013-2017_document_entier_-_copy.pdf.
16 The special representative of the secretary-general has often been assigned on paper the role of coordinator of the international political vision enshrined in Security Council resolutions, without having given the special representative the means or the necessary authority on the ground to carry out this mission. This role is all the more crucial given the number of organizations.

## References

Arthur, P., (2018) 'The Secretary-General's Sustaining Peace Report – The Peacebuilding Fund Gets a Boost', *NYU Center on International Cooperation*, 2 March.
Boutellis, A., (2013) 'Driving the System Apart? A Study of United Nations Integration and Integrated Strategic Planning', *International Peace Institute*, 28 August. [online]. Available at: Driving the System Apart? A Study of United Nations Integration and Integrated Strategic Planning | International Peace Institute (ipinst.org) (Accessed: 19 May 2021).
Boutros-Ghali, B., (1949) *Contribution à l'étude des ententes régionales*. PhD thesis. University of Paris.
Campbell, S., Chandler, D. and Sabaratnam, M., (eds.) (2011) *A Liberal Peace? The Problems and Practices of Peacebuilding*. London: Zed Books.

Cliffe, S. and Gerlach, K., (2019) 'UN Reforms – A Major Step Forward January 1, but Some Challenges Still to Overcome', *NYU Center on International Cooperation*, 28 January.

Curran, A. and Holtom, P., (2015) 'Resonating, Rejecting, Reinterpreting: Mapping the Stabilization Discourse in the United Nations Security Council, 2000–14', *Stability: International Journal of Security & Development*, 4(1), pp. 1–18.

De Coning, C., (2010) 'Clarity, Coherence and Context – Three Priorities for Sustainable Peacebuilding', *Working Paper*, NUPI, University of Ottawa.

De Coning, C., (2018) 'Sustaining Peace: Can a New Approach Change the UN?', *IPI Global Observatory*, 24 April.

De Coning, C., Aoi, C. and Karlsrud, J., (dir.) (2017) *UN Peacekeeping Doctrine in a New Era: Adapting to Stabilisation, Protection and New Threats*. London. Routledge.

Gilder, A., (2019) 'The Effect of "Stabilization" in the Mandates and Practice of UN Peace Operations', *Netherlands International Law Review*, 66(1), pp. 47–73.

Gorur, A., (2016) *Defining the Boundaries of UN Stabilization Missions*. Washington, DC: Stimson Center Report.

Guterres, A., (2016) *Vision Statement: Challenges and Opportunities for the United Nations*. [online]. Available at: Vision statement – António Guterres (antonioguterres.gov.pt) (Accessed: 19 May 2021).

Johnstone, I., (2016) 'Between Bureaucracy and Adhocracy: Crafting A Spectrum of Un Peace Operations', *Global Peace Operations Review*, 31 March.

Mahmoud, Y. and Makoond, A., (2017) 'Sustaining Peace: What Does it Mean in Practice?', *International Peace Institute*, 8 April.

Mahmoud, Y. and Ó Súilleabháin, S., (2016) 'With New Resolutions, Sustaining Peace Sits at Heart of UN Architecture', *IPI Global Observatory*, 29 April.

MONUSCO, (n.d.) *International Security and Stabilization Support Strategy, 2013–2017*. [online]. Available at: https://monusco.unmissions.org/sites/default/files/1._issss_2013-2017_document_entier_-_copy.pdf (Accessed: 19 May 2021).

Novosseloff, A., (2019) 'A Year of Reflection and Transition: Peace Operations in 2019', *Global Peace Operations Review*, NYU Center on International Cooperation.

Novosseloff, A. and Sharland, L., (2019) 'Partners and Competitors: Forces Operating in Parallel to UN Peace Operations', *International Peace Institute*, 4 November.

Novosseloff, A. et al., (2019) *Assessing the Effectiveness of the UN Missions in the DRC (MONUC-MONUSCO)*. Oslo: Norwegian Institute of International Affairs, p. 129.

Rosenthal, G., (2017) 'Reflections on the Meaning of "Sustaining Peace"', *IPI Global Observatory*, 17 July.

United Nations (UN), (n.d.a) *Countries Declared Eligible to the PBF by the Secretary-General, United Nations*. [online]. Available at: www.un.org/peacebuilding/content/list-pbf-countries-declared-eligible (Accessed: 19 May 2021).

United Nations (UN), (n.d.b) *The 17 Goals*. [online]. Available at: THE 17 GOALS | Sustainable Development (un.org) (Accessed: 19 May 2021).

United Nations, (2008) *United Nations Peacekeeping Operations: Principles and Guidelines*. New York, NY: United Nations.

United Nations, (2009) *A New Partnership Agenda: Charting a New Horizon for UN Peacekeeping*. New York, NY: United Nations.

United Nations General Assembly, (1992a) *Special Report of the Special Committee on Peacekeeping Operations*. A/47/386. New York, NY: United Nations.

United Nations General Assembly, (1992b) *Resolution Adopted by the General Assembly 47/120 A. An Agenda for Peace: Preventive Diplomacy and Related Matters*. New York, NY: United Nations.

United Nations General Assembly, (2004) *A More Secure World: Our Shared Responsibility. Report of the High-level Panel on Threats, Challenges and Change*. A/59/565. New York, NY: United Nations.

United Nations General Assembly, United Nations Security Council, (1992) *An Agenda for Peace: Preventive Diplomacy, Peacemaking, and Peace-keeping. Report of the Secretary General Pursuant to the Statement Adopted by the Summit Meeting of the Secretary Council on 31 January 1992*. A/47/277 – S/24111. New York, NY: United Nations.

United Nations General Assembly, United Nations Security Council, (1995) *Supplement to An Agenda for Peace: Position Paper of the Secretary-General on the Occasion of the Fiftieth Anniversary of the United Nations*. A/50/60 – S/1995/1. New York, NY: United Nations.

United Nations General Assembly, United Nations Security Council, (2000) *Report of the Panel on United Nations Peace Operations*. A/55/305 – S/2000/809. New York, NY: United Nations.

United Nations General Assembly, United Nations Security Council, (2009) *Report of the Secretary-General on Peacebuilding in the Immediate Aftermath of Conflict, A/63/881-S/2009/304*. New York, NY: United Nations.

United Nations Security Council, (1992) *Note by the President of the Security Council. S/23500*. New York, NY: United Nations.

United Nations Security Council, (1993) *Note by the President of the Security Council. S/25859*. New York, NY: United Nations.

United Nations Security Council, (2010) *Statement by the President of the Security Council. S/PRST/2010/7*. New York, NY: United Nations.

United Nations Security Council, (2011a) *Statement of the President of the Security Council. S/PRST-2011/1S*. New York, NY: United Nations.

United Nations Security Council, (2011b) *Statement by the President of the Security Council. S/PRST/2011/2*. New York, NY: United Nations.

United Nations Security Council, (2014) *Resolution 2177 [on Outbreak of the Ebola Virus in, and its Impact on, West Africa]*. New York, NY: United Nations.

Von der Schulenburg, M., (2014) 'Rethinking Peacebuilding: Transforming the UN Approach', *International Peace Institute*, 16 September.

Williams, P.D., (2018) *Assessing the Effectiveness of the African Union Mission in Somalia (AMISOM)*. Oslo: EPON/NUPI, p. 107.

Williams, P.D. and Boutellis, A., (2014) 'Partnership peacekeeping: Challenges and opportunities in the United Nations – African Union Relationship', *African Affairs*, 113(451), pp. 254–278.

Zondi, S., (2017) 'African Union Approaches to Peacebuilding', *ACCORD*, 12 October. [online]. Available at: www.accord.org.za/ajcr-issues/african-union-approaches-peacebuilding/ (Accessed: 19 May 2021).

# 2
# THE UNITED NATIONS AND THE AFRICAN UNION

## Partners or Rivals in Peace Operations?

*Arthur Stein and Marie-Joëlle Zahar*[1]

### Introduction

Contemporary African peacebuilding and peacekeeping feature a prominent dyad: the United Nations (UN) and the African Union (AU). Both are concerned by – and directly involved in – the search for peace, security, and development on the continent. However, even as they share similar concerns, their collaboration has neither been automatic nor easy. Ever since the failure of the UN Operation in Somalia (UNOSOM), voices in Africa have criticized UN engagement in peacekeeping and peacebuilding. These criticisms gave prominence to the phrase "African solutions to African problems," which captures the intuition that continental ownership of solutions is a requisite for their success and sustainability. On the other hand, the AU's challenges with mobilizing sufficient human and material resources to manage all of the peacekeeping and peacebuilding needs on the continent has meant that, much as the UN may have had shortcomings, the two organizations are destined to work together.

Although the UN and the AU share a "multi-dimensional and maturing relationship based on the comparative advantages of each institution" (Williams and Boutellis 2014, 256), different sources of tensions remain that sometimes hinder the effectiveness of pacification efforts. This chapter provides an analytical overview of the state of UN-AU cooperation. We argue that, although the UN and the AU have learned to recognize and make better use of each other's comparative advantages, operational and structural constraints continue to stand in the way of a real synergy in their efforts to achieve sustainable peace on the continent. The chapter opens with a brief overview of the history of UN and AU collaboration on peacekeeping and peacebuilding. It then turns to a discussion of the ways in which this collaboration has improved, followed by an analysis of unresolved operational and structural constraints. The chapter concludes with a reflection on the future of the cooperation, particularly in light of recent positive (Action for Peacekeeping) and negative (US retrenchment from the UN under the Trump administration, the impact of the COVID-19 pandemic) developments and with a set of policy recommendations.

### UN-AU Collaboration: A Brief Historical Overview

At the end of the Cold War, the unprecedented willingness of UN Security Council (UNSC) members to cooperate on matters of international peace and security translated into a growth in the number of UN-led peace operations. Increasingly, however, the organization deployed missions in unfamiliar settings, in civil rather than interstate wars, and took on a multiplicity of roles beyond the strict separation of combatants and observation of ceasefires which tested the fundamentals of UN peacekeeping (Howard 2008; Bellamy, Williams and Griffin 2010). Failures in Bosnia and Rwanda, among others, underlined the limits of UN peacekeeping and prompted the organization to review its practices. Led by UN Under-Secretary-General Lakhdar Brahimi, the 2000 Report of the Panel on United Nations Peace Operations (2000) (also called the Brahimi report) "urged improvements in strategy and doctrine, planning and management of operations, and rapid and effective deployment" (Holt and Shanahan 2005, 10). Yet, as Holt and Shanahan (2005) write, developing collaboration with regional organizations was not natural. Not only was the UN "not designed to support peace operations led or run by other multinational organizations," the Brahimi report

> offered a mere paragraph on this topic, succinctly urging more cooperation with regional organizations. The Panel . . . cautioned that many war-torn regions were unlikely to have their own robust peace operations capacities. It therefore recognized that training, equipment, logistics and resources would be needed for regional and subregional organizations to participate in UN-led missions or to conduct their own operations.

Notwithstanding the Brahimi report's cautious tone, the AU, which was established in July 2002, put matters of peace and security at the heart of its Constitutive Act. Unlike its predecessor, the Organization of African Unity, the AU established the right to "intervene in a Member State pursuant to a decision of the Assembly in respect to grave circumstances, namely: war crimes, genocide and crimes against humanity" (African Union 2000, art. 4[h]) and "the right of Member States to request intervention from the Union in order to restore peace and security" (African Union 2000, art. 4[j]). The AU also established an equivalent to the UN's peace and security institutions. An institutional framework "through which the AU and its member states envisaged to give practical application to the ideal of 'African solutions to African problems'" (Dersso 2012, 12), the African Peace and Security Architecture (APSA) included an innovative Peace and Security Council (AU PSC), a direct regional counterpart to the UNSC which became fully operational in 2004. For the AU, the launch of the APSA marked "an historic watershed in Africa's progress towards resolving its conflicts and the building of a durable peace and security order" (African Union 2004). Noteworthy is the fact that, instead of using the UN Charter's distinction between Chapters VI and VII, the AU put forward the notion of Peace Support Operations (PSOs) that "encompasses a spectrum of operations that is not defined by the level of force, impartiality, or consent, but rather by function and purpose" (De Coning 2017, 149). Almost immediately after the APSA was established, the UN General Assembly called for strengthening cooperation with the newborn AU PSC and other African organs. The General Assembly called for such regional entities to be willfully supported "in their efforts to resolve and prevent conflicts at the sub-regional and continental levels" (Weiss and Welz 2014, 891). Whereas in April 2003, the AU Mission in Burundi (AMIB) became the very first operation fully devised and executed by AU member states (Murithi 2008), in 2005 UN members approved "a ten-year AU capacity-building plan that would be supported by the UN" (Makubalo 2019, 1).

Over the years, the AU became the UN's "partner of choice" in Africa (De Coning 2017, 146). "Subcontracting" operations to regional organizations was the pattern favored by the UN in the first years of collaboration, but more complex relations developed over time. The UN increasingly deployed "missions in sequence, in parallel, or engage[d] in some degree of joint planning, shared resourcing and integrated implementation" (Spandler 2020, 187). If UN-AU collaboration in the management of peace and security in Africa has quantitatively increased over the years, the quality of the relationship has fluctuated at both the operational (where collaboration necessitates strong information-sharing and task-sharing frameworks) and strategic/institutional levels (where the main orientations for conflict resolution and peace operations are devised). Prominent and oft-cited examples of successful cooperation, as in Somalia (2009–2015), are counterbalanced by episodes of tension and acrimony, as evidenced by the transitions between AU and UN missions in Mali (2013) and the Central African Republic (CAR; 2014).

## Praxis Makes Perfect? Assessing Progress in UN-AU Cooperation

Following the 2005 World Summit, UN Secretary-General Kofi Annan and the chairperson of the AU Commission, Alpha Oumar Konaré, signed in Addis Ababa, on 16 November 2006, a declaration titled "Enhancing UN-AU Cooperation: Framework for the Ten-Year Capacity-Building Programme for the African Union." Building on previous agreements between the two organizations, the declaration reflected

> the common commitment of the United Nations and the African Union to maintaining peace and human security, promoting human rights and post-conflict reconstruction and advancing Africa's development and regional integration. . . [and] provides a holistic framework for United Nations system-wide support to the capacity-building efforts of the AU Commission and African subregional organizations (the regional economic communities).
>
> *(Annan 2006)*

The declaration was soon followed by a UN General Assembly resolution on cooperation between the UN and the AU (UN General Assembly 2007). However, it is UNSC Resolution 1809 (UN Security Council 2008) which would get the ball rolling by putting the issue of AU-UN cooperation on the Security Council agenda and thus kickstarting the development of policy frameworks to structure bilateral cooperation between the two organizations.

In parallel, the growing partnership between the UNSC and the AU PSC, as well as the varied operational collaborations in the field between UN and AU missions, established a number of practices, "socially meaningful patterns of action, which, in being performed more or less competently, simultaneously embody, act out, and possibly reify background knowledge and discourse in and on the material world" (Adler and Pouliot 2011, 119, 4). While sometimes halting and difficult, UN-AU cooperation in the management of peace and security on the continent has therefore scored noticeable progress at both operational and institutional levels. It is to a discussion of this progress that we now turn.

### *Operational Cooperation in the Field: The Logic of Comparative Advantage*

Progress in UN-AU operational cooperation is observable not only in peacekeeping but also in peacebuilding and, increasingly, in conflict management and conflict prevention settings. The growth of the collaboration has generally been explained as the result of each organization recognizing its strengths and weaknesses when it comes to establishing and preserving long-term peace in Africa. The UN's peacekeeping missions of the 1990s and the early African peacekeeping deployment experiences have indeed demonstrated that neither the UN nor the AU "could address Africa's peacekeeping burden effectively" (Williams and Boutellis 2014, 269), and that one's advantages are often the other's disadvantages.

On the one hand, as acknowledged in multiple UN reports, UN missions are "often poorly suited" to intervene when armed conflict is ongoing. This is partially a function of the principles of UN peacekeeping, which require missions to rely on the consent of the parties, be impartial, and limit the use of force to self-protection and protection of the mandate (UN 2015, 10). Even though the UN has increasingly moved away from Chapter VI operations and adopted a more robust stance under Chapter VII (Capstone doctrine 2008), the use of force remains difficult. UN involvement in peace enforcement or counterterrorism remains the exception rather than the norm as operations that clearly fall outside the UN founding ethos and traditional missions' scope (Karlsrud 2019; De Coning 2017). When there is no ceasefire or formal peace agreement – the basis of consent-based UN interventions – the UN has little choice but to allow the integration of regional partners (De Coning 2017). The inner workings of the UN also mean that the organization lacks the requisite adaptability and responsiveness to intervene quickly in a conflict (Nathan 2017). The UN's ability to respond to emerging crises is systematically curtailed, among others, by the time needed to build consensus in the Security Council to vote a resolution to establish a new mission and by the time needed, after a mission is established, to seek out troop-contributing countries (TCCs) and negotiate status of forces agreements (SOFAs).[2]

On the other hand, whereas the AU has accepted to steadily assume greater responsibility for maintaining peace in Africa, and while it certainly has the legitimacy to do so, the organization still lacks the material and organizational capabilities necessary to design and implement fully independent peace operations. Indeed, "the complexity and significant costs involved in planning, deploying, sustaining and withdrawing these operations" have persistently forced the AU to rely on external support "in the areas of training, equipment, logistics and enabling capabilities as well as financial support" (Wilén and Williams 2018, 677).

Given their respective and somewhat complementary shortcomings, both organizations acknowledge that it is in their short-term strategic interest to cooperate in the management of peace and security. The logic of comparative advantage has led to a functional division of operational tasks and to the steady development of an ad hoc sequential model of intervention. Where the UN is not willing or immediately able to deploy peacekeeping operations, the AU has acted "as the first responder to stabilize outbreaks of violent conflicts" (De Coning 2017, 146). Indeed, the AU's ability to rapidly deploy a large number of troops from neighboring African countries puts it in the best position to intervene as soon as violence occurs. When open hostilities are under control, the operations are "transferred to the UN for the peace consolidation phase," following a formal authorization from the UNSC (De Coning 2017, 146). Most of the time, the deployment of the UN mission involves the "rehatting" of AU peacekeepers who become UN peacekeepers, thus assuring the continuity of the missions (De Coning 2017, 154). Often determined on a case-by-case basis, this synergistic division of work has been seen in various recent cases.[3] In Mali, the AU deployed an African-Led International Support Mission (AFISMA) in 2012, which transferred authority to the UN Multidimensional Integrated Stabilization Mission in Mali (MINUSMA) in 2013. The African-led International Support Mission to the CAR (MISCA) likewise transferred authority to the UN Multidimensional Integrated Stabilization Mission in the CAR (MINUSCA) in 2014.

Not only have the AU and the UN developed an ad hoc sequential model of intervention, but a functional division of labor has also been established whereby AU forces have taken on counterinsurgency and counterterrorism efforts while the UN has shouldered responsibility for stabilization missions, even where such efforts are conducted in parallel, as is the case in Somalia. This division of labor does not only reflect differences in UN and AU principles of engagement. It also reflects differences between policies on authority, command, and control. Whereas UN policies requires TCCs to devolve full operational authority unto the UN, in an AU context both "civilian leadership and military command can range on a spectrum from a lead-nation approach [. . .] to a more networked approach" (De Coning 2017, 152).[4]

The oft-cited example of this synergistic and pragmatic collaboration is the UN Support Office for AMISOM (UNSOA). In Somalia, the UN and the AU acknowledged that their complementarity created a strategic interest in collaborating with one another. Recognizing that it would be "extremely difficult to launch a UN peacekeeping operation" in the conflict-riven East African country, the UN elected to empower regional actors that it felt were better equipped to create the prerequisite conditions for a proper UN peacekeeping mission in the long term (Wondemagegnehu and Kebede 2017, 205). The AU, for its part, needed logistical support to sustain its peacebuilding efforts in the country. Operating from 2009 to 2015, UNSOA was a UN-led operation mainly intended to provide "non-lethal support" ("food and water, fuel, transport, tents and medical support") to the AU Mission in Somalia (AMISOM) troops fighting al-Shabaab (New Humanitarian 2014). While challenges undoubtedly affected its effectiveness, UNSOA "overall produced positive results" and is often regarded as a successful example of operational synergy on the ground (Williams 2017, 1). UN-AU cooperation allowed the local government to regain swaths of territory from al-Shabaab, and in its public communication, the UN hailed the experience as a demonstration of success in "one of the world's most complex, challenging and cost-effective peace enforcement operations" (Kay 2015).

Before we move on to a discussion of institutional cooperation at the policy level, it is important to highlight that the development of UN-AU cooperation has also been facilitated by a parallel development which coincided with the establishment of the APSA: the implementation of a variety of capacity-building programs and the establishment of peacekeeping training schools, such as the Kofi Annan International Peacekeeping Training Centre in Ghana and the École de maintien de la paix Alioun Blondin Baye in Mali. Although criticized for catering more to the interests of donor countries (Franke and Esmenjaud 2008) and for promoting Western visions that neglect local reception of these values (Eriksen 2009), the strong focus of these programs on military training has contributed to the development of shared practices that have improved the interoperability between African TCCs and other, primarily Western TCCs in peace operations.

## *A Growing Institutional Cooperation at Higher Levels*

Since it was placed on the agenda of the UN Security Council, the UN-AU partnership has grown significantly and become more institutionalized. Unlike operational collaboration, which is "a mission-to-mission cooperation," institutional partnership requires "long-term efforts between secretariats of the organizations concerned on issues related to mission preparation and management" (Yamashita 2012, 167). Formal mechanisms and stable structures to share information and devise joint operations must be established to give a sense of stability to the relationship. Although not yet fully fleshed out, the institutionalization of UN-AU cooperation has taken three main forms in the last decade: the development of joint frameworks, the routinization of joint meetings, and the creation of new institutions.

The first indicator of deepening UN-AU institutional partnership is the development of common guidelines and principles for enhanced coordination and cooperation. Since the 2006 declaration enhancing UN-AU cooperation (UN General Assembly 2006), the institutionalization of the UN-AU partnership is illustrated first in the quantity and frequency of official documents reaffirming and framing the collaboration and cooperation between the two organizations: six Security Council Resolutions, a 2013 report of the chairperson of the Commission on the AU-UN Partnership,[5] five yearly reports of the UN secretary-general (starting in 2016), a number of Security Council presidential statements, General Assembly resolutions, and other similar milestones (see Table 2.1). These culminated in the 2017 adoption of the Joint UN-AU Framework for an Enhanced Partnership in Peace Operations, a framework of joint action on the full spectrum of conflict management through collaboration, cooperation, and financing signed on 19 April 2017, during the first UN-AU Annual Conference.

Table 2.1 List of key UN documents pertaining to cooperation with the AU since 2006

| | |
|---|---|
| *Report of the Secretary-General* on strengthening the partnership between the United Nations and the African Union on issues of peace and security in Africa, including the work of the United Nations Office to the African Union (S/2020/860) | 31 August 2020 |
| *Report of the Secretary-General* on strengthening the partnership between the United Nations and the African Union on issues of peace and security in Africa, including the work of the United Nations Office to the African Union (S/2019/759) | 19 September 2019 |
| *Security Council Resolution* 2457 (2019) | |
| *Report of the Secretary-General* on strengthening the partnership between the United Nations and the African Union on issues of peace and security in Africa, including the work of the United Nations Office to the African Union (S/2018/678) | 6 July 2018 |
| *Security Council Resolution* 2378 (2017) | |
| *Report of the Secretary-General* on strengthening the partnership between the United Nations and the African Union on issues of peace and security in Africa, including the work of the United Nations Office to the African Union (S/2017/744) | 30 August 2017 |
| *Report of the Secretary-General* on options for authorization and support for African Union peace support operations (S/2017/454) | 26 May 2017 |
| *Joint United Nations–African Union Framework for Enhanced Partnership in Peace and Security* | 19 April 2017 |
| *Security Council Resolution* 2320 (2016) | |
| *Report of the joint African Union–United Nations review* of available mechanisms to finance and support AU peace support operations authorised by the UN Security Council (S/2016/809) | 28 September 2016 |
| *First annual report of the Secretary-General* on strengthening the partnership between the United Nations and the African Union on issues of peace and security in Africa, including the work of the United Nations Office to the African Union (S/2016/780) | 13 September 2016 |
| *Report of the Secretary-General* on the future of United Nations peace operations: implementation of the recommendations of the High-level Independent Panel on Peace Operations (A/70/357-S/2015/682) | 2 September 2015 |
| *Report of the High-level Independent Panel on Peace Operations* on uniting our strengths for peace: politics, partnership and people (A/70/95-S/2015/446) | 17 June 2015 |

(*Continued*)

Table 2.1 (Continued)

| | |
|---|---|
| Security Council Presidential Statement 27 (2014) | |
| Security Council Resolution 2167 (2014) | |
| General Assembly resolution on cooperation between the United Nations and the African Union (A/RES/67/302) | 1 October 2013 |
| General Assembly resolution on the implementation of the recommendations contained in the report of the Secretary-General on the causes of conflict and the promotion of durable peace and sustainable development in Africa (A/RES/66/287) | 10 August 2012 |
| Security Council Resolution 2033 (2012) | |
| Budget for the United Nations Office to the African Union (A/64/762) | 30 April 2010 |
| Report of the African Union—United Nations panel on modalities for support to African Union peacekeeping operations (A/63/666; S/2008/813) | 31 December 2008 |
| Security Council Presidential Statement 3 | 18 March 2009 |
| Secretary-General's report to the Security Council on the relationship between the United Nations and regional organizations, in particular the African Union in the maintenance of international peace and security (S/2008/186) | 24 March 2008 |
| Security Council Resolution 1809 (2008) | |
| General Assembly resolution on cooperation between the United Nations and the African Union (A/RES/61/296) | 5 October 2007 |
| Letter from the Secretary-General addressed to the President of the General Assembly and Declaration Enhancing UN-AU Cooperation: Framework for the Ten-Year Capacity Building Programme for the African Union (A/61/630) | 11 December 2006 |

Source: https://dppa.un.org/en/african-union, accessed 3 May 2021.

The UN's Department of Peacebuilding and Political Affairs (DPPA), which leads the cooperation between the two organizations in the area of peace and security, seeks to "align and coordinate the work of the United Nations and the African Union in the area of peace and security so that their efforts become more efficient and effective in Africa" (UN Political and Peacebuilding Affairs n.d.). DPPA works with the AU Peace and Security Department and the AU Department of Political Affairs in line with the UN's 2030 Agenda, the AU's Agenda 2063 (African Union 2015),[6] and the AU's peace and security (African Union n.d.) and governance (Mccoy 2020) architectures. Thus, not only have the two organizations developed joint frameworks for action but these frameworks have expanded beyond the narrow scope of peace operations to cover both conflict resolution (including mediation) and peacebuilding. Indeed, the UN and AU have also developed joint efforts in the areas of mediation and election management. Institutionally, cooperation in mediation

> has comprised the reinforcement of the mediation capacity of the AU Commission, including support for the secretariat and the work of the Panel of the Wise, development of strategic mediation guidance, as well as documentation of mediation experiences and practices through "lessons learned" exercises.
> 
> *(UN Political and Peacebuilding Affairs n.d.)*

As was the case with peace operations, cooperation in the area of mediation began out of necessity, as the UN found itself increasingly engaged in joint mediation efforts or in support roles to regional and subregional organizations and states.[7]

The second indicator of deepening UN-AU institutional partnership is the routinization of consultative practices, chief among which are regular joint meetings. Initially made necessary by the requirements of operational cooperation in the field, regular joint meetings have provided UN and AU representatives with the opportunity to exchange views and consult one another on matters of peace and security in Africa, at different levels of the organizations' hierarchical structures (Welz 2016).

Three main institutional mechanisms have specifically been devised to help the two organizations align strategic positions and work together effectively (Forti and Singh 2019). Since 2007, an annual joint consultative meeting between members of the UNSC and the AU PSC enables the UN secretary-general and AU Commission chairperson to exchange on topics related to the maintenance of international peace and security in Africa (Forti and Singh 2019). Since 2008, a senior-level biannual Joint Task Force on peace and security brings together UN DPPA, Department of Peace Operations (DPO), and Department of Support (DOS) officials with their AU counterparts for information sharing, coordination, and cooperation in responding to regional political developments. Likewise, regular director-level video conferences and desk-to-desk exchanges enable officials to regularly discuss conflict prevention and management (Forti and Singh 2019; UN Political and Peacebuilding Affairs n.d.). The routinization of joint meetings amounts to continuous mechanisms of coordination. The desk-to-desk meetings, the Joint Task Force and the Annual Conference provide a "cohesive," multilevel approach to inter-organizational collaboration: desk-to-desk meetings lay "the groundwork for joint analysis and identify possibilities for improving joint interventions," the Joint Task Force hosts "discussions that are more sensitive or require additional political direction," and "the most sensitive and complex issues" are dealt with during the Annual Conference (Forti and Singh 2019, 16).

The third indicator of deepening UN-AU institutional partnership, and probably the most explicit and formal one, has been the UN's 2010 decision to create the UNOAU. Located in the AU headquarters in Addis Ababa, the office, which has approximately 50 staff members, plays "an important operational role in supporting the planning and management of AU peace operations" (Williams and Dersso 2015, 4). The office embodies the recognition that stable synergy, rather than ad hoc mechanisms, is required to improve peace and security prospects in Africa. Reflective of this recognition, UNOAU was given greater institutional importance in 2013, when the head of the office was granted the status of UN under-secretary-general, and its Political Affairs Section saw its institutional role upgraded (Weiss and Welz 2014). For its part, the AU has also established a permanent representation at UN headquarters in New York, the AU Permanent Observer Mission to the UN (AUPOM). Although less endowed in terms of human and material resources than its UN counterpart, the AUPOM has approximately 15 permanent staff in New York and it still plays an important role in ensuring continuous and stable working relationships between the two organizations (Forti and Singh 2019).

Altogether, the development of joint frameworks, the routinization of contacts, and the establishment of the UNOAU and AUPOM have contributed to quotidian socialization of UN and AU staff members, a daily socialization deepened by increasing opportunities for joint training and deployments which are at least as if not more important than high-level meetings for collaboration on conflict prevention and crisis management. While observers note that progress in this matter "is uneven and varies depending on the file and individual relationships" (Forti and Singh 2019, 16), these instruments have nevertheless been important vectors of socialization and the interpersonal relations that they have contributed to developing are considered as "the fulcrum of UN-AU engagement" (Forti and Singh 2019, 19).

Thus, the UN and the AU are increasingly "linked together by mutual resource constraints which are material (lack of funding) or social (deviating peacekeeping doctrines, willingness to take, or avoid risks)" (Brosig 2017a, 461), and their collaboration has indeed recorded "incremental progress" in recent years. Yet, critics note that their relationship remains undefined in terms of distribution of responsibilities (Yamashita 2012, 182). Both organizations still "coexist in a loosely defined manner that requires voluntary coordination" with no clear framework defining the real nature of their bonds (De Coning 2017, 155). The UN tends to conceive (and label) the collaboration in terms of "subsidiarity," whereas the AU prefers to speak of "complementarity" (Welz 2016, 570). As outlined in the next section, this is more than a semantic difference. It has real implications for the future of the UN-AU partnership and for current peace prospects in Africa.

## The Persistence of Structural Constraints on Cooperation

Despite the progress recorded in the past ten years, structural constraints continue to hamper the UN-AU partnership on peace and security. These constraints have been variously identified as differences in the willingness to take risks (with the UN being risk averse and the AU being risk acceptant) and in the definition of security, asymmetric capabilities, geopolitical disagreements, and ongoing competition over leadership in the management of peace and security (Weiss and Welz 2014; Brosig and Motsamai 2014). Structural constraints affect both operational cooperation and higher-level institutional cooperation, blocking the development of stable collaboration.

### *Operational Impediments in the Field*

Operational cooperation was earlier described as an ad hoc pragmatic division of labor building on comparative advantages. Often based on need, this collaboration has been hampered by doctrinal differences translating into diverging and sometimes incompatible intervention frameworks, as alluded to in the historic overview above. In addition, despite the slow but steady development of joint frameworks, other impediments to deepened cooperation remain.

That the UN and the AU jointly approve the deployment of missions does not mean that there is agreement on "enforceable sets of rules and norms that define how cooperation is to occur, and what the consequences of defecting from agreed-upon rules should be" (Albrecht and Cold-Ravnkilde 2020, 205). As discussed above, most joint operations are designed to provide a quick response to strategic imperatives in the shadow of violence. While some violent outbreaks might be more predictable than others, their timing is often difficult to pinpoint with any accuracy. Hence the sui generis nature of the response. Devised in urgency, in a context where the UN is not willing or able to authorize a traditional peacekeeping operation (as was the case in Burundi), these event-driven operations do not lend themselves to advance planning. As Paul Williams and Arthur Boutellis (2014) remark, while this may have offered a high degree of flexibility, it also favors a focus on operational issues at the expense of deepened strategic policy planning.

Given the differences between both organizations related to the conditions under which they deploy and in terms of risk acceptance, African armies often bear the human cost of peacebuilding in Africa. Even in Mali, where the French have been broadly credited for reacting quickly with deploying Operation Serval to fight terrorist groups on the morrow of the 2012 coup,

> UN officials question giving too much credit to France. Along with the United States, France provided intelligence and equipment, but apparently the bulk of fighting was

done by Chadian soldiers who were willing to endure high casualties, particularly in the mountainous area in northern Mali controlled by Islamists.

*(Weiss and Welz 2014, 897)*

Further, the sui generis nature of specific UN-AU collaborations in the field means that, while both organizations increasingly operate in parallel in conflict-riven settings, they continue to lack deep "knowledge about what the other is doing and their respective working methods" (International Crisis Group 2019, 11), something that acts as an important brake to operational effectiveness. Distinct bureaucratic procedures, different organizational cultures, dissimilar views concerning public communication, and strong inequalities in terms of resources have sometimes fostered tensions on the ground. Highly asymmetric logistical and planning capabilities have created frictions, while poor coordination has led to a "duplication of structures and waste of resources" on one side and acute tensions and growing distrust between organizations' field operatives on the other (Jentzsch 2014, 88). In extreme cases, UN support to AU operations has replaced "capacity building" with "capacity substitution," thus highlighting the profoundly unequal nature of the partnership (Williams and Boutellis 2014, 278).

If "institutional overlap" best describes the relationship between an increasingly autonomous AU and the UN (Welz 2016, 573), with overlap come questions about the nature of the relationship. Is it hierarchical, as per the UN Charter's insistence on UN supremacy, or is there room for subsidiarity, as suggested by Chapter VIII of the Charter, which addresses relations with regional organizations? The answer to this question may reside in the conundrum posed by the financing of peace operations. Indeed, and despite the real progress described in the first part of this chapter, the limits of institutionalization become apparent when looking at the distribution of financing responsibilities, as this continues to rely on informal mechanisms. While the AU has "repeatedly called on the UN to share the financial burden of its operations in support of peace and security on the continent" (International Crisis Group 2020, 2), UN financing for AU-led peace operations is generally decided on a case-by-case basis. Dependence on voluntary contributions leaves AU operational actors with little predictability. This creates dilemmas when they must adjust to changing conditions. Further, and as is often the case, pledges of support usually exceed the amounts actually disbursed; as a result, most AU-led peace operations have been mired by issues of underfunding (Jentzsch 2014).

The High-Level Independent Panel on Peace Operations in the UN addressed this recurrent issue in its June 2015 report. In its recommendations to create "a more comprehensive system of funding peace operations that would extend UN peacekeeping financing beyond its current boundaries" (Coleman 2017, 101), the Panel urged the UN to "take the decisive step to invest in and commit to the success of the African Union as a partner in addressing shared concerns" (United Nations 2015, 57). It endorsed "the use of United Nations–assessed contributions on a case-by-case basis to support African Union peace support operations authorized by the Security Council, including the costs associated with deployed uniformed personnel" (United Nations 2015, 248). The divisiveness of the issue would be reaffirmed by the UN secretary-general's implementation report which, even as it agreed with the need for sustained, predictable, and flexible funding mechanisms, remained "tentative on the issue of using UN-assessed contributions to fund AU operations" (Coleman 2017, 114). As De Carvalho (2020) notes, "resolving the financial deadlock is essential in ensuring the creation of sustainable frameworks that enable multiple international partners to effectively work together, in structures that are predictably defined with jointly agreed upon rules of the game." However, the resolution of this conundrum is heavily dependent on the goodwill of those countries that are the major

## Intractable Political and Strategic Disagreements

Ultimately, while both the UN and the AU share "similar normative commitment to peace, stability, and respect for human rights and constitutional order" (Nathan 2017, 155), their immediate objectives are often at odds. These divergences reflect a broader and more intractable strategic competition between the organizations. In this context, and in the absence of clear and formal mechanisms to apportion political responsibilities to one or the other, effective cooperation requires perpetual informal talks and negotiations. This makes it easy for each organization to blame the other for perceived failures and increases both the risk of inter-organizational disputes and, more significantly, the danger of incoherence in their responses to political crises.

Since the early days of cooperation, relations between the UNSC and the AU PSC have been "fundamentally unequal in terms of powers, authority, resources, and political status" (Forti and Singh 2019, 3). The two organizations have failed to define whether their relations are based on a "subcontracting" framework, which is defined by a clear hierarchical relation, or a real "partnering" one, which builds its strengths on the comparative advantages of each (Yamashita 2012, 183). The UN Charter is unclear on the matter. On the one hand, it acknowledges the primacy of the UNSC, emphasizing its "superior position [. . .] when it is able to act" (Weiss and Welz 2014, 903). On the other, Chapter VIII of the Charter affirms "regional responsibilities" in matters of peace and security. This has led Thomas Weiss and Martin Welz (2014, 889) to argue:

> In many ways, peace operations have increasingly come to reflect the original intention of Chapter VIII of the UN Charter, sometimes being approved by the Security Council but handed over in their entirety to regional organizations or at least involving a "hybrid" between the UN and regional organizations.
>
> Weiss and Welz (2014, 889)

The AU's Charter, for its part, also lacks textual clarity when it comes to relations with the UN. While it "upholds the primacy of the [UN] Security Council," the AU "simultaneously proclaims that the Union has the primary responsibility for ensuring peace and stability in Africa" (Nathan 2017, 158).

That both organizations want to be recognized as the primus inter pares when it comes to peace and security issues in Africa has resulted in what the International Crisis Group (2019, 11) labels "jockeying for primacy." Indeed, both UNSC and AU PSC members "have institutional interests in avoiding deferring to one another" (International Crisis Group 2019, 11). AU-UN cooperation in Mali after the 2012 coup is a case in point. Even though both organizations seemingly agreed on the ends of an intervention – eliminating jihadist groups and restoring a constitutional order – there was no agreement on means, tools, or the division of responsibilities (Weiss and Welz 2014). The AU "felt that it possessed the policy capabilities for responding to both key elements of the dual crisis – the extremist insurgency and the unconstitutional change in government – but the UN did not agree" (World Peace Foundation 2017, 4). When the time came to transition from AFISMA to MINUSMA, the AU felt sidelined by the UNSC. Whereas it had aspired to play a central role in the political response to the crisis, Resolution 2100 stated the primacy of the UN secretary-general in "*close collaboration* with the AU, ECOWAS and the EU Special Representative for the Sahel" (UN Security Council 2013, 21; emphasis added). In a rare rebuttal, the AU PSC issued a stern communiqué in which it denounced the resolution as "not in consonance with the spirit of partnership that the AU and the United Nations have been striving to promote for many years, on the basis of the provisions of Chapter VIII of the UN Charter" (Williams and Boutellis 2014, 256).

Further, there are no specific mechanisms in place to resolve conflicts that arise between both organizations, leaving the resolution of such disputes open to power dynamics. The fact that the Mission of African Union in New York lacks strong logistical and human capacities complicates the matter, leaving the AU with little leverage to defend its interests in the face of the largely endowed UN structure. To make matters worse, the A3 – the three African countries represented at the UNSC as non-permanent members – often fail to speak with a common voice (Williams and Boutellis 2014; Guerrero 2020).

## *Diverging National Interests*

It is not only organizational interests that create friction between the UN and AU. Inter-organizational disagreements are also intertwined with national rivalries and diverging national interests. In this regard, we follow Albrecht and Cold-Ravnkilde (2020, 204), who

> suggest exploring interaction and friction within missions as a practical expression of how national interests play out in organizations like the UN and AU, rather than only between or among organizations that are presumed in much analysis to be deeply political, yet still coherent units of analysis.

Even if "the UN Secretariat is more independent from its member states on day-to-day issues and can therefore have more open discussions than the AU," at all levels, both organizations undeniably represent the indirect interests of the most prominent and powerful states in their respective security councils (Forti and Singh 2019, 20). In times of crisis, this can reinforce tensions, as both entities become vectors of peculiar and intractable interests.

The AU-UN Hybrid Operation in Darfur (UNAMID) is one of the most cited examples of the way national political interests have resulted in inter-organizational tensions. Launched in 2007 as a joint initiative, the "initial optimism soon gave way to considerable disillusionment" as the operation became "mired by disputes over its mandate, failed to meet most of its goals, and encountered ongoing challenges by the Sudanese government, rebel factions and civil society groups" (Spandler 2020, 188). Western interests were a paramount cause of tensions around UNAMID. In order to have the operation accepted by the Sudanese government, UNAMID was initially mainly presented as an AU force benefiting from additional UN funding and support (Whineray 2020). However, the Western countries perceived UNAMID "as primarily a UN force that would be co-badged with the AU to make it acceptable to the Sudanese," a discrepant interpretation that fostered tensions during implementation (Whineray 2020).

Beyond UNAMID, the early 2010s was globally a period of strong dissonance in terms of political interests between Western UNSC members, the AU, and many African states. In the post-electoral crisis in Côte d'Ivoire in 2010, even though both organizations upheld the victory of Alassane Ouattara, many African states still sided with then-President Gbagbo (Rupiya 2012). In 2011, the Libyan crisis highlighted deep divisions between the UNSC and the AU PSC. Both organizations implicitly agreed that the only possible issue to the crisis would be the resignation of Libya's leader, Muammar Gaddafi, but while the AU favored a diplomatic intervention, the "UN Security Council adopted Resolution 1973, calling for 'all necessary measures . . . to protect civilians and civilian populated areas under threat of attack in [Libya]' and imposed a no-fly zone over the country" (Weiss and Welz 2014, 895). The AU denounced a "one sided interpretation of the Libyan resolution" (Rivzi 2011), and the disagreement would later be linked to veiled Western interests in overthrowing the regime. For Solomon Dersso (2012, 42), the Libyan case is an illustration of the fact that "where the interests of dominant global powers were involved, Africa cannot pursue its peace and security agenda independently."

Whether because of struggles over primacy or because of political disagreements between key member states, recurring crises in the UN-AU partnership have a deleterious impact on the prospects of peace and security on the African continent. Not only do they undermine the ideal of *Pax Africana* (Rivzi 2011; Dersso 2012), but each crisis reinforces mistrust and creates further constraints on the deepening of operational and institutional cooperation. According to the International Crisis Group's Richard Gowan (cited in Guerrero 2020), "This situation has resulted in a lot of mistrust of the Security Council in Addis Ababa [headquarters of the African Union] and among African policymakers." Together, operational and structural constraints undeniably hurt "the credibility of the United Nations in the continent," and, in definitive, are detrimental to the effectiveness of peacebuilding mechanisms (Guerrero 2020).

## Conclusion

What does our analysis suggest for the future? What are the opportunities and challenges that we can expect in terms of efforts to deepen and further institutionalize the UN-AU partnership in peacekeeping and peacebuilding? What does this mean for policymakers? There is little argument to the effect that an institutionalized UN-AU partnership is more necessary now than ever. The nature of peace and security challenges on the African continent, combined with ongoing challenges to the financing of UN peacekeeping, means that the "future of peace operations is African," to quote the title of a recent piece by Gustavo De Carvalho (2020). This is all the more true as non-UN operations are increasingly deployed in response to "threats posed by violent extremism, asymmetric warfare, transnational organized crime, as well as climate change," threats that fall outside of the traditional peace operations arrangements and mandates of the UNSC (De Carvalho 2020). Partnerships will therefore likely increase, prompting the UN to find a way to better manage the conditions of its cooperation with regional actors without undermining its main prerogatives and political ethos.

In terms of research agendas, the chapter suggests the value of approaching cooperation not only at the macro institutional level but also at the micro level. The study of practices on the ground provides a fine-grained understanding of the way collaboration or the lack thereof affects the effectiveness of peace operations. There are already pioneering studies in this realm, including the work of Séverine Autesserre (2010; 2014) and Linnéa Gelot (2017). A sociological theoretical approach to cooperation will deepen our understanding of the micro-dynamics of (non-)cooperation and of their micro-foundations. The chapter also suggests the need for a more complex analysis of not only inter- but also intra-organizational dynamics, as they affect prospects for cooperation. This is all the more important that neither the UN nor the AU has succeeded in becoming more than the sum of its parts. This means scrutinizing the role of member states with a seat in the UNSC or that of influential African member states on the AU PSC. This also means scrutinizing the role of TCCs and of the main peacekeeping donors to understand the dynamics of (non-)cooperation. There are already precedents in the work of Albrecht and Cold-Ravnkilde (2020), who focus on national interests' impact on specific peace operations, or that of Brosig (2017b), who develops the concept of "rentier peacekeeping" to account for a new form of indirect politics, or in the analysis of peacekeeping financing by Coleman (2017). More work needs to be done as well, including the various regional economic commissions into the analysis, such as the Economic Community of West African States (ECOWAS) and the Economic Community of Central African States (ECCAS). The analysis of inter- and intra-organizational dynamics would also benefit from the insights of the literature on norms and norm diffusion, which provides interesting leads to understand the conditions under which new norms come to be adopted in spite of resistance by powerful states.

In this regard, it will be interesting to follow developments regarding the May 2019 creation in Addis Ababa of the Group of Friends of the UN-AU Partnership chaired by Rwanda and Norway and the parallel launch, in February 2020, of a similar group in New York chaired by Norway and Egypt. The Group of Friends, which has the potential of becoming an instrument of norm diffusion, bills itself as

> an informal forum, supplementing the established meeting architecture and other cooperative arrangements existing between the UN and the AU with the key purpose to generate increased understanding, support and backing of member states to the UN Secretariat and the AU Commission in their efforts to deepen and widen the partnership.
> *(Group of Friends of the UN-AU Partnership 2019)*

The Group of Friends and the recent joint frameworks agreed by the UN and the AU (the Joint UN-AU Framework for Enhanced Partnership in Peace and Security in April 2017 and the AU-UN Framework for the Implementation of Agenda 2063 and the 2030 Agenda for Sustainable Development in January 2018) address one of the recurrent obstacles to deepened UN-AU collaboration; namely, the blurriness resulting from the informality of interactions and the sui generis nature of joint operations. Developed to respond to immediate threats and crises, the collaboration has long suffered from a lack of formal operational and institutional mechanisms and frameworks clearly defining roles and responsibilities. In spite of the development of joint practices and of the routinization of exchanges, the lack of formal mechanisms and frameworks has hampered collaboration in the past, making it particularly vulnerable to political interests and failing to provide the necessary predictability that is needed to develop efficient responses.

In terms of policy implications, there is growing recognition in both organizations of their need to leverage "their respective comparative advantages towards achieving the common objectives of enhancing peace and security, promoting human rights and good governance and implementing Agenda 2063: The Africa We Want and the 2030 Agenda for Sustainable Development" (UN Security Council 2019, 1). The UN recognizes that it needs to "move away from improvisation in the manner in which it worked with regional organizations" and "embrace dual roles as one partner responding politically and operationally alongside others and as an enabler and facilitator of others to play their increasingly prominent roles" (Lotze and Pietz 2015, 4; United Nations 2015, 14). To make good on this realization, the organization "should take the decisive step to invest in and commit to the success of the African Union as a partner in addressing shared concerns" (United Nations 2015, 14). The AU, for its part, also calls for "deeper collaboration [. . .] from policy formulation stage to implementation" (African Union 2020). This will require increased quotidian working-level interactions, and the collaboration would undeniably benefit from more "joint planning exercises, joint analytical reports, joint field visits, coordinated political messaging and joint statements, and staff exchanges" (Forti and Singh 2019, 19).

In closing, while it will take some time to resolve outstanding problems, iron out existing constraints, and overcome obstacles to deepened collaboration, it is also true that "some irritants to intercouncil relations" can and have to be addressed quickly (International Crisis Group 2019, 2). Given the nature of contemporary security threats in Africa, many of which fall outside the ambit of the UNSC's traditional role in maintaining international peace and security, and given the fact that "African third parties are generally more effective in resolving civil wars in Africa than non-African third parties" due to strong comparative advantages in terms of legitimacy (Duursma 2017, 611), the attainment of a Pax Africana – a peace "that is protected and maintained by Africa herself" (Mazrui 1967, 203) – is not simply an ideal. Supporting the APSA is the only way to achieve sustainable peace on the continent. The AU needs UN support, and the UN needs a strong partner in the maintenance of peace and security.

## Notes

1 We wish to thank the editors for their comments on early versions of this chapter. We are also indebted to John Karlsrud for his insights.
2 An excellent definition is provided by Sari: "Status of forces agreements (SOFAs) and status of mission agreements (SOMAs) are bilateral or multilateral treaties that define the legal position of military forces and civilian personnel deployed by one or more states or by an international organization in the territory of another state with the latter's consent" (Sari 2008, 68).
3 A similar sequential process has also been taking place, though not as regularly, in the field of mediation and conflict resolution. The UN recognized the mediation led by the AU during the post-election Kenyan crisis of 2007, contributing to its success by the provision of political and technical assistance (Juma 2009).
4 More on the distinction in De Coning (2017).
5 Titled "The Need for Greater Coherence," this report identified a number of ways to deepen AU-UN partnership.
6 Adopted by the AU Assembly in 2015, Agenda 2063 aims at achieving an "integrated, prosperous and peaceful Africa, driven by its own citizens and representing a dynamic force in the global arena."
7 Examples include the UN participation in the Algerian-led talks on Mali (2014–2015) and support for the African Initiative for Peace and Reconciliation in the CAR. The Initiative led by the AU together with the ECCAS and the International Conference of the Great Lakes Region (with the support of Angola, the Republic of the Congo, and Chad), and UN DPPA support to peace efforts led by the AU High-Level Implementation Panel in Sudan.

## References

Adler, E. and Pouliot, V., (2011) *International Practices*, Cambridge Studies in International Relations Book 119. Cambridge: Cambridge University Press.
African Union, (n.d.) *The African Peace and Security Architecture*. [online]. Available at: The African Peace and Security Architecture (APSA)-African Union – Peace and Security Department (peaceau.org) (Accessed: 6 July 2021).
African Union, (2000) *The Constitutive Act of the African Union*. Lomé: African Union.
African Union, (2004) *Statement of Commitment to Peace and Security in Africa. Issued by the Heads of State and Government of the Member States of the Peace and Security Council of the African Union*. PSC/AHG/ST.(X), 25 May. Addis Ababa: African Union.
African Union, (2015) *Agenda 2063. The Africa We Want*. Addis Ababa, Ethiopia: African Union Commission.
African Union, (2020) *African Union Calls for Closer Cooperation with the United Nations System to Achieve Agenda 2063 and the 2030 Agenda*. Victoria Falls: African Union.
Albrecht, P. and Cold-Ravnkilde, S., (2020) 'National Interests as Friction: Peacekeeping in Somalia and Mali', *Journal of Intervention and Statebuilding*, 14(2), pp. 204–220.
Annan, K.A., (2006) *Letter Dated 11 December 2006 from the Secretary-General Addressed to the President of the General Assembly*. New York, NY: United Nations General Assembly.
Autesserre, S., (2010) *The Trouble with the Congo: Local Violence and the Failure of International Peacebuilding*. New York, NY: Cambridge University Press.

Autesserre, S., (2014) *Peaceland: Conflict Resolution and the Everyday Politics of International Intervention. Problems of International Politics*. New York, NY: Cambridge University Press.

Bellamy, A.J., Williams, P.D. and Griffin, S., (2010) *Understanding Peacekeeping*. Cambridge: Polity.

Brosig, M., (2017a) 'Regime Complexity and Resource Dependence Theory in International Peacekeeping', in *Palgrave Handbook of Inter-Organizational Relations in World Politics*. London: Palgrave Macmillan, pp. 447–470.

Brosig, M., (2017b) 'Rentier Peacekeeping in Neo-Patrimonial Systems: The Examples of Burundi and Kenya', *Contemporary Security Policy*, 38(1), pp. 109–128.

Brosig, M. and Motsamai, D., (2014) 'Modeling Cooperative Peacekeeping: Exchange Theory and the African Peace and Security Regime', *Journal of International Peacekeeping*, 18(1–2), pp. 45–68.

Coleman, K.P., (2017) 'Extending UN Peacekeeping Financing Beyond UN Peacekeeping Operations? The Prospects and Challenges of Reform', *Global Governance: A Review of Multilateralism and International Organizations*, 23(1), pp. 101–120.

De Carvalho, G., (2020) 'The Future of Peace Operations Is African, and Demands Better Coordination', [Blog] *IPI Global Observatory*, 21 September. [online]. Available at: https://theglobalobservatory.org/2020/09/future-peace-operations-african-demands-better-coordination/ (Accessed: 6 July 2021).

De Coning, C., (2017) 'Peace Enforcement in Africa: Doctrinal Distinctions Between the African Union and United Nations', *Contemporary Security Policy*, 38(1), pp. 145–160.

Dersso, S.A., (2012) 'The Quest for Pax Africana: The Case of the African Union's Peace and Security Regime', *African Journal on Conflict Resolution*, 12(2), pp. 11–48.

Duursma, A., (2017) 'Partnering to Make Peace: The Effectiveness of Joint African and Non-African Mediation Efforts', *International Peacekeeping*, 24(4), pp. 590–615.

Eriksen, S.S., (2009) 'The Liberal Peace Is Neither: Peacebuilding, State Building and the Reproduction of Conflict in the Democratic Republic of Congo', *International Peacekeeping*, 16(5), pp. 652–666.

Forti, D. and Singh, P., (2019) *Toward a More Effective UN-AU Partnership on Conflict Prevention and Crisis Management*. New York: International Peace Institute.

Franke, B. and Romain Esmenjaud, R., (2008) 'Who Owns African Ownership? The Africanisation of Security and Its Limits', *South African Journal of International Affairs*, 15(2), pp. 137–158.

Gelot, L., (2017) 'Civilian Protection in Africa: How the Protection of Civilians Is Being Militarized by African Policymakers and Diplomats', *Contemporary Security Policy*, 38(1), pp. 161–173.

Group of Friends of the UN-AU Partnership, (2019) *Official Launch of the Group of Friends of the UN-AU Partnership*. Available at: https://www.google.fr/url?sa=t&rct=j&q=&esrc=s&source=web&cd=&cad=rja&uact=8&ved=2ahUKEwj3kMrV6bn1AhUFzYUKHfcpA3oQFnoECAIQAQ&url=https%3A%2F%2Fwww.norway.no%2Fen%2Fmissions%2FUN%2Fstatements%2Fother-statements%2F2020%2Flaunch-of-the-group-of-friends-of-un-au-partnership%2F&usg=AOvVaw1RWHQDCS0BgToFTLwWl-vX

Guerrero, M., (2020) 'Africans Struggle to Be a Unified Force in the UN Security Council, Complicated by the Coronavirus', *PassBlue*, 13 April. [online]. Available at: www.passblue.com/2020/04/13/africans-struggle-to-be-a-unified-force-in-the-un-security-council-complicated-by-the-coronavirus/ (Accessed: 30 June 2021).

Holt, V.K. and Shanahan, M.K., (2005) *African Capacity-Building for Peace Operations: UN Collaboration with the African Union and ECOWAS*. Washington, DC: Henry L. Stimson Center.

Howard, L.M., (2008) *UN Peacekeeping in Civil Wars*. New York, NY: Cambridge University Press.

International Crisis Group, (2019) *A Tale of Two Councils: Strengthening AU-UN Cooperation*. Brussels: International Crisis Group.

International Crisis Group, (2020) *The Price of Peace: Securing UN Financing for AU Peace Operations*. Brussels: International Crisis Group.

Jentzsch, C., (2014) 'Opportunities and Challenges to Financing African Union Peace Operations', *African Conflict and Peacebuilding Review*, 4(2), pp. 86–107.

Juma, M.K., (2009) 'African Mediation of the Kenyan Post-2007 Election Crisis', *Journal of Contemporary African Studies*, 27(3), pp. 407–430.

Karlsrud, J., (2019) 'From Liberal Peacebuilding to Stabilization and Counterterrorism', *International Peacekeeping*, 26(1), pp. 1–21.

Kay, N., (2015) 'Somalia's Year of Delivery', *Al-Jazeera*, 21 January. [online]. Available at: www.aljazeera.com/indepth/opinion/2015/01/somalia-year-delivery-201511391533903948.html (Accessed: 30 June 2021).

Lotze, W. and Pietz, T., (2015) *Trilateral Cooperation in Peace Operations: Strengthening AU, UN and EU Cooperation in Africa*. Berlin: Center for International Peace Operations (ZIF).

Makubalo, N., (2019) *Strengthening United Nations (UN) and African Union (AU) Coordination on Peace Missions*. Bruges: UNU Institute on Comparative Regional Integration Studies.

Mazrui, A.A., (1967) *Towards a Pax Africana: A Study of Ideology and Ambition*. Chicago: University of Chicago Press.

Mccoy, W., (2020) *AGA Platform*. [online]. Available at: AGA Platform (aga-platform.org) (Accessed: 30 June 2021).

Murithi, T., (2008) 'The African Union's Evolving Role in Peace Operations: The African Union Mission in Burundi, the African Union Mission in Sudan and the African Union Mission in Somalia', *African Security Studies*, 17(1), pp. 69–82.

Nathan, L., (2017) 'How to Manage Interorganizational Disputes Over Mediation in Africa', *Global Governance*, 23(2).

New Humanitarian, (2014) 'Somalia at "Risk of Relapse"', 7 May. [online]. Available at: The New Humanitarian | Somalia at "risk of relapse" (Accessed: 30 June 2021).

Rivzi, H., (2011) 'AU Concerned With One-Sided Interpretation of Libya Resolution', *Inter Press Service*, 15 June. [online]. Available at: www.ipsnews.net/2011/06/au-concerned-with-one-sided-interpretation-of-libya-resolution/ (Accessed: 30 June 2021).

Rupiya, M., (2012) 'A Review of the African Union's Experience in Facilitating Peaceful Power Transfers: Zimbabwe, Ivory Coast, Libya and Sudan: Are There Prospects for Reform?', *African Journal on Conflict Resolution*, 12(2), pp. 161–183.

Sari, A., (2008) 'Status of Forces and Status of Mission Agreements under the ESDP: The EU's Evolving Practice', *European Journal of International Law*, 19(1), pp. 67–100.

Spandler, K., (2020) 'UNAMID and the Legitimation of Global-Regional Peacekeeping Cooperation: Partnership and Friction in UN-AU Relations', *Journal of Intervention and Statebuilding*, 14(2), pp. 187–203.

United Nations, (2015) *Uniting Our Strengths for Peace – Politics, Partnership and People. Report of the High-Level Independent Panel on United Nations Peace Operations*. New York, NY: United Nations.

United Nations General Assembly, (2006) *Letter Dated 11 December 2006 from the Secretary-General Addressed to the President of the General Assembly. A/61/630*. New York, NY: United Nations.

United Nations General Assembly, (2007) *Cooperation between the United Nations and the African Union. A/RES/61/296*. New York, NY: United Nations.

United Nations General Assembly, Security Council, (2000) *Report of the Panel on United Nations Peace Operations. A/55/305-S/2000/809*, 21 August. New York, NY: United Nations.

United Nations Political and Peacebuilding Affairs, (n.d.) *African Union*. [online]. Available at: African Union | Department of Political and Peacebuilding Affairs (Accessed: 30 June 2021).

United Nations Security Council, (2008) *Peace and Security in Africa. S/RES/1809*. New York, NY: United Nations.

United Nations Security Council, (2013) *Resolution 2100. S/RES/2100*. New York, NY: United Nations.

United Nations Security Council, (2019) *Strengthening the Partnership Between the United Nations and the African Union on Issues of Peace and Security in Africa, Including on the Work of the United Nations Office to the African Union*. [online]. Available at: https://reliefweb.int/report/world/strengthening-partnership-between-united-nations-and-african-union-issues-peace-and-0 (Accessed: 30 June 2021).

Weiss, T.G. and Welz, M., (2014) 'The UN and the African Union in Mali and Beyond: A Shotgun Wedding?', *International Affairs*, 90(4), pp. 889–905.

Welz, M., (2016) 'Multi-Actor Peace Operations and Inter-Organizational Relations: Insights from the Central African Republic', *International Peacekeeping*, 23(4), pp. 568–591.

Whineray, D., (2020) 'Lessons for Peacekeeping and Peacebuilding from Darfur', [Blog] *IPI Global Observatory*, 5 February. [online]. Available at: https://theglobalobservatory.org/2020/02/lessons-for-peacekeeping-peacebuilding-from-darfur/ (Accessed: 30 June 2021).

Wilén, N. and Williams, P.D., (2018) 'The African Union and Coercive Diplomacy: The Case of Burundi', *The Journal of Modern African Studies*, 56(4), pp. 673–696.

Williams, P.D., (2017) *UN Support to Regional Peace Operations: Lessons from UNSOA*. New York: International Peace Institute (IPI).

Williams, P.D. and Boutellis, A., (2014) 'Partnership Peacekeeping: Challenges and Opportunities in the United Nations-African Union Relationship', *African Affairs*, 113(451), pp. 254–278.

Williams, P.D. and Dersso, S.A., (2015) *Saving Strangers and Neighbors: Advancing UN-AU Cooperation on Peace Operations*. New York: International Peace Institute (IPI).

Wondemagegnehu, D.Y. and Kebede, D.G., (2017) 'AMISOM: Charting a New Course for African Union Peace Missions', *African Security Review*, 26(2), pp. 199–219.

World Peace Foundation, (2017) *Mali Mission Brief*. Medford: World Peace Foundation.

Yamashita, H., (2012) 'Peacekeeping Cooperation Between the United Nations and Regional Organisations', *Review of International Studies*, 38(1), pp. 165–186.

# 3
# PEACEBUILDING VIA SECURITY SECTOR REFORM AND GOVERNANCE?
## The case of West Africa

*Niagalé Bagayoko and Eboe Hutchful*

### Introduction

Initially conceptualised by the former British Department for International Development (Short 1999; Ball 1998) in the late 1990s and then endorsed and championed by the Organisation for Economic Co-operation and Development (OECD) Development Assistance Committee (DAC; OECD 2007; Bryden 2007; OECD 2005), security sector reform (SSR) is now accepted as an indispensable component of the peacebuilding agenda (Olonisakin, Ebo and Kifle 2019), as underscored by Security Council Resolution 2151 (UN Security Council 2014).

According to the UN (General Assembly, UN Security Council 2008, 2013; UN Security Council 2014; UN 2017),[1] SSR

> describes a process of assessment, review and implementation as well as monitoring and evaluation led by national authorities that has as its goal the enhancement of effective and accountable security for the State and its peoples without discrimination and with full respect for human rights and the rule of law.
> *(General Assembly, UN Security Council 2008)*

Further, as stated by the UN Security Council, SSR "should be a nationally owned process that is rooted in the particular needs and conditions of the country in question" (Security Council 2007; Ebo and Hänggi 2020).

The European Union (EU) has also developed its own approach to SSR (European Commission 2006; Council of the European Union 2006; Council of the European Union 2016),[2] whilst the African Union (AU) Assembly adopted in January 2013 the AU Policy Framework on SSR (African Union n.d.).

The Economic Community of West African States (ECOWAS) has also proved to be responsive to building a common SSR agenda, encapsulated in a number of policy documents and protocols. The most significant of them are the 1999 Protocol relating to the Mechanism for Conflict Prevention, Management, Resolution, Peacekeeping and Security; the 2001 Supplementary Protocol on Democracy and Good Governance; the 2006 Convention on Small Arms and Light Weapons; and the ECOWAS governance-based SSR policy framework, endorsed in Dakar in June 2016 by the region's head of states and governments. An Action Plan to implement this framework was also adopted in 2018. The objective of the proposed framework is not to urge member states to engage in SSR per se but to support an enabling environment to take on SSR initiatives in each country as required.

In spite of setbacks, some progress (decrease in the number of attempts to seize power by military means, increased civilian control over the security forces, growing involvement of civil society actors to engage security establishments, international and regional protocols prohibiting unconstitutional changes of regimes) has been achieved in the West African region (Bryden and Chappui 2015). Yet, the reality is that West African states have tended to demonstrate limited compliance with international, continental and ECOWAS regional security protocols or their normative guidelines. Questions are emerging about the effectiveness of SSR and therefore its capacities to deliver for African peacebuilding. As it is presently configured and implemented, SSR faces contemporary challenges. There is a growing sentiment that SSR has failed to deliver on its promises, even as its accomplishments deserve to be preserved (Van Veen and Price 2014).

## Security sector reform and governance (SSRG): a theoretical approach

Beyond the policy-oriented approach to SSR, it is useful to take a historical and theoretical perspective on the emergence of the concept.

From the Westphalian era to the end of the Cold War period, the concept of "security" was almost exclusively understood as national and state-centric whilst being narrowly defined in militarised terms. Consequently, the security sector was commonly and widely considered as based on two pillars: on the one hand, the defence and security forces themselves (including the military forces, the police/gendarmerie, the paramilitary forces, the intelligence services, border guards, penal and corrections institutions); and on the other hand, the relevant branches of the government (in particular the head of state, the defence and interior ministries within the executive institutions) with a legal mandate to ensure the safety, the sovereignty and the integrity of the state.

Yet, a substantive widening of this traditional vision of security has become widespread in both academic and policy circles. It is increasingly recognised that security is not only about force structure, defence plans, intelligence gathering systems or the level of expenditure on any of the security bodies. Rather, as very strongly stated by the concept of "human security" (Buzan 1991; UNDP 1994; Commission on Human Security 2003), security might also be endangered by threats other than military, which include political, economic, societal and environmental aspects. According to this human security approach, individuals and communities other than the state should also be the object of security. Moreover, individuals and the general population might be endangered by the inappropriate or abusive behaviour of the defence and security forces themselves, sometimes enforcing policies emanating from an authoritarian civilian rule. As a consequence, a larger definition of the security sector (Hendrickson and Karkoszka 2002) has emerged. It not only includes the aforementioned bodies legally authorised to use force and the executive authorities responsible for managing their intervention. It also puts the stress on the crucial oversight role to be played by the elected (parliaments) and duly appointed civilian authorities (e.g. human rights commissions, audit accounts, ombudsmans, the justice sector) as well as on the role of non-state actors. Among them, some are involved in private security delivery (e.g. self-defence organisations, private security companies); others (e.g. civil society, the media) exercise public control on security provision and the protection of citizens against acts of violence and coercion. All the aforementioned actors are contributing to the "governance" of the security sector.

The concept of governance aims to reflect the fragmentation of power and authority at multiple levels and refers to the structures and processes whereby a social organisation steers itself, ranging from centralised control to self-regulation. Considering security from the perspective of governance enables emphasising how a wide array of state and non-state actors exercise power and authority over security delivery, both formally and informally, at local, national, regional and international levels. The concept of security sector governance (SSG) per se envisions the responsibilities of the government in shaping and implementing decisions about security, but it also highlights how different kinds of state and non-state actors and institutions influence security provision, management and oversight. SSG is thus an analytical concept which provides a way to understand the exercise of power and authority over state and human security in a specific national security sector. Democratic SSG (Luckham 2003; Born, Caparini and Fluri 2003) is a normative concept aimed at improving state and human security by strengthening democratic civilian control within a framework of rule of law and respect for human rights by state and non-state security providers in a national setting. It does share with the concept of human security a special focus on the safety and welfare of individuals, communities and the population at large, including legal protection of citizens' rights and personal safety as well as independence and fairness in judiciary procedures. Democratic SSG does not refer to a specific institutional model.

Promoting and establishing democratic SSG should be the goal of SSR, which is the political and technical process of improving state and human security by making security provision, management and oversight by all state and non-state actors more effective and accountable.

## SSRG challenges in West Africa

While the aforementioned international and regional SSR frameworks (UN, EU, AU, ECOWAS) share common principles of a comprehensive approach to SSR in a context of democratic SSG (Wulf 2004), "train and equip" approaches remain dominant in practice. External SSR funding tends to be short-term in spite of the recognition that SSR can only produce results through long-term processes and inclusive national dialogue (Brzoska 2003). Additionally, SSR policy documents have generally been adopted after slow validation processes without being reviewed or adapted on an ongoing basis. Consequently, emerging threats and dramatic shifts in the security environment have not really been taken into account. For instance, developments in Mali raise serious doubts about the sustainability of even well-designed and massive supported SSR efforts (ISSAT 2019, 2017; Bagayoko 2018).

Political will remains a major issue, and competing political interests beyond the security sector have not sufficiently been integrated into SSR assessments. If bilateral and multilateral donors have become convinced of the importance of SSR, such a validation has not been shared by security and civilian elites in most African countries where security cultures remain closed and narrow, and more often than not linked to regime survival.

From an operational perspective, the approach has remained too state-focused, even in contexts where there is an explosion of community-based and private security (Abrahamsen and Williams 2007) and police/justice providers (Baker 2017). Additionally, SSR has mostly been seen as related to the armed forces and to a lesser extent police forces (Hills 2007), leaving out other crucial services like customs, corrections and intelligence (Afrika 2009).

More broadly, the claimed nexus between SSR and "conflict prevention", "peacebuilding" and "development" has been less robust than hoped; all too often, countries emerging from

SSR, such as Sierra Leone (Horn, Olonisakin and Peake 2006) and Liberia, continue to be trapped in low social and development indicators, even if, on a more positive note, they are enjoying some modicum of democratic stability. Moreover, the cross-cutting dimension of SSR has yet to be fully recognised. SSR has more often than not been isolated from other political and technical processes aimed to promote peace, including peace processes (Hutchful 2009), security and democracy.

Finally, and probably even more importantly, capacity-building programmes mostly focus on security providers and administrations but not on oversight institutions, such as parliaments (see below) and rule of law institutions. Dialogue and information sharing are all aspects of SSR which have been undervalued. Similarly, local ownership is widely presented as a crucial benchmark for success; however, local perspectives and national visions of security reforms have been given little weight. The principle of local ownership (Nathan 2008) has not been extended to the process of generating ideas or approaches to reform, or to the possibility for local actors to reject wholly or in part measures supported or favoured by donors and international actors. African-led research by African academia and think tanks on SSR-related matters has tended to be limited, resulting in dire lack of an African evidence base to underpin SSR efforts. South-south knowledge transfer and experience sharing are urgently needed because the realities and contexts are similar even if the political and historical trajectories are different.

## New ways to make SSR more efficient?

Today, there is a dire need to identify creative ways to use SSR as a cross-cutting instrument to contribute to peacebuilding efforts and to the UN's Sustaining Peace Agenda (UN Security Council 2016; UN General Assembly 2016). While the present and emerging context poses a range of challenges to SSR, it also offers a number of available SSR entry points. These include maturing civil-military dialogues, improving democratic security governance, supporting civil society, incorporating the issue of hybridity and justice networks, and addressing SSR challenges in violent environments as well as in non-conflict settings.

### *Maturing civil-military relations*

For more than 30 years, the overall framework to explain security-related political matters was the civil-military relations (CMR) approach (Huntington 1957; Janowitz 1960; Finer 1962), which tried to understand the formal and (crucially) informal politics of the relationships between civilian and military authorities and was often motivated by the vexed question of how to prevent military seizure of power. This approach was centred on the military and not on the security sector as a whole. From the late 1990s, there occurred a shift from CMR to SSR and SSG, which moved the focus from the military exclusively to taking on board the other components of the security sector, as explained earlier. However, in contrast to CMR, SSR/SSG has been oriented much more toward norm development and formal institution-building, reflecting contemporary imperatives of democratisation. In the process, however, the SSR/SSG approach has tended to be overly prescriptive and misses the crucial element of power relations and realpolitik which had been core to the classical CMR scholarship, particularly in terms of better understanding the micro-politics of the security establishment itself.

It is now necessary to develop a better awareness of possible changes in the military ethos and institutional cultures as a result of new contexts and missions (in particular international and regional peace operations) and emerging/non-conventional threats (terrorism, transnational crime, corruption within the security sector itself). Indeed, differences in local and regime responses to these common challenges have stimulated a diversity of forms of civil-military relations across the African continent (Bathily and Hutchful 1998) that demand systematic analysis. Since independence, security forces in most West African countries have suffered because of poor governance. Often, political interference eroded their professionalism and led to ethnically or geographically biased recruitment. Other times, political leaders attempted to buy the loyalty of special forces at the expense of national militaries. Contrary to popular belief, military regimes tended to undermine the effectiveness of security forces, while single-party states demanded party loyalty over military professionalism. Frequently, military regimes paid relatively little attention to the role and mission of the security forces or their effective management. At times, security forces were used as an employer of the last resort, resulting in large but poorly educated and ill-trained military establishments. Given an almost complete disregard for civil security, the police usually fared even worse than the military. However, policemen and policewomen in many cases are one of the very few signs of state presence in the daily life of West Africans. These "street-level" bureaucrats, much more involved in daily governance than the military, are therefore much more visible. In most instances security, of both the state and the individual, suffered, and relations between security forces and society deteriorated.

Military academies in each West African country can also provide a relevant opportunity whilst defence reviews can also be a good tool to rethink CMR. Even if focused quite narrowly on defence-related matters, defence reviews can help developing a holistic, evidence-based and inclusive methodology, including integrating civil society into the process. If integrated into wider national security strategies based on a broader assessment of the security environment, such reviews can prove extremely significant in opening up public space and stimulating national dialogue on defence issues, as well as integrating defence budget processes into wider public policy frameworks.

Forging new civil-military relations could also mean to develop a new approach to the operationality of the defence and security forces themselves. The operational challenge does not have the same acuteness in the different West African countries. In countries such as Senegal, Ghana and Nigeria (even if in the latter massive human rights violations have historically been a matter of concern), security apparatuses appear historically as the most operational, but the commitment of armed forces in Mali, Niger and Burkina Faso in operations to fight terrorism (together with the Operation Barkhane French forces or within the G5 Sahel) might change such a situation. However, operationality of the defence and security forces should not be considered as a global concept but should rather be defined as a combination of these four elements: effectiveness of security providers, which considers operationality from a technical perspective (mission performance); efficiency of security sector institutions, which envision operationality under the lens of human and financial capacities to fulfil their missions sustainably; readiness, which is related to the state of preparedness of persons, systems, or organisations to meet a situation and carry out a planned sequence of actions; and professionalism, which refers to a normative perspective on operationality (unity, integrity, discipline, impartiality, equality). Furthermore, it is important to note that the different national security forces may not have the same record of performance from one sector or service to another; for instance, in a given country, the military can better perform than the police forces, or some forces (such as the gendarmerie in francophone countries) within the police themselves can show better results than other ones. A discriminating approach based on a distinction between different sectors or services enables to better capture the operational challenge.

The greatest challenge in West Africa remains how to move the security sector away from being a protector of regimes in the context of new and emerging forms of politicisation frequently suppressing internal discord and competitive politics, rather than true guardians of states and nations. Ethnic allegiance and promotion, and lack of professionalism, continue to harm CMR in the sub-region.

These challenges provide an opportunity to reinvigorate the CMR approach by unpacking civil-military relations and considering them through different perspectives, such as micropolitics and power relationships underlying civil-military relations; relationships between the military and the political authorities, both within the executive and the legislative branch; relations between the military and the security forces (each with their own perception of security policies and military strategies); relations between the military and civil society organisations (CSOs) and the media; relations between the military and the population at large; civil-military relationships in rural and remote areas (challenge of decentralising security beyond central elites and institutions); and civil-military relations in the context of the fight against terrorism and violent extremism. Such a perspective would bring a political economy approach to SSR, which would enable a more sociological perspective. It would be possible to avoid a one-size-fits-all and too standardised approach to security governance.

## Accountable and legitimate security through democratic governance and civilian oversight

Whilst 20 years ago there was almost no oversight of the security sector, which was the preserve of the president and of a limited number of surrounding decision makers, the institutional framework necessary to establish democratic SSG formally does exist today in most West African countries. In particular, the different security services have been created according to national legislation and regulations (e.g. laws, decrees, ministerial decrees, administrative decisions), whilst their missions and prerogatives are also legally defined; civilian control by democratically elected authorities over the defence and security forces has been theoretically instituted.

It is nevertheless important to stress the fact that SSR is well rooted in the history of democratisation in some West African countries. What can be conceptualised as "proto-SSR/G" practices were unfolding within the West African landscape, particularly manifest in the experiences of countries such as Nigeria, Ghana or Senegal in their respective processes of embracing multiparty democracy. There is a vast accumulated set of lessons to be learnt, in particular regarding the kind of balance to be struck between security and democratic governance in establishing relatively viable civil-security relationships and organs of democratic security governance.

Yet, the very existence of such control mechanisms actually has not prevented dysfunctions, gaps, deficits and failures, a large number of which still continue today. Even in contexts where democracy is relatively well rooted, West African parliaments have not played the role they are entitled or expected to play and have often served as an extension of the executive. In some countries, especially those emerging from conflict, legislative representatives may be unaware of their role. There is consequently a significant gap between the role assigned by national constitutions to legislative actors, on the one hand, and their actual role on the ground, on the other. A major challenge will be to build bridges between parliaments and CSOs. An innovative solution, for instance, might include providing CSOs with office space in parliaments to follow up the work of the Defence and Security Commission on a daily basis.

Democratic control, however, should not be reduced to parliamentary control but expanded to include other oversight institutions and actors. Judicial authorities and the justice system have key roles to play in security sector oversight by ensuring that security-related legislation does respect the constitutional order and that the defence and security forces do respect the law. Independent state authorities with focused mandates also need the willingness and capacity to include the security sector and its activities in their remit (e.g. human rights commissions, financial audit bodies, ombuds institutions, anti-corruption commissions). A final matter for consideration is what civilian democratic oversight means for local structures and people, far removed from the capitals and centres of power.

Legal reform might be a complementary entry point. Not only do laws need to be updated to ensure security sector activities respect democratic process and human rights, but people must also be aware of the rights and protections the law affords them. Thus, there is a need to make the law available to any citizen in relevant local languages and to improve awareness of the obligations of security providers. Supporting the development of more accountable standards for the classification of information under law, as well as freedom of information laws and better record keeping, can also help to raise awareness in a number of countries.

Even if all the international and regional SSR frameworks (AU, ECOWAS, UN, EU, etc.) share common principles of a comprehensive approach to SSR in a context of democratic security governance, little attention and resources have been devoted to support such a democratic SSG. Different actors of the security sector still need support to fulfil their supervisory and oversight role.

## Enhancing the role of civil society and media

Another critical factor in democratisation processes in West Africa has been the active role played by well-organised civil society (compared, for example, to Central or East Africa), many of them having benefited from support from private foundations and international development partners.

However, traditionally civil society has tended to consider security issues as the preserve of the executive, also tending to view security forces mostly as "the enemy". Consequently, CSOs have been slow to appreciate the legitimate concerns (and the genuine constraints and limitations) of the armed and security forces, even when those forces have seemed eager for greater recognition and cooperation. However, blame for the poor state of civil-security relations can be apportioned equally in most cases, and all too often the civilian political authorities have borne primary responsibility for obstructing more positive relationships between the security forces and civil society. A significant shift in prevailing culture and mindset is required on all sides to overcome the lack of dialogue and reluctance to cooperate.

Most CSOs also lack familiarity with security-related issues: CSOs as well as the population at large lack (or are often denied) access to security information, owing in large part to a lack of transparency in management of security affairs, but also to the difficulty the African media seems to experience in covering security matters (whether due to lack of expertise, self-censorship or alleged tendencies to sensationalism and indiscretion).

In a number of African countries, however (e.g. Senegal, Niger, Mali, Ghana, Liberia, Sierra Leone), civil society has developed original approaches to its oversight of the security sector, such as participation in public hearings mounted by legislators and investigative commissions set up by government, visits to police stations, meetings with police commanders and advocacy on behalf of the security services when required (e.g. by making the public aware that government had failed to invest in uniforms or hygiene facilities). In building the capacity of civil society to engage more effectively, exchange visits with other countries have proved of good value, while collaboration with international partners sometimes has given their voice added weight on the national scene. In Senegal, collaboration between the armed forces and CSOs produced positive results in fighting the proliferation of light weapons.

Organisations more often than not lack stable staff and access to resources, so they have time to build up their expertise and to engage on a long-term basis with state security providers. At the same time, external financing for civil society activities tends to skew civil society concerns towards external priorities and elite-driven projects. The concept of civil society itself can be problematic on the African continent. While Western partners may tend to idealise African CSOs, associating them with progressive thinking and civic values, the same organisations are sometimes perceived much more negatively in West Africa, where they may be viewed as politicised, partisan or even corrupt. Furthermore, far from systematically promoting human rights and democracy, CSOs advocate or defend norms and values incompatible with the principles of accountability, inclusiveness or equality.

CSOs, however, are not the only actors which suffer such weaknesses. In fact, there is a tendency to define civil society in narrow terms, based on expectations about the style and composition of ideal-type civil society actors, which misses out on contributions of other potential stakeholders. Expanding the definition of civil society beyond conventional CSOs to encompass any voluntary group that espouses a vision of the public interest can enable new SSRG entry points. Yet, the "civil society" label should not be applied so promiscuously as to encompass all and every active organisation. A clear distinction should be made between private organisations acting on the profit motive and private organisations articulating for the public interest to enable them to articulate a security agenda that serves local needs as well as those of society.

## *Security from the bottom up: hybrid security governance*

Prevailing approaches to SSR – and the associated policy literature – have tended to stress the notions of the state characterised by legal-rational norms and institutions. Thus, SSRG processes have more often than not concentrated on the formal arrangements of the state and its security and justice institutions. Yet, such approaches are fundamentally at variance with the underlying realities of the West African context, where many political and social transactions (not least in the security sector) take place in the context of informal norms and systems, and where a wide array of institutions operate alongside or within nominally formal political institutions. Security provisioning in Africa is predominantly bottom up, not top down, delivered by an array of informal institutions and actors in concert as well as in competition with the state. Yet this large and heterogeneous sector is not captured in current security governance structures or strategies. Ignorance of the non-codified norms, non-state actors and non-formal networks active in the security realm – as well as, indeed, the extent to which state policies in Africa are themselves impregnated by informal norms and practices – leads inexorably to a core element in explaining the failure of orthodox, state-centric peacebuilding and security-related policies. Such socio-cultural realities do matter in understanding African environments and tailoring solutions suited to those environments, particularly beyond the domain of the state.

This may well account for many of the limitations of efforts to reform the security sector and its governance systems. In fact, the efficiency of SSR policies conducted on the African continent often turns out to be limited because they tend to focus mostly on state institutions, governmental established stakeholders, legal frameworks and codified standards. Although understanding and controlling the state dimension remains essential, the complexity of Africa's socio-political and security dynamics calls inseparably for a deep understanding of societal realities, often informal, within which security governance in Africa is rooted. Furthermore, analysis of recent crises that have occurred in many African countries involving the security apparatus demonstrates the need to better understand the societal and cultural context within which SSR policies are implemented. Increasingly, references to the informal security and justice sector have crept into the SSR and "state-building" toolkits, although so far based upon insufficient empirical understanding of how this sector functions in the political and security marketplace, or of the complex interplay between formal and informal institutions, which determine how policies play out on the ground and impact (or not) the lives of citizens and communities. On the African continent, formal and informal systems tend to overlap, interrelate and interpenetrate at complex levels, and states and informal networks are not mutually exclusive but should rather be seen as embedded in each other.

There is consequently a need to identify this complex amalgam of formal and informal networks, actors and processes which, alongside legally established structures, influence decision-making as well as policy implementation in the security sector and which together constitute what can be seen as "hybrid security orders" (Boege, Brown and Clements 2009). The concept of hybridity (Bagayoko, Hutchful and Luckham 2016) can provide a powerful analytical tool to explain governance in West Africa, where most security networks and practices are embedded (to one degree or another) in informal institutions and beliefs. Analysis and policy have scarcely begun to touch upon the deep politics of reform or to draw in any systematic way upon the critical literatures on hybrid political orders and security.

By relying on the perspectives offered by sociology and anthropology in the daily functioning of security provision (both at the central and local levels), the analysis of hybrid security governance could provide new and refreshing insights on networks and alliances as well as on competition, tensions and conflicts within African defence and security services, which may help to explain the difficulties in implementing SSR processes. Such an approach is likely to offer decision makers a key input to understanding non-state stakeholders, non-official networks and non-codified standards, whose influences compete against or to the contrary complete the intervention perimeter of state institutions and legal frameworks. It may also serve to explain how hybrid security systems are experienced at the grassroots by supposed beneficiaries, and in particular how they impact the lives of vulnerable groups and shape citizen expectations of security and security entitlements.

In addition to contributing to strengthening the research and evidence base of SSR, this approach carries important policy implications for how we approach security governance in Africa. In this regard, the ultimate intent is going beyond the use of hybridity as an analytical tool to inquire as to the extent to which the concept can provide the underpinnings of an approach to building more effective security and security governance systems and inform the agendas of West African states and partners who wish to participate in programs aimed at reaching this objective.

## *SSRG and asymmetric threats in West Africa*

The security environment in West Africa is presently characterised by "asymmetric" threats and conflicts which existing security institutions have not been trained to deal with, as proved by the situation in the Sahel and Lake Chad region. There is almost no doctrine or security policy in West African states to address such asymmetric challenges, resulting in ad hoc and reactive responses even to increasingly complex threat environments, be they vernacular, or international or cross-border in character (ISSAT n.d.; Van Veen 2017; Bagayoko 2020). The fight against terror and radicalisation processes is of course a major new challenge for SSRG in West Africa, and their impact must be evaluated. The logic of the fight against terrorism might squeeze out whatever fragile commitment exists to democratic security governance, whilst there is increasing blurring in mandates of the armed forces, the police and the intelligence in countries undergoing counterterrorism operations. The nature of counterterrorism operations will be key to the future of the democratic governance–based approach to security reform.

Furthermore, other security challenges (sometimes emerging but also more ancient) should be seen as important as the terrorist threat, such as conflicts around resource management (between herders, farmers and fishermen); water; gold washing; maritime insecurity (e.g. piracy, armed robbery, illegal fishing); transnational organised crime; and communal conflicts. These asymmetric threats are challenges not only to the operationality of the security sector but also to its accountability and ability to provide security to the people and the states. Those emerging security risks in West Africa may well mean that SSR will become even more focused on stabilisation imperatives and counterterrorism initiatives (Charbonneau 2019) rather than longer-term governance and institution-building. More and more SSR funding will be diverted to humanitarian and migration issues; and while violent extremism is arguably leading to increased security assistance, this assistance will be guided more by donors' own security agendas rather than those of "recipient" states, along with a growing focus on capacitating security institutions (via "train-and-equip" and "robust SSR") and less focus on security governance. There also could be greater willingness to tolerate serious human rights violations (particularly in the context of asymmetric operations) and growing restrictions on political freedoms by governments. This is an adverse and unfortunately all too real development that West African states and their international partners should be particularly vigilant about if SSR is not to be gutted.

### *Fostering SSRG in a non-conflict setting*

The SSRG agenda essentially has been driven by a conflict and post-crisis perspective: most of the SSRG efforts have concentrated on the Sahel region (Mali, Burkina Faso and Niger in a lesser extent) as well as Guinea-Bissau and The Gambia. Yet, an increasingly essential challenge is to support the SSRG agenda in non-conflict settings with a much longer-term approach, particularly in post-authoritarian environments as well as stable countries. Such a perspective positions SSR as an essential component of the UN's Sustaining Peace Agenda, of the prevention-based approach promoted by the UN secretary-general (Guterres 2017) and in the UN Integrated Strategy for the Sahel (UNISS). However, distinct approaches must be developed to differentiate countries presently embracing genuine democracy from those under a more authoritarian rule.

Countries not involved in conflict face threats which transcend borders and pose unprecedented challenges, hamstrung by weak, corrupt or absent institutions. The threats posed by organised and cross border crimes; trafficking of drugs, arms, and people; money laundering; terrorism; document forgery; identity theft; online extortion/cybercriminality; and others demand not only more robust actions but also a more efficient regional and international cooperation.

## Conclusion

Much still needs to be done to improve state and human security by making more operational and accountable security provision, management and oversight by all state and non-state actors, in particular by operationalising international SSR policy frameworks and by bridging the divide between policy and practice. Today, traditional security frameworks appear as no longer relevant or adequate in responding to current challenges in both security delivery and governance in West Africa: there is a need to rethink the whole conception of SSR in the region and to root it deeply in democratisation processes throughout the region as well in "vernacular security" (Lind and Luckham 2017). The issue at stake is to consider SSR/G not only as a post-conflict instrument but also as a preventive tool (Guterres 2017) so as to define an overarching framework to enhance security delivery and accountable security, both current areas of critical weakness in the sub-region. There is also a dire need to improve understanding of SSR (whether it is civil-military relations, non-state and informal security actors, etc.) as well as rethinking accountability of the security sector and how to make it happen.

## Notes

1  These documents are at the core of the UN SSR doctrine.
2  It was endorsed by the EU Council on 14 November 2016.

## References

Abrahamsen, R. and Williams, M.C., (2007) 'Securing the City: Private Security Companies and Non-State Authority in Global Governance', *International Relations*, 21(2), pp. 237–253.

African Union, (n.d.) *Policy Framework on Security Sector Reform*. [online]. Available at: au-policy-framework-on-security-sector-reform-ae-ssr.pdf (peaceau.org) (Accessed: 25 May 2021).

Afrika, S., (2009) 'The South African Intelligence Services: A Historical Perspective', in Africa, S. and Kwadjo, J., (eds.) *Changing Intelligence Dynamics in Africa*. Birmingham, UK: Global Facilitation Network for Security Sector Reform (GFN-SSR)/African Security Sector Network (ASSN), pp. 61–94.

Bagayoko, N., (2018) 'Le processus de réforme du secteur de la sécurité au Mali', in *Centre Francopaix en résolution de conflits*. Montréal: Université Québec Montréal.

Bagayoko, N., (2020) *Étude de référence sur l'état d'avancement de la gouvernance du secteur de la sécurité (GSS) et l'inclusion de la société civile dans les processus de réforme des systèmes de sécurité (RSS) au Nigeria, au Mali, au Cameroun et dans l'espace élargi de la CEDEAO*. Friedrich-Ebert-Stiftung, and Peace and Security Centre of Competence Sub-Saharan Africa. [online]. Available at: http://library.fes.de/pdf-files/bueros/fes-pscc/16759.pdf (Accessed: 28 May 2021).

Bagayoko, N., Hutchful, E. and Luckham, R., (2016) 'Hybrid Security Governance in Africa: Rethinking the Foundations of Security, Justice and Legitimate Public Authority', *Conflict, Security & Development*, 16(1), pp. 1–32.

Baker, B., (2017) 'Policing for Conflict Zones: What Have Local Policing Groups Taught Us?', *Stability: International Journal of Security and Development*, 6(1), p. 9.

Ball, N., (1998) *Spreading Good Practices in Security Sector Reform: Policy Options for the British Government*. London: Saferworld.

Bathily, A. and Hutchful, E., (1998) *The Military and Militarism in Africa*. Dakar: Codesria.

Boege, V., Brown, M.A. and Clements, K.P., (2009) 'Hybrid Political Orders, Not Fragile States', *Peace Review*, 21(1), pp. 13–21.

Born, H., Caparini, M. and Fluri, P., (eds.) (2003). *Security Sector Reform and Democracy in Transitional Societies*. Baden-Baden: Nomos.

Bryden, A., (2007) *From Policy to Practice: The OECD's Evolving Role in Security Sector Reform*. Policy Paper 22. Geneva: DCAF Geneva Center for the Democratic Control of the Armed Forces.

Bryden, A. and Chappui, F., (2015) *Gouvernance du secteur de la sécurité: Leçons des expériences ouest-africaines*. Geneva: DCAF Geneva Center for the Democratic Control of the Armed Forces.

Brzoska, M., (2003) *Security Sector Reform in Development Donor Perspective: Origins, Theory and Practice*. Occasional Paper 4. Geneva: DCAF Geneva Center for the Democratic Control of the Armed Forces.

Buzan, B., (1991) *People, States and Fear: An Agenda for International Security Studies in the Post–Cold War Era?* Boulder, CO: Lynne Rienner Publishers.

Charbonneau, B., (2019) 'Intervention as Counter-insurgency Politics', *Conflict, Security & Development*, 19(3), pp. 309–314.

Commission on Human Security, (2003) *Human Security Now*. New York, NY: Commission on Human Security.

Council of the European Union, (2006) *Council Conclusions on a Policy Framework for Security Sector Reform*. Luxembourg: European Union.

Council of the European Union, (2016) *Council Conclusions on EU-wide Strategic Framework to Support Security Sector Reform (SSR)*. Brussels: European Union.

Ebo, A. and Hänggi, H., (eds.) (2020) *The United Nations and Security Sector Reform: Policy and Practice*. Zürich: Lit, DCAF Geneva Centre for Security Sector Governance.

European Commission, (2006) *A Concept for European Community Support for Security Sector Reform*. Brussels: European Union.

Finer, S.E., (1962) *The Man on Horseback – the Role of the Military in Politics*. London: Pall Mall Press.

Guterres, A., (2017) *Remarks to the Security Council Open Debate on "Maintenance of International Peace and Security: Conflict Prevention and Sustaining Peace"*. [online]. Available at: Remarks to the Security Council Open Debate on "Maintenance of International Peace and Security: Conflict Prevention and Sustaining Peace" | United Nations Secretary-General (Accessed: 19 May 2021).

Hendrickson, D. and Karkoszka, A., (2002) 'The Challenges of Security Sector Reform', *SIPRI Yearbook*. [online]. Available at: www.sipri.org/sites/default/files/04.pdf (Accessed: 25 May 2021).

Hills, A., (2007) 'Police Commissioners, Presidents and the Governance of Security', *Journal of Modern African Studies*, 45(3), pp. 403–423.

Horn, A., Olonisakin, F. and Peake, G., (2006) 'United Kingdom-led Security Sector Reform in Sierra Leone', *Civil Wars*, 8, pp. 109–123.

Huntington, S., (1957). *The Soldier and the State: The Theory and Politics of Civil – Military Relations*. Cambridge, MA and London: Harvard University Press.

Hutchful, E., (2009) *Security Sector Reform Provisions in Peace Agreements*. ASSN, GFN-SSR, UK: University of Birmingham.

ISSAT, (n.d.) *Governance and Security in the Sahel*. DCAF Geneva Centre for Security Sector Governance. [online]. Available at: https://issat.dcaf.ch/Learn/Resource-Library2/Podcasts/Governance-and-Security-in-the-Sahel (Accessed: 28 May 2021)

ISSAT, (2017) *Cartographie du soutien de la communauté internationale en matière de sécurité et de justice au Mali*. DCAF Geneva Centre for Security Sector Governance. [online]. Available at: https://issat.dcaf.ch/ser/download/114191/2075695/Cartographie%20Securite-Justice%20au%20Mali%20-%20Rapport%20final%20-%20Fev%202017.pdf (Accessed: 28 May 2021)

ISSAT, (2019) *Mali SSR Background Note*. DCAF Geneva Centre for Security Sector Governance. [online]. Available at: http://issat.dcaf.ch/Learn/Resource-Library/Country-Profiles/Mali-SSR-Background-Note (Accessed: 28 May 2021)

Janowitz, M., (1960) *The Professional Soldier: A Social and Political Portrait*. Glencoe, IL: Free Press.

Lind, J. and Luckham, R., (2017) 'Introduction: Security in the Vernacular and Peacebuilding at the Margins; Rethinking Violence Reduction', *Peacebuilding*, 5(2), pp. 89–98.

Luckham, R., (2003) 'Democratic Strategies for Security in Transition and Conflict', in Cawthra, G. and Luckham, R., (eds.) *Governing Insecurity*. London and New York, NY: Zed Books, pp. 3–28.

Nathan, L., (2008) 'The Challenge of Local Ownership of SSR: From Donor Rhetoric to Practice', in Donais, T., (ed.) *Local Ownership and Security Sector Reform*. DCAF Yearbook 2008. Münster: Lit, pp. 19–36.

OECD, (2005) *Security System Reform and Governance*, DAC Guidelines and Reference Series. [online]. Available at: https://doi.org/10.1787/9789264007888-en (Accessed: 25 May 2021).

OECD, (2007) *The OECD DAC Handbook on Security System Reform: Supporting Security and Justice*. [online]. Available at: https://read.oecd-ilibrary.org/development/the-oecd-dac-handbook-on-security-system-reform_9789264027862-en#page4 (Accessed: 25 May 2021).

Olonisakin, F., Ebo, A. and Kifle, A., (2019) 'From Peacebuilding to Sustaining Peace and Preventing Conflict: What Role for SSR?', in Ebo, A. and Hänggi, H., (eds.) *The United Nations and Security Sector Reform: Policy and Practice*. DCAF. Zurich: Lit.

Short, C., (1999) *Security Sector Reform and the Elimination of Poverty*. [online]. Available at: www.clareshort.org/speeches/security-sector-reform (Accessed: 25 May 2021).

United Nations, (2017) *Building Sustainable Peace for All: Synergies between the 2030 Agenda for Sustainable Development and Sustaining Peace*. New York, NY: United Nations.

United Nations Development Programme, (1994) *Human Development Report*. New York, NY: Oxford University Press.

United Nations General Assembly, (2016) *Resolution Adopted by the General Assembly on 27 April 2016. A/RES/70/262*. New York, NY: United Nations.

United Nations General Assembly, United Nations Security Council, (2008) *Securing Peace and Development: The Role of the United Nations in Supporting Security Sector Reform. A/62/659 – S/2008/39*. New York, NY: United Nations.

United Nations General Assembly, United Nations Security Council, (2013) *Securing States and Societies: Strengthening the United Nations Comprehensive Support to Security Sector Reform. A/67/970 – S/2013/480.* New York, NY: United Nations.

United Nations Security Council, (2007) *Statement by the President of the Security Council. S/PRST/2007/3.* New York, NY: United Nations.

United Nations Security Council, (2014) *Resolution 2151.* New York, NY: United Nations.

United Nations Security Council, (2016) *Resolution 2282.* New York, NY: United Nations.

Van Veen, E., (2017) 'The Politics of Security Sector Reform in the Sahel', *Clingendael Institute*, 01 May. [online]. Available at: www.clingendael.org/publication/politics-security-sector-reform-sahel (Accessed: 25 May 2021).

Van Veen, E. and Price, M., (2014) 'Securing Its Success, Justifying Its Relevance: Mapping a Way Forward for Security Sector Reform', in *Clingendael Research Unit Policy Brief.* The Hague: Clingendael.

Wulf, H., (2004) 'Security Sector Reform in Developing Countries', in McCartney, C., Fischer, M. and Wils, O., (eds.) *Security Sector Reform. Potentials and Challenges for Conflict Transformation.* Berghof Handbook Dialogue No 2. Berlin: Berghof Research Center, pp. 9–29 and 71–73.

# 4
# PREVENTING CONFLICT-INDUCED FORCED DISPLACEMENT IN AFRICA

## UNHCR, the AU and the rhetoric and realities of 'Root Causes'

*Marina Sharpe*

### Introduction

Forced internal and external displacement has reached an all-time high. At the end of 2018, there were 65,288,993 forcibly displaced persons worldwide, including refugees, people in refugee-like situations, asylum seekers and internally displaced persons (IDPs; UNHCR 2019, 68). Thirty-nine percent of these individuals were in Africa (UNHCR 2019, 68). Given the magnitude of the problem, contemporary international and regional legal and policy responses to forced displacement now almost invariably, and sensibly, mention prevention, typically in terms of 'root causes'.[1] This focus is not new. Gilbert called for a focus on root causes in 1993, and by 1995, Okoth-Obbo had already identified as 'familiar' the call to urgently 'address the root causes of refugee flows and other forms of coerced population movements' (Okoth-Obbo 1995, 283).

However, while it is difficult to establish that something has *not* happened, it seems that forced displacement actors' prevention efforts rarely move beyond rhetoric. This phenomenon in the African context was likely first identified by Okoth-Obbo. Evaluating a 1994 symposium on forced displacement in Africa convened by the Office of the United Nations High Commissioner for Refugees (UNHCR) and the Organization of African Unity (OAU), he noted that the meeting failed to tackle 'root causes with any rigour' and, as a result, 'could not etch out clearly the essential legal, policy, and operational groundmarks for tackling... [root causes] in a concrete and result-producing manner' (1995, 283). I addressed the issue in a short analysis of the Global Compact on Refugees (GCR; Sharpe 2018). Neither piece, however, considered *why* root causes are so often addressed only rhetorically by forced displacement actors in Africa. This chapter argues that it is because while forced displacement in Africa is caused primarily by violent conflict[2] (AU 2019; International Crisis Group 2016) – especially with the rise of non-international armed conflicts that increasingly target civilians (Farrell and Schmitt 2017) – the international and regional organizations (or the divisions thereof) tasked to respond do not have peacebuilding mandates. Lip service is paid to preventing forced displacement, but this does not produce meaningful efforts to stop conflict because of UNHCR's apolitical role and because the

African Union (AU) entity responsible for forced displacement is distinct from those tasked with conflict prevention and resolution, a structural problem likely to worsen with the ongoing AU reforms. UNHCR and the AU should confront these limitations head-on through meaningful inter-organizational collaboration in line with the so-called humanitarian-development-peace triple nexus that emerged from the 2016 World Humanitarian Summit or, at the very least, they should avoid proliferating empty words when the lives and well-being of so many are at stake.

This chapter begins with background on refugees and IDPs and then highlights how contemporary international and regional law and policy relating to these categories has recognized the importance of preventing forced displacement, particularly conflict-induced displacement. The chapter then addresses the structural impediments to meaningful UNHCR and AU Commission engagement with prevention in the African context, where most forced displacement stems from violent conflict. In the AU case, particular attention is paid to how the ongoing process of institutional reform might entrench the problem identified here. The chapter then suggests how notwithstanding structural impediments to their engagement with conflict prevention, UNHCR and the AU Commission might move beyond rhetoric and into reality. A final section concludes.

## Refugees and internally displaced persons

The international Convention relating to the Status of Refugees (UN 1951), as amended by article 1(2) of the Protocol relating to the Status of Refugees (UN 1967), defines a refugee as someone who,

> owing to well-founded fear of being persecuted for reasons of race, religion, nationality, membership of a particular social group or political opinion, is outside the country of his nationality and is unable or, owing to such fear, is unwilling to avail himself of the protection of that country.
>
> *(art. 1A(2))*

Because conflict rarely affects people indiscriminately, this definition applies equally to individuals in flight from armed conflict and other situations of violence (UNHCR 2016, paras. 10–39). In Africa, regional refugee law (UN 1969) adopts the international definition and also defines a refugee as

> every person who, owing to external aggression, occupation, foreign domination or events seriously disturbing public order in either part of the whole of his country of origin or nationality, is compelled to leave his place of habitual residence in order to seek refuge in another place outside his country of origin or nationality.
>
> *(art. I(2))*

This regional definition is in practice typically invoked to provide refugee protection to individuals in flight from conflict or violence (Sharpe 2017; UNHCR 2016, paras. 44–60).

The UN's 1998 Guiding Principles on Internal Displacement (ECOSOC 1998) – which restate the principles of international human rights, humanitarian and refugee law applicable to IDPs – define IDPs as

> persons or groups of persons who have been forced or obliged to flee or to leave their homes or places of habitual residence, in particular as a result of or in order to avoid

the effects of armed conflict, situations of generalized violence, violations of human rights or natural or human-made disasters, and who have not crossed an internationally recognized State border.

*(para. 2)*

## The prevention agenda in international and regional forced displacement law and policy

While neither the 1951 Convention nor the 1969 OAU Convention mentions prevention, the scale of conflict-induced forced displacement today is such that contemporary legal and policy responses do typically address it. The more recent Guiding Principles identify the obligation of all 'authorities and international actors' to 'prevent and avoid conditions that might lead to displacement of persons' (principle 5). Efforts to prevent forced displacement can avert new displacement and contribute to resolving protracted situations by creating conditions to which refugees and IDPs can return. This section illustrates the contemporary prevention trend with a non-exhaustive survey in this regard, where the 'contemporary' period is understood to cover the past decade or so.[3] The survey begins at the international level and then moves on to the regional plane; the sub-regional level is beyond the scope of this review.

### *International*

The most significant recent international initiative relating to refugees is without a doubt the GCR, including the New York Declaration for Refugees and Migrants (United Nations General Assembly 2016) that gave rise to it. In September 2016, the UN General Assembly adopted the New York Declaration, an initial set of commitments to foster a more predictable and equitable international response to human mobility. The New York Declaration includes the Comprehensive Refugee Response Framework (CRRF), which articulates best practices in refugee protection, and led to the CRRF's application in 15 initial roll-out countries.[4] Regarding prevention, the Declaration articulates states' determination to 'address the root causes of large movements of refugees and migrants, including through increased efforts aimed at early prevention of crisis situations based on preventive diplomacy', as well as through 'the prevention and peaceful resolution of conflict' and 'greater coordination of humanitarian, development and peacebuilding efforts', among others (para. 12).

The New York Declaration outlined 'steps towards the achievement of a global compact on refugees in 2018' (para. 21), thus committing states to building upon the Declaration's initial measures. UNHCR led the drafting of the GCR. Following extensive consultation, the High Commissioner presented the final draft within his September 2018 report to the General Assembly's Social, Humanitarian and Cultural Committee. The GCR was adopted in December as part of the General Assembly's annual omnibus resolution on UNHCR.

The GCR aims 'to provide a basis for predictable and equitable burden- and responsibility-sharing among all' UN member states (para. 3). It is divided into four sections, beginning with an introduction that articulates the Compact's overarching objectives, which are to ease pressures on major refugee hosting countries, enhance refugee self-reliance, expand access to third-country solutions, and support conditions for return to countries of origin. Section 2 of the GCR is the CRRF, which is incorporated by reference to the New York Declaration. Section 3 is a programme of action to support CRRF implementation, divided into two parts. The first covers specific arrangements for burden and responsibility sharing. The second part of the CRRF programme of action details specific areas in need of support: reception and admission, meeting refugee needs and supporting host communities, and solutions. Section 4 focuses on GCR follow-up and review.

The GCR's introduction includes a subsection headed 'Prevention and Addressing Root Causes'. It recognizes that 'addressing root causes is the responsibility of countries at the origin of refugee movements' but goes on to note that 'averting and resolving large refugee situations are also matters of serious concern to the international community as a whole, requiring early efforts to address their drivers and triggers' and, notably, 'improved cooperation among political, humanitarian, development and peace actors' (para. 8). The latter is perhaps in recognition of the problem identified here: the UN entity mandated to respond to forced displacement has no mandate to prevent it. The Compact goes on to call on all 'States and relevant stakeholders . . . to tackle the root causes of large refugee situations, including through heightened international efforts to prevent and resolve conflict' (para. 9). The GCR's fourth objective of supporting conditions for return in safety and dignity is tantamount to conflict resolution.

The root causes of forced displacement were also addressed at the High Commissioner's Dialogue on Protection Challenges, a Geneva meeting convened annually by UNHCR. The 2015 Dialogue focused on 'understanding and addressing root causes of displacement'. The Dialogue aimed to contribute to 'a better and more nuanced understanding of "root causes" of displacement, and their relevance to "prevention", "protection", and "solutions"', to 'generate ideas and share good practices on the institutional contributions UNHCR and other humanitarian actors can make to address root causes' and to 'identify opportunities to address root causes more strategically, collaboratively and systematically' (UNHCR 2015b, para. 3).

## *Regional*

Building on the Guiding Principles, in 2009 AU member states adopted the world's first treaty on internal displacement, the AU Convention for the Protection and Assistance of Internally Displaced Persons in Africa (AU 2009). The Kampala Convention defines an IDP in terms identical to those used in the Guiding Principles (art. 1(k)), thereby acknowledging the primacy of conflict in forcing people to flee. The Convention is framed primarily in terms of state obligations in relation to internal displacement, including state obligations of prevention (art. 4), protection and assistance obligations during displacement (art. 9) and obligations in relation to return (art. 11) and compensation (art. 12). States must protect persons from arbitrary displacement 'in situations of armed conflict' (art. 4(4)(b)), including from displacement 'intentionally used as a method of warfare' (art. 4(4)(c)).

The AU's Assembly of Heads of State and Government (Assembly) designates each calendar year with a theme. The theme of 2019 was 'The Year of Refugees, Returnees and Internally Displaced Persons: Towards Durable Solutions to Forced Displacement in Africa' (AU 2018b). The Assembly's Declaration to launch the theme of the year, adopted at its February 2019 summit, includes a section titled 'Addressing the Root Causes', in which AU member states 'recommit to address the structural root causes of protracted violent conflicts, terrorism and violent extremism' as well as other displacement drivers: 'natural disasters and calamities, climate change, governance deficit, diversity mismanagement, human rights abuses and other factors' (AU 2019a, para. 4). The Declaration goes on to commit to ensuring 'that efforts are made to guarantee sustainable peace and security, democracy and socio-economic development pursuant to the noble goals of Agenda 2063 towards silencing guns and ending all wars in Africa by the year 2020' (AU 2019a, para. 5). The Assembly's Declaration to mark the end of the Year of Refugees, Returnees and IDPs emphasized 'the importance of addressing root causes and achieving durable solutions to forced displacement in Africa in line with relevant. . . [AU] legal and policy frameworks' and called on 'Member States, humanitarian and development partners, as well as frontline responders, to scale up response beyond emergency relief' (AU 2020a, preambular para. 4).

The AU Commission, which is the regional body's Addis Ababa–based secretariat, launched the theme of the year with its 'Roundtable on Addressing Root Causes of Forced Displacement and Achieving Durable Solutions in Africa', held on the margins of the February 2019 AU summit. According to a report of the Roundtable, conflict was a principal topic of discussion. The meeting noted that

> [c]onflicts are the primary drivers of forced displacement in Africa. Addressing the structural drivers of conflict requires long-term strategies and joint ownership. The role of states in pursuing political solutions and preventive diplomacy is paramount. All stakeholders must strive to build a common understanding of these drivers and implement an integrated holistic approach to conflict prevention.
> 
> *(AU 2019b, 2)*

The meeting also acknowledged, among other things, that '[s]olutions to conflicts and other causes of displacement and humanitarian crisis is fundamentally political and, as such, political commitments are prerequisite actions in addressing root causes and ending conflicts' (AU 2019b, 6). In addition to this focus on conflict and other root causes of forced displacement at the roundtable launching the theme of the year, the role of conflict in driving displacement on the continent came up across the several meetings convened in connection with the theme of 2019.[5]

In 2020, the theme was 'Silencing the Guns: Creating Conducive Conditions for Africa's Development', aimed at ending all wars, civil conflicts, gender-based violence and violent conflict and preventing genocide on the continent. It reinforces Agenda 2063's fourth aspiration, 'a peaceful and secure Africa', which as a first step aims at 'dialogue-centred conflict prevention and resolution', such that 'by 2020 all guns will be silent' (AU 2015, 6). The AU Commission views the themes of 2019 and 2020 as inextricably linked. According to the Director of the AU Commission's Department of Political Affairs (DPA), Khabele Matlosa, 'addressing structural root causes is the key component linking the two themes together' (cited in Abebe 2020). In other words, successful 'responses to forced displacement lie not in decreasing the number of displaced persons, but in dealing with the drivers of their displacement. And conflict is the single most important driver' (Abebe 2020). To this end, in their Declaration to mark the end of the Year of Refugees, Returnees and IDPs, the Assembly urged member states to 'implement pledges and recommendations that have been made in the context of the activities of the 2019 theme of the year including by establishing stronger linkages with the 2020 theme of the year' (AU 2020a, para. 6).

The AU's Executive Council, the Union's policymaking body composed of member state foreign ministers, has addressed the importance of conflict prevention in the context of forced displacement on the continent. In 2017, for example, the Council expressed its 'deep concern . . . regarding [the] situation of refugees in Africa' and called on 'all stakeholders, Member States and international organizations to look at the root causes of refugees in Africa, working collectively on finding solutions to conflicts on the continent' (AU 2017, para. 2).

## Structural barriers to the prevention agenda

It is clear from the foregoing that contemporary law and policy on internal and external displacement in Africa is concerned with preventing the conflict that contributes to most forced displacement on the continent. What is less clear, however, is whether this concern translates into action by the major forced displacement actors in Africa: the UNHCR and the AU Commission. This section demonstrates how, despite law and policy about the importance of preventing conflict and hence forced displacement, UNHCR's mandate and the structure of the AU Commission preclude their meaningful engagement with conflict prevention.

## UNHCR

The UN General Assembly created UNHCR as one of its programmes in 1949, in light of the massive displacement caused by World War II, the UN's responsibility for the international protection of refugees and the need for a UN organization to facilitate the voluntary repatriation of refugees displaced by the war or their 'assimilation within new national communities' (UN General Assembly 1949, para. 1). UNHCR's original mandate was to last just three years (UN General Assembly 1950, para. 5); however, it was extended due to ongoing need.

In practice today, UNHCR conducts refugee status determination when states are unwilling or unable to do so, provides refugees with material and legal protection, issues doctrinal guidance on key refugee law issues and, more generally, promotes respect for the right to seek and to enjoy asylum, among other things. In its report 'UNHCR's Strategic Directions 2017–2021', the organization committed itself to focusing on protecting the rights of the forcibly displaced, responding to humanitarian emergencies, working towards the socio-economic inclusion of the forcibly displaced within host communities, empowering forcibly displaced persons to take control of the decisions that affect their lives, and resolving situations of protracted displacement (UNHCR 2017).

Notwithstanding this broad strategic direction, UNHCR is an apolitical organization. Its Statute provides that its work 'shall be of an entirely non-political character; it shall be humanitarian and social' (UN General Assembly 1950, para. 2). Furthermore, in the preamble to the 1951 Convention – which UNHCR is responsible for supervising – the contracting parties express 'the wish that all States, recognizing the social and humanitarian nature of the problem of refugees, will do everything within their power to prevent this problem from becoming a cause of tension between States' (UN 1951 preambular para. 5). Similarly, when they adopted the 1969 OAU Convention, which is the 1951 Convention's 'effective regional complement' (1969 OAU Convention, art. VIII(2)), heads of state and government were aware 'that refugee problems are a source of friction among many Member States' and were 'desirous of eliminating the source of such discord' (UN 1969, preambular para. 3). They therefore recognized 'the need for an essentially humanitarian approach towards solving the problems of refugees' (UN 1969, preambular para. 2). Additionally, according to international humanitarian law and the UN General Assembly, humanitarian action must be governed by the principles of humanity (UN 1977, art. 1(2)); neutrality; impartiality (UN General Assembly 1991); and independence (UN General Assembly 2004). UNHCR is guided by these four humanitarian principles in 'its response to *all* humanitarian crises, *whether caused by conflict, violence or natural disasters*' (UNHCR 2015a; emphasis added). The second and final principles are particularly important in the context of conflict-induced forced displacement. According to the principle of neutrality, humanitarian actors 'must not take sides in hostilities or engage in controversies of a political, racial, religious or ideological nature' (UNOCHA 2012). Under the principle of independence, humanitarian action 'must be autonomous from the political, economic, military or other objectives that any actor may hold with regard to areas where humanitarian action is being implemented' (UNOCHA 2012). Thus pursuant to its Statute, the 1951 Convention and international law more generally, UNHCR cannot become involved in the political dimensions of conflict-induced forced displacement. This precludes its formal engagement with conflict prevention.

This limitation is reflected in UNHCR's practice. For example, in the context of the GCR, UNHCR continues to forge new partnerships with development actors such as the World Bank. This contributes to the GCR's objective of promoting refugees' self-reliance, and it can contribute to preventing forced displacement where extreme poverty causes people to move. However, UNHCR has yet to forge any (or any publicly visible) partnerships with actors responsible for conflict prevention, such as the UN's Department of Political and Peacebuilding Affairs or, on the non-governmental side, organizations like the International Crisis Group. Thus while the humanitarian-development portion of the 'humanitarian-development-peace nexus' has at long last been operationalized, the humanitarian-peace portion has yet to be realized. This is addressed further in the final section of this chapter, following the discussion of structural barriers to the prevention agenda in the AU context.

## *The AU*

The AU is a continental union of all 55 states in Africa and its waters,[6] formed when it superseded the OAU in 2001. It is aimed at achieving unity and solidarity among African states and peoples; defending the sovereignty, territorial integrity and independence of its member states; accelerating African political and socio-economic integration; promoting and defending common African positions; encouraging international cooperation; promoting peace, security, stability, democracy, good governance, and human and peoples' rights; fostering strong African participation in the global economy and international relations; promoting sustainable development, the integration of African economies and cooperation in all fields of human activity; coordinating and harmonizing policies across regional economic communities; promoting research; and co-operating for public health (UN 2000, art. 3).

The AU's principal tool to advance these broad objectives is member state policy coordination. Continental policies are set by the AU's Assembly or by its Executive Council and are promoted or implemented by the Union's bureaucracy, the AU Commission. The Commission is led by a chairperson, a deputy chairperson and eight commissioners, each of whom heads a discrete department: Peace and Security; Political Affairs; Infrastructure and Energy; Social Affairs; Trade and Industry; Rural Economy and Agriculture; Human Resources, Science and Technology; and Economic Affairs. Other key AU bodies include the Permanent Representatives' Committee (PRC), which comprises member states' Addis Ababa–based AU ambassadors, and the Peace and Security Council (PSC), which makes political decisions regarding the prevention, management and resolution of conflict on the continent.

AU Commission responsibility for forced displacement resides with DPA, which is led by Commissioner for Political Affairs Minata Cessouma Samate of Burkina Faso. According to its website, DPA is responsible for 'promoting, facilitating, coordinating and encouraging democratic principles and the rule of law, respect for human rights, participation of civil society in the development process of the continent and the achievement of durable solutions for addressing humanitarian crises'; forced displacement falls under the latter. It is addressed by DPA's Division of Humanitarian Affairs, Refugees and Displaced Persons (HARDP). According to its website, HARDP provides

> continental direction to the achievement of durable solutions for addressing humanitarian crises caused by conflicts, man-made and natural disasters. This includes

*identifying and advocating for early warning and early interventions to address the root causes.* It also includes pursuing actions to alleviate the plight of refugees, returnees and [. . .] IDPs, including meeting their immediate protection and assistance needs and supporting conditions and activities for voluntary repatriation, as well as local integration and resettlement in and outside Africa.

In addition, HARDP is the secretariat of the PRC's Sub-committee on Refugees, Returnees and IDPs, and it coordinates the AU's Special Emergency Assistance Fund for Drought and Famine in Africa as well as its agenda for the continental free movement of persons.

HARDP's mandate includes addressing the root causes of forced displacement. In practice, activities in this regard take place in the context of Commissioner Samate's broader democracy, rule of law and human rights mandate, within which she can pursue diplomatic strategies to prevent or resolve conflict. These activities are not, however, central to her role, which is more focused on 'political affairs' in the traditional sense of free and fair elections. Indeed, in addition to HARDP, DPA also includes a unit for Democracy, Governance, Human Rights and Elections. True AU authority regarding conflict prevention, management and resolution resides with the political PSC and with the AU Commission's Department of Peace and Security. While there is some space for Commissioner Samate to promote negotiated solutions to conflict, the extent to which DPA/HARDP can pursue 'early interventions to address the root causes' of forced displacement is in reality limited by the fact that AU responsibility for conflict prevention is located elsewhere.

This dislocation between forced displacement on the one hand and conflict prevention on the other will be amplified by the ongoing AU reforms. In July 2016, African heads of state and government and ministers of foreign affairs and finance convened in Kigali, Rwanda, to address the AU's fitness for purpose. Thereafter, the Assembly mandated Rwandan President Paul Kagame to study and report on the institutional reform of the AU with a view to creating 'a system of governance capable of addressing the challenges facing the Union' (AU 2016, para. 2). Kagame delivered his report in January 2017. It identified several problems with the AU, including 'a fragmented organisation with a multitude of focus areas', 'underperformance of some organs and institutions due to unclear mandates or chronic underfunding' and 'inefficient working methods in both the Commission and the Assembly' (Kagame 2017, 4). The report identified four areas for action to address these and other problems: focus on key priorities with continental scope, realigning AU institutions to deliver against these priorities, efficient management at both the political and operational levels, and sustainable financing (Kagame 2017, 5). Within the second action area, Kagame recommended that the AU Commission's 'structures should be re-evaluated to ensure they have the right size and capabilities to deliver on the agreed priority areas' (Kagame 2017, 7).

Informed by Kagame's report, the Assembly convened in extraordinary session in 2018 to deliberate AU reform. They decided to reduce the number of commissioners and associated portfolios from eight to six: agriculture, rural development, blue (marine) economy and sustainable environment; economic development, trade, industry and mining; education, science, technology and innovation; infrastructure and energy; political affairs, peace and security; and health, humanitarian affairs and social development (AU 2018a, para. 3). The AU's decision to merge political affairs with peace and security followed the UN's decision to merge its Department of Political Affairs with the UN Peacebuilding Support Office (creating, on 1 January 2019, the UN's Department of Political and Peacebuilding Affairs); this may have influenced thinking within the AU.

To implement these reforms, the chairperson of the AU Commission sought input from Commission staff and from an independent firm; proposals were submitted to member states for their consideration in May 2019. At its February 2020 summit, the Assembly adopted a new structure for the AU Commission (AU 2020b, para. 3), which is being implemented over a three-year transition period that commenced in July 2020. During this time, DPA is effectively merging with the Department of Peace and Security; however, DPA's responsibility for humanitarian affairs, which includes forced displacement, is being transferred to the Department of Social Affairs, which is becoming the Department of Health, Humanitarian Affairs and Social Development (DHHS). This change officially divorces responsibility for humanitarian response to forced displacement from responsibility for preventing the conflicts that cause forced displacement: the latter will reside with the Department of Political Affairs, Peace and Security, while the former will be located in DHHS.[7] According to individuals involved in the reform process who spoke on the condition of anonymity, it was felt that humanitarian issues fit naturally within DHHS, and that situating them there would allow the Department of Political Affairs, Peace and Security to have a purely political mandate. Situating forced displacement in DHHS is reminiscent of the 'care and maintenance' approach to refugee protection that was discredited in the 1980s (Harrell-Bond 1986) and which – with the GCR's focus on self-reliance – the international community has now firmly rejected.

## 'Root causes': from rhetoric to reality

UNHCR's apolitical mandate and the structure of the AU Commission prevent these key forced displacement actors from engaging meaningfully with the prevention agenda. To deliver on the 'root causes' rhetoric they both espouse, UNHCR and the AU Commission's DPA/HARDP must collaborate with actors mandated to prevent and resolve conflict, such as the UN's Department of Political and Peacebuilding Affairs, the AU's PSC and its Department of Peace and Security and civil society actors. Such collaboration can take many forms. For example, UNHCR could share information acquired through its on-the-ground presence with political and peacebuilding actors in a position to employ it in peace processes.

The role of collaboration in transcending mandate-based silos has been recognized for some time in terms of the 'humanitarian-development nexus'. This refers to efforts to bridge the long-standing gap between humanitarian actors, who depend on independence from governments and belligerents to carry out their relief work, and development actors, whose work relies on cooperation with state actors (Stamnes 2016). The humanitarian-development nexus crystallized in 2016 at the World Humanitarian Summit. The event included a High-Level Leaders' Roundtable themed 'From Delivering Aid to Ending Need', where participants committed to 'a new way of working that meets people's immediate humanitarian needs, while at the same time reducing risk and vulnerability over multiple years through the achievement of collective outcomes' (World Humanitarian Summit 2016, 2). To achieve this, participants further committed to 'work together . . . based on the comparative advantage of a diverse range of actors' (World Humanitarian Summit 2016, 2). Further to this commitment and other Summit outcomes, following the World Humanitarian Summit the old 'humanitarian-development nexus' became the 'humanitarian-development-peace nexus', and discussion of this 'triple nexus' and 'new ways of working' became commonplace. Indeed, as mentioned above, the GCR's section on root causes calls for 'improved cooperation among political, humanitarian, development and peace actors' (United Nations General Assembly 2018, para. 8), and states commit with the GCR to addressing refugee issues through 'a multi-stakeholder and partnership approach' (United Nations General Assembly 2018, para. 33).

However, wide recognition of the triple nexus has not entrenched collaboration between humanitarian (i.e. relief) and peace (i.e. political affairs) actors to prevent conflict-induced forced displacement in Africa. There are several possible explanations in this regard – beyond the structural issues identified above, as collaboration is after all aimed at working around these – and related solutions. Regarding UNHCR, first and foremost is the scale of the crisis of forced displacement in Africa coupled with severe budgetary constraints. Resources have not kept pace with need, forcing all humanitarian organizations to do more with less. In such circumstances, it is hardly surprising that UNHCR has not expanded its programming to include collaboration with non-traditional partners. UNHCR's fundraising should recognize that the 'new ways of working' agreed at the World Humanitarian Summit and necessary to contribute to preventing conflict-induced forced displacement in Africa require dedicated resources. Second is the issue of state sovereignty and humanitarian space. UNHCR requires a country's permission to operate on its territory. This often forces the organization to make difficult choices, including perhaps decisions against becoming even tangentially involved (via collaboration) in the conflict that gave rise to the displacement it is responding to. UNHCR's root causes rhetoric should recognize that the imperative of preserving humanitarian space sometimes will (and should) preclude concomitant prevention activities.

Regarding the AU, it may be that internal AU Commission politics and poor management (Allison 2020) preclude collaboration between DPA on the one hand and peace and security entities on the other. Thus while the institutional reform process may entrench the split between humanitarian affairs and peace and security, it also presents an opportunity to promote greater collaboration, by confronting any institutional politics and mismanagement that have been preventing this. The AU Commission's new leadership must recognize that humanitarian actors cannot repeatedly raise the importance of eliminating the root causes of forced displacement without also taking meaningful action in this regard.

## Conclusion

Contemporary law and policy on forced displacement now almost always speaks to the root causes of the problem. In Africa, this means conflict. However, the principal forced displacement actors on the continent, UNHCR and the AU Commission's DPA, have no conflict-prevention mandates. UNHCR is a humanitarian organization, meaning it is bound by the principles of humanity, neutrality, impartiality and independence; furthermore, its Statute specifies that its work must be apolitical. The mandate of the AU Commission's DPA is narrowly construed; responsibility for peace and security resides elsewhere, in the bureaucratic Department of Peace and Security and with the political PSC. As a result, key forced displacement actors are structurally precluded from engaging with prevention in the African context. The way around this is collaboration with organizations with conflict-prevention mandates; the general importance of such collaboration has been widely recognized since the World Humanitarian Summit in 2016. Yet it has not occurred in the context of preventing conflict-induced forced displacement in Africa, possibly due in UNHCR's case to issues of budget and humanitarian space, and in the AU Commission's case to institutional politics. UNHCR and the AU Commission should address these issues so as to transform the root causes rhetoric into reality. The ongoing institutional reform of the AU represents both a challenge and an opportunity in this regard; the opportunity aspect should not be missed. If the humanitarian imperative prevents real collaboration between forced displacement and peace actors to prevent and resolve conflict, UNHCR and the AU Commission should nuance their messaging accordingly, to avoid empty words when the stakes are so high.

## Notes

1 This expression has been branded 'delightfully redundant' (Khazan 2020). For critical analysis of the focus on 'root causes' in human rights generally, see Marks (2011).
2 On its own or in combination with other displacement drivers, such as extreme poverty and the effects of climate change. Of the ten major source countries analysed by the International Crisis Group (2016), six were in Africa (the Central African Republic, the Democratic Republic of the Congo, Eritrea, Somalia, South Sudan and Sudan); in each African case except Eritrea, displacement was caused by violent conflict.
3 As mentioned in the introduction, the focus on prevention is not particularly new; this temporal focus should not be taken to suggest that it is.
4 The CRRF was incorporated within the GCR and is now being implemented more broadly.
5 I was involved in these meetings in my capacity as senior legal officer with UNHCR's Representation to the AU and the UN Economic Commission for Africa, a position I held during 2019.
6 This is the AU's count of its membership. It includes Western Sahara, which is not universally recognized as a state.
7 Additionally, DHHS will have less capacity to address force displacement than HARDP. The department will be split in two sections, with health and humanitarian affairs overseen by one director and social development, culture and sports overseen by another. Humanitarian affairs will have a head and five staff, which is less than the approximately eight individuals currently working at HARDP; each of the other four units within DHHS will have more staff than humanitarian affairs. This is perhaps because the AU is currently working to establish the African Humanitarian Agency as an operational AU organ.

## References

Abebe, T., (2020) 'Do the African Union's Annual Themes Deliver?', *Institute for Security Studies*, 11 February. [online]. Available at: Do the African Union's annual themes deliver? – ISS Africa (Accessed: 17 February 2020).
African Union, (2009). *African Union Convention for the Protection and Assistance of Internally Displaced Persons in Africa*, adopted 23 October, entered into force 6 December 2012.
African Union, (2015) *Agenda 2063: The Africa We Want*. [online]. Available at: https://au.int/sites/default/files/documents/36204-doc-agenda2063_popular_version_en.pdf (Accessed: 17 February 2020).
African Union (Assembly), (2016) *Decision on the Institutional Reform of the African Union*, Assembly/AU/Dec.606 (XXVII), Kigali, 17–18 July.
African Union (Assembly), (2018a) *Decision on the Institutional Reform*, Ext/Assembly/AU/Dec.1 (XI), Addis Ababa, 17–18 November.
African Union (Assembly), (2018b) *Decision on the 2019 Theme of the Year 'The Year of Refugees, Returnees and Internally Displaced Persons: Towards Durable Solutions to Forced Displacement in Africa'*, Assembly/AU/Dec.707(XXXI), Nouakchott, 1–2 July.
African Union (Assembly), (2019a) *Declaration on the African Union Theme of the Year 2019: "The Year of Refugees, Returnees and Internally Displaced Persons: Towards Durable Solutions to Forced Displacement in Africa"*, Assembly/AU/Decl.8(XXXII), Addis Ababa, 10–11 February.
African Union (Assembly), (2019b) *Summary Conclusions: Roundtable on Addressing Root Causes and Achieving Durable Solutions in Africa*. [online]. Available at: https://reliefweb.int/sites/reliefweb.int/files/resources/68798.pdf (Accessed: 11 February 2020).
African Union (Assembly), (2020a) *Declaration on the 2019 Theme of the Year on "Refugees, Returnees and Internally Displaced Persons: Towards Durable Solutions to Forced Displacement in Africa"*, Assembly/AU/Decl.1 (XXXIII), Addis Ababa, 9–10 February.
African Union (Assembly), (2020b) *Decision on the Structures of the African Union Commission, Organs and Specialized Agencies*, Assembly/AU/Dec.750 (XXXIII), Addis Ababa, 9–10 February.
African Union (Executive Council), (2017) *Decision on Humanitarian Situation in Africa*, EX.CL/Dec.968 (XXXI), Addis Ababa, 1 July.
Allison, S., (2020) 'Exclusive: A 'Mafia-style' Cartel is Running the African Union, Claim Staff', *Mail & Guardian*, 12 March. [online]. Available at: Exclusive: A 'mafia-style' cartel is running the African Union, claim staff – The Mail & Guardian (mg.co.za) (Accessed: 12 March 2020).

ECOSOC, (1998) *Guiding Principles on Internal Displacement, E/CN.4/1998/53/Add.2*, 11 February, Annex.

Farrell, T. and Schmitt, O., (2017) 'The Causes, Character and Conduct of Internal Armed Conflict and the Effects on Civilian Populations, 1990–2010', in Türk, V., Edwards, A. and Wouters, C., (eds.) *In Flight from Conflict and Violence: UNHCR's Consultations on Refugee Status and Other Forms of International Protection*. Cambridge: Cambridge University Press.

Gilbert, G., (1993) 'Root Causes and International Law: Refugee Flows in the 1990's', *Netherlands Quarterly of Human Rights*, 11(4). pp. 413–436.

Harrell-Bond, B., (1986) *Imposing Aid: Emergency Assistance to Refugees*. Oxford: Oxford University Press.

International Crisis Group (ICG), (2016) *What's Driving the Global Refugee Crisis?* 15 September. [online]. Available at: www.crisisgroup.org/global/what-s-driving-global-refugee-crisis (Accessed: 24 February 2020).

Kagame, P., (2017) *The Imperative to Strengthen our Union: Report of the Proposed Recommendations for the Institutional Reform of the African Union*, 29 January. Available at: https://au.int/sites/default/files/pages/34915-file-report-20institutional20reform20of20the20au-2.pdf.

Khazan, O., (2020) 'Corporate Buzzwords are how Workers Pretend to be Adults', *The Atlantic*, 19 February. [online]. Available at: www.theatlantic.com/health/archive/2020/02/most-annoying-corporate-buzzwords/606748/ (Accessed: 20 March 2020).

Marks, S., (2011) 'Human Rights and Root Causes', *The Modern Law Review*, 74(1), pp. 57–78.

Okoth-Obbo, G., (1995) 'The OAU/UNHCR Symposium on Refugees and Forced Population Displacements in Africa – A Review Article', *International Journal of Refugee Law*, 7, [Special Issue Summer 1995], pp. 274–299.

Sharpe, M., (2017) 'The 1969 OAU Refugee Convention in the Context of Individual Refugee Status Determination', in Türk, V., Edwards, A. and Wouters, C., (eds.) *In Flight from Conflict and Violence: UNHCR's Consultations on Refugee Status and Other Forms of International Protection*. Cambridge: Cambridge University Press.

Sharpe, M., (2018) 'The Global Compact on Refugees and Conflict Prevention in Africa: "Root Causes" and Yet Another Divide', *International Journal of Refugee Law*, 30(4), pp. 707–710.

Stamnes, E., (2016) 'Rethinking the Humanitarian-Development Nexus', *Norwegian Institute of International Affairs, Policy Brief, 24*. Oslo: NUPI.

UNHCR, (2015a) *Emergency Handbook*. [online]. Available at: https://emergency.unhcr.org/entry/44765/humanitarian-principles (Accessed: 30 January 2020).

UNHCR, (2015b) *High Commissioner's Dialogue on Protection Challenges: Background Paper*, para. 3. [online]. Available at: www.unhcr.org/564c53429.html (Accessed: 6 February 2020).

UNHCR, (2016) *Guidelines on International Protection No. 12: Claims for Refugee Status Related to Situations of Armed Conflict and Violence under Article 1A(2) of the 1951 Convention and/or 1967 Protocol relating to the Status of Refugees and the Regional Refugee Definitions, HCR/GIP/16/12*. [online]. Available at: www.refworld.org/docid/583595ff4.html (Accessed: 18 February 2020).

UNHCR, (2017) *UNHCR's Strategic Directions 2017–2021*. [online]. Available at: www.unhcr.org/excom/announce/5894558d4/unhcrs-strategic-directions-2017-2021.html (Accessed: 18 February 2020).

UNHCR, (2019) *Global Trends: Forced Displacement in 2018*. Geneva: United Nations High Commissioner for Refugees.

United Nations, (1951) *Convention Relating to the Status of Refugees*, 189 Series 137, adopted 28 July 1951, entered into force 22 April 1954.

United Nations, (1967) *Protocol Relating to the Status of Refugees*, 606 Series 267, adopted 31 January, entered into force 4 October 1967.

United Nations, (1969) *Organization of African Unity Convention Governing the Specific Aspects of Refugee Problems in Africa*, 1001 Series 45, adopted 10 September, entered into force 20 June 1974.

United Nations, (1977) *Protocol Additional to the Geneva Conventions of 12 August 1949, and Relating to the Protection of Victims of International Armed Conflicts*, 1125 Series 3, adopted 8 June, entry into force 7 December 1978.

United Nations, (2000) *Constitutive Act of the African Union*, 2158 Series 3, adopted 11 July, entered into force 26 May 2001.

United Nations General Assembly, (1949), *Refugees and Stateless Persons, A/RES/319(IV)*. New York, NY: United Nations.

United Nations General Assembly, (1950), *Statute of the Office of the United Nations High Commissioner for Refugees, A/RES/428(V)*, Annex. New York, NY: United Nations.

United Nations General Assembly, (1991) *Strengthening of the Coordination of Humanitarian Emergency Assistance of the United Nations, A/RES/ 46/182*. New York, NY: United Nations.

United Nations General Assembly, (2004) *Renforcement de la coordination de l'aide humanitaire d'urgence fournie par l'Organisation des Nations Unies, A/RES/58/114*. New York, NY: United Nations.

United Nations General Assembly, (2016) *Declaration for Refugees and Migrants, A/RES/71/1*. New York, NY: United Nations.

United Nations General Assembly, (2018) *Report of the United Nations High Commissioner for Refugees, Part II, Global Compact on Refugees, A/73/12*. New York, NY: United Nations.

UNOCHA, (2012) *What Are Humanitarian Principles*. [online]. Available at: www.unocha.org/sites/dms/Documents/OOM-humanitarianprinciples_eng_June12.pdf (Accessed: 30 January 2020).

World Humanitarian Summit, (2016) *Changing People's Lives: From Delivering Aid to Ending Need, High-Level Leaders' Roundtable, Core Responsibility Four of the Agenda for Humanity*. [online]. Available at: www.agendaforhumanity.org/sites/default/files/resources/2017/Jul/CHANGING_PEOPLE%E2%80%99S_LIVES-FROM_DELIVERING_AID_TO_ENDING_NEED.pdf (Accessed: 24 February 2020).

# PART II

# Themes and Debates

# 5
# AFRICAN MEDIATION IN HIGH-INTENSITY CONFLICT
## How African?

*Laurie Nathan*

## Introduction

Over the past three decades Africa has been the site of numerous high-intensity conflicts, which include unconstitutional changes of government, electoral disputes, political and ethnic violence and full-blown civil wars. Mediation is arguably the most common international response to these conflicts (Duursma 2017). This chapter addresses the question of whether mediation on the continent is distinctly African. On the face of it, the answer appears to be an unequivocal 'yes'. The clarion call of 'African solutions to African problems' has driven the formation, evolution and policies of multilateral institutions with a mandate for peace and security (Møller 2009). These institutions include the African Union (AU) and the sub-regional bodies known as regional economic communities (RECs), such as the Economic Community of West African States (ECOWAS), the Intergovernmental Authority on Development (IGAD) and the Southern African Development Community (SADC).[1]

In this chapter, I argue that the African character of mediation in high-intensity conflicts is not in fact clear-cut: it is strongly evident in the *identity* of the actors that lead mediation; it is not discernible in the *strategy and style* of mediation; and it is partially evident in the *content* of mediated agreements. The chapter is organized around the themes of mediation actors, mediation style and strategy, and the content of mediated agreements. It highlights a number of gaps in the literature and raises questions for further research.

## Mediation actors

Across the continent there is consensus that mediation in major conflicts should be led by African organizations. The maxim of 'African solutions to African problems' is an assertion of self-reliance, responsibility and ownership, as well as resistance to Western interventions on the continent (Nathan 2013a). In the realm of peace and security, it reflects a global tendency of regional organizations to play a prominent role in conflict prevention and resolution in their respective geographic domains. The principle of subsidiarity in peacemaking has its roots in article 52 of the United Nations (UN) Charter, which promotes regional arrangements and agencies for dealing with matters relating to the maintenance of international peace and security as are appropriate for regional action.

There is a sound motivation for subsidiarity. Regional organizations have a good understanding of the conflicts and conflict actors in their neighborhood, they have a compelling interest in regional stability, they can build affinity and trust among member states through frequent interaction, they have legitimacy in the eyes of national actors, and their mediation efforts are less likely to be perceived as external interference. Even if the RECs do not have substantial material resources, they have leverage in their ability to condemn and suspend member states that transgress regional norms.

Subsidiarity can also have drawbacks. As a result of the limited African resources for peacemaking, long-term mediations are dependent on external funding, which can lead to inappropriate donor prescriptions and pressure. In 2014 international partners covered as much as 96% of the budget for the operationalization of the African Peace and Security Architecture (APSA), which covers the AU and the RECs (Nathan et al. 2015, 81). In 2016 the AU expressed concern that external partners funded over 95% of its preventive diplomacy and mediation activities (African Union 2016a, 5). No comprehensive research has been done on the implications of this. One pattern is apparent, though. Donors often play a problematic role in pressing mediators to move hastily to produce a peace agreement before the conflict parties have achieved the consensus and reconciliation needed to make the agreement sustainable. This occurred in the AU mediation for Darfur in 2005–2006 (Nathan 2006); in the South Sudan government's mediation for the conflict in northern Uganda in 2006–2008 (Hendrickson and Tumutegyereize 2012); and in the mediation for South Sudan led by IGAD in 2013–2015 (Garang 2015).

In a study on African mediation in East Africa, Khadiagala (2007, 6) contends that escalating civil conflicts have propelled neighbors to assume responsibility for mediation even though they lack hard power, conventional leverage and the 'concrete diplomatic and political tools that make for effective mediation' (Khadiagala 2007, 6). Given their limited material resources, African interveners rely on 'organizational power' (Khadiagala 2007, 6–7). This power derives from the conflict parties' inability to resolve their predicament on their own and their consequent acceptance of the mediator as an authoritative intervener. The power is exercised through the mediator's control over the conflict resolution process and influence over the content. It encompasses creativity, persistence, patience, leadership skills, competence and knowledge about the conflict and the parties. African mediators also enjoy legitimacy and moral leverage as a result of their personal stature and the standing of the country or organization that appointed them (Khadiagala 2007, 7–9).

Over the past decade, the AU and many of the RECs have made a concerted effort to address some of the material and diplomatic deficits identified by Khadiagala (2007). They have sought to build the capacity and professionalism of their mediation activities through training, the development of policies, case studies that identify best practice, and the establishment of mediation support units (e.g. African Union 2016b; Economic Community of West African States 2018; Hartman 2013). It is not clear, however, that these efforts have had a significant impact in the field (Nathan et al. 2015, chap. 7).

African subsidiarity in peacemaking is especially problematic when the partisan interests of member states compromise mediation fairness and impartiality, prevent the AU and the RECs from acting with unity of purpose and reduce the conflict parties' confidence in the process. These problems were starkly evident in the IGAD mediation to end the civil war that broke out in South Sudan in 2013. The IGAD member states had conflicting goals and interests in that country (International Crisis Group 2015). Uganda deployed troops to defend the South Sudanese government against the armed opposition and was thus both a belligerent party and a member of the mediating body. Sudan, on the other hand, armed the opposition. Sudan and Uganda had long been engaged in proxy hostilities in the region, supporting each other's dissidents, while Kenya, Ethiopia and Uganda vied for regional influence. These divisions weakened international support for the mediation, reduced the mediators' leverage over the parties, made it hard for the IGAD Summit to reach consensus, and caused the parties to be skeptical of the process (International Crisis Group 2015).

There has often been a high degree of peacemaking cooperation between the RECs, the AU and the UN, but there have also been a number of acrimonious disputes between two or more of these organizations. As discussed by Nathan (2017a), the high-profile cases include Zimbabwe (2008), Madagascar (2009), Côte d'Ivoire (2011), Darfur (2011), Libya (2011), Guinea-Bissau (2012), Mali (2012), the Central African Republic (2013 and 2015) and Burkina Faso (2015). These disputes had extremely negative repercussions for peacemaking, undermining domestic and international confidence in the mediation initiatives and enabling the parties to play off one mediator against the other.

At a political level, the inter-organizational disputes revolved around strategy and norms. In some conflicts, the issue in contention was whether to rely on mediation or resort to military force; in other instances, the debate focused on the most appropriate mediation strategy, and there was a recurring tension between adherence to democratic principles and the imperative of peace and stability (Nathan 2017a). At a juridico-structural level, the disputes derived from a lack of clarity and consensus on which organization should lead peacemaking efforts in a given conflict. While the UN Charter endorses the principle of subsidiarity, article 24(1) asserts that the UN Security Council has primary responsibility for the maintenance of international peace and security. Article 52(4) insists, moreover, that regional efforts to resolve a conflict do not impair the Security Council's authority to intervene in that conflict. The AU similarly embraces the contradictory principles of primacy and subsidiarity (Nathan 2017a, 158–159).

The inherent contradiction between the principles of subsidiarity and primacy is not resolvable conceptually or in practice. It has therefore been argued that the most appropriate guiding principle in African mediation should be 'strategic partnerships' between the AU, the UN and the RECs (Nathan 2017a). The motivation is that each of these organizations has strengths and limitations, none of them has an exclusive or overwhelming comparative advantage in any particular case, and strategic partnerships are synergistic and mitigate the organizations' respective limitations. Since many of the inter-organizational disputes eventually evolve into a partnership, it would make sense to initiate the partnerships as the earliest possible stage.

Support for strategic partnerships in African mediation can be found in statistical research. In an analysis of mediation in African armed conflicts between 1960 and 2012, Duursma (2017) finds that African mediating bodies are far more likely than non-African mediators to succeed in getting the conflict parties to conclude a peace agreement; that the African-brokered agreements are also more likely to be durable; but that the most effective model entails joint African and non-African mediation endeavors, with African leadership. Duursma (2017) believes that the effectiveness of the joint model is due to the legitimacy that flows from the 'African solutions' norm combined with the capacity and material incentives offered by the non-African third parties.

Much of the groundwork for strategic partnerships has already been laid. The AU and the RECs have formally expressed a commitment to peace and security partnerships (e.g. African Union 2002; 2008). This is also true of the UN and the AU (e.g. African Union 2012; United Nations Security Council 2014). Over the past decade, these commitments have been effectuated through structural and programmatic arrangements (Nathan et al. 2015, chap. 8). Nonetheless, two crucial challenges remain. First, the partnership frameworks have been developed along parallel tracks, between the UN and the AU (United Nations and Africa Union 2014) and between the AU and the RECs (African Union 2014a). This is not appropriate, since peacemaking in most African conflicts requires a triadic partnership between the UN, the AU and one of the RECs.

The second challenge stems from the fact that the partnerships are being built between the organizations' secretariats and not at the vastly more important level of the member state decision-making bodies (Nathan et al. 2015, chap. 8). The major disputes in peacemaking arise because of political differences between the UN Security Council, the AU Peace and Security Council (PSC) and the equivalent entities of the RECs, typically as a result of the interests and values of their influential member states. There are no adequate mechanisms to address such differences and craft a common peacemaking stance on a given conflict. By way of illustration, the AU PSC does not consult the SADC Organ for Politics, Defence and Security Cooperation when deliberating on conflicts in Southern Africa. It simply expects SADC to follow its lead. The PSC is frustrated when the Organ fails to do this, the Organ is frustrated at the lack of consultation, and strategic divergence is more likely than it might otherwise be. It should be stressed that the consultation failure is political, not technical. It could be overcome in various technical ways if the political will existed.

## Mediation style and strategy

The relative effectiveness of different mediation styles and strategies is a major line of inquiry in international mediation studies. A prominent conceptual framework is the distinction drawn by Zartman and Touval (2007) between communicative, formulative and manipulative modes of mediation. In the first of these, the mediator is merely a conduit, carrying messages between the parties; in the second, the mediator engages with the substance of the negotiations and makes proposals for resolving the conflict; in the third, the mediator exercises leverage to push and pull the parties towards an agreement. According to Zartman and Touval (2007, 455–458), mediators have five sources of leverage: persuasion (i.e. portraying an alternative future as more favorable than the continuing conflict); extraction (i.e. producing an attractive position from each party); termination (i.e. withdrawing from the mediation); deprivation (i.e. withholding resources from one side or shifting them to the other); and gratification (i.e. adding resources to the outcome).

No systematic analyses have been done on African mediation styles and strategies in high-intensity conflict. However, a study of African mediation in response to the 14 coups that occurred in the period 2000–2014 affords a number of insights (Nathan 2017b). African actors mediated in 86% of these coups – one was led by the AU, one was led by an African state and the rest were led by a REC. After 2003, when the AU was empowered to impose sanctions on member states, it applied sanctions in 73% of the coups. External actors, such as the European Union (EU) and the United States (US), applied sanctions in 91% of the cases. After 2003 the AU suspended 91% of the countries subject to a coup. The rate of suspension from RECs was 55%, lower than the AU partly because some of the countries were not members of a REC. The threat and use of force were generally not part of the African response: force was threatened by RECs on two occasions, by the AU once and by a state once, and no force was actually used against a junta.

The strategies for ending the coups were thus both formulative and manipulative, and they were undertaken by both African and other international actors. They encompassed mediation aimed at negotiating a roadmap to restore constitutional rule through free and fair elections, as well as coercive leverage to compel the coup regime to move in that direction. The combination of strategies proved effective: with one exception, constitutional rule was restored through elections, and in 67% of these cases the elections took place within two years of the coup

(Nathan 2017b). The exception was the 2003 coup in São Tomé and Príncipe, where constitutional rule was restored quickly through the reinstatement of the ousted president.

The combination of mediation and coercive leverage has been evident not only in coups but also in armed conflicts (e.g. Darfur and South Sudan) and lower-intensity violent conflicts (e.g. Kenya and Zimbabwe). In the Darfur case in 2005–2006, the AU led the mediation while the UN Security Council imposed an arms embargo and referred the conflict to the International Criminal Court (De Waal 2007). In the South Sudan case in 2013–2018, IGAD led the mediation and decided to apply targeted sanctions against the violators of the ceasefire agreement, while the UN Security Council introduced an arms embargo and a sanctions regime (IGAD 2018; United Nations 2019). In the Kenyan electoral conflict in 2007, Kofi Annan led the AU mediation, and the EU, the United Kingdom and the US threatened sanctions (Khadiagala 2008). In the Zimbabwe mediation in 2007–2013, SADC led the mediation, international finance institutions withheld loans from the Mugabe government, and the EU and the US introduced an arms embargo and targeted sanctions (Nathan 2012, chap. 4).

Although coercion was effective in the coup cases, in other instances it has been counterproductive and militated against successful mediation (Nathan 1999). For example, the Western sanctions against Zimbabwe united the SADC states in a posture of anti-imperialist solidarity with Mugabe and intensified their opposition to UN mediation (Nathan 2012, chap. 4). The Burundi conflict provides another example. In 1996 the government collapsed and Pierre Buyoya took power in a coup. Neighboring states imposed sanctions, which were endorsed by former President Nyerere of Tanzania, the official mediator for Burundi. The Buyoya regime participated in domestic negotiations and forged a partnership with some of its internal opponents, but it boycotted Nyerere's mediation on the grounds that he was biased. The sanctions reinforced extremist positions in the army and minority community, exacerbated economic deprivation and inequality, and enabled Buyoya to claim that Nyerere was the main obstacle to ending the crisis through negotiations (International Crisis Group 1998; Mthembu-Salter 1998).

The coup mediations highlight the importance of conflict resolution mandates in shaping the process and outcome of African efforts to address major crises. The largely consistent response to the coups (i.e. condemnation, suspension, sanctions and mediation) and the largely consistent outcomes (i.e. the formation of a transitional regime followed by elections within two years) were due to policy mandates that prohibit unconstitutional change of government (Nathan 2017b). The overarching normative mandate is contained chiefly in the 2000 Declaration on the Framework for an OAU Response to Unconstitutional Changes of Government and the 2007 African Charter on Democracy, Elections and Governance. This mandate was reinforced by resolutions issued by the AU PSC and the relevant REC in response to each coup (Nathan 2017b). These resolutions affirmed an emphatic position of 'zero tolerance of coups' and provided the strategic script for implementing that position.

In 2017 the journal *African Security* broke new ground with a special edition on mediation mandates, publishing case studies on the African and UN mandates for the conflicts in The Democratic Republic Congo, Libya, Madagascar, Namibia, Sudan and Zimbabwe.[2] Two conclusions were drawn from these studies (Nathan 2017c). First, the mandates were influential in diverse ways: they projected the consensual stance of the mediating organization, which was itself a form of leverage on the conflict parties; they appointed the mediator as an agent of the organization and thereby conferred authority and legitimacy on him; they provided instructions to the mediator; they sent messages to the parties and other actors about their expected behavior; and they determined the parameters of the conflict resolution process and outcome.

Second, the mandates were especially consequential when they generated incompatibilities and tensions. The case studies revealed mandate disputes between international organizations, as discussed above; within an international organization where member states had different perspectives on a conflict and its resolution; between the mediating body and the mediator; and between the various norms covered in the mandates. Of singular importance was the tension that arose where a mandate issued by the mediating organization was biased against one of the conflict parties, causing that party to refuse to consent to the mediation.[3]

The AU's general approach to mediation is set out in a number of documents.[4] It is based on the following strategic principles: the conflict parties must own the agreement; mediation should be inclusive of all significant political actors; civil society, including women's groups, should be involved in the mediation; the mediator should help the parties develop a relationship of trust and cooperation; mediation must be a non-threatening venture for the parties; mediators should be impartial; there is no quick-fix solution to deep-rooted conflict; mediators and partners must therefore avoid pushing the parties to sign agreements prematurely; the mediator should help the parties address the root causes of the conflict; mediators should avoid a formulaic approach and instead be flexible and responsive; the drafting and implementation of peace agreements should be properly linked; mediation should be based on sound analysis, strategy and process design; and mediation should be undertaken through partnerships between the AU, the UN and the relevant REC.

Research has not been conducted on whether these principles are actually applied in practice; therefore we do not know if they are effective. Aside from the assertion that mediation should be led by African actors, the principles are not distinctly African and largely reflect the approach taken in the *United Nations Guidance for Effective Mediation* (United Nations 2012a). The *African Union Mediation Support Handbook* captures this curious situation (African Union 2014b). In a publication that runs to nearly 200 pages and covers all aspects of the mediation process, the *Handbook* does not discuss the widespread problem of ethnic conflict, the potential and limitations of African approaches to conflict resolution, or a pan-African mediation style and strategy. Instead, 'culture' is portrayed as an attribute of local communities and the conflict parties; accordingly, mediators should have a 'cultural understanding', and mediation teams should include 'cultural analysts' (African Union 2014b, 43, 66, 71, 90). The implicit and questionable assumption is that the AU itself pursues a culture-free approach to mediation.

## Content of mediated agreements

In Africa as elsewhere, mediated negotiations to end armed conflict typically seek not only to end hostilities but also to prevent a recurrence of violence in the long term. It is therefore necessary for comprehensive peace agreements (CPAs) to address the structural, political and socio-economic causes of the conflict. CPAs generally do this through provisions on governance arrangements, decentralization, human rights, the rule of law, protection of minorities and reform of the security sector, the electoral system, the judiciary and the administration (Badran 2014, 196). These provisions lay the formal foundation of the new political order, provide an agenda for post-conflict peacebuilding, and are often incorporated into a post-conflict constitution (Nathan 2020).

More specifically, African CPAs are drawn up against the backdrop of a number of seminal governance frameworks. These include the 1981 African Charter on Human and Peoples Rights, the 2002 Declaration on the Principles Governing Democratic Elections in Africa, the 2003 Protocol on the Rights of Women in Africa, and the 2007 African Charter on Democracy, Elections and Governance. In addition to enshrining universal political rights, the Charter on Human and Peoples Rights endorses the right to self-determination and the right to economic, social and cultural development (Okere 1984). The Protocol on the rights of women covers, inter alia, the rights to life, dignity, peace, access to justice and participation in the political and decision-making process. The 2007 Charter on governance endorses democracy, respect for human rights, adherence to the rule of law, the conduct of free and fair elections, and promotion and protection of an independent judiciary. Many of the RECs have promulgated similar declarations (e.g. ECOWAS 2001).

The African governance texts associate liberal democratic norms with peace. The 2007 Charter on governance, for example, conjoins democracy and peace through the notion of a composite 'culture of democracy and peace' that states are expected to promote (African Union 2007, chap. 5). The 2003 Protocol that established the AU PSC presents liberal democratic values and institutions as necessary conditions for sustainable peace: 'the development of strong democratic institutions and culture, observance of human rights and the rule of law . . . are essential for the promotion of collective security, durable peace and stability, as well as for the prevention of conflicts' (African Union 2002). Similarly, the AU Policy on Post-conflict Reconstruction and Development, which aims to consolidate peace, prevent a recurrence of violence and address the root causes of conflict, places a premium on liberal democratic principles (African Union 2006, 20–27).

Given this continental normative disposition, it is not surprising that mediated settlements in Africa frequently adopt a liberal democratic paradigm. Examples include the 1992 General Peace Agreement for Mozambique; the 1999 Lomé Agreement for Sierra Leone; the 2000 Arusha Peace and Reconciliation Agreement for Burundi; the 2003 Liberian peace agreement; the 2003 Sun City Peace Agreement for the Democratic Republic of the Congo; and the 2005 Comprehensive Peace Agreement for Sudan.[5] Such agreements usually refrain from articulating macroeconomic policy although some of them, such as the CPA for Sudan, include provisions on 'wealth-sharing'.

In contrast to the liberal frameworks of African governance policies and mediated settlements, critical theory scholars have developed a sharp critique of liberal peacebuilding (Richmond and Mac Ginty 2015). The critique derives in part from the limited success of international peacebuilding endeavors in post-conflict countries (Autesserre 2010; Doyle and Sambanis 2006). Whether liberal democratic values are in any way responsible for the limited success seems unlikely, though (Paris 2010). The failings of peacebuilding are more readily attributable to illiberal and self-serving international interventions, neoliberal economic policies, weak states, and corrupt and predatory national and local elites. At the domestic level, the central problem has little to do with the de jure liberal and democratic content of mediated settlements and post-conflict constitutions, and much to do with the illiberal and exclusionary nature of de facto governance. The insecurity and instability that are generated by state violations of liberal democratic principles highlight rather than refute the merits of these principles.

The critique of the liberal peace also derives from ideological and ontological opposition to Western, neo-colonial modes of peacebuilding intervention, knowledge, discourse and policy (Richmond and Mac Ginty 2015). Nevertheless, as noted above, liberal democratic principles are firmly embedded in the African governance frameworks and consequently do not depend for their reproduction on external actors and interventions. They are also patently preferable to illiberal authoritarian regimes and they are especially appealing to marginalized and oppressed communities whose leaders participate in mediated negotiations to end armed conflict. For all these reasons, African mediators and conflict parties generally regard the embrace of liberal democratic norms in negotiated settlements as unproblematic.

In the course of negotiations to end armed conflict, the subject of tough bargaining between the conflict parties is not the normative governance framework but rather the de jure and de facto distribution of power in the post-conflict society. The outcome of the bargaining around this issue constitutes the essence of the political settlement. In Africa, these settlements tend to eschew democratic majoritarianism in favor of interim and long-term power-sharing arrangements of various kinds (Spears 2000; Tull and Mehler 2005). This is not particular to Africa but reflects a global trend (Binningsbø 2013). In Africa, prominent examples include Burundi, the Democratic Republic of the Congo, South Africa, Sudan and, in situations that fell short of armed conflict, Kenya and Zimbabwe.

The motivation for power-sharing arrangements is compelling: in ethnically divided societies, exclusionary politics and winner-takes-all electoral systems can lead to extreme marginalization of minority groups and, consequently, to rebellion and civil war (World Bank and United Nations 2018, chap. 4). There are two further reasons for the prevalence of power-sharing in negotiated settlements. First, the settlements are intended to end conflicts where none of the parties was able to achieve an outright victory; a negotiated balance of power is consequently the only viable solution. Second, the negotiations are undertaken by elites, which naturally seek to ensure that they have access to political power and economic wealth in the post-conflict society.

Power-sharing arrangements take different forms: interim governments of national unity, decentralization of power to enable greater regional autonomy, integration of government and rebel forces, and guaranteed minority representation in the executive, the legislature, the administration and the security services. These arrangements are not inherently inconsistent with liberal democracy but, as Selby (2013) points out, in practice they can be entirely illiberal and undemocratic. One of Selby's examples is the 2004 Naivasha Agreement for Sudan, which provided that the government and the Sudan People's Liberation Movement, 'neither of which had attained their positions through elections', would 'become nondemocratic partners in ruling Sudan for a transitional six-year period', monopolize oil revenues and dominate political structures throughout the country (Selby 2013, 74).

Power-sharing does not guarantee stability. On the contrary, it can contribute to instability for several possible reasons: it might entrench ethnic or religious divisions, impeding reconciliation and national unity; constrain the ruling party and stifle the democratic will of the majority; or provide insufficient protection to minorities (e.g. Roeder and Rothchild 2005). Tull and Mehler (2005) go so far as to claim that power-sharing settlements are a cause of war in Africa. They argue that Western support for such settlements creates an incentive for 'would-be leaders' to embark on insurgency, confident that this is a viable route to gaining a share of power (Tull and Mehler 2005). According to this line of argument, the Western predilection for 'power-sharing agreements may contribute to the reproduction of insurgent violence' (Tull and Mehler 2005, 375).

This argument by Tull and Mehler (2005) ignores two elementary facts: in negotiated settlements, the government typically has no option but to share power with rebels for the pragmatic reason that it failed to defeat them; and violent conflicts arise because of exclusion, not inclusion (World Bank and United Nations 2018, chap. 4). Power-sharing will therefore remain an attractive form of conflict resolution. The research challenge is to identify the power-sharing modalities that are most likely to lead to sustainable peace and stability.

## Conclusion

Two sets of conclusions can be drawn from this chapter's discussion of African mediation in high-intensity conflict. First, the African character of the mediations is distinct in certain respects but not others. It is strong in relation to the actors that lead the mediations and that provide political direction through resolutions issued by the AU and the RECs in response to particular conflicts. It is also evident in the content of mediated settlements, which reflect the continental governance frameworks. However, the general preference for liberal democratic governance combined with power-sharing is not itself distinctly African. The African character of mediation is least evident in the style and strategy of peacemaking on the continent.

It is possible that the lack of African distinctness regarding mediation style and strategy on the continent is due to the pervasive influence of UN mediation norms and best practice guidelines. The UN's general policy on mediation, the *United Nations Guidance for Effective Mediation* (2012a), acquired global status after the UN General Assembly endorsed the document and encouraged its use by 'all relevant actors involved in mediation' (United Nations 2012b). The AU has explicitly affirmed the UN mediation norms of impartiality, consent, ownership, preparedness, quality peace agreements and inclusivity (African Union 2014b; Govender and Ngandu 2010).

It is also possible that this chapter's characterization of African mediation is inaccurate or at least incomplete in the sense that it has failed to discern mediation patterns and trends that are distinctly African. This leads to the second conclusion. It will be apparent from the scholarly work cited in the chapter that there is a dearth of research on African mediation as a subcategory of international mediation. Many studies have been conducted on specific mediation cases on the continent, but there is little research that investigates African mediation in a more general way or that compares African mediation with mediation undertaken elsewhere in the world. There is still a great deal of fruitful research to be done.

## Notes

1 The 2002 *Protocol Relating to the Establishment of the Peace and Security Council of the African Union* states that the 'regional mechanisms' for conflict prevention, management and resolution are part of the overall security architecture of the AU (AU 2002, art. 16). The nature of this architecture is developed in a 2008 memorandum of understanding between the AU and the regional mechanisms (AU 2008).
2 See Bartu (2017); Apuuli (2017); Witt (2017); Pring (2017); Saunders (2017); Melber (2017); Aeby (2017).
3 An example of this was the Madagascar regime's response to SADC's stand against the 2009 coup in that country. See Witt (2017); Nathan (2013b).
4 For example, African Union (2014b); Govender and Ngandu (2010); Nathan (2009).
5 The texts of these agreements can be found on the UN Peacemaker website at https://peacemaker.un.org/document-search.

## References

Aeby, M., (2017) 'Stability and Sovereignty at the Expense of Democracy? The SADC Mandate for Zimbabwe (2007–13)', *African Security*, 10(3–4), pp. 272–291.
African Union, (2002) *Protocol Relating to the Establishment of the Peace and Security Council of the African Union*, African Union, Durban, 9 July.
African Union, (2006) *Policy on Post-Conflict Reconstruction and Development*, African Union, Addis Ababa.
African Union, (2007) *African Charter on Democracy, Elections and Governance*, African Union, Addis Ababa, 30 January.
African Union, (2008) *Memorandum of Understanding on Cooperation in the Area of Peace and Security between the African Union, the Regional Economic Communities and the Coordinating Mechanisms of the Regional Standby Brigades of Eastern and Northern Africa*, unpublished document.
African Union, (2012) *Report of the Chairperson of the Commission on the Partnership between the African Union and the United Nations on Peace and Security: Towards Greater Strategic and Political Coherence*, 307th meeting of the PSC, 9 January.

African Union, (2014a) *Terms of Reference, Joint Task Force on Strengthening the Relations between the AU, Regional Economic Communities and Regional Mechanisms for Conflict Prevention, Management and Resolution in the Area of Peace and Security*, unpublished document.

African Union, (2014b) *African Union Mediation Support Handbook*. Durban, South Africa: African Union and ACCORD.

African Union, (2016a) *Securing Predictable and Sustainable Financing for Peace in Africa*, unpublished document.

African Union, (2016b) *Report of the Meeting on the Operationalization of the African Union Mediation Support Unit (AU MSU)*. [online]. Available at: www.peaceau.org/uploads/01-msu-meeting-report-compo site5.pdf (Accessed: 21 June 2021).

Apuuli, K.P., (2017) 'The African Union's Mediation Mandate and the Libyan Conflict (2011),' *African Security* 10(3–4), pp. 192–204.

Autesserre, S., (2010) *The Trouble with the Congo: Local Violence and the Failure of International Peacebuilding*. Cambridge: Cambridge University Press.

Badran, R., (2014) 'Intrastate Peace Agreements and the Durability of Peace', *Conflict Management and Peace Science*, 31(2), pp. 193–217.

Bartu, P., (2017) 'What Mandate? Mediating during Warfighting in the Libyan Revolution (2011)', *African Security*, 10(3–4), pp. 176–191.

Binningsbø, H., (2013) 'Power Sharing, Peace and Democracy: Any Obvious Relationships?', *International Area Studies Review*, 16(1), pp. 89–112.

De Waal, A., (eds.), (2007) *War in Darfur and the Search for Peace*. Harvard: Harvard University Press.

Doyle, M. and Sambanis, N., (2006) *Making War and Building Peace: United Nations Peace Operations*. Princeton, NJ: Princeton University Press.

Duursma, A., (2017) 'Partnering to Make Peace: The Effectiveness of Joint African and Non-African Mediation Efforts', *International Peacekeeping*, 24(4), pp. 590–615.

Economic Community of West African States (ECOWAS), (2001) *Protocol on Democracy and Good Governance*. Dakar: ECOWAS.

Economic Community of West African States (ECOWAS), (2018) *ECOWAS Mediation Policy Documents Launched in Abuja*. [online]. Available at: www.ecowas.int/ecowas-mediation-policy-documents-launched-in-abuja/ (Accessed: 21 June 2021).

Garang, A., (2015) 'The Impact of External Actors on the Prospects for a Mediated Settlement in South Sudan', presented at *the Conference on International Mediation*. University of Pretoria, 2–4 June.

Govender, K. and Ngandu, Y., (2010) *Towards Enhancing the Capacity of the African Union in Mediation*. Durban: ACCORD.

Hartman, H., (2013) 'The Evolving Mediation Capacity of the Southern African Development Community', *Conflict Trends*, 2013(1). Durban: ACCORD.

Hendrickson, D. and Tumutegyereize, K., (2012) *Dealing with Complexity in Peace Negotiations: Reflections on the Lord's Resistance Army and the Juba Talks*. London: Conciliation Resources.

Intergovernmental Authority on Development (IGAD), (2018) *Communiqué of the 61st Extra-Ordinary Session of IGAD Council of Ministers on the Situation in South Sudan*, IGAD, Addis Ababa, 26 March.

International Crisis Group, (1998) 'Burundi under Siege: Lift the Sanctions; Re-launch the Peace Process', *Burundi Report* 1, 28 April.

International Crisis Group, (2015) 'South Sudan: Keeping Faith with the IGAD Peace Process', *Africa Report*, 228, 27 July.

Khadiagala, G., (2007) *Meddlers or Mediators? African Interveners in Civil Conflicts in Eastern Africa*, International Negotiation Series, 4. Leiden: Martinus Nijhoff.

Khadiagala, G., (2008) 'Forty Days and Nights of Peacemaking in Kenya', *Journal of African Elections*, 7(2), pp. 4–32.

Melber, H., (2017) 'Mission Impossible: Hammarskjöld and the UN Mandate for the Congo (1960–61)', *African Security*, 10(3–4), pp. 254–271.

Møller, B., (2009) 'The African Union as a Security Actor: African Solutions to African Problems?', *Working Paper*, 57. Crisis States Research Center, London School of Economics.

Mthembu-Salter, G., (1998) 'A Policy Passed Its "Sell-by" Date: An Assessment of Sanctions against Burundi', report prepared for ActionAid, December.

Nathan, L., (1999) 'When Push Comes to Shove: The Failure of International Mediation in African Civil Wars', *Track Two Occasional Paper*, 8(2). Centre for Conflict Resolution, University of Cape Town.

Nathan, L., (2006) 'No Ownership, No Peace: The Darfur Peace Agreement', *Working Paper*, 5. Crisis States Research Centre, London School of Economics.

Nathan, L., (2009) 'Plan of Action to Build the AU's Mediation Capacity', report commissioned by the UN Mediation Support Unit and the AU Conflict Management Division.

Nathan, L., (2012) *Community of Insecurity: SADC's Struggle for Peace and Security in Southern Africa*. Farnham: Ashgate.

Nathan, L., (2013a) 'African Solutions to African Problems: South Africa's Foreign Policy', *WeltTrends*, 92, pp. 48–55.

Nathan, L., (2013b) 'A Clash of Norms and Strategies in Madagascar: Mediation and the AU Policy on Unconstitutional Change of Government', *Mediation Arguments*, 4, Centre for Mediation in Africa. Hatfield: University of Pretoria.

Nathan, L., (2017a) 'How to Manage Inter-Organizational Disputes over Mediation in Africa', *Global Governance*, 23(2), pp. 151–162.

Nathan, L., (2017b) 'A Survey of Mediation in African Coups', *African Peacebuilding Network Working Papers*, 15. New York, NY: Social Science Research Council.

Nathan, L., (2017c) 'Marching Orders: Exploring the Mediation Mandate', *African Security*, 10(3–4), pp. 155–175.

Nathan, L., (2020) 'The Real Deal? The Post-Conflict Constitution as a Peace Agreement', *Third World Quarterly*, 41(9).

Nathan, L., Kibochi, R., Mainge, C., Ndiaye, M. and Zoubir, Y., (2015) *African Peace and Security Architecture (APSA) Assessment Study 2014: Final Report*. AU Peace and Security Department, Addis Ababa, 16 April.

Okere, B.O., (1984) 'The Protection of Human Rights in Africa and the African Charter on Human and Peoples' Rights: A Comparative Analysis with the European and American Systems', *Human Rights Quarterly* 6(2), pp. 141–159.

Paris, R., (2010) 'Saving Liberal Peacebuilding', *Review of International Studies*, 36(2), pp. 337–365.

Pring, J., (2017) 'Including or Excluding Civil Society? The Role of the Mediation Mandate in South Sudan (2013–15) and Zimbabwe (2008–9)', *African Security*, 10(3–4), pp. 223–238.

Richmond, O. and Mac Ginty, R., (2015) 'Where Now for the Critique of the Liberal Peace?', *Cooperation and Conflict*, 50(2), pp. 171–189.

Roeder, P. and Rothchild, D., (2005) 'Dilemmas of State-Building in Divided Societies', in Roeder, P. and Rothchild, D., (eds.) *Sustainable Peace: Power and Democracy after Civil Wars*. Ithaca, NY: Cornell University Press.

Saunders, C., (2017) 'Mediation Mandates for Namibia's Independence (1977–78, 1988)', *African Security*, 10(3–4), pp. 239–253.

Selby, J., (2013) 'The Myth of Liberal Peace-Building', *Conflict, Security & Development*, 13(1), pp. 57–86.

Spears, I., (2000) 'Understanding Inclusive Peace Agreements in Africa: The Problems of Sharing Power', *Third World Quarterly*, 21(1), pp. 105–118.

Tull, D. and Mehler, A., (2005) 'The Hidden Costs of Power-Sharing: Reproducing Insurgent Violence in Africa', *African Affairs*, 104(416), pp. 375–398.

United Nations, (2012a) *United Nations Guidance for Effective Mediation*. New York, NY: United Nations.

United Nations and African Union, (2014) *Joint UN-AU Framework for an Enhanced Partnership in Peace and Security*, unpublished document.

United Nations General Assembly, (2012b) *Resolution 66/291*. New York, NY: United Nations.

United Nations Security Council, (2014) *Resolution 2167*. New York, NY: United Nations.

United Nations Security Council, (2019) *Security Council Renews Sanctions against South Sudan, Adopting Resolution 2471 (2019) by 10 Votes in Favour, with 5 Abstentions*, press statement. New York, NY: United Nations.

Witt, A., (2017) 'Mandate Impossible: Mediation and the Return to Constitutional Order in Madagascar (2009–13)', *African Security*, 10(3–4), pp. 205–222.

World Bank and United Nations, (2018) *Pathways for Peace: Inclusive Approaches to Preventing Violent Conflict*. Washington, DC: World Bank.

Zartman, I.W. and Touval, S., (2007) 'International Mediation', in Crocker, C., Hampson, F. and Aall, P., (eds.) *Leashing the Dogs of War: Conflict Management in a Divided World*. Washington, DC: US Institute for Peace, pp. 437–454.

# 6
# JUSTICE AND RECONCILIATION IN AFRICA

## The Emergence of the African Union Transitional Justice Policy

*Tim Murithi*

### Introduction

The chapter will argue that Africa has played a leading role in the transformation, innovation and diffusion of the ideas, norms and practices of justice and reconciliation. The continent of Africa has been a terrain for the innovation and experimentation in the field known as transitional justice, which has had both positive and negative consequences. Africa was not the creator of transitional justice norms: in fact, the continent borrowed a number of ideas and practices from around the world. As the field emerged and began to grow in the mid-1990s, there were efforts to import transitional justice norms into Africa. Through its experiences, the continent not only demonstrated the limits of 'traditional' transitional justice norms, but it also innovated in the implementation of a broader range of transitional justice standards, including shifting the focus from punitive to restorative justice approaches, which has in turn influenced contemporary theory and practice within the field.

More specifically, in the mid-1990s, transitional justice originated from a legalistic tradition, with a biased emphasis on the use of judicial processes to address civil and political violations in countries undergoing rebuilding processes. Africa's experience demonstrated that traditional notions of transitional justice needed to be re-thought and re-framed. Specifically, in order to effectively address the real concerns of victims of past violations, African actors pushed for the expansion of transitional justice norms beyond their narrow civil and political focus to include socio-economic and psychosocial issues. Consequently, transitional justice is now understood as involving a broad spectrum of interventions that are embedded in peacebuilding and developmental processes. These ideas have been mainstreamed into contemporary transitional justice discourses and practices.

One of the central dilemmas of transitional justice, namely the tension between peace and justice, has played itself out in the majority of post-conflict situations in Africa. Specifically, South Africa, Rwanda, Uganda, Kenya, Sierra Leone and Liberia adopted processes and institutions which sought to address the violations of the past, without allowing the potential tension that could have been generated by an orthodox approach to transitional justice to overwhelm the society and undermine efforts to build sustainable peace, through socio-economic and psychosocial redress. The truth and reconciliation commissions (TRC) of South Africa, Kenya and Sierra Leone operationalised amnesty provisions, which sought to directly address the peace versus justice dilemma faced by these countries. The experiences of these countries have been analysed, modified and adopted by other states around the world. This in effect demonstrates Africa's role in transitional justice norm-setting and norm diffusion.

The chapter will begin by contextualising norm-setting and articulating a working definition of transitional justice. It will briefly assess how the UN has framed the norms of transitional justice, prior to problematising key aspects of its processes. The chapter will then assess Africa as a terrain of norm experimentation and the continent's contribution to addressing norm divergence between the aspirations of peacebuilding and administration of justice. The chapter will discuss Africa's engagement with the amnesty norm, as well as its efforts to integrate cultural and cross-border norms into its approach to addressing the violations of the past. The chapter will analyse Africa's contribution to promotion and institutionalisation of global transitional justice norms. The chapter will conclude by suggesting that Africa will continue to innovate on the development of transitional justice norms, due to the fact that a number of countries on the continent will be emerging from conflict in the next decade and beyond. By extension, Africa will continue to be a thought leader, norm setter and norm entrepreneur in terms of transitional justice processes and institutions and the perplexing challenge of addressing the violations of the past.

## Contextualising Transitional Justice

Transitional justice strives to address challenges that emerge from historical violations and affect countries as they strive to transition from war or authoritarian rule to fair, inclusive and democratic societies (Murithi 2016). More often than not, such societies are emerging from a past of brutality, exploitation and victimisation. In this context, transitional justice does not seek to replace criminal justice, rather it strives to promote 'a deeper, richer and broader vision of justice which seeks to confront perpetrators, address the needs of victims, and start a process of reconciliation and transformation towards a more just and humane society' (Boraine 2004, 67).

The broadly accepted purpose of a process of transitional justice is to establish a quasi-judicial framework to undo the continuing effects of the past. It is also necessary not to lose sight of the fact that transitional justice is just that, a 'transitional process', and it should not be viewed as a permanent solution to addressing the atrocities of the past. It is rather a transient process that will have to give way to the rule of law and the restoration of a constitutional order that will manage and resolve the social, political and economic tensions within society. The institutional vehicles through which transitional justice is implemented, bodies such as TRCs and special courts, are temporary and time-bound institutions and should not be considered as a permanent solution.

Boraine argues that there are at least five components of a transitional justice process:

- Ensuring accountability in the fair administration of justice and restoring the rule of law;
- The use of non-judicial mechanisms to recover the truth, such as TRCs;
- Reconciliation in which a commonly agreed memory of past atrocities is acknowledged by those who created and implemented the unjust system as a prerequisite to promoting forgiveness and healing;
- The reform of institutions, including the executive, judiciary and legislative branches of government as well as the security sector to ensure that a degree of trust is restored and bridges between members of society can be rebuilt; and
- The payment of reparations to victims who had suffered human rights violations, as a way to remedy the harm suffered in the past.

Transitional justice is complicated by a number of dilemmas, including how to balance the 'competing legitimate interests in redressing the harms of victims and ensuring the democratic stability of the state' (Boraine 2004, 71). It requires the balancing of two imperatives: 'on the one hand, there is the need to return to the rule of law and the prosecution of offenders: on the other hand, there is a need for rebuilding societies and embarking on the process of reconciliation' (Boraine 2004, 72).

Reconciliation is understood as the cumulative outcome of the broad-based application of transitional justice processes. Concretely, reconciliation processes require that the affected parties:

1) recognise their *interdependence* as a prerequisite for consolidating peace;
2) engage in genuine *dialogue* about questions that have caused deep divisions in the past;
3) embrace a *democratic attitude* to creating spaces where they can disagree; and
4) work jointly to implement processes to address the legacies of *socio-economic exploitation and injustices*.

*(Du Toit 2013, 88–91)*

At the heart of reconciliation is the achievement of the principles of justice and equity (Murithi 2009, 136–159). Consequently, transitional justice is viewed as an intermediary set of processes that gradually and over time lead towards the promotion of reconciliation. Civil society in this regard can play an important function in promoting healing and reconciliation, after the TRCs and special courts have delivered their reports and issued their verdicts.

## The Evolution of Transitional Justice and Its Introduction to Africa

The processes that the field of transitional justice embodies have been implemented for as long as there have been conflicts and efforts to deal with the past. However, as a field of academic study, transitional justice began being systematically analysed during the transitions from authoritarian regimes in Latin America in the 1980s (Arthur 2009). The Latin American approaches placed an emphasis on truth recovery as a prerequisite to enabling victims and their family members to find closure for the violations that they suffered. However, efforts to promote psychosocial healing and reconciliation did not feature significantly in the Latin American experience, and the effort to integrate this agenda within Africa's processes will be discussed later. The genocides in Rwanda in 1994 and in Srebrenica in 1995 further crystallised the quest and need to understand how societies that had endured mass atrocities could establish processes and mechanisms to deal with such a brutal past and enable a society to move forward. Concurrently, in 1994, South Africa's liberation from the yoke of a white supremacist apartheid regime to a system of democratic governance also generated a broad range of insights and experiences that could be analysed and documented on how to operationalise transitional justice. South Africa introduced a number of innovations to its normative transitional justice framework, which was a significant departure from the Latin American experience, as will be discussed further later. There are still perplexing challenges, such as the issue of whether transitional justice processes can be implemented in the absence of a 'transition' or regime change (McCargo 2015, 5). There is no definitive satisfactory response to this conundrum, and more often than not, it is necessary to begin laying the foundations for transitional justice even in the absence of a transition or in the midst of a violent conflict.

The idea of transitional justice emerged from the legal sphere through a primary concern for ensuring that perpetrators of human rights violations were held accountable for their crimes and punished, ideally through a court of law and in accordance with international standards (Balasco 2013; Binningsbø 2012). The originators and custodians of these 'international standards', however, are less clear and remain unspecified in the field of transitional justice, even with the UN's framing of field. The notions that initially animated transitional justice drew heavily upon legalistic doctrines of 'the duty/right to punish' and the unitary role and function of prosecutions in the context of human rights violations (Binningsbø 2012).

The reality of implementing transitional justice through an exclusively prosecutorial framework, as was the case in Latin America and the Balkans, was soon confronted by a proliferation of social, economic and political contradictions that undermined the narrow focus of legally inspired transitional justice norms. For example, when confronted with situations in which perpetrators were also erstwhile victims, such as child soldiers who were abducted and subsequently became war-makers and violators of human rights, the knee-jerk prosecutorial approach is to punish the most recent crime. In this particular case, the historical violations committed against the now perpetrator go unpunished, and consequently a condition of injustice and moral contradiction prevails. The legal field remains ambivalent about addressing such moral conundrums and prefers to cast aside such questions in a narrow-minded commitment towards ensuring that the duty to punish is pursued above all else. As an example, a senior Lord's Resistance Army (LRA) commander, Brigadier Dominic Ongwen, was abducted, in 1999, by the LRA when he was a ten-year-old child in northern Uganda. Ongwen was a victim of the LRA militia but subsequently went on to command its ranks. As a member of the command team of the LRA, Ongwen was therefore individually culpable for the human rights violations that the militia perpetrated against innocent children whom it abducted. Therefore, Ongwen stands accused of being a perpetrator of human rights violations, yet his historical grievances for harm done to him as a child also are valid and in need of redress and accountability. Ultimately, the Ugandan government of Yoweri Museveni decided to send Ongwen to the International Criminal Court (ICC) to face charges for his most recent atrocities. However, the situation exposed the limits of a tool narrowly focused on a normative approach to transitional justice.

The legal approach to transitional justice is also generally unable to effectively provide redress for societal violations and economic crimes which historical victims have endured, because these effects are less visible to the eye and are much more complex to quantify in terms of the specific transgressions which have been perpetrated against victims. Moreover, for situations in which a particular ethnic or racial group benefited from the economic exploitation of another, the culpability is widespread across the society from the political leaders who implemented the policies to the constituencies that voted or supported them. In such a context, it is much more difficult to pinpoint the violators who should be prosecuted for economic crimes. More often than not, processes that have to be adopted to promote redress would include a broad range of interventions which are clearly located outside the scope of a punishment model of transitional justice.

At the outset, gender exclusion was also a prevalent feature in the conceptualisation and implementation of legalistic transitional justice interventions. Consequently, additional normative pressures have emerged relating to how transitional justice deals with gender issues. Authoritarian rule and violent conflict affect women and men in different and context-specific ways. Notably, gender-based violence is a common atrocity that has to be considered in a transitional justice process. Around the world, engagement has witnessed women being traditionally marginalised and excluded from defining and framing of transitional justice processes.

From the ideas relating to how to frame transitional justice processes, to legislative initiatives to codify these processes in law, to the implementation of these interventions through states and societal institutions, the phenomenon of patriarchy continues to marginalise the participation of women. Because political leadership around the world is dominated by men, when it comes to operationalising transitional justice, women's views are generally overlooked. For example, Sigsworth and Valji (2012) highlight the limitations in contemporary South Africa of transitional justice processes in entrenching accountability and preventing a recurrence of the forms of violence that were targeted at women during apartheid. Historically, transitional justice processes have tended to pay lip service to gender-sensitive interventions. Consequently, African women and men need to ensure that the voices of women are incorporated into the design and framing of transitional justice processes. This requires the active participation of African women in the political negotiations that define the orientation of transitional justice processes and the nature of their institutions.

Another defining feature of the evolving norms of the field has witnessed contemporary transitional justice processes becoming more political than legal in orientation. For example, efforts to undertake truth recovery, which are central to any effort to initiate redress for past violations, are often fraught with political manipulation. Other dimensions of transitional justice, such as accountability processes, reparations and the reform of institutions, are also subject to political interference. Consequently, the politicisation of transitional justice in some instances trumps the legal approach to dealing with the past. The challenge is one of mitigating against political interference that undermines efforts to promote democratic inclusion, heal the divisions in society and put in place measures to achieve reconciliation. For example, in Kenya, efforts to implement a truth recovery process through the Truth, Justice and Reconciliation Commission was progressively distorted by the politicisation of the work of the body (Asaala and Diker 2013). Similarly, efforts to pursue a prosecutorial path in Kenya through the ICC have similarly become hostage to the political machinations of the country's leaders (Brown and Sriram 2012).

As an overarching issue, transitional justice is understood as relating to processes that are driven by the state and state actors. Contemporary approaches to transitional justice have an almost exclusive focus on national processes. Yet the national focus of transitional justice processes is increasingly unsustainable, particularly in situations where conflicts and their effects spill over across borders. In addition, most conflicts are increasingly cross-border in nature and are in some instances sustained by cross-border support and resources. Consequently, efforts to redress violations that emerge as a result of these conflicts are incomplete if they only focus on national actors and state-driven processes. It is necessary to find a way to pursue and promote transitional justice across borders. This raises the challenge of the prospects for institutionalising cross-border and regional reconciliation approaches to transitional justice.

## *The United Nations' Foray Into Transitional Justice Norms*

The UN's foray into transitional justice was in response to the emerging conditions on the ground in countries like Rwanda, South Africa and the Balkans. Africa's experiences contributed towards the development of the emerging norms of this field. In 1997, Louis Joinet formulated the principles relating to addressing impunity in his *Final Report on the Administration of Justice and the Question of Impunity*, which he submitted to the UN sub-commission within the Commission on Human Rights. In 1999, the UN Commission on Human Rights adopted a Declaration on the Right to Restitution for Victims of Gross Human Rights Violations. It is significant that this Declaration was issued while the Ghanaian Kofi Annan was UN secretary-general, illustrating how Africans in positions of leadership have also encouraged the development of transitional justice norms.

In 2004, Secretary-General Annan issued a report titled 'The Rule of Law and Transitional Justice in Conflict and Post-conflict Societies', which defined the field as relating to 'the full range of processes and mechanisms associated with a society's attempts to come to terms with a legacy of large scale past abuses, in order to ensure accountability, serve justice and achieve reconciliation' (United Nations 2004, 4). The report further suggests that transitional justice processes 'may include both judicial and non-judicial mechanisms, with differing levels of international involvement (or none at all) and individual prosecutions, reparation, truth-seeking, institutional reform, vetting and dismissals or a combination thereof' (United Nations 2004, 4). Following this definition, transitional justice has been viewed through a legal prism and has been viewed as a special form of justice that enables societies to make the transition from authoritarian rule or violent conflict. However, all transitional justice processes should be contributing to some form of progress towards reconciliation.

In 2005, the UN Commission on Human Rights revised the Joinet principles to identify the mechanisms, modalities and procedures for the implementation of existing legal obligations under international humanitarian law and international human rights law (Sisson 2010, 12). This review was conducted by Diane Orentlicher, who enumerated what are now known as the Joinet/Orentlicher principles, which include the following:

- The right to know;
- The right to justice;
- The right to reparation; and
- The guarantee of non-recurrence.

In December 2005, the UN General Assembly adopted the Basic Principles and Guidelines on the Right to Remedy and Reparation for Victims of Gross Violations of International Human Rights Law and Serious Violations of International Humanitarian Law. These include a range of options, including prosecutions, truth commissions, reparation, memorials and institutional reforms (United Nations 2005). In December 2006, the UN General Assembly approved the Convention on the Protection of All Persons from Enforced Disappearance. In May 2012, the UN Human Rights Council appointed the first UN Special Rapporteur on the Promotion of Truth, Justice, Reparation and Guarantees of Non-recurrence to promote the engagement with these issues within member states. The UN's foray into transitional justice further concretised the normative framework for engaging with the notion, despite the fact that it remains an essentially contested terrain.

## Justice and Reconciliation in Africa: Modalities, Practices and Challenges

Transitional justice is operationalised through a wide range of institutions which seek to frame and catalyse the broad range of processes through which societies that have been affected by violent conflict or authoritarian rule can address the violations of the past as a precursor to laying the foundations for building more inclusive societies. Consequently, from its predominantly legalistic origins in the mid-1990s, transitional justice has confronted a range of societal, economic and political pressures that have precipitated a more expansive framing and understanding its normative parameters. A significant number of these pressures emerged from processes that were unfolding on the African continent, which placed the continent at the forefront of experimentation with norms of transitional justice.

The normative pressures on the legal remit of transitional justice exerted by the grassroots experiences of African societies emerging from conflict compelled the scope of transitional justice to expand significantly. Transitional justice is now faced with a broad range of challenges, including administering justice in a manner that can restore societal trust and promote reconciliation in deeply divided communities. Furthermore, the demands for socio-economic justice have pushed the normative boundaries of transitional justice beyond the confines of its historical origins within the legal sphere. The calls for reparations and restitution have demanded new approaches to operationalising transitional justice, which linked it to the peacebuilding and development fields (Murithi 2009, 136). The requirement of reforming institutions has also compelled transitional justice to expand its parameters to begin to address issues of constitutionalism and democratic governance.

Africa was not the initiator of transitional justice norms, and in fact the continent borrowed a number of ideas and practices from around the world, notably Latin America. As the field emerged and began to grow, there were efforts to import transitional justice norms into Africa. The initiatives to implement transitional justice on the African continent have challenged the traditional and legalistic framing of transitional justice norms. More specifically, African societies and countries have innovated in the implementation of a broader range of approaches and development of home-grown standards for dealing with the past, which are beginning to influence contemporary theory and practice within the field of transitional justice.

## *The Sequencing Approach to Justice and Reconciliation*

Africa's experiences have demonstrated that transitional justice processes are operationalised predominantly in post-conflict situations, in which the imperative to pursue peacebuilding is just as necessary as the demands to deliver justice to the victims. Consequently, there is a perceived norm divergence between the pursuit of peace and the requirements of justice. This means that the norms that guide the pursuit of peacebuilding, the healing of relationships and the restoration of human dignity, are in tension with the norms of administering justice, which are focused on the prosecution and punishment of former participants in wars. Peacemaking and peacebuilding is future oriented in the sense that it is striving to prevent violence that could recur and cause the death of further innocent civilians if conditions in the country remain unchanged. International criminal justice by definition is concerned with the prosecution of human rights violations that have already transpired through the application of due process, while upholding certain legal criteria and issuing a judgement for past transgressions. Consequently, there is a tension between these two processes, and trying to undertake them in tandem can occasionally generate a conundrum. Individual responsibility for mass atrocities in war situations, more often than not, resides with the leaders of factions or military organisations who might simultaneously be involved in peacemaking processes.

The notion of justice remains an essentially contested concept (Grono and O'Brien 2008). In fact, there are multiple dimensions to justice. Retributive justice seeks to ensure prosecution followed by punishment for crimes or atrocities committed (Villa-Vicencio and Doxtader 2004). Restorative justice strives to promote societal harmony through a quasi-judicial process of truth telling, acknowledgement, remorse, reparations, forgiveness, healing and reconciliation (Murithi 2010, 65). Retributive or punitive justice is generally administered by a state-sanctioned legal institution or through the remit of international law. Restorative justice draws upon a range of mechanisms including truth commissions and other societal reconciliation institutions.

Both retributive and restorative justice have a central concern with preventing the impunity of perpetrators who have committed atrocities. Retributive justice, however, has a more direct impact on the condition of the perpetrators because it summarily imposes a punitive sentence which is evident for all to witness. The impact of restorative justice is more elusive, as victims and perpetrators are often engaged in a series of face-to-face interactions designed to achieve the objectives highlighted above. The fact that the outcome of restorative justice processes is generally less dramatic than those of retributive justice means that their efficacy is generally more suspect and unquantifiable to external observers. However, both forms of justice address the issue of impunity. Impunity in this context is understood as the condition in which there has been no redress or reckoning of the past atrocities and injustices committed by a perpetrator. Retributive justice prevents the immediate impunity of the perpetrator of crime through punishment and serves as a warning for those who may be inclined to commit atrocities in the future. Restorative justice also addresses impunity by compelling the perpetrator to undergo a revelatory and confessional process of transformation, which means that he or she has not 'got away' with the crimes that they committed but rather atones for them.

The experiences in Sierra Leone and South Africa demonstrated that the debate over whether a retributive or restorative approach to justice should be deployed in the aftermath (or at the point of a conclusion) of a war has not been resolved definitively. Nor can this debate be resolved definitely because the type of justice that might be appropriate in the context of one country cannot be transplanted to another. In this regard, there is a certain degree of context specificity in the administration of justice. A combination of retributive and restorative processes of justice can be deployed to address the needs of a society in transition.

The sequence in which either retributive or restorative justice processes are initiated is also not a precise science. In the majority of cases, retributive and restorative justice processes might be instituted and operationalised simultaneously. In some instances, failure of a government or a society to embrace a restorative approach to justice and reconciliation can require the establishment of an international retributive/punitive justice process. In other instances, the demands of a restorative justice process with its emphasis on truth telling and the collective psychological transformation of promoting forgiveness and reconciliation means that efforts to administer punitive measures may need to be carefully sequenced so as not to disrupt these healing processes. In the cases of the Darfur crisis in Sudan and in the conflict in northern Uganda, individuals and leaders who have been accused of planning, financing, instigating and executing atrocities against citizens of another group – all in the name of civil war – can be investigated by the ICC if the respective country is a state party to the ICC or if the issue is referred to the Court by the UN Security Council. In the contexts of Darfur and northern Uganda, these individuals and leaders are the very same people that are called upon to engage in a peace process that will lead to the signing of an agreement and ensure its implementation. Characteristically, most peace agreements will have provisions for peacebuilding and, within this process, a framework for promoting restorative justice through the form of truth commissions as a means for promoting national reconciliation.

A punitive approach to justice cannot deal with the grievances that often underpin structural violence, identity conflict and the economic marginalisation of the majority of people in war-affected countries and thus establish a sustainable basis for peace (Meernik 2005). It will, however, prosecute key individuals who had the greatest responsibility for committing atrocities. In spite of the available option of pursuing prosecutions for the human rights violations that were committed during apartheid, South Africa deliberately chose the path of placing greater emphasis on implementing a restorative transitional justice model. The option of prosecution was available during the country's transition in the mid to late 1990s and is still viable even to this day. The fact that South Africa adopted its own unique path still distinguishes it as a norm setter. The model South Africa adopted is constantly being analysed and scrutinised for its important insights even though the country, like other countries around the world, has not yet addressed all of its challenges emanating from its past. In effect, South Africa's response to its situation advanced important transitional justice insights. The South African insights, particularly on strategy to ensure sequencing how a punitive approach is instituted in the context of transitional justice norms, have influenced prevailing transitional justice norms.

Sequencing in transitional justice requires the deliberate operationalisation of a coordinated retributive or restorative justice process in order to ensure that stability and ultimately peace is achieved in a given country context. At least two camps have emerged in the international justice fora, namely those that adopt a fundamentalist approach to prosecution and those that advocate for a more gradual approach predicated on giving time to peacebuilding and reconciliation to take root. Prosecutorial fundamentalism is not a misguided school of thought, and its intentions are noble as far as they attempt to ensure that those who bear the greatest responsibility for war crimes, crimes against humanity and genocide are summarily brought to book. However, prosecutorial fundamentalism, like all other fundamentalisms, can be blighted and become subsumed by a narrow, legalistic desire to bring the accused to justice. For example, Tunisia and Liberia placed more emphasis on adopting and implementing a restorative model rather than adhering to the prosecutorial fundamentalism which was being advocated for by external actors, notably international human rights organisations. A more nuanced approach would suggest that there is a time and a place for prosecution, and in the context of a civil war, it may not always be immediately after the cessation of hostilities between the belligerent parties. At this point in time, the tension within the country tends to be uncharacteristically high, and any attempt to prosecute individuals and leaders can often be (and sometimes is) seen as an attempt to deliberately continue the 'war by other means' by targeting the main protagonists to a conflict. Effectively what is called for in these situations is a period of time in which the belligerents can pursue the promotion of peace. In such a situation the efforts to promote peace, including its restorative justice dimension, would have to be given precedence to the administration of punitive justice. This is with a view to laying the foundations for the stability of the society. For example, the Acholi community of northern Uganda have resisted efforts to implement across-the-board prosecutions for perpetrators involved in the regional conflict and have relied extensively on the use of a culture and tradition-based justice process known as *mato oput* to frame an exchange between victims and perpetrators in the crisis. Ultimately, the perceived norm divergence between peace and justice is based on an artificially constructed false dichotomy between the pursuit of peace and the administration of justice.

## *The Amnesty Approach to Justice and Reconciliation*

One of the central dilemmas of transitional justice – namely the tension between peace and justice – has played itself out in the majority of post-war countries in Africa. Specifically, South Africa, Rwanda, Uganda, Kenya, Sierra Leone, Liberia, Tunisia, Côte d'Ivoire, the Democratic Republic of the Congo (DRC), Burundi, Mauritius, Uganda and Zimbabwe adopted processes and institutions which sought to address the violations of the past, predominantly through truth commissions, with a view to addressing the violations of the past and building societies and sustainable peace. There is also legislation to adopt the transitional justice institutions in South Sudan, following its 2013 crisis, which culminated in a 2015 peace agreement.

The TRCs in South Africa, Kenya, Sierra Leone and Liberia operationalised the amnesty norm, which sought to directly address the peace versus justice dilemma faced by these countries. These amnesty provisions were not intended to gloss over the violations of the past but were rather supposed to be granted on the basis of a confessional process of truth telling. For example, South Africa's TRC convened an Amnesty Sub-committee, whose task was to test the veracity of the claims made by those who submitted applications. The primary criterion was the need to demonstrate that the violations that individuals perpetrated were 'politically' motivated in a broad interpretation of the term. Of the close to 6,000 amnesty applications that the South African TRC sub-committee received, it only validated approximately 1,000 applications, which means that it rejected a substantial majority. Some even ended up being directed to the South African judiciary on the basis that they were not deemed to fall under the rubric of political crimes. Kenya, Sierra Leone and Liberia similarly adopted the amnesty norm in the framing of their own truth commissions, and this has contributed towards influencing how the provision is understood and implemented across the continent and around the world.

Both within Africa and internationally, amnesty has vociferous critics, notably in the legal profession that claims it encourages impunity. Yet African actors have pioneered an approach to amnesties as a part of transitional justice that addresses these charges due largely to a carefully sequenced process which includes acknowledgement of harm done, a request for mercy and a process of reparation, and then amnesty contributes directly towards addressing the impunity of the perpetrator. The fact that the perpetrator is not 'locked up' is not an indicator of the lack of veracity of a transitional justice process for redress.

The important factor is that African states' norm-setting innovations with the amnesty provision have been borrowed, modified and adopted in other countries around the world. Specifically, the TRC of the Philippines issued its report in 2016 and the Canadian TRC issued its report in 2015. These commissions drew insights from Africa's experience based on the engagement with issues that were generated by the African commissions. Sri Lanka adopted the path of convening a Lessons Learned and Reconciliation Commission, but it is now in the process of promoting a truth recovery process by drawing insights from the South African example. This in effect has demonstrated Africa's role in norm entrepreneurship and norm transfer.

## *The Cultural Approach to Justice and Reconciliation*

In contrast to other transitional justice processes in Latin America and the Balkans, for example, African states have also experimented with culturally informed processes to address the violations of the past. Due to the limitations of internationally imposed ideas of transitional justice, there was a need to draw upon Africa's knowledge systems, its traditions and culture of jurisprudence to articulate and document indigenous norms of transitional justice.

There have always been customary rules, social sanctions and ethical precepts to regulate African societies. While each society has its own specific approach to dealing with social problems, some common themes emerge across societies. In the majority of African communities, the individual is not considered a separate, autonomous entity but always part of a larger collective of human beings. Family groupings give way to the formation of clan communities and then ethnic nations. These groupings had a responsibility to maintain social harmony. Due to the importance of maintaining harmony, peaceful approaches to resolving disputes were generally preferred to more confrontational and belligerent strategies, though these were also occasionally utilised. Most African societies have developed rich cultural norms of transitional and restorative justice as well as reconciliation for preserving harmony, making and building peace and maintaining this peace by cultivating group solidarity and avoiding aggression and violence (Ake 1991).

Some of these practices have been mobilised by African states in transitional justice processes. For example, Rwanda's *gacaca* courts and Uganda's *mato oput* reconciliation framework operationalised indigenous norm restorative justice. An extensive treatment of these approaches is beyond the scope of this chapter, but as illustrated in the seminal book by Okello et al. (2012) titled *When Law Meets Reality: Forging African Transitional Justice*, the utilisation of indigenous norms of restorative justice was a significant innovation that challenged how transitional justice was predominantly conceived and understood. There have been criticisms of such inclusions, which have often included the suggestion that these cultural processes do not live up to international standards (Okello et al. 2012). However, the converse in fact has become more evident, in that African states have demonstrated that the esoteric and elusive notion of an arbitrary 'international standard' or norm should not constrain countries that are attempting to address the violations of the past in their own specific context.

Some African conceptions of the individual, and their role and place in society, can provide an alternative normative framework for establishing more harmonious political and economic relations at local, national, continental and even global levels (Wa Thiong'o 1993, 61). Through commonly found African emphasis on the value of social harmony and non-adversarial dispute resolution, there are lessons that can be learned and applied to contemporary conflict situations. It is necessary to question the notion of a universal conception of justice that can be advanced by a 'world court', like the ICC. This universalising tendency is often driven by a 'civilising' and 'modernising' imperative, which self-evidently marginalises the 'other's' conception of justice. It regrettably assumes that there is one way of conceptualising justice, which is erroneous at best and coercive and alienating at worst. Instead, we need to embrace the idea that notions of justice can be locally specific and culturally defined. As highlighted at the beginning of this chapter, the purpose of justice is to ensure accountability for harm done. If cultural forms of justice can achieve this in a way that does not rely exclusively on a prosecutorial imperative, then it is vital to draw lessons from such approaches. As discussed above, African norms of transitional justice emphasise communal harmony over the general tendency within mainstream notions of justice to prioritise individual culpability. The key point is that Africa is innovating when it comes to transitional justice norms and consequently providing normative examples of how countries can draw upon their cultural practices to address the violations of the past (see Lühe and Jones, this volume).

## *The Cross-Border Approach to Justice and Reconciliation*

In Africa as in other parts of the world, interstate wars in the region have largely been replaced by intrastate conflicts (Kaldor 2013). However, these intrastate conflicts, more often than not, have an interstate or regional dimension in the way that they are resourced and executed. In the Great Lakes region of Africa, for example, there is an intimate link between the crisis in Burundi, the eastern DRC and Rwanda, which can be situated in its historical origins in the Belgian colonisation of all three countries. Decades of misrule, combined with kleptocratic relationships between the rulers of these countries and their governmental and corporate accomplices outside the country, has generated economic crimes which have fuelled the crisis and violent conflict in the region. Attempts to address the crisis in one country in isolation of the dynamics of neighbouring countries will deliver incomplete outcomes at best (Murithi 2016). It is increasingly evident that regional reconciliation is required to ensure consolidated peace. The national focus of transitional justice processes is increasingly becoming unsustainable, particularly in situations where conflicts spill across borders, as seen in the Somali crisis conflict which has drawn in Ethiopia, Eritrea, Uganda and Kenya.

The absence of a coordinated approach to regional reconciliation in Africa has generated innovative community-based interventions which have invoked new norms of cross-border transitional justice (Murithi and Opiyo 2014). Thus even though the international focus has been on national reconciliation, there are ongoing processes across Africa which suggest the need to talk about regional reconciliation norms.

Regional reconciliation norms would require framing a way to implement processes of truth recovery, accountability and redress across borders as preliminary processes (Wallensteen 2012). The practicalities of how to operationalise regional reconciliation are challenging but not insurmountable. The reluctance of nation-states to devolve their sovereignty and adopt processes that might be seemingly outside of their sphere of authority and control through the establishment of cross-border institutions will be a primary obstacle to implementing regional reconciliation. Articulating the compelling case for a policy of regional reconciliation exposes the limitations of retaining a state-centric approach to dealing with the past and ensuring redress and accountability. This is an initial first step by African norm entrepreneurs to once again break with the constraining normative silos of the past, and regional economic communities are already engaging with this new norm through policy formulation debates, illustrated in particular by the prospective African Union Transitional Justice Policy (AUTJP).

A regional reconciliation norm would draw state actors into cross-border processes which could potentially reduce the prospects for the internal political control and manipulation of transitional justice. A regional reconciliation norm would typically require the negotiation between governments of how to frame and operationalise transitional justice processes. This requirement of cross-border negotiation would mitigate against each individual state manipulating transitional justice processes. However, such a normative shift inevitably has limits, because cross-border transitional justice processes can also become prey to interstate politics and can equally be subject to corruption. Therefore, the notion of regional reconciliation is affected by policy challenges in terms of how to operationalise the structures and institutions which can underpin its implementation.

People-to-people exchanges are already a common feature of the regional reconciliation landscape and are happening in some parts of Africa, notably in the borderlands of eastern DRC, Rwanda and Burundi, as well as historically in the Mano River Union countries of Sierra Leone, Liberia and Guinea. People-to-people approaches to regional reconciliation can be convened by civic, academic, business and cultural leaders without the approval of the states, though they can benefit from the support of governments. Consequently, people-to-people processes are developing new norms of cross-border transitional justice.

Arguably the most prominent instance of people-to-people regional reconciliation has occurred in the Horn of Africa. The region has endured the debilitating effects of violent conflict for several decades, notably as a result of the South Sudan–Northern Uganda conflict nexus and the Somali conflict system. Despite policy frameworks and the utilisation of significant resources to stabilise affected countries, conflicts in the region have remained resistant to resolution. The crises in the Horn of Africa demonstrate that conflicts have a tendency to spill across borders, affecting communities in more than one country (Karamoja Cluster Project 2005). They also demonstrate that intrastate conflicts usually have a regional dimension, as they include more than one state as either the primary or secondary actor.

While the implicated state actors have not adopted a coordinated regional strategy to promote and consolidate peace, non-state actors have taken more transnational approaches. The first approach, for example, involves the Karamoja Cluster Project, which works across the

Kenyan and Ugandan borders to promote people-to-people regional reconciliation and peacebuilding (Karamoja Cluster Project 2005). This cross-border initiative brings together the Karamoja communities of eastern Uganda and western Kenya, which have endured cyclical violence related to livestock theft and violent conflict over limited scarce resources and access to land. The initiative establishes people-to-people dialogue platforms in order to address key concerns and raise pertinent issues. These platforms can take the form of social engagement activities like cross-border sports, which draw participants from the different conflicting communities, and exchanges such as women-led cultural events. In addition, the initiative convenes educational and training programmes to raise awareness among members of the Karamoja community as to how to promote effective strategies to ensure that the livelihood of all members is protected. In addition, the people-to-people regional reconciliation initiatives are also driven by women-led peacebuilding initiatives in order to increase the focus on how the violent conflicts and the destruction of the social fabric of societies affects the women of the Karamoja Cluster differently to their male counterparts. The cross-border initiative also draws upon the convening of cross-border cultural and sports activities to increase the levels of people-to-people interaction among the Karamoja. This form of interaction creates new and innovative opportunities to engage in dialogue and deepen the understanding between communities that have traditionally engaged each other, usually through violent conflict.

The Karamoja Cluster Project should be understood as a work in progress rather than a fait accompli in terms of its efforts to promote people-to-people regional reconciliation across borders. The initiative, however, demonstrates that the adoption of regional reconciliation mechanisms is in fact already taking place, which bolsters academic and policy analysts' advocacy for the norm and thus promotes international recognition of this potentially emerging norm. If the insights drawn from the Karamoja Cluster Project can be replicated in other border regions of the Horn of Africa, this would further promote norm creation. This people-to-people initiative also demonstrates that higher-level and elite-driven regional reconciliation process can also draw normative insights from the manner in which former enemies can come together in the spirit of addressing common concerns and developing joint solutions to enhance the livelihood of citizens of the Horn of Africa.

The second kind of cross-border transitional justice process is judicial in nature and involves the Special Court of Sierra Leone in the prosecution of Charles Taylor, the former president of neighbouring Liberia. The Special Court was established by the government of Sierra Leone; however, international actors and donors played a significant role in operationalising its activities. Taylor had committed a range of human rights violations through his tacit support of armed militia in Sierra Leone. The Special Court was initially convened in Freetown, Sierra Leone, but was subsequently relocated to The Hague, where a ruling against Taylor was issued imprisoning him for up to 50 years (Government of the RSL and the RUF of SL 1999). The Taylor ruling has set a precedent for cross-border judicial redress for the victims in Sierra Leone.

Similarly, the AU's Extraordinary Chambers in Senegal were convened to prosecute the erstwhile dictator of Chad, Hissène Habré, for his individual culpability in overseeing a state system of repression and violence, which is estimated to have killed 40,000 people, and torturing and committing gender-based violence on hundreds of thousands of others. The Habré ruling has also set a precedent for cross-border judicial redress for the victims in Chad. The AU's Extraordinary Chambers in Senegal could well make a new era for pan-African justice, and it has set another normative example for the world.

The AU has sought to advance norms related to transitional justice in its bid to provide guidance to its member states emerging from conflict. Article 4(h) of the AU Constitutive Act ascribes 'the right of the Union to intervene in a member state pursuant to a decision of the Assembly in respect of grave circumstances, namely: war crimes, crimes against humanity and genocide' (African Union 2000). Furthermore, article 4(o) stipulated the AU's 'rejection of impunity' as a key normative principle. The AU was in effect ahead of its time in terms of enshrining a normative right to intervene to address these international crimes, which have since been incorporated into the framing of international transitional justice norms.

## The Adoption of the AU Transitional Justice Policy

Between 2011 and 2019, the AU became the first regional organisation to actively work on developing a specific policy relating to transitional justice. In November 2018, the AU Extraordinary Summit of Heads of State and Government in Kigali, Rwanda, formally approved the Draft AU Transitional Justice Policy. In February 2019, the AU Transitional Justice Policy (AUTJP) was formally adopted by the AU Assembly of Heads of State and Government in Addis Ababa, Ethiopia. The purpose of the AUTJP is to encourage member states to broaden their understanding of justice beyond retributive justice to encompass restorative and transformative measures found in traditional African systems (African Union 2019). The AUTJP recommends to take into account economic and social rights, with the active participation of non-state actors and beneficiaries, and designing reparations programmes that would address the structural nature of these issues. The efforts by the AU to push the boundaries of the way in which transitional justice has been conceived to include social and economic rights rectifies an oversight which was internalised by the dominant legal framework which defined the field, despite the articulation of the need for reparation. The economic and social dimension of transitional justice processes is now emerging as a key driver of sustainable transformation for societies that have experienced violations.

AUTJP recommends the promotion of

> reconciliation as a profound process which entails finding a way to live that permits a vision of the future, the rebuilding of relationships, coming to terms with the past acts and enemies, and involves societies in a long-term process of deep change.
> (African Union 2019)

The AUTJP is also path-breaking in terms of incorporating as a policy document a commitment to addressing trauma and woundedness, which is an issue that is often swept under the carpet, with the mistaken belief that the issues will remain under the carpet. Specifically, the AUTJP advocates for the importance of coming 'to terms with the traumas of slavery, colonialism, apartheid, systemic repression and civil wars' as a necessary precursor to 'achieving sustainable peace, justice, reconciliation, social cohesion and healing' (African Union 2019, para. 2, p. 1). The psychosocial dimension of peacebuilding is often underplayed, and the AUTJP tries to rectify this omission.

## Conclusion

Africa has played a leading role in the global promotion of practices and norms of justice and reconciliation. Africa in this sense has challenged the artificial normative strictures of the global discourse of transitional justice and advanced its own home-grown norms for dealing with the violations of the past. Africa's experimentation with a broad range of norms and practices has reaffirmed the interface between justice, peacebuilding and reconciliation. Several countries are emerging from conflict, and the challenge of peacebuilding is immediately confronted by the demands for justice for the victims of human rights atrocities. Traditionally, the pursuit of justice in international relations was considered detrimental to achieving peace and reconciliation, which are inherently political processes. However, Africa's experiences have challenged this presumption and demonstrated the necessary nexus between transitional justice and peacebuilding processes.

This chapter has assessed how transitional justice originated from the legal tradition, which was focused on the judicial processes to address civil and political violations during transitions. The goal was to lay the foundations for the post-transition rule of law. Africa's experience demonstrated that traditional notions of transitional justice needed to be re-thought and re-framed. Specifically, in order to address the real concerns of victims of past violations effectively, transitional justice norms had to be expanded beyond their narrow civil and political focus to include socio-economic and psychosocial issues. The chapter has discussed how transitional justice is now understood as involving a broad spectrum of interventions that are embedded in peacebuilding and developmental processes.

Culture gives distinctiveness to a particular society's way of doing things. There is a need to draw upon Africa's knowledge systems, its traditions and culture of jurisprudence to articulate and document indigenous norms of transitional justice. However, such an activity has to be informed by the fact that Africa is not a homogenous entity, and within its societies there is a vast array of different approaches to dealing with the issues of peace and justice.

Africa's experiences have also evoked the need to scale up transitional justice processes from their country-specific focus towards a normative shift based on a regionalised approach to dealing with the past. Despite the growing acknowledgment of regional conflicts, regional reconciliation has *not* been the norm. Africa will continue to innovate on the development of transitional justice norms, due to the fact that a number of countries on the continent will be emerging from conflict in the next decade and beyond. By extension, Africa will continue to be a thought leader, norm setter and norm entrepreneur in terms of transitional justice processes and institutions and the perplexing challenge of addressing the violations of the past. In effect, this chapter has argued that the notion of transitional justice is today much more expansive in terms of what is being practiced on the ground, due in part to the influence of norms and practices that were operationalised and implemented in Africa.

The AU declared 2014–2024 the Madiba Nelson Mandela Decade of Reconciliation in Africa, so it is timely that the AUTJP was adopted in 2019, almost halfway through this designated period. However, the continent still has a way to go to stabilise all of its regions and consolidate peace and security for its people. The AUTJP is a welcome addition to the arsenal of policy documents that can contribute towards the promotion of peace and security, but it is not a panacea or a magic bullet that will solve the continents problems. Governments and societies will have to undertaking the challenging, arduous, painstaking and excavational work of addressing the violations and exploitation of the past, which is vital towards building stable and peaceful communities across the continent.

## References

African Union, (2000) *Constitutive Act*. Lomé: African Union.
African Union, (2019) *African Union Transitional Justice Policy*. Addis Ababa: African Union.
Ake, C., (1991) 'Rethinking African Democracy', *Journal of Democracy*, 2(1), pp. 32–44.
Arthur, P., (2009) 'How Transitions Reshaped Human Rights: A Conceptual History of Transitional Justice', *Human Rights Quarterly*, 31, pp. 321–367.
Asaala, E. and Diker, N., (2013) 'Truth-seeking in Kenya: Assessing the Effectiveness of the Truth, Justice and Reconciliation Commission of Kenya', *Africa Nazarene University Law Journal*, 1(2).

Balasco, L., (2013) 'The Transitions of Transitional Justice: Mapping the Waves from Promise to Practice', *Journal of Human Rights*, 12, pp. 198–216.

Binningsbø, H., (2012) 'Armed Conflict and Post-Conflict Justice, 1946–2006: A Dataset', *Journal of Peace Research*, pp. 731–740.

Boraine, A.L., (2004) 'Transitional Justice', in Villa-Vicencio, C. and Doxtader, E., (eds.) *Pieces of the Puzzle: Keywords on Reconciliation and Transitional Justice*. Cape Town: Institute for Justice and Reconciliation.

Brown, S. and Sriram, C.L., (2012) 'The Big Fish Won't Fry Themselves: Criminal Accountability for Post-Election Violence in Kenya', *African Affairs*, 111(443), p. 244–260.

Du Toit, F., (2013) 'A Double-Edged Sword', in Conradie, E., (ed.) *Reconciliation: A Guiding Vision for South Africa?* Johannesburg: EFSA.

Government of the Republic of Sierra Leone and the Revolutionary United Front of Sierra Leone, (1999) *Lomé Peace Agreement between Government of Sierra Leone and Revolutionary United Front*, Lomé, 7 July.

Grono, N. and O'Brien, A., (2008) 'Justice in Conflict? The ICC and Peace Processes', in Waddell, N. and Phil Clark, P., (eds.) *Courting Conflict: Justice, Peace and the ICC in Africa*. London: Royal African Society.

International Criminal Court, *Prosecutor vs Dominic Ongwen*, December. [online]. Available at: www.icc-cpi.int/en_menus/icc/situations (Accessed: 28 January 2020). International Criminal Court: The Hague.

Kaldor, M., (2013) *New and Old Wars: Organised Violence in a Global Era*. Hoboken: Wiley.

Karamoja Cluster Project, (2005) [Facebook]. [online]. Available at: Karamoja Cluster Project | Facebook (Accessed: 20 January 2020).

McCargo, D., (2015) 'Transitional Justice and its Discontents', *Journal of Democracy*, 26(2), April, pp. 5–20.

Meernik, J., (2005) 'Justice and Peace? How the International Criminal Tribunal Affects Societal Peace in Bosnia', *Journal of Peace Research*, 42(3), pp. 271–289.

Murithi, T., (2009) *The Ethics of Peacebuilding*. Edinburgh: Edinburgh University Press.

Murithi, T., (2010) 'The Role of Security Sector Reform in Dealing with the Past', *Politorbis*, 50(3), pp. 65–70.

Murithi, T., (ed.) (2016) *The Politics of Transitional Justice in the Great Lakes Region of Africa*. Johannesburg: Jacana Media.

Murithi, T. and Opiyo, M.L., (2014) 'Regional Reconciliation in Africa', *Policy Recommendations for Cross-Border Transitional Justice Policy Brief no. 14*. Cape Town: Institute for Justice and Reconciliation.

Okello, M. et al., (2012) *Where Law Meets Reality: Forging African Transitional Justice*. Nairobi: Fahamu.

Sigsworth, R. and Valji, N., (2012) 'Continuities of Violence Against Women and the Limitations of Transitional Justice: The Case of South Africa', in Buckley-Zistel, S. and Stanley, R., (eds.) *Gender in Transitional Justice*. Basingstoke: Palgrave Macmillan.

Sisson, J., (2010) 'A Conceptual Framework for Dealing with the Past', *Politorbis – Dealing with the Past*, 50, pp. 11–15.

United Nations General Assembly, (2005) *Basic Principles and Guidelines on the Right to Remedy and Reparation for Victims of Gross Violations of International Human Rights Law and Serious Violations of International Humanitarian Law, A/RES/60/147*. New York, NY: United Nations.

United Nations Security Council, (2004) *The Rule of Law and Transitional Justice in Conflict and Post-conflict Societies: Report of the Secretary-General, S/2004/616*. New York, NY: United Nations.

Villa-Vicencio, C. and Doxtader, E., (eds.) (2004) *Pieces of the Puzzle: Keywords on Reconciliation and Transitional Justice*. Cape Town: Institute for Justice and Reconciliation.

Wallensteen, P., (2012) 'Regional Peacebuilding: A New Challenge', in *New Routes: A Journal of Peace Research and Action*, 17(4), pp. 3–5.

Wa Thiong'o, N., (1993) *Moving the Centre: The Struggle for Cultural Freedoms*. Nairobi: East African Educational Publishers.

# 7
# THE POLITICS OF KNOWLEDGE AND AN AFRICAN TRANSITIONAL JUSTICE

Analysing Africa as a Constitutive Outside

*Ulrike Lühe and Briony Jones*

### Introduction

In October 2017, the government of Burundi officially withdrew from the International Criminal Court (ICC), with Burundian spokesperson Willy Nyamitwe saying, "The ICC has shown itself to be a political instrument and weapon used by the West to enslave" (The Guardian 2017). While this decision is connected to the specific political context in Burundi, where then-President Pierre Nkurunziza sought to consolidate his increasingly authoritarian hold on power, this is not an isolated act of defiance against the ICC. Other African states have threatened to withdraw, including The Gambia, South Africa, and Kenya. They exemplify a growing public discussion over the "anti-Africa" bias of international criminal justice and calls for an "African justice". Despite the vibrant scholarly, practitioner, and policy debates that are seeking to give shape to this idea, the questions of what this would look like and what it means are far from resolved. However, whilst the content of an African transitional justice remains contested and is certainly open to (ab)use by political leaders and powerful actors, the debate itself has made important contributions to critical inquiries into the global norm of transitional justice and the politics of knowledge production in the field. This chapter unpacks that politics in order to nuance our understanding of African experiences with, approaches to, and expertise on transitional justice as co-constitutive of the global field of transitional justice.

The discussion about an African transitional justice has gained more traction with the adoption on 12 February 2019 of the African Union Transitional Justice Policy (AUTJP) in Addis Ababa. In the press release announcing its adoption, the AU (2019) stated that

> the AUTJP builds on the AU Policy on Post-Conflict Reconstruction and Development and draws lessons from past experiences, including African traditional justice systems. The AUTJP presents an African model with holistic parameters, benchmarks and practical strategic proposals for designing, implementing, monitoring and evaluating transitional justice in AU Member States based on key principles and specific indicative elements. The Policy also aims to ensure that transitional justice activities

address root causes of conflicts, legacies of violence, governance deficits and developmental challenges in Africa.

A policy ten years in the making, it reflects the culmination of a series of AU discussions, member state proposals, and research undertaken on the continent, and makes statements about African specific approaches to justice and the need for an African transitional justice policy. The policy process is but one example of the many processes, platforms, and networks in which the idea of an African transitional justice has been discussed.

While many of the elements of the recognizable global norm (Nagy 2008) of transitional justice are present in the AUTJP – justice and accountability, truth seeking, reparations, memorialization – the document nonetheless sets itself apart from this norm, or at least the actors associated with it, in making a claim to an African transitional justice. In the foreword to the policy, the AU chairperson H.E. Mr Moussa Faki Mahamat writes:

> Although the process took some time, it is gratifying to note that we now have a Transitional Justice Toolkit that is home-grown, unique to Africa, rich in its progressive methodologies and approaches, and rooted in African shared values, traditional justice systems and experiences.
>
> *(African Union 2019)*

This is a strong statement with a series of implications and assumptions, some of which will be explored in this chapter. It is a policy move which speaks to much of the critical literature on transitional justice which charts its genealogy, identifying its birth as coming

> out of the euphoria, triumphalism, and, perhaps, arrogance of the "end of history", a time in the 1980s and the 1990s when some believed, in a sort of democratic domino theory, that the world was inevitably converging, or at least normatively *should* be converging, upon Western liberal market democracy as the only plausible form of governance.
>
> *(Sharp 2018, viii)*

The AU statement also recognizes that, in a field dominated by models and replications of policies and programmes across varied geographical contexts, African events and justice interventions have been foundational for the way the field of transitional justice has evolved. The South African case, and in particular the work of the Truth and Reconciliation Commission, expanded the discourse of transitional justice in a number of fundamental ways: (1) by opening it up to a broader array of disciplines beyond the law; (2) by legitimizing calls for reconciliation not as an excuse for impunity but as a desirable goal; (3) by linking the transitional justice experiences of Africa to narratives from Latin America and Eastern Europe; and (4) by leading to a widely exported model of transitional justice with truth commissions as a key mechanism (Zunino 2019, 117–119). The statement by the AU also pushes back against what others have seen as a problematic "gaze" of transitional justice on the continent, in the case of the ICC which "prefer[s] to imagine Africa as a largely inert space in which it will easily wield its influence, rather than as an arena of vibrant agency and contestation, much of which is fundamentally opposed to external intervention" (Clark 2018, 7) and indeed denies the realities of influence by African states on the ICC (Ba 2020).

These events and dynamics say something interesting about the landscape of the politics of knowledge of transitional justice. It tells us that the expansion of the field to new contexts and actors (Hansen 2014) is also expanding in terms of epistemic inclusivity. This inclusivity suggests the possibility of different types of transitional justice approaches, values, and ways of understanding harm and its repair, and goes to the heart of legitimacy of transitional justice interventions and their claims to knowledge. These are claims to knowledge not only about the contexts in which transitional justice entrepreneurs intervene but also about themselves, who they are, and the impact of what they do. In the case of transitional justice in Africa, this is bound up in histories of colonialism and intervention and complicated by the paradox that while African experiences and justice interventions have been fundamental in shaping the field of transitional justice, the field itself is still dominated by a "core liberal-legalist narrative" (Sharp 2018, ix) seen as emanating from the Global North while all the time drawing on evidence based in the Global South.

In this chapter, we contribute to these debates and themes of the politics of knowledge by analysing Africa as a constitutive outside of transitional justice. We draw heavily on the work of Bilgin (2009) on "worlding" in the context of conflict expertise and the disjuncture between Global North and Global South knowledges. In doing so, we critically analyse the founding moments of transitional justice as well as the way Africa is cast as both absence and presence in this emergence of the field. This touches upon colonialism, ideas of the local, and the contradictions and tensions inherent in any single notion of "an African transitional justice". In the final part of the chapter, we address the implications of an African transitional justice for Africa as a constitute outside of transitional justice.

## Worlding Transitional Justice by Rendering Visible Its Constitutive Outside(s)

> "Others" have helped shape what is known as "Western" expertise even as their contributions have been overlooked by virtue of labelling it as "Western".
> *(Bilgin 2009, 87)*

In transitional justice, as in its neighboring and related fields of peacebuilding, human rights, or international relations (IR), the possibilities and limitations of local ownership have been discussed at length (for transitional justice, see Lundy and McGovern 2008; Sharp 2013, 2014, 2018; Hinton 2010; McEvoy and McGregor 2010; Wielenga 2018; Shaw, Waldorf and Hazan 2010; for peacebuilding, see Björkdahl and Höglund 2013; Millar 2014; Donais 2009). Local ownership as a lens of critique emerged largely in response to the standardized solutions that are offered by international actors from the Global North to the Global South, which are seen as undermining local ownership in terms of control, process, and substance (Sharp 2013). Focusing on the field of conflict resolution, Bilgin (2018, 77) suggests that there are two dimensions to the local ownership problem: "the prevalence of actors from the Global North in shaping conflict resolution and mediation efforts and the Eurocentric slant in the assembling of conflict expertise". Transitional justice scholarship has engaged with both dimensions in detail, as well as the associated responses. To counter the prevalence of Global North actors, one response has been to "[engage] directly with policy practitioners, seeking to render [. . .] expertise less Eurocentric by empowering [. . .] practitioners from the Global South, thereby diluting the power of Global North expertise" (Bilgin 2018, 78). In contrast, the Eurocentric slant is frequently countered by identifying differently situated expertise and assembling a new body of "expertise through tapping into already existing knowledge and techniques in the Global South" (Bilgin 2018, 78). Both responses can be found in the transitional justice literature.

However, Bilgin (2018) argues that rendering the local visible through those two strategies, which reflect the geo-cultural situatedness of knowledge, is not sufficient. She proposes worlding[1] as an additional strategy and point of analysis. Worlding is a way of "proposing epistemological equality between the West and the non-West" (Shih and Hwang 2018, 423). Whilst worlding as situatedness has its roots in feminist scholarship (Pettman 1996), it has become a broader strategy so that "the different worlds of those outside the powerful centers and classes be included in our understanding of international politics" (Bilgin 2018, 79). Shih and Hwang (2018, 426) describe worlding similarly as "practicing the given international relations and global order in a contributive identity (e.g. race, gender, class and site)". It is "the initiating West making sense of the non-West" (Shih and Hwang 2018, 426); that is, the acknowledgement of any perspective as situated, whether this be an understanding of IR or a conceptualization of transitional justice. However, as Gregory (2004) argues, and as is taken up by Bilgin, in postcolonial scholarship it is acknowledged that "focusing merely on the geo-cultural context of ideas and institutions may result in overlooking the constitutive effects of the colonial encounter in the making of the world – including the 'colonial present'" (Bilgin 2018, 80). Worlding thus has another dimension to it, that of worlding as constitutive: "[It] involve[s] becoming aware how [texts] are 'worldly', that is, how they respond to and reflect their context" (Bilgin 2018, 79). Ahluwalia and Sullivan (2001, 363) describe it similarly as the "un- or non-neglectedness of other ideologies and experiences". In other words, we are asked by this work to unpack and render visible how the periphery is co-constituted by the center *and* how the center is co-constituted by the periphery. In this, it is a step towards blurring the lines between the binaries of the West and the non-West.

In practice, this worlding as constitutive explores how ideas, in the case of Bilgin's work in IR and conflict resolution, "have been shaped through interaction with IR's 'constitutive outside'" (2018, 81); it explores the constitutive relationship between the West and the non-West. However, rather than being an actual outside, Bilgin argues that these outsides are actually "already 'inside'" – that is, they are a "constitutive outside" (2018, 86) – arguably because the "refusal to recognize how the non-West and nonmodern are already integrated as constitutive forces within the West and the modern is precisely how the colonial comes to be externalized" (Blaney and Inayatullah 2010, 670). By unpacking the outsideness of African contexts, we learn that Africa is a constitutive outsider, one that has considerable impact on the transitional justice field's ideas, norms, and principles. By making visible the constitutive role of this supposed outside, we see that in fact it is and should be considered an inside (Bilgin 2018).

Attempts at worlding transitional justice knowledge do exist in the literature. For example, the contributions in the special issue "Transition and Justice: Negotiating the Terms of New Beginnings in Africa" in the journal *Development and Change* (vol. 45, issue 3) aim at contextualizing and situating transitional justice experiences in Africa. However, this only contextualizes and situates the implementation of specific transitional justice mechanisms. What is done less often is to contextualize and situate transitional justice as a field, its origins, and the origins of its key concepts and mechanisms. When this is done, the worlding is focused on the West (see e.g. Mouralis 2013). Worlding transitional justice concepts and practices in the non-West or the interaction between the West and non-West are notably absent and thus are the focus of our contribution in this chapter.

## Interrogating Transitional Justice's Origin Myths

There are two key points to which the origins of transitional justice are assigned: post–World War II and post–Cold War, phases which have been framed as "historical moments of

Western triumphalism" (Maddison and Shepherd 2014, 260). This has led to strong normative assumptions dominating the initial developments of the field and work which seeks to unpack, deconstruct and denaturalize transitional justice (see e.g. Mouralis 2013). However, these denaturalizations have only served to highlight that transitional justice has taken a very specific, indeed limited, form because of its origins in certain events and in the pens of people with specific, Western, legal backgrounds. This denaturalization has not highlighted the contributions of the non-West to the development of these ideas and thus has not grappled with the constitutive outside of Africa.

The Nuremberg trials and the international body of law which emerged as a consequence of World War II and the Holocaust, including the Genocide Convention (1948), the Universal Declaration of Human Rights (1948) and the Geneva Convention on Laws of War (1949), are usually considered to be the starting points of transitional justice (Lundy and McGovern 2008; Teitel 2003). However, with the soon-to-start Cold War, this post–World War II phase as a "moment was short-lived" (Sharp 2013, 154). Nonetheless Teitel (2003), in her oft-cited article, "Transitional Justice Genealogy", has argued that these early legal bodies and institutions provide the purest form of transitional justice. However, the Nuremberg trials and subsequent years – the "heyday of international justice" (2003, 73) – not only established a new body of international law and a script for international criminal trials, but they also were key in "prioritizing international law over domestic law – a move that undermined the doctrine of sovereignty" (Hinton 2010, 3) which had been at the core of the international order since 1648. They laid the groundwork for the interventionist character of transitional justice, and in particular its instantiation as international criminal justice, which continues to be a major point of discontent in the field (Okafor and Ngwaba 2015; McEvoy 2007; Sriram and Pillay 2009) and which remains one of the main critiques of African states vis-à-vis the ICC.

Considering that practices of dealing with violence, establishing justice and fostering reconciliation, and transitioning societies from violence to peace existed long before this new body of law and its associated practices emerged, van der Merwe and Brinton Lykes (2018, 382) assert that transitional justice is not actually new nor was it birthed with the end of World War II, but that "it did, however, take on a new form with the global rise of universal human rights and the end of the Cold War." We also argue that the Western triumphalist narrative hides the fact that international law and the assumption of its universality was developed as a consequence of colonialist thinking and practice. The emergence of transitional justice as part of the liberal peacebuilding infrastructure (Sriram 2007) and as an international bureaucracy firmly situated in the Global North (Rubli 2012) has meant that it has been led and promoted by Western liberal democratic countries that were colonizers (Yusuf 2018, 259). Third World Approaches to International Law (TWAIL) scholarship has made important contributions in unpacking these links (Chimni 2006). Mutua (2009) has argued that international human rights law is closely associated with colonial conquest, a constitutive relationship that had been shown by Anghie (1999) already. The latter argues that in international law "even distinguished scholars [. . .] implicitly tend to treat the colonial encounter as marginal by studying it principally in terms of the effects of positivism on the colonized peoples", thus advancing a "traditional view of the discipline [that] downplays the importance of the colonial confrontation for an understanding of the subject as a whole" (Anghie 1999, 4). This calls into question the role of international law as "a heightened and important legal reference point during transitions by virtue of its externality to the parties of the conflict" (Bell, Campbell and Aoláin 2004, 308).

The assertion that transitional justice originated in the Nuremberg trials also posits transitional justice as "entirely a *post*colonial enterprise" (Maddison and Shepherd 2014, 261–262):

> The exceptionalism that defines the context of transitional justice is in itself a colonial practice of power. The imagined history of transitional justice that locates its inception at the Nuremberg Trials effectively posits that transitional justice mechanisms [were] literally brought forth into existence by the horror of the Holocaust. This discursive move allows the "international community" to reset the standard of justice and, by association, delineate a new boundary around crimes that were so severe as to require new ways of dealing with them. These crimes were considered exceptional, and thus in need of new mechanisms and new conceptual frameworks. Except such crimes were not exceptional. Such crimes were part of the everyday lexicon of colonial power. Empires such as those founded by the same powers that organised post–World War II to ensure that Nazi war criminals were brought to justice, were founded on violence, often genocidal violence.

Following the Nuremberg trials and the relative stagnation of the development of transitional justice practice during the Cold War, the third wave of transitions in Eastern Europe and Latin America has been postulated as the next phase in the development of transitional justice (Teitel 2003). Truth commissions, seen as originating in the Argentinian case, emerged as alternatives to trial justice. However, using the example of the South African Truth and Reconciliation Commission [TRC], we wish to highlight the origin of this other key mechanism of transitional justice in "the TRC's counterintuitive precedents in colonial sovereignty and governmentality" (Sitze 2013, 3). Taking South Africa's long history of indemnity jurisprudence, Sitze, in his book *The Impossible Machine*, examines the history of the TRC not as a "variation on transitional mechanisms in Germany and Latin America" but "a variation on the theory and practice of indemnity in South Africa" (2013, 4). He argues that the TRC allowed "indemnity' to survive as and in 'amnesty'" (2013, 9). Thus, not only was the TRC as an institutional form rooted in colonial governmentality practices, but it also helped perpetuate one of apartheid's crimes, that of indemnity.

In addition to these roots in practices and laws of indemnity, Sitze also traces the TRC to Commissions of Inquiry that were established (by colonial powers) in the nineteenth and twentieth centuries to investigate police and military conduct in the suppression of colonial riots and rebellion (2013). These origins are echoed in Malombe (2012), who relates the long history of commissions of inquiry to the practice of truth commissions in Kenya and on the continent more generally. Overall, Sitze's analysis aims to retrieve and comprehend "the volatile kernel of eventness that transitional justice misrecognizes when it reifies the TRC into a 'paradigm'" (2013, 20). As Pillay argues, Sitze's account "locates the TRC in a longer political and conceptual history of jurisprudence, and one that is decidedly less marvelous than the story of law as the highest form of civilization" (2013, 803). It allows us to see TRCs, considered one of the main mechanisms of Western transitional justice conceptualizations, as constituted in the interaction between the colony and the empire. The predominant discourse traces the origins of TRCs to Latin America and then South Africa in 1994, whilst simultaneously labelling them as international models, often imposed by Western stakeholders. Sitze's sidelined, but equally intriguing, proposition traces the underlying principles of truth commissions to colonial institutions that served to establish and secure governance over the colonies.

Applying a post-colonial lens to the origin myths of transitional justice highlights how the Nuremberg and post–Cold War narratives help ground transitional justice in one version of international justice that (1) blurs the interaction of transitional justice's most popular mechanisms – international law and truth commissions – and colonial governance and (2) hides previous experiences of violence that might have warranted criminal justice solutions (colonial violence). To put it in Sitze's words, one might ask,

> Why [there has] been so little analysis within transitional justice about the empirical regularity with which Truth Commissions and postcolonial orders correlate? Why have most transitional justice scholars instead interpreted these commissions according to the standard pattern of Eurocentric knowledge production?
>
> *(2013, 255)*

Maddison and Shepherd (2014) argue that the separation of historical conflict from contemporary transition in transitional justice interventions means that colonial power and colonial injustices do not fall under the gaze of transitional justice mechanisms or processes. This has relevance not only for past injustices, as we have been discussing, but also for ongoing injustices in the exercise of colonial power and its legacies. In his work on Nigeria, Yusuf (2018) describes how colonialism's predatory paradigm of governance was adopted at independence by the local political, civil, and military elite to the detriment of pursuing transitional justice. In this work we see the continuation of injustices and violations over time from colonialism to post-independence, challenging the sense of truncated time applied by transitional justice mandates concerned with specific violations occurring during a specific period. According to Yusuf, there is a tension, if not a paradox, in transitional justice:

> Conceptually, transitional justice demands a break from a past marked by injustice, harm and suffering. It also anticipates the abatement of impunity through various mechanisms as well as reformation of state institutions. Transitional justice envisages a form of revolutionary shift in the sociopolitical order. Such a shift recognizes the agency of disenfranchised or disempowered victims and ensures the authority and power of the state is reconfigured with their consent and rendered accountable to them. However, this is problematic in a context where governance is founded on the perpetuation of colonial patterns of hegemony.
>
> *(Yusuf 2018, 261)*

But this paradox arises out of an assumption about transitional justice discourse and practice that "envisages a form of revolutionary shift in the socio-political order" (Yusuf 2018, 261). This is not necessarily the case. There has been work highlighting the problematic power relations inherent in transitional justice and the way in which the international project or global norm of transitional justice is based on a continuation and perpetuation of injustice and marginalization. Indeed, the malleability of transitional justice, which can be instrumentalized by political elites (Lamont and Boujneh 2012) as well as international interveners, prompts a careful reflection over whether transitional justice – as a global norm and political project – can be or is ever intended to lead to radical and transformative change. Anders and Zenker (2014) have written, with special reference to Africa, that the convergence of peacebuilding, development, and transitional justice understands political change as transformation through individual rights and liberalism rather than structural, violent, and revolutionary, as had been the case throughout decolonization and independence movements. For Bowsher, this convergence in agendas has shaped a transitional justice project which individualizes harm and agency at the same time as delegitimizing collective struggle and the possibilities of more radical justice-seeking agendas (2018).

The founding myths, structures of practice, and discourses of transitional justice have relied on Africa as sources of both theory and practice (i.e. a constitutive outside) without always acknowledging so. Foundational texts of the academic field claim that transitional justice has developed in waves following the Nuremberg trials, and policy and practice holds up certain cases and models rendered legible through a Western gaze and decontextualized from histories of practice and justice seeking in Africa. This has led to a development of transitional justice which goes hand in hand with the colonial enterprise and a continuation of authoritarian and non-democratic practices as transitional justice is instrumentalized by new political elites in post-colonial contexts. We take this analysis into the final section of this chapter, reflecting on what the discussion about an African transitional justice means for Africa as a constitutive outside of transitional justice.

## Africa as a Constitutive Outside of Transitional Justice's Concepts and Knowledge Production Practices

Besides locating the origins of transitional justice in the Global North, there also persists a presumption in the transitional justice scholarships that many of the norms, concepts, discourses, experts, actors and institutions that shape the field are Western in their nature and origin. We provide a number of brief examples that challenge these assumptions and highlight the role which African actors, concepts, and ideas have played in shaping global norms.

A first example is provided by Vanantwerpen (2009), who has traced the concept of reconciliation from the South African TRC via the International Centre for Transitional Justice (ICTJ) and the South African Institute for Justice and Reconciliation to several South African and international scholars. This continuous reframing allowed reconciliation to become "one of the most prolific travelling theories of our time" (Vanantwerpen 2009, 97). He outlines "a profusion of competing, conflicting and at times overlapping conceptions" (Vanantwerpen 2009, 99) in which, however, the role of southern academics, non-governmental organizations (NGOs), and activists is often overlooked "as transitions and truth commissions in the Global South are taken to represent the true sites of political urgency and the essential objects of academic analysis" (Vanantwerpen 2009, 125). Whilst many authors highlight the agency of southern actors in reshaping international norms for their own agendas (e.g. Brankovic and van der Merwe 2016), Vanantwerpen's account puts the very assumption of transitional justice norms being shaped primarily in the North on its head. He shows that

> in the realm of "reconciliation", invention and innovation have developed at the periphery and the semi-periphery of the contemporary world system. Rather than being produced through an attempted mimicry of the powerful, political technologies of truth and reconciliation have arisen and circulated extensively in the Global South, being taken more seriously by intellectuals in the North only after their adoption and adaptation in Latin America and Africa.
>
> *(Vanantwerpen 2009, 125)*

A second set of examples can be found in tracing certain individuals' contributions to developing transitional justice institutions and policies around the globe. Alex Boraine, who is one of the "prominent global entrepreneurs responsible for the transnational spread of truth and reconciliation processes" (Vanantwerpen 2009, 113) is not only the co-founder of the above-mentioned ICTJ but also "the organisation Healing Through Remembering [in Northern Ireland] that has been influential in shaping the debate on dealing with the past, was created after the visit of Alex Boraine [. . .] to Northern Ireland in 1999" (All Truth Is Bitter 1999; Mourlon 2016). Similarly,

> in 2004, Paul van Zyl, Vice-President of the ICTJ [and previously Executive Secretary of the South African TRC], took advantage of the UN's efforts to outline its own approach to transitional justice issues to reframe TRCs as a central, effective element of peacebuilding (Van Zyl 2005). In so doing, he also contributed to defining TRCs as a superior standard clearly distinguishable from other types of commissions of investigation.
>
> *(Ancelovici and Jenson 2013, 303)*

Finally, Hamber, who had been working with and on the South African truth commission from a civil society perspective, used some of his experience acquired in South Africa as well as his research work and his personal involvement in the process to successfully advocate for the adoption of "a clear and more focused definition of reconciliation" in the Peace II (European Commission n.d.; European Parliament 2020)[2] Extension programme in Northern Ireland (Mourlon 2016, 9).

A third set of examples can be found in the research practices that transitional justice relies on. A 2015 evaluation of transitional justice scholarship conducted by Fletcher and Weinstein exemplifies this. Africa, at the time, was leading in terms of the geographic focus of articles published, ahead of global perspectives, Europe, Asia, the Americas, and Oceania. Yet, there is a general sense that southern voices are underrepresented in transitional justice scholarship and theorizing, leading to a narrow set of ideas and debates and limiting possibilities of critique or alternatives ways of knowing (Ní Aoláin 2015).

Thus, whilst African countries, actors, and transitions are seen as holding key insights for the field of transitional justice, as indicated in the continent's prominent role as a subject of scholarly research, little of that research is authored in Africa. This leads to extractive research practices and exemplifies a "Northern-based-researcher-South-based-practitioner model of knowledge production" (Fletcher and Weinstein 2018, 21). Both not only produce problematic power dynamics, but they are also an integral part of the continued underrepresentation of southern scholarship, whether it be authored by academics, researchers, or practitioners, in the global scholarly debate. Whilst Africa is a major source of innovation, experience, and data, this is represented by Western voices, thus furthering the impression that Africa is an outsider to the core understanding, concepts, and knowledge production practices of the field of transitional justice, when in fact it is a constitutive outsider – an insider.

## African Transitional Justice and Its Implications for Africa as a Constitutive Outside

An interesting characteristic of transitional justice as a field is its movement between universal claims and particular experience. Both the policy and study of transitional justice has tended towards a rather narrow evidence base, drawing on certain experiences and models time and again. Recent books reflecting on foundations and genealogies of transitional justice bring this into relief. Murphy, in her attempt to offer "the conceptual tools to morally evaluate options for dealing with and decisions about legacies of violence and wrongdoing", states that "All human beings care about whether justice is achieved" (2017, 6). In speaking to universal goods and values, scholars of transitional justice refer frequently to specific country experiences, and we hear more about South Africa, Rwanda, Sierra Leone and less about Côte d'Ivoire, Zimbabwe or The Gambia.[3] The prevalence of these cases is partly owed to factors such as the length of time which has passed since the transitional justice intervention took place or language (with anglophone and francophone cases being more represented). However, the field's preference for models and replicability also plays a role in determining and limiting which countries the transitional justice field engages with it (McAuliffe 2017).

The way in which African experiences have been seen as key to the development of the field of transitional justice has too often been cast in terms of the object of intervention, the beneficiaries of processes, and the marginalized in "Western" dominated discourse and practice. This is perhaps due to the excellent scholarship which has traced the links between transitional justice and colonialism, not least that which has demonstrated that the legacies of colonialism, including the impunity of the period, have shaped and conditioned later transitional justice processes which are blind to colonial histories and legacies (Yusuf 2018, 275). We have argued in this chapter to think in terms of Africa as a constitutive outside of transitional justice, not only relevant because of the absence and marginalization of African thought, experiences, and approaches from the dominant global norm of transitional justice, but because in fact African experiences and theorizations have contributed considerably to shaping the field and the way it has developed.

Transitional justice as tangled up in colonial power systems, forms of governance, and discourse is thus perhaps incapable in its current form of addressing historical or ongoing injustices. The knowledge imperialism of transitional justice (Kagoro 2012) may be challenged by initiatives such as the AUTJP or the African Commission on Human and People's Rights recent report (ACHPR 2019), which identifies African specific innovations which have contributed to expanding the mainstream approach to transitional justice:

> 1) taking local conceptions of justice into account, especially in terms of collective versus individual approaches to justice and reconciliation; 2) going beyond the mainstream focus on civil and political rights violations to address economic, social and cultural rights violations, historical and structural inequalities, and issues of sustainable development; and 3) acknowledging the differential impact of conflict on women and the need for women's participation in the design and implementation of TJ.
> 
> (ACHPR 2019, vi)

These innovations are attributed to continental policymaking around the African Charter and the Malabo Protocol (AU 2014; Clarke, Jalloh and Nmehielle 2019, 1),[4] demonstrating sustained African engagement with transitional justice which does not take the established global norm for granted. In Sirleaf's work on the Malabo Protocol, she argues that African policymaking has sought to expand accountability by including possibilities of regional efforts and to counteract Global North biases in the way international criminal law is applied (2017).

This important work on African transitional justice often refers to African experiences, African realities, and African values. It is beyond the scope of this chapter to engage in a philosophical and empirical discussion over the nature of what is "African" and indeed how this discourse can be instrumentalized and misused, but there are some important implications which deserve further reflection and are relevant for our own work on the politics of knowledge and transitional justice in Africa. Firstly, the emerging discussion on African transitional justice highlights the unresolved tension between universal human rights norms (and their application through the global transitional justice norm) and particular experiences of harms as well as expectations of justice informed by historical, geographical, and cultural contexts. Secondly, we are prompted to think carefully about continuing modes of thought and practice which place African and "the rest" on opposing sides as distinct and neat categories. As our analysis of Africa as a constitutive outside of transitional justice has shown, African and Western approaches interlink, refer to, and build upon each other. However, whilst Western contributions to and influence on African transitional justice debates is acknowledged, and often indeed foregrounded, African contributions to and influence on Western transitional justice debates is rarely acknowledged. Our proposal to think in terms of Africa as a constitutive outside – and thus in fact an inside – suggests that the centrality of Africa to the origins and implications of the global transitional justice norm has previously been obfuscated. Finally, it seems clear that the global norm of transitional justice is undergoing a series of fundamental challenges and transformations, prompted not least by African scholarship and African policymaking. All scholars of transitional justice would do well to take this seriously and to acknowledge that African contributions to global norms are far from being absent. Instead they have been rendered invisible by the field's insistence on specific narratives regarding its origins, power dynamics, and the politics and practices of its knowledge production. An African transitional justice, as promulgated by the AU policy and the vibrant debates on the continent, is an important step in rendering these contributions visible, blurring our understanding of international norms as "Western" towards a more co-constitutive understanding and making African contributions to the field more visible, and thus moving them closer to the centre to which they are integral.

## Notes

1. The concept of worlding was first discussed by Said (1978) and Spivak (1985) and developed further by scholars of post-Western IR.
2. The Peace II Programme is the Northern Ireland Peace programme of the European Union from 2000 to 2004. It was "designed to address the economic and social legacy of 30 years of conflict in the region and to take advantage of new opportunities arising from the restoration of peace."
3. A search of the *International Journal of Transitional Justice* on 11 October 2019 found 279 articles with reference to South Africa, 209 with reference to Rwanda, 166 with reference to Sierra Leone, 3 with reference to Côte d'Ivoire, 33 with reference to Zimbabwe, and 3 with reference to The Gambia.
4. The Protocol on Amendments to the Protocol on the Statute of the African Court of Justice and Human Rights (the "Malabo Protocol") was adopted by the AU in June 2014. The envisaged African Court of Justice and Human Rights anticipates a General Affairs Section, a Human and Peoples' Rights Section, and an International Criminal Law Section. Clarke et al. assess that "the merger of these three chambers addressing inter-state disputes, human rights and penal aspects into a single court with a common set of judges represents a significant development in Africa and in wider regional institution building and law making".

## References

ACHPR, (2019) *Study on Transitional Justice and Human and People's Rights in Africa*. Banjul: ACHPR. [online]. Available at: www.achpr.org/public/Document/file/English/ACHPR%20Transitional%20Justice_ENG.pdf (Accessed: 22 February 2021).

African Union, (2014) *Protocol on Amendments to the Protocol on the Statute of the African Court of Justice*. [online]. Available at: AMENDMENTS PROTOCOL AFRICAN COURT_E.pdf (au.int) (Accessed: 19 May 2021).

African Union, (2019) *African Union Adopts Transitional Justice Policy: Press Release No. 12/32nd AU Summit*. [online]. Available at: https://au.int/sites/default/files/pressreleases/36600-pr-pr_12_-_african_union_adopts_transitional_justice_policy.pdf (Accessed: 22 February 2021).

Ahluwalia, P. and Sullivan, M., (2001) 'Beyond International Relations: Edward Said and the World', in Crawford, R.M.A., (ed.) *International Relations – Still an American Social Science? Toward Diversity in International Thought*. Albany: State University of New York Press.

All Truth is Bitter. A Report of the Visit of Doctor Alex Boraine, Deputy Chairman of the South African Truth and Reconciliation Commission, to Northern Ireland (1999). [online]. Available at: https://cain.ulster.ac.uk/issues/victims/docs/alltruthisbitter99.pdf (Accessed: 14 June 2020).

Ancelovici, M. and Jenson, J., (2013) 'Standardization for Transnational Diffusion: The Case of Truth Commissions and Conditional Cash Transfers', *International Political Sociology*, 7(3), pp. 294–312.

Anders, G. and Zenker, O., (2014) 'Transition and Justice: An Introduction', *Development and Change*, 45(3), pp. 395–414.

Anghie, A., (1999) 'Finding the Peripheries: Colonialism in Nineteenth-Century International Law', *Harvard International Law Journal*, 40(1), pp. 1–71.

Ba, O., (2020) *States of Justice: The Politics of the International Criminal Court*. Cambridge: Cambridge University Press.

Bell, C., Campbell, C. and Aoláin, F.N., (2004) 'Justice Discourses in Transition', *Social & Legal Studies*, 13(3), pp. 305–328.

Bilgin, P., (2009) 'The International Political Sociology of a Not so International Discipline', *International Political Sociology*, 3, pp. 338–342.

Bilgin, P., (2018) 'Worlding Conflict Resolution and Mediation Expertise: In the "Global South"', in Leander, A. and Waever, O., (eds.) *Assembling Exclusive Expertise: Knowledge, Ignorance and Conflict Resolution in the Global South*. Oxon and New York: Routledge, pp. 77–92.

Björkdahl, A. and Höglund, K., (2013) 'Precarious Peacebuilding: Friction in Global – Local Encounters', *Peacebuilding*, 1(3), pp. 289–299.

Blaney, D.L. and Inayatullah, N., (2010) 'International Relations from Below', in Reus-Smit, C. and Snidal, D., (eds.) *The Oxford Handbook of International Relations*. Oxford: Oxford University Press, pp. 663–674.

Bowsher, J., (2018) '"Omnus et Singulatim": Establishing the Relationship between Transitional Justice and Neoliberalism', *Law Critique*, 29, pp. 83–106.

Brankovic, J. and Van der Merwe, H., (2016) 'The Role of African Civil Society in Shaping National Transitional Justice Agendas and Policies', in Williams, S. and Woolaver, H., (eds.) *Acta Juridica. Civil Society and International Criminal Justice in Africa. Challenges and Opportunities*. Claremont: Juta, pp. 225–243.

Chimni, B.S., (2006) 'Third World Approaches to International Law: A Manifesto', *International Community Law Review*, 8(1), pp. 3–27.

Clark, P., (2018) *Distant Justice. The Impact of the International Criminal Court on African Politics*. Cambridge, New York, Port Melbourne, New Delhi and Singapore: Cambridge University Press.

Clarke, K., Jalloh, C. and Nmehielle, V., (2019) 'Introduction. Origins and Issues of the African Court of Justice and Human and People's Rights', in Jalloh, C., Clarke, K. and Nmehielle, V., (eds.) *The African Court of Justice and Human and People's Rights in Context. Development and Challenges*. Cambridge and New York, NY: Cambridge University Press, pp. 1–54.

Donais, T., (2009) 'Empowerment or Imposition? Dilemmas of Local Ownership in Post-Conflict Peacebuilding Processes', *Peace & Change*, 34(1), pp. 3–26.

European Commission, (n.d.) *EU Programme for Peace and Reconciliation in Northern Ireland and the Border Region of Ireland (2000–2004) – PEACE II*. [online]. Available at: EU Programme for Peace and Reconciliation in Northern Ireland and the Border Region of Ireland (2000–2004) – PEACE II – Regional Policy – European Commission (europa.eu) (Accessed: 6 March 2020).

European Parliament, (2020) *Northern Ireland PEACE Programme*. [online]. Available at: Northern Ireland PEACE Programme | Fact Sheets on the European Union | European Parliament (europa.eu) (Accessed: 6 March 2020).

Fletcher, L.E. and Weinstein, H.M., (2018) 'How Power Dynamics Influence the "North-South" Gap in Transitional Justice', *Berkeley Journal of International Law*, 37(1), pp. 1–28.

Gregory, D., (2004) *The Colonial Present: Afghanistan, Palestine, Iraq*. Malden: Blackwell Publishing.

Guardian, (2017) *Burundi Becomes First Nation to Leave International Criminal Court*. [online]. Available at: Burundi becomes first nation to leave international criminal court | International criminal court | The Guardian (Accessed: 2 October 2019)

Hansen, T.O., (2014) 'The Vertical and Horizontal Expansion of Transitional Justice: Explanations and Implications of a Contested Field', in Buckley-Zistel, S., Koloma Beck, T., Braun, C. and Mieth, F., (eds.) *Transitional Justice Theories*. Abingdon and New York, NY: Routledge, pp. 105–124.

Hinton, A.L., (2010) 'Introduction: Toward an Anthropology of Transitional Justice', in Hinton, A.L., (ed.) *Transitional Justice: Global Mechanisms and Local Realities after Genocide and Mass Violence*. New Brunswick: Rutgers University Press, pp. 1–22.

Kagoro, B., (2012) 'The Paradox of Alien Knowledge, Narrative and Praxis: Transitional Justice and the Politics of Agenda Setting in Africa', in Okello, M.C., Dolan, C., Whande, U., Mncwabe, N., Onegi, L. and Oola, S., (eds.) *Where Law Meets Reality: Forging African Transitional Justice*. Cape Town, Dakar, Nairobi and Oxford: Pambazuka Press, pp. 4–52.

Lamont, C.K. and Boujneh, H., (2012) 'Transitional Justice in Tunisia', *Politicka Misao*, 49(5), pp. 32–49.

Lundy, P. and McGovern, M., (2008) 'Whose Justice? Rethinking Transitional Justice from the Bottom up', *Journal of Law and Society*, 35(2), pp. 265–292.

Maddison, S. and Shepherd, L.J., (2014) 'Peacebuilding and the Postcolonial Politics of Transitional Justice', *Peacebuilding*, 2(3), pp. 253–269.

Malombe, D., (2012) 'The Politics of Truth Commissions in Africa: A Case Study of Kenya', in Okello, M.C., Dolan, C., Whande, U., Mncwabe, N., Onegi, L. and Oola, S., (eds.) *Where Law Meets Reality: Forging African Transitional Justice*. Cape Town, Dakar, Nairobi and Oxford: Pambazuka Press, pp. 99–123.

McAuliffe, P., (2017) *Transformative Transitional Justice and the Malleability of Post-Conflict States*. Cheltenham and Northampton: Edward Elgar.

McEvoy, K., (2007) 'Beyond Legalism: Towards a Thicker Understanding of Transitional Justice', *Journal of Law and Society*, 34(4), pp. 411–440.

McEvoy, K. and McGregor, L., (eds.) (2010) *Transitional Justice from Below. Grassroots Activism and the Struggle for Change*. Reprinted. Oxford: Hart.

Millar, G., (2014) *An Ethnographic Approach to Peacebuilding*. Oxfordshire and New York, NY: Routledge.

Mouralis, G., (2013) 'The Invention of "Transitional Justice" in the 1990s', in Israël, L. and Mouralis, G., (eds.) *Dealing with Wars and Dictatorships: Legal Concepts and Categories in Action*. The Hague: T.M.C. Asser Press, pp. 83–100.

Mourlon, F., (2016) 'Transposition and Adaptation of Models in Post-Conflict Northern Ireland: The Personal Experience of Brandon Hamber', *Itineraires*, 2015-2, pp. 1–13.

Murphy, C., (2017) *The Conceptual Foundations of Transitional Justice*. Cambridge, New York, Port Melbourne, New Delhi and Singapore: Cambridge University Press.

Mutua, M.W., (2009) 'Politics and Human Rights: An Essential Symbiosis', in Byers, M., (ed.) *The Role of Law in International Politics: Essays in International Relations and International Law*. Reprint, Oxford: Oxford University Press, pp. 149–176.

Nagy, R., (2008) 'Transitional Justice as Global Project: Critical Reflections', *Third World Quarterly*, 29(2), pp. 275–289.

Ní Aoláin, F., (2015) 'Southern Voices in Transitional Justice. A Critical Reflection on Human Rights and Transition', in Baxi, U., McCrudden, C. and Paliwala, A., (eds.) *Law's Ethical, Global and Theoretical Contexts. Essays in Honour of William Twining*. Cambridge: Cambridge University Press, pp. 73–89.

Okafor, O.C. and Ngwaba, U., (2015) 'The International Criminal Court as a 'Transitional Justice' Mechanism in Africa: Some Critical Reflections', *International Journal of Transitional Justice*, 9(1), pp. 90–108.

Pettman, J.J., (1996) *Worlding Women: A Feminist International Politics*. London and New York, NY: Routledge.

Pillay, S., (2016) 'The Impossible Machine: A Genealogy of South Africa's Truth and Reconciliation Commission. By Adam Sitze. Michigan: University of Michigan Press, 2013.392 Pp. $70 Hardcover', *Law & Society Review*, 50(3), pp. 802–804.

Rubli, S., (2012) *Transitional Justice. Justice by Bureaucratic Means? Swisspeace Working Paper 4/2012*, Bern: Swisspeace. [online]. Available at: www.swisspeace.ch/fileadmin/user_upload/Media/Publications/WP4_2012.pdf (Accessed: 14 June 2020).

Said, E., (1978) *Orientalism*. London: Routledge and Kegan Paul.

Sharp, D.N., (2013) 'Interrogating the Peripheries: The Preoccupations of Fourth Generation Transitional Justice', *Harvard Human Rights Journal*, 26, pp. 149–178.

Sharp, D.N., (2014) 'Addressing Dilemmas of the Global and the Local in Transitional Justice', *Emory International Law Review*, 29(1), pp. 71–117.

Sharp, D.N., (2018) *Rethinking Transitional Justice for the Twenty-First Century: Beyond the End of History*. Cambridge, New York, Port Melbourne, New Delhi and Singapore: Cambridge University Press.

Shaw, R., Waldorf, L. and Hazan, P., (eds.) (2010) *Localizing Transitional Justice. Interventions and Priorities after Mass Violence*. Stanford: Stanford University Press.

Shih, C. and Hwang, Y.J., (2018) 'Re-Worlding the "West" in Post-Western IR. The Reception of Sun Zi's the Art of War in the Anglosphere', *International Relations of the Asia-Pacific*, 18, pp. 421–448.

Sitze, A., (2013) *The Impossible Machine*. Ann Arbor: University of Michigan Press.

Sirleaf, M., (2017) 'The African Justice Cascade and the Malabo Protocol', *International Journal of Transitional Justice*, 11(1), pp. 71–91.

Spivak, G.C., (1985) 'Three Women's Texts and a Critique of Imperialism', *Critical Inquiry*, 12(1), pp. 243–261.

Sriram, C.L., (2007) 'Justice as Peace? Liberal Peacebuilding and Strategies of Transitional Justice', *Global Society*, 21(4), pp. 579–591.

Sriram, C.L. and Pillay, S., (eds.) (2009) *Peace Versus Justice? The Dilemma of Transitional Justice in Africa*. Scottsville: University of KwaZulu-Natal Press.

Teitel, R.G., (2003) 'Transitional Justice Genealogy', *Harvard Human Rights Journal*, 16, pp. 69–94.

Vanantwerpen, J., (2009) 'Moral Globalization and Discursive Struggle: Reconciliation, Transitional Justice, and Cosmopolitan Discourse', in Hammack, D.C. and Heydemman, S., (eds.) *Globalization, Philanthropy and Civil Society: Projecting Institutional Logics Abroad*. Bloomington: Indiana University Press.

Van der Merwe, H. and Brinton Lykes, M., (2018) 'Idealists, Opportunists and Activists: Who Drives Transitional Justice?', *International Journal of Transitional Justice*, 12(3), pp. 381–385.

Van Zyl, P., (2005) 'Promoting Transitional Justice in Post-Conflict Societies', in Bryden, A. and Hanggi, H., (eds.) *Security Governance in Post-Conflict Peacebuilding*, pp. 209–231. [online]. Available at: www.dcaf.ch/sites/default/files/publications/documents/YB2005.pdf (Accessed: 14 June 2020).

Wielenga, C., (2018) *What Is "the Local"? Exploring Grassroots Justice Systems as a Means of Understanding the Local*. Kujenga Amani. [online]. Available at: https://kujenga-amani.ssrc.org/2018/04/17/what-is-the-local-exploring-grassroots-justice-systems-as-a-means-of-understanding-the-local/, updated on 4/17/2018 (Accessed: 14 June 2020).

Yusuf, H.O., (2018) 'Colonialism and the Dilemmas of Transitional Justice in Nigeria', *International Journal of Transitional Justice*, 12, pp. 257–276.

Zunino, M., (2019) *Justice Framed: A Genealogy of Transitional Justice*. Cambridge, New York, Port Melbourne, New Delhi and Singapore: Cambridge University Press.

# 8
# LOCAL PEACEBUILDING

## The reflexive encounter between a subaltern view and a practitioner in Côte d'Ivoire

*Jeremy Allouche and Patrick Zadi Zadi*

The aim of this chapter is to focus on the largely discussed and perhaps over-theorised issue of the local turn in peacebuilding (Mac Ginty and Richmond 2013). Recent analyses of the failures of peacebuilding have exposed the use of the local as a rhetorical tool (Leonardsson and Rudd 2015, 825). This rhetorical tool is, in part, rooted in a functionalist argument. Functionalists argue that since armed conflicts are fought at a local level, this is where solutions for peace, such as power-sharing arrangements, ultimately have to be implemented. For functionalists, peacebuilding does not work, because the local is not considered enough in creating and maintaining national political settlements (an analytical judgment; see in particular Autesserre 2017). However, the local turn as a rhetorical tool is also part of a broader agenda, which is that the local represents an alternative path beyond the states and national elites (a normative judgment). In their article on the local turn in peacebuilding, Mac Ginty and Richmond (2013) consider that there is an increased assertiveness by local actors, who are embodying critical and resistant agencies. These agencies have a stake in a subaltern view of peace[1] as opposed to the dominant one, which is the liberal, state-centered peace paradigm[2] (Baum 2008). While much of the scholarship has highlighted how peacebuilding practitioners see the limits of the liberal peacebuilding paradigm, much less has been explored about the practical meaning of the alternative paradigm. This chapter is a reflexive attempt to understand what this subaltern view of local peacebuilding means in practice for a francophone West African practitioner.

The discussion of the local turn that follows is guided by the following question: what does the local peacebuilding normative agenda, this subaltern view of peacebuilding, mean for a practitioner? To address this question, this chapter attempts to create a better dialogue between research and practice on local peacebuilding, building on Coleman's (2011) critique of the research-practice gap in conflict resolution. Such a dialogue is necessary inasmuch as this subaltern view of peace could just remain a buzzword, with no specific implications for practitioners, or conversely, that it could become mainstreamed in policy circles and lose its radical edge. This will therefore be building further on, and giving concrete meaning to, the current 'momentum' the local peacebuilding agenda is having, both intellectually and in terms of policy.

The chapter will be partly based on the experience of Patrick Zadi Zadi, a francophone West African practitioner, and Professor Jeremy Allouche, an academic specialist on Côte d'Ivoire and peacebuilding. It will also be completed with a secondary desk-based review on the practitioner-academic interactions in the peacebuilding literature, as well as a review of what the local means in the context of Côte d'Ivoire. Patrick Zadi Zadi is an Ivorian who has worked with many peacebuilding organisations, most notably the Ivorian local non-governmental organisation (NGO) Awane, the German International Cooperation Agency (GTZ) and Conciliation Resources. As the academic involved in co-producing this book chapter, Professor Allouche, whose work has focused on Côte d'Ivoire in the last 20 years, acted in some ways as a researcher-practitioner broker (Baaz and Utas 2019, 160) to enable this space and conversation and sometimes translation between the local turn in peacebuilding theory and practitioner's experience.

This book chapter is divided into six sections. While the first and second sections briefly engage with the concept of the local, the third section concentrates on local peacebuilding programmes in Côte d'Ivoire. In the fourth section, we then situate these peacebuilding initiatives in the context of the crisis of legitimacy of public authority in rural areas. We focus more specifically in the fifth section on the issue of land disputes and then identify in the final section successful local peacebuilding initiatives.

## What does the local mean and represent?

The 'local' is both an extraordinarily flexible and a highly contested term. Chabal (2009, 30) makes a strong case for turning to the local (i.e. the ground level) in order to search for complementary elements for our reflection on, and understanding of, politics in Africa. In the literature on peacebuilding, the necessity of involving the local level has also become a much-cited desideratum (Pouligny 2009, 175). This 'discovery of the local' (Chandler 2013, 22) in critical peace research has produced lively debates about the role of local agency in and the need for 'local ownership' of peacebuilding interventions (for overviews, see Leonardsson and Rudd 2015; Paffenholz 2015). Despite promises of increased legitimacy and sustainability, earlier assessments of the 'local turn' have highlighted how peacebuilding practitioners and academics may romanticise too much about local agency, disregarding how it can sometimes be violent, elitist, or illegitimate (see e.g. Meagher 2012; Hagmann and Péclard 2010; Bagayoko, Hutchful and Luckham 2016).

As Mitchell (2011) argues, the critical peacebuilding literature needs to move away from the 'local/international' dichotomy, which tends to correlate the 'everyday' and ideals of resistance to local actors and 'power/control' to international actors. Anthropologists have long de-linked the local from a given geographical territory (Gupta, Ferguson and Ferguson 1997; Hastrup and Olwig 1997). Instead, the local is understood as inherently relational and transversal, defined through its relationship to other political levels, primarily the national and the global. Mac Ginty and Richmond (2013, 770), for instance, say that the local is often much less 'local' than imagined and is the product of constant social negotiation between localised and non-localised ideas, norms and practices. Yet, what does the local mean for a practitioner if it is understood as a product of lived experience rather than through a cartographic gaze, as an interpersonal experience that connects different spatial and temporal points and networks of individuals through human agency? (see Mac Ginty 2015).

## Different interpretations of the local

The way the local has been defined in policy and practice is of direct relevance to the liberal and subaltern debates over peacebuilding.

The most conservative understanding of the local is based on large development organisations which mostly reflect a liberal understanding of state-society relations. This conservative notion of local peacebuilding is very much connected to local governance and government and entails various forms of decentralisation. This is the case, for example, of the State and Peacebuilding Fund of the World Bank (2018, 13), whose key objectives are improved institutional capacity and legitimacy of state and local governance, and to manage stresses and support prevention and recovery from conflict and fragility. Other programmes, such as the Libya Conflict, Stability and Security Fund (CSSF) Country Programme (FCO 2018), have a broader focus by also focusing on civil society. In addition to building the capacity of the Government of National Accord (GNA) through technical advisory support, the CSSF aims to ensure women's empowerment through political participation and support to civil society (FCO 2018). Large development organisations see the local in relation to democratisation and the good governance agenda (Pouligny 2005). As a key pillar to the democratisation agenda, civil society organisations (CSOs) are believed to provide a link between state and citizens, producing information and ideas; promoting democratic values; encouraging open debate; pushing for social, economic, and political change; and building social capital. This liberal conception of the local has been criticised as idealistic and not really reflecting the contextual nature of state-society relations in 'no war, no peace' countries (Richards 2005).

A different understanding of the local has been around the notion of hybridity. This approach recognises the coexistence of formal and informal institutions. The UK Department for International Development (DFID, now part of the Foreign, Commonwealth and Development Office [FCDO]) has been recognising this approach through the use of political economy analysis and country programming that would link 'traditional' authorities with local governance structures and build on already existing local formal and informal institutions. This is the case, for example, of the DFID's Yemen Peacebuilding Programme, which aims to support systems that strengthen civil society focusing on increasing local peace and security, looking in particular at local conflict and social cohesion as well as conflict sensitivity.[3] Many global peacebuilding NGOs (e.g. Peace Direct, Conciliation Resources, International Alert, Saferworld) have worked with these hybrid institutions to think about local peace councils and 'traditional' dispute resolution mechanisms (see e.g. Conciliation Resources/Centre for Humanitarian Dialogue 2020).

However, the major issue is not solely the knowledge of how the local is understood but rather its relational aspect. This aspect has been discussed in policy and practice around the question of the ownership of the peace process. Peace Direct and the Alliance for Peacebuilding (2019) distinguish between initiatives that are (1) locally led and owned, where local people and groups design the approach and set priorities while outsiders assist with resources; (2) locally managed, where the approach comes from the outside but is 'transplanted' to local management; and (3) locally implemented, primarily an outside approach, including external priorities that local people or organisations are expected to implement. International/foreign NGOs that operate in a third country generally aim to target the first type, but their experience sometimes leads them to move towards the second type. Governments, international organisations and development agencies, on the other hand, still tend to equate local peacebuilding with the third type of intervention. These three types of initiatives display the tensions/dilemmas entailed in the 'local turn' and the subaltern forms of peacebuilding, as local agency confronts significant governmental and structural power that seeks to co-opt or countermand it (Mac Ginty and Richmond 2013, 770). This also raises important questions around the legitimacy of these 'external' interventions.

As the local is being re-interpreted and negotiated in the critical peacebuilding literature, it reflects not only an epistemological shift in the theories used to 'think peace' but also brings to light the fundamental challenges of 'doing peace'. If the local is understood as relational, particular and contextual in theory, the implementation in practice (i.e. locally or externally designed, led, funded, implemented peace) raises crucial issues of legitimacy, emancipation, empowerment and resistance. A 'local turn' in peace building, Mac Ginty and Richmond (2013, 769) argue, is one framed in a way in which legitimacy in both local and international terms converges. How have these debates about the local and the nature of peacebuilding been reflected in Côte d'Ivoire?

## Local peacebuilding in Côte d'Ivoire

There is a diverse scholarship around the concept of local peacebuilding in Côte d'Ivoire (see Allouche and Jackson 2019; Ateku 2018; Bellamy and Williams 2013; Birkholz, Scherf and Schroeder 2018; Charbonneau 2012; Heitz 2009; Hudson 2009; Mvukiyehe and Samii 2009; Nwaezeigwe 2017; Piccolino 2017, 2019). On the subaltern understanding of peacebuilding, Hudson (2009), for instance, looks at how gender issues are critical for peacebuilding but that these have been sidelined in Côte d'Ivoire. She shows how women's groups contributed to build peace informally with working committees and local livelihood community action plans, but with very limited success. However, most of the literature tends to be critical about both the liberal and subaltern views of peacebuilding, mostly emphasising the notion of the local being relational and linked to the other socio-political levels nationally, regionally and globally. Heitz (2009), for instance, offers a micro-empirical analysis, offering insights into the practices of power-sharing in the local arena of western Côte d'Ivoire, in the town of Man. She argues that the local political arena is the key for a better assessment of political strategies decided at the national level and plays a much more active role in peacemaking than is commonly acknowledged. Similarly, Piccolino (2019) argues the literature on the local turn by focusing on the subaltern/margin, often neglects the role of the state and the connections between 'local' citizens and the political elite, namely the neo-patrimonial nature of local politics.

The local peacebuilding programme 'Peace and Development', funded by the German development cooperation agency (GIZ) (2007–2009), is an interesting example to reflect on these local peacebuilding efforts (see Bonnéhin and Diarrassouba 2006; Diarrassouba et al. 2006; Sissoko and Denis 2006). This programme can be described as the new generation of peacebuilding efforts, which have better integrated local peacebuilding in their operations, by supporting peace committees, councils or similar structures at village, town or provincial levels. These peace and development committees had different functions: a role in early warning and preventive action, in facilitating dialogue and enhancing community relationships, and in reconciliation. However, despite the fact that the civil war had a generational component, the role of the youths in these committees was limited, as local peace is traditionally seen as a matter for elders.

In his role as the coordinator of the Peace and Development programme in the southwestern part of the country, Zadi Zadi observed that despite its relative success (as we have argued in another paper; Allouche and Zadi Zadi 2020), the programme was negatively affecting local peacebuilding structures. By introducing a pecuniary dimension in peace programme activities with a per diem, activity funding and salary payment systems, the programmes were weakening peacebuilding structures rather than supporting them. At the county (*departement*) level, the peace committee comprised mainly retired members and was headed by the prefect and a permanent secretary, who was the only member to receive a salary. In addition, lack of funding for per diems meant that not all members could regularly participate in the activities. This system created envy among members and undermined their motivation, thus leading to a sort of privatisation of the peace committees by a handful of members.

In addition to the monetisation of peacebuilding activities, the Peace and Development programme also worked differently from the traditional peace committees. Originally, the programme aimed inter alia to strengthen traditional decision-making systems for a peaceful and lasting settlement of local and regional conflicts through the establishment of peace committees at department and sub-prefectural levels. But contrary to the objective it set for itself, the project has, by introducing new methods, weakened traditional conflict management structures.

- Firstly, the county and sub-prefectural committees, by their hierarchical positioning, overturned decisions of the village chief, who was considered biased. This then contributed to the weakening of the village chiefdom, further undermining the traditional conflict management authority.
- Secondly, the operational budget set up to facilitate the movements of committee members created a logic of demand, whereby activities were linked to the budget calendar rather than the dynamics of local conflicts. Access to membership to the peace committees and its operational budget became the focus and a source of income for the elders irrespective of the nature and situation of the local conflict.
- Thirdly, the project offered training that was aimed at improving conflict management skills in village communities. But this training with imported content could not be used by the beneficiaries. In the south-western Ivorian regions torn apart by land disputes, the protagonists sought a settlement of the conflict much more than mediation. Meanwhile, the project offered training in mediation.

A study by Interpeace/Indigo (2018, 52–55) has similar findings, showing how the capture of dividends linked to external interventions in villages, especially those of NGOs, generated increased tensions within village communities and how new institutions (such as peace committees or *Comités Villageois de Gestion du Foncier Rural* (CVGFR, i.e. Village Committees for Rural Land Management) or new conflict management models introduced by international organisations weakened the role of traditional rural authorities. The involvement in peace committees was also two-sided. As put by Interpeace/Indigo (2018, 68): 'In many communities, promoters expected committee members to be altruist, while they were seen more as individuals working for promoting their community'.[4]

Another important point in local peacebuilding programmes from a practitioner perspective is the sustainability of these external interventions designed to support the local institutions and mechanisms. During the Ebola crisis, when most organisations were focusing on the purely medical aspects of the crisis, Conciliation Resources, a UK-based charity, implemented a program aimed at resolving conflicts driven by the Ebola crisis in border regions of the Mano River Region. The project brought a new concept of District Platforms for Dialogue (DPD), which included community leaders chosen within the community by community members (Conciliation Resources 2015) Those district platforms received trainings on social cohesion and human security perspectives around transboundary relations prepared by the implementing partner, WANEP in Côte d'Ivoire, to implement activities with the financial support of Conciliation Resources. In line with the 'local turn', the social cohesion and human security activities were locally led under the supervision of the national implementing partner, and the process and the results were owned by the DPD. However, many of the DPDs were financially dependent on Conciliation Resources, which meant that only few could function after closure of the project. This example goes to show that efforts to support empowerment, training and agency at the local level nevertheless rely enormously on the international level financially. Therefore, a major challenge for the 'local turn' resides in the following question: if the key to success in peacebuilding is financial resources, how can local ownership of the peace process be ensured when ownership of the financial resources is international?

Despite good intentions, the new generation of peacebuilding efforts remained to a large extent a top-down, Western-centric external intervention, which mostly ignored the societal and human consequences on the ground, as so often pointed out in the critiques of the liberal peace paradigm (Pugh 2005; Richmond 2010). This shows a very hierarchal approach to peacebuilding which may contradict with the subaltern idea of peacebuilding, as discussed above.

More fundamentally, this new generation of peacebuilding programmes tends to assume that programmes operate according to a liberal notion of civil society, as discussed above. Rural civil society here is defined in opposition to the state. There is, of course, an important debate on the nature of civil society in sub-Saharan Africa (on the different takes of the concept of civil society in sub-Saharan Africa, see Mamdani 1997; Comaroff and Comaroff 1999; Lewis 2002). Rural society and the vitality of local institutions like chieftaincy came to be seen as made up of local communities or associational networks that were more or less egalitarian and composed of institutions representing shared interests. Rural communities were therefore presumed to possess inherent self-governing capacities. These assumptions, for instance, have been criticised by Mamdani (1997), which shows the authoritarian and even reactionary nature of these institutions. This debate is not really reflected in both the liberal and critical subaltern understanding of peacebuilding.

Policy-wise, the humanitarian-development-peacebuilding triple nexus clearly brought some important funding, and as in many other countries, façade NGOs have suddenly appeared; but civil society, at least as imagined in the Western sense through NGOs, is still weak in the Côte d'Ivoire setting. The only major national NGO that had a big and sometimes controversial influence during the civil war period and its aftermath was the *Federation ivoirienne des Droits de l'Homme*. Civil society in Côte d'Ivoire has not been operating through the grassroots in 'locally' owned, bottom-up peacebuilding processes but in practice sometimes consisting of processes that were mostly led by experts and consultants based in the capital (reproducing the origins of home-town associations which were by nature elitist; see Woods 1994). Hudson (2009), for instance, considers that civil society has always been rather divided and weak in Côte d'Ivoire, and women's movements are struggling to be the exception. The debate on civil society in Côte d'Ivoire is complex and has long historical and colonial roots. Civil society in rural areas was mainly mobilised through home-town associations (such as *mutuelles* and cooperatives), and these were established specifically to lobby the government to make their area an administrative sub-prefecture as well as a vehicle to reassert ethnicity and a means for different social groups to have some impact on the distribution and redistribution of economic resources (Woods 1994). Furthermore, the construction of 'civil society' in Côte d'Ivoire took a further dimension with the question of autochthony and land rights conflicts (Bøås 2012).

## The local and the crisis of legitimacy of public authority in rural areas in the south

These peacebuilding initiatives show limits in their effectiveness as they need to be situated and understood in relation to the crisis of legitimacy of public authority in rural areas in the south, where the plantation economy model is reaching its limits, as explained below. Rural areas in Côte d'Ivoire have been radically transformed following the colonial and then Houphouët-Boigny agricultural policies.

The various forms of public authorities in the south are of course very diverse, from the Agni territory to the east to the Wé, Bété and other groups in the west. Anthropological studies looking at the institutions in the nineteenth and early twentieth centuries divided the south in three main areas: the east, the centre and the west. In the east, the Agni territory was the most structured; localised lineage hierarchies were dominated by royal aristocracies which were centred around small and weak monarchies (see Zolberg 1971, 11), while the rest of the southern area was home to a great diversity of localised polities without administrative centralisation above the village level (see Chappell 1989). However, according to Boone (2003), this distinction between state and stateless societies that once described differences in the pre-colonial civilisations of the Ivorian south had been seriously attenuated by the weakening or breakdown of African kingdoms in this region. This is partly due to colonisation, where the French refined administrative boundaries and appointed loyal servants to them (Boone 2003, 183). This continued under Houphouët-Boigny, first with Dyula traders (and planter-traders) as agents of the Parti démocratique de Côte d'Ivoire (PDCI) in the forest zone in the 1950s and then a progressive deinstitutionalisation of the ruling party and of the limited structures of local government inherited from colonialism in the 1960s and 1970s. As put by Boone (2003, 213), 'the state's presence in localities in the South was limited almost completely to a military-style territorial administration in which rural populations were subjected to an ever-tightening grid of prefectorial control'. With the advent of multipartyism from the early 1990s, the election of chiefs and the opening up of participation of other components of the community (non-native) to notability are gradually establishing themselves as the most common current methods of village governance. But the biggest shock in the declining authority of rural institutions was the gradual return to the normalisation of local socio-political life after the war (from 2011 onwards). As documented by Interpeace/Indigo (2018), strong tensions are running between the former returned leaders and the new authorities in place. Worse, some of these leaders were imposed, either by the social cadets, the elites or even by NGOs or representatives of the state, through new methods of designation of leaders or governance (Interpeace/Indigo 2018, 52).

In conclusion, the rural south is marked by limited forms of social hierarchies, low levels of social cohesion and solidarity in village communities, and the limited powers and legitimacy of indigenous rural authorities (Boone 2003, see also Interpeace/Indigo 2018). As a result, the fragmented and atomised social structures characteristic of rural communities in the Ivorian south meant that capacities for sustained collective action were low. The local here is not only invisible as difficult to research and uncover but also invisible as a process to build collective action. This therefore creates many important dilemmas around building the idea of the local in terms of peacebuilding.

## Land disputes

Peacebuilding activities, if localised, need to reflect the local concerns, which in rural Côte d'Ivoire is mainly around issues of land tenure and policies. The origin of land conflicts is relatively complex. Agricultural reform under the government of Houphouët-Boigny mad Côte d'Ivoire one the world's major producer of cocoa beans. The plantation economy expanded in forested Côte d'Ivoire in areas of low population. Its development therefore relied on the sometimes massive arrival of immigrants from neighbouring countries, especially from Burkina Faso but also Mali and Guinea, as well as internal migrants from the Baoulé region. This was not without consequences. No rules or regulations were established, especially after Houphouët-Boigny's famous slogan, 'the land belongs to those who put it to good use'. The conditions of access to land for these immigrants varied from one region to another, and the native-migrant relationship regarding access to land was often characterised by the social embeddedness of these land transfers. Under the institution of *tutorat*, migrants gaining access to land through 'gift' or 'purchase' remained morally obligated to the native seller. Tensions and conflicts between natives and migrants frequently occur over land disputes as a result of these land transfers to migrants.

This is not new,[5] but the land tenure issue has become politicised. The legal vacuum, as well as the dualism between political and traditional authority, created the basis for the land crisis that started when young native students returned to their homes (Allouche and Zadi 2013).

Confronted with unemployment in Abidjan and other major cities[6] following structural adjustment policies, they returned to their villages only to be confronted by the reality that their families' land had been leased or sold, creating a number of tensions between the autochthones and the migrants. At the level of the social fabric, there is an underlying intergenerational tension between young indigenous people and parents.[7] These young people feel betrayed by their parents for having ceded customary land heritage, thus depriving them of means of subsistence, especially when they need it most (see Colin, Kouamé and Soro 2007). To protest the sale of the land by their parents, they question what their parents did and sell the same land to others. This situation creates a belligerence between rights holders and supposed rights holders in the struggle for control of land. The temptation by this group to regain control of what they saw as their land created a number of conflicts with the migrants. This crisis was further exacerbated by its political instrumentalisation with the concept of *Ivoirité* and the 1998 Land Law under the presidencies of Henry Konan Bédié and Laurent Gbagbo (Chauveau 2000). The law aims to transform customary land rights into private property rights regulated by the state. The law has been criticised for its legal ambiguity, an overly complicated and costly registration process and an institutional capacity that is simply too weak to implement the law. The law has also become somewhat entangled in questions of ethnicity and nationality as these concepts relate to access to land, which has fuelled some controversy regarding the law's intent.

The violence over land tenure reached its peak following the disputed presidential election in 2010. However, despite the nascent stability of the country since the war, land conflicts still represent a growing challenge to the country's political stability, as documented in many recent studies (Interpeace/Indigo 2018; Koné, Ouattara and Akindès 2017). Koné, Ouattara and Akindès (2017), for instance, show how the return of Young Patriots to the villages in the Sassandra region is linked to a new discourse aiming to recall the authority and primacy of the autochthones on the land and the various advantages attached to it. This discourse serves to disqualify the financial transactions established by their elders and 'foreigners', to legitimise new ones and also to rule out the possibility of sons of migrants to exercise various forms of power at the village and departmental level. There is therefore an urgent need to understand how various communities have managed to deal with these disputes and the extent to which these could contribute from a policy and practice lens to the subaltern views around peacebuilding.

## Identifying successful local peacebuilding initiatives

From a practitioner lens, identifying and understanding success stories is pivotal and important (inasmuch as in understanding and explaining failures as explained above in 'Local Peacebuilding in Côte d'Ivoire'). The focus of what constitutes success is very much disputed, as is what 'subaltern' could mean in this context. Our work has focused on this idea of islands of peace (Allouche and Zadi Zadi 2020; Allouche and Jackson 2019; Allouche and Zadi Zadi 2013). The main idea here is to identify zones of peace in Côte d'Ivoire where local peace processes have developed despite conflicts around them. These local initiatives are very much invisible (Mac Ginty and Richmond 2013) and difficult to research. These modes of conflict resolution mechanisms, even if socially constructed, are still prevalent (see Foucher 2007; Bagayoko and Koné 2017). They are also mostly indigenous, built on internal, domestic cultural practices, as often highlighted within the subaltern and transformative peacebuilding tradition (see e.g. Mac Ginty 2015; Paffenholz 2014). These refer in particular to the oral culture, the ritual dimensions, reference to the history and founding myths of the communities, and the sacredness and the interweaving of the spiritual and the temporal, which materialise by the prevalence of magico-religious beliefs and occult and esoteric practices. These practices are important within communities but also across communities, with interethnic alliances, that have been variously labelled 'joking kinships', 'joking relationships' and 'special affinities' (see Davidheiser 2006; Nyamba 1999). Our past research has shown that these were important in keeping social cohesion and peace at the local level in Côte d'Ivoire (see Allouche and Zadi Zadi 2020).

Realising the potential of land-related violence as soon as the war started in 2002, some rural communities put in place clear and consensual mechanisms for the usage of land given the legal vacuum, or to be more specific the tension between past practices and the new law. This was the case of the villages of Beoua and Yacoli Dabouo. These exceptions seem to be linked to more transparent systems for land transactions.

The example of Beoua, in the Guiglo sub-prefecture, clearly shows that good management of the land issue seems to be useful in preventing intercommunal violence. Indeed, the village chief of Beoua has initiated, in recent years, a kind of contract for the rental of land. All land transactions are under the control of the village chief. The latter has established a land transfer contract, which requires the signature of both parties and which specifies, among other things, the type of crop and the area to be transferred in hectares.[8] Of course, we could add other details, such as the duration of the transfer and the family's endorsement to improve it, but this document creates, despite certain shortcomings, an interesting framework that considerably limits potential disputes between the populations of this locality. Despite flaws, this document has at least the merit of defining the terms of the rental and of involving the families concerned in the land transaction. And it seems, according to our research, that there was no violence between civilian populations in Beoua during the post-electoral crisis of 2011.

Our second example is Yacoli Dabouo, a large village of 7,000 inhabitants located in the Soubré department. A village council, representing the different communities, was put in place to sensitise about the illegal nature of selling land. All the land-to-land management and tenure transactions were administered and recorded by the management committee and then sent to the sub-prefect office for registration. This means that any point of discord happening after these transactions could be arbitrated by the sub-prefect office in a more transparent and neutral way.

The village went even further, as the problem was not just about land tenure but also related to the youth returning to settle back in the area, as they were unable to find jobs in Abidjan, the country's economic capital city. Since their elders had sold land to incomers, the village council negotiated an agreement with the incomers whereby one-third of the land was given back to the youth. All the parties, whether the youth or the incomers, benefited from the NGO OUYINE (which was created by Zadi Kessy Marcel, former president of the Economic and Social Council in Côte d'Ivoire, who comes from this village). The 'big men', part of the national elite, therefore played a key role in the resolution of this conflict. OUYINE distributed hevea plans to everybody and a new rubber treatment factory was installed by Zadi Kessy Marcel, to encourage the community. As a result, since 2010 there have been no reported incidents in this community, whether between the youth groups of the different ethnic communities or when the armed forces of Ouattara were marching towards Abidjan.

This last example provides an alternative to the way local peacebuilding has been framed by the state and international organisations, inasmuch as these were mostly indigenous. Our case study on Yacoli Dabouo is interesting in that it addressed the autochthonous and allochthone conflict with a more formalised approach to land tenure and an economic livelihood program. However, it also points to the very patriarchal/patrimonial structure, which reinforces the power of traditional authorities, and the influence of big men. Does this correspond to the normative agenda around the local turn in peacebuilding? Do these examples in general really represent a subaltern view – a body of resistance – a 'little tradition' or 'hidden transcript' that operates as a constraint on the hegemonic ambitions of both state and international power? (Hughes, Öjendal and Schierenbeck 2015).

It is very difficult to qualify these initiatives as subaltern and/or transformative. Here we have focused on peace initiatives that were successful in addressing land-related violence. We considered these initiatives to be successful as they engaged directly with the structural causes of the local conflict rather than just addressing the conflict resolution as framed in the resolution of the national political settlement (very much like Autesserre 2010). Our idea of success is just based on ending the violence (in some ways, a form of negative peace), rather than a subaltern or transformative agenda.

We have broadly shown that in the south of Côte d'Ivoire, the crisis of legitimacy of public authority in rural areas and the difficult civil society landscape makes it difficult for local alternatives to emerge. However, these limited examples/case studies create further questions for the subaltern views of peacebuilding around power dynamics and legitimacy. What does this mean in terms of power for rural communities if it still relies on the connected big men from urban centres to fund their activities? What does this mean in terms of legitimacy? Is a local endeavour funded through clientelism necessarily more transformative or 'better' than if it were funded externally?

## Conclusion

The flexibility of the concept of 'local', its contested nature, its relationality and its multiscale analysis have worked in conjunction to offer both policy and intellectual responses to criticisms of liberal peacebuilding approaches. While the impetus of the local turn in peacebuilding is still very much in full swing, its normative agenda – namely, around ideas of legitimacy, emancipation, empowerment and resistance – is very difficult to translate into a relevant entry point from a practitioner perspective. The experiences of practitioner Zadi Zadi regarding local peacebuilding thinking, legitimacy crises, and land disputes in Côte d'Ivoire show some of the ways in which contextual practices challenge and complicate the dichotomic divide between notions of particularism and local variation on the one hand and universalist ideas and practices on the other hand, as laid out by Mac Ginty and Richmond (2013, 772).

In the light of the examples seen throughout this book chapter, the challenge that remains unaddressed in local peacebuilding is perhaps how to form a normative point of view of a local approach to peacebuilding, bearing in mind the fact that the notion of local itself is conceptually contested and can be locally reconfigured into actual impediments to peacebuilding. It is not just Piccolino's (2019) valid point that the local peacebuilding agenda is prone to co-optation by authoritarian and semi-authoritarian regimes, but even beyond that, the experiences of Patrick Zadi Zadi feature cases where the traditional confrontation between the international and the local destructively connects with local subversions of peacebuilding initiatives. This challenges the definition of subaltern in itself.

## Acknowledgments

The authors would like to thank Bruno Charbonneau, Tony Chafer, Camille Maubert and Dieunedort Wandji for their precious feedback.

This work was supported through the support of the UK Research and Innovation Global Challenge Research Fund under the project 'Islands of Innovation in Protracted Crises: A New Approach to Building Equitable Resilience from Below.'

## Notes

1. A subaltern view of peacebuilding is informed by Gramsci's concept of subaltern consciousness, and refers to conditions under which local actors negotiate, manipulate or reject the ideological tropes of state and international actors in pursuit of partially perceived interests of their own (Hughes, Öjendal, and Schierenbeck 2015).
2. Proponents of the liberal peacebuilding paradigm, most notably Paris (2010), argue that liberal democratic forms of governance are, whatever their limitations, still the best suited to managing and mitigating political conflict.
3. https://devtracker.dfid.gov.uk/projects/GB-GOV-1-300665 (accessed 28 May 2020).
4. Authors' own translation.
5. Land conflicts were documented already in the late 1950s in the Gagnoa and Daloa regions (Raulin 1957), again in the early 1970s between Bete and Baoule in the Gagnoa region (Boone 2003, 220), and finally in Tabou in the late 1990s (Babo 2013). This is not an exhaustive list but just to show that land conflict is recurrent.
6. According to the National Institute of Statistics, the number of unemployed aged 16–24 would have increased by around 37.5% between 1995 and 1998 (Fofona 2012, 10).
7. This generational tension is not only a rural phenomenon; in an urban setting, see Banegas 2006.
8. Interview with traditional chief, Beoua, 13 January 2011.

## References

Allouche, J. and Jackson, P., (2019) 'Zones of Peace and Local Peace Processes in Côte d'Ivoire and Sierra Leone', *Peacebuilding*, 7(1), pp. 71–87.

Allouche, J. and Zadi Zadi, P., (2013) 'The Dynamics of Restraint in Côte d'Ivoire', *IDS Bulletin*, 44(1), pp. 72–86.

Allouche, J. and Zadi Zadi, P., (2020) 'Crise post-électorale en Côte d'Ivoire et logique de la non-violence en milieu urbain: une illustration à partir des villes de Gagnoa, Guiglo et San Pedro en 2010–11', *Canadian Journal of African Studies/Revue canadienne des études africaines*, pp. 1–19.

Ateku, A.J., (2018) *Assessing the Impact of Peacebuilding on Human Security in Conflict-affected States: The Case of Côte d'Ivoire (2002–2015)*. PhD thesis. University of Nottingham.

Autesserre, S., (2010) *The Trouble with the Congo*. New York, NY: Cambridge University.

Autesserre, S., (2017) 'International Peacebuilding and Local Success: Assumptions and Effectiveness', *International Studies Review*, 19(1), pp. 114–32.

Baaz, M.E. and Utas, M., (2019) 'Exploring the Backstage: Methodological and Ethical Issues Surrounding the Role of Research Brokers in Insecure Zones', *Civil Wars*, 21(2), pp. 157–178.

Babo, A., (2013) 'The Crisis of Public Policies in Côte d'Ivoire: Land Law and the Nationality Trap in Tabou's Rural Communities', *Africa*, 83(1), pp. 100–119.

Bagayoko, N., Hutchful, E. and Luckham, R., (2016) 'Hybrid Security Governance in Africa: Rethinking the Foundations of Security, Justice and Legitimate Public Authority', *Conflict, Security & Development*, 16(1), pp. 1–32.

Bagayoko, N. and Koné, F.R., (2017) 'Les mécanismes traditionnels de gestion des conflits en Afrique Subsaharienne', *Rapport de recherche* (2). Montréal: Centre FrancoPaix, Chaire Raoul-Dandurand Centre FrancoPaix en résolution des conflits et missions de paix. [online]. Available at: https://dandurand.uqam.ca/wp-content/uploads/2017/06/Rapport_Recherche_2_FrancoPaix.pdf (Accessed: 30 June 2021).

Banegas, R., (2006) 'Côte d'Ivoire: Patriotism, Ethnonationalism and other African modes of self-writing', *African Affairs*, 105, pp. 535–552.

Baum, T., (2008) 'A Quest for Inspiration in the Liberal Peace Paradigm: Back to Bentham?', *European Journal of International Relations*, 14(3), pp. 431–453.

Bellamy, A.J. and Williams, P.D., (2013) 'Local Politics and International Partnerships: The UN Operation in Côte d'Ivoire (UNOCI)', in Druckmann, D. and Diehl, P.F., (eds.) *Peace Operation Success – A Comparative Analysis*. Leiden: Brill Nijhoff, pp. 55–84.

Birkholz, S., Scherf, T. and Schroeder, U.C., (2018) 'International Interventions Seen from the "Middle": Perceptions of Intermediary Actors in Côte d'Ivoire and Lebanon', *Cooperation and Conflict*, 53(2), pp. 173–192.

Bøås, M., (2012) 'Autochthony and Citizenship: "Civil Society" as Vernacular Architecture?', *Journal of Intervention and Statebuilding*, 6(1), pp. 91–105.

Bonnéhin, L. and Diarrassouba, M., (2006) *Femme, Conflits et Paix dans le Sud-Ouest de la Côte d'Ivoire*. Etude pour le projet 'Prévention de Crises et Consolidation de la Paix dans le Sud-Ouest de la Côte d'Ivoire', GTZ/Ministère de la Réconciliation Nationale et des Relations avec les Institutions.

Boone, C., (2003) *Political Topographies of the African State: Territorial Authority and Institutional Choice*. Cambridge: Cambridge University Press.

Chabal, P., (2009) *Africa: The Politics of Suffering and Smiling*. London: Zed.

Chandler, D., (2013) 'Peacebuilding and the Politics of Non-linearity: Rethinking 'Hidden' Agency and "Resistance"', *Peacebuilding*, 1(1), pp. 17–32.

Chappell, D.A., (1989) 'The Nation as Frontier: Ethnicity and Clientelism in Ivorian History', *The International Journal of African Historical Studies*, 22(4), pp. 671–696.

Charbonneau, B., (2012) 'War and Peace in Côte d'Ivoire: Violence, Agency, and the Local/International Line', *International Peacekeeping*, 19(4), pp. 508–524.

Chauveau, J-P., (2000) 'Question foncière et construction nationale en Côte d'Ivoire', *Politique africaine*, 2, pp. 94–125.

Coleman, P.T., (2011) *The Five Percent: Finding Solutions to Seemingly Impossible Conflicts*. New York, NY: Public Affairs.

Colin, J.P., Kouamé, G. and Soro, D., (2007) 'Outside the Autochthon-migrant Configuration: Access to Land, Land Conflicts and Inter-ethnic Relationships in a Former Pioneer Area of Lower Côte d'Ivoire', *The Journal of Modern African Studies*, 45(1), pp. 33–59.

Comaroff, J.L. and Comaroff, J., (eds.) (1999) *Civil Society and the Political Imagination in Africa: Critical Perspectives*. Chicago: University of Chicago Press.

Conciliation Resources, (2015) *Responding to Ebola Driven Conflict Dialogue Initiatives in Mano River Border Regions*. [online]. Available at: www.humanitarianresponse.info/sites/www.humanitarianresponse.info/files/assessments/responding_to_ebola_driven_conflict-_mano_river_regions_2015.pdf (Accessed: 30 June 2021).

Conciliation Resources, Centre for Humanitarian Dialogue, (2020) *Peace and Security in the Central African Republic*, Research report, London: Conciliation Resources. [online]. Available at: https://rc-services-assets.s3.eu-west-1.amazonaws.com/s3fs-public/Peace_%26_security_in_the_Central_African_Republic.pdf (Accessed: 30 June 2021).

Davidheiser, M., (2006) 'Joking for Peace: Social Organization, Tradition, and Change in Conflict Prevention and Resolution', *Cahiers d'Etudes Africaines*, 184, pp. 835–859.

Diarrassouba, N., Sissoko, A., Denis, G. and Diarrassouba, M., (2006) *Prévention de Crises et Consolidation de la Paix dans le Sud-Ouest de la Côte d'Ivoire*. Etude exploratoire pour le projet 'Prévention de Crises et Consolidation de la Paix dans le Sud-Ouest de la Côte d'Ivoire', GTZ/Ministère de la Réconciliation Nationale et des Relations avec les Institutions.

FCO, (2018) *Libya CSSF Country Programme: Annual Review – Summary Sheet*. London: Foreign and Commonwealth Office. [online]. Available at: https://assets.publishing.service.gov.uk/government/uploads/system/uploads/attachment_data/file/630386/Libya_Country_Programme_2017.pdf (Accessed: 30 June 2021).

Fofona, M., (2012) *Ethnographie des trajectoires sociales des jeunes enrôlés dans la rébellion en côte d'Ivoire*. PhD thesis, Université Alassane Ouattara.

Foucher, V., (2007) "Tradition africaine' et résolution des conflits', *Politix*, 4, pp. 59–80.

Gupta, A., Ferguson, J. and Ferguson, J.G., (eds.) (1997) *Anthropological Locations: Boundaries and Grounds of a Field Science*. Berkeley: University of California Press.

Hagmann, T. and Péclard, D., (2010) 'Negotiating Statehood: Dynamics of Power and Domination in Africa', *Development and Change*, 41(4), pp. 539–562.

Hastrup, K. and Olwig, K.F., (1997) *Siting Culture: The Shifting Anthropological Object*. Hove: Psychology Press.

Heitz, K., (2009) 'Power-Sharing in the Local Arena: Man-a Rebel-Held Town in Western Côte d'Ivoire', *Africa Spectrum*, 44(3), pp. 109–131.

Hudson, H., (2009) 'Peacebuilding through a Gender Lens and the Challenges of Implementation in Rwanda and Côte d'Ivoire', *Security Studies*, 18(2), pp. 287–318.

Hughes, C., Öjendal, J. and Schierenbeck, I., (2015) 'The Struggle versus the Song – the Local Turn in Peacebuilding: An Introduction', *Third World Quarterly*, 36(5), pp. 817–824.

Interpeace, Indigo, (2018) *L'étranger ne peut pas venir se cacher derrière une termitière et vouloir que sa tête la dépasse: Analyse locale des risques et opportunités pour la cohésion sociale à l'Ouest de la Côte d'Ivoire*. Abidjan: Janvier.

Koné, G., Ouattara, B.M. and Akindès, F., (2017) 'L'autochtonie, la terre et les jeunes à Sassandra (Ouest-Côte d'Ivoire)', *Politique africaine*, 4, pp. 69–88.

Leonardsson, H. and Rudd, G., (2015) 'The "Local Turn" in Peacebuilding: A Literature Review of Effective and Emancipatory Local Peacebuilding', *Third World Quarterly*, 36(5), pp. 825–839.

Lewis, D., (2002) 'Civil Society in African Contexts: Reflections on the Usefulness of a Concept', *Development and Change*, 33(4), pp. 569–586.

Mac Ginty, R., (2015) 'Where is the Local? Critical Localism and Peacebuilding', *Third World Quarterly*, 36(5), pp. 840–856.

Mac Ginty, R. and Richmond, O.P., (2013) 'The Local Turn in Peace Building: A Critical Agenda for Peace', *Third World Quarterly*, 34(5), pp. 763–783.

Mamdani, M., (1997) *Citizen and Subject: Decentralized Despotism and the Legacy of Late Colonialism*. Oxford: Oxford University Press.

Meagher, K., (2012), 'The Strength of Weak States? Non-state Security Forces and Hybrid Governance in Africa', *Development and Change*, 43(5), pp. 1073–1101.

Mitchell, A., (2011) 'Quality/Control: International Peace Interventions and the "Everyday"', *Review of International Studies*, 37(4), pp. 1623–1645.

Mvukiyehe, E. and Samii, C., (2009) 'Laying a Foundation for Peace: Micro-Effects of Peacekeeping in Côte d'Ivoire', *Manuscript*. New York, NY: Columbia University.

Nwaezeigwe, J.P.N., (2017) *Engaging with the 'Local Turn' in Post-conflict States: A Critical Analysis of UN Peacebuilding in Côte d'Ivoire and Libya*. Thesis submitted to Saint Mary's University, Halifax, Nova Scotia in Partial Fulfillment of the Requirements for the Degree of Bachelor of Arts (Hons.), Political Science.

Nyamba, A., (1999) 'La problématique des alliances et des parentés à plaisanterie au Burkina Faso: historique, pratique et devenir', *Les Grandes Conférences du Ministère de la Communication et de la Culture du Burkina-Faso*, Ouagadougou, pp. 73–91.

Paffenholz, T., (2014) 'International Peacebuilding Goes Local: Analysing Lederach's Conflict Transformation Theory and its Ambivalent Encounter with 20 Years of Practice', *Peacebuilding*, 2(1), pp. 11–27.

Paffenholz, T., (2015) 'Unpacking the Local Turn in Peacebuilding: A Critical Assessment towards an Agenda for Future Research', *Third World Quarterly*, 36(5), pp. 857–874.

Paris, R., (2010), 'Saving Liberal Peace-building', *Review of International Studies*, 36(2), pp. 337–365.

Peace Direct, Alliance for Peacebuilding, (2019) *Local Peacebuilding: What Works and Why*. London: Peace Direct.

Piccolino, G., (2017) 'The Discourse of Social Cohesion and the Paradoxes of Building Peace from Below in Côte d'Ivoire', *Politique africaine*, 4, pp. 49–68.

Piccolino, G., (2019) 'Local Peacebuilding in a Victor's Peace. Why Local Peace Fails Without National Reconciliation', *International Peacekeeping*, 26(3), pp. 354–379.

Pouligny, B., (2005) 'Civil Society and Post-conflict Peacebuilding: Ambiguities of International Programmes Aimed at Building "New" Societies', *Security Dialogue*, 36(4), pp. 495–510.

Pouligny, B., (2009) 'Local Ownership', in Chetail, V., (ed.) *Post-Conflict Peacebuilding: A Lexicon*. Oxford: Oxford University Press, pp. 174–187.

Pugh, M., (2005) 'The Political Economy of Peace-building: A Critical Theory Perspective', *International Journal of Peace Studies*, 10(2), pp. 23–42.

Raulin, H., (1957) *Mission d'Etudes des Groupements Immigrés en Côte d'Ivoire. Fascicule 3: Problèmes Fonciers dans les Régions de Gagnoa et de Daloa*. Paris: ORSTOM.

Richards, P., (2005) *No Peace, No War: The Anthropology of Contemporary Armed Conflicts*. London: James Currey.

Richmond, O., (ed.) (2010). *Palgrave Advances in Peace-building: Critical Developments and Approaches*. London: Palgrave Macmillan.

Sissoko, A. and Denis, G., (2006) *Gestion des Conflits dans le Sud-Ouest Ivoirien*. Etude de milieu pour le projet 'Prévention de Crises et Consolidation de la Paix dans le Sud-Ouest de la Côte d'Ivoire', GTZ/Ministère de la Réconciliation Nationale et des Relations avec les Institutions.

Woods, D., (1994) 'Elites, Ethnicity, and "Home Town" Associations in the Côte d'Ivoire: An Historical Analysis of State – Society Links', *Africa*, 64(4), pp. 465–483.

World Bank, (2018) *The State- and Peacebuilding Fund Annual Report*. Washington, DC: World Bank.

Zolberg, A., (1971) 'Political Development in the Ivory Coast since Independence. Ghana and the Ivory Coast: Perspectives on Modernization', in Foster, P. and Zolberg, A.R., (eds.) *Ghana and the Ivory Coast: Perspectives on Modernization:[Workshop Conference Held at the Center for Continuing Education of the University of Chicago, 1969]*. Chicago: University of Chicago Press, pp. 9–31.

# 9
# WOMEN, GENDER AND PEACEBUILDING IN AFRICA

*Nina Wilén*

## Introduction

How are women, their roles and functions imagined in future African post-conflict societies? What are the spaces and places that women occupy in African peace agreements? These are the questions that stand at the forefront of this chapter. Africa has seen a disproportionate number of armed conflicts on the continent since the end of the Cold War (Williams 2016, 5). A large amount of these have ended with the signing of a peace agreement. These peace agreements set out the overarching framework for the peacebuilding that is to take place in the aftermath of the armed conflict, and thus they can be understood as blueprints of the post-conflict society. In particular, they reflect how signatories perceive different groups of individuals and the roles that they should play in the post-conflict society.

The signatories to peace agreements are almost exclusively men. Only 5% of signatories in all major peace processes between 1990 and 2017 worldwide were women (CFR and UN Women 2018). This is in spite of the fact that women's groups and feminist scholars successfully pushed for the adoption of UN Security Council (UNSC) Resolution 1325 in 2000, which focused on the recognition, protection and participation of women in peace and security matters. This demand for attention and action regarding women's roles has developed into a broad-based Women, Peace and Security agenda, which has gathered academics, practitioners and civil society actors under the same (albeit very large) umbrella, where the ultimate goal is gender equality (Wilén 2017). Recognising this development, it is thus likely that the wording and space given to women in peace agreements have evolved since the adoption of UNSC 1325, despite the fact that women are not signatories to the majority of peace agreements.

In this chapter, I explore how women, their assumed roles and suggested functions are interpreted in peace agreements in Africa. Using an inductive approach, I analyse the space, wording, function and roles that peace agreements give to women and gender through a feminist lens and distinguish four categories which reflect how women are portrayed: vulnerable victims, moral peacebuilders, counting women and human rights (and women's rights). While there is a clear increase in the number of references to women and gender in the peace agreements signed after 2000, they draw strongly on essentialist understandings of women. I therefore argue that while we may have passed the stage of "gender blindness", we are still in the phase of gender dilemmas.[1] Moreover, men are still the default setting in peace agreements, while women are perceived as different, requiring special treatment or special protection.

## *Methodological and Material Reflections*

In terms of material, I have drawn the peace agreements analysed here from the University of Edinburgh's PA-X Peace Agreement database (Bell et al. 2020). For the period 1990–2019, this database contains 463 peace agreements from interstate, intrastate, and inter- and intrastate conflicts in sub-Saharan Africa. Out of these, only the 130 peace agreements which have provisions on women, girls or gender were analysed. Peace agreements are defined as formal, publicly available documents, produced after discussion between conflict protagonists and mutually agreed to by some or all of them, addressing conflict with a view to end it.

Methodologically, I carefully read all passages which have included women, girls or gender in the 130 peace agreements selected for the analysis with the aim of identifying the wording, function and roles given to women, girls and gender. Thereafter I created four categories which mirror the way in which women are portrayed in the agreements and reflect trends identified by previous feminist research in similar contexts. This may be called an inductive approach, yet the aim is not to create theory per se but to identify and underline reoccurring tendencies in official documents portraying women and gender.

Women and gender are often used interchangeably in various types of documents, including peace agreements, yet gender refers to the socially constructed roles and behaviours associated with men's and women's biological sex (Valasek 2008, 2–3). "Gender" is therefore a concept which concerns both men and women, while "women" refers only to individuals who have the biological sex of women. In this chapter, I focus specifically on how women are portrayed in the agreements, yet such a focus also entails analysing gender roles and gender stereotypes, which are reflected in the wording and spaces attributed to women.

There are methodological limitations to this analysis. Firstly, only the agreements which mention women, girls or gender are examined, which may give the reader the false impression that these provisions are part of all peace agreements. Yet only 130 out of 463 agreements signed during the period 1990–2019 contained provisions on women, girls or gender – less than a third of the agreements. Secondly, as there is no geographical comparison, it is not possible to determine whether African peace agreements represent the norm, or rather the exception, to other continents when it comes to the space and wording related to women. The overarching aim is therefore to get a broader understanding of what roles are reserved for women in the aftermath of conflict, in the peacebuilding process.

## **Women, Gender, Peacebuilding and Peace Agreements**

Women continue to be marginalised in peacekeeping missions, peace negotiations and peacebuilding processes, despite UNSC 1325 drawing attention to women's sidelining in matters related to peace and conflict. Between 1990 and 2017, women constituted only 2% of mediators, 8% of negotiators and 5% of witnesses and signatories in all major peace processes worldwide (CFR and UN Women 2018). This is in spite of the fact that there are both instrumentalist and rights-based reasons to strive for a better gender balance following the termination of conflicts. For example, feminist research has shown that states with higher levels of gender equality exhibit lower levels of violence during international crises and disputes (Caprioli 2009) and that there is a strong relationship between the physical security of women and peacefulness of states (Hudson et al. 2008/2009). In addition, newer research has found a strong link between female political empowerment and civil peace (Dahlum and Wig 2018), making women's involvement in peacebuilding crucial.

Rights-based justifications for increasing women's participation have also been put forward by academics who are pointing at women's right not only to participate but also to decide on the future of the post-conflict society in peacebuilding efforts. Both international institutions and academic scholars argue thus for women's need to be included in peace processes to build a greater post-conflict gender balance and a more inclusive and durable peace (Bouta, Frerks and Bannon 2005; Björkdahl 2012; UN Women, Krause, Krause and Bränfors 2018). As peace accords frame the society that will be built in the post-conflict environment, the inclusion of women in the negotiation of these accords is primordial (Puechguirbal 2005, 4), not only as tokens of good will but as meaningful participants who can increase representativeness, disturb the dominant masculinity and share gender-based experiences.

Often, however, international peacebuilders are likely to either bring their own template for how to build "liberal peace", or to build upon the local elites' vision of how peace should be (re)built. While hybrid versions of the two are the most likely outcome, both of these visions leave limited socio-economic status and power to women, mainly because both local elites and peacebuilders are composed, to a large majority, of men (Chinkin and Charlesworth 2006, 938). Access to peace negotiations remains therefore difficult for women, as the negotiations often tend to begin in secret venues or take place in non-public forums to which only the main protagonists of the conflict are invited (Bell 2013, 2). Out of 130 peace agreements signed worldwide between 1990 and 2014, women signed only 13[2] (Krause, Krause and Bränfors 2018, 987).

The post-conflict environment, just as the conflict, remains centred around male power systems, struggles, and identity formation (Cockburn and Zarkov 2002). It is, as Handrahan has framed it: a period where "fraternities", both national and international, compete over power (2004, 433). Here again, the distinction between public and private results in lesser influence for women: "the male, public realm is where power and authority is exercised while the private sphere is the appropriate domain of women", and by understanding peacebuilding as mainly an activity in the public sphere, women's influence in peacebuilding is limited (Björkdahl 2012, 290). Women's absence – or at best limited presence – at the negotiation table is visible in the language used in the African peace accords that have been analysed here, language being a key indicator of how men and women are defined within a given society and what roles they are expected to play (Puechguirbal 2005, 3).

## Identifying Spaces for Women and Gender in African Peace Agreements

The 130 peace agreements analysed here cover a relatively large time period (between 1990 and the end of 2019) and various types of conflicts from a whole continent. Yet the space and wording allocated to women and gender remain remarkably similar over time and between different countries and regions. Indeed, since Puechguirbal analysed women's roles in four African peace processes almost 15 years ago, very little seems to have changed when it comes to how women are being defined and the roles they are ascribed (Puechguirbal 2005). There is, however, a clear difference when it comes to the references made to women, girls and gender before and after the adoption of UNSC 1325. Out of the total of 463 peace agreements in the PA-X database which cover interstate, intrastate, and inter- and intrastate conflicts in sub-Saharan Africa, 144 were signed before 2000 and 319 after 2000. Of the 130 which mention women, girls or gender, 25 were signed before 2000 and 105 after 2000. In short, before 2000, only 17% of all peace agreements mentioned women, girls and gender, while after 2000, that number is 33%. There is thus a clear increase in the space reserved for women, girls and gender in peace agreements after the adoption of UNSC 1325.

In the months before UNSC 1325 was signed, Burundi saw a range of initiatives aimed at the inclusion of women in the negotiations leading to the Arusha Accord, which officially ended the civil war. Amongst the initiatives was UNIFEM, convening the All-Party Women's Peace Conference, which gathered two representatives from each of the warring factions. More than half of the recommendations formulated by the conference were adopted (Bell 2013, 2), giving an indication of how women's inclusion may change the content of peace accords. This also reflects research by Krause, Krause and Bränfors, which argues that linkages between women civil society groups and female signatories positively impact accord content and implementation (2018, 987).[3]

Through discourse analysis, I have identified four predominant categories in the 130 peace agreements which address women and/or gender, in the sense that I have carefully read the passages which contain mentions of women or gender. Mirroring the most prevalent interpretations of women in the agreements, and drawing on trends identified in feminist literature related to women's representation in official documents, I have labelled the categories as vulnerable victims, moral peacebuilders, counting women and human rights (and women's rights). In the coming four subsections, I analyse each of the categories separately against the literature on gender, women, peace and security.

## *Vulnerable Victims*

Women are predominantly mentioned in peace accords as part of "vulnerable" populations. Often, women are grouped in the now (in)famous "women and children" category, preceded or followed by demands to protect or to respect the "particularly vulnerable" group. In many instances, this group of vulnerable is enlarged to include different groups of populations. The Dar-es-Salaam Declaration for the Great Lakes Region from 2004 states, for example: "Protect vulnerable groups, women, children, the elderly, the disabled and the sick, the refugees and displaced persons" (p. 4, 27). Similarly, the Arusha Agreement from 2000 puts women heads of families in the same vulnerable population as "juvenile delinquents, traumatized children, child heads of families and the physically and mentally disabled" (p. 81, art. 10).

There are several consequences of framing and grouping women with vulnerable populations. Three will briefly be examined here. Firstly, portraying women as vulnerable and in need of protection reinforces gender stereotypes of women as passive and weak. This undermines their influence and power in the peacebuilding process. Secondly, by singling out women and children as civilians, the "civilians frame" becomes distorted, encompassing some combatants (female and child soldiers) and excluding some non-combatants (adult civilian men; Carpenter 2005, 296). Finally, when women are associated with groups such as the elderly, the disabled or traumatised children, there is an assumption that women constitute a minority sociological category, just as the categories based on age, color, religion or handicap. This categorisation draws attention from the fact that women constitute 50% of the population while undermining the potential of women as independent actors with rights (Puechguirbal 2005, 3).

Gender stereotypes have long portrayed women as the weaker sex, linked both to physical differences with men and to understandings of women as fragile, passive and in need of protection (Shepherd 2011, 506). While it is important not to brush aside the fact that men constitute the majority of combatants in armed conflicts, this does not equate women with being victims or as especially vulnerable. Rather, defining women as "in need of protection" or as "victims" reinforces understandings of war as masculine[4] and thereby also excludes women from fully participating in rebuilding the post-conflict society. Women and men's different experiences from war and conflict are important to recognise, and the fact that women's specific experiences from conflict, which long have remained invisible in official accounts, now gain attention is encouraging. Yet, by only singling out women as "vulnerable victims", there is a risk of associating women as dependent on a male entity, thereby buttressing the myth of women as "beautiful souls" and men as "just warriors" (Elsthtain 1987). This undermines women's capacities to act and further marginalises them in peace processes (Puechguirbal 2005, 3). In addition, it locates the responsibility for providing protection with elite political actors, who most often are constituted by a majority of men (Shepherd 2011, 506). This ultimately reinforces men's power and women's subordination.

The automatic association between women and children as civilians, vulnerable and in need of protection also distorts the "civilian frame" (Carpenter 2005). Again, it is important to acknowledge that men are the main perpetrators of violence in conflicts, and thus the automatic association between women and civilians is understandable at a first glance. However, fighters are supposed to distinguish civilians from combatants based on what they are *doing*, rather than *who* they are (Carpenter 2005, 296). This resonates with Puechguirbal's point that women often are defined according to what they are, rather than what they do; De Beauvoir phrased it eloquently in the notion "anatomy as destiny" (cited in Puechguirbal 2005, 4). This "misframing" has repercussions on how armed conflict is understood and handled. For example, men may automatically be assumed to be fighters, and treated as such, while women routinely are assumed to be civilians, even in cases when they are active fighters. This distorts responsibility during the conflict and perpetuates gender stereotypes.

Finally, grouping women into categories encompassing diverse groups, such as traumatised children, the mentally disabled and the elderly hides an assumption that women constitute a minority sociological category, rather than half the population (Puechguirbal 2005, 3). Drawing attention to the diverse experiences of different parts of the population is important, yet by putting women as a category alongside minority groups, they are seen as deviant to the norm, while men are being interpreted as the "default mode" (Cohn 2013, 16). It is also problematic to group women as a category with delinquents, the mentally disabled and traumatised individuals, as these populations often have restricted capacities (or rights) to influence the post-conflict society. Associating women with these populations undermines their possibility to act as independent individuals with a right to shape and decide on the future of the post-conflict society.

## *Moral Peacebuilders*

A recurrent trend in peace accords, as seen above, is that women are defined for what they are rather than what they do. This plays out in a paradoxical way: on the one hand, women are seen as inherently vulnerable and thus as passive victims in need of protection; on the other hand, understandings of women as innately peaceful and morally superior puts them in a position of moral responsibility for the country's post-conflict rebuilding. This takes different forms in peace accords. The Sun City Agreement for the inter-Congolese negotiations from 2003, for example, urged parties to "restore the dignity of women so that they may fully assume their noble roles of wives, mothers, educators, custodians of social values and development agents" (pp. 47–54, 21, iv). This declaration both manages to put the burden on women to be custodians of social values, and thereby regulates their behaviour and firmly establishes women's roles in the private sphere as wives and mothers – and thus outside of the public, political sphere where decisions about the peacebuilding process are taken.

Yet, while women's roles are outside the decision-making sphere in these statements, at the same time, their supposedly peaceful nature is hailed as unique for the peacebuilding process.

Burundi's Arusha Agreement from 2000 states: "Recognizing the unique potential of women to contribute to the healing, reconstruction and development of Burundian society" (p. 86, protocol V). Women are also often grouped with "young people" and civil society when it comes to the rebuilding of the post-conflict society: "recognition and promotion of cultural diversity and appreciation of the contribution made by all the people of Mali, particularly women and young people, in building the nation" (Agreement for Peace and Reconciliation in Mali Resulting from the Algiers Process 2015, 3 sec. 1, chap. 1, art. 1).

These quotes reflect the understanding of women as inherently moral individuals, bound by their roles as mothers, wives and daughters to act in ethically responsible ways to end conflicts. This interpretation is mirrored in a quote from a UN study on Women, Peace and Security: "women from the Democratic Republic of the Congo, Kenya, Liberia, Rwanda, Somalia, South Africa, Sri Lanka and the Sudan have drawn upon their moral authority as mothers, wives or daughters to call for an end to armed conflict" (UN 2002, 55). Women are hence seen as the moral vectors of the future post-conflict society. This responsibility, however, rarely materialises in a seat at the table or actual influence on the peace negotiations and the subsequent accord. As observed by Otto, the association of women with peace and moral superiority has a 'long history of keeping women out of power' (Otto quoted in Duncanson 2016, 35).

## *Counting Women*

Quotas in state institutions have become one of the methods aimed at giving women more political power and influence in the public sphere. As peace agreements design the framework which will regulate the post-conflict society, they often contain various power-sharing mechanisms, such as quotas. The Maputo Protocol (African Union 2003), which came into force in 2005, builds upon UNSC 1325 and requires state parties to promote the equal participation of women in the political life of their countries through affirmative action (African Union 2003). While many of the accords examined here do not contain explicit provisions regarding women's participation, some give detailed guidelines. In the Transnational Federal Charter of the Somali Republic, for example, it is written that the transitional federal parliament of Somalia shall "consist of Two Hundred and Seventy Five (275) Members of which at least Twelve Percent 12% shall be women" (2004, 16, art. 29). Less than ten years later, the percentage devoted to women had increased to 30% for the National Constituent Assembly in Somalia (The Garowe II Principles 2012, 3, art. 4), indicating a progression in terms of gender balance. Most accords examined here, which voice an explicit demand for women's participation in larger decision-making institutions such as a national parliament, set the number at 30%, whereas for smaller organs like expert groups, every other person is supposed to be a woman.

Adding more women to ameliorate the gender balance has at times been criticised for reducing the question of gender equality to a numbers game, bypassing the structural inequality that women face (see e.g. Eriksson Baaz and Utas 2012). Some critics have also argued that women delegates at negotiations are not representative of women in society as a whole, and they often belong to the elite (Bell 2013, 4). These are both valid points. Numbers are not enough, yet in order to change the structure, there is a need for a larger participation of women in all institutions, bypassing the often cited critical number of 30%. If women are not integrated into the decision-making institutions, these institutions remain by and for men (Wilén 2019). Similarly, criticism against the unrepresentativeness of women in politics or at the negotiation table may be valid, especially as it cannot be assumed that most women represent all women (Shepherd 2011, 510). However, this critique of not being gender representative is rarely addressed to male politicians or negotiators, who make up the majority of the individuals in negotiations and decision-making organs (Puechguirbal 2005, 9). Gaining representation for diverse women's groups is a long-term process which is likely to happen gradually.

## *Human Rights (and Women's Rights)*

The fourth and final category identified here as both constructing and reflecting upon the place for women in peace agreements is termed "human rights (and women's rights)". The reason for this is the fact that while several of the peace agreements examined here mention "human rights", some also add a specific mention of "women's rights". This gives the impression that women were not included in the overarching concept of human rights. The Protocol of Non-aggression and Mutual Defence in the Great Lakes Region, for example, states that "the primary responsibility of Member States to preserve the integrity of their sovereignty and to protect the lives and human rights of all persons and all peoples, *including women and children*" (2006, 5, art. 3; emphasis added). Whereas the Mali peace accord indicates that "no amnesty for the authors of war crimes, crimes against humanity and serious violations of Human Rights, including violence against women, girls and infants, related to the conflict" (Agreement for Peace and Reconciliation in Mali Resulting from the Algiers Process 2015, 11, art. 47).

The addition of "women's rights" to "human rights" reflects long-standing feminist critique pointing to the fact that the main international organs, established for the promotion and protection of human rights, do not deal specifically with violations of the human rights of women, except in a marginal way (Reanda 1981, 12). Feminist scholars have also demonstrated that until recently, human rights law privileged able-bodied adult men rather than women or children, as women's concerns often are submerged in more global issues (Carpenter 2005, 302; Charlesworth 2005, 1). It is thus likely that the peace agreements analysed here, which specify "women's rights" in addition to human rights, have done so to make sure that women's rights are not downplayed or neglected.

There is nevertheless a risk that this practice of adding "women's rights" to references of "human rights" backfires. Using separate instruments or concepts to deal with specific "women's rights" has, for example, resulted in a narrowing of the global human rights perspective and the relegation of questions relating to women to structures endowed with less power (Reanda 1981, 12) – in essence constructing a "women's ghetto" with fewer resources and lower priority than the "general" human rights bodies (Charlesworth 2005, 1). This can result in "human rights" being interpreted as synonymous only to "men's rights", and "women's rights" being seen as an optional add-on. This therefore appears to be another example of how the wording in peace agreements has gone from being gender blind to illustrating gender dilemmas.

## All Those "Gender Dilemmas" and the Complexity of It All

This chapter has examined the wording and context related to women and gender in African peace agreements between 1990 and 2019 from a feminist perspective. Using an inductive approach, four categories have been identified as representative of how women are portrayed in the agreements: vulnerable victims, moral peacebuilders, counting women and human rights (and women's rights). A clear increase in references to women, girls and gender can be noticed in the agreements signed after the adoption of UNSC 1325 in 2000. In addition, the difference before and after 2000 is not only quantitative but also qualitative. In the majority of the agreements signed before 2000 which mention women (none mentions gender), it is only to refer to the participation of a women's group in the negotiation, not to discuss or identify specific aspects influencing women.[5]

The increase to women and gender after 2000 implies that peace agreements have traversed the period of "gender blindness of the twentieth century to a number of gender gaps and gender dilemmas" (see Duncanson 2016). Indeed, while complete gender blindness may largely be behind us, the peace agreements signed since 2000 display a number of gender dilemmas and gender gaps. When women *are* mentioned in peace agreements, they are often portrayed in roles which draw heavily on essentialist descriptions and gender stereotypes, which risks maintaining and reinforcing gender inequality.

One gender dilemma, which is particularly evident in the texts analysed here, is the tension between identifying women's particular experiences from conflict without reducing them to passive victims. Women's experiences during and after conflict have been ignored during centuries. This includes instances of sexual- and gender-based violence, which have affected women disproportionately. The fact that women's experiences are now recognised is therefore progress towards a more gender-equal society. Yet this does not mean that women's agency should be removed and their identities narrowed down to victims. Thus, whereas the attention is important in the strive towards gender equality, it needs to be reflective of the many different aspects of women's experiences and also recognise that women are not vulnerable individuals themselves: their socio-economic positions are.

Women's roles as moral peacebuilders in the peace agreements is another example of a gender dilemma. Women clearly need to be part of the peacebuilding efforts and should play important roles in rebuilding a society. Thus, the mentions that single out women as essential to peacebuilding efforts are critical. Yet women should not bear the burden of being the moral safekeepers of the post-conflict society, nor should they be held responsible for ending wars which rarely have been started or actively maintained by them. This creates gender-stereotypical expectations on women which men do not have to bear and ultimately reinforces gender inequality.

War and armed conflicts are harmful and deeply disturbing practices which affect societies and their populations in myriad ways. Africa has been the scene of a disproportionately high number of armed conflicts over the past three decades. The peacebuilding efforts that have followed in the wake of these conflicts have often used the peace agreements as the basis from which the guiding lines of the new society have been drawn. Analysing the identities and roles attributed to women in these agreements is therefore important in order to better understand how women are seen and interpreted in peacebuilding efforts on the continent.

## Notes

1 Duncanson, asserts that "peace operations have journeyed from the gender blindness of the twentieth century to a number of gender gaps and gender dilemmas" (2016, 20) in her book *Gender and Peacebuilding*, and I apply this interpretation to this analysis of peace agreements.
2 Here it should be noted that Krause et al. (2018) are not using the same criteria for peace agreements as the authors of the PA-X database, which explains the difference in number of peace agreements.
3 The absence of women and a gender perspective from the peace accords in Côte d'Ivoire and Liberia is noteworthy, especially given the prominent roles they played in ending the conflicts.
4 Feminist scholars have long argued that war is a "masculine" practice, which is fought primarily between men and is associated with what have been considered as typical masculine traits: aggressivity, physical strength, courage and decisiveness (see e.g. Cohn 2013).
5 The only exception to this trend is the Lomé Agreement of 1999 between the government of Sierra Leone and the Revolutionary United Front (RUF), which explicitly identify women as having "been particularly victimized during the war" (Lomé Agreement 1999, p. 18, pt. 5).

## References

African Union, (2003) *The Protocol to the African Charter on Human and People's Rights on the Rights of Women (The Maputo Protocol)*, 11 July. Available at: 37077-treaty-charter_on_rights_of_women_in_africa.pdf (au.int) (Accessed: 2 July 2020).

Agreement for Peace and Reconciliation in Mali Resulting from the Algiers Process, (2015) Available at: https://www.un.org/en/pdfs/EN-ML_150620_Accord-pour-la-paix-et-la-reconciliation-au-Mali_Issu-du-Processus-d'Alger.pdf (Accessed: 24 January 2022).

Arusha Peace and Reconciliation Agreement for Burundi, (2000). [online]. Available at: Arusha peace and reconciliation agreement for Burundi, N.2 (Accessed: 2 July 2020).

Bell, C., (2013) 'Women and Peace Processes, Negotiations, and Agreements: Operational Opportunities and Challenges', *Policy Brief*, February. Oslo: Norwegian Peacebuilding Resource Centre (NOREF), pp. 1–9.

Bell, C., Badanjak, S., Forster, R., Jamar, A., Molloy, S., McNicholl, K., Nash, K., Pospisil, J. and Wise, L., (2020) *PA-X Codebook, Version 1*. Political Settlements Research Programme. Edinburgh: University of Edinburgh. [online]. Available at: www.peaceagreements.org (Accessed: 2 July 2020).

Björkdahl, A., (2012) 'A Gender-Just Peace? Exploring the Post-Dayton Peace Process in Bosnia', *Peace & Change*, 37(2), pp. 286–317.

Bouta, T., Frerks, G., and Bannon, I., (2005) *Gender, Conflict and Development*. Washington, DC: World Bank.

Caprioli, M., (2009) 'Gender Equality and State Aggression: The Impact of Domestic Gender Equality on State First Use of Force', *International Interactions*, 29(3), pp. 195–214.

Carpenter, R.C., (2005) 'Women, Children and Other Vulnerable Groups': Gender, Strategic Frames and the Protection of Civilians as a Transnational Issue', *International Studies Quarterly*, 49(2), pp. 295–334.

Charlesworth, H., (2005) 'Not Waving but Drowning: Gender Mainstreaming and Human Rights in the United Nations', *Harvard Human Rights Journal*, 18, pp. 1–18.

Chinkin, C., and Charlesworth, H., (2006) 'Building Women into Peace: The International Legal Framework', *Third World Quarterly*, 27(5), pp. 937–957.

Cockburn, C. and Zarkov, D., (2002) *The Postwar Moment. Militaries, Masculinities and International Peacekeeping*. London: Lawrence & Wishart.

Cohn, C., (2013) 'Women and Wars: Toward a Conceptual Framework', in Cohn, C., (ed.) *Women and Wars*. Cambridge: Polity, pp. 1–36.

Council of Foreign Relations and UN Women (CFR and UN Women), (2018) *Women's Participation in Peace Processes*. Available at: https://www.cfr.org/interactive/womens-participation-in-peace-processes (Accessed: 13 November 2018).

Dahlum, S., and Wig, T., (2018) 'Peace Above the Glass Ceiling: The Historical Relationship Between Female Political Empowerment and Civil Conflict', *Working Paper Series*, 77. The Varieties of Democracy Institute.

Duncanson, C., (2016) *Gender and Peacebuilding*. Cambridge: Polity.

Elsthtain, J., (1987) *Women and War*. Chicago: Chicago University Press.

Eriksson Baaz, M. and Utas, M., (eds.) (2012) 'Beyond "Gender and Stir": Reflections on Gender and SSR in the Aftermath of African Conflicts', *Policy Dialogue*, 9. Uppsala: Nordic Africa Institute.

The Garowe II Principles on Federalism, System of Government and Ending of Transition through operationalizing Garowe I, (2012). Available at: https://www.peaceagreements.org/viewmasterdocument/1680 (Accessed: 24 January 2022).

Handrahan, L., (2004) 'Conflict, Gender, Ethnicity and Post-Conflict Reconstruction', *Security Dialogue*, 35(4), pp. 429–446.

Hudson, V.M., Caprioli, M., Ballif-Spanvill, B., McDermott, R., and Emmett, C.F., (2008/2009) 'The Heart of the Matter: The Security of Women and the Security of States', *Quarterly Journal: International Security*, 33(3), pp. 7–45.

International Conference on Peace, Security, Democracy and Development in the Great Lakes Region, (2004) *Dar-Es-Salaam Declaration on Peace, Security, Democracy and Development in the Great Lakes Region*. [online]. Available at: Microsoft Word – DDFinalSigned20Nov04.doc (un.org) (Accessed: 2 July 2020).

Krause, J., Krause, W. and Bränfors, P., (2018) 'Women's Participation in Peace Negotiations and the Durability of Peace', *International Interactions*, 44(6), pp. 985–1016.

Lomé Agreement: Peace Agreement Between the Government of Sierra Leone and the Revolutionary United Front of Sierra Leone. Available at: https://peacemaker.un.org/sites/peacemaker.un.org/files/SL_990707_LomePeaceAgreement.pdf (Accessed: 24 January 2022).

The Protocol of Non-Aggression and Mutual Defence in the Great Lakes Region, (2006) Available at: https://peacemaker.un.org/greatlakes-nonagression2006 (Accessed: 24 January 2022).

Puechguirbal, N., (2004) 'Involving Women in Peace Processes: Lessons Learnt from Four African Countries (Burundi, DRC, Liberia and Sierra Leone)', in Training for Peace, *Gender and Peace-Building in Africa*. Oslo: Norwegian Institute of International Affairs.

Puechguirbal, N., (2005) 'Gender and Peace Building in Africa: Analysis of Some Structural Obstacles', in Rodriguez, D. and Natukunda-Togboa, E., (eds.) *Gender and Peace Building in Africa*. Costa Rica: University for Peace, pp. 1–13.

Reanda, L., (1981) 'Human Rights and Women's Rights: The United Nations Approach', *Human Rights Quarterly*, 3(2), pp. 11–31.

Shepherd, L.J., (2011) 'Sex, Security and Superhero(in)es: From 1325 to 1820 and Beyond', *International Feminist Journal of Politics*, 13(4), pp. 504–521.

Transnational Federal Charter of the Somali Republic, (2004) Available at: https://peacemaker.un.org/sites/peacemaker.un.org/files/SO_040129_Transitional%20Federal%20Charter%20of%20the%20Somali%20Republic.pdf (Accessed: 24 January 2022).

United Nations (UN), (2002) 'Women, Peace and Security'. Available at: https://www.un.org/ruleoflaw/files/womenpeaceandsecurity.pdf (Accessed: 24 January 2022).

Valasek, K., (2008) *Security Sector Reform and Gender*. Geneva: Geneva Centre for the Democratic Control of Armed Forces, OSCE/ODIHR/UN-INSTRAW.

Wilén, N., (2017) 'Gender and Blue Helmets', *Journal of Intervention and Statebuilding*, 11(3), pp. 382–388.

Wilén, N., (2019) 'Achieving a Gendered Transformation of the Post-conflict Military Through Security Sector Reform: Unpacking the Private-public Dynamics', *International Feminist Journal of Politics*, 22(1). [online]. Available at: Citations: Achieving a gendered transformation of the post-conflict military through security sector reform: unpacking the private – public dynamics (tandfonline.com) (Accessed: 2 July 2020).

Williams, P.D., (2016) *War and Conflict in Africa* (2nd ed.), London: Wiley.

# 10
# DEVELOPMENT AND PEACEBUILDING

*Jonathan M. Sears*

## Introduction

The peacebuilding and development paradigm is implemented by a variety of actors as appropriate for understanding and responding to complex political-economic and socio-cultural dynamics in diverse contexts across the African continent. Advanced by African leaders together with their international partners, the peacebuilding and development paradigm tends to reinforce itself and to justify and expand its domains of influence. This justification and expansion is achieved by producing knowledge about African nation-states, economies, and communities and by framing expansive, comprehensive, and holistic responses to conflict, direct and indirect violence, and impoverishment.

This chapter identifies central aspects of agendas for and approaches to the wholesale transformation of Africa. In pursuit of such transformation, knowledge is produced in ever-expanding domains to encompass security, stabilization, humanitarian relief, development, post-conflict reconstruction, conflict prevention, and peacebuilding. This chapter will detail, however, that the shortcomings of this ambitious paradigm are the shadow of its apparent strengths. The logic of the peacebuilding and development paradigm is circular and takes for granted quasi-permanent crisis conditions that invite near-permanent interventions by many different actors. The chapter then points to the role of African elites in elaborating the peacebuilding and development paradigm in the context of ongoing international cooperation and the crafting of the Millennium Development Goals (MDGs 2000–2015) and the Sustainable Development Goals (SDGs 2015–2030).

The chapter then frames processes of post-colonial, independent state formation in Africa along a "maximalist-minimalist" conceptual spectrum of state models. Although a robustly endowed, interventionist maximalist state is at odds with a light-touch minimalist state, these models coexist in governance relationships at the international-national boundary and in domestic state-society relations.

From a discussion focused on African states in their international relations, the chapter turns to the local community-based aspects of the peacebuilding and development paradigm. By augmenting the variety of actors involved and by attending to the role of culture in promoting material, emotional, and relational well-being, these community-based aspects further establish an expansive peacebuilding and development paradigm as self-evidently relevant to political-economic and socio-cultural dynamics in many African contexts. Before concluding, the chapter points to a persistent issue in international cooperation: effectiveness, in the form of demonstrable outputs and outcomes at the level of projects and discrete initiatives, brings limited structural changes, and may perpetuate the status quo. This section also points to certain issues that arise when considering how complex social change happens. The chapter's conclusion points to the continued salience of the peacebuilding and development paradigm, particularly as its features and its shortcomings relate to the place of African countries in the global political economy.

## Some conceptual landmarks

As seen elsewhere in this book, approaches to peacebuilding encompass "post-conflict reconstruction including justice, institution-building, and economic development" (McNamee and Muyangwa 2021, 6). Indeed, with its developmental dimensions, peacebuilding encompasses the wholesale transformation of societies, economies, polities, and cultures. In brief, peacebuilding and development theory links freedom from direct violence with freedom from structural violence. The concept of structural violence reflects "unequal power" and "unequal life chances" (Galtung 1969, 171). These "structures of disadvantage" are rooted in "underdevelopment as a consequence of contemporary economic structures, rather than as the original position of modernization theory" (Hughes 2016, 140). The peace to be built is more than the absence of direct violence; the development outcomes to foster are more than the absence of debilitating impoverishment (Barnett 2008; Sen 1999; Galtung 1975).

Furthermore, *development* is understood not only as *capacity-building activities* for security or prosperity outcomes but also as the outcomes themselves. Development is both an end and a means, a goal and a precondition for itself (Cowen and Shenton 1996). To achieve the SDGs, actors will do development. Moreover, ubiquitous scholarly and public statements since at least former UN Secretary-General Boutros-Ghali's remarks co-constitute peace with economic and social development (United Nations 1992). In 1994, the UN Development Programme further cemented this foundational maxim: "The peace agenda and the development agenda must finally be integrated. Without peace, there may be no development. But without development, peace is threatened" (United Nations Development Programme, *Human Development Report 1994*, iii). *Peacebuilding*, even when narrowly construed as *capacity-building for security* and focused on the kinetic capacities of defense and security actors, attends also to institutional governance (e.g. in security sector reform), and can include expansive notions of physical, material, and psychosocial security, which are all tied to development. Similarly to capacity-building activities for prosperity outcomes (the circularity of development), then, capacity-building activities for security outcomes are embedded in circular logic (the circularity of peacebuilding). This mutually reinforcing logic is reinforced further by integrative and comprehensive approaches to developmental peacebuilding, approaches that move development and peacebuilding initiatives out of their intellectual silos and exclusive areas of practice (European Union 2016; Lopez 2017; De Coning and Friis 2011).

Furthermore, developmental peacebuilding remains fraught with long-standing issues known to scholars and practitioners alike. Development/capacity-building is neither a conflict-free nor an apolitical/technocratic process, but is rather, like all forms of change, conflict-prone and highly political. Though the view that "Development Axiomatically Reduces Conflict" (Uvin 2002, 6–7) remains influential in many circles, more conflict-sensitive and politically engaged approaches are emerging (OECD 2021). These approaches seek to frame change processes themselves as conflict-prone exercises in shifting political-economic relations in zones of past, current, or potential conflict.

As Uvin also noted, the "post-conflict domain is really at the heart of the entire enterprise of integrating development and peacebuilding" (Uvin 2002, 10). Today, humanitarian relief, development, and peacebuilding activities are increasingly taking place in more shared spaces and sectors of intervention, if not always in well-coordinated ways. Scholars and practitioners alike note that "everybody wants coordination, but nobody wants to be coordinated" (Kühne 2001, 387). The expansion of security sector reform (SSR) and disarmament, demobilization, and reintegration (DDR) within post-conflict agendas is an example of linking capacity-building efforts among defense and security actors to parallel development efforts by civilian government and private sector actors as well.

With its circular logic, expansion of actors and issue areas, and "can-do zeal for intervention to promote security and development" (Hughes 2016, 144), the post-conflict domain of the 1990s has become by the 2020s a still larger domain of thinking and practice in response to quasi-permanent crises or "neither war nor peace" scenarios. Scenarios like those in Chad, South Sudan, the Central African Republic, Democratic Republic of the Congo, and Mali give developmental peacebuilding approaches ample material. Long-standing problems of structural violence that manifest as direct violence under contingent conditions are the historical dimensions of an "enormous and amorphous" post-conflict mandate, which "basically encompass[es] the entire political, economic, and social make-up of post-conflict societies" (Uvin 2002, 12). The expanding scope of the developmental peacebuilding agenda also includes extending the time horizon of initiatives and to intervene after conflict, during conflict, and before conflict.

Pragmatically, developmental peacebuilding invites more actors with more resources to engage in a greater number of potential interventions in a larger scope of sectors. In response to the increased resources, actors, and sectors, African countries' donor-partners have, since the late 1990s, sought greater coherence in their international actions through whole-of-government, comprehensive, and integrated approaches. Such donor-side pursuit of coherence involves asymmetrical bargains among military, diplomatic, development, and trade actors and "more firmly embed[s] concerns with insecurity and violence into development work," as well as "adding more attention to poverty and empowerment into high politics," where military, diplomatic, and strategic preoccupations dominate (Uvin 2002, 18). As the geostrategic stakes for donor-partners increase in African countries, whole of government approaches shift influence away from development actors and towards military and diplomatic actors.

African leaders and international actors have, overall, shown little concern about excessive interventionism. Rather, they seek to mold the developmental peacebuilding agenda to serve an expanding role for state actors (with international resources), and to adapt international intervention to their visions for their nation-states. To foster ongoing cooperation opportunities (whether from principled, pragmatic, or cynical motivations) seems to be a livable status quo. More capable, robust military and security forces suit leaders' visions of post-colonial nation-statehood in Africa. Efforts to stabilize African nation-states by building kinetic, force-projection capacities has emboldened international and national state actors to see security capacity-building as readily developmental.

## African leadership and developmental peacebuilding approaches

For at least 25 years, Africans and non-Africans in governments, international organizations, and community-based organizations have nurtured hopes for effective synergies of thinking and action where issues of security, peacebuilding, and development meet. Since the run-up to the Millennium Declaration (2000), leaders in African states and international institutions considered governance and peace issues as a significant set of cross-cutting development enablers. At the most basic level, governance is the term by which international actors acknowledge that institutions matter, and that international financial institutions' "market fundamentalism was problematic at best" (Hughes 2016, 143). What was excluded from the eight MDGs found its way into the SDGs. In 2015, the African Union (AU) urged for a "stand-alone pillar on 'peace and security' [. . .] aimed at 'addressing the root causes of conflict' by tackling a range of issues such as social inequality, exclusion, discrimination and weak democratic practices" (Laberge 2019, 65). The AU common position (African Union 2014) supported the creation of a goal on peace and security and reiterated themes present in the New Partnership for Africa's Development (African Union 2001), the African Charter on Democracy, Elections and Governance (African Union 2007), and Agenda 2063 of the AU (African Union 2015). Indeed, "African countries were instrumental in the final adoption of SDG 16, including issues related to peace and security" (Bejraoui, Gaveau and Benn 2019, 9).

African leaders have emphasized the intersectionality of conflict, impoverishment, and inequality that developmental peacebuilding approaches address. Attending to governance corrects for past neglect of the important role that states play to support enabling environments for sustainable and equitable economic development (Cling, Razafindrakoto and Roubaud 2018). Within the 2030 Agenda for Sustainable Development, SDG 16 ("Promote just, peaceful, and inclusive societies") complements the rise of governance as a focus in development policy since the 1990s (United Nations General Assembly 2015). African leaders worked to have governance as a cross-cutting issue included in the SDGs to link issues of peace and conflict, justice, and criminality (the rule of law) to the quality and capacity of national and international institutions (Laberge 2019).

African states, together with domestic civil society and community actors, work bilaterally with foreign state partners and multilaterally with international organizations and international non-governmental organizations (INGOs). As might be expected, different actors have approaches rooted in different understandings of the core issues, and they work from different types of expertise and experience with access to different kinds (and amounts) of resources. Among such diversity and asymmetry of power relations, ready agreement remains elusive about what key factors build peace and foster well-being. Agreement is made further elusive when peace and security are understood to mean the absence of direct and indirect, or structural violence, and when well-being encompasses material and non-material aspects. Even the SDG 16 targets most narrowly about direct violence (e.g. 16.1) include indicators (16.1.3, 16.1.4, 16.2.1) that are related to political economies reliant on force and threat (such as trafficking and child labor), psychological violence, and climates of fear.

Increasingly comprehensive and integrated approaches are more than an agenda imposed by international actors, donor-partners, and allies to deal with "failed" or "fragile" states. Concerns around international interference in domestic affairs and the continued securitization of development cooperation and humanitarian relief (Uvin 2002) reflect "unfinished discussions among experts on what types of peace and security activities can be considered as contributing to sustainable development" (Bejraoui, Gaveau and Benn 2019, 9). African leaders' role in countering "concerns over potential negative effects of including peace, governance and justice dimensions within the SDGs" show these leaders defining African challenges with reference to developmental peacebuilding approaches and vice versa (Bejraoui, Gaveau and Benn 2019).

The conjunction of national and international factors has helped foreground developmental peacebuilding approaches with reference especially to issues and dynamics across Africa. As an overarching concept and framework of activities across sectors of cooperation, governance links developmental peacebuilding approaches to SDG 16 and the even more expansive "SDG 16+" development goals (Cling, Razafindrakoto and Roubaud 2018). The linking of SDG 16, SDG

16+, and developmental peacebuilding agendas marks the influence of AU and African member state participants in the process of establishing the SDGs. The trend toward comprehensiveness reflects the realization by many actors that silos of policy, practice, operations, and expertise hamper effective cooperation and intervention. African elites have been putting a continental stamp on security, development, and governance agendas; thus are they recalling reinvigorating pan-Africanism, and promoting regional and continental institutions.

Incorporating governance further enlarges the already large developmental peacebuilding agenda. This expanded agenda responds to African countries' place in the late twentieth-century global political economy. In 1989, the World Bank noted,

> Sub-Saharan Africa as a whole has now witnessed more than a decade of falling per capita incomes, increasing hunger, and accelerating ecological degradation. The earlier progress made in social development is now being eroded. Overall Africans are almost as poor today as they were 30 years ago.
>
> *(World Bank 1989, 1)*

Although some analysts took this "as evidence of insufficient neoliberal reform," others "regarded Africa's crisis as signalling the failure of free-market fundamentalism and forced structural adjustment" (Hughes 2016, 141). This chapter's conclusion points to the pandemic-era parallels of eroded progress.

The developmental peacebuilding agenda comes to prominence in the context of stagnant economic and social development and associated social disruption. To address multiple internal and transnational conflicts and complex humanitarian crises around the continent, African elites stress the importance of combining developmental peacebuilding and governance issues. This emphasis resonates with citizens' views seen in multi-country opinion surveys. African publics across regime types are also preoccupied by the SDG 16 constellation of issues that African leaders stress. The priority of SDG 16 is "a close fourth (26%) in overall precedence, almost tying with health issues (SDG 3–27%) and not far from hunger issues (SDG 2–31%)" (Laberge 2019). Further, "SDG 16 in 2016–18 was the top concern for Kenyans (54%) and Malagasy (53%)," with other countries' publics ranking this as their second-highest priority, "including nearly as many Mauritians (51%), Tunisians (48%) and Cameroonians (47%)," plus Malians (45%) and South Africans (43%; Laberge 2019; Afrobarometer 2018).

From principled positions and from pragmatic calculations, African leaders and international partners construct developmental peacebuilding as well-suited to respond to conflict-prone material inequalities, uneven public services, and relational-communitarian social ethics. Furthermore, "high interest in 'SDG 16+' among Africa's political leadership" (Laberge 2019, 56–58) reflects engagement with donor-partners and allies as well as an openness to holistic understandings of well-being and to comprehensive or integrated approaches to humanitarian relief, security provision, socio-economic development, and capacity-building. Self-referential in multiple directions, SDG 16+ "underlines the fact that SDG 16 is both a goal in itself and a crucial enabler to help deliver on all other SDGs," adding to the 12 targets under SDG 16 a set of thirty-six SDG 16+ targets related to "peaceful and just societies" (Laberge 2019, 56–58). Thus, with the support of their donor-partners and allies on the continent and beyond, African leaders describe and engage with developmental peacebuilding to expand the scope of international cooperation and state-led intervention, as well as to broaden and deepen the reach of governance over all aspects of populations' lives.

*Maximalist* and *minimalist* state models are points on a conceptual spectrum, from a robustly endowed, interventionist state on the one hand to a light-touch state on the other, one that enables civil society actors (e.g. in private firms, community- and faith-based organizations, professional associations). Most African states are maximalist, in contrast to the minimalist models favored by proponents of neoliberal political economy. The legacies of colonial administration are both military and civilian, aimed to govern over all aspects of the population's lives. When African states gained independence, their leaders and populations re-established great ambitions and visions for post-colonial states, and for new Africans as citizens of these independent nation-states in a liberated and interconnected Africa. These ambitions and roles, and the capacities and authority to fill these roles, necessitated maximalist models of the state to build and shape the polity as a shared political, economic, and socio-cultural community. Nation-building functions need or presuppose a sustainable unity among the segments of the ruling class and among groups and individuals that live within the state borders. In addition to being a rational response to post-colonial ambitions, a maximalist model is also consistent with the colonial legacies toward governance by command and control. Independence rule is governance backstopped with state violence; the mitigation and containment of social disorder are paramount. Perceiving risks of conflict-prone social cleavages and possibilities of social disorder, nation-building leaders want the maximalist state to pursue and build consensus or unity by recourse to forceful persuasion as well as coercion and threat of state violence or sanction. Developmental peacebuilding is incorporated into post-colonial states working through processes of institutionalization that aim to rule states' populations as subjects as much as govern them as citizens.

On the international-national boundary of action, cooperation, and negotiation, mainstream developmental peacebuilding approaches center on the African state. International actors such as the UN embrace maximalist models for African states to pursue "a positive peace supplied from above" with top-down, comprehensive approaches that link security/military and development actors and initiatives, towards more "interventionary international policy designed to bolster the state system" (Hughes 2016, 143). Notwithstanding these legacies and ambitions, the maximalist African state, with its allied international state and International Organization actors, seeks but does not necessarily hold any of the "monopolies" that are ostensibly its defining, sovereign powers: to be the preeminent source of the goals/definitions of meaningful and durable peace and well-being as well as of the means/capacities to enable it. Where nonstate actors provide services at the community level, they may be more than simply parastatals or subcontractors. Their roles challenge both the scope of possibilities and the fundamental desirability of nation-states in Africa as European-modeled, legal-rational-bureaucratic institutions. Thus a maximalist state is a model both supported and contested by nonstate actors in Africa.

Maximalist models work well with developmental peacebuilding, and especially comprehensive approaches to cooperation and intervention, which seek "whole of government" coordination across multiple ministries/departments, which work in multiple socio-economic sectors and with a range of nonstate actors. As Mann (2014) persuasively claims with reference to states in the Sahel, the African state has for decades delegated or outsourced many of its functions to nonstate actors and organizations, often under duress of humanitarian crises and international financial institution's conditionalities, but also in an attempts to allow for or leverage traditional and customary approaches to justice, conflict mediation, and wealth redistribution. These nonstate actors and organizations, which are local and national (and may also have international nonstate partners), then become part of the larger capacity toolkit of the state. Parastatals' proliferation coincides with the 1990s emergence of donor-led "NGO-ization" of development cooperation (Rempel 2008, 145).

Parastatal actors can also contribute to and complicate the state's *legitimacy*, even as they aid in building capacity to implement initiatives. Parastatals can also influence some of the spaces and activities of daily economic, social, and cultural life, contributing positively or ambivalently to peace and well-being among the populations in which they are active. Without these international and national nonstate actors, many African states could not operate even at marginal levels for certain public services (Pritchett, Woolcock and Andrews 2012). Between the international and the local, where developmental peacebuilding initiatives are implemented and governed, the independent, post-colonial African nation-state is in an ongoing process of formation. There, developmental peacebuilding is co-constructed by African elites and their networks, and through their links to society through asymmetrical patron-client relations. To implement maximalist functional state models, state leaders have incorporated nonstate actors and organizations. Thus African states are able to aspire to and in some ways fulfill a maximalist vision without necessarily enjoying the robust capacities to fulfill all of the associated obligations, to preserve a monopoly on violence, or to be lead actors in the provision of public goods.

Some observers might consider this lack of state monopolies as evidence of the incomplete modernization and institutionalization of the post-colonial nation-state in Africa. Others see that the state in Africa "works," though not necessarily according to expectations based on Eurocentric, Westphalian, and Weberian concepts of the state. The post-colonial nation-state in Africa extends an ambitious reach, even as it struggles to grasp effectively its sovereignty and omnicompetence that leads ongoing socio-economic and military-political transformation. At issue, then, are the appropriate and viable roles of state and nonstate actors in Africa to govern all aspects of citizens' lives and pursue social transformation. Taking both views seriously – of incomplete modernization and institutionalization, and of pragmatic, adaptive, and workable arrangements (ad hoc, modus vivendi) – we see that ubiquitous clientelism and patronage politics are "a rational alternative mode of governance" with limited state resources and capacity to govern and serve the polity (Craven-Matthews and Englebert 2018, 1–3). State and nonstate actors (both domestic/national and foreign/international) fulfill roles understood as defining of and exclusive to the African state. The state's ostensible autonomy over policy and its purported monopoly over service provision are conditioned and constrained, even as the state's legal and recognized sovereignty is maintained. A model of a dependent (non-autonomous) and yet sovereign state becomes even more rational under a minimalist, neoliberal model, even if the state retains maximalist ambitions and tendencies (Mac Ginty and Sanghera 2012).

Looking to today's comprehensive approaches to developmental peacebuilding, maximalism is right at home with a model of the state as a robust, preeminent actor in all facets of citizens' lives. Even relatively basic ambitions that span the whole of life of citizens need robust, lasting capacity and cooperation among "state, private sector, faith-based, traditional, and community structures" (World Bank 2011, 106). Comprehensive approaches to cooperation and intervention fit with a maximalist state model for African countries and with colonial, post-colonial, and nation-building legacies. Maximalist visions of state functions/roles coexist with influential, neoliberal political economy discourses and practices (e.g. minimal liberal state, minimal/thin (non-economic) democracy, and deepening public-private partnerships). Comprehensive approaches run afoul, however, of low-capacity states across Africa and of minimalist state models common to liberal and neoliberal approaches to political economy. It is crucial to note that "from a development perspective, the liberal peace was specifically *neo*-liberal" and "retains the neoliberal faith in the market, when combined with a liberal service-delivering state," to enable productive engagement in the global economy (Hughes 2016, 146). The post-colonial state in Africa faces, after the 1980s, the emerging imposed vision of a minimalist state under neoliberal political economy conditions, even as the state remains, on the one hand, unevenly and incompletely institutionalized, and on the other hand, a crucial actor in service provision.

Whether in a maximalist or a minimalist model, state-centric approaches to developmental peacebuilding engage, whether explicitly or not, with post-colonial state-society relations in post-colonial states "in which the distinction between private and public power is blurry and in a state of flux" (Hameiri 2010, 33, 37; Chabal and Daloz 1999). If much of developmental peacebuilding centers on the state, there are also less mainstream ideas and less institutionalized practices that start from premises that are emphatically *not* state-centric. These community-centered approaches are gaining in influence, as we will see, in light of moves by dominant institutions and actors to "localize" their approaches to developmental peacebuilding.

## Local turn and nonstate actors in developmental peacebuilding

For at least a decade, scholars and practitioners have challenged the "approach to peacebuilding that dominates the United Nations, western governments, and the human rights community" (Philpott 2012). Approaches that are *local* happen at grassroots sites where *communities* of individuals are in *relationships* mediated by their social identities. Such localized peacebuilding starts from "an assessment of local issues – the challenges and strengths of people and communities 'on the ground' in any given conflict setting and connects them with national and international actors and institutions" (Kroc Institute for International Peace Studies 2021). Because the linkages to national and international actors come later in the community peacebuilding approach, such *relational* peacebuilding is embedded in interpersonal and inter-community relationships and aligns with traditions of thinking and practice that are, as stated, emphatically not state-centric (Lederach 1997; Galtung 1975). By starting at local community levels, and bringing local actors' perspectives, social capital, and network resources into state-centered approaches, relational peacebuilding underscores how what is called the state straddles both state and society.

When traditional authorities are afforded roles in state institutions, or when state officials act unofficially, these actors straddle, exploit, and complicate their public functions and private relationships in their networks. These public-private, official-unofficial dynamics invite different responses (Coulibaly 2016). Contrasting Côte d'Ivoire and Ghana shows that "economic development strategies that generate resources contestation along social identity lines can heighten the odds of conflict and collective violence, whereas development plans that transcend ascriptive social identities bode well for long-term peace" (McCauley 2013, 142). Further, livelihoods (land-based especially) link to identities, which can encompass interdependent or nested social and economic status cleavages. In the face of complex socio-economic cleavages, and unevenly appropriate, limited, or absent state activities and public services, individual and community survival and thriving depends not only on the resilience of nonstate actors but also on their strategic cooperation and collaboration with whatever state functions can be filled, accessed, and leveraged (Lindberg 2010). If a personal connection gains state office, then the expectation from their network is of access and resource distribution. If an official satisfies the network, then they are deemed competent; if not, then they are deemed corrupt.

Governance challenges such as corruption frame African leaders and non-African actors as needing a maximalist state to address them. In governance relationships with international actors as well as with nonstate actors, African state actors embrace comprehensive approaches to developmental peacebuilding to encompass and coordinate across relevant sectors, actors in government institutions, and civil society organizations. Comprehensive approaches value local (grassroots) actors, which enable domestic African ownership of peacebuilding and development agendas. Although comprehensive approaches tend to focus on state institution capacity-building, they also acknowledge the importance of and the need to collaborate with nonstate actors and non-governmental organizations.

The "local turn" in scholarship and practice moderates the African state's preeminence as a site of and an actor in capacity-building for peace and development (Mac Ginty and Richmond 2013). Localization agendas are only partly about international actors admitting failures and moderating their ambitions for transformation in African countries. Localization agendas, when working in tandem with neoliberal approaches, may also empower civil society actors and parastatals, to enhance public goods provision, by integrating "state, private sector, faith-based, traditional, and community structures" (World Bank 2011, 106). Further, localization also valorizes sometimes ignored grassroots approaches and capacities. For example, church organizations may play "a key role in peace-building, informing humanitarian assessments, supporting resilience and aiding in trauma recovery," but find that their roles remain unacknowledged "because churches did not take part in the [UN] cluster system and their activities were funded by small, informal sources" (Tanner and Moro 2016 in Barbelet 2018).

The local turn allows for traditional knowledge specific to a certain place to be seen in terms of pan-African ethic that privileges traditional knowledge in communities across the continent. Moreover, more radical alternatives to state-led and state-centered approaches may emerge from nonstate actors and even from counter-hegemonic social movements. Such counter-hegemonic dynamics remain part of African resilience and renaissance in the face of colonial erasure, and of ongoing independence-era struggles to participate in the benefits of globalization. Furthermore, more critical voices among Africans and non-Africans "draw attention to changing modes of capitalist production, the emergence of class-based elite and subordinate social forces, and the use of development thinking, policy and practice to manage the clash between these forces" (Hughes 2016, 147). On both sides of this clash, reference to grassroots actors and traditional knowledge is found, whether reinforcing or challenging the positions of hegemonic actors. The maxim of "African solutions for African problems" can be voiced and implemented to serve African and international elites. Conversely, it can also foreground more transformative visions for state-and-society relations, potentially drawing from perspectives that question or reject state-led development, which is seen as being anti-poor and anti-marginalized as well as neo-colonial, and driven by international elites and their domestic allies (Scott 1998; Kothari and Minogue 2002; Hout and Robison 2009).

When communities are more central in approaches to capacity-building for peace and development, relationships matter as much as institutions. Community-based approaches, by their very presence in scholars' and practitioners' toolkits, can qualify the role of the African state and can also qualify the preeminence of state-to-state alliances and bilateral partnerships. Furthermore, by refocusing attention on smaller-scale relationships, networks, and dynamics, community-based approaches can moderate or counter capacity-building efforts that are depoliticized through "technocratic approaches" preoccupied with "issue[s] of institutional design and reform implementation" (Hameiri 2010, 32). Alternative perspectives from community-based actors may complement state-centered views, help support public service capacities, and humanize otherwise technocratic approaches. Community-based actors may also work against or despite the state, whether to fill service gaps or to resist active predation and exclusion by state actors.

Most importantly, community-based actors are not bound to "see like a state" (Scott 1998). They are on the society side of state-society relationships and work with worldviews, networks, and moral economies through which security, representation, and welfare may be understood and approached – importantly – in ways not oriented to centralizing, concentrating, and monopolizing state power and authority. Viewed from the bottom up, or from the margins inward, state-led developmental peacebuilding can be seen "as a practice which marginalizes and submerges the experience and aspirations of subaltern actors, thus producing structural violence and prohibiting emancipation" (Hughes 2016, 149). By reducing the scale of activities, community-based approaches expand the scope of imagination for positive, transformative peace. At small scales, embedded in relationships, holistic approaches offer alternatives to organizational modernization and social engineering, as well as alternatives to centralization and monopolization of public service functions and of nation- and state-focused identities (Scott 1998). Local and localizing approaches can privilege otherwise marginalized understandings of and approaches to peace and well-being, can include views of youth, women, and traditional or religious leaders, and can leverage community-based knowledge, networks, and the agency of nonstate actors.

African states and their international partners make the "local turn" to legitimize neoliberal political economies. Drawing community leaders into state-led projects can leverage local capacities, knowledge, and networks for greater effectiveness of interventions. Furthermore, state-led approaches leverage grassroots mechanisms and the moral authority of community leaders to build and rebuild the legitimacy of the state, and to align grassroots actors with the ideas and interests of political and economic elites.

Even if African state and international actors harbor a largely instrumental and pragmatic interest in grassroots knowledge and agency, the turn to community-based approaches nevertheless opens a way for holistic and transformative perspectives to enter the otherwise technocratic bureaucratic world of capacity-building thinking and practice. Unlike negative peace or narrow materialism, a holistic concept of human flourishing is founded on a social-communitarian ethics of peace and well-being across sub-Saharan Africa. These concepts are undergirded and overarched with notions of political and economic justice (Gyekye 2011). A holistic approach to the sustainable well-being of individuals in community is anchored in the "relational rationality" of *Ubuntu* ("humanness") and *ukama* ("relatedness"). These terms encompass aspects of human and non-human material and non-material (psychosocial or spiritual) well-being. Figures such as Nelson Mandela and Desmond Tutu have amplified a public discourse of relational African humanism (Eze 2011; Murove 2009; Molomo 2009). In West Africa, *Manden/Bamanankan* phrases will use the word *hera* (peace, well-being) to connote good health, material security (food, clothes, shelter), and the intergenerational sustainability of these goods (Bailleul 1996, 1997).[1] Furthermore, holism welcomes comprehensive and integrated approaches to address direct and indirect violence, as well as to address material insecurity that stems from structural and stochastic factors. To pursue such an ambitious project demands a more maximalist conception of the state's roles and capacities. Furthermore, such ambitions must also link state actions and actors with "different aspects of [nonstate] groups' social and economic identities" as part of the significant ambition to transform state-society relations under conditions of conflict (and sometimes violence) across social divisions and differences (Osei-hwedie and Abu-Nimer 2009).

Comprehensive approaches, integrated across sectors and encompassing state and nonstate actors, have tremendous potential to address physical, psychological, material, and relational vulnerabilities. Peace and well-being are served by drawing on culturally based practices of conflict mediation, customary justice, and wealth redistribution, as well as on traditional knowledge about ecologies, appropriate technologies, and sustainable livelihoods. Far from a panacea, cultural approaches nevertheless "link the past, present, and future, providing comprehensive and potentially sustainable approaches to transforming conflicts [. . .] to advance peacebuilding and human development on the continent" (Osei-hwedie and Abu-Nimer 2009, 4). Yet, it is very hard to operationalize holistic well-being across diverse contexts and simultaneously to take structural violence seriously, especially when structural violence is part of political-economic and socio-cultural systems that serve elite interests and existing power relations. Moreover, as much as African cultural resources for peace and development are important considerations, especially holistic approaches to well-being, culturally sensitive approaches can remain comfortable with forms of structural violence. This comfort can maintain rather than challenge intergenerational impoverishment, gendered inequality, and identity status marginalization.

## Effectiveness, complexity, and the micro-macro paradox

In specific small-scale contexts, developmental peacebuilding shows micro-level successes. What these small scale parts add up to, however, can elude effective measurement and persuasive attribution of results in multi-sector and multi-actor initiatives in the developmental peacebuilding (and SDG 16+) domains. These difficulties of attributing demonstrable outputs and outcomes are the practical manifestations of fundamental questions of logic and causality in processes of complex social change. Under pressure from results-driven agendas and time frames, and under really existing conditions and constraints (e.g. uneven data, conflicting interests, inconsistent commitments, limited or over-extended capacities), relative success is "only possible when development and peace are approached as bottom-up processes, are rooted in local contexts, take place with local partnerships and make use of networks to pool resources and expertise" (Caparini and Reagan 2019).

Nevertheless, success is possible because of its own limited scope, and highly contextual sensitivity has limited extendibility. Success stories about highly localized initiatives show a long-standing pattern in international cooperation: good to very good micro-level results and uneven, unclear, or unchanged macro-level, structural outcomes (Degnbol-Martinussen and Engberg-Pedersen 1999, 240–241; Moseley 1986 pp. 22–27). From 25 years of international development experience, including at the World Bank and the Overseas Development Institute (UK), Alison Evans affirmed (2013), "[W]hat we didn't have is a good methodology at the [aid recipient] country level to embrace essentially complex systems. And, of course, [development] projects [. . .] were creating a little [. . .] sort of bubble within all of this complexity, holding lots of things constant, and hey, presto there was this fantastic performance rate" (Evans 2013).

Compounding such methodological difficulties are routinely acknowledged difficulties to establish reliable figures on which to base data-driven analyses and policies (Jerven 2013). In conflict zones in particular, analysts and actors rely on uneven or unreliable data and evidence, as well as on rapidly and widely disseminated rumors (Sandor 2020). Subject to actors' motivated interpretations and unintentional biases, these broad and deep knowledge problems exacerbate the difficulties of making accurate assessments and sound judgments, especially when initiatives' funding requirements and timelines demand clear and incontrovertible rationales and cause-and-effect claims. Claiming clarity about such factors remains problematic in light of the weak or absent consensus on the factors that catalyze conflict into violence, and conversely, what promotes change towards peace and well-being. Whether "quick impact" or longer-term projects, developmental peacebuilding initiatives enjoy relatively little room for maneuver or remain complicit with status quo behaviors and power structures, which maintain path dependencies that can limit even modest reforms. "[I]n so many places, after years of fighting and years of reconstructing, what emerges is often a copy of the old, against the wishes of the large majority of people involved, whether local or foreign" (Uvin 2002, 11). In this situation, repeated across the continent, developmental peacebuilding initiatives "produce positive impacts on their own terms" but "are too small, scattered, and isolated to make a fundamental difference" (Uvin 2002, 12) in the face of complex problems that invite innovative, iterative, experimental responses that are ready to learn from failure (Ramalingam 2013). Creative destruction through capitalist accumulation, periodic and chronic ecological impacts, financial shocks, and public health emergencies all amplify complexity and unpredictability. Laudable intervention outcomes, then, may or may not be evidence of broader, deeper, and sustainable transformation and can even be actively deceptive because they suggest a broader, deeper transformation that is not actually occurring.

## What next? The future of developmental peacebuilding

Does developmental peacebuilding remain well-suited to producing knowledge about and guiding initiatives in African nation-states, economies, and communities? The problems of direct and structural violence are deep and worsening (Caparini and Reagan 2019). This trend is not new and is not driven entirely by dynamics at the nation-state, regional, or continental level. Africa proves challenging for global agendas for peace and development because these agendas struggle to incorporate actors and dynamics from Africa on their own terms. In their failure to meet Africa on its own terms, these global agendas exacerbate the deep and increasing problems of direct and structural violence. If much of Africa's population are among the "bottom billion" living in countries still "missing the boat" of global capitalism (Collier 2007), then perhaps the issues are at least as much with "the boat" as with those who are chronically left out. Fundamentally, the architecture of the global political economy expects African economies to be what they mostly are not, and to leverage as yet incomplete transitions (e.g. post-agrarian, demographic, and technological).

These anticipated transitions face persistently unfavorable conditions, and augur uneven and mixed benefits. The "relatively unchanged [. . .] share of agriculture in total employment in sub-Saharan Africa" suggests a very slow pace of technology-driven transition as well as significant variation among different countries of transitions' impacts on trade and global value chains (United Nations Department of Economic and Social Affairs 2020, fig. 2.3, Polarization of labour markets, Low income countries). Innovation is also double-edged. Where labor market shifts (from agriculture to services) are at least somewhat encouraging, there is the looming threat of "jobs at risk of being lost to automation," projected at 45%–65% in Nigeria and up to 85% in Ethiopia (United Nations Department of Economic and Social Affairs 2020, fig. 2.4). Even without the pressures of climate-related crises, greater integration into the existing global economy cannot durably reduce the deepest, multidimensional vulnerabilities in African countries and communities. Deepening Africa's global integration still does little to change the structural impediments to development within the global political economy, in which African economies are marginal, with the noteworthy exceptions (e.g. Botswana, Mauritius, South Africa) proving the rule. Pre-pandemic declines in foreign direct investment (FDI), coupled with low primary commodity prices, increased economic vulnerabilities that the pandemic has since deepened (United Nations Conference on Trade and Development 2020). The COVID-19 pandemic and associated crises have again underscored long-standing and compounding inequalities of many different kinds and degrees. As UN Secretary-General Guterres said in July 2020, even the promise of technological access can seem empty when the "digital divide reinforces social and economic divides, from literacy to healthcare, from urban to rural, from kindergarten to college" (United Nations Secretary General 2020). Rising income and wealth inequality is the trend in 13 of 31 countries in Sub-Saharan Africa, where 71% of the African population lives (UNDESA 2020; Shimeles and Nabassaga 2017). Since the onset of the pandemic, living standards in a quarter of sub-Saharan African economies "are likely to be set back a decade and tens of millions of people in the region could be pushed into extreme poverty (World Bank 2021). For 2021, predicted moderate economic growth, at an average of 3%, "is essentially zero in per capita terms and well below previous projections" (World Bank 2021). Even relatively robust economies face significant challenges to do more while managing with less. Climate disruption, fueled from outside of Africa, "will affect millions of people through malnutrition, malaria and other diseases, migration, and extreme weather events" (United Nations Secretary General 2020).

Constrained at multiple levels, both internal and external, African states and societies are trying and expected to face monumental challenges and "do everything at once." Development and peacebuilding involve institutional, material, and attitudinal changes that touch social, economic, political, psychological, and cultural spheres of Africans' lives. Expansive ambitions for wholesale transformation are precisely what many different African and non-African actors (leaders, scholars, policymakers, community members) find attractive in comprehensive approaches, in which the developmental peacebuilding nexus meets the even larger suite of SDG 16+ sectors, actors, and initiatives. However, mainstream international approaches to developmental peacebuilding remain too technocratic to attend meaningfully to relevant local context (historical, political-economic, and socio-cultural). Further, despite the clear need for robustly capable states and societies in Africa to enable peace and prosperity, donor-partners are ambivalent about the roles of state and nonstate actors in pursuit of such aims, and are unevenly coherent among themselves about the appropriate means to do so. An unfinished debate is: which state in Africa, with what sorts of state-society relations for what peace and whose prosperity?

The post-colonial nation-state in Africa under neoliberal peace and development paradigms will undoubtedly continue to struggle. There is a paradox in neoliberalism and the associated liberal peace: less state, but a state better able to do all that a state should to enable global economic integration. The peacebuilding and development practice and scholarship that is centered on so-called failed or fragile states and on the need for stabilization are signs of the global order expecting states in Africa to be somehow other than states struggling to become the twenty-first-century version of themselves in a global geopolitical economy that continues to condition and constrain their fullest independence (Ezrow and Frantz 2013). The development and peacebuilding agenda shows the increasing tension between minimalist state models, which emerged largely under neoliberalism, and maximalist state models of longer standing, which appeal to African leaders in pursuit of durable peace and sustainable prosperity towards 2063 (African Union 2015).

Africa's established donor partners and allies have paradoxically moderated their transformative ambitions while multiplying areas of cooperation. African states continue to face financial and institutional constraints as well as limited policy autonomy. If state sovereignty remains intact, the autonomy of African states is constrained from within, through state-society relations, and conditioned from without, through the politics of international partnerships and cooperation (Brown 2013; Allen and Giovannetti 2011). Calls for moving beyond Eurocentric and established cooperation practices through new relationships with emerging donor-partners (the BRICS countries: Brazil, Russia, India, China, South Africa) fail to sufficiently appreciate that these relations remain steadfastly state to state, with a maximalist state model at the core of arrangements on, for example, infrastructure and industrial agribusiness (Maathai 2011; Moyo 2010).

Given some of the above-mentioned dynamics of post-colonial state formation in the post–Cold War, post-9/11 (Global War on Terror) moment, developmental peacebuilding remains highly pertinent for what it is and what it is not. As a domain of research, policy, and initiatives/interventions, and with additions and complementary elements under the banner of SDG 16+, it is expansive. Developmental peacebuilding aims at change by "basically encompassing the entire political, economic, and social make-up" of countries and communities (Uvin 2002, 12). Developmental peacebuilding is increasingly sensitive to conflict and politics, but it still neglects the larger structural harms to which intervention and cooperation may contribute. "Do no harm" approaches at the level of initiatives or projects can still overlook how changes intended to promote peace and prosperity can also catalyze or exacerbate conflict-prone relationships across existing social divisions, while deepening and widening inequalities (Hughes 2016). Even relatively uncontroversial changes (e.g. an intervention such as road-building) can have adverse material impacts, negative consequences for relationships, and "the potential to reinforce, disrupt and subvert both political borders and societal divides" (Bachmann and Schouten 2018).

Developmental peacebuilding is increasingly attentive to local, community-level dynamics and resources, but it struggles to acknowledge plainly that African and non-African beneficiaries of existing political-economic and socio-cultural arrangements may resist endeavors that may place their privileges and positions in jeopardy. Reformers resist disadvantageous reforms. The goals, actions, and resources associated with developmental peacebuilding are contested. Those involved do not necessarily share common ground. The meanings of peace or development are themselves refracted through political-economic cleavages (by whom, for whom, among whom) and further refracted through differences of identity and status categories such as generation, ancestry/family lineages, networks, gender, (dis)ability, and precarious citizenship.

Interacting cleavages (local, national, and international) place the peacebuilding and development paradigm at the center of complex and unpredictable change processes pursued by a variety of African and non-African actors. Expanding the domains of knowledge production and practice for developmental peacebuilding, these actors frame ambitious comprehensive and holistic responses to conflict, impoverishment, and violence, both direct and indirect. At stake as much as the effectiveness of responses is the future of the post-colonial states in Africa – and how they will continue their formation at the crux of maximalist and minimalist models, and at the crux of national and international interests.

## Note

1 Indigenous African concepts find resonances also in *shalom* and *salaam* (well-being and peace, wholeness) from Abrahamic/Ibrahimic religious traditions.

## References

African Union, (2001) *New Partnership for Africa's Development*. Addis Ababa: AU.
African Union, (2007) *African Charter on Democracy, Elections and Governance*. Addis Ababa: AU.
African Union, (2014) *Common Position on the Post-2015 Agenda*. [online]. Available at: Addis Ababa: AU. Available at: https://sustainabledevelopment.un.org/content/documents/1329africaposition.pdf (Accessed: 5 July 2021)
African Union, (2015) *Agenda 2063: The Africa We Want*. [online]. Available at: 33126-doc-03_popular_version.pdf (au.int) (Accessed: 17 February 2020).
Afrobarometer, (2018) 'Taking Stock: Citizen Priorities and Assessments Three Years into the SDGs', *Policy Paper*, 51, November. [online]. Available at: http://afrobarometer.org/publications/pp51-taking-stock-citizen-priorities-and-assessments-three-years-sdgs (Accessed: 5 July 2021)
Allen, F. and Giovannetti, G., (2011) 'The Effects of the Financial Crisis on Sub-Saharan Africa', *Review of Development Finance*, 1(1), pp. 1–27.
Bachmann, J. and Schouten, P., (2018) 'Concrete Approaches to Peace: Infrastructure as Peacebuilding', *International Affairs*, 94(2), pp. 381–398.
Bailleul, C., (1996) *Dictionnaire bambara-français*. Bamako: Éditions Donniya.
Bailleul, C., (1997) *Dictionnaire français-bambara*. Bamako: Éditions Donniya.
Barbelet, V., (2018) 'As Local as Possible, As International as Necessary: Understanding Capacity and Complementarity in Humanitarian Action', *HPG Working Paper*. London: Overseas Development Institute.
Barnett, J., (2008) 'Peace and Development: Towards a New Synthesis', *Journal of Peace Research*, 45, pp. 75–86.

Bejraoui, A., Gaveau, V. and Benn, J., (2019) 'TOSSD [Total Official Support for Sustainable Development] – Tracking Peace and Security Expenditures in Support of the SDGs', *OECD Development Co-operation Working Papers*, 66. Paris: OECD Publishing.

Brown, W., (2013) 'Sovereignty Matters: Africa, Donors, and the Aid Relationship', *African Affairs*, 112(447), pp. 262–282.

Caparini, M. and Reagan, A., (2019) 'Connecting the Dots on the Triple Nexus', *SIPRI Backgrounder*, 29 November. Available at: www.sipri.org/commentary/topical-backgrounder/2019/connecting-dots-triple-nexus (Accessed: 5 July 2021).

Chabal, P. and Daloz, J-P., (1999) *Africa Works: Disorder as Political Instrument*. Bloomington: Indiana University Press.

Cling, J-P, Razafindrakoto, M., and Roubaud, F., (2018) 'SDG 16 on Governance and its Measurement: Africa in the Lead', *IRD-DIAL Working Paper 2018–02*. Paris: IRD-DIAL. [online]. Available at: https://horizon.documentation.ird.fr/exl-doc/pleins_textes/divers18-03/010072517.pdf (Accessed: 5 July 2021).

Collier, P., (2007) 'On Missing the Boat: The Marginalization of the Bottom Billion in the World Economy', in *The Bottom Billion: Why the Poorest Countries Are Failing and What Can Be Done About*. Oxford: Oxford University Press.

Coulibaly, D., (2016) *Comprendre la variation de la mise en oeuvre de la participation publique entre les administrations locales: Le cas des Communes III et V du district de Bamako au Mali*. Thèse de Doctorat en études urbaines. L'Institut national de la recherche scientifique et l'Université du Québec à Montréal.

Cowen, M. and Shenton, R.W., (1996) 'The Invention of Development', in *Doctrines of Development*. London and New York, Routledge.

Craven-Matthews, C. and Englebert, P., (2018) 'A Potemkin State in the Sahel? The Empirical and the Fictional in Malian State Reconstruction', *African Security*, 11(1), pp. 1–3.

De Coning, C. and Karsten, F., (2011) 'Coherence and Coordination: The Limits of the Comprehensive Approach', *Journal of International Peacekeeping*, 15, pp. 243–272.

Degnbol-Martinussen, J. and Engberg-Pedersen, P., (1999) *Aid: Understanding International Development Cooperation*. London and New York, NY: Zed Books.

European Union, (2016) *Shared Vision, Common Action: A Stronger Europe A Global Strategy for the European Union's Foreign and Security Policy*. Brussels: EU Publications.

Evans, A., (2013) *[Remarks] Book Launch: Aid on the Edge of Chaos [B. Ramalingam]*. London: ODI offices, 12 November. [online]. Available at: https://youtu.be/ahpcMFXJWiM (Accessed: 5 July 2021).

Eze, M.O., (2011) 'I Am Because You Are – A Theory of an African Humanism', *The UNESCO Courier*. [online]. Available at: https://en.unesco.org/courier/octobre-decembre-2011/i-am-because-you-are (Accessed: 5 July 2021).

Ezrow, N. and Frantz, E., (2013) 'Revisiting the Concept of the Failed State: Bringing the State Back In', *Third World Quarterly*, 34(8), pp. 1323–1338.

Galtung, J., (1969) 'Violence, Peace and Peace Research', *Journal of Peace Research*, 6(3), pp. 167–191.

Galtung, J., (1975) 'Three Approaches to Peace: Peacekeeping, Peacemaking, and Peacebuilding', in Galtung, J., (ed.) *Peace, War and Defence – Essays in Peace Research* 2. Copenhagen: Christian Ejilers. pp. 282–304.

Gyekye, K., (2011) 'African Ethics', in Zalta, E.N., (ed.) *The Stanford Encyclopedia of Philosophy*. [online]. Available at: https://plato.stanford.edu/archives/fall2011/entries/african-ethics (Accessed: 5 July 2021).

Hameiri, S., (2010) *Regulating Statehood: State Building and the Transformation of the Global Order*. Basingstoke, UK: Palgrave Macmillan.

Hout, W. and Robison, R., (eds.) (2009) *Governance and the Depoliticization of Development*. London: Routledge.

Hughes, C., (2016) 'Peace and Development Studies', in Richmond, O.P., (ed.) *The Palgrave Handbook of Disciplinary and Regional Approaches to Peace*. New York, NY: Palgrave Macmillan.

Jerven, M., (2013) *Poor Numbers: How We Are Misled by African Development Statistics and What to Do About It*. Ithaca and London: Cornell University Press.

Kothari, U. and Minogue, M., (eds.) (2002) *Development Theory and Practice: Critical Perspectives*. New York, NY: Palgrave Macmillan.

Kroc Institute for International Peace Studies, (2021) *Strategic Peacebuilding*. Notre Dame, IN: University of Notre Dame. [online]. Available at: http://kroc.nd.edu/research/strategic-peacebuilding (Accessed: 5 July 2021).

Kühne, W., (2001) 'From Peacekeeping to Postconflict Peacebuilding', in Reychler, L. and Paffenholz, T., (eds.) *Peacebuilding: A Field Guide*. Boulder, CO: Lynne Rienner.

Laberge, M., (2019) *Is Africa Measuring Up To Its Goal 16 Commitments?* South African Institute of International Affairs (SAIIA) and UN Development Programme (UNDP).

Lederach, J.P., (1997) *Building Peace: Sustainable Reconciliation in Divided Societies*. Washington, DC: Institute of Peace Press;

Lindberg, S.I., (2010) 'What Accountability Pressures do MPs in Africa Face and How Do They Respond? Evidence from Ghana', *Journal of Modern African Studies*, 48(1), pp. 117–142.

Lopez, L.E., (2017) 'Performing EU Agency by Experimenting the "Comprehensive Approach": The European Union Sahel Strategy', *Journal of Contemporary African Studies*, 35(4), pp. 451–468.

Maathai, W., (2011) *The Challenge for Africa*. London: Springer.

Mac Ginty, R. and Richmond, O.P., (2013) 'The Local Turn in Peace Building: A Critical Agenda for Peace', *Third World Quarterly*, 34(5), pp. 763–783.

Mac Ginty, R. and Sanghera, G., (2012) 'Hybridity in Peacebuilding and Development: An Introduction', *Journal of Peacebuilding & Development*, 7(2), pp. 3–8.

Mann, G., (2014) *From Empires to NGOs in the West African Sahel: The Road to Nongovernmentality*. Cambridge: Cambridge University Press.

McCauley, J.F., (2013) 'Economic Development Strategy and Conflict: A Comparison of Côte d'Ivoire and Ghana 50 Years after Independence' in Ascher, W. and Mirovitskaya, N., (eds.) *The Economic Roots of Conflict and Cooperation in Africa*. New York, NY: Palgrave Macmillan, pp. 141–166.

McNamee, T. and Muyangwa, M., (eds.) (2021) *The State of Peacebuilding in Africa: Lessons Learned for Policymakers and Practitioners*. Cham: Palgrave Macmillan.

Molomo, M.G., (2009) 'Building a Culture of Peace in Africa: Toward a Trajectory of Using Traditional Knowledge Systems', *Journal of Peacebuilding & Development*, 4(3), pp. 57–69.

Moseley, P., (1986) 'Aid-effectiveness: The Micro-Macro Paradox', *IDS Bulletin*, 17(2), pp. 22–27.

Moyo, D., (2010) *Dead Aid: Why Aid Is Not Working How There Is Another Way for Africa*. Harmondsworth: Penguin.

Murove, M.F., (2009) 'An African Environmental Ethic Based on the Concepts of Ukama and Ubuntu', in Murove, M.F., (ed.) *African Ethics: An Anthology for Comparative and Applied Ethics*. Pietermaritzburg: University of Kwazulu-Natal Press, pp. 315–330.

Organization for Economic Cooperation and Development, (2021) *DAC Recommendation on the Humanitarian Development Peace Nexus*, OECD/LEGAL/5019. Paris: OECD.

Osei-Hwedie, B.Z. and Abu-Nimer, M., (2009) 'Enhancing the Positive Contributions of African Culture in Peacebuilding and Development', *Journal of Peacebuilding & Development*, 4(3), pp. 1–5.

Philpott, D., (2012) *Just and Unjust Peace: An Ethic of Political Reconciliation*. New York, NY: Oxford University Press.

Pritchett, L., Woolcock, M. and Andrews, M., (2012) 'Looking Like a State: Techniques of Persistent Failure in State Capability for Implementation', *Journal of Development Studies*, 49(1), pp. 7–9.

Ramalingam, B., (2013) *Aid on the Edge of Chaos*. Oxford: Oxford University Press.

Rempel, R., (2008) 'Periodizing African Development History', *African Economic History*, 36, pp. 125–158.

Sandor, A., (2020) 'The Power of Rumour(s) in International Interventions: MINUSMA's Management of Mali's Rumour Mill', *International Affairs*, 96(4), pp. 913–934.

Scott, James C., (1998). *Seeing Like a State: How Certain Schemes to Improve the Human Condition Have Failed*. New Haven, CT: Yale University Press.

Sen, Amartya. 1999 *Development as Freedom*. New York, NY: Alfred Knopf.

Shimeles, A. and Nabassaga, T., (2017) 'Why is Inequality High in Africa?', *Working Paper Series 246*. Abidjan: African Development. [online]. Available at: Bank:.www.afdb.org/fileadmin/uploads/afdb/Documents/Publications/WPS_No_246_Why_is_inequality_high_in_Africa_A.pdf (Accessed: 5 July 2021).

Tanner, L. and Leben, M., (2016) *Missed Out: The Role of Local Actors in the Humanitarian Response in the South Sudan Conflict*. CAFOD/Trocaire/Christian Aid/Tearfund/Oxfam, GB. [online]. Available at: Missed Out: The role of local actors in the humanitarian response in the South Sudan conflict (open-repository.com) (Accessed: 5 July 2021).

United Nations Conference on Trade and Development, (2020) *World Investment Report 2020*. New York, NY: United Nations. [online]. Available at: https://unctad.org/system/files/official-document/wir2020_en.pdf (Accessed: 5 July 2021).

United Nations Department of Economic and Social Affairs, (2020) *World Social Report 2020 Inequality in a Rapidly Changing World*. New York, NY: United Nations.

United Nations Development Programme, (1994) *Human Development Report*. New York, NY: United Nations.

United Nations General Assembly, (2015) *Transforming Our World: The 2030 Agenda for Sustainable Development, A/RES/70/1*. New York, NY: United Nations.

United Nations General Assembly, United Nations Security Council, (1992) *An Agenda for Peace: Preventive Diplomacy, Peacemaking, and Peace-keeping. Report of the Secretary General Pursuant to the Statement Adopted by the Summit Meeting of the Secretary Council on 31 January 1992. A/47/277 – S/24111*. New York, NY: United Nations.

United Nations Secretary General, (2020) *Tackling the Inequality Pandemic: A New Social Contract for a New Era. Secretary-General's Nelson Mandela Lecture 18 July*. [online]. Available at: www.un.org/sg/en/content/sg/statement/2020-07-18/secretary-generals-nelson-mandela-lecture-%E2%80%9Ctackling-the-inequality-pandemic-new-social-contract-for-new-era%E2%80%9D-delivered (Accessed: 5 July 2021).

Uvin, P., (2002) 'The Development/Peacebuilding Nexus: A Typology and History of Changing Paradigms', *Journal of Peacebuilding & Development*, 1(1), pp. 5–24.

World Bank, (1989) *Sub-Saharan Africa: From Crisis to Sustainable Growth*. Washington, DC: World Bank.

World Bank, (2011) *World Development Report 2011: Conflict, Security, and Development*. Washington, DC: World Bank.

World Bank, (2021) *Global Economic Prospects: Sub-Saharan Africa*. Washington, DC: World Bank. [online]. Available at: https://pubdocs.worldbank.org/en/389631599838727666/Global-Economic-Prospects-January-2021-Analysis-SSA.pdf (Accessed: 5 July 2021).

# 11
# PEACEBUILDING AND DEMOCRACY IN AFRICA

*Daniel Eizenga*

## Introduction

Democracy became an essential component of peacebuilding efforts across the world during the 1990s in the wake of the Soviet Union's collapse. This was especially the case in Africa, where political transitions to democracy occurred at a rapid rate during this time. This not only occurred in countries suffering from conflict, but also in stable countries seeking legitimacy domestically and internationally that had come under pressure from their citizens and the political exigencies of the times. In Africa's post-conflict settings, international peacebuilding initiatives often supported and expedited political transitions to democracy under the assumption that building the foundations for democratic governance would help to restore peace and maintain it.

The legacy of these initiatives persists today through international interventions that pressure governments to organize elections and partake in democratic institution-building. Given the wide array of different regimes in Africa, the results of these interventions in post-conflict settings are somewhat mixed. This is true in cases where conflict erupted in the 1990s, such as Somalia, just as it is the case for the Central African Republic (CAR), the most recent African country to host a UN peacekeeping mission. Indeed, scheduled elections in both countries were set to proceed within months of one another (December 2020 in CAR and February 2021 in Somalia), yet both electoral processes experienced major setbacks, heightening the risks for renewed conflict. There are also peacebuilding and democracy success stories on the African continent, such as Liberia, Sierra Leone, and Mozambique, where multiparty elections have become routine and conflict largely averted, though a militant Islamist insurgency in northern Mozambique appeared to be gaining momentum in 2021.

Democracy, of course, is more than routine multiparty elections. For conceptual purposes, this chapter borrows from Mainwaring, Brinks and Perez-Liñán's (2007) to define democracy as a regime type with four key features: regular free and fair elections, political and civil rights that ensure the former, including adult suffrage without regard to identity characteristics, and effective authority for those elected. Similarly, peacebuilding encompasses more than international peacekeeping interventions. Borrowing from McNamee and Muyangwa (2021, 6), this chapter adopts a broad understanding of peacebuilding to include several actions such as conflict prevention and resolution, high-level mediation efforts through special envoys and meetings, peace enforcement, and post-conflict reconstruction including justice, institution-building, and economic development. Given these broad definitions, the contents of this chapter will focus on post-conflict reconstruction and peacebuilding, and particularly on the efforts to establish and reinforce the liberal political institutions that typify democratic governance.

Ideally, international and domestic commitments to deepen democratic governance in post-conflict settings persist long after initial cessations in fighting. Peacebuilding requires time and is prone to setbacks, and even reversals, due to myriad obstacles. Additionally, while the international community presents virtually uniform agreement on the desirability of and pathways to achieve sustainable peace, the significant resources and lengthy commitments required to transform conflict-prone societies have often proven challenging to obtain (McNamee and Muyangwa 2021, 9). The experience of democratization in Africa reveals that, like sustainable peace, democratic consolidation rarely follows a linear trajectory of accumulation, and even when democratic gains occur, they remain vulnerable to erosion and degradation when neglected or circumvented by erstwhile authoritarian elites. Nevertheless, the 30-year experience of African countries, both those recovering from conflict and those that remain at peace, suggests that where peacebuilding and democracy initiatives receive domestic and international support, they result in improved governance, peace, and prosperity over the long term.

This chapter discusses the relationship of democracy and peacebuilding in Africa in four sections. First, it reviews the historical underpinnings of peacebuilding and democracy on the international stage and their joining during the 1990s, offering a discussion of their origins. The next section reviews the theoretical assumptions behind liberal or democratic peace theory, which provides the foundation for democracy promotion within peacebuilding initiatives and then briefly engages with common critiques of these initiatives. The chapter then reviews two essential topics for understanding democracy and peacebuilding, by first investigating the role of elections and then examining the risks posed by democratic backsliding in contemporary Africa. Finally, the chapter concludes with a brief reflection on the state of democracy and peacebuilding on the continent and what it might mean for the future of African democracy.

## The International Origins of Democracy and Peacebuilding in Africa

Democracy promotion and peacebuilding as policy tools gained momentum within the international community following the fall of the Berlin Wall. Indeed, by the beginning of the 1990s, the discourse of "democratic conditionality" became integrated into the Bretton Woods institutions' larger package of structural adjustment reforms (Colleta, Kostner and Wiederhofer 1996). Beyond simply the promotion of democratic institutions, adherence to this type of political system became a precondition to development aid and other international support as part of broader Western-led international agenda (see Sears, this volume). Without Soviet support and competition, advocates for liberal democracy and capitalism more forcefully mediated and imposed conditions within peace agreements in countries such as Angola, Mozambique, Nicaragua, El Salvador, and Cambodia. These agreements typically stipulated that a multiparty electoral system be established, a process that Ottaway (2003) refers to as the "democratic reconstruction model." This new model of international intervention initially consisted of two components that, 30 years later, seem ubiquitous in their application to post-conflict peacebuilding efforts. The first component included, the surrender and disarmament of former combatants, followed by efforts to return them to civilian life and then the creation of a national armed forces (Colleta, Kostner and Wiederhofer 1996). The formalization of these policies has become commonly referred to as demobilization, disarmament, and reintegration programs. The second component included the organization of inclusive national conferences to draft new constitutions and to lay the groundwork for multiparty electoral systems (i.e. a political package that established the electoral institutions of a democratic political system and provided post-conflict transitional governments with a roadmap to multiparty elections).

International organizations, funded largely by Western governments, pursued the democratic reconstruction model in post-conflict settings by attempting to operationalize the theoretical assumptions of the "liberal peace" or "democratic peace" thesis into policy (Doyle 2005; Wallis 2018).[1] Yet, as officials refined the democratic reconstruction model over the course of the 1990s in response to the growing need for international interventions in post-conflict countries, the theorized feedback loop that would result in democratic peace proved elusive.

By the end of the 1990s, a consensus surfaced: following founding elections, new democracies needed support to bolster the essential components of democratic governance. In response, distinct programs evolved to boost civil society, to strengthen independent media, to promote the rule of law, and to reinforce regional and local governments through decentralization (Ottaway 2003, 316). Such programs became commonplace as Western governments invested heavily in democracy promotion around the world. Gradually, this view spread to include the continued transformation of the security sector, particularly regarding issues of security governance such as civilian oversight and accountability, thereby resulting in a set of policies commonly known as security sector reform (Ball 2001). These peacebuilding initiatives (marrying post-conflict reconstruction to democracy promotion) became pervasive across Africa, as civil conflicts had become more widespread and complex during the 1990s and 2000s.

Democracy promotion and support for improving governance and accountability were greeted with a great deal of initial optimism. Many observers suggested that these democratizing initiatives marked a "second wave of liberation" in Africa that would invigorate experimentation with political institutions across the continent to expand representative governance (Osaghae 2005). This optimism for the democratization efforts waned, however, as it became apparent that many countries on the continent continued to display authoritarian characteristics. Explanations for this lack of democratization range from the absence of a capable African state (Joseph 1999) and legacies of endemic conflict and instability (Cheeseman 2015) to entrenched neopatrimonial relations (Bratton and van de Walle 1994) and a lack of "modernization," a civic culture, and social capital – components several scholars understand as crucial for democracy.

Yet, these accounts fail to address why most African countries successfully undertook at least some liberalizing reforms, and moreover, why many of the "flawed" and "blocked" transitions resulted in dramatically different regime trajectories rather than quick returns to authoritarianism.[2] Indeed, a systematic review of Africa's 1990s political transitions reveals significant variation in the trajectories of their subsequent regimes (Villalón and VonDoepp 2005). While regimes in the CAR, the Republic of the Congo, Madagascar, and Guinea-Bissau became typified by an entrenched ruling elite committed to restoring authoritarian rule often producing instability, others such as Mali, Benin, Malawi, and Zambia exhibited significant liberalization and routinely held legitimate elections. Still others, such as Senegal, Ghana, Mauritius, Namibia, and Cape Verde, exemplified the ways in which political elites harnessed early moments of institution-building and political transition to negotiate the rules over new electoral systems and have since renegotiated these rules through compromise and coalition building in accordance with their constituencies, the very core of democratic adaptation (Halperin, Siegle and Weinstein 2010). Quite contrary to analyses of failed democratization efforts in Africa, there was and continues to be significant evolution and revolution in the "electoral" (if not fully democratic) regimes that emerged during the 1990s.

Since the 1990s, several post-conflict countries, such as Côte d'Ivoire, Sierra Leone, Liberia, and Mozambique, have embraced peacebuilding efforts to expand and deepen democratic governance, albeit incompletely, and have subsequently enjoyed tenuous peace and stability in the aftermath of conflict. Others with a growing track record of democratic consolidation such as Senegal, Ghana, Malawi, and Namibia – each of which underwent some form of democratic transition during the 1990s – continue to remain among the most stable countries on the continent. Similarly, conflict in Africa remains connected to countries lacking democratic governance. In 2020, of those countries grappling with civil conflict (excluding militant Islamist insurgencies), nine out of ten lacked constitutional term limits on the executive and, of those, eight were among the top ten African countries of origin for forcibly displaced persons (Siegle and Cook 2020). These dynamics suggest that the relationship between peacebuilding and democracy remains robust in Africa. The following section addresses this relationship's theoretical foundations and then examines various critiques to understand possible explanations for continued conflict.

## Democratic Peace Theory and Liberal Democratic Peacebuilding

The ideas behind democratic peace theory have been vital to the policies that comprise liberal democratic peacebuilding. Building on the core tenets of the "democratic peace theory," policymakers aimed to establish political institutions that would support democracy, the rule of law, and universal human rights in post-conflict settings that would then provide the necessary conditions for capitalist market economies to develop. Simplistically, this hypothesized positive feedback loop or virtuous circle might be described as follows: once conflict has ended, first establish and promote democratic governance; democratic governance will engender a more peaceful society helping to advance economic development, which in turn will further stabilize and sustain peace, and thereby promote continued democratic governance. This notion of a positive feedback loop assumes that liberalism – as an ideology as well as economic and political policy – espouses an inherent attractiveness, as it offers the most likely path to peace and prosperity (Wallis 2018, 83). The concomitant argument that expanding liberalism also helps end and prevent conflict between other liberal democracies adds to its allure.

The liberal democratic peace theory, as presented by Doyle (2005), claims that three necessary conditions when taken together are sufficient for sustained peace between and within countries.[3] Doyle's three conditions are (1) republican representative democratic government, (2) a legally enshrined appreciation for the legitimate rights of all individuals, and (3) economic incentives that sustain commitments between other liberal governments (2005, 464). The relationship between these three pillars can be briefly summarized as follows: representative democratic institutions enable citizens to hold their elected officials accountable, thereby tempering policy and allowing for governments to self-correct over the long term (Halperin, Siegle and Weinstein 2010, 51–52). Similarly, the liberal norms enshrining respect for individual rights guide public policy to be just; elected officials are judged by the principles they profess and whether these principles accord with their constituents' interests through representative government (Doyle 2005, 464). Economic development flourishes through institutions of shared power, widespread access to information, and rule of law that respects property and enforces legal exchange, helping to mitigate economic shocks or crises (Halperin, Siegle and Weinstein 2010, 64). Finally, at the international level, these three pillars of liberal institutions, ideas, and economics promote a sustainable peace, or "liberal peace," because those countries adhering to these pillars share in the mutual benefits of collaborating with other liberal societies and thus remain at peace with one another. Embracing liberalism, however, does not eliminate illiberal governments nor the insecurity caused by anarchy in the international system, and thus it does not in itself eliminate the possibility of conflict (Doyle 2005, 465). Based on the theory, however, the greater number of liberal democracies in the world, the less likely interstate conflict becomes.

The postulated relationships briefly discussed above form the basis for the international community's post-conflict reconstruction efforts to build liberal democratic institutions, as well as the more general effort to promote democracy in Africa. Liberal democratic peace theory has generated volumes of debate and scholarly attention. Rather than attempting to recount all the various theoretical and academic disputes, the remainder of this section proceeds by briefly discussing some prominent critiques of democratic peace theory as they pertain to the deployment of liberal democratic peacebuilding initiatives.

At first, these initiatives aimed to refashion post-conflict states into functioning democracies in only a few short months. Given the time and resources necessary to accomplish these goals effectively, it should come as no surprise that in some countries, such as Angola and Cambodia, peace agreements and subsequent electoral outcomes quickly fell apart and conflict reemerged. These initial setbacks led the international community to reallocate greater time and resources to transforming armed groups into political parties, something that occurred with greater success, though still imperfectly, in Mozambique (Turner, Nelson and Mahling-Clark 1998). It became increasingly clear, however, that long-term international assistance and intervention remained vital for transforming political systems into self-sustaining democracies buttressed by a strong civil society and free press. Consequently, questions emerged regarding the feasibility and suitability of internationally mandated, and largely Western-backed, democratic transformations, which for some smacked of hubris, particularly in the post-colonial context of Africa (Ottaway 1997).

The overambitious posture of the international community led to several critical assessments of the democratic reconstruction model's effectiveness. The international community's store of political will and financial resources diminished as the number of international interventions increased, which invariably reduced the effectiveness of the interventions themselves (Ottaway 2003). This inverse relationship led critics to deem the reconstruction efforts unrealistic and to call for a dramatic rethinking of their scale (Ottaway 2003). Some, seeking to offer a more optimistic perspective, suggested that reducing expectations in the short term by extending the time given to interim governments to organize elections and by incorporating locally supported transitional governance structures might yield more success (Call and Cook 2003, 243). This marks the beginning of an explosion of interest in the local dimensions of peacebuilding, referred to as the "local turn" in peacebuilding literature. Growing recognition of the arguably more successful roles of local actors vis-à-vis their international counterparts provided momentum for this view of peacebuilding (Mac Ginty and Richmond 2013). Ultimately, these perspectives coalesced around a common call for more modest interventions by the international community in post-conflict settings, arguing that such an approach stood a better chance of stabilizing countries and igniting a political process that would lead to democracy.

The push for a more restrained approach gained traction in the wake of liberal democratic peacebuilding's apparent failures during the 2000s. Western governments, the UN, and other international institutions shifted their expectations and overall goals towards enhancing (rather than transforming) service delivery to populations through a mixture of "state, private sector, faith-based, traditional, and community structures" (World Bank 2011, 106). This lowering of expectations for liberal democratic peacebuilding reduced the duration and cost of the international commitment to political transformation by accepting the organization of credible multi-party elections in place of stringently free and fair ones (Wallis 2018, 84).

This change also reflects a reaction to an academic critique of democracy promotion and peacebuilding, based on the concept of hybrid peacebuilding. Born out of the dual push for a shift in expectations and a greater degree of local level engagement, hybrid peacebuilding aims to locally embed aspects of liberal democracy by encouraging "mediation between local and international scales and norms, institutions, law, rights, needs and interests, depending on both power and legitimacy" (Richmond 2015, 51). Executed appropriately, a "positive hybrid peace ... rooted in accommodation, reconciliation, emancipation, autonomy, social justice and a sense of liberation" results at the local and individual levels (Richmond 2015, 60). While critical of early attempts at liberal democratic peacebuilding, this perspective is not necessarily incommensurate with the theoretical foundations or tenets of this approach.

Hybrid peacebuilding seeks to bridge a divide between the elite/international level peacebuilding that characterized the early liberal democratic peacebuilding, and the local peacebuilding initiatives that experienced a greater degree of success, even if less dramatic in transformation. Indeed, when liberal notions of popular sovereignty are applied to peacebuilding, people at the local level decide the extent to which liberal and local principles guide peacebuilding efforts and the extent to which this occurs through state and local institutions (Wallis 2018, 97). Bringing liberalism back into peacebuilding in a participatory fashion entails an assessment of existing pluralism in political and legal institutions and their ability to allow for liberal norms to be renegotiated within their context, thus producing hybridity (Richmond 2015, 56). Under the appropriate circumstances, an inclusive and participatory constitution-making process that allows for debate and dialogue among multiple actors may provide an opportunity for this form of negotiation to take place (Wallis 2014). There are, of course, several forums during which such negotiations can take place including during transitional justice processes and elections for their new institutions (Wallis 2018, 97). As these perspectives underscore, calls for hybrid peacebuilding and their implicit critiques of liberal democratic peacebuilding rarely contradict the presumed relationships between democratic governance, peace, and prosperity, and instead offer criticisms regarding the process and policy implementation of liberal democratic peacebuilding.

These theoretical critiques regarding the process and implementation of peacebuilding are consistent with more policy-oriented critiques that focus on the technical application of institution-building and its shortcomings. Such critiques, focus on the timing of elections, the capacity of transitional governments to successfully organize and hold elections, the sequence of reform efforts, the human capacity to staff newly established institutions, and so forth. While these critiques no doubt have merits on a case-by-case basis, a review of just how successful the adoption of regular multiparty elections in Africa has been since the 1990s suggests technical critiques over process and implementation may overlook the degree of political change that has occurred.

## The Role of Elections

Elections play a key role both in democratic governance and peacebuilding. As discussed above, regular free and fair elections allow for citizens to hold their elected officials accountable. This provides the foundation for representative democratic governance and helps periodically to improve policy and political performance. Regular elections also contribute to peacebuilding by granting political legitimacy to leaders, enabling predictable and peaceful transfers of power and enhancing the overall inclusion and participation of citizens in governance (Oduro 2021, 163). Following ceasefires and peace agreements, evidence indicates that elections also strengthen the durability of peace when rebel and government parties follow the electoral process and outside observers remain in place to enforce the process as necessary (Matanock 2018). Elections, of course, are only one component of democratic governance and peacebuilding, but given the centrality of elections to both, this section proceeds by examining their role in the African context.

By the 2010s, virtually every African country organized regular multiparty elections. According to Morse (2017, 115), by 2014, only four sub-Saharan African countries (Eritrea, Somalia, Eswatini, and South Sudan) did not hold regular elections to national office. The adoption of regular multiparty elections in previously authoritarian contexts has generated significant debate over the effects of elections on regimes and political leaders in Africa. Certainly, incumbent presidents and ruling parties across much of the continent have proven themselves to be stubbornly entrenched, in many cases avoiding turnovers at the ballot box and remaining in power following transitions to democracy. In that respect, Africa has followed global trends toward electoral authoritarianism with nearly half of African regimes classified as either "competitive" or "hegemonic" electoral authoritarian regimes (Howard and Roessler 2006).[4] Despite their democratic deficits, electoral processes continue in these regimes.

Repetitive elections, even those that fail to be completely free and fair, may still lay the groundwork for improving elections over time and thus increase prospects for democratization. Looking exclusively at African regimes, Lindberg argues that the explosion of electoral activity in the 1990s produced a new form of political transition, "democratization by elections," through which repeated elections shape voter expectations and improve electoral systems (2006, 143). This then bolsters the chances for freer and fairer elections and eventually democratic consolidation thanks to mutually reinforcing processes of political learning and increased accountability (Lindberg 2006, 161). Others have viewed this "electoral mode of transition" skeptically, as it has not been observed in other parts of the world, and further analysis of the evidence for Africa suggests that uninterrupted electoral cycles do not necessarily lead to a greater number of democratic regimes (Bogaards 2013). Still, the essentially complete adoption of multiparty elections across the continent represents a transformation of politics and deserves to be analysed as a moment of significant political change capable of long-lasting effects.

The degree to which experience with elections improves the electoral process remains an open debate and one for which African examples may offer insight. Research on opposition parties in Africa demonstrates that when they openly contest elections over several iterations, their participation fundamentally alters the political system through a self-reinforcing form of democratic socialization (Edgell et al. 2018). In some cases, by participating in elections, opposition parties educate their constituents about the standards of the electoral process which may then gradually enhance the democratic quality of electoral regimes by enhancing degrees of electoral competition (Edgell et al. 2018). This, of course, depends on the ability of other institutions to ensure the integrity of the electoral process.

Regular elections and the institution-building efforts of establishing electoral management bodies, such as national electoral commissions and their subnational counterparts, have raised the technical capacity of election officials. With each electoral cycle, these bodies have become more professionalized answering calls for greater transparency in the administration of elections and helping to build social trust in the electoral process (Oduro 2021, 166). In some post-conflict settings, arguably the least likely contexts for this to occur, independent national electoral commissions have been essential to upholding the integrity of elections. In both Liberia and Sierra Leone, multiple electoral cycles eventually produced electoral upsets (2017 in Liberia and 2018 in Sierra Leone), resulting in peaceful turnovers of power (Pailey and Harris 2020, 769). The Liberian and Sierra Leonian electoral commissions played a key role in validating the results and maintaining a relatively peaceful atmosphere before, during, and after their respective elections, as have other electoral commissions in Africa that have helped adjudicate opposition victories (Oduro 2021, 166). On this front, recent elections in Nigeria (2019), Ghana (2016),

Kenya (2017), Liberia (2017), Sierra Leone (2018), and Malawi (2019) have yielded improvements to the litigation of election disputes through independent commissions as well as judicial institutions (Oduro 2021, 170). These improvements to the electoral process suggest that, at least in some cases, the regular and repetitive organization of elections may benefit democratizing governments as well as peacebuilding efforts in post-conflict settings.

These incremental advances, however, have also coincided with a growing number of cases where efforts to improve the electoral process have resulted in consequences that counteract their intended positive effects. These efforts include the adoption of new digital and biometric technology, use of peace messaging around electoral cycles, and an increasingly entrenched, "winner-take-all" attitude among politicians (McNamee and Muyangwa 2021, 11). The adoption of new technologies intended to add layers of transparency to the democratic process have at times contributed to an increase in corruption and entrenchment of ruling parties (Cheeseman, Lynch and Wallis 2018; Debos 2018).[5] Similarly, peace messaging attempting to reduce the chance of electoral violence has been shown to have the counterintuitive effect of depoliticizing electoral campaigns and thus offering de facto support to those in power, a phenomenon referred to as "peaceocracy" (Lynch, Cheeseman and Willis 2019).[6] Finally, as elections have grown increasingly competitive, the stakes for political elites have also increased, causing a turn to sometimes violent tactics against opponents and their supporters (Oduro 2021, 168). Such politics in post-conflict settings risk reigniting violence and destabilizing these fragile countries, rather than advancing democracy or peace.

These observations highlight that elections and electoral processes can become flashpoints for heightened violence when subverted by authoritarians. This raises several challenges for countries seeking to advance democracy and peacebuilding initiatives without the support of domestic political elites or greater support from the international community. It also helps to explain how, despite a growing number of countries that organize regular national elections, prosperity remains elusive, peace tenuous, and democratic gains stymied in Africa. Indeed, some have even termed an alternative trajectory: "illiberal peacebuilding" (Soares de Oliveira 2011).

In countries such as Angola, Rwanda, and Eritrea, elites have flouted the liberal peacebuilding democratic model deploying a much more controlled approach. This process of post-war reconstruction offers little expansion of civil liberties, support for the rule of law, or interest in economic freedoms and poverty alleviation; rather, local elites manage reconstruction with a view to centralize power and dominate the political economy (Soares de Oliveira 2011, 288). Ultimately, the illiberal tactics of would-be authoritarian elites hamper the democratic potential of many African countries and contribute to a broader environment in which the international community has become more permissive toward authoritarianism. This constitutes not only a challenge to liberal democracy as a model for peacebuilding but a threat to the democratic institutions and norms that help maintain peace and stability.

## The Threat of Democratic Backsliding

If the 1990s represent years of democratic progress, then the 2010s might be best characterized as an incremental resurgence of authoritarianism in Africa. Scholars have described this turn toward more illiberal politics as "democratic backsliding" to characterize the erosion of the institutional safeguards for democratic governance (Bermeo 2016). This has particularly perverse effects in Africa because of the many young democracies on the continent as well as the many countries struggling to overcome legacies of political violence. Democratic backsliding may take many different forms. Bermeo (2016) discusses three effects worth exploring in greater detail, as they constitute threats to peacebuilding efforts seeking to bolster democratic institutions.

Encapsulating a variety of techniques, "executive aggrandizement" refers to the weakening of accountability mechanisms on the executive branch of government (Bermeo 2016, 10). This often occurs through piecemeal reforms after the ruling party wins presidential elections and holds a dominant majority in the legislature, allowing the government to claim a popular mandate for reforms that weaken institutional checks and balances. These institutional changes impede the ability of the political opposition and other institutions, such as inspectors general, to constrain executive power. Executive aggrandizement often subversively employs legal mechanisms such as newly elected constitutional assemblies, referenda, or other legally decreed acts to frame such reforms as having a democratic mandate (Bermeo 2016, 11). Several cases across the African continent showcase executive aggrandizement. Two recent and egregious examples are Tanzania and Zambia, which had both previously been considered stable African democracies and have thus far avoided conflict.

Following the 2016 elections of John Magufuli in Tanzania and Edgar Lungu in Zambia, political space for opposition parties and civil society shrunk dramatically and at times violently. In Tanzania, this occurred as the ruling party passed eight reforms using a legal maneuver to avoid constitutionally mandated public debate and giving the authorities discretionary powers to suspend civil society organizations (Africa Center for Strategic Studies 2019). Magufuli subsequently banned public demonstrations and assembly using the security forces to crack down on opposition gatherings. In Zambia, Lungu has used the courts to circumvent constraints on his office by pressuring the Independent Broadcasting Authority and bringing a defamation suit against the Law Association of Zambia (Africa Center for Strategic Studies 2019). Lungu has also used a stacked constitutional court to win a ruling that he can contest elections for a third presidential term despite a constitutional two-term limit.

Weakening, evading, or at times eliminating presidential term limits is one of the most significant forms of executive aggrandizement. Of the 34 presidential elections scheduled between 2019 and 2021 in Africa, approximately one-third are grappling with the issue of leaders challenging term limits (Siegle and Cook 2021). Since 2015, African presidents increasingly have eliminated or avoided constitutional term limits through reforms, legal arguments, or referenda and have thus undermined the legitimacy that democratic electoral processes are intended to generate. This growing pattern of evading term limits in Africa carries far-reaching consequences for the continent's governance, security, and development, undercutting the potential benefits of democracy and peacebuilding.

Another form of democratic backsliding regards the changing nature of military coups. It is no longer common for military juntas to remain in power, although events in Mali and Chad in 2021 cast doubts on this trend. Instead, military leaders have shifted to executing "promissory coups that frame the ouster of an elected government as a defense of democratic legality," after which the putschists "promise" to organize elections and return the country to civilian rule (Bermeo 2016, 8). Whether the military subsequently agrees to return political power to elected civilian leaders is irrelevant, as in the interim citizens have effectively lost their democratic rights following the illegal seizure of power (Siegle and Eizenga 2020). Once coup leaders have taken control, the constitutional protections and civil liberties afforded to citizens in a democracy vanish and what is legal or enforced is now up to those who have seized power, a reality that Egyptians and Zimbabweans experienced after 2014 and 2017, respectively. In both cases, the coup leaders (Abdel Fattah al-Sisi and Emerson Mnangagwa, respectively) ultimately did organize elections, but each did so to ensure their victory at the polls.

Ironically, the shift in strategy by military coup leaders to quickly promise a return to elected civilian rule suggests that democracy and peacebuilding efforts have had some partial impact. Military leaders recognize they must at least install the window dressing of and pay lip service to democracy following a coup d'état. These tendencies suggest that backsliding in form of the promissory coups is a logical reaction to international pressure. Evidence confirms that sanctions on international assistance following the extraconstitutional removal of democratically elected governments have reduced the frequency of coups (Marinov and Goemans 2014). The few successful coups that do occur typically frame themselves as promissory to escape or limit sanctions (Bermeo 2016, 15). When coup leaders agree to organize elections, it is rarely without exerting some degree of influence over the process, which overlaps with Bermeo's third form of backsliding, "strategic election manipulation" (Bermeo 2016, 13).

Often performed in tandem with executive aggrandizement, strategic election manipulation refers to a range of actions intended to advantage incumbents in elections. Indeed, many of these strategies are observed in Magufuli's Tanzania and Lungu's Zambia, including among others abusing independent media, financing incumbent campaigns with government funds, harassing opposition candidates or excluding them from the ballot, and packing electoral commissions (Africa Center for Strategic Studies 2019). These tactics are "strategic," since they avoid the scrutiny of international elections observers (Beaulieu and Hyde 2009, 393). The increase in opposition harassment and legal tactics to exclude opposition leaders and parties from contesting elections has obvious deleterious effects on democratic competition (Bermeo 2016, 14). Some studies suggest that, like promissory coups, this form of backsliding has emerged as an unintended consequence to international pressures through election monitoring by forcing politicians to employ new methods to guarantee victory at the ballot box (Hyde and O'Mahony 2010).

Benin offers a recent and blatant example of such tactics. On 28 April 2019, Benin elected a new National Assembly, but only parties loyal to President Talon participated in the election. Talon's government enacted a series of eleventh-hour hurdles, effectively disqualifying all opposition parties (Duerksen 2019). As one of the more flagrant examples of strategic elections manipulation in Africa, it is all the more brazen given that Benin has long been heralded as one of Africa's beacons of democracy. Even more worryingly, Benin joins its West African neighbors Côte d'Ivoire, Guinea, Togo, Burkina Faso, and Niger, which all exhibited varying degrees of democratic backsliding ahead of their elections in 2020 and 2021 (Patuel 2020). Such events should not be overlooked, as they emphasize how pernicious this threat may become. In post-conflict settings, democratic backsliding presents an even more serious threat to often fragile political situations.

Mali provides an illustrative example of the serious effects that democratic backsliding poses as it plummeted from being West Africa's "democratic darling" into years of conflict. In Mali, democratic backsliding crept slowly under the administration of President Amadou Toumani Touré. As an independent candidate, Touré formed "consensus government" coalitions to satisfy his political opposition. This reduced electoral accountability (perhaps inadvertently) and served to embed a form of governance that failed to respond citizens' demands or preform effectively (Bleck and van de Walle 2011). When popular discontent eventually spread to the armed forces, which were simultaneously engaged in a nascent low-grade secession conflict, junior officer Captain Amadou Haya Sanogo staged a coup d'état in March 2012. This would be the first of three such coups within a decade and triggered dynamics which exacerbated conflict in Mali.

Ultimately, after the 2012 coup, little progress was made toward restoring Mali's democratic character or resolving its conflict. Despite a return to elected government in 2013, the government avoided significant democratic reform (Bleck and Michelitch 2015). This was facilitated in part due international interventions that sought to restore the status quo ante but failed to recognize its democratic deficits, and thus at least a partial cause for Mali's conflict (Charbonneau and Sears 2014). Consequently, the conflict persisted, evolved, worsened, and spread, claiming the lives of thousands and displacing millions in the region by the end of 2020, despite significant peacebuilding efforts by the international community, including a UN peacekeeping mission.

The failure to recognize that democratic backsliding in Mali contributed to an onset of conflict, the subsequent failure of peacekeeping and peacebuilding interventions to recognize the need to rebuild fundamentally Mali's democratic institutions has contributed to a state of permanent crisis (Charbonneau 2017). Reflecting on how international interventions in Mali have contributed to this, Charbonneau (2020) describes these dynamics as global counterinsurgency governance in which the international community seeks to separate itself from "national" or domestic politics purportedly only engaging in conflict resolution. This stance ignores the political implications of such interventions, however, and fails to acknowledge how such actions as peacekeeping and counterterrorism operations openly undermine democratic peacebuilding by empowering uninterested domestic political actors.

It is within this context that a military junta in Mali staged a coup in August 2020 and subsequently engineered an influential role for itself with an 18-month political transition. When civilian authorities in the transition sought to reduce the junta's influence, the soldiers retained control over the political transition by staging their second coup in May 2021. Rather than reprimand the junta and demand the restoration of constitutional order, the international community, remaining out of politics, condemned the coups without any serious repercussions for the putschists. The irony of condemning the coups but then effectively letting the coup leaders remain in power might stoke laughter, if it did not simultaneously perpetuate Mali's devastating conflict.

The Malian case dramatically underscores the threat that democratic backsliding presents for conflict generally, but even more so, it highlights the importance of substantive democracy promotion within peacebuilding contexts, which in post-conflict settings requires explicit international support and engagement. Without consequences for backsliding and concrete actions that strengthen democratic institutions, there can be little expectation that long-term peacebuilding initiatives will succeed.

## Conclusion

Peacebuilding and democracy exhibit a robust relationship on the African continent. Many post-conflict countries have managed to embrace democratic governance and have enjoyed a tenuous peace. In other contexts, African countries that have worked to deepen their democratic performance have benefited over the long term from stability and increased prosperity. Conversely, 10 of the 14 African countries facing armed conflict in 2021 exhibited authoritarian-leaning governments, and those conflicts in Africa's authoritarian-leaning countries have persisted twice as long, on average, as those in democratizing countries (Africa Center for Strategic Studies 2021). This makes efforts to erode democratic institutions especially alarming as they threaten to reignite former hostilities or unleash new conflicts.

Democratic backsliding, consequently, poses serious challenges to scholars and policymakers alike. One challenge is analytical. Those wishing to advance democracy must view it as "a collage" of institutions vulnerable to the tinkering and re-tinkering of those in power (Bermeo 2010, 1120). This harkens back to the early dismissals of the democratic reconstruction model as unrealistic and shallow. However, rather than causing democracy promoters to abandon their endeavor and avoid politics, contemporary democratic backsliding suggests that democracy promotion has made an impact on governance and peacebuilding. Thus, democratization might be best viewed as an iterative process across near, middle, and long terms. Scholars and policymakers committed to understanding and deepening democracy, therefore, should consider what options exist that might incentivize democratic flows and forestall democratic recessions.

Democracy and peacebuilding should remain top policy priorities for the international community. Polling from Afrobarometer clearly and consistently demonstrates strong support for elections and democracy across the continent, especially when elections produce change and are seen by citizens as free and fair. Crucial to this type of engagement will be to counter disillusionment and disengagement by citizens suffering under authoritarian regimes.

Where democratic gains are undone it can result in perpetual conflict, as the Malian case tragically reveals. Yet, elections and democratic reforms in Mozambique, Liberia, and Sierra Leone helped end violent conflicts in those countries, and elections marked major milestones for peacebuilding efforts in other contexts like Côte d'Ivoire and the Democratic Republic of the Congo (Doss 2020). Where democratization processes have been derailed or sidestepped, leaders have clung to power, corruption has flourished, and elected officials have failed to build social trust (Doss 2020). This has too often foreshadowed the onset of conflict or renewed hostilities in post-conflict contexts. To prevent such outcomes, the international community will need to build up the resolve to engage in politics and once again promote substantive democracy and peacebuilding in Africa.

## Notes

1 This chapter discusses the essential theoretical foundations of liberal peace theory in the subsequent section. There is substantial scholarly literature devoted to democratic peace theory and/or liberal peace theory, but for the purposes of this chapter, these bodies of work are referred to interchangeably as they hinge on the notion that liberal democratic governments are far less likely to engage in interstate conflict or to experience civil conflicts.
2 The terms "flawed" and "blocked" refer to Bratton and van de Walle's distinctions (1997, 120).
3 Doyle (2005) offers the most succinct treatment of democratic peace theory, though there are several other in-depth discussions including by Doyle himself. There is a substantial body of work testing the democratic peace theory and its hypothesized relationships across quantitative and qualitative studies. For an empirically based assessment of democratic peace theory and its effects on governance, development, and conflict in poor countries, see Halperin, Siegle, and Weinstein (2010).
4 In 2018, using Roessler and Howard's (2006) regime typology, 21 out of 48 regimes in Africa for which data were accessible were classified as "hegemonic" or "competitive" authoritarian regimes within which regular elections occurred. For more details, see Eizenga (2018).
5 Debos (2018) observes these trends in Chad; Cheeseman, Lynch, and Wallis (2018) observe them in Kenya, Ghana, and Uganda.
6 Lynch, Cheeseman, and Willis (2019) compare experiences of electoral violence and subsequent peace messaging used by ruling parties in Ghana, Kenya, and Uganda.

## References

Africa Center for Strategic Studies, (2019) 'Subverting Democracy in Tanzania and Zambia', *Spotlight*, 17 September. [online]. Available at: https://africacenter.org/spotlight/circumvention-of-term-limits-weakens-governance-in-africa/ (Accessed: 1 July 2021).
Africa Center for Strategic Studies, (2021) 'Autocracy and Instability in Africa', *Infographic*, 9 March. [online]. Available at: https://africacenter.org/spotlight/autocracy-and-instability-in-africa/ (Accessed: 1 July 2021).
Ball, N., (2001) 'Transforming Security Sectors: The IMF and World Bank Approaches', *Conflict, Security & Development*, 1(1), pp. 45–66.

Beaulieu, E. and Hyde, S.D., (2009) 'In the Shadow of Democracy Promotion: Strategic Manipulation, International Observers, and Election Boycotts', *Comparative Political Studies*, 42(3), pp. 392–415.

Bermeo, N., (2010) 'Interests, Inequality, and Illusion in the Choice for Fair Elections', *Comparative Political Studies*, 43(8–9), pp. 1119–1147.

Bermeo, N., (2016). 'On Democratic Backsliding', *Journal of Democracy*, 27(1), pp. 5–19.

Bleck, J. and Michelitch, K., (2015) 'The 2012 Crisis in Mali: Ongoing Empirical State Failure', *African Affairs*, 114(457), pp. 598–623.

Bleck, J. and Van de Walle, N., (2011) 'Parties and Issues in Francophone West Africa: Towards a Theory of Non-mobilization', *Democratization*, 18(5), pp. 1125–1145.

Bogaards, M., (2013) 'Reexamining African Elections', *Journal of Democracy*, 24(4), pp. 151–160.

Bratton, M. and Van de Walle, N., (1994) 'Neopatrimonial Regimes and Political Transitions in Africa', *World Politics*, 46(4), pp. 453–489.

Bratton, M. and Van de Walle, N., (1997) *Democratic Experiments in Africa: Regime Transitions in Comparative Perspective*. Cambridge: Cambridge University Press.

Call, C.T. and Cook, S.E., (2003) 'On Democratization and Peacebuilding', *Global Governance*, 9(2), pp. 233–246.

Charbonneau, B., (2017) 'Intervention in Mali: Building Peace between Peacekeeping and Counterterrorism', *Journal of Contemporary African Studies*, 35(4), pp. 415–431.

Charbonneau, B., (2020) 'Counterinsurgency Governance in the Sahel', *Bulletin FrancoPaix*, 5, 1, pp. 3–6. [online]. Available at: https://ffm-online.org/wp-content/uploads/2020/04/Charbonneau-Bulletin-FrancoPaix-vol5n1_eng.pdf (Accessed: 1 July 2021).

Charbonneau, B. and Sears, J., (2014) 'Faire la guerre pour un Mali démocratique: l'intervention militaire française et la gestion des possibilités politiques contestées', *Canadian Journal of Political Science*, 47(3), pp. 597–619.

Cheeseman, N., (2015) *Democracy in Africa: Successes, Failures, and the Struggle for Political Reform*. Cambridge: Cambridge University Press.

Cheeseman, N., Lynch, G. and Wallis, J., (2018) 'Digital Dilemmas: The Unintended Consequences of Election Technology', *Democratization*, 25(8), pp. 1397–1418.

Colleta, N.J., Kostner, M. and Wiederhofer, I., (1996). *The Transition from War to Peace in sub-Saharan Africa*. World Bank Series on Directions in Development. Washington, DC: World Bank.

Debos, M., (2018) 'Electoral Biometrics in Chad: Techno-Political Controversies and Imaginaries of Modernity', *Politique Africaine*, 4(152), pp. 101–120.

Doss, A., (2020) *A Peacekeeper in Africa: Learning from UN Interventions in Other People's Wars*. Boulder, CO: Lynne Rienner.

Doyle, M.W., (2005) 'Three Pillars of the Liberal Peace', *American Political Science Review*, 99(3), pp. 463–466.

Duerksen, M., (2019) 'The Testing of Benin's Democracy', *Spotlight Africa Center for Strategic Studies*, 29 May. [online]. Available at: https://africacenter.org/spotlight/the-testing-of-benin-democracy/ (Accessed: 1 July 2021).

Edgell, A.B., Mechkova, V., Altman, D., Bernhard, M., Lindberg, S.I., (2018) 'When and Where Do Elections Matter? A Global Test of the Democratization by Elections Hypothesis, 1900–2010', *Democratization*, 25(3), pp. 422–444.

Eizenga, D., (2018) *Managing Political Liberalization after Multiparty Elections: Regime Trajectories in Burkina Faso, Chad, and Senegal*. PhD diss., University of Florida.

Halperin, M.H., Siegle, J.T. and Weinstein, M.M., (2010) *The Democracy Advantage: How Democracies Promote Prosperity and Peace*. New York, NY: Routledge.

Howard, M.M. and Roessler, P.G., (2006) 'Liberalizing Electoral Outcomes in Competitive Authoritarian Regimes', *American Journal of Political Science*, 50(2), pp. 365–381.

Hyde, S.D. and O'Mahony, A., (2010) 'International Scrutiny and Pre-Electoral Fiscal Manipulation in Developing Countries', *Journal of Politics*, 72, pp. 690–704.

Joseph, R., (eds.) 1999) *State, Conflict, and Democracy in Africa*. Boulder, CO: Lynne Rienner Publishers.

Lindberg, S.I., (2006) *Democracy and Elections in Africa*. Baltimore, MD: Johns Hopkins University Press.

Lynch, G., Cheeseman, N. and Willis, J., (2019) 'From Peace Campaigns to Peaceocracy: Elections, Order and Authority in Africa', *African Affairs*, 118(473), pp. 603–627.

Mac Ginty, R. and Richmond, O.P., (2013) 'The Local Turn in Peace Building: A Critical Agenda for Peace', *Third World Quarterly*, 34(5), pp. 763–783.

Mainwaring, S., Brinks, D. and Pérez-Liñán, A., (2007) 'Classifying Political Regimes in Latin America, 1945–2004', in Munck, G.L., (ed.) *Regimes and Democracy in Latin America: Theories and Methods*. New York, NY: Oxford University Press, pp. 123–160.

Marinov, N. and Goemans, H., (2014) 'Coups and Democracy', *British Journal of Political Science*, 44, pp. 799–825.

Matanock, A.M., (2018) *Electing Peace: from Civil Conflict to Political Participation*. New York, NY: Cambridge University Press.

McNamee, T. and Muyangwa, M., (eds.) (2021) *The State of Peacebuilding in Africa: Lessons Learned for Policymakers and Practitioners*. Cham, Switzerland: Palgrave Macmillan.

Morse, Y.L., (2017) 'Electoral Authoritarianism and Weak States in Africa: The Role of Parties Versus Presidents in Tanzania and Cameroon', *International Political Science Review*, 39(1), pp. 114–129.

Oduro, F., (2021) 'The Changing Nature of Elections in Africa: Impact on Peacebuilding', in Mcnamee, T. and Muyangwa, M., (eds.) *The State of Peacebuilding in Africa: Lessons Learned for Policymakers and Practitioners*. Cham, Switzerland: Palgrave Macmillan.

Osaghae, E.E., (2005) 'The State of Africa's Second Liberation', *Interventions: International Journal of Postcolonial Studies*, 7(1), pp. 1–20.

Ottaway, M., (1997) 'African Democratization and the Leninist Option', *The Journal of Modern African Studies*, 35(1), pp. 1–15.

Ottaway, M., (2003) 'Promoting Democracy After Conflict: The Difficult Choices', *International Studies Perspectives*, 4, pp. 314–322.

Pailey, R. N., and Harris, D., (2020) '"We Don't Know Who Be Who": Post-party Politics, Forum Shopping and Liberia's 2017 Elections', *Democratization*, 27(5), pp. 50–68.

Patuel, F., (2020) 'Civic Space Backsliding Ahead of Elections in Francophone West Africa Case Studies: Benin, Côte d'Ivoire, Guinea, Niger and Togo', *CIVICUS*, October, pp. 1–61.

Richmond, O.P., (2015) 'The Dilemmas of a Hybrid Peace: Negative or Positive?', *Cooperation and Conflict*, 50(1), pp. 50–68.

Siegle, J. and Cook, C., (2020) 'Circumvention of Term Limits Weakens Governance in Africa', *Infographic*, Africa Center for Strategic Studies, 14 September. [online]. Available at: https://africacenter.org/spotlight/circumvention-of-term-limits-weakens-governance-in-africa/ (Accessed: 1 July 2021).

Siegle, J., and Cook, C., (2021) 'Presidential Term Limits Key to Democratic Progress and Security in Africa', *Orbis*, 65(3), pp. 467–482.

Siegle, J. and Eizenga, D., (2020) 'Mali: Beware the "Popular" Coup', *AllAfrica.com*, 31 August. [online]. Available at: https://allafrica.com/stories/202008310790.html (Accessed: 1 July 2021).

Soares de Oliveira, R., (2011) 'Illiberal Peacebuilding in Angola', *Journal of Modern African Studies*, 49(2), pp. 287–314.

Turner, J.M., Nelson, S. and Mahling-Clark, K., (1998) 'Mozambique's Vote for Democratic Governance', in Kumar, K., (ed.) *Post-Conflict Elections, Democratization, and International Assistance*. Boulder, CO: Lynne Rienner, pp. 153–176.

Villalón, L.A. and VonDoepp, P., (eds.) (2005) *The Fate of Africa's Democratic Experiments: Elites and Institutions*. Bloomington, IN: Indiana University Press.

Wallis, J., (2014) *Constitution Making during State Building*. Cambridge: Cambridge University Press.

Wallis, J., (2018) 'Is There Still a Place for Liberal Peacebuilding?' in Wallis, J., Kent, L., Forsyth, M., Dinnen, S. and Bose, S., (eds.) *Hybridity on the Ground in Peacebuilding and Development: Critical Conversations*. Canberra, Australia: Australian National University Press, pp. 83–98.

World Bank, (2011) *World Development Report 2011: Conflict, Security, and Development*. Washington, DC: World Bank.

# 12
# THE CLIMATE CRISIS AND ITS CHALLENGES FOR AFRICAN PEACEBUILDING

*Bruno Charbonneau, Peter Läderach, Marc-André Boisvert, Tatiana Smirnova, Grazia Pacillo, Alessandro Craparo, and Ignacio Madurga*

## Introduction

Studies on the connections between climate change and security, conflict dynamics, conflict resolution, and environmental peacebuilding have steadily increased since the mid-2000s. This interest reflects how climate change has been increasingly characterized as a security issue. The UN Security Council acknowledges that climate change can act as a "threat multiplier", aggravating certain stresses that are often at the heart of conflicts such as poverty, weak institutions, inadequate access to information or resources, and high unemployment (UN Secretary-General 2009). There is a general and vague consensus on the effects of climate change on social systems and on security, but the relationship largely depends on how one defines security and whose security one is concerned about. Academics have focused on whether climate change leads to armed conflict, but there is no consensus on what climate security means for practice, policy, and intervention. Policy statements, think tank reports, and academic debates depict different conceptions and understandings of the relationship and thus often disagree on what constitute appropriate policy responses (Busby 2021; McDonald 2013). Scholars of environmental peacebuilding have sought to escape the narrow analytical focus on environmental- or climate-induced conflicts by positing that cooperation on environmental problems can contribute to peacebuilding (Ide et al. 2021). Yet, environmental peacebuilding does not come without adverse effects or a "dark side" (Ide 2020).

This chapter brings together conflict analysts and climate scientists to examine the challenges and risks that the climate crisis represents for conflict, violence, and system fragility. We proceed from the general to the specific. First, we briefly examine the literature on the relationship between climate change and armed conflicts, and then on that relationship in the context of the West African Sahel. This allows us to insert an abstract discussion of climate-conflict debates into the historical context of the Sahel, thus highlighting the inherent politics of the academic and policy fields of "climate security" and how it can inform practices of intervention. Second, we present an overview of the multiple impact pathways through which climate change and variability have or can act as a threat multiplier in the case of Niger. We emphasize the effects of climate change and variability on local governance practices and mechanisms, on how Nigerien adaptation, mitigation, and resilience to climate change affect or transform Nigerien conflict management mechanisms, processes, and practices. These mechanisms, processes, and practices were built historically through consensus, collaboration, competition, and/or conflict, but the climate crisis imposes new stresses as it also accelerates the timeline for their necessary transformation. Next, we analyse the last few years of a deteriorating security situation. The regional context of the increasing destabilizing effects of transnational armed group activities and significant international military forces (French, American, European, UN) engaging these armed groups has strained or ruined local conflict resolution mechanisms, which does not bode well for building a climate resilient peace. Addressing the relationship between the climate crisis and conflict dynamics must be planned in a context where modes of governance are called into question, if not outright being transformed, by violent extremist groups or by the military interventions of international actors.

Our method is a case study of Niger, with a focus on the regions of Tillaberi and Tahoua. These regions depend on rain-fed agriculture and livestock, making Nigerien pastoralists and smallholders particularly vulnerable to climate variability, especially droughts and floods. They also face high fragility, conflict, and violence (FCV) risks with local, national, and regional roots that are found in the transnational dynamics of the Malian conflict that began in 2012. Niger's Tillaberi and Tahoua regions present a critical case study on the relationship between climate change and FCV risks in West Africa, connecting local grievances to transnational threats. They also provide an original case study beyond the usual suspects of climate security research: Darfur, Syria, and South Sudan. We describe the multifactorial processes and dynamics of regional destabilization and climate change in Niger, where actors threaten local resilience, peacebuilding efforts, and conflict management mechanisms.

We conclude that despite the role of climate change as a potential factor of FCV risks, historical legacies and political processes and practices have a crucial impact on how state and local communities face, respond to, or overlook climate variability. A climate-change focus should thus not overshadow politico-historical analyses. The Niger example demonstrates that climate-induced tensions do not lead necessarily to armed conflict. It illustrates how state, people, and communities react to climate variability largely depends on structures and relationships of power. Yet, Niger also shows that a significant challenge comes from transnational conflicts meshing with local dynamics, which interferes with efforts at addressing the climate crisis.

## Brief Literature Review on the Interlink Between Climate and Conflict

A prominent approach emphasizes the threat that climate change poses to the security of the state. From a national security (or state-centric) perspective, this approach draws from early 1990s research that emphasized climate, demography, resource scarcity, and environmental stresses as conducive to armed conflict (see Kaplan 1994; Homer-Dixon 1999; for a critical engagement with its evolution, see Dalby 2009, 2020; Swain and Öjendal 2018). The approach was embraced by the United States (the Pentagon) and several US think tanks that pointed to the notion of "threat multiplier". Others talk in terms of "risk multiplier", "risk amplifier", or "conflict catalyst" (Ivleva et al. 2019; CNA Military Advisory Board 2014; Dion 2016). Overall, the "threat multiplier" approach focuses on how states could or should adapt to the effects of climate change (CNA 2007; Busby 2007). Several academics challenged this approach on the basis that it emphasizes military threats and responses, and thus carries the danger of securitization or militarization. Hence, it is often considered ill-suited to address the complex relationships and dynamics between climate and security (van Schaik et al. 2020; Brzoska 2009), while critics argue that it might even lead to powerful states waging endless wars in fragile states (Rogers 2021).

Experts have criticized the "threat multiplier" approach for its inaccuracies and its recourse to causal explanations (see e.g. the debate on Syria; Selby et al. 2017). While the policy and think tank worlds at times still draw from, and policymakers justify decisions based on, causal models (Charbonneau and Smirnova 2021), there is greater awareness of the risks both of climate change and of searching for direct causal links. Climate change can exacerbate existing socio-economic and political conditions, vulnerabilities, and risks that are generally linked to conflict and violence. Indirect causal pathways are another approach that points to the effects of climate change on agriculture, economic growth, migration flows, or state capacity (Koubi 2019; Barnett and Adger 2007; Mobjork, Krampe and Taris 2020). Yet, the identification of indirect causal pathways is only a first step that must be followed by in-depth conflict analyses given that conflict can occur without links to climate change, while climate change challenges and stresses do not necessarily lead to conflict (Burke, Hsiang and Miguel 2015).

For instance, adverse climatic conditions and extreme weather events can reduce economic output and growth and negatively impact agricultural production and productivity, which then have detrimental effects on socio-economic and socio-political relations (Hidalgo et al. 2010; Burke, Hsiang and Miguel 2015; Schlenker and Lobell 2010; Hsiang, Meng and Cane 2011; Lobell, Schlenker and Costa-Roberts 2011). Developing countries that are highly dependent on the agricultural or livestock sectors are thus more at risk (Burke, Hsiang and Miguel 2015; Dell, Jones and Olken 2012; 2014). Another example are climate-related disasters that have become the most relevant factor influencing migration, accounting for 61.5% of total displacements, while 38.5% were induced by armed conflict (Institute for Economics and Peace 2019). Migration is an adaptation strategy for people to cope with changing climate conditions (Mobjork, Krampe and Taris 2020; Reuveny 2007), but the community and policy response to such migration has been argued to factor into conflict dynamics (Barnett and Adger 2007; Reuveny 2007; Swain 1996).

The responses to (and the effects on human security of) climate change partly depend on state capacity and preparedness (Ubelejit 2014; Barnett and Adger 2007). Climate change and variability are likely to hinder the administrative capacity of the state to act, increasing the costs of the public provision of goods and services, the state's ability to analyse and manage risks and crises and to respond to the needs of citizens and to resolve social conflicts. In those contexts, the provision of essential goods and services such as water, education, or healthcare could be curtailed, further impacting human security (Barnett and Adger 2007; Adger et al. 2014; Ubelejit 2014). In several ways, this can induce a feedback loop, as fragile states that cannot respond effectively to climate variability could see their vulnerabilities worsen (Ndaruzaniye et al. 2010) and their capacities to resolve or prevent conflict deteriorate (Adger et al. 2014; Stewart and Fitzgerald 2001; Ndaruzaniye et al. 2010; Ivleva et al. 2019).

## Brief Literature Review on Climate and Conflict in Sahelian Countries

Despite greater awareness of the relationship between climate change, security, armed conflict, and the prospects for peace, the academic field of climate security has yet to offer insights into what to do about it precisely, notably in the context of fragile states with low capacity and fragmented political systems (Busby 2021; McDonald 2021). In the case of Sahelian countries,[1] this lack of insight is evident both in policy terms (or often lack of policy) and in the reactions to the climate war/security narrative of many Sahelian specialists. Yet, the increasing attention to climate change is not without consequences.

For several Sahelian country experts (in the social sciences and humanities), the climate-change or climate-security narrative overshadows other causes and crowds out politico-historical analyses (Benjaminsen 2016). Even the International Crisis Group (ICG) published a briefing that argued that in Mali, Niger, and Burkina Faso, the theory "that global warming is leading to a reduction in available resources and, consequently, an increase in violence" does not seem supported by the evidence. The ICG accepts that climate change contributes to the transformation of the region's agro-pastoral systems, but "the direct relationship sometimes posited between global warming and dwindling resources, on one hand, and growing violence, on the other, does not help policymakers formulate appropriate responses" (ICG 2020b).

Yet, among policymakers, the Sahelian climate-desertification-conflict nexus still resonates, as it sustains and contributes to the securitization of climate change and "threat multiplier" approaches (Benjaminsen and Svarstad 2021, 184–201; also Selby and Hoffman 2014). Climate-induced resource scarcity and biosphere degradation and overexploitation are commonly associated with conflict. However, as shown by Nobel Prize winner and economist Elinor Ostrom – who studied the interaction of people and ecosystems throughout her career – the management of scarce resources can lead to cooperation between groups of people, even without government intervention (Ostrom 1990). Conflict is far from preordained.

The idea that "the Sahel is caught in a vicious cycle of land degradation and drought" dates back to the colonial period (Benjaminsen and Hiernaux 2019) and was consolidated during the droughts of the 1970s and 1980s, notably by international humanitarian non-governmental organizations (NGOs; Mann 2015). It should not be surprising, then, that when it comes to discussing climate change and policy in the Sahel, the climate-desertification-conflict narrative endures, despite the climate research that shows increasing rain patterns since the big drought of the mid-1980s and the greening of the Sahel (Fensholt et al. 2017). The scepticism to the climate security narrative of Sahelian specialists comes partly from the resilience of the Sahelian vegetation to drought (Hiernaux et al. 2021), partly from the securitization effect that it has on understandings of intercommunal conflict (Kulesza 2021), and partly from the oversimplification that can gloss over historical roots, political dynamics, power relationships, and the political economy of conflicts (ICG 2020b).

As the following section shows, using the case of Niger, farmer-herder or intercommunal conflicts in the Sahel have not been primarily driven by increasing resource scarcity, identity politics, demographics, climate change, or their combination. While these variables play a role, and while climate change is and will transform the physical environment, the biosphere, and human structural conditions (for agriculture, water access, grazing rights, land tenure, etc.), ultimately for conflicts to turn violent, Sahelian specialists argue that it is necessary to analyse their historical roots; the political economy of land tenure and governance; the power relations and structure that frame and manage social, economic, and political conflicts; and the political ecology of local governance (Benjaminsen and Ba 2019; Bøås and Strazzari 2020).

## Niger: An Impact Pathway Analysis

Niger is highly vulnerable to climate disruptions with relative low levels of readiness (University of Notre Dame 2019). The climate in Niger is expected to become more erratic and is projected to see rises in temperatures, increases in rainfall variability, intensity, and the number of floods (BMZ 2017; USAID 2017). These climate stressors will critically impact Niger's political economy, which is dependent on climate-sensitive sectors such as agriculture, livestock, and fisheries (USAID 2014b; FEWS-NET 2005).

Indeed, agriculture alone contributes to 39.2% of Niger's GDP and employs more than 80% of the workforce (BMZ 2017). Rainfall variability is impacting crop production which, in turn, is having a negative effect on food availability (FEWS-NET 2019). Increase in temperatures and rainfall variability negatively impact water availability as well as forage (water points) and pasture production, which reduces livestock productivity and calving rates (USAID 2017; FEWS-NET 2019). Some of Niger's main staple crops will be affected by climate disruptions, as the large majority is rain-fed agriculture while less than 1% of the cropland is irrigated (BMZ 2017). The production of millet and sorghum will continue to be negatively affected by rainfall variability and rising temperatures (USAID 2017; 2018; FAO 2020; Ben Mohamed, Van Duivenbooden and Abdoussallam 2002). This is particularly worrisome, considering that millet and sorghum represent around 85% of Niger's total food production and provide 80%–90% of the energy requirements of Nigeriens (Ben Mohamed, Van Duivenbooden and Abdoussallam 2002). Likewise, the yields of certain cash crops like groundnut and cowpea are likely to decrease in the coming years (Duivenbooden, Abdoussallam and Ben Mohamed 2002).

Climate change and variability will continue impacting farmers and pastoralist communities in north-western Niger, where they already live with other vulnerabilities such as food insecurity, poverty, and high levels of violence. Agadez, Tillaberi, and Tahoua are among the regions most affected by food insecurity and malnutrition, with the northern pastoralist zones of Tillaberi and Tahoua and the western part of Agadez being the most affected by food consumption quality and quantity deficits (FAO 2019). Poverty rates in Tillaberi and Tahoua are 43.2% and 38.5%, respectively (Razafimandimby, Nguyen and Nshimiyimana 2020).

## *Impact Pathways*

The analysis of the consequences of climate disruptions on agriculture, livestock, and fisheries must be combined with an analysis of Niger's political economy and its history, punctuated by military coups (1974, 1996, 1999, 2010) and armed rebellions (Tuareg in 1990–1995 and 2007–2009; Toubou uprisings in the mid-1990s, 2006, and 2016). The colonial history of Niger and post-colonial struggles for power (at local, national, regional, and international levels) explain the durability of structures of social and regional inequalities. These struggles have left bordering areas (such as the Diffa, Tillaberi, Tahoua, and Agadez regions) relatively marginalized, with limited access to basic state services, but deeply integrated within regional political economies of borderlands and peripheries with Mali, Burkina Faso, Libya, and Algeria (and countries of the Lake Chad region for the region of Diffa). Marginalization from central state authority (Niamey) also meant the reinforcement of processes and structures of localized and transnational systems of governance and conflict resolution mechanisms (Mohamadou 2018; De Sardan and Tidjani Alou 2009).

One of the most important and politically sensitive issues for communities living in these areas is the access to land and water points. They represent critical resources both for farmers and herders. Pastoralist communities have historically coped with climate variability by migrating southwards during the dry season in search of better pasture, while staying or moving back north during the rainy season. Transhumance is a means of livelihood but also an important form and source of identity, a set of practices that reinforce social ties between different pastoralist communities like Peul (Fulani), Tuareg, Arabs, and Toubou, but also between pastoralists and farmers. The access to land and water points has been regulated by public policies and traditional customary law. The latter is important in cases of disagreement and inter- or intra-community conflicts. However, government policies have tended to favour the development of agriculture, thus often undermining pastoralists' access to land and partly impeding their mobility as an essential tool of adaptation (De Sardan and Mohamadou 2019; Mohamadou 2004; McKune and Silva 2013; Thébaud and Batterbury 2001).

Law No. 61–5 of 1961 established a demarcation for pastoralist activities (the so-called pastoral zone), forbidding agriculture in that area. Yet, increasing land pressure in the south and the rise in rainfall in the 1960s and 1990s pushed farmers northwards, leading to an expansion of agriculture (USAID 2014b), and thus creating contested de facto "grey" areas. The expansion of agriculture was often done at the expense of livestock corridors and pastureland that were delineated in the Law No. 61–5, leading to tensions (USAID 2014a; 2014b; UNOWAS 2018). A Rural Code was developed in 1993 to institutionalize a legal framework that would manage natural resources and mitigate the effects of climate variability. However, its implementation was highly deficient, and led to herder communities (especially Tuareg and Peul) believing that Niamey could not or did not want to protect their livelihoods (USAID 2014a; 2014b). These issues combined with frustrations over political representation and economic policy (notably revenue sharing from uranium production and the effects of the pollution on local communities; Benjaminsen 2008; Grégoire 2011; MALOCA 2016; Mongay Font and Meneses 2002).

The political stage was thus set decades before the Tuareg uprising of the 1990s. Though the historical context explains much about the roots of the 1990s rebellion, the immediate causes were the unequal distribution of social, economic, and political resources coming from the uranium extractive industry. It was also a moment of important political transformation for Niger. Following the military suppression of the student demonstration of 9 February 1990, political authorities announced the beginning of a *multipartisme* system (December 1990) and the organization of the National Conference (July–November 1991). The 1995 peace agreement promised financial and technical support for the northern regions as an integral part of the decentralization process. However, its implementation met with serious difficulties and exacerbated feelings of abandonment. Another rebellion broke out in 2007 that was settled in 2009.

The rebellions in the Agadez region, the uprisings of Toubou pastoralists in the areas of Manga and Kawar, and the relative instability of the Tillaberi region in the mid-1990s led to the formation of Peul self-defense groups that also felt politically and economically marginalized. Years of consultations were needed to adopt Ordinance No. 2010–029 of 20 May 2010 on pastoralism. One of its major contributions was the recognition of pastoral mobility by article 3, stipulating that "mobility is a fundamental right of pastoralists, nomadic pastoralists and transhumant herders" and that "this right is recognized and guaranteed by the State and the local authorities". However, the Ordinance is still poorly implemented. As of 2017, only 14 decrees had been passed. Furthermore, definitions of *point d'attache* or "the right to land" remain unclear in practice. Judgements on the "right to land" or access to water points are at times done on a case-by-case basis by local chiefs whose legitimacy may be in dispute. Local chiefs are perceived as instruments of the central government, a political party, or armed groups. Questions over the legitimacy of national and local authorities are particularly problematic in the Tillaberi and Tahoua regions (ICG 2020a).

Since 2010, both the security and the climate situations have continued to deteriorate. Adverse climate conditions affected fodder production in 2019, leading to a 11.3 million tonne fodder deficit that especially impacted the centre-west of Tillaberi and Tahoua (FAO 2020). The scarcity of pasture increasingly forces certain herders to sell some of their livestock during the dry season at a lower price in order to buy fodder to feed their animals; this temporarily solves the problem but depletes the income of pastoralists in the long term. Considering the existing imbalance between supply and demand of animal feed, rising prices negatively impact herders' income (Bøås, Cissé and Mahamane 2020; UNOWAS 2018). It should be underlined that the trend in the Sahel and West Africa region is an expansion of agricultural land from 3% to 6% per year, which usually affects grazing areas and the *couloirs de passage* that are progressively being reduced (Kamuanga et al. 2008). Reducing pasture areas can force pastoralists to move southwards earlier, into agricultural zones before harvest, damaging the crops and contributing to the increase in farmer-herder tensions (UNOWAS 2018).

In this context, there are several pathways that can exacerbate existing socio-economic risks and vulnerabilities and potentially aggravating FCV risks in Niger, but there are also several points of intervention for adaptation strategies (see Figure 12.1). Hence, there is an enormous need for developing adaptation strategies that reduce people's climate vulnerability as it affects livelihoods (Heinrigs 2010). However, as we elaborate in the next section, the capacity to adapt to the effects of climate change and variability has been undermined by the levels of violence and insecurity that frustrate the coping capacity of states, communities, and individuals (Adger et al. 2014; Stewart and Fitzgerald 2001; Ndaruzaniye et al. 2010). The ongoing transnational violence in the western regions of Tillaberi and Tahoua and the state's reliance on counterterrorist tactics are undermining the efforts of local communities to implement survival strategies and conflict resolution (DNPGCA 2020; FAO 2020). Among other things, the influx of refugees from Mali (around 60,000) as well as a subsequent increase of internally displaced persons in the Tillaberi and Tahoua regions (up to almost 140,000) adds important pressure to social systems (UNHCR 2021b).

## Conflict Analysis of Tillaberi and Tahoua

This section is dedicated to understanding how conflict dynamics has impacted modes of governance in the regions of Tillaberi and Tahoua, two neighboring yet separate administrative regions that share a social, political, and economic context and that face similar conflict dynamics (see Table 12.1). Risks and vulnerabilities in these regions, despite local roots, are tied to transnational dynamics that are more complex than an opposition between local and global. In this context, prior to diving into an in-depth dynamic of the two regions, it is important to understand the transnational and transregional dynamics that influenced the conflict.

First, the meaning of "local" cannot be limited to the political borders set at independence (Boilley 2019). The division of communities along the Mali-Niger border has not cut important social and economic ties that communities maintain. On several occasions, just as humans and cattle cross borders daily, conflict between communities crossed and spread beyond the official border. In 2018, the Malian region of Menaka saw a spike in violence: from June to December 2018, 32% of the violent incidents and 27% of the civilians killed were carried out and spilled over into Niger as kin communities protected themselves (ACLED 2021).

Second, conflict actors are often also "violent entrepreneurs" (Bøås, Cissé and Mahamane 2020) with transnational connections and reach. In the Tillaberi and Tahoua regions, armed groups affiliated to the Islamic State in the Greater Sahara (ISGS) and to a lesser extent to al-Qaeda in the Islamic Maghreb (AQIM) provide limited governance in their areas of operations (Raineri 2020). Their presence can be perceived as "glocal" (Marret 2008), given that despite their adherence to global jihad, they maintain and rely on solid connections to the local, pulling strings and influencing local dynamics. They can use violence, but they also exploit existing fault lines to pursue their objectives and build local legitimacy. They depend on the proximity or connections between strongholds: they spread slowly like rhizomes, moving from stronghold to stronghold in attempts at expanding into new areas (Frowd 2020).

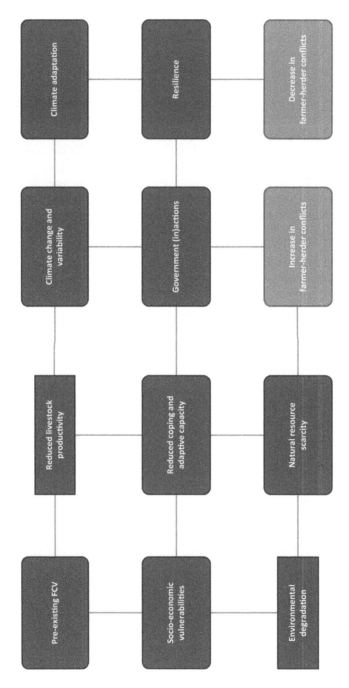

Figure 12.1 Conflict impact pathways

Table 12.1 Sources of conflict in the Tahoua and Tillaberi regions

| | |
|---|---|
| **Local level** | |
| Access to resources | Access to water points and grazing lands carries potential conflict for herder-farmer relations, while the water points and grazing land "change/move" due to climate change. |
| Struggles for local governance | Modes of governance are being challenged by changing power relations, notably due to new actors, especially armed groups. |
| **National level** | |
| Defending sovereignty | Niger's government faces insurgencies and conflicts in the tri-border area, in the south-east (Nigeria-Chad), and to the north-east (Libya). |
| Insecurity and the state's policy autonomy | Niger's government is working to contain or eliminate the threat of armed groups, partly through numerous partnerships with international and regional states that can limit its policy autonomy. |
| Civil-military relations | More international security intervention and actors translate into more "security rents" over which Nigerien military and political compete. Overall, such rents have encouraged counterterrorist approaches and solutions, at times leading to the indiscriminate use of force by Nigerien security forces against civilian populations. |
| **Transnational level** | |
| Fighting jihadist groups | ISGS and JNIM compete for control over territories and population, offer (to some extent) alternative modes of governance, and thus challenge the state's legitimacy. |
| Curbing international migration | Increasing external pressure (from Europe) on Niger to control, manage, and reduce migration flows is transforming patterns of mobility in north-western Africa. |
| Defense of kin communities | Borderland communities and livelihoods transcend borders, requiring interstate cooperation and regional conflict management and resolution mechanisms. |
| Control of traffic routes | The regional political economy is dependent on changing traffic routes for both licit and illicit goods. Control over those routes involve, in part, a game of hide-and-seek between criminal and armed groups and state and state and international security forces (with the increasing use of drones for ISR activities). |

Third, and following on from the above, conflict dynamics in the Tillaberi and the Tahoua regions are linked to other conflicts and transnational dynamics. Agadez is one key site, as it attracts merchants, traffickers, criminals, and terrorist groups and is a center for funding and recruitment (Raineri 2018; Raineri and Strazzari 2021; Harmon 2014). The centrality of Agadez in regional and transborder dynamics – as a pole along the Libya-North Mali corridor – partly explains why international actors have focused their efforts on "stabilizing" Agadez through interrupting vital routes between Mali and Agadez as they go through Tillaberi and Tahoua. In this context, transnational and transregional dynamics means that actors that have no interests or limited footprint in the Tillaberi and Tahoua regions still impact local dynamics, even if they have no intention to do so. Few global actors understood this impact on local dynamics in the two regions until the conflict became salient (Harmon 2015; Frowd 2020; Raineri and Strazzari 2021). The existence of a transnational dimension is crucial to understanding the deterioration of the situation.

## *Tillaberi and Tahoua: A Chronology of Conflict*

As described in the previous section, the Tillaberi and Tahoua regions have developed at the periphery of state governance, meaning that governance, infrastructure, and security gaps remain (Bøås, Cissé and Mahamane 2020). Yet they have also developed local modes of governance that are potential sources or mechanisms of resilience to climate change but that have been challenged by transregional and transnational actors.

Data shows that the Tillaberi and Tahoua have been at the forefront of extreme weather (Fiorillo et al. 2018), with decades of cycles of droughts and floods that have progressively worsened. The Palmer Drought Severity Index (Figure 12.2) illustrates the extent and severity of drought in Tahoua from 1958, with both metrics increasing in intensity from the year 2000 onwards. The index captures temperature, precipitation, and evapotranspiration, which are particularly relevant for both farmers and herders. Before 2012, their communities had developed numerous tools to mitigate inter and intra-community conflicts. Local communities built and managed their own conflict resolution mechanisms and governance instruments. Since the 1990s, tensions have led to cycles of violence between the Tuareg, Dahoussak, Peul, and Zarma communities. On multiple occasions, local youth took arms to defend their respective community's grievances regarding resource management (especially land and water access; ICG 2019; Interviews with community leaders, 12 November 2018). National peace settlement mechanisms, including the Haute autorité pour la Consolidation de la Paix (HACP), observed these crises but remained largely uninvolved, as traditional leaders took the lead in solving disputes (Interview with governmental officials, Niamey, November 2018). Thus, customary and religious leaders have been at the center of a governance system that ensures a fair share of resources and conflict settlement mechanisms – even though these local modes of governance are not infallible.

While communities have known conflicts, prior to 2016 they were contained and short-lived. In Niger, armed conflict and violence exploded when the Malian conflict started spilling over, notably from Menaka and Gao. New sources of tension came from the Menaka border in early 2016, as rumours of attacks setting Dahoussaks against Peuls in Mali spread to Niger (Interview with local chief, Niamey, 13 November 2018). While tensions were simmering between communities, violence became apparent on 11 July 2017, when two Malian armed groups – the Mouvement pour le Salut de l'Azawad (MSA) and the Groupe d'Autodéfense Touareg Imghad et Allié (GATIA)[2] – launched a series of deadly transborder raids against Nigerien Peul communities, notably one in the Aderamboukane market. Operation Akawal was presented as an action to contain terrorism (Interviews with local leaders, Niamey, 12 November 2018). From that moment on, Niger's Peul leaders accused the government and international forces of supporting Malian armed groups to the detriment of Nigerien citizens.

At the time, in 2017–2018, the collaborative actions of the French Barkhane military force were increasingly interpreted and perceived by local communities as partial and supportive of the GATIA and MSA. In May 2018, Tuaregs allegedly linked to the GATIA kidnapped and killed Peul herders. The resulting chain reaction benefited ISGS, whose recruitment among Peul communities skyrocketed. In November 2018, Nigerien soldiers kidnapped a Tuareg leader with alleged links to ISGS, showing the complexity of affiliations of armed actors. ISGS launched another wave of retaliation that led to the attack of the Inates military base in April 2019. From November 2018 to March 2019, reported fatalities from attacks against civilians rose by a "startling" 500% compared to the same period in 2017 (ACLED 2019a).

Conflict moved from isolated villages to more densely populated places. On 10 December 2019, an attack against a military post near Inates brought the conflict to new heights. With

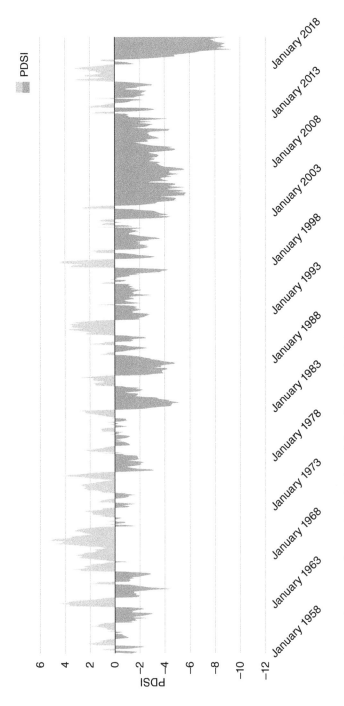

*Figure 12.2* Palmer Drought Severity Index (PDSI) for Tahoua, 1958–2020

30,000 inhabitants, the attack on Inates was a significant transformation of conflict dynamics and levels of violence (Crisis Group 2019). Several weeks later, in January 2020, another attack occurred on a military position in Chinagodrar, killing at least 89 soldiers. Both attacks were claimed by the ISGS. This launched a cycle of retaliation. In July 2020, the Commission Nationale des Droits de l'Homme (CNDH) reported more than 100 summary executions by the Niger military (CNDH 2020). The civilian toll increased, as communities faced attacks from both security forces and armed groups. In January–March 2021, several violent security incidents implicating armed militias groups were reported both in the Tillaberi and Tahoua regions (WhatsApp discussions, Protection Cluster/Niger officer, June 2021). In March 2021, an attack by the ISGS in Banibangou killed an estimated 58 civilians. It was followed by several others that led to significant internal displacements as the crisis spread quickly, notably in the Tahoua region where violence had remained rare until then.

## *Fragile Conflict Resolution Mechanisms*

Prior to the start of the Malian conflict in 2012, intercommunal conflicts were rooted in livelihood concerns between herders and farmers, and between herders who must share grazing fields and water points. Cattle theft was perceived by locals as the most important security threat, as the economic impact could ruin a family (Interview with Peul leaders, Niamey, 13 November 2018; WhatsApp conversation, 12 February 2021). Distribution and sharing resources processes are a crucial purpose of local governance with, in some instances, codified practices interpreted by traditional leaders. Governance, in this context, intends to ensure a fair allocation of resources among competing livelihoods.

Security actors have emphasized ethnicity as a narrative that pretends to explain the violence and conflicts. Nigerien authorities have focused and instrumentalized ethnic identities, often pointing out that ISGS predominantly recruits among Peuls. Soldiers taking part in one of the several Niger Armed Forces missions, Operation Dongo,[3] have been accused of eagerly "seeking vengeance" rather than trying to appease communities (Jeune Afrique 2017), thus contributing to the growing alienation of Peul communities. From our field interviews and research, divisions along ethnic lines can be distractions, often simplistic, and obscuring the ideological and political instrumentalization of ethnicity. Several leaders of ISGS are Dahoussak and Djerma, among other examples of diversity within groups (ICG 2020a, local analyst WhatsApp conversation, 12 October 2019). While ISGS recruitment occurs primarily in herding communities, jihadists have been efficient in identifying contentions within farming communities for recruitment purposes. Identifying and targeting existing tensions over allocation of resources has been the core recruitment strategy of the ISGS. ISGS has succeeded in instrumentalizing tensions over resources, the youth's lack of economic opportunities, and generational divides to offer alternatives, including the use of violence, to traditional conflict mechanisms. Malian armed groups have also taken sides and re-enforced ethnic cleavages, thus nurturing widening gaps between communities and enabling narratives of ethnic revenge.

The Tillaberi and Tahoua regions faced jihadist attacks before 2017, but they were scarce and external to local dynamics. They targeted governmental offices or military bases, not civilians. From 2013 until 2016, alleged MUJAO[4] elements were accused of conducting several strikes, notably against the Ouallam prison in 2014. Things started to drastically change when Malian-based armed groups, the MSA and GATIA, crossed the Nigerien border to chase alleged terrorists in the summer of 2017. While taking sides for Dahoussaks, they committed several abuses that exacerbated intercommunal tensions and helped ISGS local recruitment in northern Tillaberi (Molenaar and El Kamouni-Janssen 2017; New Humanitarian 2019).

Increasing competition about access to water and grazing lands had already created significant frictions (Communauté Peul, communiqué 2018, in possession of authors). While the MSA and GATIA acquired military experience and weapons from the Malian conflict, the ISGS had also refined its tactics on the Lake Chad "front". This was reflected in the use of improvised explosive devices (IEDs). Scarcely used before 2019, the number of exploding engines increased significantly in the Tillaberi region, with strong operational and device similarities with those found in eastern Niger and Nigeria (ACLED 2019b; Niger military, WhatsApp conversation, 2021).

The Nigerien government has struggled to adequately respond and prevent the deterioration of the security situation, while its armed forces are being accused of exactions against civilians. The state's limited presence and failure to curb violence have had the adverse side effect of contributing to the dynamics of violence and conflict. The Nigerien military has even proved unable to stop attacks on its positions, suffering important casualties. The Nigerien state has committed important resources and launched several military operations, including Operation Kouffra 3,[5] in collaboration with Barkhane, GATIA, and the MSA. Its military is allowed to pursue terrorist groups into Mali as part of the G5 Sahel. Yet, Nigerien security forces have maintained a minimal presence in the tri-border area, while being constantly accused of supporting one community against another. Rather than alleviating violence, the central government became the main target of jihadist attacks, with multiple deadly attacks against military positions. A Nigerien officer summarized the situation by stating: "we end up with this kind of situation when politicians do not take decisions" (Nigerien officer, Niamey, 15 November 2018). In the early 2010s, the Nigerien government passed several ordinances and decrees to protect pastoralist access to resources but ultimately continued to select who was deemed a legitimate actor for negotiation, thus often bypassing local and traditional actors who might have more legitimacy in the eye of local communities. Under these conditions, HACP mediation has struggled to execute and succeed in conflict resolution (Interview, Niger analyst, WhatsApp conversation, 19 September 2019).

## Competing Modes of Governance?

The climate crisis brings peculiar challenges to Niger's conflict management and resolution mechanisms. The post-2012 conflicts and increasing violence are the matter of immediate policy concerns but carry dire consequences for the resilience of regions like Tillaberi and Tahoua. More precisely, armed conflicts and the worsening of the regional security situation point to the transformation of modes of governance (Charbonneau 2021). National and local systems of governance have been largely unable to respond to violent extremist actors who have corroded social contracts and destabilized intercommunal relations of power.

So far, ISGS maintains its influence through terrorist activities, delivering little in terms of governance beyond the promise of protection. The killing of the chief of Tchomabangou in November 2019 represented a shift in local perception, as the Djerma community leader refused to pay zakat to the ISGS. Since then, the ISGS lost ground in Tillaberi and Tahoua to rival jihadist group JNIM, while Barkhane's airstrikes seriously decapitated the organization's leadership. Several reports show that the ISGS does not have the capacity or the ambition to enforce governance beyond the zakat, but still sees muzzling local opposition and terrorizing local as a viable strategy to remain dominant in the area (ICG 2020a). Meanwhile, civilian deaths at the border increased, with a rising percentage of the population believing that the Nigerien state also deploys terrorist-like tactics, thus contributing to intercommunal tensions (Local leader, WhatsApp conversation, 12 July 2021).

Traditional chieftaincies have, on several occasions, attempted to stop Nigerien youth from taking arms and joining the ISGS, but so far, such efforts have failed at curbing the spiral of violence. The call for conflict resolution is drowned by the violence of the ISGS and Malian armed groups. In the Tahoua region, the inability of both traditional leaders and national government to guarantee the protection of communities, especially as cattle theft has increased, has led to the creation of several self-defense militias whose loosely organized role became a serious alternative to consensual method or tool of governance (WhatsApp conversation, 28 July 2021). Thus, local actors demonstrate that they are not without agency, that they are not passive victims or silent bystanders, and that they can show resilience by adapting and creating new modes of governance.

## Conclusion

One of the key challenges is integrating climate security concerns peacebuilding activities. What does it mean to do peacebuilding under the transforming conditions brought on by climate change? The immediate concerns of peacebuilding and related conflict management practices are not readily compatible with the temporality of the climate crisis, the latter demanding long-term planning and prevention mechanisms and a fundamental transformation (or at least a rethinking) of academic research, policymaking, and program implementation.

As this chapter suggests, the extent to which climate variability and stresses affect conflict dynamics in Niger's Tillaberi and Tahoua regions is difficult to assess, given that (1) Sahelian countries have lived with and endured climate variability for centuries and (2) that Niger's recent instability, insecurity, and armed violence find their immediate causes in the ongoing Malian conflict. Climate variability has always been the background context of the political and economic development of post-colonial Niger and thus difficult to distinguish analytically.

Nevertheless, based on our analysis of conflict dynamics and the security situation, it seems reasonable to assume that the climate change–induced transformation of that background can sustain or exacerbate current conflict dynamics, just as it can create new ones – or at the very least, cause mass human suffering and misery. To resolve or prevent armed conflicts will require building *ecosystem resilience* based on the complex interrelationships of biosphere and human systems. Given that there is some degree of climate change that is "locked in", it is imperative to develop FCV risk analyses that inform policies and programs for ecosystem resilience (i.e. the capacity of ecosystems to sustain life across time and space). The focus on ecosystems would allow to formulate policies and programs that bridge the biosphere and human systems.

Yet, one of the key challenges remains the translation of this sort of analysis into peacebuilding activities. It is the problem of implementation: so what if climate change is another possible cause of conflict? We think that there are at least three things that must be done. One is to encourage further research – and fine-grained case studies (not only quantitative) – into unveiling the complexity of climate and security for informed decision-making. This requires not only regular and detailed analyses of the main impact pathways but also the creation of decision support tools that provide real-time and high temporal and spatial resolution evidence on the climate-security nexus.[6]

A second is the need to increase climate security sensitiveness of peacebuilding programs and investments. The lack of (or limited) implementation is particularly problematic because solutions that do not directly consider climate security risks can negatively impact people and communities, reinforcing vulnerabilities and inequalities and increasing conflict potential

(Krampe 2019). There is the need for developing regional, national, and subnational guidelines to integrate climate security risks into programmatic planning. These guidelines could help in gaining an adequate understanding of the contexts and identify appropriate climate security–sensitive strategies that integrate climate adaptation and peacebuilding approaches in environmental programming. Moreover, these guidelines will inform the design and implementation of integrated programming recommendations for specific contexts, improving interventions, research, policies, and investments to mitigate and prevent conflicts and reduce people's inequalities and vulnerabilities.

Last, and perhaps most relevant for African peacebuilding, there is an urgent need to better articulate the role of food systems in the climate crisis. For policies seeking to address pre-existing social, economic, or political insecurities to remain responsive to shifting climatic and ecological contexts – and to increase climate resilience – it is imperative that policy frameworks detect and evaluate how insecurities interact with climate change and variability. The New Climate for Peace report commissioned by the G7 foreign ministries identifies the unintended effects of climate policies as one of its seven core climate-fragility risks. It argues that adaptation projects bear the risk of leading to unintended negative effects on the economy and political stability, particularly in already fragile settings. The integration of a climate security–sensitive land, food, and water systems lens is crucial in ensuring coherence in these contexts. Climate Security Policy Coherence guidelines could support national and local policymakers on how to increase coherence across climate and peace programming to enhance the effectiveness of climate adaptation strategies in a gender-sensitive and socially equitable manner.

## Notes

1 The Sahel is defined in different ways by different people, governments, and organizations. For our discussion, we limit it to the G5 Sahel organization, comprising Burkina Faso, Mali, Niger, Mauritania, and Chad.
2 GATIA is a Malian Tuareg-led armed group and a signatory of the 2015 peace agreement as part of the Plateforme, the pro-government umbrella. MSA was created in 2016 as a splinter group of the Mouvement National pour la Libération de l'Azawad (MNLA), one of the Tuareg armed groups that started the 2011–2012 Tuareg rebellion.
3 This operation was launched in 2016 in collaboration with US special forces to curtail jihadist activities.
4 The Movement for the Unicity of Jihad in West Africa (MUJAO from its French acronym) was one of the several jihadist movements that controlled the north. MUJAO was an al-Qaeda-affiliated group that successfully controlled Gao and its region from March 2012 until the French Operation Serval forced them to abandon their position. MUJAO was believed to recruit primarily among local Peul and Songhay communities.
5 Kouffra 3 is one of the many operations involving different actors. These includes Operations Haw-Bi and Kouffra 1 and 2 as well as ad hoc operations in collaboration with US forces, G5 Sahel and Nigerien troops.
6 One set of tools responding to the need for rapid, real-time, but also accessible data and evidence is the Climate Security Observatory (CSO), one of the solutions proposed in Action Track 5 of the UN Food Systems Summit (UNFSS) Humanitarian-Development-Peace nexus, to be developed by CGIAR in partnership with multiple international and national stakeholders across Latin and Central America, Africa, and Southeast Asia.

## References

ACLED, (2019a) 'Political Violence Skyrockets In The Sahel According To Latest ACLED Data', *Press Release.* [online]. Available at: https://acleddata.com/2019/03/28/press-release-political-violence-skyrockets-in-the-sahel-according-to-latest-acled-data/ (Accessed: 24 October 2021).

ACLED, (2019b) 'Insecurity in Southwestern Burkina Faso in the Context of an Expanding Insurgency', *Press Release*. [online]. Available at: https://acleddata.com/2019/01/17/insecurity-in-southwestern-burkina-faso-in-the-context-of-an-expanding-insurgency/ (Accessed: 24 October 2021).

ACLED, (2021) 'Sahel 2021: Communal Wars, Broken Ceasefires, and Shifting Frontlines', *Report*. [online]. Available at: https://acleddata.com/2021/06/17/sahel-2021-communal-wars-broken-ceasefires-and-shifting-frontlines/ (Accessed: 24 October 2021).

Adger, W.N., Pulhin, J.M., Barnett, J., Dabelko, G.D., Hovelsrud, G.K., Levy, M., Oswald Spring, Ú. and Vogel, C.H., (2014) 'Human Security', in *Climate Change 2014: Impacts, Adaptation, and Vulnerability. Part A: Global and Sectoral Aspects. Contribution of Working Group II to the Fifth Assessment Report of the Intergovernmental Panel on Climate Change*. Cambridge and New York, NY: Cambridge University Press, pp. 755–791. [online]. Available at: www.ipcc.ch/pdf/assessment-report/ar5/wg2/WGIIAR5-Chap12_FINAL.pdf (Accessed: 24 October 2021).

Barnett, J. and Neil Adger, W., (2007) 'Climate Change, Human Security and Violent Conflict', *Political Geography*, 26(6), pp. 639–655. [online]. Available at: https://doi.org/10.1016/j.polgeo.2007.03.003 (Accessed: 24 October 2021).

Benjaminsen, T.A., (2008) 'Does Supply-Induced Scarcity Drive Violent Conflicts in the African Sahel? The Case of the Tuareg Rebellion in Northern Mali', *Journal of Peace Research*, 45(6), pp. 819–836.

Benjaminsen, T.A., (2016) 'Is Climate Change Causing Conflict in the Sahel?', *Climate Home News*, 8 September. [online]. Available at: Is climate change causing conflict in the Sahel? (climatechangenews.com) (Accessed: 24 October 2021).

Benjaminsen, T.A. and Ba, B., (2019) 'Why Do Pastoralists in Mali join jihadist Groups? A Political Ecological Explanation', *The Journal of Peasant Studies*, 46(1), pp. 1–20.

Benjaminsen, T.A. and Hiernaux, P., (2019) 'From Desiccation to Global Climate Change: A History of the Desertification Narrative in the West African Sahel, 1900–2018', *Global Environment*, 12, pp. 206–236.

Benjaminsen, T.A. and Svarstad, H., (2021) *Political Ecology: A Critical Engagement with Global Environmental Issues*. Cham: Palgrave Macmillan.

Ben Mohamed, A., Van Duivenbooden, N. and Abdoussallam, S., (2002) 'Impact of Climate Change on Agricultural Production in the Sahel – Part 1. Methodological Approach and Case Study for Millet in Niger', *Climatic Change*, 54(3), pp. 327–348. [online]. Available at: https://doi.org/10.1023/A:1016189605188 (Accessed: 25 October 2021).

BMZ, (2017) 'Climate Risk in Food for Peace Geographies: Niger'. [online]. Available at: 2017_USAID ATLAS_Climate Risks in Food for Peace Geographies Niger.pdf (climatelinks.org) (Accessed: 25 October 2021).

Bøås, M., Cissé, A.W. and Mahamane, L., (2020) 'Explaining Violence in Tillabéri: Insurgent Appropriation of Local Grievances?', *The International Spectator*, 55(4), pp. 118–132. [online]. Available at: https://doi.org/10.1080/03932729.2020.1833567 (Accessed: 25 October 2021).

Bøås, M. and Strazzari, F., (2020) 'Governance, Fragility and Insurgency in the Sahel: A Hybrid Political Order in the Making', *The International Spectator*, 55(4), pp. 1–17.

Boilley, P., (2019) 'Nord-Mali: Les Frontières Coloniales de l'Azawad', *Canadian Journal of African Studies/Revue Canadienne Des Études Africaines*, 53(3), pp. 469–484. [online]. Available at: https://doi.org/10.1080/00083968.2019.1667840 (Accessed: 25 October 2021).

Brzoska, M., (2009) 'The Securitization of Climate Change and the Power of Conceptions of Security', *Security and Peace*, 27, pp. 137–145.

Burke, M., Hsiang, S.M. and Miguel, E., (2015) 'Climate and Conflict', *Annual Review of Economics*, 7(1), pp. 577–617. [online]. Available at: https://doi.org/10.1146/annurev-economics-080614-115430 (Accessed: 25 October 2021).

Busby, J.W., (2007) *Climate Change and National Security: An Agenda for Action*. New York, NY: Council on Foreign Relations CSR 32.

Busby, J.W., (2021) 'Beyond Internal Conflict: The Emergent Practice of Climate Security', *Journal of Peace Research*, 58(1), pp. 186–194. [online]. Available at: https://doi.org/10.1177/0022343320971019 (Accessed: 25 October 2021).

Charbonneau, B., (2021) 'Counter-insurgency Governance in the Sahel', *International Affairs*, 97(6), pp. 1805–1823.

Charbonneau, B. and Smirnova, T., (2021) 'La sécurité climatique au Sahel: pour qui et pour quoi?', *Bulletin FrancoPaix*, 6(6), pp. 1–6.

CNA Corporation, (2007) *National Security and the Threat of Climate Change*. Alexandria: CNA Corporation.

CNA Military Advisory Board, (2014) *National Security and the Accelerating Risks of Climate Change*. Alexandria: CNA Corporation.

Commission Nationale des Droits de l'Homme (CNDH), (2020) *Rapport de mission d'enquête, d'investigation, de vérification et d'établissement des faits relatifs aux allégations portant sur la disparition de 102 personnes dans le département d'Ayorou, Région De Tillabéri*, Report. Niamey: CNDH Niger.

Dalby, S., (2009) *Security and Environmental Change*. Cambridge: Polity Press.

Dalby, S., (2020) *Anthropocene Geopolitics: Globalization, Security, Sustainability*. Ottawa: University of Ottawa Press.

Dell, M., Jones, B.F. and Olken, B.A., (2012) 'Temperature Shocks and Economic Growth: Evidence from the Last Half Century', *American Economic Journal: Macroeconomics*, 4(3), pp. 66–95. [online]. Available at: https://doi.org/10.1257/mac.4.3.66 (Accessed: 25 October 2021).

Dell, M., Jones, B.F. and Olken, B.A., (2014) 'What Do We Learn from the Weather? The New Climate-Economy Literature', *Journal of Economic Literature*, 52(3), pp. 740–798. [online]. Available at: https://doi.org/10.1257/jel.52.3.740 (Accessed: 25 October 2021).

De Sardan, J.-P.O. and Mohamadou, A., (2019) 'Eau Et Pâturages Au Niger: Conflits, Marchandisation Et Modes De Gouvernance', *Nomadic Peoples*, 23(2), pp. 303–321.

De Sardan, J.-P.O. and Tidjani Alou, M., (2009) *Les Pouvoirs locaux au Niger à la veille de la décentralisation*. Paris: Karthala.

Dion, S., (2016) 'Keynote: The Security Implications of Climate Change in Fragile States', *Climate-Diplomacy*. [online]. Available at: https://climate-diplomacy.org/magazine/environment/keynote-security-implications-climate-change-fragile-states (Accessed: 25 October 2021).

DNPGCA, (2020) *Résultats de l'analyse de l'impact de la Pandémie COVID-19 sur la sécurité alimentaire et nutritionnelle au Niger*. [online]. Available at: https://reca-niger.org/spip.php?article1463 (Accessed: 17 January 2022).

Duivenbooden, N.V., Abdoussallam, S. and Ben Mohamed, A., (2002) 'Impact of Climate Change on Agricultural Production in the Sahel – Part 2. Case Study for Groundnut and Cowpea in Niger', *Climatic Change*, 54(3), pp. 349–368. [online]. Available at: https://doi.org/10.1023/A:1016188522934 (Accessed: 25 October 2021).

FAO, (2019) *The Niger: Response Overview*. Rome: FAO Office of Emergencies and Resilience. [online]. Available at: The Niger – response overview – December 2019 (fao.org) (Accessed: 25 October 2021).

FAO, (2020) *The Niger: Response Overview*. Rome: FAO Office of Emergencies and Resilience. [online]. Available at: The Niger | Response overview (March 2020) (fao.org) (Accessed: 25 October 2021).

Fensholt, R., Mbow, C., Brandt, M. and Rasmussen, K., (2017) 'Desertification and Re-Greening of the Sahel', in *Oxford Research Encyclopedias. Climate Science*. [online]. Available at: https://doi.org/10.1093/acrefore/9780190228620.013.553 (Accessed: 17 January 2022).

FEWS-NET, (2005) *Niger Livelihood Profiles*. Washington, DC: FEWS NET.

FEWS-NET, (2019) *Assessment of Chronic Food Insecurity in Niger*. Washington, DC: FEWS NET.

Fiorillo, E., Crisci, A., Issa, H., Maracchi, G., Morabito, M. and Tarchiani, V., (2018) 'Recent Changes of Floods and Related Impacts in Niger Based on the ANADIA Niger Flood Database', *Climate*, 6(3). [online]. Available at: https://doi.org/10.3390/cli6030059 (Accessed: 25 October 2021).

Frowd, P.M., (2020) 'Producing the "Transit" Migration State: International Security Intervention in Niger', *Third World Quarterly*, 41(2), pp. 340–358, [online]. Available at: DOI: 10.1080/01436597.2019.1660633 (Accessed: 25 October 2021).

Grégoire, E., (2011) 'Niger: A State Rich in Uranium', *Hérodote*, 142, pp. 206–225.

Harmon, S., (2014) *Terror and Insurgency in the Sahara-Sahel Region: Corruption, Contraband, Jihad and the Mali War of 2012–2013*. London: Ashgate.

Harmon, S., (2015) 'Securitization Initiatives in the Sahara-Sahel Region in the Twenty-First Century', *African Security*, 8(4), pp. 227–248.

Heinrigs, P., (2010) *Security Implications of Climate Change in the Sahel Region: Policy Considerations*. Issy-les-Moulineaux: OECD. [online]. Available at: www.oecd.org/swac/climatechange (Accessed: 25 October 2021).

Hidalgo, F.D., Naidu, S., Nichter, S. and Richardson, N., (2010) 'Economic Determinants of Land Invasions', *Review of Economics and Statistics*, 92(3), pp. 505–523. [online]. Available at: https://doi.org/10.1162/REST_a_00007 (Accessed: 25 October 2021).

Hiernaux, P., Turner, M.D., Eggen, M., Marie, J. and Haywood, M., (2021) 'Resilience of Wetland Vegetation to Recurrent Drought in the Inland Niger Delta of Mali from 1982 to 2014', *Wetlands Ecology and Management.* [online]. Available at: https://doi.org/10.1007/s11273-021-09822-8 (Accessed: 25 October 2021).

Homer-Dixon, T., (1999) *Environment, Scarcity, and Violence*. Princeton: Princeton University Press.

Hsiang, S.M., Meng, K.C. and Cane, M.A., (2011) 'Civil Conflicts Are Associated with the Global Climate', *Nature*, 476(7361), pp. 438–441. [online]. Available at: https://doi.org/10.1038/nature10311 (Accessed: 25 October 2021).

Ide, T., (2020) 'The Dark Side of Environmental Peacebuilding', *World Development*, 127. [online]. Available at: https://doi.org/10.1016/j.worlddev.2019.104777 (Accessed: 25 October 2021).

Ide, T., Bruch, C., Carius, A., Conca, K., Dabelko, G., Matthew, R. and Weinthal, E., (2021) 'The Past and Future(s) of Environmental Peacebuilding', *International Affairs*, 97(1), pp. 1–16.

Institute for Economics & Peace, (2019) 'Global Peace Index: Measuring Peace in a Complex World', *Institute for Economics & Peace*, 1–99.

International Crisis Group (ICG), (2020a) *Sidelining the Islamic State in Niger's Tillabery*, Report 289, 3 June. [online]. Available at: Sidelining the Islamic State in Niger's Tillabery | Crisis Group (Accessed: 25 October 2021).

International Crisis Group (ICG), (2020b) *The Central Sahel: Scene of New Climate Wars?* Briefing 154, 24 April. [online]. Available at: The Central Sahel: Scene of New Climate Wars? | Crisis Group (Accessed: 25 October 2021).

Ivleva, D., Schaller, S., Pohl, B. and Vivekananda, J., (2019) *Climate Change and Security: A Short Q&A*, Berlin: Adelphi Research GmbH. [online]. Available at: CLIMATE CHANGE – Questions and Answers (climate-diplomacy.org) (Accessed: 25 October 2021).

Jeune Afrique, (2017) *Niger: nouvelle opération contre les "terroristes" venus du Mali*. 17 June. [online]. Available at: www.jeuneafrique.com/depeches/448775/politique/niger-nouvelle-operation-contre-terroristes-venus-mali/ (Accessed: 25 October 2021).

Kamuanga, M.J.B, Somda, J., Sanon, Y. and Kagoné, H., (2008) *Livestock and Regional Market in the Sahel and West Africa – Potentials and Challenges*. Issy-les-Moulineaux: OECD. [online]. Available at: www.oecd.org/swac/publications/41848366.pdf (Accessed: 25 October 2021).

Kaplan, R.D., (1994) 'The Coming Anarchy', *The Atlantic*, February Issue. [online]. Available at: https://www.theatlantic.com/magazine/archive/1994/02/the-coming-anarchy/304670/ (Accessed: 17 January 2022).

Koubi, V., (2019) 'Climate Change and Conflict', *Annual Review of Political Science*, 22, pp. 343–360. [online]. Available at: https://doi.org/10.1146/annurev-polisci-050317-070830 (Accessed: 25 October 2021).

Krampe, F., (2019) 'Climate Change, Peacebuilding, and Sustaining Peace', *IPI Global Observatory*, 13 September. [online]. Available at: https://theglobalobservatory.org/2019/09/climate-change-peacebuilding-and-sustaining-peace/ (Accessed: 17 January 2022).

Kulesza, P., (eds.) (2021) *Pasteurs Peuls nomads et transhumants. Quel avenir?* Paris: L'Harmattan.

Lobell, D.B., Schlenker, W. and Costa-Roberts, J., (2011) 'Climate Trends and Global Crop Production Since 1980', *Science*, 333, pp. 616–621. [online]. Available at: https://doi.org/10.5040/9780755621101.0007 (Accessed: 25 October 2021).

Maloca Internationale, (2016) 'Atteintes à l'environnement et désagrégation du milieu socioéconomique des touaregs du Niger: l'industrie de l'uranium mise en cause', in *Rapport pour le Deuxième Examen Periodique Universel du Niger*. Genève: Nations Unies.

Mann, G., (2015) *From Empires to NGOs in the West African Sahel: The Road to Nongovernmentality*. Cambridge: Cambridge University Press.

Marret, J-L., (2008) 'Al-Qaeda in Islamic Maghreb: A 'Global' Organization', *Studies in Conflict and Terrorism*, 31(6), pp. 541–552.

McDonald, M., (2013) 'Discourses of Climate Security', *Political Geography*, 33(1), pp. 42–51.

McDonald, M., (2021) *Ecological Security: Climate Change and the Construction of Security*. Cambridge: Cambridge University Press.

McKune, S. and Silva, J.A., (2013) 'Pastoralists under Pressure: Double Exposure to Economic and Environmental Change in Niger', *The Journal of Development Studies*, 49(12), pp. 1711–1727.

Mobjork, M., Krampe, F. and Taris, K., (2020) *Pathways of Climate Insecurity: Guidance for Policymakers*. Stockholm: SIPRI.

Mohamadou, A., (2004) *Foncier agro – pastoral, conflits et gestion des aléas climatiques au Niger. Cas de Dakoro et Abalak*. Niamey: LASDEL.

Mohamadou, A., (2018) 'État, pouvoirs locaux et insécurités au Sahel: L'intégration différenciée des communautés locales dans la construction de l'État-nation au Niger et au Mali', *Afrique contemporaine*, 265, pp. 77–97.

Molenaar, F. and El Kamouni-Janssen, F., (2017) *Turning the Tide. The Politics of Irregular Migration in the Sahel and Libya*. The Hague: Clingendael Institute.

Mongay Font, A. and Meneses, G.A., (2002) 'Los Tuareg: La Resistencia de Un Pueblo Del Sáhara', in *Más Allá Del Estado: Pueblos Al Margen Del Poder*. Barcelona: Edicions Bellaterra, pp. 109–131.

Ndaruzaniye, V., Lipper, L., Fiott, D., Flavell, A. and Clover, J., (2010) *Climate Change and Security in Africa – Vulnerability Discussion Paper*. [online]. Available at: https://africa-eu-partnership.org/sites/default/files/documents/doc_climate_vulnerability_discussion_paper.pdf (Accessed: 25 October 2021).

New Humanitarian, (2019) *Niger, Part 1: At the Centre of a Brewing Militant Storm*, 28 March. [online]. Available at: www.thenewhumanitarian.org/2019/03/28/niger-part-1-centre-brewing-militant-storm (Accessed: 28 October 2021).

Ostrom, E., (1990) *Governing the Commons: The Evolution of Institutions for Collective Action*. Cambridge: Cambridge University Press.

Raineri, L., (2018) 'Human Smuggling across Niger: State-Sponsored Protection Rackets and Contradictory Security Imperatives', *The Journal of Modern African Studies*, 56, pp. 63–86. [online]. Available at: https://doi.org/10.1017/S0022278X17000520 (Accessed: 25 October 2021).

Raineri, L., (2020) 'Explaining the Rise of Jihadism in Africa: The Crucial Case of the Islamic State of the Greater Sahara', *Terrorism and Political Violence*, pp. 1–15. [online]. Available at: https://doi.org/10.1080/09546553.2020.1828078 (Accessed: 25 October 2021).

Raineri, L. and Strazzari, F., (2021) 'Drug Smuggling and the Stability of Fragile States. The Diverging Trajectories of Mali and Niger', *Journal of Intervention and Statebuilding*, pp. 1–18. [online]. Available at: https://doi.org/10.1080/17502977.2021.1896207 (Accessed: 25 October 2021).

Razafimandimby, L., Nguyen, N.T.V. and Nshimiyimana, M., (2020) *Niger: Note Sur La Situation de l'économie et de La Pauvreté Au Temps de La COVID-19*. Washington, DC: World Bank Group.

Reuveny, R., (2007) 'Climate Change-Induced Migration and Violent Conflict', *Political Geography*, 26, pp. 656–673. [online]. Available at: https://doi.org/10.1016/j.polgeo.2007.05.001 (Accessed: 25 October 2021).

Rogers, P., (2021) *Losing Control. Global Security in the Twenty-first Century*. 4th ed. London: Pluto Press.

Schlenker, W. and Lobell, D.B., (2010) 'Robust Negative Impacts of Climate Change on African Agriculture', *Environmental Research Letters*, 5(1). [online]. Available at: https://doi.org/10.1088/1748-9326/5/1/014010 (Accessed: 25 October 2021).

Selby, J., Dahi, O.S., Fröhlich, C. and Hulme, M., (2017) 'Climate Change and the Syrian civil War Revisited', *Political Geography*, 60, pp. 232–244. [online]. Available at: https://doi.org/10.1016/j.polgeo.2017.05.007 (Accessed: 25 October 2021).

Selby, J. and Hoffman, C., (2014) 'Rethinking Climate Change, Conflict and Security', *Geopolitics*, 19, pp. 747–756.

Stewart, F. and Fitzgerald, V., (2001) *War and Underdevelopment: Volume 1: The Economic and Social Consequences of Conflict. War and Underdevelopment*. Oxford University Press. [online]. Available at: https://doi.org/10.1093/ACPROF:OSO/9780199241866.001.0001 (Accessed: 28 October 2021).

Swain, A., (1996) 'Environmental Migration and Conflict Dynamics: Focus on Developing Regions', *Third World Quarterly*, 17(5), pp. 959–973.

Swain, A. and Öjendal, J., (eds.) (2018) *Routledge Handbook of Environmental Conflict and Peacebuilding*. New York, NY: Routledge.

Thébaud, B. and Batterbury, S., (2001) 'Sahel Pastoralists: Opportunism, Struggle, Conflict and Negotiation. A Case Study from Eastern Niger', *Global Environmental Change*, 11(1), pp. 69–78.

Ubelejit, N.T., (2014) 'The Undermining of State Capacity By Climate Change and Vulnerabilities', *Global Journal of Political Science and Administration*, 2(3), pp. 1–10.

UNHCR, (2021b) *Sahel Situation (Tillbéri and Tahoua Regions)*. Geneva: UNHCR.

United Nations Secretary-General, (2009) *Climate Change and Its Possible Security Implications-Report of the Secretary-General*. New York, NY: United Nations.

University of Notre Dame, (2019) *Country Rankings – Notre Dame Global Adaptation Initiative (ND-GAIN)*. [online]. Available at: https://gain.nd.edu/our-work/country-index/rankings/ (Accessed: 28 October 2021).

UNOWAS, (2018) *Pastoralism and Security in West Africa and the Sahel: Towards Peaceful Coexistence*. [online]. Available at: https://unowas.unmissions.org/sites/default/files/rapport_pastoralisme_eng-april_2019_-_online.pdf (Accessed: 28 October 2021).

USAID, (2014a) *Climate Change and Conflict : Findings and Lessons Learned From Five Case Studies in Seven Countries*. Washington DC: USAID.

USAID, (2014b) *Climate Change and Conflict in the Sahel: A Policy Brief on Findings from Niger and Burkina Faso*. Washington, DC: USAID.

USAID, (2017) *Climate Change Risk Profile: West Africa Sahel*. [online]. Available at: www.climatelinks.org/sites/default/files/asset/document/2017 April_USAID ATLAS_Climate Change Risk Profile – Sahel.pdf (Accessed: 28 October 2021).

USAID, (2018) *Climate Risk Profile: West Africa*. [online]. Available at: www.climatelinks.org/sites/default/files/asset/document/West_Africa_CRP_Final.pdf (Accessed: 28 October 2021).

Van Schaik, L., Von Lossow, T., Yassin, M. and Schrijver, A., (2020) *Fears for Militarisation of Climate Change: Should We Be Concerned?* The Hague: Clingendael Institute.

# PART III

# Case Studies

# 13
# PEACE BY DELEGATION?
## The G5 Sahel's quest to build sustainable peace

*Ousmane Diallo*

### Introduction

The African continent hosts half of the current UN peace operations[1] worldwide and a variety of security interventions aiming to address conflict and restore peace in different countries. Various initiatives motivated by different logics are at play, leading to multiple and overlapping coordination processes between state actors and regional organizations (De Carvalho 2020). In these interactions, African actors navigate between global norms and local practices on governing peace and security, which they appropriate and redefine, to meet their political objectives. These often mirror the shift at the global level, as is the case with the concept of peacebuilding, which has meant different things for different actors since the UN's *Agenda for Peace* (Donais 2012; De Coning 2017, 2018; Karlsrud 2019). Initially, it focused on actions aiming to bring structural changes in societies to prevent the relapse into conflict (Barnett et al. 2007, 37) by linking development and security (Tschirgi 2013, 197). Over the past two decades, peacebuilding has broadened to include various activities for countries coming out of conflicts, or trying to come out of conflicts, which may or may not have to do with the state.

These developments are also reflected in the peace and security regime in the African continent. Following a decades-long process, the Organization of African Unity (OAU) became the African Union (AU) in 2002, a shift that entailed a greater interest in building peace through the promotion of democratic norms, human rights, and the rule of law. The African Peace and Security Architecture (APSA), encapsulated in the Protocol on the Peace and Security Council (PSC), reflects this ambition. As a set of structures, principles and institutions directing the relations between the AU, regional economic communities (RECs)/regional mechanisms (RMs) and national governments, the APSA serves as a guiding compass on security governance and peacebuilding. But over the years, the APSA, as a project to govern peace and security, has been under stress due to the gaps between the expectations it raises, and its capacity to execute them (Babarinde 2011; Williams 2016) has had a mixed record since its development (Williams 2009; 2016). This is mainly due to the proliferation of conflict in the continent and the challenges posed by hybrid orders of governance,[2] which is not captured in the logic of the APSA, and to the competing and overlapping security mechanisms it coexists with.

Perhaps nothing is as illustrative of the trends and challenges to an African way of "making peace" than the different intervention strategies to manage and contain the multidimensional crisis affecting the Sahel. Long simmering since the 2000s, the Sahel has received greater regional and international attention following the conflict in Mali (2012–), where the fear of a state collapse was rampant among national, regional, and international actors. One of the lessons learnt was the lack of a "Sahelian organization" to coordinate and lead the international action in an integrated way. This fear has led to an overhaul of the regional cartography of security governance with the development of new initiatives by the AU, but also at the level of the Sahelian states. Thus, the Group of Five for the Sahel (G5 Sahel) was created in February 2014 by Mali, Burkina Faso, Niger, Chad, and Mauritania as a way of pooling their capacities in order to address their development and security challenges, especially in their peripheral regions. The objective of the new organization is to prevent a relapse into conflict in Mali and the establishment of a lasting peace in the Sahel through increased military and developmental cooperation. These ambitions also met the concerns of various international actors active in the Sahel, where they developed different strategies and policies to deal with the Islamist insurgency, trafficking, and irregular migration, among others. While fairly recent, the G5 Sahel's understanding of building peace has trumped existing regional initiatives and is essentially rooted in filling the gap of its member-states, whether by consolidating its presence in all of its territory or through the provision of public services, often with the support of its development partners. In this sense, the G5 Sahel's approach prioritizes a state-driven approach to building peace, hinged on strengthening the Westphalian features of the state without really engaging with societal actors or the hybrid orders of governance who are key actors in its domestic governance. This is rather devolved to the member-states based on their political choices and different historical trajectories.

In the context of the Sahel, a region heavily securitized by international actors and their local partners, there is a growing tendency to conflate peacebuilding and state-building. This reflects a "problem-solving paradigm to peacebuilding" (Mac Ginty 2013, 3) interested in addressing urgent problems in regions, in a crisis, that overlooks the fundamental drivers of conflict in those regions. This is epitomized by the G5 Sahel's approach to building peace in its regional space, which ties security concerns with the Sahelian state's many failings, through the pooling of capacities and the support of international partners, while each state, depending on its historical trajectories and governance preferences, determines its own peacebuilding path. In the case of this organization, peace goes by strengthening the capacities of the state in delivering public services and in its regalian attributes, without always addressing the social tensions at the root of conflict in the five countries.

This chapter will explore the location of African actors in the international system through a careful study of the G5 Sahel's activities since 2014. In more prosaic terms, I try to identify how the G5 Sahel understands its role as a peacebuilding actor in a crowded region where it is an emerging security actor. Is the G5 Sahel geared towards building peace or restoring state authority? The argument I am making is that the G5 Sahel's approach to building peace reflects a state-centric perspective in which peace is sustained by filling the state's gaps in terms of securing its territory and the provision of public goods. This ambition rejoins the various development strategies and initiative in the region by international partners, who see in the G5 Sahel the "best fit" organization to secure the Sahel. The first section of this chapter will provide a background on the emergence of the G5 Sahel in 2014 and its progressive institutionalization over the subsequent three years. The second section will analyze the G5 Sahel's development framework and demonstrate and highlight its links with preexisting strategies developed by the organization's technical and financial partners centered around the security-development nexus.[3] I will demonstrate that the G5 Sahel has not been very successful in claiming its voice because it reproduced in several instances the same policies that were conceived by the European Union

(EU) and other international actors. This is also compounded by the organization's increased dependence on its international partners for funding and military support but also knowledge production, a dependence that puts it in a subaltern position in this dynamic. The last section will contrast the Joint Force of the G5 Sahel with the local dynamics of violence, fueled by the erosion of social trust between communities and towards the state, since 2013. If the G5 Sahel focuses on peacebuilding, then the task of engaging with societal actors must be taken by the member-states at different levels for it to be sustainable.

## The G5 Sahel and its environment

The G5 Sahel emerged in the wake of the Malian conflict for the purpose of preventing another challenge to state authority by non-state armed groups. Following a rebellion in January 2012 and a coup d'état in March, the northern regions of Mali were quickly overrun and governed by a coalition of armed groups including irredentist movements and groups affiliated with al-Qaida in the Islamic Maghreb (AQIM). The first phase of the conflict exposed the limitations of the APSA, the continental framework governing security governance spearheaded by the AU PSC, and the need for a regional organization legitimate enough to coordinate regional and international action in the Sahel. The Economic Community of West African States (ECOWAS) and the AU led most of the regional initiatives to defuse the multidimensional crisis in Mali from the March 2012 coup to Operation Serval, the French-led military intervention that rolled back the jihadist conquests of the northern region in January 2013 (Bagayoko 2019, 29). This paved the way to the deployment of the UN International Mission for Stabilization in Mali (MINUSMA) and to a greater international presence in Mali and its immediate environment. While the UN mission aimed to contribute to a lasting peace in Mali by favoring dialogue with the parties and addressing the structural causes of conflict, Operation Serval was exclusively military and focused on neutralizing jihadist groups and restoring state authority, where it has lapsed. It is in this double context of unclear regional leadership, and interest by the international community, that the G5 Sahel was formed by Mali, Mauritania, Burkina Faso, Chad, and Niger in February 2014. The new organization reflected a commitment to play an important role on peacebuilding by addressing the root causes of conflict, which were perceived as being linked to security and development challenges (ICG 2017; Châtaigner and Chevalier 2019). These challenges were understood to be transnational and acute in these countries' peripheral regions where state authority was wavering.

From the beginning, the G5 Sahel demarcated itself from existing African regional actors but also manifested its interest in playing a substantial role in the region by positioning itself as the interlocutor of international partners in addressing joint security and development challenges faced by its member-states. The G5 Sahel became a key partner as the role of the AU and ECOWAS waned in Mali and the Sahel.

From the origins, it has been tied with the concerns in the Sahel of several extra-continental actors such as the EU and the UN at a moment where a repetition of the Malian state collapse was feared by many. For the G5 Sahel, peace in the region goes by strengthening the capacities of its five member-states and fostering avenues for cooperation on security and development issues. In this regard, the ambitions of the five Sahelian states coincided with the concerns of international interventions in the region, which created room for a comprehensive partnership. But the dynamic between the G5 Sahel and its partners was unequal from the start, due to the differences in wealth, capacity and institutionalization.

Security and development, the two objectives of the G5 Sahel, are characteristic of the peacebuilding priorities of many interventions since the 2000s to stabilize post-conflict theatres (Karlsrud 2019). In this regard, the G5 Sahel embraces the discourse on the security-development nexus that has been central to the strategies of its international partners, such as the EU, in the Sahel. From its creation, the G5 Sahel has been closely associated with international peacebuilding efforts in the region, and in particular France's counterterrorist operation in the Sahel. The founding meeting of February 2014 in Nouakchott occurred three months after a multi-stakeholder visit by the heads of the UN, World Bank, the EU and the Organization of Islamic Cooperation (OIC) to discuss and assess development issues in the region and to operationalize the UN integrated strategy for the Sahel. Five of the six countries visited during that international mission formed the G5 Sahel, the key partner of international organizations and Western governments in the region.[4]

The formation of the G5 Sahel has been ascribed to the political deadlock of the Nouakchott Process, an initiative that went beyond the AU's attempt to operationalize the APSA in the Sahel in March 2013. Despite their agreement on fostering intelligence cooperation among Sahelian countries, the member-states in the process could not decide on the deployment of a regional counterterrorist force in Mali, leading several countries, hard-pressed by security challenges, to unite together in order "to move faster forward and together".[5]

Considering the makeup of the G5 Sahel, an AU senior military official involved in the APSA opined that G5 Sahel does not include all Sahelian countries. There are 13 countries in the Nouakchott Process (which includes all Sahelian countries, per the AU) and among those, five decided to work together due to the specific challenges they faced within the process, mainly security and counterterrorism. It was a legitimate decision to see that nucleus within the group work together in a tighter framework.[6]

The AU sees itself as the primary actor on peace and security in Africa, especially in relation with extra-continental actors. This is based on article 16.1 of the Protocol of the PSC of the AU, which if it includes regional mechanisms in the continental architecture stresses that the AU has the primary responsibility for promoting peace, security and stability on the continent. This is most manifest in the AU's claim to be the interlocutor of the UN Security Council (UNSC) on peacebuilding in the continent, a claim that has been challenged from time to time by the regional economic communities and also by some states at the UNSC. In the Sahelian context, the G5 Sahel's formation constituted a disavowal of the initiatives developed by the AU in reaction to the experiences of the African-led International Support Mission in Mali (AFISMA), such as the Nouakchott Process and the African Capacity for Immediate Response to Crises (ACIRC).

This perspective, although viewed with skepticism at the formation of the G5 Sahel (Slate Afrique 2014), has come to be more accepted at the AU. The G5 Sahel is part of a current trend in peace operations in the continent, in which ad hoc coalitions are formed by countries outside of the framework of the APSA to respond to their common security challenges. Further east in the Lake Chad region, the Multinational Joint Task Force (MNJTF) was formed by the members of the Lake Chad Basin Commission (LCBC) to deal with the Boko Haram insurgency.

Over the years, the dynamic between the AU and G5 Sahel has gone from mistrust to cautious collaboration as the continental organization realizes the imperative of supporting peacebuilding efforts in the Sahel. Rivalry between regional organizations, heavily dependent on external funding for their programs, in a region that has seen a dramatic interest by international partners was one of the reasons for the fractious relation.[7] Beyond this, other questions have beset the G5 Sahel membership since 2014; the absence of Algeria from the regional mechanism has been a regular question mark among observers. Algeria's absence might be due to differing perspectives on how to establish lasting peace in the region and the failure of previous Sahelian initiatives in which Algiers played a major role: the promises of the Algerian-led CEMOC

(Joint Military Staff Committee) formed in 2010 never came to be, and this was felt especially during the conflict in Mali, frustrating Mali, Mauritania and Niger, the other member-states. Algeria's traditional reluctance to deploy military troops outside of its territory could become a hindrance for the newer organization.[8] This is despite the country's experience with dealing with Islamic insurgency in the 1990s and its influence on political, commercial and security dynamics affecting northern Mali (Scheele 2009; Cantens and Raballand 2017; International Crisis Group 2015; Bensassi et al. 2015).

While there are still lingering issues between the two organizations, the AU has been vocal about its support to the G5 Sahel's activities and has joined the chorus of actors asking for more international support towards the organization. The AU PSC has endorsed the military initiative of the G5 Sahel and called for an increased cooperation with the different ad hoc coalition in the continent, such as the MNJTF. Although the endorsement is a matter of courtesy and not legally binding (Williams 2019), it reflects the progressive institutionalization of the G5 Sahel and affirmation as an important actor in a region characterized by the plurality of interventions (ICG 2017). Thus, the G5 constitutes a rupture in the cartography of security by African actors but also continuity of the different stabilization policies preferred by international partners in the region. This is particularly apparent with the unequal relationship of the EU and the AU towards the G5 Sahel: while the EU has played an important supportive role in the development of the G5 Sahel and even in its strategic orientations, the AU has had a fractious relationship with the new organization, especially at its beginning.[9]

## Peacebuilding by proxy? The G5 Sahel's development pillar

The G5 Sahel operates in an environment where, since its formation, various armed groups challenge state authority. This informs G5 Sahel's problem-solving approach to peacebuilding, which is focused on addressing the immediate security and development challenges singled out as the causes of regional instability and fostering greater cooperation between the five countries. Peacebuilding, when it occurs, is very securitized and reflects a state-centric posture rather than a societal process. This posture is also facilitated by the interventions in the region by partners with greater resources and capacities, which, if they are willing to support the G5 Sahel in addressing its security and development challenges for the sake of stability, do not necessarily have the leverage to direct their long-term engagement on societal processes.

Like several other African organizations, the G5 Sahel's relation with its international partners is marked by the imbalance between their financial and military capabilities, which create an unequal partnership. This is apparent in the organization's actualization of its development pillar. To address it, the G5 Sahel submitted a priority investment plan (PIP) to its international partners to address the short-, medium-, and long-term governance and development challenges. The initial PIP was developed in a hurry under the pressure of the organization's heads of state in a moment where there was great interest by the UN, the EU and France, among other actors, in stabilizing the Sahel. The PIP was designed as a framework document to engage with technical and financial partners and preceded the formulation of the organization's development strategy (Desgrais 2019, 100). It is structured around four pillars: governance, infrastructures, security and resilience. The initial document was less an integrated regional approach than the amalgamation of five national perspectives. A G5 Sahel official stressed:

> The Heads of State pressured us because there were many funding pledges for the Sahel following Ban Ki-Moon's visit. The Heads of State believed that they had to capture the pledges quickly: "Ministers had to meet and establish an investment program that

will be presented to partners". The first plan amounting to XOF 7000 bn reflected the funding pledges made by Ban Ki-Moon.

*(Desgrais 2019, 102)*

The PIP has been revised several times since 2014 to make it more coherent, integrated and in order to meet the concerns and priorities of the donor countries whose financial support the G5 Sahel expects. While the G5 Sahel has pledged to fund 10% of its PIP, the remaining 90% are scheduled to be funded by bilateral and multilateral partners (Bertrand and Cheeseman 2019, 11), and despite pledges, funds have been slow to be disbursed by donors. Beyond the PIP, the G5 Sahel has also spearheaded initiatives on mainstreaming gender considerations into conflict prevention and countering violent extremism (CVE), protection of civilians and political governance, and by promoting the Women, Peace and Security Agenda of the UN at the regional and national levels (G5 Sahel 2017; 2020). But these activities are yet to take off and, as with the PIP, remain hinged on the support of international partners.

The securitized approach to peacebuilding favored by the G5 Sahel is heavily dependent on the international support of its development partners, bilateral and multilateral, leading to the conflation of considerations linked to official development assistance (ODA) and what the G5 Sahel aims to achieve in terms of development. Indeed, one of the trends in the peacebuilding agenda has been the inclusion of stabilization and counterterrorism as ODA, a change most manifest in OECD's guidelines (Karlsrud 2019, 5). G5 Sahel's partners can therefore fund security-related activities that prop up the organization's governments through training and military equipment, as part of ODA.

To support development in G5 Sahel countries, the Alliance Sahel was formed by several bilateral and multilateral organizations as a forum to coordinate their development projects and prevent the duplications of efforts in July 2017. Six fields were identified as priority in tandem with the Permanent Secretariat of the G5 Sahel:

- Education and youth employment;
- Agriculture, rural development, food security;
- Energy and climate;
- Governance;
- Decentralization and basic services; and
- Internal security.

The Alliance Sahel (see Table 13.1 below) is coordinated by the EU, which has been long present in the region and has a strategic partnership with the G5 Sahel. The partnership reflects a delegation of development initiatives from the G5 Sahel to its international partners. While the platform facilitates the coordination and the rapid implementation of development and humanitarian projects, it is the G5 Sahel that defines the projects and objectives to be achieved. These goals are met through innovative and flexible financing methods that may involve subcontracting to non-governmental organizations, local authorities and private actors. Peacebuilding in this format obeys a securitized logic that does not question its ontological assumptions on whether the nature of the state and the modes of governance could be central to the absence of peace, but on the necessity of redeploying state authority and ensuring its provision of public goods towards the citizens, who play a marginal role in this process. Most of the Alliance Sahel's activities are concentrated in remote areas, considered fragile and vulnerable to the alternative projects of spoiler groups such as the jihadists (Châtaigner and Chevalier 2019, 32). While the G5 Sahel, through its Permanent Secretariat, is involved in the selection of the development

*Table 13.1* Members of the Alliance Sahel

| | |
|---|---|
| France | French Development Agency (AFD) |
| Germany | Federal Ministry for Economic Cooperation and Development |
| European Union | European Union/EU Investment Bank |
| World Bank | World Bank (WB) |
| Africa | African Development Bank (AfDB) |
| United Nations | UN Development Programme |
| Italy | Italian Agency for Cooperation and Development (AICS) |
| Spain | Spanish Agency for International Cooperation and Development (AECID) |
| United Kingdom | UK Aid |
| Luxembourg | Luxembourg Aid and Development |
| Denmark | *Observer Status* |
| The Netherlands | *Observer Status* |

projects of the Alliance Sahel, this choice is constrained by the different priorities and objectives of the Alliance's members. Yet the Alliance Sahel reflects the donor priorities on issues that are relevant to them (and to Sahelian countries), such as migration and trafficking, and that they are attempting to contain through their development programs.

Following the decision to deploy a Joint Force in February 2017, the G5 Sahel member countries decided to revise their PIP and to resubmit it to their partners. The last version of the PIP (June 2017) reflects the hierarchization of the projects as outlined by the G5 Sahel and the Alliance Sahel. Top priority projects were selected based on five criteria:

- Their *transboundary nature*: projects that would cover the governance issues on the Mali/Mauritania border (western sector), Mali/Burkina/Niger borderlands (central sector) and Niger/Chad border (eastern sector);
- Their *impact*: in the model of the UN's Quick Impact Projects (QIPs), with the view of showcasing the positive presence of the state in marginalized areas through short-term projects.
- Their *feasibility* in the two-year period (2019–2021) based on their convergence and the degree of agreement with international partners in the Alliance Sahel.
- Their *subsidiarity*, through the comparative advantage of the G5 Sahel in complementing the actions of national governments and other regional organizations; and
- Their *convergence with security needs*, based on the impact they have on addressing security issues in the space. (G5 Sahel 2018, 3)

The latest PIP of the G5 Sahel still reflects its outward posture towards its international partners. Although sensibly less expensive than its first version, the different projects of the PIP for 2019–2021 amount to XOF 1.996 billion, out of which 87% of the funding (about XOF 728 billion) is yet to be found (G5 Sahel 2018, 3). Different donor conferences have led to important pledges to the G5 Sahel on issues of development, but the disbursement of these funds has been slow so far, and even when they were timely, they may not necessarily fit into the 40 projects outlined in the latest version of the PIP. By January 2019, the Alliance Sahel announced the availability of EUR 11 billion for its strategic objectives in the Sahel, but despite the close collaboration, they may differ with the projects identified in the updated PIP.

There is a tension inherent in the G5 Sahel's approach to peacebuilding. If the organization was set up to move forward faster and has progressively become a key player in the region, it is yet to find its voice amid the different interventions in its region. The emphasis on the security-development nexus reproduces the EU's different strategies in the Sahel since 2011, while the securitized responses remain heavily dependent on the support of France but also of MINUSMA, contributing to blurring the rigid line between peacekeeping and counterterrorism (Charbonneau 2017; Karlsrud 2017; 2019).

## The G5 Sahel's Joint Force and the local dynamics of violence

If the G5 Sahel's development plans has been hinged on its PIPs and the activities by proxy of its development partners through the Alliance Sahel, it has made the most progress in its project to sustain peace and stability through the consolidation of state authority by the securing of its shared borders. Established in February 2017, the Joint Force is composed of the contingent from the five member-states and aims to neutralize all spoiler groups in its shared regional space through coordinated actions in their shared borders. The possibility of a regional military force was raised soon after the organization's formation in 2014, but it only became effective in 2017 when it was authorized successively by the AU PSC and the UNSC.

Initially announced to include 10,000 personnel (RFI 2017) before being reduced to 5,000, the activities of the Joint Force are structured around transborder cooperation in three sectors. The central command of the force was initially based in Sévaré in the Mopti region of Mali, where transborder operations are planned. Beyond the central command, seven battalions consisting of 650 troops[10] are deployed in three transborder sectors:

- The western sector, which consists of the border region between Mali and Mauritania, with its headquarters in Nbeiket el Ahouach, Mauritania;
- The central sector, which consists of the border between Burkina, Mali and Niger, with its tactical headquarters in Niamey, Niger; and
- The eastern sector, which is the border between Niger and Chad, with its tactical headquarters in Wour, Chad.

During the joint operations in these corridors, the relevant national components of the G5 Sahel would have the right to "hot pursuit" of terrorists and other spoiler elements within up to 50 km of each border, pending an approval of their request by the Joint Force commander, from its headquarters in Sévaré in central Mali (United Nations 2017, 6).

The Joint Force operates in a heavily militarized environment, which hosts a plurality of interventions, all aiming to neutralize jihadist and other spoiler groups, restoring state authority and legitimacy via impactful development projects. Mali has been hosting a UN stabilization mission (MINUSMA) since July 2013, mandated with supporting a 2015 peace agreement with rebel factions, and operating in an environment characterized by the blurriness between peacekeeping and counterinsurgency operations (Charbonneau 2017; Karlsrud 2019).

Beyond the UN mission which supports its activities in Mali, the Joint Force is also closely supported by France, which checked the jihadist advance to southern Mali in January 2013 with Operation Serval. This operation (2013–2014) was merged with another long-standing one in Chad (Épervier, 1986–2014) and became Barkhane (2014–), a regional counterterrorist force in August 2014. Barkhane has played a major role in supporting the Joint Force of the G5 Sahel through targeted strikes against jihadist leaders and intelligence collection/sharing. Barkhane also supports the operations in these countries' so-called ungoverned spaces and denies spoiler groups safe havens, logistical caches and mobility.[11] The dynamic between the Joint Force and France is definitely post-colonial, since they are definitely marked by the colonial past between France on one hand, and Mali and the four other members of the G5 Sahel on the other hand. France has maintained intricate security and political links with its former colonies, such as Chad, with whom it intervened in the reconquest of northern Mali. Burkina Faso, Chad and Mali have had historically more distant links with France compared to Chad, but the 2013 intervention shifted their dynamics, as the insurgency progressively spread beyond Mali. Barkhane's support preceded the establishment of the Joint Force. In partnership with Barkhane, the five countries were already conducting transborder operations to showcase their presence in remote areas, to win the hearts of its populations, and to destroy the logistical base of jihadist groups since November 2013, when Operation Roussette was launched in the Mali/Niger border region (Robinet 2018). A multilateral military coordination mechanism, with quarterly strategic meetings between the G5 Sahel chief of staff and the commander of the French Operation Barkhane, prior to the authorization of the Joint Force by the AU PSC and the UNSC in March and June 2017.

The G5 Sahel constituted for France, an ideal and crucial partner for the stabilization of the Sahel in an environment characterized by a plurality of African regional actors. For General de Villiers, the then French joint chief of staff, G5 Sahel was "the best framework to push forward security in the region" (Tisseron 2015, n. 1). The proximity of the Joint Force and Barkhane cannot be overstated: between August 2014 and October 2017, "more than 5,300 military personnel from G-5 Sahel have taken part in 250 joint operational instructions with Operation Barkhane" (United Nations 2017, 7).

The EU has also deployed three missions under its Common Security and Defense Policy. The first one, the European Union Capacity Building Mission in Niger (EUCAP Sahel Niger) was deployed in 2012 with the goal of fighting terrorism and organized crime, through EU assistance to Nigerien security services (police, gendarmerie and national guard), and to facilitate their interoperability and coordination. EUCAP Sahel Mali was deployed in January 2015 as part of the EU's contribution to reforming the security services of Mali in the wake of the 2012 conflict. The mission is tasked with supporting the Malian security forces (police, gendarmerie and national guard) and ensuring constitutional and democratic order, putting in place the conditions for lasting peace as well as maintaining state authority throughout the entire territory. Beyond these two civilian missions, the EU has also deployed a military mission, the EU Training Mission in Mali (EUTM Mali) in February 2013 to support security sector reform (SSR) especially on command and control, international humanitarian law and training of the Malian troops. Since 2015, the EUTM Mali also participates in MINUSMA's work on disarmament, demobilization, and reintegration (DDR) as part of the 2015 peace agreement. This support consists of training sessions of the different belligerents for the purpose of establishing an inclusive Malian army. Beyond Mali, the EUTM Mali also supports the G5 Sahel in the coordination and interoperability of their national armies.

The different programs on SSR and capacity-building of defense of security forces have so far been disconnected from the dynamic at the local level, especially in Mali (Tull 2017, 2) and hampered by the poor coordination and diverging views between Sahelian armies and their international partners. For Tull (2017, 2019, 2020), SSR efforts in Mali are beset by the urgency of the current context, in which national armies have to reform while fighting against an insurgency threatening the state, by the lack of input of the Malian authorities in designing its nature, and by the poor coordination between international partners. Despite the initial enthusiasm, the military response has failed to take into account the local dimensions to the peacebuilding challenges in the G5 Sahel may have contributed to neglecting local tensions that mushroomed into communitarian conflicts. The Joint Force aims to police shared border regions and deny sanctuary to spoiler groups through the regular projection of military force.

Most of its activities have focused so far on the central corridor, where there has been a spike of communitarian violence since 2013. Since 2014, the area of operations of the insurgent groups expanded from northern Mali to the central region, and soon spilled over to northern and eastern Burkina Faso and western Niger. More importantly, the Islamist insurgency grafted on preexisting tensions between pastoralist and agricultural communities, leading to the rise of self-defense groups and communitarian violence. Land issues have regularly opposed Fulani pastoralist and Dogon communities in central Mali, but these issues have taken a deadlier turn since 2013 with the presence of Katiba Macina, a Fulani-dominated Islamist brigade, and Dan Na Ambassagou (i.e. "The hunters who trust in God"), a Dogon-dominated that was formed in response to the insecurity. There is therefore a disconnect between the macro response in the form of the Joint Force, and the micro-dynamics of conflict in which ethnic militias arise to complement the security vacuum left by the state with the support of local communities and even sometimes state officials. In this context of eroding trust between communities and towards the state, the G5 Sahel's approach has focused on strengthening security cooperation and state redeployment while delegating the complexities of local politics leading to violence, to the governments of its different member-states. While this constitutes a clear division of labor between the regional organization and its constituent member, the lack of synergy between the regional effort and the five approaches to engaging with the micropolitics of violence hamper the ultimate objective of securing borders and strengthening the trust of communities towards their national government. So far, the Joint Force has proved ineffective on its own, in alleviating these fears and to contain communitarian conflicts for various reasons. First, the force is conceptualized at the central level and structured around joint transborder operations in the different sectors to conduct security operations. Structural issues related to land management and local governance are neglected in this approach. Furthermore, violence perpetrated by regular military forces contribute to the widening distrust and defiance towards the state. For example, the Malian contingent of the G5 Sahel is responsible for the mass killing of 16 civilians in Nantaka and 22 civilians in Koumaga, in the Mopti region, on 16 and 23 June 2018, respectively, after an altercation opposed a soldier and a herdsman in Nantaka. State violence and the lack of accountability are two challenges that the G5 Sahel must overcome in its peacebuilding efforts. This is despite the implementation of a human rights compliance framework in the activities of the Joint Force, developed by the Office of the High Commission for Human Rights (OHCHR), aiming to better protect civilians, to prevent human rights violations and to report on the impact of operations on civilians in transborder communities.

Between its authorization by the UNSC in June 2017 and March 2019, the Joint Force has launched ten joint border operations for a mixed result due to training and equipment shortfalls. If these operations contributed to making the five national armies working better together, their impact on the situation was very limited, they had a limited strategic impact on the broader insecurity in Mali and in the Sahel and reflected the tactical limitations and prudent commitment of the Sahelian armies.[12] Some of the mission's mandates were also hampered by the poor equipment of the different battalions, whose capacities in intelligence, transmissions and rapid response remain slow.[13] The ability of the different battalions to cover the scale of territory around the border has also been questioned: the two to three battalions scheduled to police each of the three sectors were deemed as not enough military presence to deter in the long-term, spoiler groups. To supplement this deployment, several member-states tend to delegate security prerogatives to non-state armed groups, a decision that facilitates the expansion of communitarian conflict.[14]

The limits of the military dimension of the G5 Sahel were demonstrated in dramatic fashion in June 2018, when the headquarters of the force in Sévaré were attacked by the Group for the

Support of Islam and Muslims (GSIM), a coalition of armed groups active in Mali and constituting the main spoiler to the peace process. The attack occurred while G5 Sahel Joint Force Operation Ir Go Ka was active in the central sector and hampered the activities of the Joint Force for half a year. The complex attack by GSIM, which involved the use of suicide vehicle–borne improvised explosive device (SVBIEDs) and fighters, occurred on 29 June 2018 and targeted the central command of the Joint Force in Sévaré. It caused ten casualties (six dead and four wounded) and "dealt a significant blow to efforts aimed at accelerating the full operationalization of the Joint Force and led to a temporary halt of its operations" (United Nations 2018, 1). The attack led to the total destruction of the headquarters and had immediate consequences on the military leadership in the planification and the procurement for the regional force.[15] The force commander, General Didier Dacko from Mali, was relieved two weeks later by the heads of state during a summit and replaced by the Mauritanian Hanena Ould Sidi. General Dacko's deputy commander, Burkina's Colonel-Major Yaya Séré, was also replaced by the Chadian Oumar Bikimo. The decision, far from surprising, was preceded by the declaration of Mauritania's president, who denounced the "failures" of the Joint Force command and stressed the necessity of addressing these issues that led to the attack, if there was any chance of "stabilizing the Sahel" (Le Monde avec AFP 2018).

Since this attack, the Joint Force does not have a permanent headquarters and its command structure is spread out between Sévaré and Bamako, where MINUSMA and the EU support them in their activities. In October 2018, the Defense and Security Committee decided to permanently relocate the headquarters of the force in Bamako (United Nations 2018), a decision that has fostered anger and resentment among the civilian populations in Sévaré and Bamako, who have become even more critical of the force. This attack was also a financial setback for the G5 Sahel, whose funding schemes have always been one of its main weaknesses. The funding of the force was estimated to be at "423 million euros at the beginning, and then 115 million euros per year" by the Mauritanian representative to the UN, Ambassador Ousmane Ba, in December 2017 (Conseil de sécurité de l'ONU 2017). With the destruction of the headquarters of Sévaré in June 2018, another financial burden was to identify and build a secure and fortified base in Bamako and beyond that would secure the force's personnel, arms, ammunitions and supplies. The cost was estimated at "approximatively 80 million euros" by the new force commander in September 2018 (United Nations 2018), and the heaviest contribution was expected to come from the G5 Sahel's financial partners, namely the EU, while the five states would contribute to the tune of EUR 50 million each, a contribution that was estimated to be minimal by one Malian political actor.[16]

The security response to the dynamics of violence has not been effective so far. Violence in the region has increased between 2017 and 2020, with regular reports of violence against civilians perpetrated by non-state armed groups and Sahelian armies (ACLED 2019; United Nations 2019b; Nsaibia 2020) and to mass displacement and the closures of education facilities (UNICEF 2019; UNHCR 2020).

Building peace must involve a consideration of local governance politics and engaging with local communities on issues such as justice, accountability, and their relationships with governments and security forces. The G5 Sahel's extraverted posture towards its international partners limits its possibility organization to have a distinct voice in this debate. Since 2014, the organization has progressively claimed its place in the regional landscape, but its approach to peacebuilding has been very conservative, with an emphasis on strengthening state capacity, with mixed results. Peacebuilding initiatives aiming to restore trust between communities have been led by civil society and other local actors, who have at times engaged with some of the armed groups excluded from the formal peace processes. These parallel initiatives must converge and complement each other in order to increase the possibilities of long-term conflict transformation.

## Conclusion

The experience in peacebuilding of the G5 Sahel shows that if new actors are emerging on the continent, their location in determining the peacebuilding agenda remains subaltern to the objectives of their international partners and suffers from its disconnect to the initiative led within its member-states. The G5 Sahel was formed in reaction to the AU's mixed record in the Sahel and to act as an interlocutor to the plurality of international initiatives in the region, following Operation Serval. In this dynamic, there is a contrast between the responses of African actors and the micropolitics of violence at the subnational level. If the states have responded by pooling their capacities and by seeking convergence with the interests and priorities of their international partners, they have only engaged in a limited way with local-level community dynamics, thus leaving an important dimension to transforming conflict in the Sahel. In the Liptako-Gourma region, communities are still grappling with the 2012 conflict and the transformations it engendered in state-society relationships, such as the eroding trust between communities and increased interethnic violence perpetrated by local Islamist brigades and self-defense groups. Meanwhile the organization remains heavily dependent on its international partners for its development projects, while its security actions have proved ineffective so far. The full operational capability (FOC) of the regional force was scheduled for March 2018, but by May 2019, it had only attained 75% of its FOC after having been delayed twice (United Nations 2019a). The security response has been a failure so far despite the heavy international investment for its success.

The G5 Sahel will have to look inward and foster greater synergy between the regional response to security and development challenges and the processes initiated at the national and subnational levels. Self-defense militias have been set up with the support of local communities where state authority is weak and where jihadist factions operate. This has contributed to ethnic polarization and to the increasing massacres in 2019, such as Yirgou (1–2 January) in Burkina Faso and Ogossagou (23 March) and Sobame Da (10 June) in Mali. There must be greater synergy between the G5 Sahel's emphasis on sustaining peace by consolidating state authority and local peacebuilding initiatives initiated by its member-states and non-state actors.

## Notes

1 Seven out of fourteen current peace operations. See https://peacekeeping.un.org/en/current-peace keeping-operations
2 By hybrid orders of governance, I refer to the "multiple sites of political authority and governance where security is enacted and negotiated" (Luckham and Kirk 2013, 7), in which formal features linked to the rational-modern logic of the modern state coexist with informal processes leveraging "traditional, personal, kin-based and clientelistic [sic] logics" particular to specific historical and national trajectories (Bagayoko, Hutchful, and Luckham 2016, 6).
3 The security-development nexus refers to the overlapping of security and development concerns in the stabilization activities and projects of external actors rooted in the assumption on their mutually reinforcing linkages (Chandler 2007; Stern and Öjendal 2010).
4 The six countries are Burkina Faso, Chad, Mali, Mauritania, Niger and Senegal. Senegal is not part of the G5 Sahel.
5 Interview with former official of the French Barkhane Operation (Skype/Dakar, January 2018).
6 Interview with senior AU military official (Addis Ababa, 30 May 2019).
7 Interview with AU officials, Peace and Security Department (Addis Ababa, May–June 2019).

8 Interview with Malian diplomat involved in the Algiers peace process (Bamako, October 2017). This is echoed in another interview I had with an AU official, who said that "Algeria was interested in joining Sahelian mechanisms in order to control them rather than see them forward" (Addis Ababa, June 2019).
9 Interview with several AU officials of the PSD (Addis Ababa, June 2019).
10 Each battalion is composed of 650 troops divided into 550 soldiers and 100 police officers (or gendarmerie).
11 The support was in planning, transmissions, aerial support, medical evacuation and through the deployment of Special Forces (Robinet 2018).
12 Interview with EU military adviser (Skype/Abuja, August 2019).
13 Interview with senior AU military officer (Addis Ababa, June 2019).
14 Interview with senior AU military officer (Addis Ababa, June 2019).
15 Interview with EU military adviser (Skype/Abuja, August 2019).
16 Interview with Malian senior government leader (Bamako, October 2017).

# References

ACLED, (2019) 'Political Violence Skyrockets in the Sahel According to Latest ACLED Data', [Blog] *ACLED*, 28 March. [online]. Available at: https://acleddata.com/2019/03/28/press-release-political-violence-skyrockets-in-the-sahel-according-to-latest-acled-data/ (Accessed: 19 May 2021).

Babarinde, O., (2011) 'The African Union and the Quest for Security Governance in Africa', in Kirchner, E. and Dominguez, R., (eds.) *The Security Governance of Regional Organizations*. London and New York, NY: Routledge, pp. 273–299.

Bagayoko, N., (2019) "Le multilatéralisme sécuritaire africain à l'épreuve de la crise sahélienne", Centre Franco-Paix/Université du Québec à Montréal, (rapport), juin. Available at: https://dandurand.uqam.ca/wp-content/uploads/2019/06/Rapport_Bagayoko_Multilateralisme_Securitaire_Africain.pdf.

Bagayoko, N., Hutchful, E. and Robin Luckham, R., (2016) 'Hybrid Security Governance in Africa: Rethinking the Foundations of Security, Justice and Legitimate Public Authority', *Conflict, Security & Development*, 16(1), pp. 1–32.

Barnett, M., Hunjoon, K., O'Donnell, M. and Sitea, L., (2007) 'Peacebuilding: What Is in a Name?', *Global Governance*, 13(1), pp. 35–58. [online]. Available at: www.jstor.org/stable/27800641 (Accessed: 19 May 2021).

Bensassi, S., Brockmeyer, A., Pellerin, M. and Raballand, G., (2015) 'Commerce Algérie-Mali. La Normalité de l'Informalité', *Working Paper*. Washington, DC: World Bank Group.

Bertrand, E. and Cheeseman, N., (2019) 'Understanding the G5: Governance, Development and Security in the Sahel', *Open Publications*, 3(2). Brussels: NATO. [online]. Available at: www.act.nato.int/images/stories/media/doclibrary/open201902-understanding-g5-sahel.pdf (Accessed: 19 May 2021).

Cantens, T. and Raballand, G., (2017) 'Cross-Border Trade, Insecurity and the Role of Customs: Some Lessons from Six Field Studies', in *(Post-) Conflict Regions. Institute of Development Studies*. [online]. Available at: https://opendocs.ids.ac.uk/opendocs/handle/123456789/13379 (Accessed: 19 May 2021).

Chandler, D., (2007) 'The Security – Development Nexus and the Rise of "Anti-Foreign Policy"', *Journal of International Relations and Development*, 10(4), pp. 362–386.

Charbonneau, B., (2017) 'Intervention in Mali: Building Peace between Peacekeeping and Counterterrorism', *Journal of Contemporary African Studies*, 35(4), pp. 415–431.

Châtaigner, J-M. and Chevalier, C., (2019) 'Enjeux de paix et de développement: comment sortir le Sahel de la trappe à pauvreté ?', *Réalités Industrielles*, pp. 29–37, 91–92, 94. [online]. Available at: http://search.proquest.com/docview/2277920163/abstract/4CB5EDFDF40842ADPQ/2 (Accessed: 19 May 2021).

Conseil de sécurité de l'ONU, (2017) *Pour Appuyer La Force Conjointe Des États Du G5 Sahel, Le Conseil de Sécurité Propose Un Accord Technique Avec l'ONU et l'Union Européenne, via La MINUSMA*. New York, NY: Organisation des Nations Unies. [online]. Available at: www.un.org/press/fr/2017/cs13112.doc.htm (Accessed: 19 May 2021).

De Carvalho, G., (2020) 'The Future of Peace Operations Is African and Demands Better Coordination', [Blog] *IPI Global Observatory*, 21 September. [online]. Available at: https://theglobalobservatory.org/2020/09/future-peace-operations-african-demands-better-coordination/ (Accessed: 19 May 2021).

De Coning, C., (2017) 'Peace Enforcement in Africa: Doctrinal Distinctions between the African Union and United Nations', *Contemporary Security Policy*, 38(1), pp. 145–160.

De Coning, C., (2018) 'Adaptive Peacebuilding', *International Affairs*, 94(2), pp. 301–317.

Desgrais, N., (2019) *Cinq Ans Après, Une Radioscopie Du G5 Sahel Des Réformes Nécessaires de l'architecture et Du Processus Décisionnel*. Paris: Fondation pour la recherche stratégique. [online]. Available at: www.frstrategie.org/web/documents/programmes/observatoire-du-monde-arabo-musulman-et-du-sahel/publications/201913.pdf (Accessed: 19 May 2021).

Donais, T., (2012) *Peacebuilding and Local Ownership: Post-Conflict and Consensus-Building*. New York, NY: Routledge.

G5 Sahel, (2017) *Plaidoyer pour la promotion du leadership des femmes en matière de prévention et de lutte contre l'extrémisme violent dans les pays du G5 Sahel*. [online]. Available at: https://admin.g5sahel.org/wp-content/uploads/2017/03/images_Docs_DOCUMENT_DE_PLAIDOYER_VF.pdf (Accessed: 19 May 2021).

G5 Sahel, (2018) *Programme d'investissements prioritaires (PIP/G5 Sahel): première phase (2019–2021)*. G5 Sahel/Secrétariat Permanent. [online]. Available at: www.g5sahel.org/images/DOCPIP/PIP_G5S_2019_2021_FR_VF.pdf (Accessed: 19 May 2021).

G5 Sahel, (2020) *Le Plan Stratégique de La Plateforme Des Femmes Du G5 Sahel Finalisé et Validé*. [online]. Available at: www.g5sahel.org/article/le-plan-strategique-de-la-plateforme-des-femmes-du-g5-sahel-finalise-et-valide (Accessed: 19 May 2021).

International Crisis Group, (2015) 'Algeria and Its Neighbors', *Middle East and North Africa Report*, 164. Dakar, Brussels: International Crisis Group. [online]. Available at: www.refworld.org/pdfid/561cd6294.pdf (Accessed: 19 May 2021).

International Crisis Group, (2017) 'Finding the Right Role for the G5 Sahel Joint Force', Africa Report, 258. [online]. Available at: https://d2071andvip0wj.cloudfront.net/258-finding-the-right-role-for-the-g5-sahel-joint-force.pdf (Accessed: 19 May 2021).

Karlsrud, J., (2017) 'Towards UN Counter-Terrorism Operations?', *Third World Quarterly*, 38(6), pp. 1215–1231.

Karlsrud, J., (2019) 'From Liberal Peacebuilding to Stabilization and Counterterrorism', *International Peacekeeping*, 26(1), pp. 1–21.

Le Monde avec AFP, (2018) *Un général mauritanien et un adjoint tchadien prennent la tête de la force du G5 Sahel*, 16 Juillet. [online]. Available at: www.lemonde.fr/afrique/article/2018/07/16/un-general-mauritanien-et-un-adjoint-tchadien-prennent-la-tete-de-la-force-du-g5-sahel_5331960_3212.html (Accessed: 19 May 2021).

Luckham, R. and Kirk, T., (2013) 'The Two Faces of Security in Hybrid Political Orders: A Framework for Analysis and Research', *Stability: International Journal of Security and Development*, 2(2), Art. 44.

Mac Ginty, R., (ed.) (2013) *Routledge Handbook of Peacebuilding*. New York, NY: Routledge.

Nsaibia, H., (2020) 'State Atrocities in the Sahel: The Impetus for Counterinsurgency Results Is Fueling Government Attacks on Civilians', [Blog] *ACLED*, 20 May. [online]. Available at: https://acleddata.com/2020/05/20/state-atrocities-in-the-sahel-the-impetus-for-counter-insurgency-results-is-fueling-government-attacks-on-civilians/ (Accessed: 19 May 2021).

RFI, (2017) 'Mali: 10 000 hommes et 50 millions d'euros pour la force commune du G5 Sahel – RFI', *RFI Afrique*, 5 June. [online]. Available at: www.rfi.fr/afrique/20170605-mali-force-commune-g5-sahel-dix-mille-soldats-50-millions-euros-union-europeenne (Accessed: 19 May 2021).

Robinet, C., (2018) 'Genèse de La Force Conjointe Du G5 Sahel', [Blog] *Ultima Ratio*, 16 January. [online]. Available at: http://ultimaratio-blog.org/archives/8650 (Accessed: 19 May 2021).

Scheele, J., (2009) 'Tribus, États et Fraude: La Région Frontalière Algéro-Malienne', *Études Rurales*, 184(2), pp. 79–94.

Slate Afrique, (2014) *G5 du Sahel: à quoi ça sert vraiment?* [online]. Available at: www.slateafrique.com/441755/g5-sahel-initiative-floue-objectifs-mysterieux (Accessed: 19 May 2021).

Stern, M. and Öjendal, J., (2010) 'Mapping the Security – Development Nexus: Conflict, Complexity, Cacophony, Convergence?', *Security Dialogue*, 41(1), pp. 5–29.

Tisseron, A., (2015) *G5 Sahel : Une Simple Organisation de Plus ?* Bruxelles: Groupe de recherche et d'information sur la paix et la sécurité (GRIP). [online]. Available at: EC_2015–03–25_FR_A-TISSERON.pdf (grip.org) (Accessed: 19 May 2021).

Tschirgi, N., (2013) 'Securitization and Peacebuilding', in Mac Ginty, R., (ed.) *The Routledge Handbook of Peacebuilding*. London and New York, NY: Routledge, pp. 197–211.

Tull, D., (2017) *Mali, the G5 and Security Sector Assistance: Political Obstacles to Effective Cooperation*. SWP Comments 4. Berlin: German Institute for International and Security Affairs.

Tull, D., (2019) 'Rebuilding Mali's Army: The Dissonant Relationship between Mali and Its International Partners', *International Affairs*, 95(2), pp. 405–422.

Tull, D., (2020) *The European Union Training Mission and the Struggle for a New Model Army in Mali*. Research Paper 89. Paris: Institut de recherche stratégique et militaire (IRSEM).

UNHCR, (2020) *Sahel Crisis: Responding to the Urgent Needs of Refugees, Internally Displaced, Returnees and Others of Concern*. Geneva: UNHCR. [online]. Available at: https://reporting.unhcr.org/sites/default/files/UNHCR%20Appeal%20for%20the%20Sahel%20Crisis_June%202020.pdf (Accessed: 19 May 2021).

UNICEF, (2019) *School Closures in the Sahel Double in the Last Two Years Due to Growing Insecurity*, 27 February. [online]. Available at: www.unicef.org/press-releases/school-closures-sahel-double-last-two-years-due-growing-insecurity-unicef (Accessed: 19 May 2021).

United Nations, (2017) *Report of the Secretary-General on the Joint Force of the Group of Five for the Sahel*. S/2017/869. New York, NY: United Nations. [online]. Available at: www.securitycouncilreport.org/atf/cf/%7B65BFCF9B-6D27-4E9C-8CD3-CF6E4FF96FF9%7D/s_2017_869.pdf (Accessed: 19 May 2021).

United Nations, (2018) *Joint Force of the Group of Five for the Sahel: Report of the Secretary-General*. UN Secretary General Report to the UN Security Council. S/2018/1006. New York, NY: United Nations. [online]. Available at: www.securitycouncilreport.org/atf/cf/%7B65BFCF9B-6D27-4E9C-8CD3-CF6E4FF96FF9%7D/s_2018_1006.pdf (Accessed: 19 May 2021).

United Nations, (2019a) *Joint Force of the Group of Five for the Sahel: Report of the Secretary-General*. Report of the Secretary-General. S/2019/371. New York, NY: United Nations. [online]. Available at: https://reliefweb.int/sites/reliefweb.int/files/resources/S_2019_371_E.pdf (Accessed: 19 May 2021).

United Nations, (2019b) *Report of the UN Secretary-General on the Joint Force of the G5 Sahel*. New York, NY: United Nations. [online]. Available at: www.securitycouncilreport.org/atf/cf/%7B65BFCF9B-6D27-4E9C-8CD3-CF6E4FF96FF9%7D/S_2019_868.pdf (Accessed: 19 May 2021).

Williams, P.D., (2009) 'The African Union's Peace Operations: A Comparative Analysis', *African Security*, 2(2–3), pp. 97–118.

Williams, P.D., (2016) *War and Conflict in Africa*. 2nd ed. Malden, MA: Polity.

Williams, P.D., (2019) 'Can Ad Hoc Security Coalitions in Africa Bring Stability?', [Blog] *IPI Global Observatory*, 14 January. [online]. Available at: https://theglobalobservatory.org/2019/01/can-ad-hoc-security-coalitions-africa-bring-stability/ (Accessed: 19 May 2021).

World Bank, (2009) *Securing Development*. [online]. Available at: http://siteresources.worldbank.org/NEWS/Resources/RBZUSIPSpeech010809.pdf (Accessed: 19 May 2021).

# 14
# COUNTERINSURGENCY AND PEACEBUILDING IN SOMALIA AND MALI

*Bruno Charbonneau and Louise Wiuff Moe*

## Introduction

Reflecting on the limitations of the post-9/11 campaigns in Afghanistan and Iraq, David Kilcullen – one of the most influential contemporary counterinsurgency thinkers – in his 2010 book *Counterinsurgency* argued for a rethink of international military strategy toward a more 'population-centric' approach, coupling hard power (coercion) with soft power (consent and reconstruction). To do so, Kilcullen argued, 'counterinsurgency and counterterrorism people . . . need to start talking more with the peacebuilding and development community, and they both need to talk much more with the rule-of-law community' (Kilcullen 2010, 160).

Integrating military objectives with goals commonly associated with peacebuilding – including security sector reform (SSR), rule of law, and support to 'civil society' – has been a key policy trend in the 2000s and arguably since the end of the Cold War. The interventions in Afghanistan and Iraq marked the trend as they exposed, for military strategists, the limitations of a conventional military approach for fighting unconventional wars (Moe and Müller 2017). They paved the way for a renaissance of counterinsurgency. Colonial and Cold War lessons in fighting irregular enemies were revived, while counterinsurgency was reframed and updated to better align with post–Cold War normative goals related to the promotion of good governance, rule of law, and sustainable peace (Moe and Müller 2018).

Post-9/11 American war experiences were certainly very influential in fashioning and disseminating counterinsurgency thinking. The US Army counterinsurgency field manual *FM 3–24*, first published in 2006, was instrumental in promoting a form of enlightened 'armed social work', aiming 'to redress basic social and political problems while being shot at' (US Army 2014). This doctrine of and for new wars promised the advantages of lessons learned from anti-guerrilla warfare while writing out the controversies of Cold War and colonial strategies, instead co-articulating itself with discourses of peace- and nation-building. The re-emergence of counterinsurgency in an allegedly more enlightened, population-centric version represents a significant moment of growing convergence between stabilization mandates, counterinsurgency, and peacebuilding (Turner 2015; Charbonneau 2017; Moe 2018), between military logics and various conflict management mechanisms.

For Dierk Walter (2017, 108), counterinsurgency is a form of politics that, instead of creating military conditions for political victory, 'incorporates political measures into the military sphere, subjects them to military logic, and makes them into ancillary methods for achieving a military victory'. In other words, counterinsurgency is not a technical tool, a professional practice without ideological underpinnings, or an objective science for conflict management, for quelling rebellions, or for eliminating terrorists. It is more than the military tactics of conquest or stabilization. In the words of Patricia Owens, counterinsurgency wars played a significant role in the 'dissemination of social governance': 'If the conflict between insurgents and counterinsurgents is a "competition in government", a form of "applied political science", and victory is achieved through social administration, then what is the nature of the government offered through counterinsurgency rule?' During the late colonial wars, 'military strategists sought to create units of rule over local populations as a means to the end of defeating insurgents' using the 'correct combination of force and politics [in order to] socialise, pacify and domesticate a population into regulating itself'. For Owens, the essence of counterinsurgency is thus the creation of governable populations (Owens 2015, 24, 45, 157).

While Afghanistan and Iraq are the main reference points, the influence of counterinsurgency thinking has spread far and wide, including on the African continent. Counterinsurgency practices expanded substantially beyond the grand-scale campaigns of the post-9/11 world to a number of 'secondary fronts' (Moe and Müller 2017). They also informed American military training programs to African states (Africa Contingency Operations Training and Assistance [ACOTA]). The Global War on Terror and subsequent NATO military deployments contributed to the prioritization of counterterrorism and counterinsurgency in multilateral operations and brought them into the UN system (Curran and Holtom 2015) and UN peacekeeping and peacebuilding missions (Karlsrud 2018). The think tank Saferworld argues that the rise of the countering or preventing violent extremism agenda, and the creation of a stand-alone UN Office of Counter-Terrorism, constitutes the UN's 'fourth pillar' which risks undermining the integrity and effectiveness of the other three (i.e. human rights, peace and security, and development; Altiok and Street 2020). Certainly, within the UN system, the tensions were apparent. The 2015 Report of the Independent High-level Panel on Peace Operations (HIPPO), for instance, was largely the result of, and a contribution to, the debates over the use of force in UN peacekeeping, the intrusion of counterterrorism, the ambiguity of stabilization mandates, and what it might mean for the future of UN peace operations – a report that was informed by the cases of Somalia and Mali.

In this chapter, we examine the two cases of Somalia and Mali, as both examples have been at the heart of relevant discussions and debates about the use of force in peacebuilding and peacekeeping. In both Somalia and Mali, peacebuilding and peacekeeping practices and principles came under stress through the pressures of stabilization, counterterrorism, and counterinsurgency agendas. In this chapter, we consider counterinsurgency and stabilization to be synonyms in doctrinal texts, as 'ultimately stabilisation means different things to different actors engaged in the same process. . . . The United States . . . views stabilisation as being a subset of COIN, whereas UK doctrine views the relationship in entirely the opposite terms' (Tripodi 2021, 41). Yet, the relationship between the two concepts goes beyond the doctrinal texts. On the one hand, there are numerous books and articles on the meanings, purposes, and practices of counterinsurgency. On the other hand, there are almost as many on UN stabilization mandates and militarization of UN peacekeeping. However, there is very little on the relationship between the rise of counterinsurgency in the post-9/11 era and the rise of stabilization in UN mandates, and how this relationship has affected peacebuilding and conflict management mechanisms. If there is one starting point, though, it is that there is no agreed upon definition of 'stabilization', whether in the academic or policy world. Stabilization sounds more neutral than counterinsurgency, less military, yet malleable enough to mean everything and anything, a hodgepodge of words merging with other terms in better defined areas of practice like peacebuilding (Mac Ginty 2012, 24).

As David Curran and Charles Hunt argue, the point is not about the robustness or militarization of UN peacekeeping. What matters more is the political impact of stabilization mandates (Curran and Hunt 2020). In the cases of Somalia and Mali, what matters most is how counterinsurgency thinking and stabilization mandates impact the possibilities of peacebuilding and conflict resolution. This chapter analyses the political logic and effects of such military and strategic thinking on conflict management mechanisms and processes, on the possibilities of conflict resolution in Mali and Somalia, by interrogating the assumptions that sustain the ideas about the use and the utility of military force. The theoretical perspectives, the narrative frames, the discursive strategies, and the conceptual issues of or inspired by counterinsurgency do not simply respond to 'threats' somehow, somewhere. Practices of security, including the military use of force, contribute to the production or constitution of the objects and subjects that ought to be secured and governed, in the formation of states, regions, regional security communities, and regional dynamics of conflicts (Charbonneau 2017; Moe 2017). Put another way, counterinsurgency is more than a technique of warfare: it is a form of social thought that is co-constituted by resistance to its practices (Owens 2015).

In Mali and Somalia, what we observe is how military intervention incorporates peacebuilding and holistic approaches into its logic only to the extent that it normalizes and legitimizes the use of force, perpetually.

## Stabilization mandates and counterinsurgency

The 2015 HIPPO Report lamented the lack of clarity in the interpretation of stabilization mandates. It recommended a clear division of labour between UN forces engaged in peacekeeping and other parallel military forces. Yet, neither conceptual clarity nor a coherent stabilization practice has materialized: 'Instead, the [UN] Security Council [has] continued to use stabilization in a flexible manner precisely because it was politically useful to have it fit the distinct needs of unique local contexts' (Williams and Bellamy 2021, 200). Stabilization has also proven useful for parallel forces and non-UN forces.

Indeed, diplomats, politicians, and diverse practitioners understand the advantages of conceptual murkiness. As Susan Woodward showed, the ideology of the failed states plays an important role in intervention politics. The concept of the failed state facilitates and justifies external intervention. As Woodward argues, it is an ideology that works *for* the international system and third-party actors, and not to explain what goes on in conflict environments. It is used to overcome the political, legal, and operational constraints on international actors and interventions (Woodward 2017). Scholars generally agree that the concept of stabilization is connected to, if not synonymous with, the restoration or extension of state authority in failed states (Gorur 2016). They have shown, time and again, that the concept of failed/fragile states makes no sense theoretically and empirically. It does not tell us anything useful about the states so labelled (Hameiri 2009). It still has its political use.

The relationship between the concepts of stabilization and failed/fragile states is thus crucial both as a justification mechanism and as carrier of an implicit solution to conflicts (i.e. to capacity build the state). Stabilization connects the roadmap for implementing peace processes to the restoration of legitimate state authority (Gorur 2016). Political and institutional reforms, support for SSR and disarmament, demobilization, and reintegration (DDR) programs, for reconciliation and justice measures, and for the organization of elections, and more, are conceived as building the necessary state capacity for (re)asserting its authority. Unburdened by a precise definition, stabilization is nevertheless dependent on the legitimacy of the state's authority. It is thus both logically and practically tied to the state's armed security forces and to the inevitability of countering non-state armed groups that violently challenge host governments.

The link between stabilization and the restoration of state authority is an indication of the influence of counterinsurgency doctrine, or certainly the thin line between stabilization and counterinsurgency. State-building is a central pillar of counterinsurgency thought (Moe and Müller 2017). Counterinsurgents seek to establish and impose the state's monopoly on the use of legitimate force upon the enemies of the state (Porch 2013), while the failure of the post-colonial state to monopolize the use of legitimate force forms the space where international military intervention and its associated politics can exist and take shape (Charbonneau 2019).

Counterinsurgency doctrine incorporates development and holistic approaches into its logic to the extent that it normalizes and legitimizes the use of force.[1] Military operations are conceived as largely distinct from the political sphere. The population is conceived as the vulnerable social body at risk and in need of protection and as a body from which risks, dangers, and threats emerge (Owens 2015; Charbonneau 2021a). In other words, the emphasis on civilians is not anathema to counterinsurgency or stabilization; it is central to the logic of military operations:

> while the centre of gravity is the civilian population, operationalized through protection of civilians, this is not based on a moral imperative of protecting human rights or on notions of human security, as in the UN context . . . it is a means to an end; to reduce popular support for insurgents.
>
> (Friis 2010, 52)

If the focus on civilians or civilian attempts at peacebuilding do not work, military forces can go back to the use of force and counterterrorist tactics (Turner 2015).

From 'the legacy of Bosnia and Rwanda' and 'the rise of an increasingly strong anti-atrocity turn in international law and policy' emerged the push for more proactive and robust UN peacekeeping forces willing to increase the scale and the regularity of the use of force to protect civilians (Mégret 2015). In this context, peacekeeping became more coercive in terms of becoming more humanitarian, to protect human rights and for human protection (Curran 2017; Fjelde, Hultman and Nilsson 2019; Foley 2017; Williams 2013; Willmot et al. 2016). At the same time, the principle that the host state is first and foremost responsible for protecting civilians – which is part of both the agendas of the Responsibility to Protect (R2P) and the Protection of Civilians (POC)[2] – the UN's protection agenda has expanded to entail building and strengthening state capacity and reforming state-level security institutions and forces (Donais and Tanguay 2020).

This is the merger of the human rights, peacebuilding, and security rationales from the 1990s. As UN peacekeepers became increasingly involved in state-building and stabilization efforts, 'the relationship between military force and peacebuilding activities was overtly codified through their fusion in peace support operations' (Turner 2015). The rapprochement between the respective doctrines and discourses of peacekeeping, counterinsurgency, and counterterrorism under the various labels of 'stabilization', 'complex humanitarian emergencies' or 'peace support operations' have led many scholars to point out the parallels to colonial pacification campaigns and global counterinsurgency strategies.

By virtue of its conceptual malleability, stabilization allows the rapprochement of peacekeeping, counterinsurgency, and counterterrorism practices and doctrines. Stabilization enables and allows the link between violent coercion and enmity by supporting the host state's authority and building its security capacity, or by allowing parallel forces to implement their strategic vision of the conflict. Therefore, and prior to any mediation or peace negotiation, stabilization designates state actors as worthy of UN peacekeeping protection and non-state actors as those against whom coercive force can be used. There are several implications for UN peacekeeping, not least in terms of undermining UN legitimacy, impartiality, and potential for peacebuilding and conflict resolution (Curran and Hunt 2020).

The following sections examine the cases of Somalia and Mali. Both conflicts have been and continue to be central testing grounds for the practices of stabilization, counterinsurgency, and counterterrorism (Charbonneau 2017; Moe 2016, 2017). In analysing the key dynamics and consequences of the increasing blur between stabilization, counterinsurgency, and peacebuilding practices, we challenge the legitimating depictions of the 'new' counterinsurgency as a more enlightened and benign hearts and mind approach that enables and sustains stability and peace. Indeed, we demonstrate how the influence of counterinsurgency doctrine within the vocabulary and practices of peacebuilding in fact contributes to turning the latter into 'another layer of pacification techniques' (Turner 2015), centred on governing 'unruly' or subversive others – or at least to contain them.

## Somalia: tangled ties of military intervention and politics

Since the collapse of the state in 1991, Somalia has been the site of numerous international and regional efforts of reviving government institutions, countering insurgents, and enforcing peace. Thus, the context paradigmatically illustrates how the ideology of 'failed states' legitimizes intervention. Since the mid-2000s, Somalia has also become a key testing ground for a post-Iraq and post-Afghanistan reworked approach to counterinsurgency, departing from large-scale internationally led military occupation and nation-building attempts, focusing instead on international support toward enabling regional forces to counter insurgents, and to stabilize the country so as to allegedly pave the way for political solutions and to revive state authority. The latter outcomes, however, have not materialized. Rather than safeguarding the space for politics and peacemaking, counterinsurgency efforts in Somalia have become integral to, and defining of, politics, with the result that the arenas of governance, local orders, and institutions have been subsumed under the logic of infinite military intervention (Moe 2017, 2018).

### *Political crisis, military responses and the rise of al-Shabaab*

While the 'Black Hawk Down' battle in Mogadishu in 1993 significantly deterred international intervention in Somalia, the country nonetheless came to occupy an ever more central position on the international counterterrorism agenda. One important event in this regard was the 1998 bombings of the US embassies in Nairobi and Dar es Salaam, which brought Somalia into focus as key actors implicated in the bombings, were understood to have had their base within Somalia. After 9/11, Americans established the Combined Joint Task Force–Horn of Africa, based in Djibouti, to better coordinate its operations in East Africa and, reportedly, special forces were deployed into Somalia. Americans channeled substantial support to the Alliance for the Restoration of Peace and Counterterrorism, which was essentially a coalition of warlords seeking to bolster their elite networks through catering for CIA interests. In turn, in 2006 the Union of Islamic Courts (UIC), opposing the coalitions of US-supported warlords and the Transitional Federal Government (TFG), took control over most areas of south-central Somalia. This was followed by a surge of military intervention, as hostilities between UIC and Ethiopia led the latter to launch a major military campaign, strongly backed by the US, and to the defeat of the UIC. Before this defeat, the courts had managed to establish a level of peace and order that neither the Transitional National Government, nor its predecessor, the warlord-dominated TFG, had been able or willing to provide (Samatar 2006). While the US-backed Ethiopian intervention against the courts, as well as the subsequent military occupation, were justified as necessary steps in the war on terror, they arguably became part of producing exactly the violent extremism they set out to defeat (Menkhaus 2009). While the UIC dissolved, its small, hard-line al-Shabaab factions hid in the interior of Somalia, and in the aftermath of the Ethiopian intervention – where Ethiopian and TFG security forces became the key sources of insecurity and terror for the population – al-Shabaab was able to mobilize an armed insurgency. The TFG and the Ethiopian forces responded by stepping up heavy-handed counterinsurgency operations, resulting in escalating violence and displacement. The ensuing humanitarian crisis – wherein the impacts of armed conflict were compounded by hyperinflation and drought – played to the benefit of al-Shabaab and its mobilization against Ethiopia, the TFG, and international forces (Menkhaus 2009, 8).

## *AMISOM and the fallacy of 'clear hold build'*

The establishment of the African Union Mission in Somalia (AMISOM) in January 2007 was a means for replacing Ethiopian occupation and countering al-Shabaab. The mission deployed into a context not only of armed conflict but also of profound contestation of the government. The latter was shaped by the lack of popular backing to what was but a shell of a state, the presence of resented Ethiopian forces collaborating with state forces in combatting insurgents. In turn, insurgents forged considerable support networks and governance arrangements in large swatches of the country.

AMISOM was established by the African Union (AU) and authorized by the UN Security Council (UNSC) in 2007. Funding for the mission was primarily provided by the European Union (EU), with supplementary contributions from UN and AU funds as well as additional sources of bilateral support. The establishment of AMISOM also allowed international interveners to pursue a low 'footprint' approach by channelling various forms of support – centred around train and equip and special operations – through local and regional partners.

AMISOM aligns with tenets of an 'integrated' stabilization approach, mandating the military use of force to create conditions for peace and state-building. The mission profile also resonates with much of the reasoning informing the 'new' counterinsurgency thinking of the 2000s and 2010s, stressing 'light footprint' involvement of internationals, the primacy of local and regional ownership or alliances, and the need for combining coercion and military approaches with civilian, peacebuilding, and humanitarian components. AMISOM thereby also reflects a wider trend: the combination of coercion and reconstruction that involves a division of labour, according to which regional actors take the lead of the riskier and more controversial enforcement and clear activities that sit uneasy with the UN's and EU's institutional identities and capacities. Thus, this logic envisions regional actors as first responders who, through military means, clear the ground for international 'hold' and 'build' efforts gravitating around peace- and state-building.

While initially AMISOM comprised only one battle group of Ugandan forces, airlifted into Somalia's capital Mogadishu, it grew to become the largest AU operation – and indeed, by 2017, it had become the 'largest deployment of uniformed peacekeepers in the world' (Williams 2018a, 2). Against the backdrop of advances against al-Shabaab from 2009 onwards, AMISOM gained the status of a model for reworked security approaches, demonstrating the potentials of the new 'innovative, low-cost, and small-footprint approaches' called for in the American Defense Strategy released in early 2012 (Pham 2013; Parrish 2013). During this period the rapprochement between counterinsurgency and counterterrorism, on the one hand, and 'peace support', on the other, significantly shaped the AMISOM model and its strategic communication. While according to the official representation of AMISOM the mission was transformed from 'conventional combat forces into a much more sophisticated peace-support operations capability', in practice, at that stage, it had evolved into a veritable 'war-fighting mission with an admixture of VIP protection tasks' (Williams 2018a, 104).

During the years that followed, it has become increasingly clear, however, that war-fighting advances against al-Shabaab were not accompanied by advances in peacebuilding. Politics has remained profoundly tense, with little if any progress being made on the fundamental questions of governance and reconciliation (Williams 2018b). The failures to conduct scheduled elections in 2020 and 2021 – due to power struggles between the Somalia federal government and its federal member states – and the resulting increase in armed clashes and instability are illustrations of the highly strained political climate (Diatta et al. 2021). Meanwhile, al-Shabaab expanded its transnational networks, adopted more asymmetric tactics (Williams 2018a, 13), and increased the frequency of its attacks after August 2020 (Diatta et al. 2021). In addition, al-Shabaab substantially expanded its governance practices. The group raised at least as much revenues as the state authorities, not only in the large swatches of territory it controlled in south-central Somalia but also in Mogadishu, where the group was able to extend its influence (Harper 2020).

The political impasse and resilience of al-Shabaab has undercut any viable exit strategy for AMISOM. In 2017, a thousand troops were withdrawn as a first step in AMISOM's planned drawdown. The UNSC voted for further drawdown, but during the COVID-19 pandemic it authorized AMISOM's deployment until the end of March 2022. Several experts warned that the Somali government was likely to collapse in the face of a full AMISOM withdrawal, while also recognizing that AMISOM is effectively 'caught in a situation of political and development failures [. . .] with seemingly no viable political projects for Somalia, and consequently no sustainable peace to be achieved' (Thomas Mandrup, quoted in Diatta et al. 2021).

Thus, Somalia and the AMISOM model have become illustrative cases of how the promise of counterinsurgency – that clear and hold military efforts will pave the way for 'a happy homestretch' (Ucko 2013, 55) of building sustainable peace and order – is rarely if ever achieved.

## *Beyond 'getting politics right'*

Some observers pointed to the lack of sufficient resourcing of AMISOM as a key factor behind the lack of progress in stabilizing Somalia. Indeed, there is an evident gap between allocated resources and AMISOM's ambitious mandate of combatting al-Shabaab, supporting effective and legitimate government, building the capacity of state institutions, and fostering reconciliation. In 2021, discussions on extending AMISOM's mandate pointed to the need to move beyond a narrow focus on security and place greater priority on 'getting politics right' (Diatta et al. 2021).

Questions of resources and the importance of 'political solutions' vis-à-vis military objectives are both valid and important perspectives. Yet, they leave unaddressed core questions concerning how military strategy itself gets to define and, indeed, becomes integral to defining the legitimate parameters of politics. This deep military-political linkage has been a constant undercurrent of intervention in Somalia: from the US and Ethiopian military backing of the warlord-based Alliance for the Restoration of Peace and Counterterrorism, prompting the rise of the UIC, to the ensuing US-supported Ethiopian invasion and the eventual deployment of AMISOM. This backdrop of events highlights how the challenge facing AMISOM and its effort to counter insurgents were not simply about resources or about the balance between military and political solutions. Instead, a core predicament stems from a history of intervention whereby military logic has penetrated and thereby put distinct limits to politics and peace.

The political consequences of military strategy are conveyed by the political economy that has developed around intervention, whereby political elites (at national and local levels) have a vested interest in the perpetual military engagements and the derived security rents available for counterinsurgency allies. These dynamics also involve centrifugal forces whereby support to federalism and local administrations have become entwined with bolstering local coercion wielders against al-Shabaab, in some cases leading to an outright decentring of sovereignty and the outsourcing of the administration of force (Moe 2017, 2018).

In turn, the rise in US airstrikes and targeted killings in Somalia conveyed the willingness of counterterrorist strategists to eventually bracket 'politics' (and civilian protection) altogether in the wake of the mounting limitations of counterinsurgency approaches.

## Counterinsurgency and peacebuilding in Mali

In January 2012, Tuareg rebels allied with jihadist armed groups conquered the northern territories of Mali. Later in March, humiliated and angry at the state's incompetent management of the crisis, elements of the Malian army, led by Captain Sanogo, toppled the government in Bamako. The UNSC reacted with much prudence, notably because of US reticence or reluctance to admitting that there was an emergency. The Economic Community of West African States (ECOWAS) and the AU responded more swiftly but were unable to reach an agreement over a course of action that would convince the UNSC to authorize the deployment of an African force. After months of negotiations, the prudent Resolution 2085 was passed in December 2012, authorizing an African force to be operational by September 2013. The resolution seemingly prompted the now-jihadist armed groups to move south towards Mopti, which in turn provoked the French Serval intervention in January 2013.

Arguing that Mali was a destabilizing threat to the West African region and to the 'close neighbourhood' of Europe, French President François Hollande ordered the launch of Operation Serval, which drastically changed the momentum of and perspectives on the situation. The military intervention was to be a short-term affair meant to stabilize the situation by eradicating the jihadist terrorist groups that threatened, according to the French government, the territorial integrity, the state, and the capital of Mali. The French troops were ordered to seek and destroy the jihadists so that they could then pass the mantle to the UN and African partner organizations which would do the difficult work of political reconciliation and reconstruction of the Malian state and army.[3] With the French military intervention, Mali and the Sahel became the newest terrorist hotspots and counterterrorist battleground, attracting the typical counterterrorist, peacekeeping, peacebuilding, and development communities.

In the spring of 2014, it had become increasingly clear that if French forces left Mali, the UN would be in serious trouble, the Malian state and army would not be able to respond to a resurgence of armed groups, and Serval's tactical victories would be wasted. So the French army stayed. The French government declared Serval a success and fused it with Operation Épervier (in Chad since 1986) to create Operation Barkhane. French military operations would no longer be limited by Malian borders, as Barkhane's area of operation covered the territories of the countries of what has become known as the G5 Sahel: Mali, Niger, Burkina Faso, Chad, and Mauritania. The G5 Sahel was also created in 2014 as a new African regional organization.

Following Serval, the multiplication of regional and international strategies and actions directed at stabilizing Mali and the Sahel, at countering and preventing violent extremism, at capacity-building local actors, and so on was impressive. It was not long before academics talked of a security traffic jam in the Sahel, where 'international actors often emphasize synergies between what are commonly framed as multidimensional and comprehensive approaches, aimed sometimes at rebuilding "failed" states and sometimes at stabilizing the entire region' (Cold-Ravnkilde and Jacobsen 2020, 857). None of it has improved the situation so far and, arguably, some of it has made things worse (International Crisis Group 2021; UN Security Council 2020).[4]

Indeed, the 2015 Bamako Peace and Reconciliation Accords signed by the government of Bamako, the Coordination des Mouvements de l'Azawad (CMA), and the Plateforme expired in 2017 to little objection, as everyone knew that the Accords were going nowhere and disputes over territories, rents, drug routes, and influence between the signatory non-state groups and their respective allies continued to disrupt the peace process. By then, the central regions of Mali had imploded in late 2016. These areas had been suffering from the lack of state services, the fragmentation of social relations, the dismantling of conflict resolution mechanisms, the weakening of social trust, and increasing tensions over land use, which all participated in escalating ethnicized violence (Jourde, Brossier and Cissé 2019). As jihadist armed groups resurged in 2017 and continued operating, multiplied, and regionalized to Niger and Burkina Faso, the implementation of the expired Accords remained the glimmer of hope to hang on to for lack of a better alternative.

No matter the unit of measurement, the worsening situation trend is unequivocal, be it the increasing number of violent events, of victims, of displaced persons and refugees, the level and nature of the violence incurred (notably the 2019 Ogossagou massacre), the increased sophistication of attacks targeting national armed forces (e.g. the attack against the Nigerien Armed Forces at Inates), or the number of violent acts spreading to Niger and Burkina Faso. In spite of the notable growth in national military budgets and increases in troop levels for Mali, Burkina Faso, and Niger, combined with the resilience and determination of French and UN troops stationed across the Sahel, the security situation has grown steadily worse.

## *Peacebuilding as a containment strategy*

When French President Hollande ordered the execution of Operation Serval in 2013, he did not plan for a long-term military engagement. Serval was meant to establish the military control of the country and to recover the territorial integrity of the Malian state. French soldiers were to liberate and secure the necessary space and time required for the Malian Armed Forces, the UN, and other actors involved in peace talks to elaborate and put into place political solutions. The UN was meant to quickly replace French forces. By 2014, Serval had become the regional Operation Barkhane, a French counterterrorist and long-term presence that oversaw a regional space, with a view of accompanying and training (provided by the EU) African troops that would eventually deploy and replace French forces. Nevertheless, the military strategy remained the same: fighting terrorists in order to ensure the required time and space needed to implement political solutions.

Military chief of staff of the French Armed Forces, Army General François Lecointre, described France's 'Global Approach' for the Sahel 'as a crisis management strategy centred on the Sahel's own populations and their perceptions regarding the development of the crisis. This concept has been inherited from our colonial adventure'. The general continued by referencing 'French know-how' inherited through colonial conquests 'from Gallieni to Lyautey', during which counterinsurgency thought was developed. In the past as it is today, he argued, victory consists of 'winning the hearts and minds of the populations to whose aid we come in the regions we seek to stabilize' (Assemblée nationale 2019).

He could hardly be clearer. Since its inception, the international military engagement in the Sahel[5] is rooted in this French framework, a division of labour between counterterrorist troops and UN peacekeepers and peacebuilders (Charbonneau 2017). Its conception is based on counterinsurgency thinking, which is largely inspired by French military experiences in Africa, revised by the experience gained in Afghanistan, and largely approved by the European troops serving in the UN Malian mission.[6] Tactically and operationally, the French military and its allies speak of counter- or anti-terrorist missions, but the strategy is counterinsurgency. French military officers as much as their UN counterparts openly speak of securing populations and developing zones of stability like 'oil spots', from which it would be possible to construct or consolidate peace, notably through working to spatially spread such spaces in order to control larger sections of territory (Charbonneau 2019). Recurring references to the security-development nexus is the hallmark of this discourse: the military creates space for development and peace practitioners, and thus for political solutions, who then are supposed to take advantage of military successes and comply with the requirements of military strategy. As declared by General Lecointre, 'military gains we obtain will be worth nothing if they don't result in political agreements and tangible actions leading to economic and social development' (Assemblée nationale 2019).

In 2019, the limits of the approach became evident for everyone to see. It was the deadliest and most violent year the Sahel had faced since the start of the Malian crisis in 2012. It was also a year of increasing public critiques of the French military strategy and its emphasis on the threat of terrorism (specifically of the jihadist variant). Critiques were expressed more openly and ardently, explored multiple angles, and originated from diverse social milieus (politicians, journalists, academics, civil society). The International Crisis Group even dared to suggest a dialogue with jihadist armed groups (International Crisis Group 2019).[7]

Mediatized critiques, notably by organized groups from Mali, were especially directed at the French government to the point that President Emmanuel Macron summoned his G5 Sahel counterparts to a summit held at Pau on 13 January 2020. The diplomatic spectacle intended to put these critiques to bed. The summit allowed Macron's allied heads of state to reiterate their common interest to continue their collaboration to neutralize the Sahel's terrorist threat. They reaffirmed the necessity for a continued French military presence and again prioritized continued counterterrorist operations. Thus, they endorsed the French military strategy, while repeating clichéd rhetoric that a military solution could not solve the crisis and that political solutions like development and peacebuilding ought to be prioritized.

Meanwhile, the Malian state and army had become entities in a permanent state of being 'capacity-built'.[8] This did not prevent elements of the army to organize another coup d'état in August 2020, arguably embarrassing international actors and underlining the failure of their approach to stabilizing Mali. International organizations and governments of the world denounced the coup, but beyond the rhetoric, and except for ECOWAS, the coup was largely swept under the rug. The French government called to maintain constitutional order and declared its commitment to Malian sovereignty and democracy. Yet, President Macron, Minister of the Armed Forces Florence Parly, and Minister for Europe and Foreign Affairs Jean-Yves Le Drian reiterated their priorities of stabilization and counterterrorism and, above all, that the coup would not disrupt France's military operations (Charbonneau 2021b). Since then, Sahelian armies (especially the Malian army) have been shown to be more deadly to civilians than terrorist groups (Nsaibia 2020), and the French have been accused of atrocities in the Bounti incident (MINUSMA 2021).

Despite all, what has remained constant are the international engagements and committed Sahelian actors claiming to combat terrorism and/or prevent violent extremism in the name of stability, security, peace, and development. Despite the 'bitter harvest of French interventionism' (Guichaoua 2020), the increasing number of critiques of the security-focused approach, and the numerous calls for refocusing conflict resolution efforts on peacebuilding, dialogue, and reconstruction, there is no end in sight to military intervention in the Sahel. Under a permanent state of military intervention, a form of counterinsurgency governance manages the effects of instability, conflict, and violence in the Sahel (Charbonneau 2021a).

## Drawing lessons from Somalia and Mali

Counterinsurgency, conceived and presented as a military doctrine and a theory of practice in military operations, has a controversial history in military settings. The principles it promotes, for instance the primacy of politics, the need for development gains, and the centrality of tight civil-military relations, are now cliché of the genre.[9] Nevertheless, as Jean-Hervé Jezequel reminds us in the context of the Sahel, inasmuch as everyone knows that we must find and implement political solutions, 'few have drawn concrete consequences for how military action and political action should be co-articulated. . . . [while] military contingents advance . . . development has stalled and governance components continue to lag far behind' (Jezequel 2020).

We have argued that military operations should not be viewed as technical activities distinct from the political sphere that (according to the theory) facilitate the development of a space and time for political action. Rather, military strategy must be considered in its action and its political consequences, at least if one hopes to understand its failures and its limits in Somalia and Mali.

Counterinsurgency efforts have enrolled non-state armed groups in both Somalia and Mali. A range of armed groups of varied legitimacy govern large swathes of territory in both contexts. Links between these groups, and between them and the state, have certainly diverged and fluctuated, but it is clear that internationally led or backed counterterrorism and counterinsurgency operations have contributed to some of their coercive power and moral authority (Moe 2018; Carayol 2016).

It is well established that one of the effects of these counterterrorism collaborations has been an increase in inter-communal tensions (Jourde, Brossier and Cissé 2019). However, the consequences extend beyond the rise of local tensions. In both Somalia and Mali, counterinsurgency practice contributed to the fragmentation of the national territory. Spheres of influence more or less officially recognized were established and consolidated through these actions (e.g. Jubaland in Somalia, Kidal and Ménaka in Mali). Each of these spaces is governed by context-specific rules and norms, a form of governance sustained through paramilitary actions and forces, and power concentrated in the hands of dominant elites that shape a wartime political economy rooted in transnational trafficking and international counterterrorism rents.

In other words, as practiced in Somalia and Mali, counterinsurgency contributes to the construction and consolidation of local and regional political orders of violence. While such political orders are always in construction and are locally contested, their existence is certainly in contradiction to the stated objectives of restoring the authority of the Somali and Malian states, maintaining their territorial integrity, and the political work of facilitating national reconciliation. The political field and spaces of intervention that counterinsurgency theory supposedly preserves and secures are in fact fundamentally transformed, therein producing political dynamics that evade counterinsurgency practice.

These transformations eliminate or at least diminish needs and motivations to engage in political negotiation or to implement any sort of peace agreement. Instead, a 'counterterror' war economy is developed. More widely, the distinctive characteristic of 'the global approach' is its perpetuity in the name of fighting terrorism. In this context, counterinsurgency cannot resolve conflict since it requires an unending military engagement in order to manage instability.[10] It becomes a mode of governance through which international military operations become integral parts of the states where they take place.

Military interventions (and development) condition the majority, if not all, of national relations of power: negotiations and pacts between elites, patronage systems, multiparty elections, resource management, the development and consolidation of government institutions, constitutional reforms, and more. Military questions are therefore intrinsically connected to the political. Military logic does not precede politics sequentially through the establishment of a monopoly on the use of violence that authorizes politics. Instead, military intervention conditions, dictates, and imposes limits on the political.

Undoubtedly, the beginning of a solution must come from within Somalia or Mali (Devermont 2019) or develop out of an African reflection that fully considers a continental perspective (Bagayoko 2020). Nevertheless, any so-called political solution must detach itself from the counterinsurgency security paradigm and its colonial heritage and, more generally, the international obsession with stabilization as the only horizon for international conflict management.

For some scholars, the answer to the issues raised by the increasing connections between peace operations and other kinds of military operations is the explicit elaboration of a UN stabilization doctrine or the clarification of boundaries: 'where the threat to stability is an insurgency and a decision is made to counter it, stabilization becomes counterinsurgency', and 'when the threat to stability is terrorism, stabilization include elements of counterterrorism' (Aoi, De Coning and Karlsrud 2017b, 296; Gorur 2016). Yet, the call for a precise typology of UN missions underestimates the constraints and difficulties of clarifying the boundaries.

First, in practice, UN peace operations have not engaged much, if at all, in counterinsurgent or counterterrorist kinetic actions. At the least, they engage in counterterrorism in the limited meaning of the term as tactical measures to protect UN peacekeeping personnel (Charbonneau 2017). Yet, UN missions have enabled counterinsurgent or counterterrorist actions through stabilization mandates that authorize and support parallel forces to do so. Parallel forces deployed alongside UN missions are the ones identifying and responding to insurgent or terrorist threats. Since the end of the Cold War, more than 40 parallel forces deployed alongside UN peace operations have blurred the division of labour between missions, 'their goals hav[ing] sometimes come into conflict'. Parallel forces are conceived as filling a gap in the capabilities of UN forces, usually where the use of force is needed, but they often bring in competing or contradictory priorities and objectives (Novosseloff and Sharland 2019).

Second, both the elaboration of UN stabilization doctrine and the division of labour between UN peace operations and parallel forces are premised on the possibility, the ability, and the authority to distinguish between conflict actors. In practice, however, how do you distinguish civilians from combatants? How do you differentiate insurgents, rebels, criminals, fighters, and terrorists? In conflict settings from Democratic Republic of the Congo, Somalia, Mali, and the Central African Republic to Chad, Libya, and Sudan, scholars have demonstrated how individuals have fluid and multiple identities and allegiances. They can shift between non-state armed formations and government forces. Armed groups drift between countries. These patterns of mobility shape local political and moral economies and notions of authority and legitimacy (Ahram and King 2012; Briscoe 2014; Debos 2016; Dowd 2015; Sandor 2017; Scheele 2012).

The 'division of labour' or parallel forces arrangements work on paper as a broader strategy of legitimizing the use of force, because they address the legal aspects of having two international military forces operating in the same theater, of separating UN peacekeepers from combat troops. The challenges that emerge come from the competing logic, ethics, and purpose of peacekeeping, counterinsurgency, and counterterrorism. The latter two are grounded in enmity, practices that need to identify an enemy to destroy (Charbonneau 2017). By definition, UN peacekeepers are not supposed to have or identify enemies (Levine 2014). Otherwise, they become just like all the other combatants, lose what makes their presence unique, and might as well just go to war. Impartiality is, for some analysts, the bedrock principle of UN peacekeeping and peacebuilding missions because it plays a fundamental function in drawing the limits to the use of force and its purpose (Aoi, De Coning and Karlsrud 2017a, 6). Impartiality does not prohibit peacekeepers from using military force, but it severs the link between violent coercion and enmity, between the use of military force and the identification of an enemy.

## Notes

1. On the merging of security and development, see Duffield (2001).
2. On R2P and POC, see Rhoads and Welsh (2019).
3. On Serval and the initial French engagement, see Notin (2014).
4. According to the quarterly reports of the UN secretary-general on Mali, the situation has continued to steadily deteriorate since 2015. This recurring sentence is found again in the latest report: 'The security situation continued to deteriorate during the reporting period, in particular in the centre of Mali'.
5. Including MINUSMA, Barkhane, European Union Training Mission in Mali (EUTM), G5 Sahel, and European and American forces in Niger and elsewhere, while recognizing the central strategic role played by French military operations which influence and structure the various military strategies of its allies and partners.
6. The influence of counterinsurgency, as deployed in Afghanistan in particular, is either implicit or fully recognized by military officers. Observations or interviews with more than 20 American, French, Dutch, German or Canadian officers deployed in Mali, between 2015 and 2019.
7. Since 2017, Centre FrancoPaix reports have proposed engaging in political dialogue as a possibility to explore, while the Malian state secretly pursued this option under the leadership of Prime Minister Abdoulaye Idrissa Maïga. See Campana (2018).
8. On the Malian army, see Tull (2019).
9. For instance, see Kilcullen (2010).
10. When the generals speak of a French engagement of 20 to 30 years, we consider such a horizon to be 'permanent'. See remarks of General Lecointre in Assemblée nationale (2019).

## References

Ahram, A. and King, C., (2012) 'The Warlord as Arbitrageur', *Theory and Society*, 41, pp. 169–186.
Altiok, A. and Street, J., (2020) *A Fourth Pillar for the United Nations? The Rise of Counter-terrorism*. London: Saferworld.
Aoi, C., De Coning, C. and Karlsrud, J., (2017a) 'Addressing the Emerging Gap between Concepts, Doctrine, and Practice in UN Peacekeeping Operation', in De Coning, C., Aoi, C. and Karlsrud, J., (eds.) *UN Peacekeeping Doctrine in a New Era*. New York: Routledge.
Aoi, C., De Coning, C. and Karlsrud, J., (2017b) 'Towards a United Nations Stabilization Doctrine: Stabilization as an Emerging UN Practice', in De Coning, C., Aoi, C. and Karlsrud, J., (eds.) *UN Peacekeeping Doctrine in a New Era*. New York: Routledge.
Assemblée nationale (France), (2019) *Compte rendu 12*, Commission des affaires étrangères, 6 November. [online]. Available at: www.assemblee-nationale.fr/dyn/15/comptes-rendus/cion_afetr/l15cion_afetr1920012_compte-rendu (Accessed: 6 July 2021).
Bagayoko, N., (2020) 'Sahel: Il faut repenser la sécurité du continent selon une perspective stratégique africaine', *Le Monde*, 10 January.
Briscoe, Y., (2014) 'Mali: A Colonel in His Labyrinth', *Open Democracy*, 27 June. [online]. Available at: Mali: a colonel in his labyrinth | openDemocracy (Accessed: 6 July 2021).
Campana, A., (2018) *Entre déstabilisation et enracinement local: les groupes djihadistes dans le conflit malien depuis 2015*. Montréal: Centre FrancoPaix, Chaire Raoul-Dandurand en études stratégiques et diplomatiques.

Carayol, R., (2016) 'Mali: les troupes de l'opération Barkhane prennent leurs distances avec les ex-rebelles touaregs', *Jeune Afrique*, 26 September.

Charbonneau, B., (2017) 'Intervention in Mali: Building Peace between Peacekeeping and Counterterrorism', *Journal of Contemporary African Studies*, 35(4), pp. 415–431.

Charbonneau, B., (2019) 'Intervention as Counter-insurgency Politics', *Conflict, Security and Development*, 19(3), pp. 309–314.

Charbonneau, B., (2021a) 'Counterinsurgency Governance in the Sahel', *International Affairs*, 97(6), pp. 1805–1823.

Charbonneau, B., (2021b), 'Le coup d'état au Mali n'a pas eu lieu', *Bulletin FrancoPaix*, 6(1–2), pp. 3–4.

Cold-Ravnkilde, S.M. and Jacobsen, K.L., (2020) 'Disentangling the Security Traffic Jam in the Sahel: Constitutive Effects of Contemporary Interventionism', *International Affairs*, 96(4), pp. 855–874.

Curran, D., (2017) 'Muddling on Through? Cosmopolitan Peacekeeping and the Protection of Civilians', *International Peacekeeping*, 24(1), pp. 63–85.

Curran, D. and Holtom, P., (2015) 'Resonating, Rejecting, Reinterpreting: Mapping the Stabilization Discourse in the United Nations Security Council, 2000–14', *Stability: International Journal of Security & Development*, 40(1), pp. 1–18.

Curran, D. and Hunt C., (2020) 'Stabilization at the Expense of Peacebuilding in UN Peacekeeping Operations', *Global Governance*, 26(1), pp. 46–68.

Debos, M., (2016) *Living by the Gun in Chad. Combatants, Impunity and State Formation*. London: Zed Books.

Devermont, J., (2019) 'Politics at the Heart of the Crisis in the Sahel', *CSIS Briefs*, 6 December. [online]. Available at: 191206_Devermont_SahelCrisis_layout_v5.pdf (csis-website-prod.s3.amazonaws.com) (Accessed: 6 July 2021).

Diatta, M., et al., (2021) 'AMISOM Should Provide More Than Security in Somalia', *ISS Peace and Security Council Report 2021*, 133, pp. 11–12.

Donais, T. and Tanguay, E., (2020) 'Doing Less with Less? Peacekeeping Retrenchment and the UN's Protection of Civilians Agenda', *International Journal*, 75(1), pp. 65–82.

Dowd, C., (2015) 'Grievances, Governance and Islamist Violence in Sub-Saharan Africa', *The Journal of Modern African Studies*, 53(4), pp. 505–531.

Duffield, M., (2001) *Global Governance and the New Wars: The Merging of Development and Security*. London and New York, NY: Zed books.

Fjelde, H., Hultman, L. and Nilsson, D., (2019) 'Protection through Presence: UN Peacekeeping and the Costs of Targeting Civilians', *International Organization*, 73(Winter), pp. 103–131.

Foley, C., (2017) *UN Peacekeeping Operations and the Protection of Civilians*. New York, NY: Cambridge University Press.

Friis, K., (2010) 'Peacekeeping and Counter-insurgency – Two of a Kind?', *International Peacekeeping*, 17(1), pp. 49–66.

Gorur, A., (2016) *Defining the Boundaries of UN Stabilization Missions*. Washington, DC: Stimson Center.

Guichaoua, Y., (2020) 'The Bitter Harvest of French Interventionism in the Sahel', *International Affairs*, 96(4), pp. 895–911.

Hameiri, S., (2009) 'Capacity and its Fallacies: International State Building as State Transformation', *Millennium: Journal of International Studies*, 38(1), pp. 55–81.

Harper, M., (2020). 'Somalia Conflict: Al-Shabab "Collects More Revenue Than Government"', *BBC News*, 26 October. [online]. Available at: www.bbc.com/news/world-africa-54690561 (Accessed: 6 July 2021).

International Crisis Group (ICG), (2019) *Parler aux jihadistes au centre du Mali: le dialogue est-il possible?* Rapport Afrique 276, 28 mai, Brussels. [online]. Available at: Parler aux jihadistes au centre du Mali: le dialogue est-il possible? | Crisis Group (Accessed: 6 July 2021).

International Crisis Group (ICG), (2021) *A Course Correction for the Sahel Stabilisation Strategy*, Africa Report 299, Brussels.

Jezequel, J-H., (2020) *Engager le dialogue au Sahel: à Pau un revirement stratégique est nécessaire*, 13 January. Bruxelles: Commentary, International Crisis Group.

Jourde, C., Brossier, M. and Cissé, M.G., (2019) 'Prédation et violence au Mali: élites statutaires peules et logiques de domination dans la région de Mopti', *Revue canadienne des études africaines*, 53(3), pp. 431–446.

Karlsrud, J., (2018) *The UN at War: Peace Operations in a New Era*. Middletown: Palgrave Macmillan.

Kilcullen, D., (2010) *Counterinsurgency*. New York, NY: Oxford University Press.

Levine, D.H., (2014) *The Morality of Peacekeeping*. Edinburgh: University Press.

Mac Ginty, R., (2012) 'Against Stabilization', *Stability: International Journal of Security and Development*, 1(1), pp. 20–30.

Mégret, F., (2015) 'Between R2P and the ICC: "Robust Peacekeeping" and the Quest for Civilian Protection', *Criminal Law Forum*, 26, pp. 101–151.

Menkhaus, K., (2009) 'Somalia: What Went Wrong?', *The RUSI Journal*, 154(4), pp. 6–12.

MINUSMA, (2021) *Rapport sur l'incident de Bounty du 3 janvier 2021*, Division des droits de l'homme et de la protection, March.

Moe, L.W., (2016) 'The Strange Wars of Liberal Peace: Hybridity, Complexity and the Governing Rationalities of Counterinsurgency in Somalia', *Peacebuilding*, 4(1), pp. 99–117.

Moe, L.W., (2017) 'Counterinsurgent Warfare and the Decentering of Sovereignty in Somalia', in Moe, L.W. and Müller, M.M., (eds.) *Reconfiguring Intervention: Complexity, Resilience and the 'Local Turn' in Counterinsurgent Warfare*. London: Palgrave Macmillan, pp. 119–140.

Moe, L.W., (2018) 'Counterinsurgency in the Somali Territories: The "Grey Zone" between Peace and Pacification', *International Affairs*, 94(2), pp. 319–341.

Moe, L.W. and Müller, M-M., (2017) 'Introduction: Complexity, Resilience and the "Local Turn" in Counterinsurgency', in Moe, L.W. and Müller, M-M., (eds.) *Reconfiguring Intervention: Complexity, Resilience and the 'Local Turn' in Counterinsurgent Warfare*. London: Palgrave Macmillan.

Moe, L.W and Müller, M-M., (2018) 'Counterinsurgency, Knowledge Production and the Travelling of Coercive Realpolitik between Colombia and Somalia', *Cooperation & Conflict*, 53(2), pp. 193–215.

Notin, J-C., (2014) *La guerre de la France au Mali*. Paris: Tallandier.

Novosseloff, A. and Sharland, L., (2019) *Partners and Competitors: Forces Operating in Parallel to UN Peace Operations*, International Peace Institute.

Nsaibia, H., (2020) 'State Atrocities in the Sahel: The Impetus for Counterinsurgency Results is Fueling Government Attacks on Civilians', *ACLED*, 20 May. [online]. Available at: https://acleddata.com/2020/05/20/state-atrocities-in-the-sahel-the-impetus-for-counter-insurgency-results-is-fueling-government-attacks-on-civilians/ (Accessed: 30 June 2021).

Owens, P., (2015) *Economy of Force: Counterinsurgency and the Historical Rise of the Social*, New York, NY: Cambridge University Press.

Parrish, K., (2013) '"Small-Footprint" Operations Effective, Official Says', *DoD News*, 31 January. [online]. Available at: http://archive.defense.gov/news/newsarticle.aspx?id=119150 (Accessed: 30 June 2021).

Pham, J.P., (2013) *State Collapse, Insurgency, and Counterinsurgency: Lessons from Somalia*, Report for US Army War College. [online]. Available at: www.globalsecurity.org/military/library/report/2013/ssi_pham.pdf (Accessed: 30 June 2021).

Porch, D., (2013) *Counterinsurgency: Exposing the Myths of the New Way of War*. New York, NY: Cambridge University Press.

Rhoads, E.P. and Welsh, J., (2019) 'Close Cousins in Protection: The Evolution of Two Norms', *International Affairs*, 95(3), pp. 597–617.

Samatar, A.I., (2006) 'The Miracle of Mogadishu', *Review of African Political Economy*, 33(109), pp. 581–587.

Sandor, A., (2017) *Insecurity, the Breakdown of Social Trust, and Armed Actor Governance in Central and Northern Mali*. Montréal: Centre FrancoPaix, Chaire Raoul-Dandurand en études stratégiques et diplomatiques.

Scheele, J., (2012) *Smugglers and Saints of the Sahara: Regional Connectivity in the Twentieth Century*. New York, NY: Cambridge University Press.

Tripodi, C., (2021) *The Unknown Enemy: Counterinsurgency and the Illusion of Control*. Cambridge: Cambridge University Press.

Tull, D.M., (2019) 'Rebuilding Mali's Army: The Dissonant Relationship between Mali and its International Partners', *International Affairs*, 95(2), pp. 405–422.

Turner, M., (2015) 'Peacebuilding as Counterinsurgency in the Occupied Palestinian Territory', *Review of International Studies*, 41(1), pp. 73–98.

Ucko, D.H., (2013) 'The Five Fallacies of Clear-Hold-Build: Counter-Insurgency, Governance and Development at the Local Level', *The RUSI Journal*, 158(3), pp. 54–61.

United Nations Security Council, (2020) *Situation in Mali. Report of the Secretary-General, S/2020/1281*, 28 December. New York, NY: United Nations.

US Army, (2014) *Insurgencies and Counter Insurgencies*, Field Manual (FM) 3–24/MCWP 3–33.5, 13 May. Washington DC: US Government Printing Office [GPO].

Walter, D., (2017) *Colonial Violence: European Empires and the Use of Force.* Oxford/New York: Oxford University Press.

Williams, P., (2013) 'Protection, Resilience and Empowerment: United Nations Peacekeeping and Violence against Civilians in Contemporary War Zones', *Politics*, 33(4), pp. 287–298.

Williams, P., (2018a) *Fighting for Peace in Somalia: A History and Analysis of the African Union Mission (AMISOM), 2007–2017.* Oxford/New York: Oxford University Press.

Williams, P., (2018b) 'Subduing al-Shabaab: The Somalia Model of Counterterrorism and Its Limits', *The Washington Quarterly*, 41(2), pp. 95–111.

Williams, P. and Bellamy, A., (2021) *Understanding Peacekeeping* (3rd ed.). Cambridge: Polity Press.

Willmot, H., Mamiya, R., Sheeran, S. and Weller, M., (eds.) (2016) *Protection of Civilians.* Oxford/New York: Oxford University Press.

Woodward, S., (2017) *The Ideology of Failed States. Why Intervention Fails.* New York, NY: Cambridge University Press.

# 15

# PEACEBUILDING IN THE GAMBIA

## Sustaining the Gains and Addressing Potential Threats to the Process

*Festus Kofi Aubyn*

### Introduction

Until January 2017, The Gambia was led by former President Yahya Jammeh, who ruled for 22 years with an iron fist and little regard for human rights principles. His Alliance for Patriotic Reorientation and Construction (APRC) government was implicated in several cases of abuse of power, gross human rights violations, and total disregard for the rule of law (Government of The Gambia 2017). Gambians were subjected to 22 years of dictatorship. Jammeh was successfully replaced in January 2017 by President Adama Barrow following the latter's electoral victory on 2 December 2016 and subsequent resolution of the ensuing political stalemate which almost plunged the country into a civil war (Connolly and He 2018). As aptly captured in the National Development Plan (2018–2021) of The Gambia, this historic transition heralded a new chapter and offered a renewed opportunity for the country to build a state based on the foundations of democracy, good governance, respect for human rights, security, and prosperity for all (Government of The Gambia 2017, 3).

However, the historic political transition not only magnified old problems but also presented a new set of challenges that the new administration had to grapple with. Prior to the regime change, the country was faced with a stalled economy arising from several fiscal shocks and economic mismanagement, an acute electricity crisis, and low productivity in the agricultural and tourism sectors. Furthermore, there was increasing poverty, corruption, a poor healthcare system, a failing educational sector, gender inequality, and rising youth unemployment (Government of The Gambia 2017, 5–6). Some of these challenges were captured in the October 2017 World Bank Macro Poverty Outlook for The Gambia, which among other things noted a range of socio-economic challenges including increasing poverty, a growing rural-urban divide, a decreasing literacy rate, and high unemployment (World Bank 2017). On the security front, the military and the police were politicized and turned into adjuncts of Jammeh's APRC regime. The divisive tactics of the former regime also affected the social fabric, resulting in an antagonistic relation between ethnic groups.

In order to address the inherited challenges to promote good governance, social cohesion, national reconciliation, and a revitalized economy, the new administration developed a National Development Plan (NDP) in 2017. As a forward-looking peacebuilding agenda, the plan emphasizes a comprehensive approach in tackling the aforementioned challenges (Government of the Gambia 2017). Since its adoption, the government has implemented several initiatives aimed at restoring democratic governance, reforming key sectors and promoting the rule of law with the assistance of civil society organizations (CSOs) and international, regional, and bilateral partners. This chapter assesses the implementation of the peacebuilding agenda in The Gambia, the role being played by international partners, and the potential threats to the process (Petesch 2020). The chapter also highlights the peacebuilding progress made so far and how the achievements can be consolidated to build sustainable peace.

The chapter begins with the context of peacebuilding in The Gambia, underscoring its importance in the aftermath of Yahya Jammeh. The next section examines the key components of the peacebuilding process and the level of implementation. Here, particular emphasis is placed on security sector reform (SSR), constitutional reforms, judicial reforms, transitional justice and reconciliation, and socio-economic development. The role of international actors including the United Nations (UN), the African Union (AU), the Economic Community of West African States (ECOWAS), and the European Union (EU) in the peacebuilding process is analyzed in the subsequent section. Thereafter, the potential threats to the peacebuilding process are discussed especially in the midst of the COVID-19 pandemic, which has had a multidimensional effect on every sector of the economy. The chapter concludes with some ideas on how the government of The Gambia can further consolidate the country's relative peace.

## Context of Peacebuilding in The Gambia

The Gambia is a small country in West Africa, bordered by the Republic of Senegal on the north, south, and east and by the Atlantic Ocean on the west. The capital is Banjul, and the country has five administrative regions: Central River Region, Lower River Region, North Bank Region, Upper River Region, and West Coast Region (Gambia Investment and Export Promotion Agency 2020). The Gambia has an estimated population of about 2.1 million, and the main ethnic groups are the Mandinka (42%), Fula (18%), Wolof (16%), Jola (10%), Serahuli (9%), other Africans (4%), and non-Africans (1%). The main religions are Islam (90%), Christian (8%), and indigenous beliefs (2%; GIEPA 2020). The Gambian economy is dominated by agriculture but is also known for tourism because of its beautiful beaches, warm water, and nature retreats.

The country gained independence in 1965 with Dawda Jawara, then prime minister and later president after a referendum in 1970. He ruled The Gambia until 1994, when he was ousted in a bloodless coup led by Lieutenant Yahya Jammeh (BBC News 2020). Following the promulgation of a new constitution in 1996 and subsequent election, Jammeh was elected a civilian president after banning three major political parties (BBC News 2020). Consequently, Jammeh ruled for four consecutive terms with an iron fist until his defeat in the December 2016 elections by the United Democratic Party (UDP), made up of a coalition of seven political parties led by Adama Barrow. At the end of the 2016 elections, Barrow won with 263,515 votes (45.5%) against 212,099 (36.7%) for Jammeh (Connolly and He 2018). Jammeh's defeat came as a huge surprise to the international community and Gambians because most people expected the status quo to prevail.

After initially conceding defeat, Jammeh later contested the results and declared a state of emergency, exacerbating political tensions across the country. Sensing danger, ECOWAS, with the support of the UN and AU, responded swiftly by deploying the heads of state of Ghana, Liberia, and Nigeria to convey its support for a peaceful political transition in conformity with the election results. Subsequently, the regional body deployed the ECOWAS Mission in The Gambia (ECOMIG) to the Senegalese border to intervene and remove Jammeh after his refusal to relinquish power. On 21 January 2017, Jammeh peacefully relinquished power after several weeks of mounting pressure and went into exile in Equatorial Guinea with his family, trusted military officers, and a fleet of luxury cars (UN 2017). His departure allowed President-elect Adama Barrow to take political leadership of the country after his swearing-in ceremony in the city of Bakau (DW 2020).

However, the legacy of the former autocratic regime posed a set of peculiar challenges to sustaining peace in what has been described as the new Gambia. On Jammeh's exit, the national coffers were nearly empty and a legacy of human rights abuses and institutional dysfunction had been created. For 22 years, the people of The Gambia lived under a culture of fear and silence with a very oppressive defence and security apparatus. Several reports of Human Rights Watch (2015) showed widespread abuses, including emasculation of political opponents, forced disappearances, extrajudicial killings, rape, and arbitrary detention under Jammeh's rule. Many political figures, journalists, civil society activists, and students were allegedly detained, tortured, and murdered, while others were forced into exile. Jammeh was implicated in the 2004 murder of journalist Deyda Hydara, who was the editor and co-founder of the independent daily *The Point* as well as a correspondent for the Agence France-Presse (AFP) news agency and Reporters Without Borders (RSF; Aljazeera 2019). The Gambia's National Intelligence Agency (NIA), a paramilitary group known as the "Jungulers," and the armed units of the Gambian Police Force were frequently implicated in these abuses (Human Rights Watch 2015).

The Jammeh era was also tainted by restriction of freedom of expression, association, and assembly (UNICEF 2018). The spaces for political expression, dialogue, and inclusive processes in which constructive political debate and conversations could take place were circumscribed. Apart from media censorship, many media houses were closed down to silence criticism and suppress negative information about the country to the outside world. The institutions of state, including the judiciary, parliament, military, and police as well as local administrative structures were all politicized and made appendages of the ruling APRC regime with outdated policies and infrastructures (UN 2017). In the judiciary, for instance, there was constant political interference by Jammeh and his cohorts to preserve the oppressive regime (Jagger 2020). Independent-minded judges were arbitrarily removed from office. The slow pace of the justice delivery system and lack of access to justice was also a huge problem, mainly in semi-urban and rural areas.

On the security front, the security sector itself was a victim of the regime. According to Jagger (2020), security institutions were kept weak and refused opportunities to professionalize, train, or equip to better deliver people-centric security. The APRC regime fomented a culture of nepotism, corruption, tribalism, distrust, and suspicion between and within security agencies in order to manipulate their work and maintain control. Security personnel who refused to succumb to the control of Jammeh were sidelined, intimidated, and coerced. The tribal patronage scheme in particular contributed to the deterioration of standards of discipline, professionalism, and deep-seated tribal mistrust within the military, police, and other security forces (UN 2017; Jagger 2020). Respect for human rights and the rule of law was alien to most members of the security forces, who carried out several unlawful killings, torture, arbitrary arrest, and detention of political opponents/critics. The institutional frailties caused by the politicization and excessive control of the executive affected public sense of trust and confidence, resulting in a weak state-society relationship.

Another concern which attracted the attention of the new government was the embedded patterns of mistrust and divisions amongst ethno-linguistic groups caused by unequal access to goods and services, and active fomenting of divisions based on ethnicity, tribal, and political affiliation (UNICEF 2018). Under Jammeh, the Jola ethnic group (of which he is a member) received most privileges within the state administration (Toupane, Faye and Kanté 2019). The country's largest ethnic group, the Mandinkas (to which his predecessor Dawda Jawara and main opponent Ousainou Darboe belong), were marginalized. In a political rally in Tallinding in 2016, Jammeh threatened the Mandinkas with extinction. He is reported as having said that "since 1994, all the troublemakers have been the Mandinkas. If you don't behave I will bury you nine feet deep. . . . I will kill you like ants and no western country can do darn thing about it" (Freedom Newspaper 2016). Although the speech was widely condemned (UN News 2016), it showed vividly the legacy of political fractures based on identities, which threatened peaceful coexistence amongst communities and families. The new administration also inherited a country with severe socio-economic and developmental challenges (Anya and Palmer 2014). In the UN Development Programme (UNDP) Human Development Report of 2016, The Gambia was ranked as one of the poorest countries in the world, ranking 173 out of 188 (UNDP 2016).

## Components of the Peacebuilding Process

Although The Gambia is not a post-conflict country, the ills of the former regime have necessitated an effective peacebuilding process. Therefore, soon after coming into office, the new administration with the support of partners undertook a joint assessment of state institutions to determine their current state and immediate needs (Africa Center for Strategic Studies 2018). The findings of the assessment have led to the rollout of several reforms in different sectors since 2017. This section focuses on five of the sectors; namely, security sector reform (SSR), constitutional review, judicial reforms, transitional justice and reconciliation, and socio-economic development. These areas have been the major preoccupation of the Gambian government in the efforts to build lasting peace.

### *Constitutional Review Process*

There is an ongoing constitutional review process as part of comprehensive legal reform aimed at rebuilding the foundations of the democratic system and good governance. The purpose is to review the current 1997 constitution of the Republic of The Gambia, which had undergone more than 50 amendments during the previous regime, with the view to develop a new constitution that met the hopes and aspirations of Gambians. The 1997 constitution replaced the country's founding constitution of 1970. However, it was amended several times to manipulate the political process to enable Jammeh to dominate the political landscape (Afrobarometer 2018). One amendment allowed for the removal of presidential term limits to enable him to run for re-election, and in 2001, the electoral system was changed to require only a plurality, rather than an absolute majority, to win a presidential election (Constitutional Review Commission 2020). Other flaws identified were the constitutional provisions that conferred too much power on the president, lacked clarity or created uncertainty, conflict of interest, and granted unwarranted broad immunity on the president (Asemota 2017).

Accordingly, in December 2017, the Gambian National Assembly established the Constitutional Review Commission (CRC) to draft the country's third constitution. The Commission's main functions was to review and analyze the current 1997 constitution and draft a new constitution. After a lengthy and unprecedented public consultation to solicit inputs from Gambians both at home and abroad, the 11-member CRC in November 2019 released its first draft constitution and invited the public to provide comments and suggestions (Constitutional Review Commission 2020). On 30 March 2020, the CRC submitted the long-awaited "new constitution" to President Adama Barrow in accordance with Section 21 of the Constitutional Review Commission Act 2017.

Among the key issues covered include presidential term limits, the definition of citizenship, separation of powers, a quota system for women's representation in the National Assembly, political independence for members of the national electoral commission, issues of accountability and respect for human rights of state institutions, as well as the democratic pluralism of The Gambia, which put to rest the contentious secularism debate of guaranteeing fair treatment to all faiths. However, the new constitution has provoked different reactions, with mixed feelings of hope, national accomplishment, and scepticism. While some analysts like Sainey Bah describe it as a very ambitious constitution, some skeptics have described it as a "carbon copy" of the 2010 Kenyan Constitution due to some related provisions (Bah 2020). But, of course, these reactions are not unexpected given the universal principles and values that cut across most constitutions, such as democratic pluralism, administrative fairness, separation of powers, transparency, accountability, and human rights.

## *Judicial Reform Process*

Sections 120 to 148 of the 1997 Constitution of The Gambia provide for the structure, composition, and jurisdiction of the courts. Section 120(3) of the Constitution states:

> In the exercise of their judicial functions, the courts, the judges and other holders of judicial office shall be independent and shall be subject only to this Constitution and the law and, save as provided in this Chapter, shall not be subject to the control or direction of any other person or authority.

Despite the widely acclaimed notion of judicial independence, the Jammeh regime never accorded such autonomy to the courts. The constitutional provisions (section 138) that accorded the president the power to appoint the chief justice and senior judges and to terminate their appointments (section 142(2)I) was significantly abused to undermine judicial independence. Yahya Jammeh controlled the courts and used them as a tool to consolidate his grip of power. He hired judges from abroad and frequently fired them at his whims and caprices (Nabaneh 2018). Political interferences in the judiciary, coupled with the slow justice delivery and lack of access to justice, greatly influenced the legitimacy and public confidence in the courts.

Against this backdrop, some important steps have been made by the government to reform the judiciary to make it more independent and accountable and effectively deliver justice. The reform started with the appointment of new senior judges to the supreme court and other courts. President Barrow appointed a Gambian, Hassan Jallow, who was a former prosecutor of the International Criminal Tribunal for Rwanda in Arusha, Tanzania, as the new chief justice. This is a major departure from the past, where Jammeh appointed foreigners to the position (Sowe and Nabaneh 2018). Furthermore, all the foreign judges who were appointed by the previous regime have also been replaced with Gambian judges at all levels of the judiciary. Vetting, training of judicial staff, and recruitment of new personnel is ongoing with the support of UNDP to strengthen the human resource base of the judiciary.

The government has started the process of reviewing laws restricting political and civic freedoms to repeal them. The government also signed a UN treaty committing The Gambia to abolish the death penalty. Guidelines to strengthen the Office of the Ombudsman, which was established in 1997 with the mandate to investigate the abuse of power, have also been developed. This is expected to strengthen the governance process by enhancing the accountability of government institutions and officials. As part of the judicial reforms, the government has also embarked on some prison reforms to reduce overcrowding in the prisons and improve the welfare of prisoners. There are also ongoing initiatives to improve housing, food, sanitation, and medical care of prisoners. The president has pardoned over 250 prisoners, including political prisoners (Africa Center for Strategic Studies 2018), which has greatly reduced prison overcrowding.

## *Transitional Justice and Reconciliation*

As part of the transitional justice and reconciliation process, the National Assembly passed new bills creating a National Human Rights Commission and a Truth, Reconciliation, and Reparations Commission (TRRC). The TRRC was officially launched on 5 October 2018, and its main task is to conduct research and investigations into human rights violations committed from 1994 to January 2017 under the former regime (Truth, Reconciliation, and Reparations Commission 2020b). The TRRC is also mandated to determine the scope of future prosecutions and possible amnesties, pursue truth-seeking, advance community and national reconciliation, educate the public on peace and justice, and deliver individual and communal reparations. The goal of the TRRC's work is to prevent a repeat of the violations and abuses suffered under the previous regime by making recommendations to government aimed at ensuring the crimes of the past never reoccur. The TRCC's work is complemented by a separate judicial commission of inquiry that is holding public hearings into the mismanagement of public funds under the previous administration. Jammeh left behind a legacy of corruption, and he is estimated to have stolen upwards of $50 million from national coffers (International Centre for Transitional Justice 2020a). As a result, the assets belonging to Jammeh have been frozen to allow for the investigations into the alleged abuses of public finances. The commission also began hearing evidence in public sessions in August 2018.

As indicated by Amnesty International, the start of the TRRC demonstrated a strong commitment by the government to break with a past of systematic human rights violations (Amnesty International 2019). It is difficult to know exactly how many human rights violations occurred or to quantify them, but in January 2019 the TRRC began recording testimonies from victims and perpetrators to understand the magnitude of the problem (Trial International 2020). In the first year of its work, 188 witnesses, including 51 women, appeared before the commission. While some of the hearings were open, others were held behind closed doors and through live video link especially for Gambians living abroad. So far, there have been testimonies of victims of torture and rape as well as stunning confessions of perpetrators from senior members of the former regime. Among the most important issues covered were the execution of soldiers during the 1994 military coup, the killings of West African migrants in 2005, the murders of journalist Deyda Hydara in 2004 and former Finance Minister Ousman Koro Ceesay in 2005, the crackdown on the media and journalists, and cases of sexual and gender-based violence (Truth, Reconciliation, and Reparations Commission 2019). Others include the killing of students in the April 2000 demonstrations; arbitrary arrests, detentions, and tortures; and the 2009 Jammeh-led witch-hunt in which hundreds of people were forced to drink dangerous liquids.

The evidence from both victims and perpetrators since 2019 is quite poignant. The following quote by Dr Baba Galleh Jallow, the executive secretary of the TRRC, shows the unspeakable nature of the abuses:

> the evidence shows widespread instances of arbitrary arrests, detentions, horrible prison conditions, tortures, killings, sexual abuses, and the incomprehensible practice

of accusing innocent people of witchcraft, subjecting them to cruel, inhuman and degrading treatment, forcing them to drink health-destroying concoctions, and subjecting them and their families to a life of stigma and public ridicule.

*(Darboe 2020a)*

Indeed, the testimonies given so far implicate most state institutions of wrongdoing, making the task of redressing past abuses very complex. The work of the TRRC is still ongoing, but it is imperative that Gambians go through this painful process, and they will emerge stronger after justice is delivered to victims whose rights and dignities were violated with impunity. Beyond the official TRRC mechanism, it is also important to ensure the active participation of civil society, youth, women, and other citizens in the process which is currently weak to make it more participatory and inclusive. Victims who appear before the court must be protected against stigmatization, and their safety and well-being should also be guaranteed.

## *Security Sector Reform*

SSR in The Gambia is considered fundamental for the future stability of the country. It forms part of the stabilization process and the wider reform agenda, which was launched on 12 September 2017 by President Barrow with the support of the UN, ECOWAS, AU, EU, CSOs, and other partners. In his speech during the launch, the president stated that his administration inherited a security sector that was deeply politicized, "polluted", and unresponsive to people's needs (Republic of The Gambia 2017). This is why he requested ECOMIG to provide security in The Gambia for his first six months in office. He had limited trust in the loyalty of the Gambian Armed Forces, the police, and the intelligence agencies (Dwyer 2017). Many Gambians also lacked confidence in the security actors and their capabilities due to their past legacies (Serrano 2020). SSR was therefore necessary to depoliticize the security institutions and render them more accessible and responsive to the needs and rights of The Gambian people (UNOWAS 2020).

SSR in The Gambia is aimed at transforming the security sector into institutions that are well organized, ethical, effective, professional, and accountable to the state and the people (Manneh 2019a). The goal is to make the security sector institutions – especially the military, intelligence, and law enforcement agencies – perform their constitutional mandate with full respect for human rights and in line with the rule of law and democratic principles of transparency and accountability. The reform is focused on the gaps and malfunctions within the security apparatus, which include inadequate legal and policy frameworks, lack of civilian oversight to direct security sector governance, lack of training and logistics capabilities, politicization and tribalism, and downsizing the security services (Jagger 2020). The implementation of SSR is coordinated from the Office of the National Security Advisor (ONS). There is a steering committee consisting of ONS; the ministries of justice, defence, finance, and foreign affairs; civil society representatives; and the UN, AU, EU, and ECOWAS, which provide strategic guidance and oversight responsibilities.

The implementation of the SSR is supported by international partners including the AU, UN, ECOWAS, EU, Turkey, Qatar, the US, France, and China, as well as CSOs and international institutions such as the Geneva Centre for the Democratic Control of Armed Forces (DCAF). These partners provide funding, technical support, military equipment, and logistic support. In 2019, for example, Turkey provided $1.4 million worth of logistic aid to the country and donated equipment to the military (Alam 2019). So far, the SSR implementation has been slow. The process has mainly focused on the internal reforms of all the security institutions including the police, military, immigration, correction service, and intelligence agencies. There has been a change of leadership, review of their capabilities, and development of new norms and policies to enhance their governance system. The heads of the army, police, intelligence, and correction services have all been replaced. There is also an ongoing capacity-building exercise both at home and abroad to enhance the technical competence of personnel and strengthen their operational preparedness to respond to crisis situations, especially terrorism. There are training programmes focused on building the skills of the security and intelligence community's ability to conduct deep research, analysis, and assessment of threats to the security of the country. Others include human rights, rule of law, crime prevention, and VIP and presidential protection training (Manneh 2019b).

A reorientation process is also ongoing to rebuild trust among personnel and bolster the confidence of the political elites and citizens in the security institutions. The military, for example, is still divided between Jammeh and Barrow loyalists, and already some narratives are going round that personnel from Jammeh's minority Jola community are being discriminated against by the new administration (Afrobarometer 2019). Building trust among security personnel is therefore essential. Furthermore, the oversight body for the security sector is also being reviewed. For instance, NIA, which oversaw arbitrary detentions and torture during the Jammeh era, has been changed to the State Intelligence Service, which is overseen by Parliament. The service's powers of detention have also been eroded (Human Rights Watch 2017). That notwithstanding, the operational systems and agents of the NIA remain unchanged. For instance, a former Gambian anti-narcotics agent arrested by the NIA in 2009 lamented during the public hearings of the TRRC that one of his former torturers, Jim Drammeh, is now his boss at the anti-narcotics agency (Darboe 2020b).

Efforts are also being made to downsize the security forces through a national vetting process, but up to now, few personnel have been vetted across the country to determine their status. There are fears among personnel from Jammeh's Jola community that they may be targeted in the downsizing. The government is yet to also determine clear exit plans and appropriate reintegration packages for veterans to return to civilian life (ISS 2019). Some personnel accused of human rights violations are still on active duty, and their continued presence is causing unease among personnel and is undermining SSR implementation. Nevertheless, it must be stated that some accused personnel are currently on trial. As of 2019, there were nine former NIA officers on trial (Human Rights Watch 2017). As a precautionary measure, the ONS has introduced a policy to ensure that people seeking jobs in the security sector acquire security clearance instead of a certificate of character before taking up their posts (Gambiana 2019). Essentially, this is to ensure that the right persons with unblemished records are recruited into the security sector.

## *Socio-economic Recovery and Development*

With the support of the international partners, the government has implemented several initiatives based on the NDP 2018–2021 to improve the economic outlook of the country. As a result, the GDP growth rate in 2018 accelerated to 6.6%, driven by a recovery in agriculture, tourism, construction, and trade (African Development Bank Group n.d.); however, it then fell to an estimated 5.4% in 2019 due to weak fiscal management and delays in budget support disbursements. Inflation subsided due to a stable exchange rate, strong food supply, and declining commodity prices. Improvements in net services, private capital flows, and remittances from the diaspora also helped to mitigate the current account deficits in the past years (World Bank in The Gambia 2020). Nonetheless, the high public debt and limited fiscal space have kept poverty stagnant and unemployment high. There are also major challenges in the energy, infrastructure, and agriculture sectors.

The global COVID-19 pandemic is also straining the economy, as it has halted tourism, disrupted trade, and reduced remittances and private capital inflows (UNDP 2020a). Already, The Gambia is facing an employment crisis, with an unemployment rate of 35.2% and half (48.6%) of the country's 2.1 million population living below the poverty line (World Bank in The Gambia 2020). Safeguarding the vulnerable people, especially women, youth, children, and people with disabilities, has been a challenging task. To augment its budget resources, the International Monetary Fund (IMF) approved a $21.3 million financial assistance for the country under the Rapid Credit Facility (IMF 2020) and also granted debt service relief under the Catastrophe Containment and Relief Trust. This financial assistance, together with support from other development partners including the UN system, has helped the government to kick-start recovery efforts, mainly to safeguard livelihoods and sustainable development progress.

## Role of International Partners in the Peacebuilding Process

The role of international partners has been central to the peacebuilding agenda of the government. Since the initial intervention of ECOMIG in 2016 (Williams 2017) and the subsequent exile of Jammeh, international partners (including the UN, AU, EU, IMF, World Bank, the UK, the US, France, Turkey, Qatar, and China) have become crucial sources of support. ECOMIG has been providing vital security services to the government while the country's security forces are being trained and capacitated (Mutangadura 2018), but according to an Afrobarometer survey, it is gradually becoming unpopular because most Gambians want the mission to exit amid frustration over the slow pace of the SSR process (Afrobarometer 2018). This is in spite of the fact that the role of ECOMIG has provided the AU and other international actors the enabling security environment to implement their various programmes.

In 2018, the AU also deployed the AU Technical Support to The Gambia (AUTSTG) to provide advice to the government on the rule of law, democracy, transitional justice, and security sector transformation. Experts from the AUTSTG are currently embedded within state institutions including the Gambian Armed Forces, National Security Agency, National Human Rights Commission, and the Ministry of Interior. The incorporation of the AUTSTG team in the state institutions is helping to compensate for the lack of institutional capacity without undermining local ownership of the process (Mutangadura 2020). The UN system in The Gambia is also supporting national efforts for sustainable human development in diverse ways in line with the NDP, which is aligned with the 2030 Agenda for Sustainable Development and the African Union Agenda 2063. The UN is providing financial and technical support to strengthen institutional capacities, promote evidence-based policy formulation, resource mobilization, and mainstreaming of relevant issues into national policies and implementation (UNDP 2020b) – for example, through the UN Peacebuilding Fund.

The EU, the World Bank, and the IMF have all been providing budgetary support and technical assistance to the government. As of December 2019, the EU, which is the biggest development cooperation partner in The Gambia, had transferred a total amount of €77 million in grant financial assistance to support reforms to improve governance, public financial management, and service delivery (European Union 2020; Jeffang 2019). The UK, the US, China, Turkey, Qatar, and France are also providing varied bilateral assistance to the government. For example, in 2018 France gave €30 million in aid, comprising €5 million for budgetary support, €20 million for drinking water projects, and €5 million for agriculture (Irish 2018). Indeed, the varied international support has been overwhelming as compared to the previous regime. However, coordination among the various international stakeholders is key to prevent duplication of efforts. Strong accountability mechanisms are also essential to prevent corruption and mismanagement of the funds.

## Potential Threats to the Peacebuilding Process

One of the most obvious threats to the peacebuilding process is the impact of the COVID-19 pandemic (Ministry of Health, The Gambia 2020). The outbreak has slowed down stabilization efforts by redirecting attention from the ongoing peacebuilding processes to the country's strategic response to the pandemic. The projected GDP growth rate of 6.3% in 2020 is expected to shrink to 3.3% and the economic loss is estimated at GMD 2.5 billion, according to the Minister of Finance and Economic Affairs (UNDP 2020a). This will have implications for the country's budget and net domestic borrowing, which will also affect the concessionary fiscal stance undertaken by the government in recent years. As noted earlier, the COVID-19 pandemic is likely to move the vulnerable populations back into poverty and unemployment. For the international partners providing technical assistance, the pandemic has delayed the deployment of additional experts to the country. Given the uncertainties about the future spread of the virus, the government will have to navigate the ongoing peacebuilding efforts and the fallout of the pandemic.

The changing political landscape in the country is a second potential threat to peacebuilding. The United Democratic Party (UDP) that brought President Adama Barrow to power has disintegrated since 2019 over his refusal to call for new elections (Darboe 2020b). Before coming into office, there was a supposed agreement among the coalition parties that Barrow would serve a three-year term and call for a new election in case he won the 2016 elections. There was outrage following the president's decision to serve a full five-year term until 2021, as allowed by the 1997 constitution; some members of the coalition took to the streets to protest on different occasions in 2019, leading to mass arrests and violence (BBC News 2019). Although the COVID-19 pandemic has prevented further protests, President Barrow has left the UDP and formed his own political party, the National People's Party, to seek a new political constituency to allow him to contest future elections unhindered (Mukabana 2020). Many of his critics have also accused him of softening his position on Yahya Jammeh as a way of attracting the former ruler's support base or possibly forming an alliance with his party, APRC. They will also potentially hamstring the political consensus and commitments required to implement the various reforms to building peace.

The government came to power on the back of significant institutional decay, which poses major challenges to the reform process. Some of the issues like tribalism, politicization, corruption, unprofessionalism, and weak institutional capacity are deeply entrenched in the wake of the 22-year Jammeh regime. Although there has been limited progress in the reformation of state institutions, it may take a significant amount of time and years to completely transform the institutions, instill new norms, and nurture their independence and professionalism. This is especially the case for the military, intelligence agencies, and the judiciary which faces immense public pressure to deliver quickly on its mandate.

Finally, the peacebuilding agenda of The Gambia is very ambitious due to the number of ongoing reforms. Adequate funding to implement all the peacebuilding interventions may prove challenging in the years ahead. External financial support from development partners may be limited, especially in this period of COVID-19 when most advanced economies are suffering with internal problems to take care of. Besides, the capacity of the government to generate internal funding from taxes and exports is also severely hampered by internal shocks partly attributed to the COVID-19 pandemic, financial mismanagement, and corruption.

## Conclusion

The successful political transition in January 2017 in The Gambia offered the country a renewed opportunity to rebuild the state. The new administration has made steady progress towards building durable peace through the implementation of the NDP and the various peacebuilding programmes in the areas of SSR, constitutional reforms, judicial reforms, transitional justice and reconciliation, and socio-economic development. The support of CSOs and non-governmental organizations, the UN, AU, ECOWAS, EU, and other international partners has been crucial in these efforts. While the peacebuilding processes are still ongoing, making it impractical to give a definitive verdict on whether they are achieving their intended objectives, it is crucial for the Gambian authorities and the various stakeholders to pay particular attention to the potential threats or challenges that could hinder the implementation process. Critical among them is the impact of COVID-19 on socio-economic development, the changing political dynamics in the country, and issues of adequate funding and the deep antagonistic relations between ethnic groups that manifest at the political and institutional levels. Additionally, it is important to strengthen nationwide sensitization of the various reform processes in a bid to make the peacebuilding process more visible, more participatory, and more inclusive to promote local ownership at the grassroots level of society to ensure sustainability. It is also crucial going forward to deal with the complex issue of bringing Yahya Jammeh and his accomplices from exile to face justice. To this end, the ongoing investigations by Swiss authorities into crimes against humanity allegedly committed by former Minister of the Interior Ousman Sonko, who fled the country in September 2016, is a step in the right direction (Trial International 2020).

## References

Africa Center for Strategic Studies, (2018) *Gambia's Road to Democratic Reform*. [online]. Available at: https://africacenter.org/spotlight/gambia (Accessed: 16 May 2020).

African Development Bank Group, (n.d.) *Gambia*. [online]. Available at: www.afdb.org/en/countries/west-africa/gambia/ (Accessed: 3 June 2020).

Afrobarometer, (2018) *Gambia's Draft Constitution Reflects Citizens Preference, Term Limits, Gender Quota*. [online]. Available at: AD338: The Gambia's draft Constitution reflects citizens' preference for term limits, gender quota | Afrobarometer (Accessed: 3 June 2020).

Afrobarometer, (2019) *Gambians Trust the Armed Forces but Are Split over the Presence of ECOMIG*. [online]. Available at: AD317: Gambians trust the armed forces but are split over the presence of ECOMIG | Afrobarometer (Accessed: 20 May 2020).

Alam, S., (2019) 'Turkey Plays Key Role in Gambia Military Training', *Anadolu Agency*. [online]. Available at: www.aa.com.tr/en/africa/turkey (Accessed: 1 June 2020).

Aljazeera, (2019) *Gambian Soldier Names Ex-president in Reporter's 2004 Murder*. 23 July. [online]. Available at: Gambian soldier names ex-president in reporter's 2004 murder | Freedom of the Press News | Al Jazeera (Accessed: 10 April 2020).

Amnesty International, (2019) *Gambia: Truth Commission Hearings an Important Step Towards Justice and Reparations*. [online]. Available at: Gambia: Truth Commission hearings an important step towards justice and reparations | Amnesty International (Accessed: 24 May 2020).

Anya, S.E. and Palmer, A., (2014) *The Gambia National Human Development Report on Youth Employment*. Banjul: UNDP.

Asemota, B., (2017) *Gambia Needs New Constitution*. 1 June. [online]. Available at: Gambia needs new constitution – The Point (Accessed: 20 May 2020).

Bah, S., (2020) *Commentary on the Landmarks in the 2020 Draft Constitution of The Gambia*. [online]. Available at: www.lawhubgambia.com/lawhug-.(Accessed: 26 May 2020).

BBC News, (2019) *Gambians Protest to Push for Fresh Elections*. [online]. Available at: www.bbc.com/news/live/world-africa-47639452?ns_ (Accessed: 30 May 2020).

BBC News, (2020) *The Gambia Profile -Timeline*. 14 February. [online]. Available at: www.bbc.com/news/world-africa-13380407 (Accessed: 10 May 2020).

Connolly, L. and He, C., (2018) 'Toward a New Gambia: Linking Peace and Development', *International Peace Institute*, 1 January.

Constitutional Review Commission, (2020) *Report of the Constitutional Review Commission on The Draft Constitution for The Third Republic of The Gambia*. Banjul: CRC.

Darboe, M.K., (2020a) *One Year of Truth-telling in the Gambia*. 13 January. [online]. Available at: One year of truth-telling in the Gambia – JusticeInfo.net (Accessed: 24 May 2020).

Darboe, M.K., (2020b) *Gambia: Finger Pointing in the Security Forces*. 25 February. [online]. Available at: Gambia: Finger pointing in the security forces – JusticeInfo.net (Accessed: 28 May 2020).

Deutsche Welle (DW) (2020) *Gambia's New President Barrow Sworn in, for Second Time*. [online]. Available at: Gambia's new President Barrow sworn in, for second time | News | DW | 18.02.2017 (Accessed: 10 May 2020).

Dwyer, M., (2017) 'Fragmented Forces: The Development of the Gambian Military', *African Security Review*, 26(4), pp. 362–377.

European Union, (2020) *EU Projects in The Gambia. Delegation of European Union to The Gambia*. Banjul: Delegation of the European Union to The Gambia.

Freedom Newspaper, (2016) *The Gambia Is Not A Mandinka Country, Jammeh, As Jammeh Brands Gambian Mandinkas as 'Foreigners'*. [online]. Available at: www.freedomnewspaper.com/2016/06/04/ (Accessed: 1 May 2020).

Gambia Investment and Export Promotion Agency, (GIEPA), (2020) *Country Profile*. [online]. Available at: Country Profile | GIEPA (Accessed: 20 May 2020).

Gambiana, (2019) *Office of National Security to Introduce Security Checks for Government Job Seekers*. [online]. Available at: Office of National Security to introduce security checks for government job seekers (gambiana.com) (Accessed: 23 May 2020).

Government of the Gambia, (2017) *The Gambia National Development Plan (2018–2021)*. Banjul: The Government of the Gambia.

Human Right Watch, (2015) *Gambia: Two Decades of Fear and Repression*. [online]. Available at: www.hrw.org/news/2015/09/17/gambia-two-decades-fear-and (Accessed: 1 May 2020).

Human Rights Watch, (2017) *Gambia – Events of 2017*. [online]. Available at: World Report 2018: Gambia | Human Rights Watch (hrw.org) (Accessed: 28 May 2020).

International Centre for Transitional Justice, (2020) *Background: Transitional Justice in the Gambia*. [online]. Available at: www.ictj.org/our-work/regions-and (Accessed: 15 May 2020).

International Monetary Fund, (2020) 'IMF Executive Board Approves a US$21.3 Million Disbursement to The Gambia to Address the COVID-19 Pandemic', *Press Release*, 20(164).

Irish, J., (2018) 'In Push for Stability, France Gives 30-million-euro Aid to Gambia', *Reuters*, 5 November. [online]. Available at: www.reuters.com/article/france-gambia/in-push-for (Accessed: 2 June 2020).

ISS PSC Report, (2019) *The Democratisation Process in the Gambia Remains Fragile*. 24 July. [online]. Available at: https://issafrica.org/pscreport/psc-insights/the- (Accessed: 2 June 2020).

Jagger, C., (2020) 'Restoring Trust: Toward a People-Centric Security Sector in The Gambia', *DAI*, [online]. Available at: Restoring Trust: Toward a People-Centric Security Sector in The Gambia (dai-global-developments.com) (Accessed: 23 April 2020).

Jeffang, K., (2019) 'EU Disburses 22 Million Euros of Budget Support to The Gambia', *The Chronicle*. [online]. Available at: www.chronicle.gm/eu-disburses-22-million-euros-ofia/ (Accessed: 2 June 2020).

Manneh, K.A., (2019a) 'Gambia's March Towards Security Sector Reform Gains Momentum: NSA Calls on Citizens to Take Ownership', *The Chronicle*. [online]. Available at: www.chronicle.gm/gambias (Accessed: 20 April 2020).

Manneh, M., (2019b) 'Gambia: Soldiers Deployed for VIP Training in Senegal', *All Africa*. [online]. Available at: https://allafrica.com/stories/201908230288.html (Accessed: 10 May 2020).

Ministry of Health, The Gambia, (2020) *Coronavirus, Gambia: COVID-19 Case Update*. Banjul: Ministry of Health, The Gambia.

Mukabana, S., (2020) 'Gambia President Forms New Political Party', *CGTN Africa*, 1 January. [online]. Available at: https://africa.cgtn.com/2020/01/01/gambia-president-forms-new-political-party/ (Accessed: 30 May 2020).

Mutangadura, C., (2018) 'Hard times ahead for the African Union in The Gambia', *ISS Today*, 21 April.

Mutangadura, C., (2020) 'Will The Gambia be a Turning Point for AU Peace Efforts?', *ISS Today*, 13 May. [online]. Available at: https://issafrica.org/iss-today/will-the-gambia-be-a-turning (Accessed: 27 May 2020).

Nabaneh, S., (2018) *The Need for an Independent Gambian Judiciary*, Law Hub Gambia. [online]. Available at: www.lawhubgambia.com/lawhug (Accessed: 23 May 2020).

Petesch, C., (2020) 'Gambia Arrests 137 in Protests Urging President to Step Down', *AP News*, 27 January. [online]. Available at: https://apnews.com/b2424ca2a010691532761a051c8dc954 (Accessed: 20 May 2020).

Republic of the Gambia, (2017) *President Barrow Launches Gambia's Security Sector Reform Project*. [online]. Available at: www.statehouse.gm/president-barrow (Accessed: 20 May 2020).

Serrano, L., (2020) *Gender and the Security Sector: A Survey of the Security Services of the Gambia*. Geneva: DCAF.

Sowe, G. and Nabaneh, S., (2018) 'The Gambia: The State of Liberal Democracy' in Albert, R., Landau, D., Faraguna, P. and Drugda, Š., (eds.) *Global Review of Constitutional Law*. Boston: The I·CONnect-Clough Center.

Toupane, P.M., Faye, A.K. and Kanté, A., (2019) 'The Gambia Must Heal its Social and Political Divisions', *ISS Today*.

Trial International, (2020) *The Gambia*. [online]. Available at: https://trialinternational.org/countries-post/gambia/ (Accessed: 20 May 2020).

Truth, Reconciliation, and Reparations Commission (TRRC), (2019) *Interim Report, 2018–2019*. Banjul: TRRC.

Truth, Reconciliation, and Reparations commission (TRRC), (2020a) *Statement by the Chair, Dr. Lamin J. Sise, at the Opening of the 11th Session of the TRRC's Public Hearings*. [online]. Available at: www.trrc.gm/updates/ (Accessed: 24 May 2020).

Truth, Reconciliation, and Reparations Commission (TRRC), (2020b) *Welcome To The TRRC*. [online]. Available at: viewed 10 May 2020, www.trrc.gm/ (Accessed: 24 May 2020).

UNDP, (2016) *Human Development Report of 2016*. Gambia: UNDP.

UNDP, (2020a) 'Update on The Socio-Economic Situation Following Covid-19 Outbreak in the Gambia', *Brief #1*, 27 March.

UNDP, (2020b), *The Gambia*. [online]. Available at: www.gm.undp.org/ (Accessed: 24 April 2020).

UNICEF The Gambia, (2018) *Conflict Analysis of The Gambia for Peacebuilding Education and Advocacy*. UNICEF, Banjul.

United Nations, (2017) *IRF-Project Document for the Gambia, UN Peacebuilding Support Office/Peacebuilding Fund*. Gambia: United Nations.

UN News, (2016) *Gambia: UN Adviser Condemns President's Reported Threats Against Ethnic Group*. [online]. Available at: https://news.un.org/en/story/2016/06/531822- (Accessed: 24 April 2020).

UNOWAS, (2020) *Launch of the Security Sector Reform process in The Gambia*. [online]. Available at: https://unowas.unmissions.org/launch-security-sector-reform (Accessed: 20 May 2020).

Williams, P.D., (2017) 'A New African Model of Coercion? Assessing the ECOWAS Mission in The Gambia', *IPI Global Observatory*.

World Bank, (2017), *Macro Poverty Outlook for Sub-Saharan Africa: The Gambia*. [online]. Available at: http://pubdocs.worldbank.org/en/214601492188159621/mpo- (Accessed: 20 May 2020).

World Bank in The Gambia (2020) *The Gambia: Overview*. [online]. Available at: www.worldbank.org/en/country/gambia/overview (Accessed: 3 June 2020).

# 16
# THE POLITICS OF TRANSITIONAL JUSTICE AND PEACEMAKING IN A NON-TRANSITION CONTEXT

## The Case of South Sudan

*Kuyang Harriet Logo*

### Introduction and Background

South Sudan became independent in July 2011, and in 2013 a civil war erupted. The immediate causes of the 2013 civil war centered on political disagreements over party leadership and the future of the Sudan People's Liberation Movement (SPLM; Knopf 2018). Internal debates of the SPLM and the leadership's failure to prioritize national issues, governance and reforms, party elections and the future of the South Sudan state began to increase opposition towards President Salva Kiir Mayardit's rule and his inner circle (International Crisis Group 2014). During the negotiation of the Comprehensive Peace Agreement (CPA)[1] of 2005, many southern groups were absorbed into the SPLM without due consideration to the diverse identities and affiliations of the groups beforehand. The groups were absorbed as part of the SPLM, yet each maintained its identity and varied objectives. In the absence of a joint platform for representation of its diverse membership, the SPLM became superficially representative of the diverse interests of its membership and only pursued one ideal agenda, to attain independence from Sudan and nothing else (International Crisis Group 2014).

Additionally, negotiations of the CPA in early 2000 only focused on ending the north-south conflict and failed to deal with internal rivalries within the SPLM, ethnic dominance by those who felt the party belonged to them and a tendency to lead the movement in a non-democratic manner (Nyadera 2018). The 2013 conflict, just like the 1991 Nassir split[2] of the SPLM, focused on ethnic identities and became brutal. Consequently, the political stalemate resulting from the firing of Dr Riek Machar from the position of vice president by President Salva Kiir in early 2013 quickly degenerated into a civil war where certain ethnicities – the Nuer and Dinka – targeted each other at the start of the conflict in 2013 and in 2014 (Rolandsen 2015). From December 2013 onwards, the conflict spread to other parts of Greater Upper Nile, Greater Bahr el Ghazel, and Greater Equatoria, resulting in large-scale violence and the targeting of civilians in the most brutal way. The African Union (AU), in furthering its subsidiary role of supporting regional organizations, such as the Intergovernmental Authority on Development (IGAD), established a commission of inquiry on South Sudan to conduct investigations into allegations of massive human rights violations. Eventually, an AU report of inquiry into the violence in South Sudan documented the massive human rights violations, crimes against humanity and other brutal crimes committed by the Sudan People's Liberation Army and by the opposition forces (African Union 2014). Other entities, such as the UN Mission in South Sudan (UNMISS), the South Sudan Human Rights Commission and the International Crisis Group, documented similar human rights violations and crimes against humanity committed by both the parties to the conflict (UNHCR 2020). The reports made recommendations on how IGAD, the Troika countries, the UN and the AU could deal with reconciliation, reparations and, most importantly, criminal accountability through a hybrid court to deal with the massive impunity.

Dealing with impunity became central to the resolution of the conflict in South Sudan and central to dealing with the past. It would be recalled that the CPA of 2005 was preoccupied with ending the Sudanese civil war, one of the longest civil wars in Africa, and paid little attention to issues of justice and the primacy of holding both the Sudanese government and the SPLM accountable for atrocities committed against civilians during the 21-year war (Mamdani 2016). IGAD, with the engagement of international stakeholders (i.e. the Troika countries), brokered the 2005 agreement with the sole purpose of ending the war and completely undermined commitments to democratic change and including justice provisions as part of the 2005 peace deal (Young 2007). Consequently, the SPLM political leadership that emerged in charge of South Sudan were not held accountable for human rights violations that occurred during the liberation war (Mamdani 2016).

The exclusion of justice by IGAD and Troika in 2005 relegated the significance of justice as a peacebuilding tool to a less significant position in South Sudan. So when civilians were once more subjected to the worst form of violence in 2013, IGAD rethought its peacemaking approach in South Sudan and sought to include justice through a hybrid court (Carroll 2013). However, the inclusion of transitional justice as a mechanism to dealing with issues of the past and impunity not only complicated the mediation, but it made the South Sudanese parties to the conflict resist the process altogether (Kumalo and Lucey 2017). Eventually, IGAD expanded the mediation to include other key stakeholders that were already supporting the process informally and from the periphery. The reconstituted body, IGAD PLUS,[3] reinvigorated the mediation but had to contend with several challenges originating from the disinterest of the South Sudanese parties to the peace process itself, particularly disinterest in criminal accountability (Amnesty International 2019). This is therefore a context of non-transition, one where no form of political and criminal change has taken place. Against this backdrop, the chapter makes two arguments. First, while transitional justice, especially criminal accountability, was regarded crucial in South Sudan, its inclusion in peacemaking in a context where no political and democratic developments have taken place resulted in political games played by the elites in Juba to frustrate the whole process, and their actions significantly lowered the prospects for justice. Second, the chapter argues that in the absence of a transition, political elites put on a façade giving the impression that the pursuance of justice is important, but with the intention to manipulate these processes and play politics to suit the agenda of avoiding justice altogether while pursuing alternative aims (Loyle and Davenport 2015). The outcome of the political games eventually denied justice to victims, and the likelihood of renewed conflict remains high. The chapter concludes that in extremely fragile contexts like South Sudan, an empirical assessment (Skaar, Gianella Malca and Eide 2016) remains vital to determine which of the transitional justice mechanisms would sustain peace and keep justice on the agenda for a suitable time.

## Making the Case for Transitional Justice in a Non-transition Context Like South Sudan

UN reports (UNMISS 2015), the report of the African Union Commission of Inquiry on South Sudan (African Union 2014) and independent reports authored by research institutions (International Crisis Group 2014), recommended key stakeholders (i.e. the IGAD PLUS) to consider holding perpetrators of human rights violations accountable for acts committed during the civil war from 2013 onwards (Kumalo and Lucey 2017). In 2014, the AU commissioned an investigation into allegations of gross human rights violations by both the Sudan People's Liberation Army and the opposition groups, especially the SPLM (the dominant opposition). The findings of the AU report of inquiry pointed to large-scale abuses by the parties to the conflict (African Union 2014). A monitoring and verification mechanism was created in 2014 to monitor the parties' compliance with the 2015 agreement and was later reconstituted in compliance with the 2018 revitalized agreement. The monitoring and verification mechanisms faced barriers such as "limited access in areas where violations have occurred and most importantly, the impact of the monitors' presence in changing the parties behavior was uncertain" (Verjee 2019). It was assumed that regular reports on the status of the parties' compliance to ceasefire arrangements in 2015 and later in the revitalized 2018 agreement would deter violations (Verjee 2019). However, due to a lack of consequences for serious violations, the monitoring and verification report had little impact on the conduct of the parties, who continued to violate ceasefire arrangements while disregarding warnings of punitive action by IGAD PLUS (Verjee 2019).

The UNMISS produced reports (UNMISS 2015) detailing massive human rights violations against civilians, including the killing of civilians in hospitals and places of worship. The reports detail several incidents where civilians were targeted based on their ethnicity (UNMISS 2014). The UN Commission on Human Rights in South Sudan reported incidents of human rights violations by the parties and continues to collect and preserve evidence and clarify responsibility for alleged gross human rights violations in South Sudan (UNHCR 2020). Therefore, evidence of large-scale human rights violations as collated in several reports prompted key stakeholders to consider the inclusion of transitional justice, especially a hybrid court in the peace agreements of 2015 and the revitalized agreement of 2018. Considering the enormous targeting of innocent civilians by the parties to the agreement, justice for victims of human rights violations became significant in dealing with the legacies of human rights violations and dealing with the past (Booth 2016).

Eventually, transitional justice including a criminal accountability mechanism through a hybrid court became an integral part of both the 2015 and 2018 agreements on the resolution of the conflict in South Sudan (Tombe 2019). While the parties to the agreement were receptive to truth telling and reparations mechanisms, they despised the hybrid court. Therefore, by arguing that in situations where no apparent political and democratic transitions have taken place, criminal accountability would be strongly resisted by the political elite who are part of the transitional government in place, the chapter touches on complex dilemmas in the South Sudan context (Booth 2016). Transitional justice itself emerged after the periods following the end of World War II, preceded by the Nuremburg trials and a wave of democratization and political transitions in Latin America in the 1980s. Key questions regarding criminal trials during these periods were raised and with relative success were attributed to both the political and democratic transitions (Teitel 2003). While transitions were considered key to the pursuance of criminal prosecutions, there were concerns regarding introducing criminal prosecutions in precarious political contexts (Arthur 2009) and the imperative to balance competing moral imperatives to reconcile legitimate claims for justice and claims for stability and for peace (Loyle and Davenport 2015).

Despite the growth of the field and its application in a range of contexts, it lacks a clear theoretical agenda and is now being applied in different contexts, sometimes in a context where no form of political and democratic changes occurred (Buckley-Zistel et al. 2014). Importantly so, introducing transitional justice in South Sudan demonstrates that criminal prosecutions will encounter difficulties because the incumbent elites remain those who are implicated in wrongdoing (Loyle and Davenport 2015). For instance, to illustrate the confusion here and some of the challenges being encountered in South Sudan, there are claims that justice aims could further the goal of reconciliation, peace and liberal democratic change (Loyle and Davenport 2015), and that lasting peace and the rule of law are contingent on the mechanisms of transitional justice, including criminal prosecutions. Yet a thorough review of these claims in contexts of conflict and where no transitions occurred show that criminal prosecutions could lead to state failure and renewal of the conflict (Loyle and Davenport 2015). Perhaps the argument that justice could facilitate reconciliation, liberal peace and advance the rule of law influenced IGAD PLUS to include transitional justice, especially criminal prosecutions, as part of the two peace agreements in South Sudan (Booth 2016). Alongside the claims of the field of transitional justice, the massive human rights violations and the culture of impunity prompted IGAD PLUS to embed transitional justice as part of peacemaking (International Crisis Group 2014).

The inclusion of justice mechanisms as part of peace accords may prompt incumbent political leadership, implicated in wrongdoing, to resist the implementation of the provisions on justice (Darch 2018). The inclusion of justice mechanisms in peace agreements remains important, but the scale is limited due to anticipated rejection (Vinjamuri and Boesenecker 2007). Embedding transitional justice, especially justice mechanisms, as part of the two agreements in South Sudan resulted in several complexities arising from the role of the incumbents trying to frustrate the implementation of justice mechanisms. The incumbent political leadership took advantage of insecurity and ongoing conflict to frustrate the criminal accountability demands (Vertin 2018). The very inclusion of transitional justice during the mediation of the 2015 and 2018 negotiations sparked resistance by the political leadership of South Sudan (Vertin 2018), and even when the agreements were eventually signed, the parties are yet to make good on their promise to establish the Hybrid Court of South Sudan (HCSS; IGAD 2018).

The inclusion of transitional justice was also critical in dealing with the past and correcting the mistakes of the CPA, which had avoided justice in the Sudans (Mamdani 2016). The ambitious and ambiguous goal of achieving justice in transition and balancing the need for peace and stability present significant challenges (Maddison and Shepherd 2014). The basis for peacebuilding and recently transitional justice hinged on plans to assist fragile states to transition to peace, democracy and the rule of law (Merlingen and Ostrauskaite 2005). This intention remains the primary driver of external stakeholders' engagements in fragile and war-torn states, but an assessment of a context like South Sudan would prove that justice remains extremely difficult (Merlingen and Ostrauskaite 2005).

## Politics of Sabotaging Justice: The Role of the Politicians and of the Context

As soon as the 2015 agreement was signed and the transitional government was formed in April 2016, the presidency allegedly authored an opinion piece in the *New York Times*, stating South Sudan's desirability for truths and not trials (Kiir and Machar 2016). The conduct of the political leadership of South Sudan raised questions regarding the viability of justice in a context of non-transition and also the role that the political leadership plays in frustrating the initiation of justice mechanisms (Kumalo and Lucey 2017). Even in the era where transitional justice took shape, in the 1980s, it was hard for states emerging from dictatorships and conflict to prosecute former perpetrators (Hinton 2010). While the *New York Times* article was largely regarded as an attempt to sidestep the establishment of the court, it also pointed to the political leaderships' attempt to relegate the significance of holding perpetrators accountable for human rights violations (Booth 2016). The predicament in South Sudan points to observable trends that transitional justice initiatives of justice, adopted in contexts where no form of political or democratic transitions took place (Vertin 2018), will encounter resistance from the incumbent elites. The conceptualization of transitional justice scored mixed results, especially justice as part of political transitions and the inclusion of human rights accountability as a requirement for democratization (Bell 2009). Also in the absence of empirical assessment of non-transitional context, goals of justice might not be met (Bell 2009). For instance, in the South Sudan context, the political leadership showed their disinterest in criminal prosecution of perpetrators during the mediation of the peace agreement (Amnesty International 2019).

The inclusion of transitional justice as a peacebuilding model, especially criminal accountability through the HCSS, offset the political leadership and resulted in several delays and complexities during the entire peace mediation (Owiso 2018). The South Sudan political leadership engaged in extensive foot-dragging and often stuck to irreconcilable differences during the 2015 peace negotiations. The crisis that occurred in 2016, barely two months after the agreement, was a sign that the parties were not interested in the transitional justice mechanisms (Burke 2016). The 2015 agreement collapsed in 2016, and a High-Level Revitalization Forum (HLRF) was eventually convened to discuss some provisions of the agreement, engage other political actors who were initially left out of the 2015 process, and take stock of political and security realities on the ground (Verjee 2017). The peace revitalization process convened in Khartoum faced significant obstacles and was only possible due to pressure exerted on the parties by the president of Uganda and the former president of Sudan, Al Bashir (Tombe 2019). Additionally, some of the challenges of making peace in South Sudan are linked to the bad blood between the political leadership in the opposition and in government, and much of the difficulty in making peace is a result of the tensions arising from unresolved issues at the top political leadership level (Knopf 2018). The internal political tensions amongst the political leadership and unresolved underlying root causes of the conflict continued to frustrate both peacebuilding and transitional justice (de Vries and Schomerus 2017). While transitional justice, especially criminal accountability through the hybrid court, was considered central to dealing with impunity and massive human rights violations, the incumbent political leadership in South Sudan remains uninterested in the prospects of justice and what it would achieve in South Sudan (Young 2015). The resistance to justice and to the holding of perpetrators accountable by the political elite remain linked to an attempt to avoid being held accountable for human rights violations (Amnesty International 2019).

As witnessed in contexts where the same political leadership implicated in wrongdoing remains the same one making decisions regarding peace and justice, the South Sudanese elites are poised to frustrate the establishment of the court, because they would not establish a court that would try them (Amnesty International 2019). The security of the context also remains unconducive for documentation of human rights violations and preservation of evidence to prosecute those who hold responsibility for human rights violations (Verjee 2019). The national security agency, with the approval of the political leadership, denies verification teams' access to sites where human rights violations occurred. In situations where victims could be accessed, they remain afraid to speak for fear of reprisals from the security agents (Burke 2016). In some situations, local-level insecurity became a significant barrier to human rights monitors to access sites and victims (Human Rights Watch 2019). Transitional justice scholarship touches on some of the challenges in enforcing criminal accountability in contexts where no transitions occurred and the possibility of actors pursuing transitional justice mechanisms for alternative political goals (Loyle and Davenport 2015).

There are claims that justice in a non-transition context may raise new problems. While transitional justice scholarship asserts there could be no peace without justice, the inclusion of justice as a peacebuilding model is not that simple in non-transition contexts (Fourlas 2015). While victims' rights rest at the center of demands for justice and claim that just and democratic transition to peace requires a process of legal and political accountability, the political elites of the old order resist justice demands for fear of being held accountable (McGrattan 2009). While criminal accountability remains crucial in dealing with human rights violations, the myriad of contexts within which prosecutions have been enforced presented mixed results. Adopting a similar mechanism of justice in contexts different from those of the origins of the field remain difficult and complex (Lawther, Moffett and Jacobs 2019). In recent years, far from the years of its development, transitional justice mandate broadened to include conflict and post-conflict settings with the goal to achieving peace and democracy. However much of this development remains largely in part a theoretical development devoid of empirical assessments of each context (Turner 2013).

## Alternatives to Achieving Lasting Peace Within the Framework of the 2018 Agreement

After the collapse of the 2016 peace agreement, the HLRF was convened to take stock of changes in the implementation environment and political developments and to renegotiate certain aspects of the failed agreement of 2015. The 2018 agreement signed in Khartoum, Sudan, is the current agreement under implementation. As it stands, the transitional justice mechanism of justice through the HCSS will not be implemented in the current context, where the political leadership remains uninterested in pursing justice for victims and where the same elites implicated in wrongdoing lead decisions on the court (Kumalo and Lucey 2017). Hence, while key stakeholders within IGAD PLUS work with the political leadership to push for criminal accountability, they could leverage some of the transitional justice mechanisms on truth telling and reparations. Chapter V of the revitalized 2018 agreement provides for the establishment of the Commission for Truth, Reconciliation and Healing and a reparations authority (IGAD 2018). Before the collapse of the 2015 peace agreement (IGAD 2015), South Sudan had launched countrywide consultations on the establishment of the commission (Xinhua 2018). A technical committee was formed by the national Ministry of Justice to consult the people on the framework of the commission. The stakeholders within IGAD PLUS could leverage some of their efforts to some of the acceptable mechanisms of truth telling and reparations for the time being, while keeping the justice demands on the hold (Xinhua 2018).

It is believed that undertaking a national healing process could bring relative stability, peace and reconciliation to the people of South Sudan (Sansculotte-Greenidge, Yanaki Taban and Gogol 2013). Reconciliation, in the current context, could be a first step to promote individual responsibility and, importantly, to task ring leaders and perpetrators of violence to find peace within themselves and lead others towards peace. It is believed that a national reconciliation process could significantly reduce the ongoing violence (Sansculotte-Greenidge, Yanaki Taban and Gogol 2013). The people of South Sudan have on several occasions and in several forums demanded that the perpetrators of human rights violations be brought to book for their wrongs, but that remains tricky in the current context (Carroll 2013). That said, the masses also demanded reconciliation, healing and reparations in situations where criminal accountability may not be possible (UNDP 2015). Since there are significant obstacles to achieving justice, IGAD PLUS and the political leadership in South Sudan could harness their calls on the formation of the Commission for Truth, Reconciliation and Healing and a reparations authority as a first step (UNDP 2015). Once the more acceptable mechanism of transitional justice of reconciliation is commenced, then linkages to the proposed hybrid court could be established (Carroll 2013). Additionally evidence emanating from testimonies and truths being expressed during the commission's hearings could be used to build a case for the need to try some of the perpetrators who bore significant responsibility (UNDP 2015).

Evidence emerging from transitional justice literature shows that local actors often resist internationally designed forms of criminal accountability and prefer to adopt a localized approach to justice and peacebuilding. As much as there is limited international discussion on local mechanisms of reconciliation and restoration, its contributions could help stabilize fragile states. The outcomes of justice and its expectations may not necessarily provide the much-needed relief in a deeply divided society but could result in more turmoil (Subotic 2015). For instance, in South Sudan, the political leadership views the push for the hybrid court as an attempt by IGAD PLUS to impose foreign norms of justice and to push for a regime change (Amnesty International 2019). Additionally, in the demand for justice in South Sudan, several complexities do arise from a simple conceptualization of what is a perpetrator and a victim, and what individual guilt means (UNDP 2015).

The political leadership in late 2015 and early 2016 before the collapse of the agreement, progressed to the level of signing a memorandum of understanding (MoU) with the AU to pave way for the establishment of the court. However, after the collapse of the 2015 agreement in July 2016, the political leadership and the justice institutions in South Sudan failed to provide information on the status of the MoU that was initially signed with the AU and also constantly informed IGAD PLUS that the court was only viable if a transitional government of national unity was in place and in accordance with provisions of the revitalized agreement (Owiso 2018). Therefore, since reconciliation and reparations are more acceptable to the current political leadership in Juba, IGAD PLUS could proceed on that basis and eventually establish links to broader justice aims and also perhaps hope that in the event that a transition occurs, then the new era could permit the pursuit of perpetuators of human rights violations (de Vries and Schomerus 2017). It is also important to note here that the transitional justice framework of the 2018 agreement combined criminal accountability, reconciliation and reparations. Therefore, in the absence of an environment that allows for the implementation of criminal accountability mechanisms, the other two mechanisms for reconciliation and reparations could still play a part in fostering peace and stability for the time being (Sansculotte-Greenidge, Yanaki Taban and Gogol 2013).

Recommendations from truth commissions had in some contexts paved the way for the discussion of criminal accountability, especially where support for truth commissions could be seen as alternatives to prosecutions (Seils 2002). The mandate of the truth commission could be crafted to include possibilities for trials for perpetrators (Seils 2002). Additionally, it remains critical to consider local realities and hybridized mechanisms of justice in very complex contexts (Betts 2007). For instance, in Rwanda, at the domestic level the Gacaca derived its legitimacy from being regarded as home-grown and the International Tribunal for Rwanda as far from the victims. In this case, just as it is now in South Sudan, after massive atrocities are committed, domestic mechanisms of transitional justice could be better placed to deal with collective guilt, where nearly everybody was complacent in one way or the other for committing human rights violations (Betts 2007). Furthermore, the insistence on the hybrid court is likely to heighten the political leadership's resistance not only to justice but also to the other transitional justice mechanism that was acceptable to the leadership. So devising intelligent alternatives around the proposed commission for truth and reparations authority could provide the much-needed incentive to kick start the process (Carroll 2013).

Lessons for South Sudan could be drawn from the South African approach to healing and reconciliation. The South African truth commission gained prominence as a key element of a model which advances a social political transformation, healing and reconciliation (Colvin 2000). IGAD PLUS worries that if justice is denied to victims in South Sudan, the likelihood that people and communities will continue to engage in revenge attacks and killings will remain high (Amnesty International 2019). Therefore, in such situations healing and recovery remain important and will not only be dependent on criminal accountability mechanisms but also on what the context and political leadership will allow for now, which is reconciliation and healing. It is often also understandable that formal peace agreements and those that include justice mechanisms do not often lead to lasting peace, and a more comprehensive search for better peacebuilding approaches led to the discovery of mechanisms of reconciliation and memorialization (Keynan 2014). Once achieved, reconciliation could permit the restoration of genuine peaceful relationships (Keynan 2014). The arguments raised above could benefit South Sudan's transitional justice path and peacebuilding (Arthur 2009). Equally important in South Sudan would be an attempt to establish links between a commission for truth and the traditional mechanism of peacebuilding and reconciliation (Huyse and Salter 2008). Experiences of the international community's engagement in reconciliation in African could equally benefit IGAD PLUS and the political leadership in South Sudan (Huyse and Salter 2008).

## Conclusions and Ways Forward

Principally, the inclusion of transitional justice as part of the 2015 agreement and the revitalized agreement of 2018 was hinged on a concrete foundation to ensure that impunity is curtailed and justice served for the victims of gross human rights violations occurring from 2013 to date (Burke 2016). Reports authored and evidence of human rights violations influenced the demand for justice as part of the peace trajectory (International Crisis Group 2014). IGAD PLUS convinced the political leadership of South Sudan to accept a transitional justice chapter detailing truth telling processes, reparations and justice through the HCSS as part of the peace agreement (Booth 2016). The political leadership was receptive of the establishment of a truth commission and a reparations authority but continues to stall and play political games on the issue of the HCSS (Kiir and Machar 2016), and after the political leadership in South Sudan had agreed for the court to be included as part of the agreement, they continue to avoid its establishment (Kumalo and Lucey 2017). This chapter made the argument that in the absence of both political and democratic transition, the political leadership in South Sudan engaged in politics to frustrate the establishment of the court and also gave the impression that they would prosecute perpetrators, while their intention was to pursue alternative political aims. The reasons for the rejection of criminal accountability remains linked to the fact that the same political leadership implicated in wrongdoing and massive human rights violations became the same leaders making decisions on transitional justice under the framework of the 2018 agreement. In the absence of a transition, the political leadership was seen as engaging in discussions about the court with the AU. The political leadership was falsely pretending support for justice, when in fact they had no intention of proceeding as expected.

The political leadership also took advantage of a complex and insecure context to undermine the work of monitoring and verification teams who attempted to access victims and sites of human rights violations across the country (Verjee 2019). In light of the foregoing conclusions, it remains vital that acceptable alternatives of mechanism of transitional justice within the framework of the revitalized 2018 peace agreement are pursued to reconcile and heal communities (Betts 2007). For instance, a commission for truth, reconciliation and healing could equally place responsibility on perpetuators to tell the truth and to apologize communities for wrongs committed during the conflict (Sansculotte-Greenidge, Yanaki Taban and Gogol 2013). After successfully operationalizing the Commission for Truth, Reconciliation and Healing, links to criminal accountability could be established as the truth-telling processes progress. Equally imperative would be a continuous empirical assessment of the context to determine whether context-specific difficulties changed, such as insecurity, conflict and the attitude of leadership. An assessment on whether the attitude of the political leadership changed or whether a transition occurred takes time, and dealing with other acceptable forms of transitional justice is critical as a starting point (Skaar, Gianella Malca and Eide 2016). Consequently, as a non-transition context, attempts at justice in South Sudan demonstrated that as much as transitional justice scholarship made a case for the implementation of justice mechanisms, things play out differently. Implementation of justice mechanisms in contexts where no transitions occurred in order to foster a transition to democracy, peace and stability, proved difficult in South Sudan (De Vries and Schomerus 2017).

The assumptions of the transitional justice field regarding its viability in non-transition contexts lacks empirical assessment to take stock of the realities on the ground (Skaar, Gianella Malca and Eide 2016). It is therefore imperative that before initiatives of justice are included as part of peace agreements, an assessment of the context should be done (Loyle and Davenport 2015). For now, and as reinforced by advocates of reconciliation and other local initiatives, South Sudan should proceed with a transitional justice mechanism of reconciliation that is acceptable by the leadership, because the current impasse about the court could lead to renewed conflict (Booth 2016).

## Notes

1 The CPA was signed between the SPLM and the National Islamic Front in 2005. The agreement established a semi-autonomous government in South(ern) Sudan (Warner 2016).
2 This was a spilt that occurred within the SPLM. Dr Riek Machar, who became disgruntled by the way the SPLM leadership under Dr John Garang, led the movement, rebelled and formed his own movement called the Nasir faction. He was followed by some prominent Southern Sudanese leadership, prominent amongst whom were Dr Lam Akol Ajawin and Dr Peter Adwok Nyaba (Carney 2007).
3 The Assembly of Heads of State and Government IGAD and the African Union Ad Hoc Committee on South Sudan. AU High-Level Ad Hoc Committee of Heads of State and Government is composed of Algeria, Chad, Nigeria, Rwanda and South Africa, to strengthen Africa's support to IGAD and assist South Sudanese Parties and stakeholders to achieve durable peace. The Sudan People's Liberation Movement and the Sudan People's Liberation Movement in the Opposition are the main parties to the agreement. IGAD PLUS is composed of the United Nations, the African Union, The Intergovernmental Authority on Development, the European Union, the TROIKA countries, i.e., The United States of America, the United Kingdom, and Norway.

## References

African Union, (2014). *Final Report of the African Union Commission of Inquiry on South Sudan*. Addis Ababa: African Union. [online]. Available at: Final report of the African Union Commission of Inquiry on South Sudan (reliefweb.int) (Accessed: 8 July 2021).

Amnesty International, (2019) *"Do You Think We Will Prosecute Ourselves?" No Prospects for Accountability in South Sudan*. London: Amnesty International. [online]. Available at: "Do You Think We Will Prosecute Ourselves?" No Prospects for Accountability in South Sudan (amnesty.org) (Accessed: 8 July 2021).

Arthur, P., (2009) 'How "Transitions" Reshaped Human Rights: A Conceptual History of Transitional Justice', *Human Rights Quarterly*, 31(2), pp. 321–367.

Bell, C., (2009) 'Transitional Justice, Interdisciplinarity and the State of the "Field" or "Non-Field"', *The International Journal of Transitional Justice*, 3(1), pp. 5–27.

Betts, A., (2007) 'Should Approaches to Post-conflict Justice and Reconciliation be Determined Globally, Nationally or Locally?', *The European Journal of Development Research*, 17(4), pp. 735–752.

Booth, D., (2016) *South Sudan's Peace Process: Reinvigorating the Transition*. London: Chatham House, Royal Institute of International Affairs. [online]. Available at: South Sudan's Peace Process: Reinvigorating the Transition (chathamhouse.org) (Accessed: 8 July 2021).

Buckley-Zistel, S., Koloma Beck, T., Braun, C. and Mieth, F., (eds.) (2014) *Transitional Justice Theories*. New York, NY: Routledge.

Burke, J., (2016) 'More than 300 Dead as South Sudan Capital is Rocked by Violence', *The Guardian*, 11 July. [online]. Available at: More than 300 dead as South Sudan capital is rocked by violence (theguardian.com) (Accessed: 8 July 2021).

Carney, T., (2007) *Some Assembly Required: Sudan's Comprehensive Peace Agreement, USIP*. Available at: http://www.usip.org.

Carroll, C.E., (2013) *Hybrid Tribunals are the Most Effective Structures for Adjudicating International Crimes Occurring Within a Domestic State*. South Orange: Seton Hall University. [online]. Available at: Hybrid Tribunals are the Most Effective Structures for Adjudicating International Crimes Occurring Within a Domestic State (scholarship.shu.edu) (Accessed: 8 July 2021).

Colvin, C.J., (2000) *'We Are Still Struggling': Storytelling, Reparations and Reconciliation after the TRC*. Cape Town: Centre for the Study of Violence and Reconciliation. [online]. Available at: 'We Are Still Struggling': Storytelling, Reparations and Reconciliation after the TRC (csvr.org.za) (Accessed: 8 July 2021).

Darch, C., (2018) *A Success Story Gone Wrong? The Mozambican Conflict and the Peace Process in Historical perspective*. Maputo: Friedrich-Ebert Stiftung. [online]. Available at: A Success Story Gone Wrong? The Mozambican Conflict and the Peace Process in Historical Perspective (library.fes.de) (Accessed: 8 July 2021).

De Vries, L. and Schomerus, M., (2017) 'South Sudan's Civil War Will Not End with a Peace Deal', *A Journal of Social Justice*, 29(3), pp. 333–340.

Fourlas, G.N., (2015) 'No Future without Transition: A Critique of Liberal Peace', *International Journal of Transitional Justice*, 9(1), pp. 109–126.

Hinton, A.L., (ed.) (2010) *Transitional Justice: Global Mechanisms and Local Realities after Genocide and Mass Violence*. Brunswick: Rutgers University Press.

Human Rights Watch (HRW), (2019) *South Sudan Events of 2018*. [online]. Available at: South Sudan Events of 2018 (hrw.org) (Accessed: 8 July 2021).

Huyse, L. and Salter, M., (eds.) (2008) *Traditional Justice and Reconciliation after Violent Conflict: Learning from African Experiences*. Stockholm: International Institute for Democracy and Electoral Assistance (IDEA).

Intergovernmental Authority on Development (IGAD), (2015) *Agreement on the Resolution of the Conflict in the Republic of South Sudan*. Addis Ababa: IGAD. [online]. Available at: Document Retrieval Agreement on the Resolution of the Conflict in South Sudan (peacemaker.un.org) (Accessed: 8 July 2021).

Intergovernmental Authority on Development (IGAD), (2018) *Revitalised Agreement on the Resolution of the Conflict in the Republic of South Sudan*. Addis Ababa: IGAD. [online]. Available at: Revitalised Agreement on the Resolution of the Conflict in the Republic of South Sudan (R-ARCSS) (docs.pca-pca.org) (Accessed: 8 July 2021).

International Crisis Group (ICG), (2014) *South Sudan: A Civil War by Any Other Name*, Africa Report no. 217, 10 April 2014. Belgium: International Crisis Group. [online] Available at: South Sudan: A Civil War by Any Other Name (crisisgroup.org) (Accessed: 8 July 2021).

Keynan, I., (2014) 'Between Past and Future: Persistent Conflicts, Collective Memory, and Reconciliation', *International Journal of Social Sciences*, 3(1), pp. 19–28.

Kiir, S. and Machar, R., (2016) 'South Sudan Needs Truths, Not Trials', *New York Times*, 7 June. [online]. Available at: South Sudan Needs Truth, Not Trials (nytimes.com) (Accessed: 8 July 2021).

Knopf, P., (2018) *South Sudan's Civil War and the Conflict Dynamics in the Red Sea*. Washington, DC: The United States Institute of Peace. [online]. Available at: South Sudan's Civil War and Conflict Dynamics in the Red Sea (usip.org) (Accessed: 6 July 2021).

Kumalo, L. and Lucey, A., (2017) *How the AU Can Promote Transitional Justice in South Sudan*. Pretoria: Institute for Security Studies. [online]. Available at: How the AU can promote transitional justice in South Sudan (issafrica.org) (Accessed: 6 July 2021).

Lawther, C., Moffett, L. and Jacobs, D., (eds.) (2019) *Research Handbook on Transitional Justice: The Development of Transitional Justice*. Cheltenham: Edward Elgar.

Loyle, C.E. and Davenport, C., (2015) 'Transitional Injustice: Subverting Justice in Transition and Post conflict Societies', *Journal of Human Rights*, 15(1), pp. 126–149.

Maddison, S. and Shepherd, L.J., (2014) 'Peacebuilding and the Postcolonial Politics of Transitional Justice', *Peacebuilding*, 2(3), pp. 253–269.

Mamdani, M., (2016) *Who's to Blame in South Sudan?* Cambridge: Boston Review. [online] Available at: Global Justice Who's to Blame in South Sudan? (bostonreview.net) (Accessed: 6 July 2021).

McGrattan, C., (2009) "Order Out of Chaos': The Politics of Transitional Justice', *Politics*, 29(3), pp. 164–172.

Merlingen, M. and Ostrauskaite, R., (2005) 'Power/Knowledge in International Peacebuilding: The Case of the EU Police Mission in Bosnia', *Alternatives: Global, Local, Political*, 30(3), pp. 297–323.

Nyadera, I.N., (2018) 'South Sudan Conflict from 2013 to 2018: Rethinking the Causes, Situation and Solutions', *African Journal on Conflict Resolution*, 18(2), pp. 59–86.

Owiso, O., (2018) *The Proposed Hybrid Court for South Sudan: Moving South Sudan and the African Union to Action against Impunity*. Durban: ACCORD. [online]. Available at: The proposed hybrid court for South Sudan: Moving South Sudan and the African Union to action against impunity (accord.org.za) (Accessed: 6 July 2021).

Rolandsen, Ø.H., (2015) 'Another Civil War in South Sudan: The Failure of Guerrilla Government?', *Journal of Eastern African Studies*, 9(1), pp. 163–174.

Sansculotte-Greenidge, K., Yanaki Taban, E. and Gogol, N., (2013) *Reconciliation without Regret: National healing and reconciliation in South Sudan*. Durban: ACCORD. [online]. Available at: Reconciliation without Regret: National healing and reconciliation in South Sudan (accord.org.za) (Accessed: 6 July 2021).

Seils, P.F., (2002) 'Reconciliation in Guatemala: The Role of Intelligent Justice', *Race & Class*, 44(1), pp. 33–59.

Skaar, E., Gianella Malca, C. and Eide, T., (2016) *After Violence: Transitional Justice, Peace and Democracy*. New York, NY: Routledge.

Subotic, J., (2015) 'Truth, Justice, and Reconciliation on the Ground: Normative Divergence in the Western Balkans', *Journal of International Relations & Development*, 18(3), pp. 361–382.

Teitel, R.G., (2003) 'Transitional Justice Genealogy', *Harvard Human Rights journal*, 16, pp. 69–94.

Tombe, S., (2019) *Revitalising the Peace in South Sudan: Assessing the State of the Pre – transitional Phase*. Durban: ACCORD. [online]. Available at: Revitalising the peace in South Sudan: Assessing the state of the pre-transitional phase (accord.org.za) (Accessed: 6 July 2021).

Turner, C., (2013) 'Deconstructing Transitional Justice', *Law and Critique*, 24(2), pp. 193–209.

United Nations Development Programme (UNDP), (2015) *Search for a New Beginning: Perception Survey on Truth, Justice, Reconciliation and Healing in South Sudan*. New York, NY: United Nations Development Programme. [online]. Available at: Search for a New Beginning: Perception Survey on Truth, Justice, Reconciliation and Healing in South Sudan (ss.undp.org) (Accessed: 8 July 2021).

United Nations Human Rights Council (UNHCR), (2020) *Report of the Commission on Human Rights in South Sudan*. Geneva: United Nations Human Rights Council. [online]. Available at: Report of the Commission on Human Rights in South Sudan (digitallibrary.un.org) (Accessed: 8 July 2021).

United Nations Mission in South Sudan (UNMISS), (2014) *Attacks on Civilians in Bentiu & Bor*. Juba: United Nations Mission in South Sudan. [online]. Available at: Attacks on Civilians in Bentiu & Bor April 2014 (Reliefweb.int) (Accessed: 8 July 2021).

United Nations Mission in South Sudan (UNMISS), (2015) *The State of Human Rights in the Protracted Conflict in South Sudan*. Juba: United Nations Mission in South Sudan. [online] Available at: The State of Human Rights in the Protracted Conflict in South Sudan (ohchr.org) (Accessed: 8 July 2021).

Verjee, A., (2017) *South Sudan's High Revitalisation Forum: Identifying Conditions for Success*. Washington, DC: The United States Institute of Peace. [online]. Available at: South Sudan's High Level Revitalization Forum: Identifying Conditions for Success (usip.org) (Accessed: 8 July 2021).

Verjee, A., (2019) *Ceasefire Monitoring in South Sudan 2014–2019: "A Very Ugly Mission"*. Washington, DC: United States Institute for Peace. [online]. Available at: Ceasefire Monitoring in South Sudan 2014–2019: "A very Ugly Mission" (usip.org) (Accessed: 8 July 2021).

Vertin, Z., (2018) *A Poisoned Well: Lessons in Mediation from South Sudan's Troubled Peace Process*. New York, NY: International Peace Institute. [online] Available at: A Poisoned Well: Lessons in Mediation from South Sudan's Troubled Peace Process (ipinst.org) (Accessed: 8 July 2021).

Vinjamuri, A. and Boesenecker, A.P., (2007) *Accountability and Peace Agreements: Mapping Trends from 1980 to 2006*. Geneva: Henry Dunant Centre for Humanitarian Dialogue. [online] Available at: Accountability and Peace Agreements: Mapping trends from 1980 to 2006 (files.ethz.ch) (Accessed: 8 July 2021).

Warner, L.A., (2016) 'The Disintegration of the Military Integration Process in South Sudan (2006–2013)', *Stability: International Journal of Security and Development*, 5(1), p. 12. http://doi.org/10.5334/sta.460.

Xinhua, (2018) 'South Sudan Launches Consultations on Truth and Reconciliation', *Xinhua*, 5 June. [online]. Available at: South Sudan launches consultations on truth and reconciliation (Accessed: 8 July 2021).

Young, J., (2007). *Sudan IGAD Peace Process: An Evaluation*. [online] Available at: Sudan IGAD Peace Process: An Evaluation (sudantribune.com) (Accessed: 8 July 2021).

Young, J., (2015). *A Fractious Rebellion: Inside the SPLM/IO*. Geneva: The Small Arms Survey, Graduate Institute of International and Development Studies. [online]. Available at: A Fractious Rebellion: Inside the SPLM/IO (files.ethz.ch) (Accessed: 8 July 2021).

# 17
# PEACEBUILDING IN GUINEA-BISSAU

Challenges and the Way Forward to Sustaining Peace and Security

*Fiifi Edu-Afful and Ruth Adwoa Frimpong*

### Introduction

As one of the world's most fragile countries, Guinea-Bissau has suffered from frequent political upheavals since independence from Portugal in 1974. Nearly four decades of power struggles and unconstitutional changes of power have led many to label the country a 'failed state', although this concept has been much criticized over the years. The chaotic course of events demonstrated by the successful overthrow of a colonial regime, the inception of structural adjustment programs and the introduction of multiparty elections have exposed the assurance of nonviolent political transitions and post-colonial development. As the World Bank notes, recurrent coups d'état and political instability has reversed the country's development and democratic gains over the years (ECOWAS, 2004; Bodea, 2012). Guinea-Bissau has the most recent of these coups occurring in April 2012, following an electoral impasse between Carlos Gomes Jr of the African Party for the Independence of Guinea and Cape Verde (PAIGC) and Kamba Yale of the Party for Social Renovation (PRS) after the first round of presidential elections. While the motivation underlying the coup was the opposition parties, including Yale's PRS allegations of massive electoral fraud by PAIGC, the major reason was to bar Gomes, who was then the prime minister from rising to power. Prior to the elections, Gomes had a tense relationship with the military hierarchy about the presence and activities of the Angolan Mission for Military and Security Assistance to Guinea-Bissau (MISSANG), who were seen as his pretorian guard (African Union 2014). As a result, when the military saw the possibility of him winning the second round of the presidential elections after leading the first round with 48.97% of the vote, against his close rival, Kamba Yale, who had 23.36%, the coup was staged on 12 April 2012 to interrupt the electoral process (African Union 2014). In the end, the military achieved their aim by forcing him into exile and completely disrupting the activities of MISSANG.

Following that, in May 2012, the Economic Community of West African States (ECOWAS) signed a political accord and established a one-year transitional administration in close consultation with the UN, the European Union (EU), the African Union (AU) and the Community of Portuguese Language Countries (CPLP; UN Security Council 2012a). Sheriff Nhamadjo, then acting speaker of the National People's Assembly (ANP) as interim president, headed the transitional government. The transitional government had the mandate to carry out some proposed reforms and organize credible presidential and legislative elections within a 12-month period. It was within this context that the ECOWAS Mission in Guinea-Bissau (ECOMIB) was deployed on 16 May 2012 to support the transition processes. Since its deployment, ECOMIB has supervised the conduct of relatively peaceful elections in 2014 and served as an effective deterrent to political interference by the Guinea-Bissau armed forces. Although it was initially deployed for a period of 12 months, the political realities on the ground necessitated the extension of the mission's mandate every year until its exit in December 2020. ECOWAS leaders justified ECOMIB's withdrawal from Guinea-Bissau on the premise of 'improved functioning of the *Assembleia Nacional Popular* (parliament) and the government'. This optimism notwithstanding, the unsolved accusations of flawed presidential elections of 2019 and the autocratic nature of the Umaro Cissoko Embaló regime presents serious weaknesses to political stability in the country.

Since the end of the last coup d'état, the main priorities for repeated international attention in Guinea-Bissau have focused on poverty alleviation, democratic consolidation (multiparty elections) and peacebuilding. These priorities have led to various peacebuilding initiatives from the international community, including a joint UN, EU, AU, ECOWAS, CPLP and government of Guinea-Bissau national strategy on national reconciliation, restructuring and modernization defense and security sector reforms (DSSR) and the reactivation of the national economy. Strategically, the international community together with ECOWAS, under the 'Guinea-Bissau P5' formula, has offered considerable assistance to the political process and the national reform agenda. The high-level meetings of the resident coordinators of these five organizations increasingly accompanied by bilateral and multilateral exchanges have succeeded in the relatively calm atmosphere being enjoyed in the country. For instance, in May 2016 the P-5 meetings contributed significantly to the amicable resolution of the political standoff between the dismissed former Prime Minister Carlos Correia and members of his cabinet, following the refusal to relinquish their political positions. Initially, the government of President José Mário Vaz had wanted to use military action to eject the deposed Correia and his group. Such an action could have resulted in chaos and bloodshed. However, following mediation and negotiation efforts of the P-5 group, the standoff ended on 9 June 2016 with the former government and supporters of the PAIGC agreeing to leave the palace without a single violent incident.

Despite these initiatives and achievements, Guinea-Bissau battles with internal political divisions, authoritarian governance, power struggles between the military and civilians, infighting within the armed forces and other security agencies, and lack of public investment in the economy while pervasive corruption and trafficking of arms and drugs remain the bane of continuing social inequality. Undoubtedly, ensuring sustainable peace in such context requires a number of key issues to be tackled at the national, regional and global levels using a comprehensive and composite approach. The other factor relates to the recurrent gap in the top-down model of peacebuilding being practiced in Guinea-Bissau and the need for it to be replaced by a grassroots approach (Havoc 2015). There is less systematic evaluation of the nature, impact and challenges as well as lessons learnt of such an intractable peacebuilding venture.

This chapter attempts to fill these enumerated gaps by focusing on the realities and pitfalls of peacebuilding in Guinea-Bissau. Specifically, it examines the nature, relevance and challenges of peacebuilding initiatives in Guinea-Bissau and explores measures that could be taken to further enhance the effectiveness of the cooperative ventures between multiple actors in bringing sustained peace to a troubled country. The chapter is set in five sections, beginning with the political context of Guinea-Bissau and followed by the discussion of the liberal peacebuilding agenda versus the African lens. The third section examines the many phases of peacebuilding in the country, where particular attention is given to the experiences and roles of international actors. The fourth section discusses the pitfalls and challenges involved in the collaborative efforts of the multiple actors. The final section suggests measures needed to consolidate the gains made so far, as many of the international interveners continue to exit the country.

## Political Context of Guinea-Bissau

The canvas of Guinea-Bissau is painted with power struggles over four decades. The country was involved in a war of liberation between 1963 and 1974 and has been the target of repeated international attention for the implementation of programs geared towards inclusive peace (Havoc 2015). Guinea-Bissau's political economy suffered from military coups, mutinies, assassinations and a civil war after independence from Portugal in 1974. The resultant effect of Guinea-Bissau's political discord and instability was an impoverished economy, leading the World Bank to list the country as one of the poorest in the world.

In April 2012, the political compass of Guinea-Bissau went south with the army's arrest of the soon to be elected president, Prime Minister Carlos Gomes Jr. The arrest resulted in a break in constitutional rule and the second round of presidential elections. A year later, a transitional structure was put in place by international actors to facilitate elections in April 2013. In 2014, ECOWAS played a critical role in reducing political tensions by organizing elections and providing security and finances to the transition government and electoral commission. Under the banner of the country's main political party, José Mário Vaz was elected president and Domingos Simões Pereira was elected prime minister (Bappah 2017). Two former prime ministers (Pereira and Embaló) and incumbent President Vaz contested the presidential elections held on 24 November 2019. However, in a turn of events, the incumbent president was taken out of the presidential race and a run-off election between the two former presidents was held on 29 December 2019. The outcome of the run-off election saw Embaló winning a majority (54%) of the total votes cast. The relative peace and order was short-lived, as a bitter political rivalry broke out after the 2019 presidential elections, dividing the country's road to political recovery. The PAIGC alleged that the party was cheated out of victory and demanded that Embaló wait for the Supreme Court's decision on annulling the elections (Shryock 2020). Since then, the country has had two presidents and two prime ministers until President Cipriano Cassamá stepped down, citing fears for his safety. According to the founder of the West African think tank WATHI, the political class of Guinea-Bissau remains the main hindrance to the country's attainment of peace and stability. To muddy the waters, the political class of Guinea-Bissau is at the centre of the operations of international drug trafficking, illegal arms/weapons and the insurgency of armed groups. It should be stressed that political situation in Guinea-Bissau is the consequence of a complex web of internal, regional and international factors.

## Liberal Peacebuilding Agenda Versus the African Lens

Enshrined in Boutros-Ghali's 1992 *An Agenda for Peace*, peacebuilding comprises one of four approaches that are aimed at fostering peace (Karbo and Virk 2018). The liberal peace thesis was postulated based on the assumptions that the rule of law, democracy and a free-market economy were catalysts in creating sustainable peace, especially in post-conflict settings. The ideology promotes a universalist vision of emancipation through political and economic liberalization, but it also embraces an ethic of individual and group choice or self-government, which might be incompatible with universalist formulations (Campbell, Chandler and Sabaratnam 2011). This theoretical-political framework was later to become the cornerstone of most peacebuilding interventions carried out by the UN in the nineteenth to twentieth centuries.

Described as fundamentally destructive or illegitimate, the liberal peacebuilding (LPB) agenda, according to critics, has become difficult and more unpredictable than expected. It hinges on four strands of thoughts of peace: victor's peace, constitutional peace, civil peace and institutional peace. While this may be so, it is important to re-evaluate and clarify the debates about the post–Cold War peacebuilding agenda.

In the case of Guinea-Bissau, the UN has employed the LBP agenda since the 1990s. It played a pivotal role in the peace process after the signing of the Abuja agreement. The UN peacebuilding project echoes liberalist values and ideals in the layout of activities undertaken to sustain peace. As part of its consolidated activities, it established the United Nations Integrated Peacebuilding Office in Guinea-Bissau (UNIOGBIS) in March 1999 (Cavalcante 2014). The mandates of this office were streamlined to sustain peace, democracy, the rule of law and ensuring free and fair elections. While these are necessary catalysts in recovering from political instability, the context specificity varies. The decades-old approach to peacebuilding has been heavily centred on diplomatic and political initiatives involving international actors and national authorities. It lacked local ownership of the peace process. The interlocutors, who were a representation of Bissau-Guinean society, were hardly involved in the UN peacebuilding project (Cavalcante 2014), although involvement of local actors is crucial to the peace process of post-conflict societies because it consolidates the peace process and restores trust between local and national authorities. Lack of ownership of the peace process may account for relapses into conflict despite efforts made by international actors.

It is imperative to bring into the limelight the African perspective and approach to peacebuilding as part of the discussions on peacebuilding in Guinea-Bissau. As Ali Mazrui succinctly puts it:

> The peace of Africa is to be assured by the exertions of Africans themselves.
> *(Mazrui 1967, 35, as cited in Karbo and Virk 2018)*

Africans can best solve problems created by Africans, an epistle preached by scholars like Ali Mazrui, Ngugi wa Thiong'o, Patrice Lumumba and the like. Prior to peacebuilding being heavily dominated by Western ideologies, there were indigenous approaches in restoring peace, order and development to post-conflict societies in Africa. The effectiveness of indigenous approaches to building peace is evident in post-conflict societies such as Liberia, where the *palaver hut* was employed; the use of *ubuntu* in South Africa; the use of *gacaca* in Rwanda; and the use of Islamic courts (Muslim peacebuilding) in Somalia (McNamee and Muyangwa 2021). These society-centred mechanisms of peacebuilding are effective in preventing retaliation; geared towards instilling the values of solidarity, truth, social cohesion and justice in societies; and are affordable and accessible to all factions of the conflict (Wanis St-John 2013). In recent times, international actors in conjunction with regional actors (e.g. the African Union [AU], the Economic Community of West African States [ECOWAS], the Southern African Development Community [SADC], the East African Community [EAC]) and the former, mostly wielding greater financial and technical influence, undertake peacebuilding on the continent.

As part of regional efforts towards peacebuilding, the AU's African Post-conflict Reconstruction Policy Framework (NEPAD 2005) seeks to restore security, facilitate political transition, resuscitate socio-economic development and promote human rights and justice and resource mobilization (Zondi 2017). This strategic policy framework has been instrumental in peace formation in Burundi, Somalia and Sudan. AU's policies on peacebuilding have been backed by local initiatives by non-governmental organizations (NGOs) and civil society organizations (CSOs). Coordinated with UN Security Council (UNSC) Resolution 1325, a number of these peacebuilding activities have included women-driven efforts. Increasingly, women have shown enthusiasm in issues regarding peace and security, especially in war-torn societies. A stellar example is the role Liberian women played in restoring peace in the post-Taylor setting, which led to the creation of women peacebuilding groups such as the Women in Peacebuilding Network (WIPNET) and the Mano River Women's Peace Network (MARWONET).

One of the greatest hurdles to post-conflict reconstruction in Africa is the use of peacebuilding projects to rekindle neo-patrimonial accumulation, breed nepotism and appease rebel leaders and their constituencies (Zondi 2017). There is the consensus to remodel peacebuilding in Africa to address historical experiences which are mostly the root causes of political discord of post-conflict states. Other challenges to African-led peacebuilding projects and activities include the lack of coordination between AU and international actors such as the UN, uneven performance between the vertical coordination of the AU and regional economic communities (RECs) and the multiplicity of actors in the post-conflict setting. Another way of thinking is that both local and international peacebuilding mechanisms need synchronization to create a hybrid approach which addresses both structural and root causes of conflict and promotes social order and retributive accountability.

## Phases of Peacebuilding in Guinea-Bissau

The trajectory of peacebuilding in Guinea-Bissau has seen several facelifts since the country was added to the UN Peacebuilding Commission (PBC) in 2007. One striking feature of the myriad peacebuilding activities in the former Portuguese colony is the presence of multiple actors: UN, AU, European Union (EU), ECOWAS and the CPLP. There have also been initiatives and mechanisms by traditional and local actors in the quest to restore peace and security. In an attempt to restore security, ECOWAS in 1998 deployed its ceasefire monitoring group (ECOMOG) to Guinea-Bissau. ECOMOG's presence resulted in the facilitation of a ceasefire agreement, which in turn led to the restoration of legitimate power to President João Bernardo Vieira. Essentially, ECOWAS employed negotiation, mediation and dialogue talks between the political elite and military factions. International actors undertook other efforts targeted at restoring security in the country. These included stabilization attempts by the AU, the EU, the West African Economic and Monetary Union (UEMOA), the Organisation Internationale de la Francophonie (OIF) and the CPLP (World Peace Foundation n.d.). ECOWAS has been consistent in standing by the country each time the political or security situation deteriorated (Yabi 2010). Its response and strategies contributed to security sector reforms, the fight against drug trafficking and organized crime in Guinea-Bissau.

Over the years, the UN has played various roles in Guinea-Bissau's road to political and socio-economic recovery. In 2008, the country was placed under the PBF, which consists of a number of mutually reinforcing sectors including dialogue and national reconciliation, formal and informal justice sector development, women and youth empowerment, and professional and conflict-sensitive media strengthening as a cross-cutting issue (UN Peacebuilding n.d.). The Peacebuilding Fund came with an allocation of $6 million in 2009 for the purposes of conducting legislative elections and establishing rehabilitation centres and military barracks (UNIOG-BIS 2009a; United Nations Peacebuilding n.d.a). Another disbursement of $16.8 million was allocated for security sector reforms (SSRs), youth employment and national dialogues in the country (UNIOGBIS 2009a; United Nations Peacebuilding n.d.b).

To spearhead governance and political process, the Special Representative of the Secretary-General (SRSG) in 2015 began extensive work on institutional and constitutional reforms. This was done in consultation with important national stakeholders, civil society, youth organizations, religious leaders, trade unions, private sector representatives and international and regional actors. Another notable activity is the organization of a number of political dialogue and reconciliation meetings. A national dialogue conference was organized in November 2016 to address the impunities of the civil war and a dysfunctional civil-military relation along human rights, security and justice dimensions (UNIOGBIS 2009c). The PBF in Guinea-Bissau also sought to strengthen the country's ailing democratic institutions. This was done through the provision of capacity-building, development of legal frameworks and policies, promotion of information exchange and monitoring the function of democratic institutions at the national and regional levels.

In addition, UNIOGBIS peacebuilding activities included human rights protection and gender mainstreaming. These are crucial areas in consolidating peace and stability in a country constantly beset by coups d'état and assassinations. UNIOGBIS and the Office of the High Commission for Human Rights (OHCHR) supported the formation of the Human Rights Defenders Network of Guinea-Bissau (HRDN) in 2017 with technical and financial assistance (UNIOGBIS 2009c). Cumulatively, the network had a representation of about 900 human rights defenders, including 343 women, from 61 organizations countrywide (UNIOGBIS 2009c). Also, UNIOGBIS forged a partnership with Guinea-Bissau's Ministry of Education and the Institution of Educational Development (INDE) to incorporate human rights education in the curricula of schools in the country (UNIOGBIS 2009b). This partnership has resulted in the sensitization of students on their human rights and the respect for the rights of others. A commendable milestone is the implementation of initiatives that are directed at mainstreaming women in the defence and security sectors of Guinea-Bissau. Periodically, youth and women representatives are invited to participate in SSR conferences.

Despite these efforts, the proliferation of drug networks and organized crime groups remained a security threat to consolidating peace and security in the country. Thus, it was strategic to include the combat of drug trafficking and organized crimes in peacebuilding activities in Guinea-Bissau. Together with the UN Office of Rule of Law and Security Institutions (OROLSI) and the UN Office on Drugs and Crime (UNODC), national plans on the fight against organized crime and drug trafficking were implemented, and the SSR-mainstreamed West Africa Coast Initiative (WACI) Transnational Crime Unit was established (UNIOGBIS 2009d). In the previous year, two separate operations were undertaken around the country, resulting in the seizure of unlawful Bissau-Guineans and foreign passports as well as drug seizures and multiple detentions (UNIOGBIS 2009d).

Peacebuilding activities rounded up on 31 December 2020 with the closure of UNIOGBIS. Prior to this, there were engagements with CSOs, leading to a number of peace initiatives. In 2020, CSOs approved the Agenda for Sustainable Development. This agenda sought to promote discussions between political actors, the rule of law, justice, and the fight against impunity. To promote transparency and fight corruption and to improve CSO collaboration in the fight against COVID-19, prior pledges for stability should be promoted and monitored. What other peace stakeholders, especially in Africa, can take home from the context of Guinea-Bissau is the importance of working through civil society partners, when the government institutions are paralyzed and there is the need for shorter, more flexible projects in contexts of high political volatility and risk.

## The Role of International Actors/Partners

The peacebuilding process in Guinea-Bissau has been characterized by a variety of actors, international actors inclusive. Following the power friction between then President Vieira and the military chief of staff, Ansumane Mané, and the subsequent fallout from the Casamance conflict, ECOWAS brokered a peace agreement (the Abuja Accord) between the parties, specifying the discontinuation of Guinean and Senegalese forces (World Peace Foundation n.d.). Complementing this, the peacekeeping arm of ECOWAS and ECOMOG provided troops to monitor the agreement (Yabi 2010).

In 1999, the near deadlock of the Abuja Accord, due to the coup staged by Mané's military faction and the fallouts of the accord, had the UN intervene under UNSC Resolution 1233 (UN Security Council 1999). This led to the creation of the United Nations Peacebuilding Support Office in Guinea-Bissau (UNOGBIS, which in the secretary General's Report 2005 had the oversight responsibility to implement the Abuja Agreement using a modest $19 million annual budget (UN Security Council 1999). Likewise, these literatures accredited UNOGBIS for its successful supervision of Guinea-Bissau's subsequent parliamentary and presidential elections that brought President Yala into office when it assumed position after the withdrawal of ECOMOG. Before the 2005 election of President Vieira there was a military coup in 2003 amidst infractions within the military and later a military takeover (World Peace Foundation n.d.). This necessitated the joint body of ECOWAS-AU and the UN in attempts to stabilize and bring change to the country, following its numerous precarious coups, resorted to preventive diplomacy, sent delegations and used on-the-spot mediation to convince the candidates and other parties with keen interest to accept the electoral results (World Peace Foundation n.d.).

In early 2006, UK advisors formed an inter-ministerial committee on security sector reform observed by the UN and ECOWAS and the prime minister based on their assessment work (World Peace Foundation n.d.). Within the same era ECOWAS, with the intent to manage and streamline the multiplicity of proposed or foreseen international donors' interventions, also established an International Contact Group (ICG) on Guinea-Bissau, one that later earned Guinea-Bissau and its government millions of dollars to discharge its immediate responsibilities (Yabi 2010). The intent for interventions by the international donors was to suppress illicit drug trafficking caused by the state's weakness (Yabi 2010). The mandate of UNOGBIS in 2008 was extended to also include countering drug trafficking and organized crime owing to the increasingly international attention and the state's own interest to free the country of the ongoing drug traffic crisis (Vulliamy 2008). Ahead of the November 2008 parliamentary elections, which proved successful, ECOWAS had earlier been involved in the monitoring of the voter registration exercise and other electoral preparatory processes, held meetings with the ICG and deployed a mission of about 45 election observers to every part of the country.

Other complementary deployments came from the notable Guinea-Bissau P5, comprising the AU, EU, UEMOA, OIF and the CPSC (Fiott 2008). The group mobilized the international community to rally strongly and provide support towards Guinea-Bissau's political process and national reform agenda (Fiott 2008).

Until its withdrawal, the 2008 EU Advisory Mission for Security Sector Reform, under the auspices of the EU, provided instrumental support to the Technical Committee of the PBC and 15 military and civilian advisors (Fiott 2008). With their absence, Angola, the chair of the CPLP, assumed position while it bilaterally confronted SSR gaps and also undertook agreement under MISSANG to deploy about 200 technical Angolan military (World Peace Foundation n.d.). Again, MISSANG later assisted with SSR and the implementation of the SSR roadmap by ECOWAS-CPLP; World Peace Foundation n.d.). In March 2009, President Vieira and other prominent figures were assassinated, and the Minister for Defence was killed by security services when he allegedly resisted arrest for his alleged plotting of another coup (Helly 2009). Following that, UNOGBIS reasoned to shift its focus to intervene in issues of SSR, human rights, the rule of law and building a working partnership with Guinea-Bissau (Vulliamy 2008; Helly 2009). By

2010, UNOGBIS was replaced by UNIOGBIS under the UNSC Resolution 1987 mandate and was supported with about 18 international civilian personnel, a lone military expert and 13 local civilians (World Peace Foundation n.d.). The entity further attended to related issues on SSR, human rights, political affairs, public information and gender. By December 2011, MISSANG was widely acknowledged for its most significant achievement in the prevention of another plotted coup against President Malam Bacai Sanhá, which consequentially fuelled a rivalry between Angola and Guinea-Bissau's military (World Peace Foundation n.d.).

President Sanhá's natural death in 2012 called for another election, but with the rampant assassinations of important military and intelligent individuals, allegations of rigging and the near boycotting of the April 2012 elections, the AU, ECOWAS and UN quickly aided the country's rescue before the issues escalated to any further crises (UN Security Council 2012a). In the same period when the army orchestrated a coup, these bodies came together and responded by chartering a peace agenda with ECOWAS, deploying its standby force to Guinea-Bissau and leading mediation processes.

ECOWAS again significantly deployed about 683 troops, which was later renamed as the ECOMIB to replace the impromptu exit of MISSANG (UN Security Council 2012b). ECOMIB then superintended over the implementation of the SSR roadmap of ECOWAS-CPLP, the transition of the newly formed (coup-led) government, the preparation for joint patrols with the national troops of Guinea-Bissau, the establishment of the Guinea-Bissau Sanctions Committee and the imposition of sanctions on the five coup leaders under UNSC Resolution 2048. Later, ECOWAS sponsored a mediation process, and the coup leaders agreed to the Agreement on Stabilization and Maintenance of Constitutional and Democratic Order, which required them to surrender power to civilian administration for a period of 12 months until elections could be conducted (UN Security Council 2012b). However, due to a failed mediation and with an unstable interim government, the UN, EU, AU, ECOWAS and CPLP then consented to proceed on undertaking a joint assessment mission to Guinea-Bissau (UN Security Council 2012b).

Moving on, the recent elections in Guinea-Bissau can be argued to have been relatively peaceful owing to the fact that, if any, most recorded cases of violence during those periods were insignificant. For example, there were fears of a possible coup that was bound to happen during the 2014 presidential and parliamentary elections, yet evidence provided through election monitoring by the UN, EU, AU, ECOWAS and the CPLP showed the elections were relatively free and fair, with unprecedented records of high voter turnout in fact (Galamas 2014). These incidents arguably induced ECOWAS's move to fulfil its pledge through a readmission of Guinea-Bissau, especially as there were no records of strong military involvement in the country's elections, as was often suspected. In relation to ECOMIB, the mission was equally applauded for its efforts in the prevention of attacks on the government by the military and championing dialogues to support the financing of the country's numerous retired demobilized soldiers (World Peace Foundation n.d.). Moreover, in February 2015 a renewal and extension of UNIOGBIS's mandate under UNSC Resolution 2203 was made to 29 February 2016 (UN Security Council 2015). International actors for leading initiatives that led to the Conakry Agreement of 10 September 2016 and the six-point roadmap of October 2016 (World Peace Foundation n.d.; Albert and Eze 2017) have since applauded ECOWAS as the sole implementer of SSR in Guinea.

Until the withdrawal of ECOMIB, established by the heads of states and governments in the region on 7 September 2020, the body had assisted the country to secure election-related centres, infrastructures, and transportation of election kits, voters, ballots and other election materials during its 2019 legislative presidential elections. Through its contribution, the EU ensured that ECOMIB also discharged its responsibility to support Guinea-Bissau's government and its authority, assisted its security, provided humanitarian support wherever needed and safeguarded citizens and institutions. It is evident, although debatable, that these peacebuilding efforts by many of the cited international actors since the inception of violent conflicts in Guinea-Bissau have played tremendous roles towards helping the country to experience a modest peaceful growth. For instance, the country has been enjoying a medium state of peace and is amongst the countries with the greatest improvement on political terror according to the Global Peace Index (Institute for Economics and Peace 2019).

## Challenges to Peacebuilding in Guinea-Bissau

Since independence in 1973, Guinea-Bissau post-independence has been marred with a few strongmen oppressing multitudes of poor people in unconnected hinterlands, with military coups leading to civil wars and a series of incomplete presidential terms (World Peace Foundation n.d.). Arguably, prolonged political instability poses great threats to the political and socio-economic development of states. In Guinea-Bissau, however, peace seems almost impossible to achieve for a litany of reasons. At the inception of the peace process, the famous 1998 Abuja Accord between Vieira and Mané did not fully serve its purpose. The effort to broker peace was faced with financial and logistical impediments; the deployment of only 600 troops as in March 1999 and the later withdrawal of ECOMOG's forces. The early days of UNOGBIS also failed to make significant impact on profound issues, such as disarmament and SSR, particularly due to meagre budgetary allocations (World Peace Foundation n.d.; Fiott 2008). Another impediment to SSR was the unsuccessful implementation of the policies by the Security Sector Reform Committee led by UK advisors and its allies. This was due to domestic political deadlock, inaccurate data on its enlisted forms and the fact that up until 2008, a basic census of army personnel was not feasible. In addition, there were contrasting perspectives from the donor and recipient, together with the misunderstanding of local needs and interests. Kohl (2015) argued that SSR in its present form is flawed and is lacking in coordination, integration, flexibility and continuity among the various reform strategies. The implication of this is that SSR becomes rigid and short-term (Kohl 2015).

Peacebuilding in Guinea-Bissau has been hampered by sporadic conflicts between political elites and the military leaders. In April 2010, the kidnapping of Army Chief of Staff Zamora Induta and Prime Minister Carlos Gomes Jr by soldiers crippled political stability. This was followed by the appointment of the mastermind behind the kidnappings, Antonio Indjai, as army chief of staff (Yabi 2010). Due to this, the EU abrogated its 2008 inaugural EU Advisory Mission for Security Sector Reform in the Republic of Guinea-Bissau, specifically over dissatisfaction with the absence of relevant national commitment (Fiott 2008). Tensions further mounted from the imprisonment of the former prime minister (the highly tipped winner of the elections of the 2012 elections) and the interim president and proceeded with its orchestrated coup despite the appointment of President Alpha Condé of Guinea as a mediator over the country's electoral concerns. Subsequently in 2014, the peacebuilding efforts for implementation under the government's Terra Ranka program was also forestalled by disputes between critical political actors (seven prime ministers) during the legislative period in the country (UN n.d.). These disputes not only stifled the country's peaceful progress but also affected the cooperation between international actors and the government, and further made the work of the Peacebuilding Fund Committee tedious (UN no date.). Also notable are the unresolved issues related to the 2015 political tensions between the civilian and military leadership, mingled with a vicious cycle of institutional crises that equally served as barriers to Guinea-Bissau's quest for peacebuilding.

Local ownership, commitment and strong political will in the peace process of any country are important in achieving durable peace. In the situation of Guinea-Bissau, the lack of commitment and national ownership stalled the implementation of the best alternative to broker peace for the political impasses between political actors, the mediation process of the Conakry Agreement of 10 September 2016 and the six-point roadmap of October 2016 (Albert and Eze 2017). Havik (2015, para. 11) proposes that local ownership of the peace process will only be effective if the top-down model of peacebuilding and peacekeeping is replaced by a 'grassroots approach based, upon existing social and cultural institutions that could provide a broad framework for dialogue and conflict resolution'. Following on from this, political leaders who must hit the ground running with the reconstruction of the peace infrastructure and state institutions portray weak political will. A report by the UN Secretary-General's Special Rapporteur on the independence of judges and lawyers on Guinea-Bissau stated that state structures were absent at the local level. It highlighted that the political elites and military had misdirected their political will in consolidating their power base in a bid to accumulate political advantage (Institute for Peace and Security Studies 2019) at the expense of building strong state institutions and infrastructure for peace. Advancing this further, scholars have warned that the continuous absence of social and political platforms to give people a sense of participation and space to express their frustrations for redress, limited support for local peacebuilding mechanisms as huge blockages to reducing civil unrest, and persistent youth demonstrations, among others, make Guinea-Bissau more vulnerable to protracted violence (Albert and Eze 2017).

Socio-economic recovery forms a pivotal part of the peacebuilding processes. This is because social and economic factors form structural causes of conflict, and in the case of Guinea-Bissau, its socio-economic development has been derailed due to prolonged political crisis. The emergence of the COVID-19 pandemic stifled the ongoing peacebuilding process in Guinea-Bissau. Like the rest of the world, the socio-economic development of the country has not been spared by the global health pandemic. A UN Development Programme (UNDP) report in 2020 stated that Guinea-Bissau is ill-prepared to absorb the shocks of the pandemic on some of the development gains obtained during the past decades. The pandemic has taken a toll on the sustenance and livelihood of Bissau-Guinean citizens, thereby causing a level of economic vulnerability and high dependency on coping mechanisms. For example, the closure of two main export markets for cashews in the country stifled the 2020 cashew campaign and poses risks for 2021, as demand for the nuts decreased significantly (UN Development Programme 2020). Another challenge the pandemic poses to socio-economic recovery is its impact on education and employment in Guinea-Bissau. The closure of schools and folding of companies have the potential to increase the level of unemployment in the country. Relatedly, the relative deprivation theory of conflict posits that the more people are deprived of basic needs and opportunities, the higher the tendency for them to damage the source of the barrier. This results in incidences of frustration, which metamorphose into aggression. This may be potentially dangerous for Guinea-Bissau given the existing political instability in the country. According to the executive director of the UNODC, Ghada Fathi Waly, COVID-19 is a wake-up call to international, national and local actors involved in peacebuilding to unite behind crucial socio-economic reforms (UN 2020).

The fight against drug trafficking in Guinea-Bissau was one of the priorities and mandates of UNIOGBIS. The factors that necessitated the flourishing of the drug trade are the geographical position of the country, poverty, lack of social opportunities, unemployment and the administrative collapse of state institutions (Madeira, Laurent and Roque 2011). UNIOGBIS, together with UNODC, formulated policies, mechanisms and national plans to address the bane of drug trafficking. The growth of drug cartels and its resultant effect on crime rates and proliferation of violent groups threatened both international and sub-regional efforts to stabilize and develop political and social institutions in Guinea-Bissau. The involvement of the political and military elite, such as Vieira and Indjai, in drug operations undermined the collective efforts aimed at combatting drug trade. Money from the drug trade has been used to fuel illicit activities, which had the ability to interfere with ongoing peacebuilding activities. For example, the aftermath of the 2012 coup revealed that the protection network at the heart of the military had diversified into a range of other illicit activities such as smuggling of people and the illegal exploitation of the country's timber resources (Shaw 2015). With the closure of the UN mission, it is with great expectation that coordinated national and sub-regional efforts would tackle the menace of drug trade.

## The Way Forward

Peacebuilding is a multifaceted and long-term process. The coordinated efforts of state and non-state actors are vital in achieving the overall goals of durable peace, justice, reconciliation and socio-economic development. The inception and closure of the UN mission in Guinea-Bissau may have watered down the heated sparks that existed prior to the international intervention. The drawdown of UNIOGBIS gives the green light to national and local actors to establish home-grown mechanisms for sustaining peace and stability in Guinea-Bissau. To consolidate the fragile peace situation, there needs to be a rebuilding of state institutions with strong political will. This is necessary for restoring citizens' trust and confidence in state institutions and government leaders. Connected and committed national action as well as continuous international community support are required to resolve structural factors contributing to violence. The purging must begin from home. Drug trafficking, a main catalyst in the political discord in Guinea-Bissau, must be addressed at the political level. Finally, investment in civil society and non-governmental organizations as well as the building blocks for political resilience are critical in creating a bulwark against autocracy. It is hoped that national and local actors in Guinea-Bissau will capitalize on the international efforts that have been made in its peace process over the years in dealing with the root causes of the country's political instability and will work for the peace of the country.

## References

African Union, (2014) *Report of the Chairperson of the Commission on the Situation in the Central African Republic and the Activities of the African-Led International Support Mission in the Central African Republic*. [online]. Available at: https://archive.au.int/handle/123456789/8652 (Accessed: 8 April 2021).

Albert, I.O., Eze, C.B., (2017) 'Resolving the Protracted Political Crises in Guinea-Bissau. The need for a peace infrastructure', *Conflict Trends*, 2, ACCORD.

Bappah, Y.H., (2017) 'Why Peace Fails in Guinea-Bissau. A Political Economy Analysis of the ECOWAS-brokered Conakry Accord', *Friedrich-Ebert-Stiftung Peace and Security*. [online]. Available at: https://library.fes.de/pdf-files/bueros/fes-pscc/14166.pdf (Accessed: 9 April 2021).

Bodea, C., (2012) Natural Resources, Weak States and Civil War Can Rents Stabilize Coup Prone Regimes? *Policy Research Working Paper 6071*. The World Bank. Available at: https://documents1.worldbank.org/curated/en/992791468156573552/pdf/WPS6071.pdf.

Campbell, S., Chandler, D. and Sabaratnam, M., (eds.) (2011) *A Liberal Peace?* London and New York, NY: Zed Books.

Cavalcante, F., (2014) 'The Influence of the Liberal Peace Framework on the United Nations Approach to Peacebuilding in Guinea-Bissau', *RCCS Annual Review*, 6, pp. 141–161, [online]. Available at: https://doi.org/10.4000/rccsar.564 (Accessed: 8 April 2021).

ECOWAS (2004) *Is There a Risk of a New Coup in Guinea-Bissau?* The ECOWAS Peace and Security Report, 8, Institute for Security Studies. [online]. Available at: Is There a Risk of a New Coup in Guinea-Bissau? (ethz.ch) (Accessed: 22 April 2021).

Fiott, D., (2008) 'European Union Security Sector Reform Missions: The Case of Guinea-Bissau', *European Security Review*, 38. [online]. Available at: www.ies.be/files/Fiott%20%282008%29%20EU%20SSR%20and%20Guinea%20Bissau.pdf (Accessed: 22 April 2021).

Galamas, F., (2014) 'Elections Give Guinea-Bissau a Chance to Emerge from Turmoil', *World Politics Review*. Available at: www.worldpoliticsreview.com.ezproxy.library.tufts.edu/articles/13763/elections-give-guinea-bissau-a-chance-to-emerge-from-turmoil (Accessed: 25 April 2021).

Havik, P., (2015) *A Short History of Peacebuilding in Guinea-Bissau*. Peace Direct. [online]. Available at: www.peaceinsight.org/en/articles/a-short-history-of-peacebuilding-in-guinea-bissau/ (Accessed: 17 April 2021).

Havoc, P., (2015) 'A Short History of Peacebuilding in Guinea-Bissau', *Peace Insight*. [online]. Available at: www.peaceinsight.org/en/articles/a-short-history-of-peacebuilding-in-guinea-bissau/?location=guinea-bissau&theme (Accessed: 7 April 2021).

Helly, D., (2009) *EU SSR Guinea-Bissau the EU Mission in Support of Security Sector Reform in Guinea-Bissau (EU SSR Guinea-Bissau)*. Brussels: European Security and Defence Policy.

Institute for Economics and Peace, (2019) *Global Peace Index 2019: Measuring Peace in a Complex World*. Sydney.

Institute for Peace and Security Studies, (2019) 'Guinea Bissau Conflict Insight', *Peace and Security Report*, 1 July. Addis Ababa University. [online]. Available at: https://media.africaportal.org/documents/guinea_bissau_conflict_insights_vol_1-_conflict_insight.pdf (Accessed: 17 April 2021).

Karbo, T. and Virk, K., (eds.) (2018) *The Palgrave Handbook of Peacebuilding in Africa*. Cham: Palgrave Macmillan.

Kohl, C., (2015) 'Guinea-Bissau's Security Sector: Challenges and Lessons', [Blog] *Peace Direct*, 2 July. [online]. Available at: www.peaceinsight.org/en/articles/guinea-bissaus-security-sector-challenges-lessons/ (Accessed: 17 June 2021).

Madeira, F.L., Laurent, S. and Roque, S., (2011) 'The International Cocaine Trade in Guinea-Bissau: Current Trends and Risks', *Norwegian Peacebuilding Centre*. [online]. Available at: www.files.ethz.ch/isn/137866/international%20cocaine%20trade.pdf (Accessed: 17 April 2021).

Mazrui, A., (1967) *Towards a Pax Africana: A Study of Ideology and Ambition*. Chicago: University of Chicago.

McNamee, T. and Muyangwa, M., (eds.) (2021) *The State of Peacebuilding in Africa. Lessons Learned for Policymakers and Practitioners*. Cham: Palgrave Macmillan. [online]. Available at: https://doi.org/10.1007/978-3-030-46636-7 (Accessed: 19 April 2021).

NEPAD, (2005) *African Post-Conflict Reconstruction Policy Framework*. NEPAD, African Post-Conflict. Midrand: NEPAD Secretariat.

Shaw, M., (2015) 'Drug Trafficking in Guinea-Bissau, 1998–2014: The Evolution of an Elite Protection Network', *The Journal of Modern African Studies*, 53(3), pp. 339–364, [online]. Available at: www.jstor.org/stable/pdf/26309823.pdf?refreqid=excelsior%3A61b4b8df97d1fe9de073c8c84ce49d80 (Accessed: 18 April 2021).

Shryock, R., (2020) 'Guinea Bissau: Political Chaos Could Boost Cocaine Trade', *BBC News*, March 12. [online]. Available at: www.bbc.com/news/world-africa-51833073 (Accessed: 8 April 2021).

UNIOGBIS, (2009a) *Fund to Spend $6 Million on Peacebuilding Efforts*. [online]. Available at: https://uniogbis.unmissions.org/en/april-28-2008-un-fund-spend-6-million-peacebuilding-efforts (Accessed: 21 April 2021).

UNIOGBIS, (2009b) *Governance and Political Process*. [online]. Available at: https://uniogbis.unmissions.org/en/governance-and-political-process (Accessed: 21 April 2021).

UNIOGBIS, (2009c) *Human Rights and Gender Mainstreaming*. [online]. Available at: https://uniogbis.unmissions.org/en/human-rights-and-gender-mainstreaming (Accessed: 21 April 2021).

UNIOGBIS, (2009d) *Drug Trafficking and Organized Crime Combat*. [online]. Available at: https://uniogbis.unmissions.org/en/drug-trafficking-and-organized-crime-combat (Accessed: 21 April 2021).

United Nations, (2020) *Amid Rising Political Tensions, Economic Woes, Ongoing International Support Key for Maintaining Stability in Guinea-Bissau, Top Officials Warns Security Council*. [online]. Available at: www.un.org/press/en/2020/sc14274.doc.htm (Accessed: 17 April 2021).

United Nations Development Programme, (2020) *Building Back Better Starts Now. Covid-19 Socio Economic Impact Analysis for Guinea-Bissau*. [online]. Available at: www.greengrowthknowledge.org/sites/default/files/downloads/resource/Guinea_Bissau_SocioEconomicImpact_UN.pdf (Accessed: 17 June 2021).

United Nations Peacebuilding, (n.d.a) *The PBF in Guinea Bissau*. [online]. Available at: www.un.org/peacebuilding/sites/www.un.org.peacebuilding/files/documents/guinea-bissau_two-pager.pdf (Accessed: 26 April 2021).

United Nations Peacebuilding, (n.d.b) *The PBF in Guinea Bissau*. [online]. Available at: https://un-peace building.tumblr.com/post/173266231395/the-pbf-in-guinea-bissau (Accessed: 21 April 2021).

United Nations Security Council, (1999) *Security Council Resolution 1233 on Implementation of the Abuja Agreement and on Establishment of a Post-Conflict Peace Building Support Office in Guinea-Bissau (UNOGBIS), S/RES/1233*, 6 April. [online]. Available at: https://digitallibrary.un.org/record/1491738?ln=ar (Accessed: 22 April 2021).

United Nations Security Council, (2012a) *Report of the Secretary-General on the restoration of constitutional order in Guinea-Bissau Report of the Secretary-General on the restoration of constitutional order in Guinea-Bissau. S/2012/704*. New York, NY: United Nations.

United Nations Security Council, (2012b) *Resolution 2048*. S/RES/2048. New York, NY: United Nations.

United Nations Security Council, (2015) *Resolution 2203*. S/RES/2203. New York, NY: United Nations.

Vulliamy, E., (2008) 'How a Tiny West African Country Became the world's First Narco State', *The Guardian*. March 9. [online]. Available at: www.theguardian.com/world/2008/mar/09/drugstrade (Accessed: 22 April 2021).

Wanis St-John, A., (2013) 'Indigenous Peacebuilding', in Mac Ginty, R., (ed.) *Routledge Handbook on Peacebuilding*. New York, NY: Routledge, pp. 360–374. [online]. Available at: www.researchgate.net/publication/262179622_Indigenous_Peacebuilding (Accessed: 17 April 2021).

World Peace Foundation, (n.d.) *African, Peace and Politics. Guinea-Bissau Short Brief*. [online]. Available at: https://sites.tufts.edu/wpf/files/2017/07/Guinea-Bassau-brief.pdf (Accessed: 20 April 2021).

Yabi, G.O., (2010) 'The Role of ECOWAS in Managing Political Crisis and Conflict', *FES Peace and Security Series*. [online]. Available at: https://library.fes.de/pdf-files/bueros/nigeria/07448.pdf (Accessed: 19 April 2021).

Zondi, S., (2017) 'African Union Approaches to Peacebuilding: Efforts at Shifting the Continent towards Decolonial peace', *African Journal on Conflict Resolution*, 17(1), pp. 105–131. [online]. Available at: www.ajol.info/index.php/ajcr/article/view/160586(Accessed: 17 April 2021).

# 18
# STABILITY FOR WHOM AND FOR WHAT?

## The Ivorian peacebuilding experience under Alassane Ouattara

*Maxime Ricard*

Most of the literature on international peacebuilding focuses on the failure of interventions to build peace, but the case of Côte d'Ivoire appears to represent a counterexample. At the end of the United Nations Operation in Côte d'Ivoire (UNOCI), the members of the UN security council claimed that the UN mission was a "success story" (UNSC 2017), and others said that the country's economy might be "at the gates of paradise" (World Bank 2018a). Following the violent resolution of the conflict through the removal of Laurent Gbagbo in 2011, Alassane Ouattara had apparently succeeded in building a form of political "stability." The gross domestic product was growing 8% per annum on average. Governing elites and international actors celebrated the 2015 re-election of Ouattara as proof that the country was on the long-term path to sustainable peace.

But as the end of Ouattara's second term approached, it was clear that something was not quite right. The situation with respect to democratic and human rights, although relatively better than during the previous decade of conflicts, appeared precarious and even to be regressing in some respects as the 2020 presidential election got closer (Amnesty International 2018, 2019). The benefits of the reconciliation process were close to non-existent (Akindès 2017), and the political scene was tense and volatile (Bensimon 2019). Moreover, there was an important disconnect between macroeconomic results and socio-economic progress for Ivorian citizens (Berrou et al. 2017, 10), the life expectancy of Ivorians remaining similar to that of Somalians and South Sudanese (World Bank 2018b). Coupled with a tightening of authoritarian measures (Ricard 2020), the president's decision to run for a third term in August 2020 set the country on fire, with electoral violence causing nearly 100 deaths before and after a "non-inclusive" presidential election (Carter Center 2020). The goal of international actors was to restore the authority of the post-conflict state (Chandler and Sisk 2013). But there was a failure to ask for whom – and for what. Indeed, the important questions were never seriously raised. How does international peacebuilding in post-conflict Côte d'Ivoire contribute to a particular vision of peace and socio-political order? And to reflect more broadly, what does this "Ivorian experience" tell us about the nature of contemporary international peacebuilding?

Arising out of a political rupture after the fall of Laurent Gbagbo, international peacebuilding under Alassane Ouattara amounted to supporting a cosmetic process of reconciliation through forgetting and a fixation on economic growth. Under the watch of international actors with little room for manoeuvre, Côte d'Ivoire, which was neither a miracle nor a mirage, highlighted instead "contrasting and complex chiaroscuro realities" (Miran-Guyon 2017, 13). It demonstrated the limits of a clear dichotomy between war and peace (Richards 2005; Debos 2016), with the enduring presence of past governing practices and various forms of violence, which did not disappear simply because the guns had been silenced. Supposedly "weak" or "failing" after a decade of socio-political conflict (Bilgin and Morton 2002), national elites proved to the contrary that they had the ability to move rapidly to seize the opportunities provided by the violent resolution of the conflict and by unwavering international support. A partly Franco-African nexus of national elites and international actors built a common project, which was not, as declared, a positive peace or reconciliation process but a form of "stability" whose sustainability was, to say the least, questionable.

The "post-conflict" Ivorian experience has demonstrated what is at stake in contemporary peacebuilding: "status quo aspirations, concerned with regulatory stability and regional and domestic security, rather than transformation" (Chandler 2017, 34). Peacebuilding becomes the pragmatic management of effects, "enabling organic systems and existing knowledges, practices and capacities" (Chandler 2017, 201) that are in line with the contemporary governance strategies of international financial institutions (Best 2013, 38). The qualitative enquiry presented here was undertaken with Professor Hyacinthe Digbeugby Bley[1] in November and December 2017 in the cities of Abidjan and Bouaké. We interviewed 57 individuals, some in the context of a focus group. These individuals were from UN agencies and major embassies, the international development and finance sector, local human rights groups, transparency and civil society non-governmental organizations (NGOs), ex-combatants' associations, the public service in Côte d'Ivoire, political parties and the offices of elected officials, and research centres in the social sciences.

## Imposed peace, illusions of reconciliation and justice

The fall of Laurent Gbagbo was a turning point that provided the shifting ground on which post-conflict international peacebuilding was initiated. Alassane Ouattara promoted a biased, cosmetic vision of political reconciliation and transitional justice in Côte d'Ivoire without encountering any real opposition from international actors. The results were meagre and not counterbalanced by any of the limited, last-minute gestures toward the opposition during his second term, with the situation worsening closer to, during, and after the presidential election of 31 October 2020, which gave him a controversial third term. Forgetting (Akindès 2017, 15) was therefore the main strategy of national elites, an approach that was not without risks for Ivorian society.

### *No going back: the rupture of the post-electoral crisis*

The Ivorian post-electoral crisis of 2010–2011 was the endgame after a decade characterized by neither war nor peace (McGovern 2011). After an attempted coup d'état in 2002, the country was de facto divided until 2011, with the Forces Nouvelles rebel coalition controlling the northern part of the country. The Ouagadougou Political Accords (OPA) in 2007 were perceived as a decisive step toward the election process, which had been delayed multiple times. President Gbagbo perceived that the time was ripe for him to win re-election. During the years of the de facto partition of the country, Gbagbo's main tactics revolved around manipulating the local/international line of alliances and interests using political nationalism and divisions between international actors (Charbonneau 2012). After the crisis of November 2004, France discharged most of its peacemaking, peacekeeping, and peacebuilding efforts to the UNOCI, but the former colonial power kept active its military base and its Security Council sanctioned Operation Licorne in Côte d'Ivoire.

After years of using delaying tactics to postpone the presidential election, Laurent Gbagbo gave no clear indication that he would be willing to accept defeat. In a runoff, the disputed election of 2010 opposed the incumbent to former Prime Minister Ouattara, who Gbagbo had always perceived as one of the co-conspirators of the failed 2002 coup attempt. Under diplomatic pressure, particularly from France, the US, and the UK, Special Representative to the Secretary-General (SRSG) Choi Young-jin certified the election results of the Independent Electoral Commission, which had declared Ouattara the winner on 2 December 2010, in line with the view of numerous international electoral observers. The following day, the highest court in the land, the Constitutional Council, headed by a Gbagbo ally, invalidated the results in the northern regions, where Ouattara was popular, and declared Gbagbo the winner. This time, with the certification of the victory of Alassane Ouattara by the UN (Charbonneau 2014), Laurent Gbagbo's astute political tactics and his populist mobilization skills failed to achieve the result he desired. Under the same diplomatic pressures, especially from France, the UNOCI fully backed Ouattara in the post-electoral conflict, raising questions with regard to one of the pillars of UN peacekeeping policy, the norm of impartiality (Paddon Rhoads 2016; Novosseloff 2018, 30).

This decision was a major turning point in the Ivorian conflict, as was the decision of the leader of the former rebel coalition Forces Nouvelles, Guillaume Soro, who was appointed prime minister after the OPA in 2007, to back Alassane Ouattara both politically and militarily. In the face of a stalled process and increasing violence, UN Security Council Resolution 1975 invoked the controversial Responsibility to Protect, authorizing France and the UNOCI to "violently resolve" the post-electoral standoff in Abidjan (Bellamy and Williams 2011). Laurent Gbagbo was arrested at his presidential palace on 11 April 2011. The post-electoral crisis resulted in at least 3,000 deaths, thereby transforming the meaning of peacebuilding in Côte d'Ivoire.

### *Transitional justice: cosmetic forgiveness and truth, victor's justice*

Transitional justice is presented as a central element of international peacebuilding policies (see Murithi, this volume). Since 2011, Alassane Ouattara has theoretically supported two of its key components (Hazan 2017): the policy of truth and forgiveness and the policy of punishment (international and national criminal justice). This vision for peacebuilding has been described as reconciliation constructed through a new "hegemonic articulation" (Renner 2014). The Dialogue, Truth, and Reconciliation Commission (CDVR) was central to this ambition. From the beginning, the nomination of a politician to head the institution, former Prime Minister Charles Konan Banny, was perceived as a mistake. The CDVR eventually turned into "unfinished business" in a context where it had come to "reflect a post-crisis image"[2] after undertaking some serious but underutilized investigations.[3] Moreover, contrary to the South African experience, the government never allowed the commission's hearings to be televised.

Faced with an avalanche of criticism regarding its policy of truth and forgiveness, the Ivorian government created the National Program of Social Cohesion (PNCS) in 2012, an institution in de facto competition with the CDVR. The strategy, quickly adopted by the government, was to face down the criticism by promoting "social cohesion." This strategy was also promoted by international actors through numerous international peacebuilding projects, so that it became a depoliticizing tool at the service of the government (Piccolino 2018). In 2015, a few months before the presidential election, the president set up the National Commission for Reconciliation and Compensation of Victims (CONARIV). Among local actors in Bouaké and international or national actors in Abidjan, disillusionment with these initiatives was widespread. A process that sacrificed care for victims to clientelist politics and reduced reconciliation to the selective distribution of money was denounced.[4] This lack of confidence in the national policy of truth and forgiveness led major donors such as the EU to refuse the government's request to participate in the financing of reparations,[5] which was seen as a blatant attempt to buy votes before the 2015 presidential election. According to a high-level official who participated in the CDVR and the CONARIV, there was a clear lack of political will when it came to making genuine gestures of reconciliation toward the Gbagbo camp.[6] It was a cosmetic approach from a domestic perspective, and also a form of extraversion (Ricard 2017b) to convince outsiders that the "checklist"[7] of international peacebuilding policies was being respected.

The punitive dimension of transitional justice entrenched political inequalities. One hundred and twenty-eight pro-Gbagbo military and civilian personnel were charged with 22 criminal offences, and 10 international arrest warrants were issued (Akindès 2017, 12). Only two dozen soldiers from the Ouattara camp were arraigned on preliminary charges, and rather conveniently, this occurred a couple of months before the 2015 presidential election (RFI 2015). These later indictments were never followed up. Indeed, some of the high-profile former commanders of the rebellion who were charged are still in the upper echelons of the Ivorian state. In short, it was a form of two-tier justice involving biased and politicized trials of former officials from the Gbagbo regime (HRW 2016). As the Ivorian regime started to become more confident and less reliant on international support, mentioning impartial justice even became a "taboo"[8] in discussions with international actors, who were nevertheless lobbying for credible accountability.

Contrary to political leaders in other countries such as Angola, Sudan, and Rwanda, where the regime came out the winner after a socio-political conflict, Alassane Ouattara owed a great deal to a former rebel movement, Forces Nouvelles (Akindès 2017, 16). As a result, he had little room to manoeuvre and was politically fragile, a situation that was clearly revealed by the 2017 mutinies (Martin 2018). Moreover, the two-tier approach to punitive justice was reinforced by the choice of the International Criminal Court (ICC) to indict only Laurent Gbagbo and his camp. The extradition of Laurent Gbagbo to The Hague was also a form of extraversion payment for the government, which could use the legitimacy of an international justice process to get rid of a very complicated opponent by collaborating in the extradition. After several limited initiatives to liberate prisoners from the opposing camp, a turning point occurred in August 2018: the release and amnesty of 800 pro-Gbagbo prisoners (including Simone Gbagbo, whom Alassane Ouattara maintained would not be sent to the ICC despite an arrest warrant from the court). According to opposition members who were interviewed, including one of the opposition leaders, reconciliation initiatives and transitional justice "did nothing to ease the bruises."[9] This was echoed by international actors who spoke of "an operation of charm without substance [and] no real will"[10] in "a society that is in total denial about its history."[11] In a word, this victor's peace (Piccolino 2018) was discursively justified as "national reconciliation," but in reality it was an empty universal (Renner 2014).

## A reaffirmation of the state, but to what end?

The goal of international actors in post-conflict Côte d'Ivoire was to "restore the state's authority," the principal leitmotif of contemporary state-building, but they had little room to manoeuvre when it came to influencing a state that was not as weak as might appear at first sight.

During this nine-year process, no substantial progress was made on fundamental problems such as the authoritarian exercise of power, widespread poverty, and vast social inequalities.

## *Supporting the Ivorian state*

The post-conflict disarmament, demobilization, and reintegration (DDR) process was clearly directed and managed by the Ivorian state, which funded 75% of the program Autorité pour le Désarmement, Demobilisation et Réintégration (ADDR). Officially completed in 2015, with its representatives claiming to have reintegrated nearly 60,000 ex-combatants, the ADDR became a central issue with important debates on its effectiveness. Although the UNOCI had a DDR section, it did little to monitor its activities, which was "a strategic mistake,"[12] according to several of our interviewees. International actors (the UNOCI as well as major international donors such as the EU) participated in selling these results with "laudatory and sheltered acclaims."[13] Other actors stressed positive points, in particular the rapid achievements of the program during its brief three-year existence. According to international and national actors we interviewed and to ex-combatants we met in Bouaké, the main problem was the dynamics of co-optation in the profiling process. The nine ex-combatants we met in Bouaké stressed their bitterness about the program, which they considered insufficient for proper reintegration. When ex-combatants began to organize for what they saw as their rights, state forces started to arrest the leaders of ex-combatant associations. Some were abducted in the middle of the night with no legal proceedings.[14] We met one who said that he had spent a year in prison "because [he] talked too much."[15] Our field work at the end of 2017 in Bouaké highlighted a climate of fear, one interviewee stating poignantly that "we're afraid of our own brothers in power."[16] Following the army mutinies in January and May 2017, which mainly involved soldiers based in Bouaké, there were ex-combatants who demanded the same bonuses granted to the mutineers, since many of them had fought in the same units as these soldiers during the rebellion. The response was brutally clear: four ex-combatants were shot dead (Jeune Afrique 2017).

Although a thorough review of the UNOCI is not possible here,[17] there is no question that the impact of the UNOCI on DDR and on security sector reform (SSR) was very limited. The UN wished to stand back and support the elected government, but this may have limited its ability to assert itself and caused it to lose its political voice.[18] After 2011, the UNOCI was in a peculiar situation in several ways. Staff turnover was low, national elites and UN officials were too close to one another, a form of opacity was required in published reports critical of the government, and press communications were subject to very strict controls:

> We always remained superficial, we always touched on the problems [knowing] we shouldn't say things that could be upsetting. Even when a report was going to be published, we were always betting on what the government's response would be.[19]

The government even successfully fought the establishment of a bureau of the Office of the High Commissioner for Human Rights (OHCHR) that would have monitored these issues and allowed for a period of transition after the UNOCI.[20] However, the work of the UNOCI during the post-conflict era was helpful from the perspective of human rights and civil society organizations in Bouaké. Most of the persons interviewed stated that the departure of the UNOCI was rushed. The UN military presence and human rights monitoring allowed for some form of check on the government: "I regret the departure of the UNOCI. . . . [It] was a way of redressing the balance of power."[21]

## *Reaffirmation of the state and Houphouëtist practices*

In both rhetoric and practice, the Ivorian post-conflict period has been characterized by a reaffirmation of state authority. The goal has been to treat the post-conflict reconstruction as an assertion of a position of strength vis-à-vis international actors so as to erase the image of a state under the control of international intervention (Akindès and Toit 2017, 21).

The average annual economic growth of 8% between 2012 and 2019 was overseen by two consecutive National Development Plans (NDPs). This major articulation of the logic of state reaffirmation aimed to show that the government was no longer managing an emergency but instead investing in the economy. This economic investment was based on a "bureaucratization of the economy"[22] that operated through calls for tenders, often a source of corruption, particularly in the case of direct contracting (World Bank 2015): "Procurement is a real issue [because] the level of corruption is very high."[23] Nevertheless, many actors in the field of international development finance have highlighted the clarity and predictability that the NDPs have brought. Besides the return of the African Development Bank during the first term of Ouattara, another symbol of the economic recovery and reaffirmation of Côte d'Ivoire was the establishment of the headquarters of the International Cocoa Organization in Abidjan. Moreover, partnering with Ghana, Côte d'Ivoire achieved some success in the struggle against the world markets. Lobbying together as a form of cartel (WSJ 2020), the two African nations succeeded in increasing producers' prices for cocoa, a rare victory for agricultural producing countries.

Just as during the Houphouët-Boigny era (1960–1993), a carrot-and-stick approach was used with the political opposition, a strategy of wavering back and forth between negotiation and coercion (Ricard 2020). However, after the disintegration of the political alliance that had allowed for the easy re-election of Ouattara in 2015 and with the 2020 presidential election approaching, the regime gradually increased its use of the coercive resources of the state to ensure that it remained in control. Alassane Ouattara is known for having a technocratic style of governing, but he is also someone who learned politics under Félix Houphouët-Boigny (Ricard 2017a). Thus, through the alliance that became the political party Rassemblement des Houphouëtistes pour la Démocratie et la Paix (RHDP), the president partially resumed the policy of the reciprocal assimilation of elites (Bayart 2009). The party regularly co-opted "independents" before or after elections (Konan 2018). After the break-up of the Parti démocratique de Côte d'Ivoire (PDCI) and the end of Guillaume Soro's alliance with the RHDP (2018–2019), elites in power began suppressing or harassing those in the senior public service or in local governments who did not pledge allegiance to the RHDP. Similarly, Ouattara's main reform of a political institution, the adoption of the new constitution through the 2016 referendum, demonstrated that he was more interested in finding ways to make his party hegemonic than in opening up Ivorian society to democratic mechanisms.

Since Alassane Ouattara came to power in 2011, "illiberal" tools, including arbitrary detentions, temporary suspensions of opposition newspapers, and strategic bans on demonstrations, have been used by national elites to assert their power. Therefore, the balance sheet for democratic and human rights is disappointing (HRW 2016). The degradation of civic space was evident during the years before the presidential election of 2020 (CIVICUS 2020), with coercion increasingly used against civil society activists and journalists. However, when Ouattara declared in March 2020 that he would not seek a third term and that he had chosen then Prime Minister Amadou Gon Coulibaly to run as his successor, there was hope that 30 years after the introduction of a multiparty system, the first peaceful transfer of power in Côte d'Ivoire was in sight. But everything fell apart when Gon Coulibaly died unexpectedly just before the start of the presidential campaign in July 2020. Afraid that his party would lose without him, Ouattara decided to run for a third term, contradicting his previous declaration. While the constitution clearly states that the president is re-eligible only once, Ouattara used the controversial argument that the vote for the adoption of a new constitution acted as a "reset button" and therefore allowed him to run a third time.

## Social inequalities and tensions

Ivorian citizens overcame the situation of the early 2000s when there was "neither war nor peace." But the symbolic and material violence of poverty continued during Ouattara's two terms (2011–2020), which brought more despair and death to the country than any armed groups did. This enduring violence indicates that in stark opposition to "exceptionalist" visions of the transition from war to peace (Grajales and Jouhanneau 2019), the case of post-conflict Côte d'Ivoire highlights complex realities.

The post-conflict economic growth of Côte d'Ivoire is impressive, but the completely inadequate social redistribution of this wealth may be the most important impediment to the country's stability. On the human development index, the country is ranked 34th out of 54 African countries, and 165th out of 189 countries in the world, despite being the first economy of the West African Economic and Monetary Union (UEMOA). By 2020 the GDP of Côte d'Ivoire had doubled under Alassane Ouattara, but there was only a very slight decrease in the poverty rate compared to 2008, with half the population living with daily consumption expenditures of less than $1.20. Under pressure from international actors, the government seemed to be receptive to these arguments and increased the education and health budgets in Outtara's second term. Abidjan, the economic capital, epitomizes these contrasts and disparities in a society of high income inequality (Cogneau, Czajka and Houngbedji 2017, 224). This situation constitutes a social risk that an Ivorian intellectual has described as the construction of an "economic apartheid" (Niakaté 2018).

Thus it is no surprise that profound tensions exist in contemporary Côte d'Ivoire. In rural areas, where land conflicts have continued, in part as a historical feature of the Ivorian socio-political economy, tensions erupted many times during the second mandate of Alassane Ouattara. For example, in the western part of Côte d'Ivoire, multiple persons were killed or displaced in 2017 (Indigo and Interpeace 2018, 38–39), and in the central part of the country, there were also tensions between social groups (Konan 2019). In the end, using economic growth as the main criterion for evaluating post-conflict Côte d'Ivoire conceals profound tensions related to what economists used to call "growth without development" (Amin 1967), a phenomenon linked to the continued primary focus on the country's performance on world markets. This is a clear indication that the discourse of emergence is merely performative (Nubukpo 2019).

## Peacebuilding or building stability?

Official Development Assistance (ODA)[24] flows and relations "are influenced both by donor interests and priorities, and by recipients' agency and autonomy" (Hagmann and Reyntjens 2016, 13). What we saw in Côte d'Ivoire is an embedded national and international strategy, a nexus constructed by Alassane Ouattara, with his ability to attract international support, and by donors seduced by a technocratic approach. Moreover, the entire nexus is reinforced by the specific context of Franco-African relations. However, over time, international actors have become more and more aware of the limitations of the discourse of stability.

## Betting on Ouattara: a nexus of national and international actors

Côte d'Ivoire has sold the country well, but behind the mirror it's something else.[25] Alassane Ouattara developed various strategies of extraversion (Bayart 2000). These strategies involved discursive and symbolic performances (Jourde 2007), with both ideational and material dimensions to attract international financial support. The performances were related to building emergence, good governance, reconciliation, and international justice but also to national and regional security concerns (Ricard 2017b). We discussed these performances earlier in the section on reconciliation and justice. Ouattara was determined to create symbolic and material practices that would improve the ranking of Côte d'Ivoire on the Doing Business Index of the World Bank or that would make the country eligible for support from the American Millennium Challenge Corporation. These practices were created through the production of legislative and regulatory texts as well as through institutions that met a "checklist" of requirements primarily intended to respond to external requests. This is in line with the governance strategies promoted by international financial institutions in their relations with poor countries (Best 2013). For instance, the High Authority for Good Governance is an institution that was created in 2013 "by a request from the IMF to obtain loans"[26] in order "to play to the gallery,"[27] as one interviewee put it. In other words, it is one of many examples of an institutional "empty shell."[28] The success of the government strategy was also related to the attraction to technocrats like Alassane Ouattara. After abandoning earlier commitments to promote democracy and to reward transparency (Alesina and Weder 2002), aid donors have become more and more focused on the importance of top-down expertise and planning (Van de Walle 2016, 164). This fetishism for technocrats who can "deliver results" is inspired by theories of developmental patrimonialism (Hagmann and Reyntjens 2016, 6).

In the post-conflict years, the influence of France was more discreet.[29] There was a quasi-symbiosis between the two governments, which may have been a mistake.[30] This relationship should be understood both in terms of the contingency of the "bet" on Alassane Ouattara's project and in terms of the historicity of relations between France and Côte d'Ivoire in the context of a transnational Franco-Ivorian and francophone space (Charbonneau and Chafer 2014). The decision makers in the UNOCI exemplified this second aspect of the relationship.[31] Between 2011 and 2015, the International Monetary Fund's Heavily Indebted Poor Country (HIPC) initiative reduced Ivorian public debt from over 90% of GDP to around 40% of GDP. A major portion of this debt was held by France, which adopted an approach to debt reduction that was different from the one adopted by other creditors. Debt reduction was achieved through several Debt Reduction and Development Contracts (C2Ds) piloted by the French Development Agency (AFD), which made some major investments in education and health. In addition, separate French concessional loans have provided key support to major projects. Construction of the Abidjan Metro transit network is being carried out by a consortium of French companies, a project financed by a concessional loan of €1.4 billion, the largest ever made by France. There is also the Third Bridge of Abidjan, built by a French entrepreneur and personal friend of Alassane Ouattara, Martin Bouygues. French companies account for 50% of the state's tax revenues and tens of thousands of jobs.[32] Thus this "bet" on Ouattara has also been made by French capitalists, with support from the French government.

Strategically, Abidjan has remained the French army's gateway to West Africa. Even before the launch of Operation Serval in Mali, Alassane Ouattara was already justifying the maintenance of the French military base and its troops in the name of the fight against terrorism (Le Monde 2012). The attacks in the seaside resort Grand-Bassam near Abidjan in 2016, in which 22 persons were killed, have obviously reinforced this discourse. French entrepreneurs in Côte d'Ivoire have also appreciated the maintenance of this base.³³ From 2013 onward, it is the contingency of French investment in the fight against terrorism in the Sahel and the importance of the historicity of Ivorian security extraversion that underlie the strategic interest post-conflict Côte d'Ivoire represents for France. The political and security difficulties in the Sahel have given an important dimension to Côte d'Ivoire:

> The country has had a central role since the Burkinabe lock was broken.³⁴
> 
> The stability of the country is an important element, especially since the Sahel is going into a tailspin. France does not want Côte d'Ivoire, in this context, to fail.³⁵

Abidjan is seen as an anchor of stability for the global fight against terrorism in West Africa, which may explain why it was chosen as the location for a regional training school for counterterrorism. Regional fears of terrorism and of intrusion into the northern Ivorian border area became tangible when in June 2020, 11 Ivorian soldiers were killed by an armed group at a border post near Burkina Faso (France 24 2020). The two mutinies of 2017 reinforced the focus on these issues. Indeed, France appointed a new ambassador with a "security" profile, Gilles Huberson, who has a military background and who was the ambassador to Mali from 2013 to 2016. Huberson was involved in the reform of the army after the mutinies. Recalled at the end of 2019, he was in the habit of saying bluntly that "France's interest is stability. And that's Ouattara" (Bensimon et al. 2020).

## *"Normalizing" a country and the limits of the discourse on "stability"*

After the stabilization of 2012–2013, the main objective of the Ivorian elites in power was to bring the UNOCI to a close in order to normalize the country. It was essential to build a post-conflict image "to please the West or the international community."³⁶ The international actors interviewed were aware of this. This departure had been "in the air since 2013–2014."³⁷ Announced after the 2015 presidential election, it was a "nice political signal but at the same time really brutal at a time when the whole Ivorian system almost collapsed because of the mutinies."³⁸ Others blamed the "trap of economism,"³⁹ claiming that donors, blinded by impressive macroeconomic results, did not seem to understand that the implementation of their programs could be significantly impacted by the institutional nexus of corruption and concentrated power.⁴⁰

Beyond the economic growth and the global perception of "good" macroeconomic management, it is undeniable that Côte d'Ivoire retrieved the regional and international influence that it had lost during the early 2000s. Symbolically, the election of Alassane Ouattara as president of the Economic Community of West African States (ECOWAS), a position that he held from 2012 to 2014, demonstrated a return to normalcy in terms of the important influence of the country in West Africa. During Ouattara's mandate as president of the ECOWAS, the organization managed difficult crises in Mali and Guinea-Bissau but also adopted a common external tariff. Despite the mutinies, Côte d'Ivoire sent peacekeepers to Mali just a year after the closing of the UNOCI. On the international scene, obtaining a non-permanent seat on the UN Security Council in 2017 was an important success for the government as well as a recognition of its "return," although this achievement should also be understood as an asset for France in the UN political game.⁴¹

However, as the last peacekeepers were leaving the country at the beginning of 2017, what was sold in New York as a success story became more and more unpredictable. The mutinies of January and May 2017, which were extremely disturbing to Ivorian elites (Hervieu 2017) and deeply affected Bouaké,[42] were the first signs. In addition, the various crises in the power alliance revealed a certain disenchantment, one that was palpable in almost all of our interviews with international actors in 2017. Against a backdrop of corruption and wealth-grabbing, it was difficult for these actors to accept a generally authoritarian exercise of power that is not conducive to political reconciliation, especially in a context of deepening economic and social inequalities.[43] The amount of political violence was limited during the presidential election campaign of 2015, but just days before Ivorians were supposed to go to the polls, most high-profile candidates called for the election to be boycotted, for it was clear that the campaign had not been taking place on a level-playing field (Piccolino 2016, 103). These concerns led to growing tensions with international actors. This was highlighted by the case of the EU ambassadors' report (Le Monde 2018), which caused a stir in Côte d'Ivoire. The report is credited with helping to put pressure on the government to make a major gesture of political reconciliation, one that was symbolized by the previously mentioned amnesty in August 2018 of pro-Gbagbo prisoners. Coupled with a tightening of authoritarian measures (Ricard 2020), the president's decision to run for a third term in August 2020 set the country on fire. International actors were powerless in the face of the deteriorating situation during the 2020 election campaign. The opposition repeatedly called for the postponement of the vote so that negotiations could take place, as did organizations such as the International Crisis Group (ICG 2020) and the French diplomatic corps (Banda 2020). Several rulings of the African Court on Human and Peoples' Rights highlighted the lack of respect for the rule of law in the organization of the presidential election. For example, there was a failure to adhere to the decision of the Ivorian Constitutional Council requiring that 4 candidates out of 44 be selected for the presidential election. Tensions rose with the call for an "active boycott" of the opposition during the election campaign. On 17 October 2020, individuals burned the residence of Affi N'Guessan, one of the opposition leaders and a presidential candidate. Pre-electoral violence caused at least 30 deaths between August 2020 and October 2020. Between 31 October 2020 (election day) and 10 November 2020, 55 persons were killed and 282 injured as a result of post-electoral violence (CNDH 2020). Moreover, according to the United Nations High Commissioner for Refugees, 8,000 refugees fled the country during this period (UNHCR 2020).

## Conclusion

The end of Alassane Ouattara's second term and his controversial bid for re-election for a third term have pushed this political regime deeper and deeper into an increasingly risky logic of "electoral autocracy" (Van de Walle 2016, 161), as close to 100 Ivorians died in electoral violence before, during, and after the 2020 presidential election. Ivorians have seen these episodes before. Indeed, the civil war of the early 2000s was partly caused by the refusal of the Ivorian elites in power to allow Alassane Ouattara to run in the presidential elections of 1995 and 2000. In the face of this logic, just how far the political elites in power are willing to repress protests is a central issue that raises the question of the legitimacy of the president for his third term. After this tightening of authoritarian measures, will there be a loosening? With the end of the ICC proceedings against him, Laurent Gbagbo is expected to return to Côte d'Ivoire, and this may be an opportunity to calm tensions, at the same time as the president has opened a dialogue with Henri Konan Bédié. Just as during the Houphouët era, a carrot-and-stick approach is being used strategically. However, the deep-seated problems are still unresolved.

Although the guns have been silenced in Côte d'Ivoire, and although in this process international actors such as the UNOCI have clearly helped the country take a step toward some form of "stability" or negative peace, the post-conflict Ivorian experience demonstrates the important limitations of projects to build stability. It highlights the difficulties faced by international peacebuilding in contexts in which there are deeply political issues, such as reconciliation that can be a tool for elites in power to impose a very particular vision of what "peace" means; however, it also sheds light on the sometimes successful but mostly limited achievements of state elites with authoritarian impulses who attempt to build sustainable peace. The Ivorian regime became a form of "illiberal" peacebuilding (Soares de Oliveira 2011; Jones, Soares de Oliveira and Verhoeven 2013) in which international actors tolerate authoritarianism in the name of perceived "good" macroeconomic management. But this "bet," similar to the ones made in many parts of the world during the Cold War era of modernization (Van de Walle 2016), is far from being a safe one.

## Notes

1 Université Félix Houphouët-Boigny, Abidjan, Côte d'Ivoire. I also thank Paul Lorentz for his assistance. This study was part of the research project (with Bruno Charbonneau as principal investigator), "A New Theory of Post-Conflict Governance: Transforming the State at the Security-Development Nexus of Intervention" (2015–2017), funded by the Social Sciences and Humanities Research Council of Canada.
2 Interview, head of a human rights organization, Abidjan, December 2017.
3 Interview, head of a civil society and human rights organization, Bouaké, November 2017.
4 Interview, local politician and municipal councillor no. 2, Bouaké, November 2017.
5 Interview, embassy official no. 1, Abidjan, December 2017.
6 Interview, former national official at the CDVR and CONARIV, Bouaké, November 2017.
7 Interview, international organization official no. 1, Abidjan, December 2017.
8 Interview, embassy official no. 2, Abidjan, December 2017.
9 Interview, high-level politician from the opposition, Abidjan, December 2017.
10 Interview, president of a national human and civil rights organization, Abidjan, December 2017.
11 Interview, embassy official no. 3, Abidjan, December 2017.
12 Interview, embassy official no. 3, Abidjan, December 2017.
13 Interview, embassy official no. 1, Abidjan, December 2017.
14 Interview, human rights specialist no. 2, Bouaké, November 2017.
15 Focus group, six ex-combatants, Bouaké, November 2017.
16 Interview, ex-combatant no. 3, Bouaké, November 2017.
17 See e.g. Novosseloff (2018).
18 Interview, embassy official no. 3, Abidjan, December 2017.
19 Interview, former UNOCI official, Abidjan, December 2017.
20 Interview, international organization official no. 1, Abidjan, December 2017.
21 Interview, human rights specialist no. 2, Bouaké, November 2017.
22 Interview, social science professor, Bouaké, November 2017.
23 Interview, international development specialist no. 2, Abidjan, December 2017.
24 As defined by the Organisation for Economic Co-operation and Development (OECD).
25 Interview, embassy official no. 4, Abidjan, December 2017.
26 Interview, embassy official no. 2, Abidjan, December 2017.
27 Interview, international development specialist no. 1, Abidjan, December 2017.
28 Interview, international development specialist no. 2, Abidjan, December 2017.
29 Interview, embassy official no. 3, Abidjan, December 2017.
30 Interview, international development specialist no. 1, Abidjan, December 2017.
31 Interview, former UNOCI official, Abidjan, December 2017.
32 Interview, embassy official no. 4, Abidjan, December 2017.
33 Interview (from previous research), French military officer, Abidjan, May 2015.
34 Interview, embassy official no. 4, Abidjan, December 2017.
35 Interview, international development specialist no. 2, Abidjan, December 2017.
36 Interview, president of a national human and civil rights organization, Abidjan, December 2017.
37 Interview, former UNOCI official, Abidjan, December 2017.
38 Interview, embassy official no. 3, Abidjan, December 2017.

39 Interview, international organization official no. 3, Abidjan, December 2017.
40 Interview, international organization official no. 1, Abidjan, December 2017.
41 Interview, embassy official no. 4, Abidjan, December 2017.
42 Interview, local politician and municipal councillor no. 1, Bouaké, November 2017: "The mutinies, we were very scared, we didn't know who was who, we didn't know in the morning if we'd be alive in the evening."
43 See the qualitative interviews in Berrou et al. (2017).

# References

Akindès, F., (2017) 'On ne mange pas les ponts et le goudron': les sentiers sinueux d'une sortie de crise en Côte d'Ivoire', *Politique africaine*, 148, pp. 5–26.

Akindès, F. and Toit, V., (2017) 'Introduction. La transition humanitaire en Côte d'Ivoire, éléments de cadrage', in Fouquet, T. and Toit, V., (eds.) *Transition humanitaire en Côte d'Ivoire*. Paris: Khartala, pp. 1–25.

Alesina, A. and Weder, B., (2002) 'Do Corrupt Governments Receive Less Foreign Aid?', *American Economic Review*, 92(4), pp. 1126–1137.

Amin, S., (1967) *Le Développement du Capitalisme en Côte d'Ivoire*. Paris: Éditions de Minuit.

Amnesty International, (2018) *Côte d'Ivoire: A fragile human rights situation*. London: Amnesty International. [online]. Available at: Cote d'Ivoire: A fragile human rights situation: Amnesty International submission for the UN Universal Periodic Review – 33rd Session of the UPR Working Group, May 2019 (Accessed: 23 June 2021)

Amnesty International, (2019) *Côte d'Ivoire: Growing attacks on activists and opposition ahead of elections*. London: Amnesty International. 6 August. [online]. Available at: Côte d'Ivoire. Les attaques se multiplient contre les militants et les opposants à l'approche des élections | Amnesty International (Accessed: 23 June 2021).

Banda, H., (2020) 'Côte d'Ivoire/France: Ouattara Refuses Macron's Request to Delay Polls', *The Africa Report*, 8 September. [online]. Available at: Côte d'Ivoire/France: Ouattara refuses Macron's request to delay polls (theafricareport.com) (Accessed: 23 June 2021).

Bayart, J.-F., (2000) 'Africa in the World: A History of Extraversion', *African Affairs*, 99, pp. 217–267.

Bayart, J-F., (2009) *The State in Africa: The Politics of the Belly*. 2nd ed. Cambridge: Polity.

Bellamy, A. and Williams, P., (2011) 'The New Politics of Protection? Côte d'Ivoire, Libya and the Responsibility to Protect', *International Affairs*, 87(4), pp. 825–850.

Bensimon, C., (2019) 'La Côte d'Ivoire prisonnière de ses chefs', *Le Monde*, 27 December. [online]. Available at: La Côte d'Ivoire prisonnière de ses chefs (lemonde.fr) (Accessed: 23 June 2021).

Bensimon, C. et al., (2020) 'Violences sexistes et sexuelles: l'ancien ambassadeur de France en Côte d'Ivoire prépare sa défense', *Le Monde Afrique*. [online]. Available at: Violences sexistes et sexuelles: l'ancien ambassadeur de France en Côte d'Ivoire prépare sa défense (lemonde.fr) (Accessed: 23 June 2021).

Berrou, J-P et al., (2017) 'Le réveil des classes moyennes ivoiriennes? Identification, caractérisation et implications pour les politiques publiques', *Papiers de recherche AFD*, 71.

Best, J., (2013) *Governing Failure: Provisional Expertise and the Transformation of Global Development Finance*. Cambridge: Cambridge University Press.

Bilgin, P. and Morton, A.D., (2002) 'Historicising Representations of "Failed States": Beyond the Cold-war Annexation of the Social Sciences?', *Third World Quarterly*, 23(1), pp. 55–80.

Carter Center, (2020) *International Election Observation Mission Côte d'Ivoire 2020: Preliminary Statement*, 2 November. [online]. Available at: cote-divoire-prelim-110220.pdf (cartercenter.org) (Accessed: 30 June 2021).

Chandler, D., (2017) *Peacebuilding: The Twenty Years' Crisis, 1997–2017*. Basingstoke: Palgrave Macmillan.

Chandler, D. and Sisk, T.D., (eds.) (2013) *Routledge Handbook of International Statebuilding*. Oxon and New York, NY: Routledge.

Charbonneau, B., (2012) 'War and Peace in Côte d'Ivoire: Violence, Agency, and the Local/International Line', *International Peacekeeping*, 19(4), pp. 508–524.

Charbonneau, B. and Chafer, T., (eds.) (2014) *Peace Operations in the Francophone World: Global Governance Meets Post-colonialism*. London: Routledge.

CIVICUS, (2020) *Civic Space Backsliding Ahead of Elections in Francophone West Africa*. [online]. Available at: west-africa-report-2020_en.pdf (civicus.org) (Accessed: 30 June 2021).

Cogneau, D., Czajka, L. and Houngbedji, K., (2017) 'Le retour de l'éléphant triomphant? Croissance et inégalités de revenu en Côte d'Ivoire (1988–2015)', *Afrique contemporaine*, 263–264(3), pp. 221–225.

Conseil national des Droits de l'Homme (CNDH), (2020) *Déclaration no 6 relative aux atteintes aux droits de l'homme, aux actes d'incivisme et de destructions de biens*. Abidjan: Conseil national des Droits de l'Homme, 10 November.

Debos, M., (2016) *Living by the Gun in Chad. Governing Africa's Inter-Wars*. London: Zed Books.

France 24, (2020) *Ivory Coast Soldiers Killed in Attack at Border Post Near Burkina Faso*, 11 June. [online]. Available at: Ivory Coast soldiers killed in attack at border post near Burkina Faso (france24.com) (Accessed: 30 June 2021).

Grajales, J. and Jouhanneau, C., (2019) 'L'ordinaire de la sortie de guerre: sociologie de l'action publique après la violence armée', *Gouvernement et action publique*, 8(4), pp. 7–23.

Hagmann, T. and Reyntjens, F., (2016) 'Introduction: Aid and Authoritarianism in sub-Saharan Africa after 1990', in Hagmann, T. and Reyntjens, F., (eds.) *Aid and Authoritarianism in Africa: Development without Democracy*. Uppsala and London: Zed Books, pp. 1–20.

Hazan, P., (2017) *Juger la guerre, juger l'histoire. Du bon usage des commissions Vérité et de la justice internationale*. Paris: Presses Universitaires de France.

Hervieu, S., (2017) 'Côte d'Ivoire: comment les mutins ont fait plier le gouvernement', *Le Monde Afrique*, 26 May. [online]. Available at: Côte d'Ivoire: comment les mutins ont fait plier le gouvernement (lemonde.fr) (Accessed: 30 June 2021).

Human Rights Watch (HRW), (2016) *'Justice Reestablishes Balance': Delivering Credible Accountability for Serious Abuses in Côte d'Ivoire*. [online]. Available at: www.hrw.org/sites/default/files/report_pdf/cotedivoire0316_web.pdf (Accessed: 30 June 2021).

Indigo Côte d'Ivoire and Interpeace, (2018) *'L'étranger ne peut pas venir se cacher derrière une termitière et vouloir que sa tête la dépasse': Analyse locale des risques et opportunités pour la cohésion sociale à l'ouest de la Côte d'Ivoire*. Abidjan: Bureau regional d'Interpeace. [online]. Available at: "L'étranger ne peut pas venir se cacher derrière une termitière et vouloir que sa tête la dépasse" (interpeace.org) (Accessed: 30 June 2021).

International Crisis Group (ICG), (2020) *Côte d'Ivoire: An Election Delay for Dialogue*, Briefing 161, 29 September. [online]. Available at: Côte d'Ivoire: An Election Delay for Dialogue | Crisis Group (Accessed: 30 June 2021).

Jeune Afrique with Agence France Press, (2017) *Côte d'Ivoire: 4 morts dans des affrontements à Bouaké entre démobilisés et policiers*, 23 May. [online]. Available at: Côte d'Ivoire: 4 morts dans des affrontements à Bouaké entre démobilisés et policiers – Jeune Afrique (Accessed: 30 June 2021).

Jones, W., Soares de Oliveira, R. and Verhoeven, H., (2013). *Africa's Illiberal State-builders. Refugee Studies Centre Paper Series no 89*. Oxford: University of Oxford.

Jourde, C., (2007) 'The International Relations of Small Neoauthoritarian States: Islamism, Warlordism, and the Framing of Stability', *International Studies Quarterly*, 51, pp. 481–503.

Konan, A.S., (2018) 'Côte d'Ivoire: confusion autour des ralliements d'élus indépendants au RHDP', *Jeune Afrique*, 25 October. [online]. Available at: Côte d'Ivoire: confusion autour des ralliements d'élus indépendants au RHDP – Jeune Afrique (Accessed: 30 June 2021).

Konan, A.S., (2019) 'Côte d'Ivoire: 18 interpellations après les violences intercommunautaires à Béoumi', *Jeune Afrique*, 24 May. [online]. Available at: Côte d'Ivoire: 18 interpellations après les violences intercommunautaires à Béoumi – Jeune Afrique (Accessed: 30 June 2021).

Le Monde, (2012) *Entretien avec le Président Alassane Ouattara*, 26 January.

Le Monde and AFP, (2018) *La Côte d'Ivoire 'moins solide et démocratique' qu'on pourrait le penser, selon l'UE*, 2 August. [online]. Available at: La Côte d'Ivoire "moins solide et démocratique" qu'on pourrait le penser, selon l'UE (lemonde.fr) (Accessed: 30 June 2021).

Martin, P.A., (2018) 'Security Sector Reform and Civil-military Relations in Postwar Côte d'Ivoire', *African Affairs*, 117(468), pp. 522–533.

McGovern, M., (2011) *Making War in Côte d'Ivoire*. Chicago, IL: Chicago University Press.

Miran-Guyon, M., (2017) 'Côte d'Ivoire, le retour de l'éléphant: Introduction thématique', *Afrique contemporaine*, 263–264(3), pp. 11–23.

Niakaté, H., (2018) 'Les enfants 'microbes' sont un signe de l'apartheid économique qui s'installe en Côte d'Ivoire. Entretien avec Francis Akindès', *Le Monde Afrique*, 1 April. [online]. Available at: "Les enfants "microbes" sont un signe de l'apartheid économique qui s'installe en Côte d'Ivoire" (lemonde.fr) (Accessed: 30 June 2021).

Novosseloff, A., (2018) *The Many Lives of a Peacekeeping Mission: The UN Operation in Côte d'Ivoire*. New York, NY: International Peace Institute. [online]. Available at: The UN Operation in Côte d'Ivoire (ipinst.org) (Accessed: 30 June 2021).

Nubukpo, K., (2019) *L'Urgence africaine: Changeons le modèle de croissance!* Paris: Odile Jacob.

Paddon Rhoads, E., (2016) *Impartiality and the Future of the United Nations*. New York, NY: Oxford University Press.

Piccolino, G., (2016) 'One Step Forward, Two Steps Back? Côte d'Ivoire's 2015 Presidential Polls', *Africa Spectrum*, 51(1), pp. 97–110.

Piccolino, G., (2018) 'Peacebuilding and Statebuilding in Post-2011 Côte d'Ivoire: A Victor's Peace?', *African Affairs*, 117(468), pp. 485–508.

Radio France Internationale (RFI), (2015) *Côte d'Ivoire: les réactions aux inculpations d'ex-chefs rebelles*, 8 July. [online]. Available at: Côte d'Ivoire: les réactions aux inculpations d'ex-chefs rebelles (rfi.fr) (Accessed: 30 June 2021).

Renner, J., (2014) 'The Local Roots of the Global Politics of Reconciliation: The Articulation of 'Reconciliation' as an Empty Universal in the South African Transition to Democracy', *Millennium: Journal of International Studies*, 42(2), pp. 263–285.

Ricard, M., (2017a) 'Gouverner le "post-conflit" en Côte d'Ivoire', in *Annuaire français de relations internationales*, XVIII. Paris: Université Panthéon-Sorbonne, pp. 551–567.

Ricard, M., (2017b) 'Historicity of Extraversion in Côte d'Ivoire and the "Post-conflict"', *Journal of Contemporary African Studies*, 35(4), pp. 506–524.

Ricard, M., (2020) "Mon président, on dit quoi?': le resserrement autoritaire en Côte d'Ivoire', *Bulletin FrancoPaix*, 5(9). Montréal: Centre FrancoPaix, Chaire Raoul-Dandurand, pp. 2–8.

Richards, P., (ed.) (2005) *No Peace No War: An Anthropology of Contemporary Armed Conflicts*. Oxford: James Currey.

Soares de Oliveira, R., (2011) 'Illiberal Peacebuilding in Angola', *Journal of Modern African Studies*, 49(2), pp. 287–314.

UNHCR, (2020) *UNHCR Expands Aid as Ivorian Refugee Numbers Top 8,000*, 10 November. [online]. Available at: UNHCR – UNHCR expands aid as Ivorian refugee numbers top 8,000 (Accessed: 30 June 2021).

United Nations Security Council, (2017) *Lors d'une réunion 'historique', le Conseil de sécurité salue la 'success story' de la mission de l'ONU en Côte d'Ivoire, à quelques jours de sa clôture*, CS/12852, Meetings coverage, 2 June. New York, NY: United Nations.

Van de Walle, N., (2016) 'Conclusion: Democracy Fatigue and the Ghost of Modernization Theory', in Hagmann, T. and Reyntjens, F., (eds.) *Aid and Authoritarianism in Africa: Development without Democracy*. Uppsala et London: Zed Books, pp. 161–178.

*Wall Street Journal*, (2020) *Cocoa Cartel Stirs Up Global Chocolate Market*, 5 January. [online]. Available at: Cocoa Cartel Stirs Up Global Chocolate Market – WSJ (Accessed: 30 June 2021).

World Bank, (2015). *La Force de l'Éléphant: pour que sa croissance génère plus d'emplois de qualité*. Rapport sur la situation économique en Côte d'Ivoire. [online]. Available at: World Bank Document (Accessed: 30 June 2021).

World Bank, (2018a) *Aux portes du paradis – Comment la Côte d'Ivoire peut rattraper son retard technologique?* Rapport sur la situation économique en Côte d'Ivoire. [online]. Available at: Aux portes du paradis – Comment la Côte d'Ivoire peut rattraper son retard technologique? (worldbank.org) (Accessed: 30 June 2021).

World Bank, (2018b) *Life Expectancy at Birth, Total (Years) – Cote d'Ivoire, Somalia, South Sudan*. [online]. Available at: Espérance de vie à la naissance, total (années) – Cote d'Ivoire, Somalia, South Sudan | Data (banquemondiale.org) (Accessed: 30 June 2021).

# CONCLUSION

## African Peacebuilding for Whom and for What? Bringing the People Back In

*Cyril Obi*

This book is partly hinged on "the centrality of African experiences in the ways international politics position Africa as an object and subject of international interventions." By engaging in a critical exploration and interrogation of African ideas, conceptions and approaches to conflict management and peace, and an international politics that routinely seek to intervene on its own terms in African conflicts, the contributors to this important book draw attention to how multiple factors and relationships shape peacebuilding on the continent. The book makes several compelling points about the institutionalization and practices underpinning peacebuilding in Africa. These include Africa's key location in international interventions, the various contested meanings and different framings and practices of peacebuilding and how these reflect on its instrumentalization by various actors, including the United Nations (UN) and the African Union (AU). The book builds on earlier works to link African peacebuilding to African thinking, norms, frameworks and practices of intervening in conflicts on the continent.

The point of departure of this book is its focus on the contested nature of the concepts and practices underpinning peacebuilding in Africa. Beyond the critical observation that peacebuilding in Africa is a "work in progress" and a political contest of ideas and practices, it interrogates the fundamental basis of intervention by asking the all-important question: whose peace? This opens to the door to a critical examination of African and external approaches to the institutionalization and practices of peacebuilding. This, for example, provides a basis for analyzing the role and impact of the politics and practices of the UN, UN-AU partnership, the AU and other African regional economic communities (RECs) that have intervened in African conflicts and sought to institutionalize peace on the continent with varying degrees of success or failure. The chapters shift the debate away from the binary of African agency versus international intervention to the nature of the various conceptualizations, practices and institutional approaches and actors jostling for space, influence and power over the peacebuilding terrain, facilitating a deeper understanding of their evolution, but better still, the nature of the contestations that will continue to drive the structure and processes of peace interventions for some time to come.

The issues raised by the editors and contributors to the *Routledge Handbook of African Peacebuilding* as to "Whose peacebuilding?" will continue to be central to the politics of peacebuilding and resonate across the worlds of theory, policy and practice. This critical intellectual intervention makes it clear that it is no longer "business as usual" to treat African peacebuilding as being a homogenous concept or one that is marginal to the practice of international interventions on the continent. The book goes a long way in demonstrating the centrality of African agency, ideas and practices to peacebuilding on the continent and why these matter to knowledge and actions.

## Post–Cold War Africa's First-Generation Peacebuilding

African peacebuilding could be said to have received a fillip following the end of the Cold War, particularly after Boutros Boutros-Ghali, the first African UN secretary-general, launched *An Agenda for Peace* in 1992 (UN 1992), followed by the *Supplement to an Agenda for Peace* (UN 1997), in opening the door to UN peacebuilding. This was about the same time that the Organization of African Unity (OAU), the precursor to the African Union (AU) that was launched in 2002, laid down the Continental Mechanism for Conflict Prevention, Management and Resolution, which later culminated in the African Peace and Security Architecture (APSA) as an African-owned peace intervention framework. While African peacebuilding from an institutionalist perspective has evolved in terms of normative innovativeness, it also has faced some challenges in terms of international collaboration. However, has at best yielded mixed results. While progress with African ownership of the peacebuilding agenda has assumed a rather strong normative profile replete with institutional frameworks at the sub-regional and regional levels, including a working partnership with the United Nations (UN), actual practices and actions reveal a real gap between rhetoric and reality. Thus, the continent continues to experience a mix of limited success and outright failure in addressing conflict. Several chapters of this book explore the structural and institutional issues of UN, UN-AU collaboration, security sector reform (SSR) and governance international law, rightly noting how competing interests and policies impede the effective implementation of peacebuilding actions.

The book opens with an analysis of the evolution from UN peacekeeping to peacebuilding by Alexandra Novosseloff. This is followed by the chapter by Arthur Stein and Marie-Joëlle Zahar, who note that UN-AU collaboration has been hobbled by "structural constraints," "operational impediments" and "intractable political and strategic disagreements." This is not fundamentally different from the challenges facing SSR, another aspect of peacebuilding, which Niagalé Bagayoko and Eboe Hutchful observe faces several challenges including poor linkages with the UN's "peace agenda" and the eclipsing of SSR by "stabilization and counterterrorism initiatives and training." Marina Sharpe takes the analysis of international peacebuilding a step further, linking the UN and AU's poor performance in addressing the root causes of conflict in terms of their practices towards problems of forced displacement and refugeeism (fallouts of violent conflict). She makes a case for better and more effective UN-AU coordination on conflict prevention and management.

Despite claims to African agency and ownership, partly captured by the phraseology of "African Solutions to African Problems" (ASAP), a term coined by George Ayittey in the early 1990s but later appropriated by the AU to emphasize the need for the continent to exercise greater agency and step up to fill the gaps left by the international community in response to multiple challenges facing the continent, additional effort still needs to be made to theorize African peacebuilding. Omeje (2019, 10) is unsparing in his critique of ASAP as a self-serving device, noting among others that "for African elites, ASAP is a convenient rhetoric for evading sensible accountability." He is equally critical of "local ownership" of peacebuilding as an "empty buzzword" usually deployed by the international community to undermine and marginalize peacebuilding purposes.

The foregoing speaks to some of the constraints and challenges linked to the unfinished business of nation-statism and the citizenship question, and regional frameworks that tend to privilege state-led and elite-centered approaches to the politics and practices of African peacebuilding. This includes the recognition of the framing of international peacebuilding within a "colonial/neo-colonial" framing and how this has shaped contending perspectives to peacebuilding on the continent, including the gaps that impinge on the fundamental question, "Whose peacebuilding?" and the dynamics of power, politics and actions underlining the quest for conflict transformation.

Some of the critical issues such as financing and coordination across contributing countries and agencies to peacekeeping/peace support operations are likely to continue to pose challenges to UN-AU collaboration as well as peacebuilding practices. As the contributors to Part I of the book rightly note, more needs to be done to overcome the structural constraints by addressing areas of disagreement, focusing on long-term institutionalization and sustainability of peacebuilding. They also recognize the need to pay much closer attention to the root causes of violent conflict on the continent rather than the symptoms, short-term gains and quick exit strategies. By drawing attention to these issues, we can better recognize the urgent need for radical thinking on a more integrated and equitable African-rooted institutional reforms aimed towards greater people-centeredness, cohesiveness, sustainability and effective peacebuilding.

The chapters in Part I help illustrate the point that ownership of a peace architecture bereft of control over the reproduction of conditions for self-sustaining economic production, integration and development limits the effectiveness of African peace interventions. With international peacebuilding processes in Africa largely dependent on external financing and disconnected from the daily struggles and aspirations of the majority, it is not clear what claims to African ownership really amount to. The evidence suggests that the rhetoric of African leaders on lofty AU initiatives, such as "Silencing the Guns by 2020" (now postponed till 2030; AU 2013) and "Agenda 2063: The Africa We Want" (AU 2015), aimed at ending all wars and "building a prosperous and peaceful Africa," is neither backed by adequate Africa's resources nor political will.

The foregoing points are further elaborated upon in Part II, on the impact of themes and debates on African peacebuilding. Laurie Nathan's chapter interrogates the issue of whether mediation on the continent has "distinct African characteristics," noting the ways it reflects liberal democratic values, which are contradicted by illiberal practices typified by resorting to "power-sharing arrangements" that tend to privilege the interests of squabbling elites. Chapters by Tim Murithi and by Ulrike Lühe and Briony Jones offer insights into how African innovativeness is reshaping contemporary approaches to transitional justice and demonstrating some of its complementarities with peacebuilding, and how the influence of the colonial moorings of transitional justice shapes contemporary practices and makes it imperative for African norms to play a significant role in transforming global transitional justice. The same logic can be applied towards defining role for African (local) contributions to international peacebuilding. Jeremy Allouche and Patrick Zadi Zadi are critical of liberalism-infused peacebuilding approaches and draw on two case studies to demonstrate how local engagement of structural issues led to successful examples of local peacebuilding. In terms of the overall focus of the book, it lends credence to the view of the effectiveness of local rather than international peacebuilding approaches.

The chapters add to existing knowledge by other scholars and research organizations that have criticized the liberal model of peacebuilding (Omeje 2019; Zambakari 2016; Mustapha and Tar 2019) or produced research-based knowledge by drawing on African traditional/cultural forms or approaches to peacebuilding. However, most such efforts have been marked by "relatively little writing on epistemological and methodological approaches" (Rashid and Niang 2021, 2). This would require more scholarly engagements and reflexivity on the part of scholars to move what Omeje (2019, 4–6), refers to as "orthodox peacebuilding" processes at the regional and national levels beyond the current dominance by Western/liberal values, elitism and international interventionist models. In this regard, there is an urgent need to conduct more research aimed at expanding the knowledge bases of African peacebuilding.

Chapters by Nina Wilén, Jonathan Sears and Daniel Eizenga remind us of the salience of gender dilemmas and the need to avoid gendered stereotypes and the peacebuilding-development and democracy-peacebuilding nexus. These call attention to the ways the structures of dominant international peacebuilding in Africa marginalize and render women invisible, how the peacebuilding-development nexus feeds into recurring interventions in Africa and how the connection between democracy and peacebuilding exhibits a "robust relationship," even if the former has been "vulnerable to authoritarian elites." These are germane in explaining how African concepts and approaches shape peacebuilding and the impact of international politics on international interventions in African conflicts. By unpacking the varied ways in which one impacts on and shapes the other, we are better informed on the content of and relations of power underpinning African peacebuilding, particularly in the ways it has tended to favor elites and global powers (traditional and emerging) and the need to critically examine the prospects for the future.

The case studies in Part III provide empirical support for the issues that undergird the ways "international politics position Africa as an object and subject of international interventions." Drawing on cases such as the G5 Sahel organization (Ousmane Diallo), Mali and Somalia (Bruno Charbonneau and Louise Wiuff Moe), The Gambia (Festus Kofi Aubyn), South Sudan (Kuyang Harriet Logo), Guinea-Bissau (Fiifi Edu-Afful and Ruth Adwoa Fripong), and Côte d'Ivoire (Maxine Ricard), contributors explore various dimensions of the international politics of intervention such as dependency on international donors and securitization – how "counterinsurgency and stabilization" overshadow conflict prevention and conflict management on African peacebuilding. Other findings point to the shortcomings of regional and international peacebuilding which marginalize local people, the failed attempt to foist a transitional justice agenda on South Sudan that had not gone through an inclusive democratic transition, the inability of international peacebuilding approaches to address the roots of conflict in Guinea-Bissau and Côte d'Ivoire, creating forms of peace that hardly touch the underlying issues of inequality, injustice and widespread poverty. Thus, as Africa transits from what may be described as first- to second-generation post–Cold War peacebuilding, the issues covered by this book help us to navigate and unpack the nature of African peacebuilding as a distinct scholarly enterprise and practice. Beyond this, contributors to the book promote a better understanding of the emerging contours of next-generation peacebuilding and begin to rethink the possibilities for the politics and practice of international interventions in the coming decades.

## Post–Cold War Africa's Second-Generation Peacebuilding?

After three decades of post–Cold War peacebuilding, Africa seems to be caught between the promise of next-generation peacebuilding and the hard reality that internationally driven and regionally led policies and actions have largely remained "complex, multifaceted and messy" (Africa 2020). Undergirded by mainstream Western ideologies, interests and resources, dominant peacebuilding templates and practices have tended to reify and legitimize state authority and the interests of powerful elites – local, regional and global. Peacebuilding has been characterized by a set of technical and managerial actions leading to the establishment of a patchwork of exigent but brittle peace arrangements that are thrown overboard once the leading protagonists and conflict entrepreneurs feel they no longer serve their narrow interests. Despite billions of dollars spent on international interventions, the trends in peacebuilding in Africa, represented by a motley cast of largely incoherent international, state, non-state actors continue to pursue an agenda of international interventionism in the face of the persistence of structural and violent forms of conflict, widespread poverty and crises of citizenship.

While achieving some economic growth before the outbreak of the COVID-19 pandemic, which has had a rather devastating socio-economic impact, the continent has continued to be roiled by structural, insurgent and low-intensity violent conflicts at a rate that seems to outpace the capacity of its peace, security and governance architectures to cope. Existing peacebuilding approaches, mechanisms and practices lag behind the emerging trajectories of conflict on the continent, while the dominant relations of power continue to favor dominant local elites and members of the international community in fostering forms of interventions that hardly address the structural roots of conflict. According to Nshimbi (2020), the ongoing "civil wars in Libya and South Sudan, insurgency and banditry in Cameroun, regional conflicts in the Sahel affecting Mali, Burkina Faso, Northern Nigeria, Chad, Sudan and Eritrea, and the Horn of Africa, including Somalia, Sudan, South Sudan, and Kenya, and the Great Lakes Region, including Burundi, the Democratic Republic of the Congo (DRC) and the emergence of an Islamist Insurgency in Cabo Delgado region of Mozambique" continue to undermine peace and security on the continent.

Apart from these cases, parts of the Central African Republic (CAR), Southeast Nigeria, South Sudan, the anglophone region of Cameroon and the Tigray province of Ethiopia are either unstable or in the grip of insurgent violence. At the same time, democratic governance based on free and fair elections, multipartyism and nonviolent constitutional changes of power is under threat, as seen from the recent upsurge in military coup d'états in several African countries, including Mali, Guinea and, more recently, Sudan and the elongation of presidential tenures of long-serving presidents in several other countries.

Insights provided in these chapters revisit some of the debates animating peacebuilding in Africa. Given the ways liberal values are shaping African mediation, transitional justice, reconciliation and the focus of international interveners on stabilization and political order – with limited results – we are better able to appreciate the challenges facing African peacebuilding. The chapters in Part III remind us of the need to pay closer attention to the ways the international politics of peacebuilding intersect local or grassroots initiatives and how in some respects lend themselves to a better understanding of the extent to which such approaches effectively address the roots of local conflict. Whether international and elite-dominated approaches to peacebuilding connect to locally embedded ideas and practices or not, the broader question remains how to drive a paradigm shift in African peacebuilding based on the interests and priorities of most African citizens, rather than by those of few elites colluding with hegemonic transnational actors and states to impose peace from above on their conflict-affected societies.

The current travails of democracy across the continent in which some gains from previous decades are gradually being eroded and replaced by varying degrees of authoritarianism should also be placed in the context of the current global moment characterized by the rise of populist and right-wing movements in the Global North and the surging domestic pressures linked to post-COVID-19 economic recovery. The prioritization of domestic challenges in the immediate post-COVID-19 period suggest that Western powers are unlikely to offer anything more than the usual symbolic gestures towards democracy promotion while securing their national and strategic interests in Africa. A logical question that arises is the likely impact of other international peace interventions based on the "no strings attached" rhetoric of non-Western emerging powers on Africa's peace and security terrain. The early indicators suggest that so far, such engagements show that beyond replacing the emphasis on "democracy promotion" with "development promotion," the politics of such international interventions does not provide a radically different alternative, as it reflects the same structure of power relations that exclude ordinary African people from building their own version(s) of peace (from the grassroots).

The connection between democracy and peacebuilding on the continent will continue to be tenuous, as Africa's political elites subvert democratic principles and structures of inclusion by engaging in zero-sum struggles for power and resources. Also, the prospects for peace are limited in contexts where several long-term presidents have successfully extended their stay in office by manipulating their country's constitution. Global double standards or tolerance of such anti-democratic behavior implies that most citizens are disempowered and alienated from politics and any democratic dividends. In some cases, this has led to prolonged mass protests or even violent challenges to the legitimacy of the state. Another outcome of democratic regression has been a gradual slide backwards to either authoritarianism, various forms of insurgency or low intensity conflicts. As Rashid and Niang (2021, 2) note, there has "been an emergence of new terrains and actors in the political economy of violence, the proliferation of 'structures of conflict,'" and geopolitical complexity of so-called local conflicts. While such conflicts are rooted in the complex histories of diverse locales, their effects are increasingly being felt on a much wider scale, drawing in a range of state, national and transnational actors.

## Peacebuilding for What?

While a lot has been said about the limitations of international peacebuilding and the need for a "local turn" capable of centering African agency and ownership of interventions, the question of "Whose peacebuilding?" will be with us for a long time to come. This book reaffirms this point, noting that Africa has become a space for multiple peacebuilding interventions and possibilities that simultaneously reflect relations of power that are predominantly skewed against African people. Yet, to seek an answer to the rhetorical question of whose peacebuilding in the coming decades will require going back to the "original sins" of colonialism to the non-transformative neo-colonialism that followed, which in turn undergirds the question, "Peacebuilding for what?" In the future, the complementarity between the "whose" and "what" questions would be key to the much-needed paradigm shift to which African peacebuilding will remain central. The politics of peacebuilding will in the years to come continue to reflect the relations of power between the "international" and "Africa," and what it would take to define or transform the relationship. While those who have the hegemonic power and resources to shape African peacebuilding may be keen on forms of peace that are protective of their interests, the real issue may lie in a deeper question of what that peace represents, and for whom. "Peacebuilding for what?" is a question present and future generations will have to address.

In doing so, current forms and trajectories of peacebuilding will have to be systematically unpacked. Much is also happening below the radar in the form of peacebuilding from below. As the changing trajectories of conflict increasingly shift from the macro towards the micro level, low intensity or regionally networked wars, the emerging truism to the effect that all peacebuilding is local is bound to assume more complex forms that connect the local to the national, regional and transnational. It is a world in which peacebuilding – broken into poorly coordinated components lodged between the spectrum of conflict to peace and compartmentalized into various "technical" components of early warning such as peacekeeping; security sector reform (SSR); disarmament, demobilization, and reintegration (DDR); reconciliation; and reconstruction – calls for more a more holistic, integrated, inclusive and equitable approach.

The evidence from regionally brokered mediation missions aimed at resolving post-election crises, violent conflict or negotiating the return to constitutional rule after illegal seizures of power in various countries suggests the need to rethink elite bargains or power-sharing arrangements as part of the orthodox peacebuilding toolkit. If anything, the rate at which such contrived "governments of national unity" or "transitional unity governments" are proving to be unstable or unravelling in post-conflict contexts – as the cases of recent events in Mali and the Sudan show – is instructive. This shows that such attempts amount to no more than palliatives aimed at restoring the status quo, rather than creating conditions for addressing the deeper roots of conflict embedded in histories of domination, grievance, injustice, inequality and exploitation of the majority by a select few.

The question of peacebuilding for what gains more prominence when we consider the ways in which mainstream agendas of peacebuilding are securitizing African conflict-affected terrains as "ungoverned spaces," for incubating terrorist/extremist groups, proliferation of small arms, human and drug trafficking, illicit transfers and so forth. Securitization and instrumentalization of peace in the current context often undermine democratic freedoms and prioritizes military and special joint training and surveillance operations over inclusive, community-led and participatory approaches. It also effectively excludes ordinary citizens for whom peace can best be experienced within a radically new and equitable social contract with their leaders. It is by empowering the people to reclaim their rights and freedoms as equal citizens capable of realizing their full potential, and freely choosing and holding their leaders accountable, that Africans can reclaim the peacebuilding agenda on its own terms.

Already there are signs that the continent is experiencing episodic outbursts of demands for an alternate, next-generation peacebuilding in which young people in various countries are demanding change: social emancipation, protection of the rights of minorities, an end to authoritarianism by corrupt and self-serving leadership, and the depredations of international extractivism and neo-colonialism(s). These include uprisings by youth, women and identity groups innovatively combining street protests with digital technologies in the struggle for social justice, equality and peace, and numerous peace initiatives both at the community and grassroots levels. These have come up against the forces of the status quo, sometimes resulting in wanton repression, as in the case of the Lekki toll gate killing of protesters by the military in Lagos, Nigeria (Busari et al. 2020), and the shooting of protesters against the military coup d'état in Khartoum, Sudan (Abdelaziz 2021).

Other elements of next-generation peacebuilding are evident from the resilience being demonstrated across many conflict-affected communities on the continent where people are finding innovative ways of thriving and rebuilding their lives in conflict-affected settings, organizing everyday peace and security and addressing structural drivers of conflict. Although local resilience is not entirely free from international interventionism and has become an object of its programming, more research is required to unpack African success stories based on the innovativeness and ingenuity of local people.

In the unfolding scenario, it appears African peacebuilding is at the crossroads between what could be termed the structural imperatives of post–Cold War, first-generation peacebuilding and the transition to the second-generation peacebuilding in which young people, grassroots organizations, social movements and new/digital technologies are bound to play key roles. The fundamental issue will be the extent to which we would expect continuity or change. In the unfolding dialectics, peace to regimes seeking to cling to power at all costs, war entrepreneurs and international interveners seeking to perpetuate the status quo lies in the ability to block the possibilities for social transformation and disempower those groups mobilizing for a different kind of peace based on equality, social equity, justice, harmony and freedom.

Another aspect that should not be overlooked is the need for a research agenda for unpacking the emerging trends and for producing new knowledge on African peacebuilding. This would address both the need for a paradigm shift and the transformation of Africa's peace and security agenda. Even as we acknowledge the centrality of African experiences of an international politics that places the continent at the center of interventionism, a new research agenda will help to broaden the scope for rethinking African ideas and practices and explore possibilities for transforming the structure of international interventions. It will require both a keen sense of interdisciplinary approaches to peacebuilding concepts, institutionalization and practices on the continent. Part of the research agenda should also include unearthing more information on African success stories, giving voice to the otherwise marginalized or invisible local peacebuilders, and generating innovative ideas to guide African-rooted practices and institutionalization.

One of the lessons of the COVID-19 pandemic for Africa is its disastrous socio-economic impact on the continent and how it has deepened the cleavages, inequalities and grievances of the majority who have been marginalized and excluded from the social contract. The pandemic has also meant a reduction in the flow of resources in support of international peacebuilding, including UN peace operations (De Coning 2020), on the continent at a time when some conflict-affected regions are facing increased levels of tension or experiencing a sharp decline in livelihoods. Other aspects that have been adversely affected include the diversion of national resources from other sectors to address the pandemic, rising food insecurity and impoverishment of certain sections of the populace.

The pandemic has also brought to the fore the continued centrality of the state to the quest to resolve the myriad challenges facing the continent. A lot has been written about the nature of the African state, including its role in relation to peacebuilding, but this will not delay us here. With the distancing of international peacebuilding from an international state-building agenda (but not a state-centric securitization agenda), following rather problematic results in Iraq, Afghanistan and elsewhere, the African state must be brought back into the debate about the future of peacebuilding on the continent. A crucial element in the unfolding scenario is the wide gap between the state and the people across African countries. State power and politics remain central to peacebuilding in Africa. Evolving state forms, not entirely immune from the jostling of fractions of dominant elites and their international allies but detached from the collective interests and aspirations of the people remain a force of control, repression and extraction, conditions that work against a people-owned peace that is inclusive, fair and sustainable. What emerges from the scenario is the constant push and pull between social forces seeking to retain or redefine the direction of peace, either from above or from below. The future of peace will fundamentally be shaped by what African peacebuilding represents for the continent's peoples, particularly in terms of bringing them back in and reconnecting them to the current struggles for emancipation, equal citizenship, participatory, equitable and sustainable development, and human dignity.

## References

Abdelaziz, Khalid, (2021) 'Three People Shot Dead during Huge Protest against Sudan Coup, Doctors Say', *Reuters*, 31 October 2021. Available at: www.reuters.com/world/africa/sudanese-set-nationwide-protests-against-military-coup-2021-10-29/.

African Union, (2013) *Silencing the Guns*. Available at: https://au.int/en/flagships/silencing-guns-2020.

African Union, (2015) *Agenda 2063*. Available at: https://au.int/en/agenda2063/overview

Busari, Stephanie et al., (2020) 'The Pointed Their Guns at Us and Started Shooting: How a Cruel Night of Bullets and Brutality Quashed a Young Protest Movement', *CNN*, 2020. Available at: www.cnn.com/2020/11/18/africa/lagos-nigeria-lekki-toll-gate-feature-intl/index.html

De Coning, Cedric, (2020) 'The Impact of Covid-19 on Peace Operations in Africa', *Conflict Trends*, ACCORD, 2020.

Mustapha, Raufu and Tar, Usman, (2019) 'The Peacebuilding and Development Debate: Is Contemporary Peacebuilding Development in Disguise?', in Omeje, Kenneth, (ed.) *Peacebuilding in Contemporary Africa: In Search of Alternative Strategies*. London and New York, NY: Routledge.

Nshimbi, Christopher, (2020) 'Why the African Union Has Failed to "Silence the Guns," and Some Solutions', *The Conversation*, June 2020. Available at: https://theconversation.com/why-the-african-union-has-failed-to-silence-the-guns-and-some-solutions-139567.

Omeje, Kenneth (ed.), (2019) 'Introduction: Peacebuilding in Contemporary Africa', in *Peacebuilding in Contemporary Africa: In Search of Alternative Strategies*. London and New York, NY: Routledge.

Rashid, Ismail and Niang, Amy (eds.), (2021) 'Introduction', in *Researching Peacebuilding in Africa: Reflections on Theory, Fieldwork and Context*. London and New York, NY: Routledge.

United Nations, (1992) *An Agenda for Peace*. New York, NY: UN. Available at: https://digitallibrary.un.org/record/145749?ln=en

United Nations, (1997) *Supplement to an Agenda for Peace*. New York, NY: UN. Available at: https://digitallibrary.un.org/record/244655?ln=en

Zambakari, Christopher, (2016) 'Challenges of Liberal Peace and Statebuilding in Divided Societies', *Conflict Trends*, ACCORD, February 2016. Available at: www.accord.org.za/conflict-trends/challenges-liberal-peace-statebuilding-divided-societies/.

# AFTERWORD

This book was conceived in another era. It was construed and planned, and the authors were recruited, before the outbreak of the COVID-19 pandemic. Its chapters were written and revised during a health crisis that affected every contributor. The global crisis intruded into the authors' lives and disrupted their academic focus, albeit in ways that depended on geography and racial, gender, and class hierarchies. Then the book was published into a world that was trying to recover from the viral shock, but the post-2020 rebound was, and will remain, deeply uneven. Advanced economies were forecast to return to their pre-pandemic trend levels during 2022, while emerging markets and developing economies, and the low-income countries, saw the growth gap increase, as the poorer countries of the world – many of them African – could not expect to be properly vaccinated before 2023 or 2024. The shocks of the pandemic in many parts of Africa reflected an unequal access to vaccines, asymmetric impacts on economies largely dependent on the tourist industry, remittances or informal labour markets, a relative incapacity to provide fiscal and monetary stimulus, and timid debt relief measures (Tooze 2021, 251–268). Put another way, the COVID-19 pandemic has exacerbated the structural realities of deep inequalities, state failures, and inadequate prevention and management mechanisms and capabilities.

This book was also completed during the Conference of the Parties (COP26) that was held in Glasgow on 31 October–12 November 2021. The expected rhetoric of Global North state leaders calling for climate action – or as Greta Thunberg put it, the 'blah, blah, blah' – was on full display. Many words were voiced and promises were made, but there were limited commitments and actions. The effects of climate change on Africa are hard to quantify, but the picture is grim. Among other attempts, the Institute for Economics and Peace identified three ecological hotspots that 'are particularly susceptible to collapse' and conflict. Two are in Africa: the Sahel–Horn of Africa belt, from Mauritania to Somalia, and the Southern African belt, from Angola to Madagascar (the third stretches from Syria to Pakistan; IEP 2021). While climate change is an ecological crisis, as David Wallace-Wells (2021) put it, it can also be conceived 'as a moral catastrophe, engineered by the sheltered nations of the global North in the recent past, and suffered by those, in the global South, least responsible for it and least prepared.'

Climate change will be central to the future of African peacebuilding. There is no option for peacebuilding that doesn't run into the reality of the climate crisis. And if COVID-19 was a first 'test' for multilateral cooperation and global solidarity in the face of global crisis, the results were far from convincing. This (post-)pandemic and climate-changing world is and will be the context of peacebuilding research and practice in the decades to come. Yet, this (ongoing) transformation of context will occur under the circumstances of pragmatic crisis management in the form of peacebuilding and peacekeeping missions, whose institutions, legacies, and entrenched interests and practices will at best inform, and at worse impede, necessary transformations.

This book located many of the structural and power asymmetries in the practices, institutions, and relations of African peacebuilding, arguing that they are inextricable from the international politics of intervention in African armed conflicts. The study of African peacebuilding is thus an endeavor that cannot avoid problems arising from structural forces and conditions. Despite various attempts at escaping or obscuring its politics, building peace inevitably encounters the question of what and whose 'peace' ought to be built. Thus, peacebuilding as practice confronts issues and problems arising from power asymmetries, colonial legacies, discrimination, marginalization, (in)justice, uneven development, democratization, state formation, and so on – but also in the twenty-first century a future of climate emergency and ecological disasters. What we must be suspicious of, however, are the casual assumptions that presume to know what structural forces and conditions define a particular situation or peacebuilding intervention.

Indeed, the contributions to this book point to several structural realities that, put together, offer a bleak picture. Part I demonstrated how structural constraints and competing agendas and interests often undermine – or at the very least restrict – the formal objectives of peacebuilding. Alexandra Novosseloff showed how both the ambitious goals and the ambiguity of what constitutes peacebuilding activities amplify institutional and operational barriers, notably when and where it encounters other UN activities like peacekeeping. Arthur Stein and Marie-Joëlle Zahar argued that despite increasing cooperation and joint frameworks and practices, the UN-AU partnership faces the limitations of intractable disagreements over policy and strategy. It follows that peacebuilding practices like security sector reforms can be captured by stabilization and counterterrorism agendas or initiatives, as Niagalé Bagayoko and Eboe Hutchful demonstrated. Marina Sharpe showed how the root causes of conflict are often tackled only rhetorically because of the restrictions found in the mandate of the UN High Commissioner for Refugees (UNHCR) and the structure of the African Union (AU) Commission that impede their engagement in conflict prevention and peacebuilding.

Part II emphasized how the study of the workings and evolution of African peacebuilding must be understood both within context-specific conditions and broader global dynamics. In the domain of conflict mediation, Laurie Nathan argued that the African inclination for de jure liberal and democratic content is contradicted for a preference for stabilization through power-sharing arrangements, thus reflecting the global preference for pragmatism and stability over conflict resolution. Tim Murithi analysed Africa's role in establishing, transforming, and mobilizing transitional justice norms in ways that pushed its boundaries beyond the legal sphere and into the fields of peacebuilding and development. Yet, Ulrike Lühe and Briony Jones pointed to the limits of such African contributions by examining the historical origins of the concept of transitional justice. Conceptualized as a field of knowledge, transitional justice is found to be tangled up with colonial power systems and ideologies that sustain the authoritarian and non-democratic practices and preferences of (some) African political elites.

The following chapters analysed several common assumptions about peacebuilding and its relationship to related concepts, institutions, and practices, again highlighting the structural constraints and competing agendas and interests that inform African peacebuilding. The 'local' is often an expression used by academic experts or international practitioners to emphasize African contributions to peacebuilding and as a normative statement about the legitimate parameters of peacebuilding practice. Yet, as Jeremy Allouche and Patrick Zadi Zadi argued, the 'local' is both a highly flexible and contested term. It cannot escape the politics of legitimacy, emancipation, empowerment, and resistance that come from top-down and Western-centric policies. In similar ways, Nina Wilén analysed how the integration of gender into peacebuilding theory and practice has led to greater representativity of women in peace accords but has yet to address the structural inequalities and obstacles that women face. Just like the 'local', the gender norm has been mainstreamed, but its implementation – its concrete consequences in and for practice – has left much to be desired as gender dilemmas and gaps remain.

If there are ideological constraints or parameters that inform African peacebuilding, they have strong foundations in the concepts of development and democracy. While peacebuilding advocates argue that peace and security are impossible without development, Jonathan Sears contended that the peacebuilding-development paradigm is circular and, thus, invites near-permanent interventions into African states and societies. Framed within the confines of global capitalism, the peacebuilding-development nexus can only deliver micro-level successes, as it does not call into question the structural forces and relations of dependencies that bind African economies. Daniel Eizenga argued that despite the shortcomings of democracy and peacebuilding, the relationship between African peacebuilding and democracy has been strong, pointing to long-term improvements in governance, peace, and prosperity for those African states that chose the path of durable democratization. And yet, he also called attention to how democratic gains are stymied by an international context that has become more permissive of authoritarian governments and measures. Bruno Charbonneau, Peter Läderach, Marc-André Boisvert, Tatiana Smirnova, Grazia Pacillo, Alessandro Craparo, and Ignacio Madurga pointed to how climate change and variability stress human systems and conflict dynamics, arguing that climate-induced transformation can sustain or exacerbate conflict dynamics, just as it can create new ones and cause mass human suffering and misery.

Part III offered case studies that point to the shortcomings of peacebuilding missions, practices, and institutions and to the structural conditions that make peace a set of contested ideas and practices that are intertwined with numerous layers of dependency relations. Yet, fine-grained analyses of context-specific socio-political trajectories also reveal the agency of African actors in the (un)making of peace. Ousmane Diallo examined the example of Sahelian post-colonial elites who set up a regional organization that aims to tackle development and security challenges in the region. His analysis showed that the G5 Sahel focused mainly on the capacity-building of Sahelian states. Hence, he argued that African post-colonial elites have sustained or reproduced structural impediments to sustainable peace by creating an organization that is financially and militarily dependent on international donors. Similarly, counterinsurgency and counterterrorism are domains where transnational elites can find common ground. According to Bruno Charbonneau and Louise Wiuff Moe, such military interventions incorporate 'peacebuilding' into a logic that normalizes and legitimizes the use of force in African politics and conflict management. The field of peacebuilding is thus transformed as a political order that primarily seeks to contain the effects of conflict and violence.

Building sustainable peace in a context of persistent authoritarian practices is an important structural impediment for peacebuilding. Festus Kofi Aubyn demonstrated how in The Gambia the legacy of long-term autocracy makes it difficult to advance meaningful peacebuilding, socio-economic development, and reconciliation. Likewise, in the case of one of Africa's longest civil wars, Kuyang Harriet Logo asserted that South Sudanese elites, socialized during decades of conflicts, reproduce power practices of unaccountability and injustices which hinders long-term peace. Fiifi Edu-Afful and Ruth Adwoa Frimpong highlighted that in one of Africa's most fragile states, Guinea-Bissau, efforts at building durable peace are also hindered by a mix of deep socio-economic challenges and authoritarian governance, with elites deeply involved in global drug trafficking. These analyses of post-conflict peacebuilding in Africa also suggest solutions that emphasize the promotion of local ownership and measures to render elites accountable. Maxime Ricard argued that the Ivorian experience shows that status quo aspirations and 'stabilization' are drivers of such contemporary focuses. Peacebuilding in Africa has given up on the transformation of conflicts and society, as practices shifted to building 'resilience' and to the 'pragmatic management of effects' (Chandler 2017, 201).

Our analyses of institutions, power relations, practices, themes, and debates about the limits of African peacebuilding should not overshadow some progress in terms of human development and democratization since the 2000s, with, for example, a clear decline in civil war casualties (Palik et al. 2020). Yet, arguably the most potent way to achieve peace and security, and to improve peacebuilding practices and their effects on societies, is to seriously address structural conditions, impediments, and power relations. While some indicators (e.g. economic growth) might point to some positive future(s), African possibilities remain constrained by numerous legacies of structural power inequalities and imbalances. War and conflicts are not spared or outside such realities. For instance, while since 2012 Mali and Burkina Faso have been destabilized by terrorist attacks, their respective states and security forces are unable or unwilling to protect their citizens, and being largely dependent on external intervention and support, they have nevertheless experienced sustained and high levels of economic growth. Moreover, in the era of the global war on terror, many 'illiberal' peacebuilding experiences in countries like Angola and Rwanda (Soares de Oliveira 2011) demonstrate that international actors tolerate authoritarianism in the name of 'good enough' governance, economic management and growth, and political 'stability' (Van de Walle 2016). Most African countries remain in a state of dependency in relation to the global capitalist system as the location of transnational extractive industries, as exporters of commodities, as recipients of international aid, and/or as a space of permanent international interventions. Even the AU, as the supposed champion of *Pax Africana*, cannot function without external funding.

African peacebuilding does not and cannot evade international hierarchies (Pingeot 2019). It is partly built on, with, around or despite them. As this book's chapters showed, African peacebuilding is a political contest over the meaning of peace, over who should be at peace and under what conditions. Thus, it is also a contest between moral claims. And considering what is coming, it is and will be a moral tale about whose future matters. It is and will continue to be a necessary struggle.

Bruno Charbonneau and Maxime Ricard

## References

Chandler, D., (2017) *Peacebuilding: The Twenty Years' Crisis, 1997–2017*. Basingstoke: Palgrave Macmillan.
Institute of Economics and Peace, (2021). *Ecological Threat Report 2021: Understanding Ecological Threats, Resilience and Peace*. Sydney: IEP.
Palik, L., et al., (2020) 'Conflict Trends in Africa, 1989–2019', Peace Research Institute Oslo Paper.
Pingeot, L., (2019) 'International Peacebuilding as a Case of Structural Injustice', *International Peacekeeping*, 27(2), pp. 263–288.
Soares de Oliveira, R., (2011) 'Illiberal Peacebuilding in Angola', *Journal of Modern African Studies*, 49(2), pp. 287–314.
Tooze, A., (2021) *Shutdown: How Covid Shook the World's Economy*. New York, NY: Viking.
Van de Walle, N., (2016) 'Conclusion: Democracy Fatigue and the Ghost of Modernization Theory', in Hagmann, T. and Reyntjens, F., (eds.) *Aid and Authoritarianism in Africa: Development without Democracy*. Uppsala et London: Zed Books, pp. 161–178.
Wallace-Wells, D., (2021) 'Climate Reparations', *Intelligencer*, 1 November. Available at: https://nymag.com/intelligencer/2021/11/climate-change-reparations.html?s=09.286

# INDEX

Page numbers in *italic* indicate a figure; page numbers in **bold** indicate a table; and n indicates a note on the corresponding page.

Abidjan 267–268
Abuja Accord 253, 255
activities of peacebuilding 1–2, 18
African Commission on Human and People's Rights recent report (ACHPR) 109
African elites 142, 146
African-Led International Support Mission (AFISMA) 29
African Party for the Independence of Guinea and Cape Verde (PAIGC) 247
African Peace and Security Architecture (APSA) 27, 191, 275
African Solutions to African Problems (ASAP) 275
African transitional justice: constitutive outside 103, 107–108; implications of 108–110; introduction 100–102
African Union (AU) 60–61; Charter 36; construction of 2; effectiveness of 3; forced displacement and 58, 63–65, 66; G5 Sahel and 194–195; mediation approach 78; origins of 191, 275; peacebuilding approach of 3; role of 194; *see* UN/AU relationship
African Union Commission of Inquiry on South Sudan 237
*African Union Mediation Support Handbook* (AU) 78
African Union Mission in Somalia (AMISOM) 10, 30, 211–212
African Union's Peace and Security Council (AU PSC) 27
African Union Transitional Justice Policy 96–97, 98, 100–101
Agadez 177
agency 107, 115, 116, 147, 274

Agenda 2063 39, 40n6
*Agenda for Peace, An* (Boutros-Ghali) 1, 2, 4, 16–18, 191, 249, 275
Ahluwalia, P. 103
Ajawin, L.A. 243n2
Akindès, F. 121
Albrecht, P. 38
Alliance Sahel 196–197, **197**
Allouche, J. 7, 114, 115, 276, 284
All-Party Women's Peace Conference 131
amnesty approach 92–93
Ancelovici, M. 108
Anders, G. 106
Annan, K. 28, 77, 88–89
Arusha Accord 131, 133
Aubyn, F.K. 10, 222, 277, 285
AU Mission in Somalia (AMISOM) () 10
Autesserre, S. 38
authoritarians/authoritarianism: in Burundi 100; conflict and 165; in Côte d'Ivoire 260, 264, 269; democratic backsliding 8; gender and 87; in Guinea-Bassau 248; local peacebuilding and 119, 157; resurgence of 162, 279; transitional justice and 107
AU-UN Hybrid Operation in Darfur (UNAMID) 37
Ayittey, G. 275

Bagayoko, N. 5, 44, 275, 284
Bah, S. 226
Banny, C. K. 262
Ba, O. 201
Barkhane 198, 199, 213, 214
Barrow, A. 10, 222, 223, 224, 228, 231

Bédié, H.K. 121
Benin 164
Beoua, Côte d'Ivoire 122
Bermeo, N. 162
Bilgin, P. 102, 103
Bley, H.D. 261
Boisvert, M.-A. 8, 169, 285
Boone, C. 120
Boraine, A. L. 85, 107
bottom-up approaches 51–52; *see also* local peacebuilding
Boutellis, A. 34
Boutros-Ghali, B. 1, 2, 4, 249, 275
Bowsher, J. 106
Brahimi, L. 27
Brahimi report 1, 18, 27
Bränfors, P. 131
Bratton, M. 166n2
Brinks, D. 155
Brinton Lykes, M. 104
Brosig, M. 38
Burundi 100
Buyoya, P. 77

capacity-building 139
case studies: G5 Sahel 191–205; Gambia, The 222–234; Guinea-Bissau 247–259; Mali 213–218; Somalia 210–213, 216–218; South Sudan 235–246
Ceesay, K. 227
Central African Republic (CAR) 155
Chabal, P. 115
Chad 96
Chafer, T. 123
Charbonneau, B. 1, 8, 9, 123, 165, 169, 206, 277, 285
Charter of the African Union 36
Charter of the United Nations 36
Cheeseman, N. 166n5, 166n6
civil–military relations 47–49
class 3, 146, 249
climate change/crisis 8–9, 283–284; conflict and 170–172; introduction 169–170; in Niger 172–181; peacebuilding activities and 182–183; in Sahelian countries 170; as security issue 169
climate security 169
climate variability 9, 170, 171, 174, 182
coercion 10, 77, 206, 209, 211, 213, 265
Cold-Ravnkilde, S. 37, 38
Coleman, K.P. 38
Coleman, P.T. 114
colonialism 106
community-based approaches *see* local peacebuilding
comparative advantage 28–30
Comprehensive Peace Agreement (CPA) 235, 236

Comprehensive Refugee Response Framework (CRRF) 59
Conakry Agreement 256
conflict analysis 175–181
conflict catalyst 170
constitutive outside 103, 107–108
containment strategy 214–216
contextual/contextualisation 85–86, 103, 116, 123
Continental Mechanism for Conflict Prevention, Management, and Resolution 2
Correia, C. 248
Côte d'Ivoire 11, 145; Houphouëtist practices 265–266; imposed peace 261–263; introduction 117–119, 260–261; land disputes 120–121, 124n5; legitimacy of public authority 119–120; national and international actors 267–268, 269; normalisation 268–269; post-electoral crisis 261–262; reaffirmation of the state 263–266; social inequalities and tensions 266; successful initiatives 121–123; transitional justice 262–263
counterinsurgency 198; influence of 218n6; introduction 206–208; Mali 213–218; Somalia 210–213, 216–218; stabilisation mandates and 208–210
*Counterinsurgency* (Kilcullen) 206
counterterrorism 194, 196, 198
COVID-19 pandemic 230, 231, 232, 256, 278, 281
Craparo, A. 8, 169, 285
crisis management: as continuum 16–18; from stabilisation to sustaining peace 20–22; as unified whole 18–20
cross-border approach 94–97
cultural approach 93–94
Curran, D. 207
Curtis, D. 2

Darboe, M.K. 228
Darfur 37, 74, 77, 91
Debos, M. 166n5
De Carvalho, G. 38
De Coning, C. 40n4
definition of peacebuilding 18, 19, 23n11
definitions 17, 18
delegation, peace by: G5 Sahel Joint force 198–202; G5 Sahel's development pillar 195–198; introduction 191–193
democracy 8; backsliding 162–165, 279; definition 155; elections, role of 160–162; international origins 156–158; introduction 155–156; liberal democratic peacebuilding 158–160, 166n3; peace theory 158–160, 166n3; promotion of 156–158
democratic consolidation 8, 156, 158, 161
democratic SSG 46

## Index

Department of Health, Humanitarian Affairs and Social Development (DHHS) 65, 67n7
Department of Peacebuilding and Political Affairs (DPPA) 32, 63–64
Dersso, S.A. 38
Desgrais, N. 196
development: African leadership 140–145; capacity-building 139; complexity of 148–149; conceptual landmarks 139–140; definition 139; effectiveness of 148–149; future of 149–151; in The Gambia 229–230; governance and 140–141, 142; introduction 138–139; local turn and nonstate actors 145–148; micro-macro paradox 148–149
Diallo, O. 9, 191, 277, 285
Dialogue, Truth, and Reconciliation Commission (CDVR) 262
displaced persons 5, 57–69; African Union 63–65; definition of 60; HARDP 63–64, 65, 67n7; internal displacement 58–59, 60; international initiatives 59–60; introduction 57–58; prevention agenda 59–65; refugees 58–59; regional initiatives 60–61; root causes 57, 60, 65–66; structural barriers to prevention 61–65; UNHCR 62–63, 65, 66
division of labour 215, 217
Doyle, M.W. 158, 166n3
Duncanson, C. 135n1
Duursma, A. 75

East Africa 74
Ebola 23n7, 118
École de maintien de la paix Alioun Blondin Baye 30
Economic Community of West African States (ECOWAS) 10, 44, 73, 193
ECOWAS Mission in Guinea-Bissau (ECOMIB) 11
Edu-Afful, F. 11, 247, 277, 285
Eizenga, D. 8, 155, 277, 285
elections: role of 160–162; strategic manipulation 163–164
electoral autocracy 269
emancipation 146, 249
"Enhancing UN-AU Cooperation" 28
essentialist descriptions 7, 128, 135
Eurocentric thinking 2–3
European Union 199
Evans, A. 148
executive aggrandizement 163
external influences 2–3

failed state 3
feminist approach 7
*Final Report on the Administration of Justice and the Question of Impunity* (Joinet) 88
first-generation peacebuilding 275–277

Fletcher, L.E. 108
forced displacement *see* displaced persons
France: in Côte d'Ivoire 262, 267–268; in Mali 34–35, 198–199, 213; in Sahel 214–215
francophone space 267–268
Friis, K. 209
Frimpong, R.A. 11, 247, 285
functionalists/functionalism 114

G5 Sahel 9, 213; African Union and 194–195; Alliance Sahel 196–197, **197**; environment of 193–195; introduction 191–193; Joint force 198–202; origins of 193–194; priority investment plan 195–198; *see also* Sahel
Gambia, The 10; components of peacebuilding 225–230; constitutional review 225–226; context 223–225; international partners 230–231; introduction 222–223; judicial reform 226–227; security sector reform 228–229; socio-economic recovery and development 229–230; threats to peacebuilding 231; transitional justice and reconciliation 227–228
Garang, J. 243n2
Gbagbo, L. 11, 121, 260, 261–262, 263, 269
Gelot, L. 38
gender 7; balance 133; complexity of 134–135; in subaltern view 117; transitional justice and 87–88; *see also* women
Ghana 145
Gilbert, G. 57
global capitalism 8, 149, 285
Global Compact on Refugees (GCR) 5, 57
global integration 8, 149
Gomes, C. Jr 247, 249
Gon Coulibaly, A. 265
governance 46; challenges 145; development and 140–141, 142; hybrid orders of 202n2; modes of 8, 142–143, 181–182; *see also* security sector reform and governance (SSG)
Gowan, R. 38
Gregory, D. 103
Group of Friends of the UN-AU Partnership 39
Guinea-Bissau 11; challenges to peacebuilding 255–257; drug trafficking 256–7; international actors/partners 252–255; introduction 247–249; liberal peacebuilding versus African lens 249–251; phases of peacebuilding 251–252; political context 249; socio-economic recovery 256; way forward 257
Guterres, A. 22, 149

Habré, H. 96
Halperin, M.H. 166n3
Hamber, B. 108
Handrahan, L. 130
Heitz, K. 117

*hera* (peace, well-being) 147
High-Level Independent Panel on Peace Operations 35
High-level Panel on Peace Operations (HIPPO) 207, 208
history 2
holistic approaches 147
Hollande, F. 213, 214
Holt, V.K. 27
Horn of Africa 95–96
Houphouët-Boigny, F. 120, 265–266
Howard, M.M. 166n4
Huberson, G. 268
Hudson, H. 117
Humanitarian Affairs, Refugees and Displaced Persons (HARDP) 63–64, 65, 67n7
Hunt C. 207
Hutchful, E. 5, 44, 275, 284
Hwang, Y.J. 103
hybrid orders of governance 202n2
hybrid peacebuilding 116, 159–160
hybrid security governance 51–52
Hydara, D. 224, 227

illiberal peacebuilding 162, 265, 286
illiberal politics 79, 80, 265, 276
*Impossible Machine, The* (Sitze) 105
indigenous approaches 250
indigenous norm restorative justice 94
Indjai, A. 255
institution-building 47, 155, 157, 160, 161
institutions 4–6; African Union (AU) *see* African Union (AU); cooperation at higher levels 30–34; overlap 35; United Nations *see* United Nations (UN)
instrumental approach 2
Intergovernmental Authority on Development (IGAD) 73, 74, 235, 236, 243n3
International Criminal Court (ICC) 100
International Crisis Group (ICG) 172, 215
international system 192, 208
Interpeace/Indingo 118
intervention 140, 143

Jagger, C. 224
Jallow, B.G. 227
Jammeh, Y. 10, 222, 223–224, 226, 232
Jeng, A. 2
Jenson, J. 108
Jezequel, J-H. 216
Joinet, L. 88
Joinet/Orentlicher principles 89
Joint Task Force 33
Jones, B. 6, 98, 276, 284
justice: indigenous norm restorative 94; restorative 90–91; retributive 90–91; transitional *see* transitional justice; universalizing tendency 94

Kagame, P. 64
Karamoja Cluster Project 95–96
Karbo, T. 3
Kenneth, O. 275
Kenya 88, 96
Khadiagala, G.M. 2, 74
Kiir, S. 235
Kilcullen, D. 206
Kofi Annan International Peacekeeping Training Centre 30
Kohl, C. 255
Konaré, A.O. 28
Koné, G. 121
Krause, J. 131, 135n2
Krause, W. 131

Läderach, P. 8, 169, 285
land disputes 120–121, 124n5
Lecointre, F. 214
Le Drian, J.-Y. 215
leverage, sources of 76
liberal peacebuilding 79; versus African lens 249–251; liberal democratic peace theory 158–160
Lindberg, S.I. 161
local and regional dynamics of violence 198–202
local peacebuilding 7, 145–148; in Côte d'Ivoire 117–123; District Platforms for Dialogue (DPD) 118; interpretations of 115–117; introduction 114–115; land disputes 120–121, 124n5; legitimacy of public authority 119–120; meaning of local 115; successful initiatives 121–123
Logo, K.H. 10, 235, 277, 285
Lomé Agreement 135n5
Lorentz, P. 270n1
Lühe, U. 6, 98, 276, 284
Lungu, E. 163
Lynch, G. 166n5, 166n6

Mac Ginty, R. 114, 115, 117, 123
Machar, R. 235, 243n2
Macron, E. 215
Maddison, S. 106
Madurga, I. 8, 169, 285
Magufuli, J. 163
Mahamat, M.F. 101
Mahmoud, Y. 20
Maïga, A.I. 218n7
Mainwaring, S. 155
Makoond, A. 20
Malabo Protocol 109, 110n4
Mali 9–10; AU Mission in 29; counterinsurgency in 213–218; democratic backsliding 164–165; France in 34–35, 198–199; G5 Sahel and 193, 198; UN Mission in 29, 198
Malombe, D. 105

Mamdani, M. 119
Mann, G. 143
Maputo Protocol 133
Marcel, Z.K. 122
Maubert, C. 123
maximalist model of state 8, 142–143, 144
Mazrui, A. 2, 250
McNamee, T. 155
mediation 6, 160; actors in 73–76; content of agreements 78–80; in East Africa 74; introduction 73; style and strategy 76–78
Mehler, A. 80
military coups 163–164
Millennium Development Goals (MDGs) 141
minimalist model of state 8, 142–143, 144
Mitchell, A. 115
modes of governance 8, 142–143, 181–182
Moe, L.W. 9, 206, 277, 285
Morse, Y.L. 161
Multidimensional Integrated Stabilization Mission in Mali (MINUSMA) 29
Murithi, T. 6, 276, 284
Murphy, C. 108
Museveni, Y. 87
Mutua, M.W. 104
Muyangwa, M. 155

Nathan, L. 6, 73, 75, 276, 284
National Commission for Reconciliation and Compensation of Victims (CONARIV) 263
National Program of Social Cohesion (PNCS) 262
NATO 17
New Horizon initiative 19
New York Declaration for Refugees and Migrants 59
next-generation peacebuilding 280
Nhamadjo, S. 247
Niang, A. 279
Niger 9, 170; Agadez 177; conflict chronology 178–180; conflict resolution mechanisms 180–181; conflict sources **177**; governance, modes of 181–182; impact pathway analysis 172–175, *176*; Tahoua 175–181, **177**; Tillaberi 175–181, **177**
Nkurunziza, P. 100
norm setting and diffusion 6
Novosseloff, A. 4, 15, 275, 284
Nshimbi, C. 278
Nuremberg Trials 104, 105
Nyaba, P.A. 243n2
Nyamitwe, W. 100
Nyerere, J. 77

Obi, C. 274
obstacles 22
Okello, M. 94

Okoth-Obbo, G. 57
Ongwen, D. 87
operational impediments 34–36
operational peacebuilding 19, 20, 28–30
Operation Restore Hope 17
Operation Serval 193, 198, 213, 214
Orentlicher, D. 89
Organization of African Unity (OAU) 2, 57
orientalism 3
Ostrom, E. 172
Ottaway, M. 156
Ouattara, A. 11, 260–273
Ouattara, B.M. 121
Owens, P. 207

Pacillo, G. 8, 169, 285
Palmer Drought Severity Index (PDSI) 178, **179**
parastatals 143–144
partnerships, strategic 75–76
Party for Social Renovation (PRS) 247
*Pax Africana* 2, 38, 40
Peace and Development 117–118
Peace and Security Council (AU PSC) 27, 191
peace continuum 4, 15–24
peacekeeping 1, 17, 18, 18–19
peacemaking 1, 17
Peace Support Operations (PSOs) 27
Pérez-Liñán, A. 155
Piccolino, G. 117, 123
Pillay, S. 105
politics of knowledge 102
post–cold war era 10, 18, 105–106, 206, 250, 275–279
post-colonial situation 103, 105–106, 144, 150, 198–199
post-conflict environment 19, 130, 139, 140, 157, 250, 261, 265–266, 267
power relations 106, 141, 279
power-sharing arrangements 80
preventive diplomacy 17
prosecutorial fundamentalism 92
Puechguirbal, N. 130, 132

Rashid, I. 279
reconciliation: amnesty approach 92–93; cross-border approach 94–97; cultural approach 93–94; definition 86; introduction 84–85; regional 95; sequencing approach 90–92
refugees: definition 58; *see also* displaced persons
regional economic communities (RECs) 73, 74, 83n1
regional reconciliation 95, 279–280
relational peacebuilding 145
relational rationality 147
research, need for 280–1
resistance 115, 123, 208, 239, 242
restorative justice 90–91

retributive justice 90–91
Ricard, M. 1, 11, 260, 277, 286
Richmond, O.P. 114, 115, 117, 123
risk amplifier 170
risk multiplier 170
Roessler, P.G. 166n4
'Rule of Law and Transitional Justice in Conflict and Post-conflict Societies, The' (Annan) 89

Sahel: climate and conflict in 171–172; definition 183n1; international system in 214–215; Niger 172–181; *see also* G5 Sahel
Said, E. 110n1
Salim, S.A. 2
Sanhá, M.B. 254
Sanogo, A.H. 164
Sears, J. 8
Sears, J.M. 138, 277, 285
second-generation peacebuilding 277–279
security-development nexus 192, 202n3
security sector reform and governance (SSG) 5; asymmetric threats in West Africa 52–53; civil–military relations 47–49; civil society role 50–51; democratic governance and civilian oversight 49–50; efficiency improvements 47–53; in The Gambia 228–229; in Guinea-Bassau 255; hybrid security governance 51–52; introduction 44–45; media role 50; in non-conflict setting 53; theoretical approach 45–46; West African challenges 46–47
sequencing approach 90–92
Serval *see* Operation Serval
Shanahan, M.K. 27
Sharp, D.N. 101
Sharpe, M. 5, 57, 275, 284
Shepherd, L.J. 106
Shih, C. 103
Siegle, J.T. 166n3
Sierra Leone 96
Sigsworth, R. 88
Sirleaf, M. 109
Sitze, A. 105, 106
*Sky Monitor* 17
Smirnova, T. 8, 169, 285
social change 8, 139, 148
Somalia 9–10, 133, 155; al-Shabaab 211, 212; AU Mission in 10, 30, 211–212; counterinsurgency 210–213, 216–218; UN/AU collaboration 30
South Africa 91–92, 101, 105, 107
Southern African Development Community (SADC) 73
South Sudan 10, 74, 77; 2018 peace agreement 240–242; introduction 235–236; sabotaging justice 238–240; transitional justice 236, 237–238; ways forward 242–243
sovereignty 4, 66, 95, 104, 105, 134, 144, 150, 160

Spivak, G.C. 110n1
stabilisation 20–22, 207–210, 260–273
state-building 209
state-centric perspective 192
state formation 142–145
state–society relations 115, 116, 145, 146, 147
Stein, A. 5, 26, 275, 284
strategic election manipulation 163–164
strategic partnerships 75–76
structural relations 3
subaltern view 114, 117, 124n1
subsidiarity 73–74
Sudan 10, 37
Sudan People's Liberation Movement (SPLM) 10, 235, 243n2
Sullivan, M. 103
*Supplement to An Agenda for Peace* (Boutros-Ghali) 1, 16–18, 275
Sustainable Development Goals (SDGs) 141, 142
sustainable peace 20–22, 247–259
system fragility 8, 169

Tahoua 175–181, **177**
Talon, P. 164
Tanzania 163, 164
Taylor, C. 96
Teitel, R.G. 104
threat multiplier 170–171, 172
Tieku, T.K. 3
Tillaberi 175–181, **177**
top-down approaches 7
Toumani, A. 164
Touval, S. 76
transitional justice 6–7; African *see* African transitional justice; amnesty approach 92–93; components of 85; contextualisaton 85–86; in Côte d'Ivoire 262–263; cross-border approach 94–97; cultural approach 93–94; evolution of 86–89; in The Gambia 227–228; introduction 84–85; local ownership 102–103; origin myths 103–107; political interference and 88; pressures on 89–90; sequencing approach 90–92; in South Sudan 235–246; United Nations 88–89; worlding 103
Truth and Reconciliation Commission (TRC) 84, 101, 105
Truth, Reconciliation, and Reparations Commission (TRRC) 227
Tull, D. 80, 199

*Ubuntu* ("humanness") 147
Uganda 74, 87, 91, 92, 96
*ukama* ("relatedness") 147
UN/AU relationship 5, 15, 37; cooperation at higher levels 30–34; disagreements 36–37; diverging national interests 37–38; documents on cooperation **31–32**; historical overview

26–28; operational cooperation 28–30; operational impediments 34–36; progress assessment 28–34; structural constraints 34–38
UN High-Level Panel on Threats, Challenges and Change 18
UNIFEM 131
United Nations Department of Peacebuilding and Political Affairs (DPPA) 32, 63–64
*United Nations Guidance for Effective Mediation* (UN) 78, 81
United Nations High Commissioner for Refugees (UNHCR) 57–58, 62–63, 65
United Nations Integrated Peacebuilding Office in Guinea-Bissau (UNIOGBIS) 250, 252
United Nations Peacebuilding Support Office in Guinea-Bissau (UNOGBIS) 253, 254, 255
United Nations (UN): AU relationship and *see* UN/AU relationship; Charter 36; in Côte d'Ivoire 260, 264; Department of Peacebuilding and Political Affairs 32; on development 139; fourth pillar 207; in Guinea-Bassau 250, 251, 252; High-Level Independent Panel on Peace Operations 35; towards a peace continuum 15–24; transitional justice and 88–89
United Task Force (UNITAF) 17
UNOAU 33
UN Operation in Somalia (UNOSOM ()) 17
UN Peacebuilding Commission 19
UNSC 1325 129, 130–131, 133, 134
UN Support Office for AMISOM (UNSOA) 30
Uvin, P. 140

Valji, N. 88
Vanantwerpen, J. 107
van der Merwe, H. 104
van de Walle, N. 166n2
van Zyl, P. 108
Vaz, J.M. 248, 249
Vieira, J.B. 251

Wai, Z. 3
Wallace-Wells, D. 283
Wallis, J. 166n5, 166n6
Walter, D. 206
Wandji, D. 123
Weinstein, H.M. 108
Weinstein, M.M. 166n3
Weiss, T.G. 35, 36
Welz, M. 35, 36
West Africa: asymmetric threats 52–53; civil–military relations 47–49; civil society role 50–51; democratic governance and civilian oversight 49–50; hybrid security governance 51–52; introduction 44–45; media role 50; SSRG challenges 46–47; SSRG in non-conflict setting 53; terrorism in 268
Western-centric policies 7, 119, 285
*When Law Meets Reality* (Okello) 94
Wilén, N. 7, 128, 277, 285
Williams, P. 1
Williams, P.D. 34
women 7; counting 133–134; human rights and 134; identifying spaces for 130–134; introduction 128–129; marginalisation in peacebuilding 129–130; as moral peacebuilders 132–133, 135; peacebuilding groups 251; as vulnerable victims 131–132; *see also* gender
Women, Peace and Security Agenda 128, 196
Woodward, S. 208
World Bank 142
worlding 110n1

Yacoli Dabouo, Côte d'Ivoire 122
Yale, K. 247
Yusuf, H.O. 106

Zadi, P.Z. 7
Zadi Zadi, P. 114, 115, 117, 123, 276, 284
Zahar, M.-J. 5, 26, 275, 284
Zambia 163, 164
Zartman, I.W. 76
Zenker, O. 106
Zimbabwe 77
Zondi, S. 3

Milton Keynes UK
Ingram Content Group UK Ltd.
UKHW020756230624
444299UK00015B/15